PAUL HAM

SANDAKAN

THE UNTOLD STORY OF THE SANDAKAN DEATH MARCHES

Doubleday

LONDON · TORONTO · SYDNEY · AUCKLAND · JOHANNESBURG

TRANSWORLD PUBLISHERS
61–63 Uxbridge Road, London W5 5SA
A Random House Group Company
www.transworldbooks.co.uk

First published in Australia
in 2012 by William Heinemann

First published in Great Britain
in 2013 by Doubleday
an imprint of Transworld Publishers

Maps on pp. xiv–xvi by Laurie Whiddon, Map Illustrations.
The Death March route on pp. xiv–xv is based on the map published by the
Australian Government Department of Defence in April 2012
Internal design by Xou Creative, Australia

A CIP catalogue record for this book
is available from the British Library.

ISBN 9780857521033 (cased)
9780857521040 (tpb)

Addresses for Random House Group Ltd companies outside the UK
can be found at: www.randomhouse.co.uk
The Random House Group Ltd Reg. No. 954009

The Random House Group Limited supports the Forest Stewardship Council® (FSC®),
the leading international forest-certification organisation. Our books carrying the FSC label
are printed on FSC®-certified paper. FSC is the only forest-certification scheme supported
by the leading environmental organisations, including Greenpeace. Our paper procurement
policy can be found at www.randomhouse.co.uk/environment

Typeset in Adobe Garamond
Printed and bound in Great Britain by
CPI Group (UK) Ltd, Croydon, CR0 4YY

2 4 6 8 10 9 7 5 3 1

Dedicated to the Australian and British prisoners of war in Borneo who never came home, the few who did, and the local people who tried to save them

Paul Ham
Sydney
Australia

Tennō Heika (天皇陛下)
His Imperial Majesty The Emperor of Japan
The Imperial Palace
Tokyo
Japan

October 2012

Your Majesty,

You may think it impertinent of me, an Australian historian, to presume to address the Emperor of Japan. No doubt, many of your countrymen will think so and urge you to ignore this unsolicited letter.

But I write to you in an effort to find some connection between our countries beyond trade, tourism and the memory of the most terrible conflict our world has known. We are still recovering from that experience. Of the 50 million people who died in the Second World War, more than half were Asian people and Allied servicemen and women, the victims of Japanese aggression.

I write not in anger or bitterness, but rather in the spirit of respect and friendship. I do not share in the slightest degree the racial intolerance of some of my countrymen and women, whose hatred of the Japanese people festers decades after the last drop of blood fell to earth in the dying months of the Pacific War. But it is absurd and wrong to 'hate' a whole people, as Robert Menzies, a former Australian prime minister, reminded us in 1942. Few Australians seem to realise that Japan was our ally during the First World War, and treated German and Russian prisoners of war with exemplary care and restraint.

I therefore appeal to our shared sense of humanity, which recognises no social or cultural distinctions, transcends race, religion and the colour of our skin, and reaches out to embrace the higher attributes of human nature: justice, compassion and mutual goodwill. It is in this spirit that I present you with my book, *Sandakan: The Untold Story of the Sandakan Death Marches* (Random House, 2012), the history of a little-known war crime that occurred between 1942 and 1945 in Borneo, when the island was an outpost of the Japanese Empire. It is the story of the agonising last days and needless deaths of more than 2400 Australian and British prisoners of war. Enslaved for three years in a Japanese prison camp at Sandakan, many died of disease, malnutrition and appalling treatment. Some 1100 survivors were then force-marched into the heart of the island. Of these, six came home – a 99.5 per cent death rate, the worst of any prisoner-of-war camp in the Pacific or European theatres of the Second World War.

The victims of Borneo were starved, tortured, shot, bayoneted or beheaded. Many died of untreated illnesses or starvation. One was crucified and disembowelled, according to a witness. The Death Marches were the biggest killer: sick and hungry men were forced to carry heavy loads through jungle and swamp, and over mountains, until they collapsed from exhaustion or disease or hunger, whereupon the guards shot or clubbed them to death. It was a policy of mass extermination. The killing continued until 27 August 1945, nearly a fortnight after the armistice. These crimes were committed in the name of the military regime over which your father held supreme command, under Article 6 of the Imperial Japanese Constitution.

The facts only partly convey the horror of the individual stories – stories of men who experienced unearthly suffering. Chaplain Harold Wardale-Greenwood, for instance, was an officer who led his troops on the Death Marches with his Christian god in his heart and hope for his men in his head, but he lost his faith in the face of such cruelty days before he succumbed to sickness. Captain Lionel Matthews, arrested for running an underground smuggling operation in Sandakan Prison Camp, was tortured to within an inch of his life but never broke. After each torture session, he would tap Morse signals on his knee to warn his fellow prisoners of what they were about to endure at the hands of the Kempei-tai. Added to this were the countless acts of bravery and resistance by soldiers beaten, starved and exhausted beyond reach of hope or deliverance, prodded at bayonet point to a lonely death in the sodden jungles of Borneo.

These facts were laid before the War Crimes Tribunal, which convened in a tent on a beach in Labuan in January 1946. They outraged every scrap of humanity enshrined in the Geneva Convention, to which Japan was not a signatory, but by the terms of which your country had promised to abide. Many of the perpetrators, Japanese and Formosan, were executed; most were imprisoned and then freed, in the 1950s, under a general amnesty.

Since the end of the war, no Japanese government has

recognised or accepted historic responsibility for the Death Marches in Borneo. None has apologised to, recognised or made an effort to compensate the Australian and British families and the native people of Borneo for the atrocities that left behind so many widows, fatherless children and families in mourning for their boys. Of course, nothing can 'compensate' a family for the loss of a father, son, husband or brother – except his return.

Japan's silence on these crimes – crimes that will disgust every human heart capable of feeling – implies a reluctance to accept responsibility for them and redounds to the disgrace of the Japanese nation.

That does not mean the victors are immune from the same charge. Any honest analysis of the Pacific War accepts that the Allies committed unconscionable acts of wanton barbarity. I am the author of *Hiroshima Nagasaki*, a history of the atomic bombs. Only the wilfully ignorant or prejudiced could fail to conclude, after examining the evidence, that the nuclear attacks on your country were not only crimes against humanity but also militarily unnecessary. Was the breaking, burning or irradiation of hundreds of thousands of Japanese civilians justified as revenge for Pearl Harbor, as the American Government claimed at the time? We debase ourselves, and the history of civilisation, if we accept that Japanese atrocities warranted an American atrocity in reply.

Crimes against humanity, war crimes, atrocities – whatever legal name we choose to give them – affront everything we hold dear as human beings. They do not admit of justification or excuse or qualification. 'Revenge' is no defence. They are singularly abhorrent. They revolt us.

Many people would prefer to let these issues wither unread in the dusty chronicles of war. Let the past be, they cry, dimly unable to see that ignorance of the past dooms us to repeat it. Many resort to facile banalities, and excuses, for such acts, that of 'victor's justice' and 'all nations commit war crimes'; or, from the Allied perspective, the Old Testament equation of an 'eye for an eye', or the infantile 'Japan started it'. But there are absolutes in the realm of human cruelty, which transcend the special pleading of nations and tribunals – and bring me to the point of this letter.

What happened to the tens of thousands enslaved on the Burma–Siam Railway, to the 'comfort women', to the citizens of Nanking, to the Koreans and Chinese and millions of people throughout the Pacific, from 1931 to 1945, and indeed to the victims of Hiroshima and Nagasaki and of the firebombing of Japanese cities will appal all fair-minded people in perpetuity. Their story is part of our collective human history.

I do not presume to speak for them – others are better qualified to do so. But I do feel entitled to speak on behalf of the families of the victims of the Sandakan Prisoner of War Camp and Death Marches, many of whom I have met. And I make a simple request of you, as the ultimate representative of your people: that you publicly recognise these events and apologise on behalf of the Japanese nation for the crimes committed in Borneo in 1942–45.

Japan has not hitherto apologised *as a nation*. Individual Japanese officials have expressed personal remorse for 'mistakes' made in the war, or used the term *'owabi'*, which, as I understand it, means an apology that is not heartfelt. The most sincere form of Japanese apology is, I believe, rendered by the phrase '*moshiwake gozaimasen*'. Yet the world has never heard a Japanese leader say this on behalf of the Japanese people in relation to Pacific War crimes.

A sincere apology from the Emperor would express, on behalf of all Japanese people, a genuine acknowledgement of these crimes, and that Japan recognises them as uniquely heinous and abhorrent. As our former prime minister, Paul Keating – whose uncle died on the Death Marches – has stated: 'Sandakan should be remembered because it was more than a battle between nations and . . . conflicting ideologies; it was a war between human decency and human depravity.'

No apology can alleviate the terrible losses suffered by thousands of families. But it can atone for Japan's silence and obfuscation, and render these events in the true light of history rather than as forgettable ephemera, untaught in Japanese schools and unacknowledged by the nation that perpetrated them. And your words – coming from the highest moral authority in Japan – would bring our two countries a step closer to that most elusive quality in the affairs of people, mutual understanding, which is surely the beginning of true forgiveness and friendship.

Yours sincerely,

Paul Ham

CONTENTS

Part 3: Resistance

Part 4: They March

Part 5: Revelation

Appendices

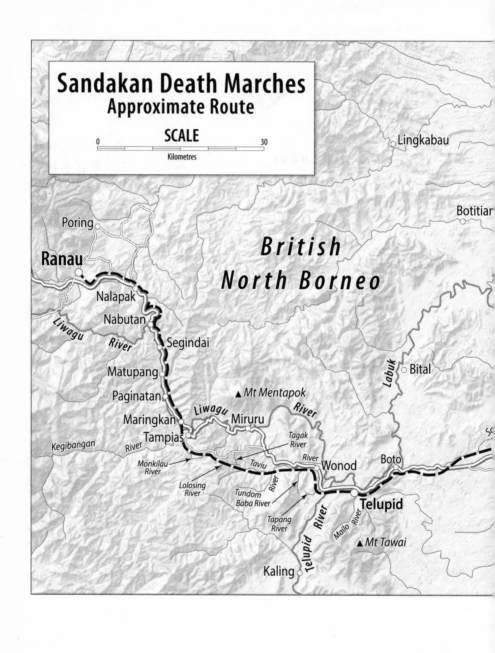

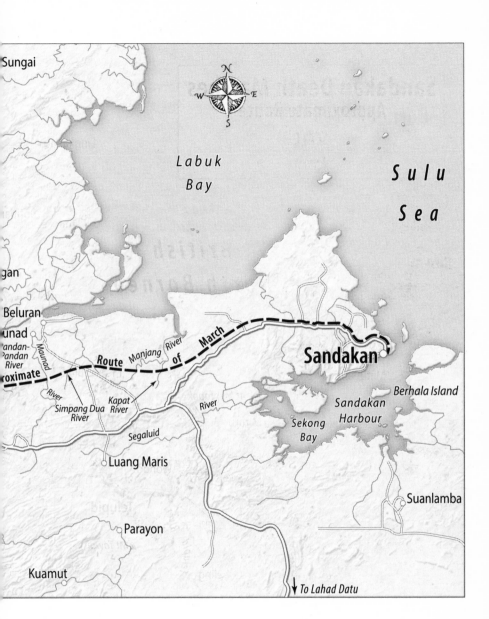

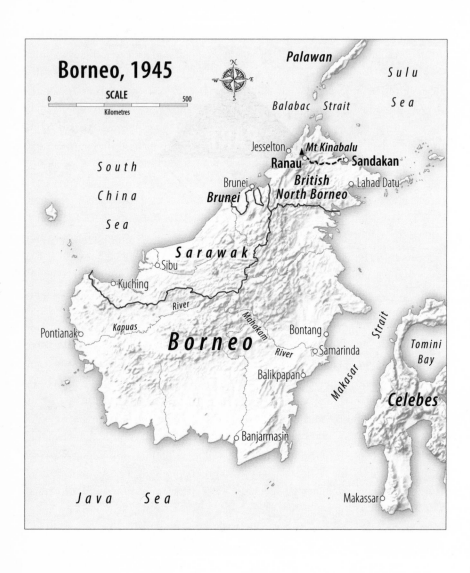

Borneo, 1945

SCALE

0   500

Kilometres

Palawan

Sulu

Sea

Balabac Strait

Jesselton

Mt Kinabalu

Ranau

Sandakan

Brunei

South

British

Lahad Datu

China

Brunei

North Borneo

Sea

S a r a w a k

Sibu

Kuching

River

Kapuas

Mahakam

Bontang

Strait

Pontianak

B o r n e o

River

Samarinda

Tomini

Bay

Balikpapan

Makasar

Celebes

Banjarmasin

J a v a   S e a

Makassar

PART

1

BEFORE

1

SINGAPORE LOST

[F]urther resistance would not only serve to inflict direct harms
[sic] and injuries to thousands of non-combatants living in
the city, throwing them into further miseries and horrors of
war, but also would not add anything to the honour of your
Army and result in annihilation of the city and civilians.
Japanese leaflet, signed by General Yamashita Tomoyuki, dropped on
Allied positions in Singapore days before the British surrender

---

THE WAR COMES TO SINGAPORE with a bloody, terrible
suddenness that shocks the British and Australian forces who
garrison the city's naval base. In their field offices, on the outskirts
of town, Allied war diarists record Britain's greatest military
humiliation in short, handwritten phrases, like taps on a snare
drum pacing the approach of oblivion.

'Civilians,' warns an Australian diarist of the 8th Division
General Staff, on 2 February 1942, may hear 'war-like noises
– range practice etc' – a ruse conceived by the Allies to prevent
civilian hysteria.[1] To further this illusion of safety, the British
commander Lieutenant General Arthur Percival postpones plans
to build proper land fortifications along the coast. But those 'war-
like noises' hammering Singapore's north coast are *actual* war

noises, writes the Australian war diarist. Real Japanese guns and bombs are destroying the naval fortress, whose huge new docks have not contained a warship for weeks.

Defeat is everywhere: in the smell of encroaching shellfire, the cries of terrified Chinese, and the bewildered eyes of Allied soldiers and commanders, who fall back on the island beneath the rampaging forces of Nippon. The Japanese control the Johore Peninsula and since January have turned their sights on the little island to the south, Fortress Singapore, hitherto thought impregnable. With their backs to the sea, British and Australian troops prepare to fight to the last man in defence of this sumptuous colony, the pride of the Empire. Just weeks earlier, pink gin, linen suits, croquet and the calm of Raffles Hotel seemed the unassailable constituents of civilisation. Today, these trinkets of colonial life have vanished in the cordite-filled stench of defeat. Everyone knows Singapore's surrender is imminent.

Churchill is already resigned to the fact, having lost hope of the colony's salvation after the sinking of the *Repulse* and the *Prince of Wales* the previous December; he will later describe the Fall of Singapore as the 'worst disaster' and 'greatest capitulation' in British history. Reasons beyond his control, he implies at the time, have forced the defeat. Yet the responsibility is the British Government's, in its inability to reinforce the colony, chiefly with crucial aircraft. Stretched to the limit fighting Germany, Britain simply hasn't the resources to defend its Far Eastern garrison. The prime minister will never forgive the Japanese for the loss of Singapore, which envenoms his mind against 'the Wops of the East', the deaths of whom he later demands in great numbers to avenge British honour.[2] If the voyage of Christopher Columbus marked the dawn of the European colonial era, the great clanking sound of the retreat of Western imperialism has surely started here.

◆

No doubt, there is great bravery in the path of defeat, isolated acts that do little to stanch the downward rush of Japan. No fair account of the withdrawal could overlook the stoic role of Australia's 22nd Brigade, whose 2/30th Battalion at Gemas on 14 January inflicted a tactical blow distinctly absent from the rest of the Malayan campaign. Ordered to 'stop' the enemy, as part of the wider fighting withdrawal from Muar, the battalion's commanding officer, Lieutenant Colonel Frederick 'Black Jack' Galleghan, commanded his men to set an ambush at a wooden bridge over the Sungei Gemencheh River. At 4 pm that day, as the Japanese crossed on bicycles, the Australians blew the bridge and turned their machine guns, rifles and grenades on the enemy. The initiative was short-lived: unable to call in artillery because the Japanese had broken their telephone lines, the Australians fought on for two bloody days before withdrawing, during which they inflicted several hundred Japanese casualties (not a thousand, as popularly claimed) and destroyed a few Japanese tanks, for the loss of 81 men.

It was a fleeting tactical victory. Yet if the action achieved little, it was not the fault of Captain Lionel Matthews, an Australian signaller, who ran into no-man's-land several times to reconnect broken communications lines, for which he would earn every shred of his Military Cross. (Matthews would later perform the same feat, 'laying a cable over ground strongly patrolled by the enemy and thus restoring communication' between his divisional headquarters and a brigade during the battle for Singapore.)

The stand at Gemas was but a straw in the wind. At Bakri, from 18 to 22 January, Lieutenant Colonel Charles Anderson, a South African-born Australian, earned the only Victoria Cross of the Malayan campaign. Anderson, commanding Australia's 2/19th Battalion, was ordered to halt the Japanese near Parit Sulong Village. Cut off deep inside enemy territory, without air or artillery support, Anderson repelled 'persistent attacks on his position from air and ground forces, and forced his way through the enemy lines to a depth of fifteen miles', his citation would state.[3] Suffering severe casualties, 'he personally led an attack with great gallantry on the enemy who were holding a bridge, and succeeded in destroying four guns . . . throughout all this fighting, [he] protected his wounded and refused to leave them'. Captured, Anderson and a few survivors were doomed to spend years on the Thai–Burma Railway; to his fury, the Japanese would massacre all the Australian wounded.

A great assortment of British forces engaged in the biggest and most sustained battles during the 'fighting withdrawal' (a noble euphemism, disguising what had become a hasty and disorganised Allied retreat) down the Malayan Peninsula: the 2nd Argyll and Sutherland Highlanders, 2nd Gordon Highlanders, regiments raised in Cambridgeshire, Norfolk, Suffolk, Bedfordshire and Hertfordshire, Lanarkshire, East Surrey, as well as anti-tank, anti-aircraft and artillery units. The measureless courage of a few failed to inhibit the onrush. Near the end, the Scots bore the brunt of combat – fighting, pulling back and regrouping to fight again – during which the Argylls were decimated. A handful of bloody survivors, led by their kilted pipers, staggered across the Causeway, the last troops over this 1100-yard sea bridge linking

Singapore island to Johore Peninsula, before the Royal Navy blew it up on the morning of 31 January.

And then there were the Indians. The heroic failure of several Indian units confounds later reports of wholesale cowardice and disloyalty. Denouncing their 'low morale' after the war,[4] the Australian commander Lieutenant General Gordon Bennett (Major General at the time of the fall) – himself in no position to condemn others – would spare the performance of the 11th Indian Division, who endured the hellish four-day battle of Kampar. None who lived through it would forget the performance of the Sikh units of the 6/15th Brigade, and the hair-raising war cries of 1/18th Punjab Regiment, who fell on the Japanese with bayonets fixed and eyes ablaze. Just 30 survived the carnage.

Against this, the Japanese proved an unstoppable force. Superbly led, jungle-trained, phenomenally brave and driven to the limits of endurance by Tokyo's craving for raw materials, the soldiers are easily the better and more experienced. Psychologically programmed to scorn death, they present the terrifying aspect of an army utterly indifferent to its own preservation, in accordance with the revitalised code of the samurai, the bushido, whose opening words, '. . . to die!' ring in the heads of thousands of screaming young men swarming up the beaches.[5] Indeed, they relish the prospect, in battle and captivity, of self-annihilation in the name of the Emperor.

◆

The last days of Singapore are a frenzy of blood and iron. The Australian war diarist, seemingly oblivious to his own coming doom, dutifully completes his chronicle: on 4 February, the civil authorities order 'all natives living within one mile of foreshores' to evacuate. The reason appears overhead, in a squadron of triumphant, low-flying Zeros, rolling and diving like flocks of playful birds, in complete control of the sky. A million terrified people are now crammed onto the little island.

That night, unmolested, the Zeros bomb the precincts of the Causeway. On 8 February, they strafe the town centre. Panic is open and everywhere, amid reports of Japanese landings on the island's north-west shore and manifestly *not* in the east, where Allied commanders had expected them. In fact, that day, one and a half divisions, some 30,000 Japanese troops, heave ashore directly in the sights of Australia's vastly outnumbered and thinly spread 22nd Brigade, who mount a desperate, if futile, resistance before being utterly overwhelmed, as the diarist glibly notes: '2330 . . . situation very confused . . . Penetration has occurred'.

The Australian forces are being 'pushed back', notes the 8th Division war diary. Their British comrades, occupying the same poorly fortified positions, are similarly routed – a direct consequence of British commander General Arthur Percival's refusal to build proper coastal defences. This eases the task of the Japanese shock troops, who fall on the shallow Allied defences in a screaming, seemingly limitless tide; they blow holes in the thinning lines and charge through, shooting or butchering the wan face of resistance.

The news resonates at the command centre in the city: the Allies' tactic of spreading the men thinly around the shores rather than concentrating them at likely landing points has failed. Percival anticipated an enemy force of at least five divisions, some 100,000 troops; in fact, the Japanese attack the island with just 30,000 strike troops and 35,000 in reserve, against total Allied forces of some 88,000. The latter include tens of thousands of dozy 'base wallahs' – staff and supporting units – who are more likely to raise a glass of crème de menthe than a rifle. By contrast, *all* Japanese personnel – the cooks, batmen, medics and drivers – double as combat troops.

At 4.30 am on 9 February, the situation rapidly deteriorates. 'Brigade disorganised and comm[unications] extremely difficult,' the Australian scribbles. 'HQ withdrawing . . . Situation in Brigade area not clear . . . unknown where actual front of brigade [is] situated . . .' At 8 am, the Western Area HQ moves its Operations Room to underground dugouts, and British and Australian troops fall back on the city. Lieutenant Tony White, an Australian officer, looks into the clear blue sky: nothing. 'In the last days it was rumoured the skies were going to be black with American planes,' he recalls.[6] Today, only the dismal sound of the oncoming Zeros can be heard.

The last charter plane, packed with startled civilians, leaves Singapore that day. That night, some 2000 Australians are reported to be holed up in the Anzac Club – a figure later found to be 'grossly exaggerated', the diarist notes. In truth, British and Australian morale has plummeted. Whole units crack, and their soldiers, unable to bear the shame of defeat and the horror of what awaits them, desert. Australian and British stragglers – most cut off from their units – wander the city's precincts in disbelief that it has come to this. '[T]hroughout Singapore,' writes another witness, 'small bands of British and Australian troops could be seen wandering aimlessly about, with a very dispirited demeanour'.[7]

◆

In the command bunker at Allied HQ Western Area, west of the town, General Archibald Wavell, commander-in-chief, Far East, General Percival, general officer commanding Malaya, and Lieutenant General Gordon Bennett, commander of Australia's 8th Division, confer.

Wavell, imperturbable, possessed of charm and intelligence, is sent to Singapore with failure howling in his head, after Rommel's forces chased the British out of Crete and Greece and destroyed their offensive in North Africa. Removed by Churchill after that debacle, Wavell arrives in Asia to confront another.

Percival cuts an ungainly figure in his baggy shorts, snub moustache and buck teeth, the epitome of the chinless Pom in the eyes of resentful Australians. In fact, he is a brave officer, the recipient of the Military Cross in the Great War, and a sound administrator. But he is not equipped for his present challenge. In Singapore, Percival's unpromising appearance, timid grip on command and indecisiveness fail to inspire his subordinates – and hasten the colony's doom.

Bennett, nominally Percival's most senior subordinate, is an insufferably proud Australian, decorated at Gallipoli, where he led 300 men in an attack south of Lone Pine, and Pozières, the worst Australian clash on the Western Front. Bennett is a front-line commander, prickly to the point of insubordination and utterly unsuited to working with his British superiors. He makes little effort to disguise his contempt for Percival, and their relationship is 'devoid of harmony'[8] – a serious mark against Bennett's attitude and any hope of smooth and decisive command in Singapore.

These are the men charged with leading the defence of the colony. In early February 1942, they deliberate inside a heavily fortified bunker beneath Japanese aerial bombardment. With every shuddering blow, the obvious outcome stares them in the face: surrender, or face obliteration. Outside the bunker, the casualties of the air attack are 'light', the 8th Division diarist wishfully writes. Inside, the British generals exhibit 'exemplary coolness', Bennett records.[9]

Wavell delivers the message he has been sent to convey: British and Australian forces must hold the island to the last man. '[O]ur whole fighting reputation is at stake and the honour of the British Empire,' he declares[10] – echoing Churchill's grim injunction, sent via a personal signal, that there must be 'no thought of saving the troops or sparing the population'. The battle for Singapore, Churchill insists, must be fought to the bitter end 'at all costs'. Britain's 18th Division 'has a chance to make its name in history. Commanders and senior officers should die with their troops . . . I rely on you to show no mercy or weakness in any form.'[11] Percival accepts the order; Bennett grumpily demurs.

◆

That night, Wavell dines with the governor Sir Shenton and Lady Daisy Thomas at Government House. Premonitions of the end obsess him; in his mind, British Singapore, this Gibraltar of the East, is a thing of the past. He sits 'thumping his knees with his fists' (as Sir Shenton observes in his diary), saying over and over, '"It should never have happened."'[12] But his work is done here – he has delivered his instructions, assessed the situation – and he prepares to leave Percival and his embattled men. His duty is elsewhere, in the vast amphitheatre of the Pacific, the defeat of which now threatens not only whole nations but also his very career. Lady Thomas, sick with dysentery, declines Wavell's invitation to accompany him to Java – a last, perfunctory act of chivalry. The general leaves Singapore after midnight.

On 10 February, British and Australian commanders order the destruction of the island's petrol reserves and all classified documents, while Allied units withdraw to the outskirts of the city. Australian units in the vicinity of the village of BT Panjang are ordered to hold the line. That night, a large Japanese force with tanks attacks the area. A British counter-offensive fails, or never occurs, as reported, and the Allies resume the withdrawal, 'in confusion after suffering heavy casualties'.[13]

The Australian diarist ends the day on a plaintive note: 'It appeared that there was little of our force on the road to stop any breakthrough by the enemy SOUTH . . . towards SINGAPORE.' The very breakthrough occurs that night. Australia's 2/29th Battalion becomes 'disintegrated': 'Bn HQ and one coy and stragglers move back to HALL ROAD.' The Japanese grab control of the food, petrol and supply dumps in the area, as the Allies retreat in a loose semicircle around the heart of town.

On the morning of 11 February, Japanese planes scatter leaflets signed by General Yamashita Tomoyuki calling on all British forces to surrender:

> [F]urther resistance would not only serve to inflict direct harms [*sic*] and injuries to thousands of non-combatants living in the city, throwing them into further miseries and horrors of war, but also would not add anything to the honour of your Army and result in annihilation of the city and civilians.[14]

If the Allies continue to resist, 'I shall be obliged though reluctantly from humanitarian considerations to order my army to make annihilating attacks on Singapore'.

Countless Chinese towns can attest to the seriousness of the threat; Nanking offers the apotheosis. The Allied forces converge on the racecourse and the city's precincts. Incidents of lawlessness and looting erupt in the city; small groups of soldiers are found 'searching the waterfront for some means of escape'.[15] That day, British military police block at least two attempts by drunken troops to rush the last ships, designated for white women, children and nurses. Discipline severely lapses, as drunk and nerve-racked troops undermine the stoic example of most soldiers, no less anxious and exhausted.

The most potent symbol of the colony's end is the destruction of its financial reserves. The sight of Captain Hartley James Walker towing out to sea and throwing overboard the banks' bullion coinage astonishes the local people.[16] Walker casts a stern eye on those who attempt to board the ship. Elsewhere, he sees cowardice and defeatism at the highest levels: officers at the Union Jack Club – 'hopeless cases' – are heard whining, 'They gave them a chance at Dunkirk and Greece and Crete! What about us!'[17] It is too late to evacuate the remaining civilians, who nervously await the invader in the churches and clubs, their grand old homes and the ballroom and lobby of the Raffles Hotel. Hundreds sing hymns in the beautiful cathedral and pray. God is their only weapon left.

◆

There follows an atrocity committed by the invading Japanese that bears out the Allies' worst reports of the enemy's incomprehensible cruelty. On 13 February, Japanese advance troops strike along the Pasir Panjang Ridge west of town. They penetrate Alexandra, where a military hospital contains 900 sick and wounded patients.

At 2 pm, they cut the water supply to the city; the reservoirs promise just a few days' flow. 'There are now one million people within radius of three miles,' Governor Thomas cables London. 'Many dead lying in the streets and burial impossible. We are faced with total deprivation of water, which must result in pestilence . . .'[18]

On 14 February, at 1.40 p.m., the first Japanese troops enter the hospital, where a British female officer presents them with a white flag. They reply by bayoneting her, burst into the main hospital and proceed to slaughter the medical staff and patients. According to one witness, '[The Japanese] ran amok on the ground floor. They were very excitable and jumpy; neither pointing to the RED CROSS brassard nor shouting the word HOSPITAL had any effect.'[19] In the operating theatre, they run through five doctors and nurses with their swords, as well as an anaesthetised corporal on the operating table.[20] Hundreds are herded into tiny cells in a nearby industrial site and left there overnight, where many die of heat or thirst; the survivors are bayoneted the next day. Over two days of inexplicable slaughter, the Japanese forces massacre 320 staff and patients at Alexandra Hospital.

◆

At that hour, Percival confers with senior officers at Fort Canning. All are 'unanimous' that further resistance is 'hopeless',[21] writes Bennett, and the question arises: are we to fight to the death? In deference to his orders, Percival favours continued resistance – at least until his men can resist no more. The Australian officers disagree: 'did Singapore still have a strategic value to justify the sacrifice of 720,000 civilians?' Brigadier Jim Thyer, general staff officer commanding the 8th Australian Division, later writes.[22] Bennett, similarly, believes surrender is inevitable and escape a senior officer's duty.

The next day, Percival orders the artillery to fire only on 'observed targets' due to an acute shortage of Allied shells. 'There was practically no ammunition left,' Lieutenant Colonel Charles Kappe, commanding the Australian 8th Division Signals, later writes while a prisoner in Changi.[23] The water reserves are almost drained, with at best 48 hours' supply. Yet still Percival vows to fight on – for as long as the water lasts. Bennett, however, has made up his mind. Without informing his British counterpart, he cables Australia's prime minister John Curtin that he intends to surrender to avoid further, needless loss of life.[24] The message enrages Percival when he later hears of it.

On 15 February, at 11 am, brandishing a telegram from Wavell, Percival summons his senior commanders for their last conference as free men. The telegram qualifies Churchill's Armageddon strategy. 'So long,' Wavell writes, 'as you are in a position to inflict losses and damage to [the] enemy and your troops are physically capable of doing so you must fight on . . . When you are fully satisfied that this is no longer possible I give you discretion to cease resistance.'[25] The exhaustion of the men and the lack of water and ammunition make up Percival's mind. 'Unable therefore [to] continue the fight any longer,' he replies. 'All ranks have done their best and grateful for your help.'[26]

◆

The Japanese celebrate the Allied surrender with shouts of *'Banzai!'* and a clatter of swords. The world, too, must share in the British humiliation, see and feel it, their commanders decide. The abjection of the white man must be milked for all it's worth, insists General Yamashita Tomoyuki, the big, bullet-headed commander of the Japanese armies in Johore. Revelling in his nickname, the 'Tiger of Malaya', Yamashita orders the British commanders to prostrate themselves before him.

And so, a little after 4 pm, Percival and his staff, bearing a Union Jack and the white flag of truce drive north along the Bukit Timah road to the Japanese lines, whereupon they begin the walk of infamy to Yamashita's headquarters. Photographs of this terrible procession are broadcast around the world. At the same time, the Rising Sun flag appears over the Cathay Pacific Building, Singapore's tallest. The British commanders enter the Ford Automobile company, where Yamashita sits at his desk and lays down the terms of unconditional surrender.

Ignoring the thudding demands for his signature, Percival quietly peruses the surrender document and dares to request a ceasefire instead of a surrender; he asks as well that 1000 British troops be allowed to maintain order in the town and protect civilians. Yamashita ignores him, to which Percival replies that the Japanese commander must accept full responsibility for the lives of the troops and civilians remaining in Singapore. To such impertinence, Yamashita bangs his fist and declares that 'Bushido would look after these things'.[27] (In the event, Yamashita, while still in charge, restrains the Guards division of the Imperial Army from entering the city centre; and yet, had Percival not surrendered – as Yamashita later admits – the Japanese Army would have razed the town and subjected half a million citizens to the treatment of Nanking.)[28] The Allies are committed to the unconditional surrender of Singapore.

The Australian war diary concludes with the pitiable realisation: 'Captured enemy maps [show] all our dispositions and HQs.' In short, the Japanese know everything – the fruit of busy, local fifth-columnists. Later that night, the Australian 8th Division makes a crueller discovery. Bennett, their commander, is missing, apparently absent without leave: 'General Gordon Bennett was not seen at HQ after this hour.'[29]

Vowing never to be caught, Bennett flees with two subordinates, Major Charles Moses and Lieutenant Gordon Walker. Their exit is distinctly unedifying: having burnt their papers, downed last drinks with a few Gordon Highlanders, who share the Australians' loathing of the English, Bennett and his staff commandeer a Chinese sampan and pitch into the sea. A witness later describes the ensuing fiasco, of Bennett screaming 'like a young girl' as pandemonium erupts on the crowded vessel.[30] That night, while the crew argue over the best route to Sumatra, the sampan crashes into a series of exposed fishing stakes. Despite these mishaps, the three Australian officers eventually get home. Their flight later attaches ignominy to the Australian commander's name, which his fussy, self-serving memoir does little to dispel.

For his part, Percival is sent to Changi, to spend years in a Japanese prisoner-of-war camp, unable to defend himself from the charges, *in absentia*, of responsibility for the disgrace. He provides, sadly, a perfect scapegoat for the failures of Whitehall.

The general ceasefire takes effect at 8.30 that night, with the surrender of all arms and ammunition. The Japanese troops, delirious on the shoreline, fling their arms in the air and continue their interminable '*Banzai*'s. The ferocity, speed and strategic brilliance of Yamashita's descent on Singapore has stunned the Allies, who were assuredly 'outwitted, outgeneralled and outfought', in the devastating summary of Wavell's chief of staff, Sir Henry Pownall.[31] Not since the defeat of Russia in 1905 has Japan inflicted so humiliating a punishment on a foreign foe; not since their invasion of Manchuria has Nippon devoured so much territory in one fell swoop. And not only the Johore Peninsula – a month earlier Japanese forces digested all of Borneo, the nuggety island to the south-east, along with its great tin mines, rubber plantations and oilfields, which are set to fuel the southerly advance of Japan's 'Greater East Asian Co-Prosperity Sphere'.

The Allied troops – British, Australian, Indian, Dutch – are at once furious and coldly defiant. Many were willing to give their lives for Singapore, the last citadel in the defence of New Guinea and Australia; many feel betrayed by their commanders, and betrayers of the people they were sent here to defend. In reality, they have been abandoned, their actions bold if futile gestures in the gale of the Japanese onslaught, their flesh and blood the price of others' mistakes. Of the 88,000 soldiers at Percival's disposal, many are reinforcements, bright-eyed volunteers rushed up from Australia weeks before the capitulation. Some 15,000 are British and Australian support staff, who rarely left the palm-fringed comfort of the Singapore Turf Club and the dazzling whiteness of Raffles, from whose grand ballroom the strains of 'There'll Always Be an England' die forever. Still thousands more lie sick, wounded and weapon-less in the island's hospitals.

Of all the melancholy reasons advanced for the fall of Singapore – Japan's combat strength; Percival's inadequate defences; the island's south-pointing guns (a false legend); the colony's 'Dollar Arsenal', which valued commerce (rubber, tin) over military efficiency; the failure of 'the Indians' (Bennett's personal bête noire); Japan's monopoly of tanks; the 'betrayal' by High Command; or sheer Anglo-Saxon/Celtic laziness and unreadiness – by far the most persuasive is the lack of Allied aircraft. The absence of fighters and heavy bombers, then needed in Europe, freed the Japanese Zeros to sink Churchill's finest symbols of resistance, the battleships *Repulse* and *Prince of Wales*, and to lacerate Allied troop entrenchment and retreating columns unhindered by the Spitfires that Whitehall promised but failed to deliver. The effect of Japanese air supremacy was 'tremendous', Bennett will tell a meeting with the Australian prime minister and chiefs of staff on 2 March 1942. The unchallenged Zeros pulverised the island's defences and severely damaged civilian morale. 'The Japanese won the campaign with bicycles,' Bennett avers. 'They had no artillery,' he concludes – a devastating, if self-serving, verdict.[32]

And there are the less tangible 'human' factors: the mutual loathing of Percival and Bennett, who 'disagreed about almost everything';[33] the ill-adjusted relationships between the Australians and British, Gurkhas and Indians; and what Bennett describes as the 'retreat complex', surely an own goal. '[L]eaders allowed their fatigue to be communicated to their men,' he reports, 'units withdrew without a fight, frequently without orders, and sometimes in the face of imaginary threats. Many senior officers regarded retreat as inevitable.'[34]

Allied commanders are less inclined to acknowledge the

success of the Japanese and the extraordinary generalship of Yamashita, commander of the Imperial 25th Army. The Tiger of Malaya conquered 685 miles of the Malayan Peninsula in just 70 days; his detractors warned it would take one and a half years. For this achievement, his Tokyo superiors forgive Yamashita's rebellious and somewhat eccentric methods. He treats prisoners, for example, relatively humanely; he sends gifts to the governor and to British women and children; and he punishes any troops who loot and rape. Bemoaning the lack of moral fibre in the Japanese forces, he later remarks in his diary, 'I regret that staff officers have no sense of propriety.'[35] And yet, Tokyo sees his comparative restraint (which failed, shockingly, at Alexandra Hospital) as a weakness, and within six months Yamashita will be redeployed to Manchuria, a sign of Tokyo's displeasure at his lenience.

With the capture of Singapore, Japan's strategic offensive radiates throughout the Pacific along three axes: one speeds north to Rangoon and consolidates the Japanese grip on Burma; a second drives hard against Java and Sumatra and reinforces Borneo – the great oil-breathing island; and a third continues further south to Rabaul, the Solomon Islands, New Guinea – and the very edge of Australia.[36] Singapore is the strategic wheel on which this vast military apparatus turns, and the 130,000 Anglo-Saxon, Chinese and Indian prisoners held here are to provide a great pool of slave labour for the Empire of the Sun.

2

THE BOAT

Down it would come, lowered from above, a cut-down steel
barrel full of . . . putrid, sour, sticky, lime-green rice!
Private Billy Young recalls feeding time
aboard the hell ship to Sandakan

[E]very dog has his day and I do hope it's not long
before [the Japanese] will be praying for mercy . . .
Private Tom Burns, after the experience at sea

THE DAY AFTER THE FALL, thousands of Japanese troops
march through the streets of Singapore shouting 'Banzai' and
'Long live the Emperor', to appalled English ears. The Rising
Sun flutters over the city and the Union Jack lies in shreds as the
occupying forces transform Singapore into a Japanese colony.
Yen replaces the local currency; the streets, shops and hotels are
renamed; all inward and outward trade seized and controlled;
farmlands and local manufacturing operations appropriated.

Some 50,000 British, Australian and Indian troops are
rounded up and marched off to prison. Most of the Indians are

taken to camps west of the island, and the British and Australians to Changi, a military base built by the British, 17 miles east. White civilians soon join them. The captured soldiers walk through the streets in shock and yet defiant, singing and joking and dressed in a motley array of torn and ragged fatigues, mufti and headgear – caps, pork-pie hats, toupees and the occasional turban – keen to impress upon the Japanese and frightened local witnesses a sense of careless defiance.

As the foreigners leave, the Chinese and Malays wait in huddled terror. The Chinese well know the fate of their countrymen and women in Nanking, Shanghai and Manchuria. Their worst fears are soon realised. Within days, agents of the secret police, the Kempei-tai – a name that will forever desecrate the annals of human history – arrive to subject Singapore's Chinese community to a policy of 'purification by elimination', starting with the interrogation and slaughter of communists, collaborators and other perceived subversives. Yamashita imposes a three-day limit on routine arrests and executions. On its expiry, his director of operations, Colonel Tsuji Masunobu, nicknamed 'The Wolf', casts aside his commanding officer's restraint in sparing the rest of the Chinese male population. Tsuji amply lives up to his moniker, later chiding fellow officers in Burma for refusing to share his dinner – the liver of a dead Allied pilot[1] – and embarks on the wholesale massacre of Chinese males aged between 15 and 50. In the coming months, more than 70,000 Chinese Singaporean civilians will be incarcerated and enslaved, and 6000–10,000 executed. Australian and British prisoners, consigned to gravedigging parties, are burying the Chinese dead well into March 1942.

◆

While the Japanese treat the Singaporean Chinese with routine brutality, their approach to their Anglo-Saxon captives is initially confused. This relationship is new, untested; the master–subordinate assumption has been turned upside down. The clash of military cultures creates bizarre and unpredictable reactions. At one extreme, many, better-educated Japanese – senior officers such as Yamashita – jealously admire the British Empire and its economic and industrial achievements, are conscious of international protocols on the treatment of prisoners and urge their men to observe restraint. At the other extreme, fiery junior officers and non-commissioned men, anxious to impress their superiors, display a vindictive and puerile hatred for the white man, manifesting itself in sudden, extreme violence – the source of which seems to be a mixture of indoctrination, poor education and an ingrained sense of inferiority.

Older Japanese soldiers remember the incarceration of Russian prisoners in the war of 1904–05, and Germans in the Great War in 1916 – who were in fact dealt with humanely, in a manner befitting the rules of war.[2] But the modern Japanese regime is different. For one thing, younger Japanese troops have no precedent for dealing with white prisoners, tens of thousands of whom have fallen into their hands for the first time. These young men behave in the sway of a reinterpretation of the Samurai tradition of self-sacrifice. Its modern incarnation is a bastardised version of the original text, glorifying death for its own sake and condemning as unfit to live any Japanese soldier who fails to destroy himself in captivity. The Japanese regime extends this culture of death to the enemy and inculcates in its young firebrands the maxim that *any* prisoner should honourably destroy himself in the Samurai way. A man who fails to do so hardly deserves respect as a soldier.

Indeed, the junior Japanese officers find something especially abhorrent in the *sight* of British and Australians cheerfully trying to adapt to captivity. The Western instinct to live, the simple, overwhelming urge to *go home*, are incomprehensible to Japanese troops raised on a bogus philosophy of death, for whom the worst kind of shame attaches to being captured. Were the positions reversed, Japanese prisoners who failed to kill themselves would return home in disgrace. And so a new-found contempt insinuates itself into the heads of these simple, 'born-again' Samurai – brutish, insensible young men, easy prey for Tokyo's banal propaganda, who metamorphose into warriors on the receipt of their first sword. In time, Japanese soldiers – and, by extension, their Formosan and Korean underlings – will come to see the prisoners as loathsome curiosities, deserving of no more consideration than a beast of burden.

◆

Official policy towards the prisoners has not yet drawn on this well of hatred, and the conditions at Changi are initially tolerable. The Japanese look askance at the proceedings inside the camp. 'When we were marched out to Changi we hadn't seen a Jap. Nobody guarded us. The Japs said, "You administer yourselves,"' recalls Lieutenant Russ Ewin.[3] The white prisoners are rather surprised to find themselves living unguarded – at first – in spacious British-built barracks, houses and drill grounds covering 30 square miles set in lush tropical gardens and bounded on three sides by the sea. Some 14,860 Australians occupy Selarang Barracks; 37,000 British and other nationalities are sent further east to Roberts, India and Kitchener Barracks. The echoes of colonial grandeur may ring hollow here, but the prison camp is indeed a pleasant surprise. The prisoners are allowed to wander about, chat, sing and smoke. Their quarters are big and airy. The food – at first a kind of sloppy, rice-based bilge – greatly improves as the prisoner–cooks grasp the rudiments of cooking rice and vegetables.

And yet, in those first few weeks, morale and discipline lapses in circumstances where thousands of disgruntled troops hold the commanders, rightly or wrongly, to blame for an acute sense of having disgraced themselves and their units. In the early stages of captivity, many soldiers see no point in upholding the army's strict hierarchy and deeply resent junior officers who attempt to reimpose discipline – including the salute. For their part, the officers, sensing the psychological levelling effect of wholesale capture, are anxious not to let military order dissolve. The rift between the officers and other ranks – particularly in the British Army – deepens, which the preferential treatment the Japanese extend to the officers does little to heal.

The prisoners nonetheless adopt a kind of self-imposed order. The shock and fury of defeat yields to a cautious awareness of their strange new circumstances, and an eerie state of limbo ensues, during which the prisoners' thoughts oscillate between the hope of rescue, the possibility of escape, the likelihood of a long incarceration and the fear of brutal reprisals.

In town, volunteer clean-up parties witness the mediaeval handiwork of the Japanese: weeks after the surrender, Chinese and Malayan civilians continue to be rounded up, tortured, imprisoned and executed. Their headless bodies are put on display and the heads impaled on pikes throughout the town as a warning to anyone opposing the new regime. Chinese suspected of having resisted the Japanese during the final battles are lined up on the beaches and 'machine-gunned by the hundreds', according to an Australian report in 1944.[4]

◆

In the early months, the Japanese dragoon the prisoners into working parties to rebuild Singapore. They must construct roads, bridges, homes – and even erect a large monument to the Japanese war dead. The prisoners' enslavement is a flagrant breach of the spirit, and letter, of the Third Geneva Convention on the treatment of prisoners of war (1929); Japan, however, has conveniently refused to sign the relevant protocol. In any case, the humanity of the treaty's intent has little traction on minds that bend only to written diktat from Tokyo.

The prisoners swiftly adapt to their circumstances in Changi. The officers organise work parties and strive to maintain order and discipline. An immediate priority is digging deeper ditches covered in thunder boxes to control disease-bearing flies that gather in clouds around the shallow latrines. They hurriedly plant vegetable gardens, in response to Japanese orders, as they're told the food supply is likely to run out within six weeks. They set up a camp 'university' that offers a wide range of courses, from agriculture, cooking and bricklaying to philosophy, literature and law – using textbooks the former British occupants left behind. By April/May, the camp cooks are turning out tolerable meals of rice, vegetables and occasionally fish, Anglican and Catholic chapels are built, and an arts and crafts show organised. In time, the prisoners stage plays and musicals, and procure rugby and Aussie Rules balls, cricket bats, tennis racquets and boxing gloves.

In the first half of 1942, the invaders, flush with victory, treat the prisoners of war relatively well. No doubt, the Japanese guards bash 'scroungers' and anyone suspected of 'going slow' on working parties. But the prisoners' entertainments, musicals, sporting events and even gambling operations flourish; in fact, British and Australian officers seek to stamp out gambling with greater thoroughness than the Japanese. They fail. The Changi Frog Races are hugely popular. And while their food is poor – the camp gardens nonetheless yield spinach, soya beans and other vegetables – Changi is not nearly as dreadful as most other prison camps in the Japanese Empire.

Indeed, Gunner Owen Campbell of the 2/10th Field Regiment praises the conditions, at least in the first six months:

> Lived in halls. Stalls and shops. Had sheets and nets. Good conditions. Did own cooking. Showers and plenty of water. No soap. Latrines – municipal pan service – twice daily. As much rice as wanted and vegetables. Very little meat. Flour available. Stole a lot of tinned food from dumps on which we worked. Best rations of PW's army life. Excellent canteen. Could buy anything including bottled beer.

The guards are 'well behaved' and their treatment of the prisoners, 'good. Hardly knew they were there.'[5] Church services and concerts (twice weekly) are permitted, as well as sporting activities, chiefly boxing.

Indeed, the popular image of Changi as a hellhole of hideous suffering is misplaced: the guards are generally lenient and the conditions exceptional, when compared with the horror that soon descends on prisoners sent elsewhere. In fact, the Japanese guards even play football with the Australians and British, and attend boxing matches, as Gunner Eric Cooper of the Victorian 4th Anti-Tank Regiment recounts. 'A keen sportsman', the Japanese camp commandant would attend POW boxing matches bearing gifts:

> His aides carried baskets laden with all sorts of wonderful 'trophies' – pineapples, bananas, canned foods, soft drinks, cigarettes and even bottles of cold Tiger beer. He took great pride in presenting these awards at the end of each bout, not only to the winner but to the loser as well.

Basketball was also popular at Changi, as one prisoner remembers:

> By today's standards, our team was not all that tall but some had good experience with Australian rules football, so the ball was kept in the air, where we could outmark the Japs. When it was over, we sat down on a grassy patch adjoining the court and the Japs put on buckets of tea . . . and handed around cigarettes.

Professor Kevin Blackburn, a historian at Nanyang Technological University in Singapore, records many similar stories in his history, *The Sportsmen of Changi*:

> Even POWs themselves say Changi was like heaven compared with elsewhere. Some 87,000 POWs went through Changi – only 809 died. Actually, you have got a very low death rate. It's sort of like a myth that Changi was a hellhole.[6]

One severe deficiency, however, is medical care. The Japanese supply neither medicines nor clothing and appropriate the most valuable foreign aid donations for themselves; later that year, Japanese personnel are seen wearing Red Cross boots and clothing meant for the prisoners. The lack of proper medicines produces tropical conditions such as 'Changi balls', a severe scrotal itch, and 'happy feet', shooting pains in the feet caused by vitamin deficiency. Dysentery is widespread, and beriberi and malaria will later become common. In neglecting medical care, the Japanese forces defy even Tokyo's interpretation of the 1929 Geneva Convention, which they refuse to ratify but whose spirit they apparently agree to honour, as outlined in a telegram from Japan to the Allies on 29 January 1942. The cable notes:

> The Imperial Government has not ratified the agreement concerning the treatment of prisoners of war dated 27 July 1929, and therefore, it would not be bound to any extent by the said agreement, but would apply 'mutatis mutandis' [the necessary changes] of the said agreement toward the British, Canadian, Australian and New Zealand prisoners of war under Japanese control.[7]

This leaves wide open the interpretation of 'necessary': by their actions, the Japanese clearly regard medicines and adequate clothing as 'unnecessary'.

The prisoners are allowed to send a card or two home – invariably a few stock phrases, written in child-like capitals by a dictation-taker, such as: 'I AM A PRISONER OF WAR. I AM FIT AND WELL. LOVE TO YOU AND THE CHILDREN' (as Albert Anderson wrote to his wife, Dot). Ray Carlson and John Barnier inform their families, 'I WAS NOT WOUNDED.

I AM WELL.'[8] Similarly, Russ Ewin, on 20 June: 'WE ARE
WELL CARED FOR AND I AM QUITE HAPPY.'[9] The letters
might arrive months, sometimes years later, and prisoners may
neither send nor receive parcels. British and Australian families,
immensely relieved to find their sons, brothers or husbands alive,
will attempt to reply, or send food and other items, unaware that
the Japanese destroy or confiscate the lot.

◆

These comparatively benign circumstances are about to change
dramatically. The extremities of the Japanese Empire have a great
need of slave labour, to strip the conquered territories of raw
materials, build airfields and ports, and cement the Empire's grip
on the Western Pacific in the face of the expected Allied counter-
offensive. Airfields are particularly coveted, as control of the air
will determine victory in the Pacific.

The supply of Chinese 'coolies' is not enough to meet these
requirements. The Japanese need more men, and they have few
compunctions about enslaving their white prisoners, in Changi,
which serves as a vast new source of labour. In May 1942, some
3000 Australians (named 'A Force') and similar numbers of
British and Dutch and Indians are selected for work in an
unidentified northern location, said to offer better conditions and
plentiful food. These unfortunate men shortly find themselves in
Japanese-occupied South Burma, building an airfield; and, later,
slogging and dying at a huge rate on the Thai–Burma Railway,
the completion of which is expected to deliver reinforcements
and supplies to the Japanese forces in China. In prosecuting this
impossible task, the Japanese guards will intentionally work the

prisoners to death: at least 16,000 Allied soldiers (26 per cent of the total enslaved) and 90,000 Asian civilians (50 per cent) will perish on the Thai–Burma Railway, of disease, starvation, murder and exhaustion.

Prisoners selected from among the volunteers for another work detachment – designated 'B Force' – are similarly in the dark about their destination. In July, rumours suggest British North Borneo and its capital, Sandakan. Few know where this is, or what they will be doing there, but many men are eager to exchange Changi for a location that, their Japanese guards assure them, offers better food and conditions. Talk of lush southern climes closer to Australia convince many to join B Force, which is drawn mostly from the three infantry battalions of Australia's 22nd Brigade, and 'bits and pieces of practically every AIF unit in Malaya'.[10] Their commanding officer, Lieutenant Colonel Arthur Walsh, of the 2/10th Field Regiment – an unpopular man and a stickler for discipline – will shortly earn the men's respect in the most testing of circumstances.

The men of B Force look forward to leaving Singapore, the wretched symbol of their defeat and humiliation. They are unaware of their relative comfort, as conditions deteriorate and medical supplies grow scarce. 'A big outbreak of dysentery' sweeps through the camp in the week before their departure, Private Tom Burns, a 33-year-old storeman from Queensland, writes in his secret diary. 'It is all over in the Pommies camp; they are dying at the rate of five men per day. There are about 300 buried in Changi cemetery in such a short time.'[11] This spurs more to volunteer for B Force.

To limit numbers, the Japanese order Australian medical officers to select the 1500 or so fittest soldiers in the days before departure. One, Captain Rod Jeffrey, looks forward to 'a pleasant voyage' and hopes 'to see us all back in Aussie in the near future'. An unnamed brigadier offers a grim-spirited 'good luck'. 'I think,' Burns writes, 'he had an idea where we were going and said it would be the last time he would see us.'

◆

At 3 am on 8 July 1942, the 1494 men of B Force (145 officers, 312 non-commissioned officers and 1037 enlisted men) assemble on Changi parade ground together with their few belongings – a blanket, razor, mess tin, groundsheet, perhaps a second shirt or kitbag. After a breakfast of rice porridge with milk, sugar and half a slice of bread, they move off to the waiting trucks. The convoy rumbles through town, past the rotting heads of murdered Chinese civilians impaled on pikes on the sides of the road – often, at dusk in the city's parks, Japanese troops may be seen playing soccer with Chinese skulls[12] – and down to Keppel Harbour.

These gruesome scenes are among the soldiers' last memories of Singapore as they board the *Yubi Maru*, a 3300-ton iron tramp steamer (sometimes confused with the *Ume Maru*). Machine guns cover the long line of men coming aboard. All 1500 are herded onto the deck, where they sit until dusk. As the ship prepares to sail, crowds of Chinese line the shore with 'a sorrowful look on their faces to see us leaving Singapore', Burns writes.[13] That night, the *Yubi Maru* releases its ties and pulls away from the wharves into submarine-infested seas; the men are sent below.

The vessel never lives up to its designation as a 'cargo-passenger ship'. To the soldiers, it answers, in every degree imaginable, to the name 'hell ship'. For Private Burns, it resembles 'one of those pictures from the slave ship days . . . nothing can compare with this dreadful boat. I am sure there will be a lot of sickness before the voyage is over.'

There are three holds – forward (for the artillery units), aft (infantry) and amidships (medical and support units) – entered via steel hatches on the main deck and down steep wooden stairways or steel ladders. Below, the holds are split into two iron 'sleeping' decks. Crammed inside, roasting in the equatorial heat, each man is allocated a rectangle of straw-covered iron measuring five feet six inches by one foot six inches. The straw throws up dust into the foul air.

There are no portholes, or ventilation, just a few air shafts. Later in the voyage, with some men on the verge of death, a canvas chute is inserted to carry air to the lower hold, 'if the ship is moving'. The officers are better served. 'I slept on top of rice bags,' recalls Lieutenant Tony White.[14] The Japanese guards allow two scheduled visits per day to the main deck, which Australian officers, anxious not to provoke them, stiffly enforce.

They sail east through long nights of stifling heat and fetid air, their prospects as ominous as the grey swell. The prisoners are fed twice a day, on weevilly rice, recalls Lieutenant White, and on a watery stew 'containing a few shreds of what looked like grass and a smell of meat', cooked in huge cauldrons on the upper deck and lowered into the holds.[15] 'Down it would come,' remembers Private Billy Young, of the 2/29th Battalion, 'lowered from above, a cut-down steel barrel full of . . . putrid, sour, sticky, lime-green rice!'[16] Lieutenant Rod Wells later recalls, 'They merely put boiled water into this rice and boiled the lot and as a result it could hardly be eaten. We were hungry all the time . . .'[17]

Water is severely rationed, at 1.5 litres per man per day. There is no salt. A daily allowance of lukewarm brown liquid, described as tea, does nothing to replenish body salts lost in the sweltering atmosphere. At night, it is impossible to reach the toilets – wooden planks suspended over the water on either side – without stepping on prostrate bodies, usually eliciting a punch or kick. In any case, many of the troops, now sick with dysentery, are unable to rise to go to the toilet, and the hold is soon awash in human waste.

◆

The memory will never leave those who experience this 11-day voyage: the long, rolling nights in the darkened belly, a playground for rats; the intolerable stench and oven-like atmosphere; and the sound of the sick. 'My God this is dreadful . . . We are all just lost soldiers,' writes Private Burns.[18] Beatings are common, often on a whim. Burns witnesses one man screaming in pain as the Japanese laugh, but 'every dog has his day and I do hope it's not long before [they] will be praying for mercy'. The brief visits to the deck – where the sick are laid under steam-driven machinery to benefit from the drops of condensation[19] – provide fresh air and sunshine, and the sight of blue sea and silver flying fish. Below deck, card games, stories and the odd song eat up the time and lift morale in men determined to deny Japanese efforts to break them.

On the third or fourth night, a submarine alert terrifies the Japanese guards, who 'started banging on the roof above us', Lieutenant White recalls. He adds, 'The Japs were very nervous about American submarines.'[20] In a few days, the boat reaches the west coast of Borneo and stops at Miri, the oil depot in Sarawak, to refuel. It stays for two nights, during which the prisoners are forced to remain below while the Japanese go ashore to relax and to purchase supplies, chiefly tropical fruit.

On a brief visit to the deck, at least two Australian soldiers – Billy Young and Joey Crome – contemplate jumping in and swimming for it, but the sight of sharks, drawn to the swill thrown overboard and clinging to the hull, restrains them. Landfall nonetheless raises their spirits. The sick lift their heads from the straw mats, and the sound of singing wafts across the water. Remarkably, no one has yet died of illness – but many are only a couple of days away from death, Bombardier Richard Braithwaite later recalls.[21]

The ship sails north. The few bored guards stand listlessly about. Their inattention tempts some prisoners to rise en masse and overwhelm their captors. Australian officers frown on the idea – and the sight of a Japanese submarine scotches any further talk of seizing the ship. They steam along the island's west coast, past Jesselton (now Kota Kinabalu), the British colonial outpost, renamed Api by the Japanese in a nod towards native history. In the distance, Mount Kinabalu, the highest in Malaya, rises 13,000 feet to a needlepoint shrouded in mist. The surrounding tribes live in the shadow of this sacred peak, chiefly in the jungle-clad foothills near the town of Ranau, on the mountain's eastern flank, invisible from the sea.

Today is Lieutenant White's 22nd birthday. 'I felt aggrieved,' he writes, 'as we passed that massive peak.'

The ship steams on, hugs the coastline around the Balabac Straits – to avoid detection by American submarines – rounds the tip and turns south towards Sandakan, former capital of British North Borneo, now in Japanese hands.

◆

At dawn on 18 July, the ship passes the red chalk cliffs of Berhala
Island – home of a leper colony established under the British, now
also an internment camp for civilians – and enters the harbour of
Sandakan. 'We landed at last and God I am so pleased that trip is
over,' writes young Burns when he glimpses the 'very picturesque'
bay, where Japanese and Malayan vessels rock inoffensively at
anchor near the wooden pylons of Government Wharf.[22] 'It
looked really beautiful,' Richard Braithwaite later recalls. 'It was
green and planned . . . the little islands with palm trees on . . .
and I'm thinking to myself, this is pretty good, and we noticed
some white women in some houses up the back as we were being
disembarked and they waved to us and I thought, oh well, things
can't be too bad here.'[23]

On either side of the pier runs a stone sea wall lined with low-
slung, red-roofed buildings, ending on the left in a beach. Palm-
thatched native huts are perched on bamboo stilts in the sandy
grey shallows. On the green hills above the town stand the two-
storey homes of wealthy Europeans, now the residences and
offices of Japanese officials and the local Kempei-tai. Over everything flies the conqueror's red-orbed standard, announcing the
new power in the land.

In the centre of town, a green common – or padang – runs to
the sea wall. The prisoners assemble here as they disembark. As
they step off the gangplank, their feet and legs are sprayed with a
carbolic-acid solution, supposedly to control dysentery. The artillery and support troops are the first to leave the ship; the infantry remain on board for another night and sing away the hours,
accompanied by a major on an accordion.[24]

The sight of hundreds of dirty, unshaven white men filing into
town evokes uneasy feelings in the crowds of curious Malayans

and Chinese. Many do as they're told and taunt the prisoners by waving Japanese flags. Some believe in it; others do so to avoid Japanese suspicion. Braver Chinese, and sympathetic Malayans and Europeans, do nothing: they just watch, quietly, the line of prisoners disembarking – an act of self-condemnation in the eyes of their new masters, for whom silence and inaction are themselves forms of resistance.

3

BRITISH NORTH BORNEO

*The natives of Borneo are in a certain sense savages, but they are
savages of a high order, possessed of a civilization far above what is
usually implied by the term . . . One of their gravest faults, however,
is their embarrassing tenacity to the* fad *of head-hunting . . .*

William Furness, American scientist, *Folk-Lore in Borneo*

IN LATE 1941 – in the months leading up to the fall of Singapore
– Sandakan was a scene of listless colonial peace, of prettified
bungalows, Englishmen in whites on the padang and well-dressed
ladies at card or garden parties. Some 17,000 people occupied
the capital of British North Borneo in the early 1940s, of whom
a few thousand were British or 'European'. Their leisure time
revolved around the Sandakan Recreation Club and the Sandakan
Turf Club, the oldest in Borneo. The indefatigable Social Sub-
Committee excelled at tea parties, dances and debates ('That This
House Would Welcome the Taxation of Bachelors' was one of the
more daring subjects of debate in July 1941). Tennis matches, ideally
between single and married doubles partners, were a local favourite;
so, too, were football, cricket and horse racing. It was all done in
the lap of tropical luxury; and forever at the pooh-bahs' service were
their 'boys', or coolies, usually of Malay or Chinese origin.

England was never far away. *The British North Borneo Herald* advertised delightful echoes of home: Bovril, Nestlé Powdered Milk and Allsopp's beer, 'The Drink of Good Taste'. And if any white man or woman lapsed in asserting his or her superior status in the 'Far East', the *Herald*'s pages offered bracing reminders. 'For Your Servants' Quarters, For Your Coolie Lines,' runs one typical ad on 1 May 1941, 'Use Coconut Oil Lamps . . .'; or this, aimed at white wives: 'Do you find that . . . managing your servants is a strain? Do you find that entertaining has become an intolerable drudge? If so . . . you are very much in need of a tonic. Start taking Wincarnis at once – a wineglassful once or twice a day . . . will send rich young blood once more coursing through your veins.'[1]

The paper's letters pages were a lively forum for vexatious spirits, such as one 'R. R. M.', who wrote in 1941 to complain of the 'odious' comparison a correspondent had drawn between people of English and Australian stock; apparently, the Australians were judged coarse and uncultured, and their accents incomprehensible. The mysterious R. R. M. was determined to set the matter to rights: 'Let the writer remember when he (or she) writes disparagingly of the Australian that he writes of those born from the same stock as himself and that they left England to seek greater prosperity for her.'[2] As for the Australians being misunderstood, R. R. M. wondered whether English was actually spoken in some of the outer Home Counties.

The civilian residents – white and 'coloured' – of Sandakan were a wealthy little community, but also a charitable one; they gave generously, for example, to the leper colony on Berhala Island. A list of donors to the lepers, published regularly in the *North Borneo Herald*, was a little 'Who's Who' of the township.

They included, in May 1941: His Excellency R. C. Smith (the governor) and Mrs R. C. Smith, the Directors of the North Borneo Chartered Company, the Malayan Tobacco Distributors, Borneo Fishing Company, Reverend Henthorn, Right Reverend Monsignor A. Wachter, Reverend Mother Rose, Mr and Mrs Keith, Dr James Taylor, the surgeon-general, Gerald Mavor, a manager at Sandakan Light and Power, and a great number of prominent Chinese, coastal Malays, mixed-race burghers and business people, such as the Fatt family, Messrs Funk & Sons, Mr Lo Pak Kat, Mr Lan Thau Seng, Heng Joo Ming, Hiap Hong and dozens more. Thanks to the donation of seeds, textiles and home goods, the Berhala lepers found themselves able to plant fruit and vegetable gardens, knit, crochet and keep 'their own little huts so clean', noted the eminently satisfied English matron who organised the monthly charitable drive.[3]

In mid-1941, the white residents appeared more concerned about the war in Europe than about the threat in the Pacific. Singapore would hold, they believed. *The British North Borneo Herald* concentrated its columns on the air war over France and Germany, paying desultory interest to the danger in the north. In May 1941, the residents read of RAF bombers flying daily sorties across Northern France, of Hurricanes and Spitfires 'sweeping the skies' of German fighters, and of rationing in England. Meanwhile, two English cricket teams, according to one article, unable to afford white flannels, were seen playing in their 'pyjamas'.[4] Such a thing could never have happened in Sandakan, the locals smiled.

This portrait of a colonial idyll belied another reality in the interior and remote coastal areas of Borneo, on the great plantations and oilfields to the west, where thousands of coolie workers grunted and sweated in the equatorial heat under the control of their mostly white masters. Commercial exploitation had drawn the Europeans to Kalimantan and put the 'British' into British North Borneo. The Japanese forces gathering to the north, for whom the colony's richness had not gone unnoticed, were determined to remove it.

◆

Before the war, North Borneo – or Sabah, to use its pre- and post-colonial name – was a thriving British protectorate, under the administrative control of the British North Borneo Company. With a population of 285,000 people in the late 1930s, it spanned the northern slice of the world's third-biggest island.

Borneo was a complex society, understandable only by appreciating its extraordinary racial and cultural diversity, as wittily described in the American writer Agnes Newton Keith's book *Land Below the Wind*. In 1941, most Europeans lived in the coastal towns; few had ventured into the dark heart of the island that the natives called Kalimantan, a land of steaming jungles, wild rivers and mountainous ascents.

At the outbreak of war, the island comprised three British protectorates – British North Borneo, Sarawak and Brunei, created by treaties in 1888 – a western chunk controlled by the Dutch East Indies, whose borders were agreed with Britain in 1891, and the little offshore island of Labuan, a Crown colony. For almost a century, the English Brooke family – the 'White Rajahs' – who ruled Sarawak (the last Rajah's rein ended in September 1941), and British and Dutch traders had exploited the island's great oil, rubber and palm resources.

This colonial facade was comparatively recent, beneath which lay a dazzlingly complex, ancient society. Indeed, Borneo may be said to resemble a giant onion, whose shells represent centuries of human occupation and interference. Until the Japanese arrived, the British, in terms of wealth and influence, occupied the outermost shell. The next layer down were the Chinese and their commercial interests, then the Malays and larger ethnic groupings, and at the heart were the tribal people, the original inhabitants, infrequently seen or heard in the British towns, unless as coolie labour.

The indigenous people encompassed a great spectrum of ethnic groups, the survivors of centuries of internecine struggle over scarce resources. The Dusun, Murut, Dyak, Tulun and Kayan were skilled with the blowpipe, supreme in their knowledge of the jungle, and, until relatively recently, some had been active in the ancient rite of headhunting. A well-known local essay, *Folklore in Borneo*, published in 1899, offers a colourful white man's impression of the tribal composition at the time:

> The island is large and the people, scattered and isolated
> by constant inter-tribal warfare, differ from one another,
> in language, customs and appearance almost more than do
> Germans, French, or English . . . A greater drawback to any
> universality, in legend or custom, is that there is no written
> language, not even so much as picture-drawings on rocks to
> give us a clue to ancient myths and traditions. The natives of
> Borneo are in a certain sense savages, but they are savages
> of a high order, possessed of a civilization far above what is
> usually implied by the term; they live together in what almost
> might be called cooperative communities, they practise the

art of weaving, they forge rough implements of iron, they cultivate rice and esculent plants, and in all their work, such as house building, boat building, manufacture of cloth and weapons of warfare, they show an ambitious desire . . . to ornament their work and add . . . pleasure to the eye.

One of their gravest faults, however, is their embarrassing tenacity to the *fad* of head-hunting, and a strict adherence to the principle of an eye for an eye and a tooth for a tooth. This keeps the different households, even of the same tribe, at constant war and makes inevitable an uncomfortable yet pleasing interchange of heads during the tedious months of the rainy reason, when time hangs heavy on the warriors' hands, and disused swords might get rusty.[5]

Fifty years later, some things had changed. Human heads were no longer hunted or traded – although shrivelled skulls were sometimes seen strung on the rafters of village huts in remote parts, relics of a belief that human heads sanctified the home and helped the family to attain the happy state of *Apo Leggan*, the abode of the spirits.[6] Nor was the skill of centuries entirely forgotten: the Japanese invasion re-awoke the tribes' headhunting days, as Captain Athol Moffitt would discover on a journey into the Dyak country in Sarawak soon after the war. The Australian lawyer would witness, in a village hut, 'thirteen Japanese skulls', some with hair on them, threaded together with rattan: 'I queried the identity of one who had some gold in his teeth. The head man said he was the Japanese doctor from Brunei. When asked why he was killed, he replied, with a twinkle in his eye, "He didn't give us any medicines."'[7]

◆

Understandably, the white colonisers tended to stick to the coastal towns – in Sabah, under the watchful eye of the ubiquitous British North Borneo charter company. This effective monopoly ran the country more like a mercantile entrepôt than a state; commerce, not democracy, was the lubricant of civil life in British Sabah and Sarawak and the Dutch East Indies. If their methods were more humane, European commercial claims on the country scarcely differed from those of their Japanese successors. Oil was the main prize, chiefly in the oilfields of Miri in Sarawak and Seria in Brunei, with great petroleum-exploration potential around Tarakan, Balikpapan and Banjarmasin. In North Borneo, rubber, timber and coconuts accounted for the enduring British presence.[8] To this end, the British had established plantations along the fertile hinterland; and as long as the profits continued to roll in, and their Malay and Chinese coolies continued to work without protest, few complained, least of all the British Government.

Indeed, the British administrators of Borneo were more likely 'managers' – auditors, engineers and accountants – than politicians or soldiers. In fact, there were no British soldiers in the colony just months before the outbreak of war. Hardier than their Singaporean kinsmen, the civilian authorities in Borneo were here less for the parties, pink gins and cricket than to make their fortunes. Nonetheless, a robust civil infrastructure propped up the commercial life of Sandakan, Labuan and Jesselton, the main coastal towns.

Alongside the titles of government surveyor, general manager (Sandakan Light and Power), mills manager (BBT Co. Ltd), and similar that drove British mercantilism were the adornments of any civilised colony: a chief police officer, chief justice, archdeacon, priest, nun, headmaster, matron and doctor. Many of those men and women – and companies – were alert to the coming threat from the north. In time, they would show astonishing resilience in the face of Japanese brutality, which is all the more remarkable given the homely callings of Dr James Taylor, Gerald Mavor, the Cohen family of local grocers, the Keith family from America and Dr Val Stookes, the local GP. No less courageous, and just as formidably determined to resist the Japanese, were scores of local Chinese, Indians, Malays and indigenous tribes, notably the Funk and Lagan families, and individuals too numerous to list here (see Appendix 3).

◆

The prevalence of the Chinese, the next onion ring, gave Sandakan its nickname, Little Hong Kong. Following the example of their British bosses, the Chinese diaspora in Borneo tended to regard the island as a business opportunity. Chinese shop-holders, small exporters and pawnbrokers proliferated. These Chinese were less overtly anti-Japanese than their counterparts on the Malayan Peninsula, preferring, at first, a supine adherence to business over the political cudgels of resistance. The outbreak of war with Japan in 1937 prompted little local hostility, and certainly not a Chinese boycott on Japanese goods. 'Everywhere [in Sabah] the Japanese have ingratiated themselves with the Chinese and have contacted [*sic*] friendships with leading Japanese . . .' according to one North Borneo Company official.[9]

Their carefree attitude changed with news of the bombing of Pearl Harbor and Japan's invasion of Malaya in December 1941. In response, Chinese shops in Jesselton dared to sell newspapers depicting scenes of Japanese aggression against mainland China (e.g. the bombing of Shanghai); Chinese bus drivers refused to carry Japanese passengers; and two Chinese-language newspapers were severely censured for running anti-Japanese material.[10] North Borneo's Chinese community even started raising money for their stricken countrymen, through local fetes with 'hoopla stalls', curry and sati shops, and Chinese singers and dancers. Thus Clarissa Tuxford, honorary organiser of one such event, wrote to *The North Borneo Herald* full of haughty praise for the local Chinese who had helped to raise $2600 for the British and China War Relief Funds: 'Our small landholders, smiling, hot and heavy laden, gave us baskets of vegetables and fruits, fowls and ducks, to say nothing of a small puppy.'[11]

◆

Responsibility for defending this peaceful entrepôt lay not with the white civilians, of course, but with the Far East Command of the British Imperial Defence Plan, based in Singapore. By late 1941, this was plainly a tragic irrelevance, with the general officer in command of Malaya besieged by the Japanese onslaught. In any case, unlike Sarawak, which paraded a proud detachment of Punjabi fighters loyal to Britain, and the fierce Free Dutch Forces of the Dutch East Indies – who vowed to fight on despite the Nazis occupying their country – there were no troops stationed in Sabah. The slovenly English thinking that so drastically underplayed the threat to the Malayan Peninsula was alive and flourishing in North Borneo.

A British Foreign Office official breezily informed the War Office at the time:

We consider it unlikely that the Japanese would stage a
major attack on North Borneo, and it is considered at present
impossible for them to undertake two major offensives in
Southeast Asia, eg North Borneo and Malaya. It is for these
reasons that it has been decided not to defend North Borneo
against a major attack.[12]

The Foreign Office thus completely misread its enemy's
determination and strength – and more or less abandoned North
Borneo 'to face the Japanese threat on its own', according to
Danny Wong Tze Ken, professor of history at the University of
Malaya.[13]

To meet the Japanese threat, British civilian officials in Borneo
depended on the locals – chiefly the Chinese and Malays – and
chose rather desultorily to organise them into a token defensive
unit. The Legislative Council convened in 1938 to revive the
old North Borneo Volunteer Force, which had served in 1916
before disbanding in the 1920s. A motley collection of Chinese,
Malays, Indians and indigenous ethnic groups were urged to
'volunteer' for the revived force; and while social pressure exerted
some compulsion, most did so of their own volition. These were
courageous young men who loved their country.

Their two companies formed an attractive force of eager
fighters, many of whom hailed from prominent local families,
resplendently turned out in khaki shirts and riding breeches,
puttees, boots and 'pigsticker' helmets, naively defiant and
inordinately brave. Their designation as an official combat unit
would, of course, pitch them against battle-hardened, jungle-
trained enemy troops vastly superior in number and skill.
Nonetheless, it was felt that the Volunteers should at least offer

a gesture of resistance. They received rudimentary training, requiring them to 'pass as efficient' in 'musketry' and attain 'such simple drill as may be decided on'.[14] If captured, as seemed inevitable, their combat status should ensure their 'honourable treatment as prisoners' under international law, according to the colony's doe-eyed *Official Gazette*.[15]

The Borneo Volunteers were lambs to the slaughter. Many of their number would perish during the coming occupation; others would join the underground resistance and experience first-hand the quality of Japanese mercy. In time, the names of those Volunteers – notably Johnny, Paddy and Alex Funk (sons of a first-class magistrate, one of the few locals to attain that position), Ernesto Lagan, Osman bin Usop, Khoo Siak Chiew and many others – would resonate in the villages and towns as heroes of the resistance, symbols of the selfless dedication to liberty.

Alas, in 1941, the Volunteers managed to raise just one combat platoon in defence of the east coast around Sandakan, and another in defence of the west coast at Jesselton. Complementing them was an 'auxiliary force' of 31 more or less itinerant Britons, who cheerfully fanned out to 'garrison' four 'strategic points' in the country. In short, British North Borneo's preparations for the coming invasion were pathetic: the island was left utterly naked to the storm.

◆

Meanwhile, the small Japanese diaspora in Borneo helped to ease the Imperial Army's conquest of the colony. The community had existed in Sabah since the 1890s. In the 1930s, they numbered almost 2000, most of whom the British suspected of being fifth-columnists. As war tensions rose, the British Administration curbed Japanese activities on the island, and, from October 1938, banned Japanese immigrants from settling on the strategically useful north-west coast. These restrictions did little to inhibit Taniguchi Taku, the Japanese consul at Sandakan, from launching a state-wide tour of Sabah, Sarawak and Brunei in October 1940. Billed as an innocent perambulation among his people, his journey was almost certainly a spying mission to identify suitable landing sites for the coming invasion.[16] Indeed, diplomatic traffic between Japanese government officials and Sabah greatly increased throughout 1940.

The invasion fell on this defenceless British protectorate with the suddenness of a hammer-blow. There was little resistance. Intimations of the approaching strike provoked panic in the coastal towns. On the morning of 9 December 1941, the day after Pearl Harbor, the longest road train ever assembled in Sabah pulled out of Jesselton packed with Chinese desperate to reach the high country and the interior. The Japanese attacked the island of Labuan on New Year's Day 1942 and entered Jesselton unopposed on 9 January – a month before the fall of Singapore. They occupied the Armed Constabulary Headquarters and demanded the Volunteers' disbandment. The Volunteers disbanded, but not without burying much of their weaponry and ammunition for future use. In the event, their British masters ordered the Volunteers not to resist, as any stand by their puny numbers was deemed suicidal.

The Japanese marched into Jesselton virtually unopposed. The town was soon bedecked in fluttering, rising suns, which energetic local entrepreneurs sold for $2 each.[17] The coastal communities of Tarakan, Balikpapan and Pontianak fell in quick succession, and the whole island was in Japanese hands by the end of January 1942. Two weeks later, Singapore followed.

Sandakan offered a more robust account of itself. The locals anticipated the Japanese arrival and hoped to impede the occupation at every stage. In December, the governor of North Borneo, Robert Smith, ordered local industries to stop work and the Sandakan mint to destroy some $900,000 in unissued local currency. 'All stocks of aviation spirit have already been destroyed,' he cabled the secretary of state for the colonies in London on 23 December.[18] Three days later, stocks of jute bags and scrap metal were dumped in the sea and most vessels, with the exception of small local fishing craft, sunk. And on 4 January, with the enemy's landing imminent, the governor circulated an edict that, 'No person should engage in production and processing of any commodity that may assist the enemy's war effort. Europeans are relied upon to set the example.'[19]

Himself a model of non-cooperation with the Japanese, the governor sought the War Council's advice on how best to meet the enemy: 'I consider that I and my offices should decline to take any part in the governing of the country and should surrender ourselves for immediate internment and demand protection of all civilians, especially women and children.'[20] To which the War Council agreed 'that you should refuse to co-operate in any way with the enemy'.[21] Local volunteer forces should not resist the Japanese and instead maintain internal law and order, advised the colonial secretary on 6 January.[22]

A week later, with the Japanese landing expected at any moment, London received word that all secret and confidential records in Sandakan had been burnt, and the wireless station and surplus weapons and ammunition destroyed. The local timber mills were preserved, as burning them, the governor argued, 'would almost certainly result in wide conflagration of Asiatic habitations'.[23] Food stocks were dispersed among the locals, as 'any destruction will cause starvation and serious local disturbances, bloodshed. We could not control the population and we would make them actively and permanently hostile.'[24]

The Japanese entered Sandakan Bay on 19 January 1942. Unlike their smooth reception at Jesselton and elsewhere, the landing party encountered a deeply resistant community. The denial of basic services, administration and cash seriously frustrated the invaders, who immediately ordered the internment of Europeans in a quarantine station – a few squat huts – near the leper colony on Berhala, the flat, malarial atoll surrounded by muddy mangroves and shreds of beach less than a mile off Sandakan. This was supposed to be a temporary incarceration; it was in fact an open-ended act of retribution. The British had interned Japanese civilians on the island in the early weeks of the war – a point not lost on the arriving Kempei-tai.

◆

The occupying forces immediately set themselves the task of 'Nipponising' North Borneo. Within days, the Japanese flag flew atop every building, all clocks were put back an hour, in line with Japanese time, and the working day extended. The Japanese leaders made a show of ingratiating themselves with the non-white communities – with crude propaganda, presenting themselves as 'liberators' from the European oppressors. Liberty, the locals soon discovered, meant learning Japanese and embracing Japanese culture: Japanese language classes were mandatory, as was the honouring of Japanese public holidays. Jesselton, for example, received its first taste of the new order on 11 February 1942 – four days before the fall of Singapore – when the locals found themselves celebrating the 2602nd 'Empire Day' with 'a big parade', as George Woolley, the former commissioner of land in Jesselton, recorded in his wartime diary: 'Jap troops in uniform with rifles, about 100, then Jap ladies and other columns of Chinese school children, Dusuns, etc . . . Then all columns, troops, officers, Chinese etc, moved off in a procession around the town.'[25]

A linguistic re-colonisation accompanied the invasion: Sandakan was renamed 'Elopura', its original native name; Jesselton 'Api'; and so on. North Borneo was subdivided into provinces, or *shui*, governed by the military's placemen. Elopura became the regional capital of Tokai Shui, the eastern province. In quick succession, the conquerors similarly Nipponified Java, Sumatra, Rabaul and many smaller atolls throughout the Pacific. This hardly squared with the letter and spirit of Japanese propaganda, which promised self-determination to Asian people under the warm embrace of the Greater East Asian Co-Prosperity Sphere. On the contrary, as many Asians soon found, one imperialist had merely replaced another, and the new rulers seemed immeasurably more intrusive than the old.

The commanders of the Imperial Army knew the truth behind the posters: taking Borneo amounted to the routine acquisition of another South Pacific outpost, another grab for the spoils of the great downward thrust of Hirohito's armies, which had conquered most of China and all of Indochina and Malaya with little serious opposition. In the army's wake arrived the real force in the land, in the form of the Kempei-tai, the Japanese secret police, whose interrogation and torture cells swiftly become a loathsome feature of every occupied city in Asia.

With the capture of Singapore, Borneo and Rabaul, the Japanese forces set their sights on locking up the South-West Pacific and completing the occupation of Burma, Java and Papua New Guinea. Australia loomed in the soldiers' sights as the ultimate prize, but Premier Tojo Hideki decided in March 1942 against the invasion of the great southern land, planning instead to isolate it – and sever any links with American ships – through air supremacy. That goal would, however, require the possession of the airfields of Port Moresby, which the Japanese first attempted to capture by sea, in the Battle of the Coral Sea, in May 1942. When this failed, the Imperial Army consolidated its hold on the Solomon Islands, as a natural citadel against US vessels approaching Australia. In July, the army attempted the capture of Port Moresby, through a brazen land assault over the Kokoda Track, which passed through the Owen Stanley Mountains. At about this time, the prisoners of B Force were disembarking at Sandakan.

4

NO. 1 PRISONER OF WAR CAMP

I tell you, I have powers of life and death over you,
and you will build this aerodrome if you stay here
until your bones rot under the tropical sun.

Captain Hoshijima Susumi, first commandant
of the Sandakan POW camp

SIX MONTHS HAVE ELAPSED between the Japanese invasion of Borneo and the arrival of the first prisoners, from Singapore, in July 1942. The Imperial Army has pressed doggedly south, consolidated its strength in the main towns of Sabah and Sarawak, commandeered the wide-verandahed bungalows of former British rajahs and installed Japanese high officials in the best and most spacious of them. Kuching, in south-western Sarawak, has become the headquarters of the Borneo prison network, in which the prison camp of Sandakan will play a vital role.

On the afternoon of 18 July 1942, the men of B Force assemble on the padang by the foreshore – a shifting, bemused crowd of Australian soldiers. Some fraternise with locals who loiter nearby and disabuse them of the Japanese lie that Australia is under enemy occupation – before being severely admonished by the guards: fraternising with the locals is forbidden. Many soldiers still cannot quite believe their circumstances, unable to dislodge the notion of their capture as some kind of surreal joke against the natural order of things – a state of mind the fiercely proud Japanese commanders are determined, in time, to crush.

After a meal of rice, dispensed from buckets, some of the prisoners are marched up the hill to a large Anglican church. They spend their first night in Borneo under the sway of hurricane lamps and the gaze of stained-glass saints. They sleep on the stone floor, on pews, or in the church grounds. Roused before dawn, they regroup with the rest, who slept on the ship, or camped in the padang, and prepare for the march west, to the prison camp.

◆

The steady tramp of boots to the strains of 'Waltzing Matilda' and 'Along the Road to Gundagai' alerts the locals to the approaching column of white men, laden with kitbags, moving cheerfully through town. They proceed up a steep gradient and pass the turn-off to the former governor's residence, now the home of the local Japanese commander.

The mood even seems to lift the spirits of the Japanese, thinks Lieutenant Leslie Bunn ('Bunny') Glover, who observes the guards strutting alongside.[1] The sick follow, in trucks, with the gear. They pass the outskirts of town, lined by the kampongs (very small hamlets) of local people, who chatter and point. Willing collaborators or fearful locals wave Japanese flags. Some gloat at the dirty white man, fallen symbol of the erstwhile colonial power. Others watch in mute awe, scarcely able to believe the sight. The shrill cries of children and barks of dogs mingle with the gruff orders of the Japanese and Formosan guards, pressing the column on. Encountering a farmer asleep on his ox-drawn cart, someone turns the cart around in the opposite direction. '[E]ven the Japs laughed at that,' Braithwaite later recalls, 'that cheered everyone up a bit.'[2]

The prisoners march west, along a dirt road past lines of rubber trees and dense jungle. Within a few hours, they reach the eight-mile marker, near a crossroads, and turn right, past a small police station and a once government-run experimental farm. They halt before a hollow off the side of the road that rises gradually to a hill. A noticeboard on the padlocked gate says, 'NO. 1 PRISONERS OF WAR CAMP, BRITISH NORTH BORNEO', with the name of the ultimate authority, 'HQ Kuching'.[3]

The prisoners devour the features of their new homes, the quicker to assess the conditions – and possible escape routes. The camp compound itself covers about five acres. On the periphery are coils of barbed wire, barricades and sentry towers; to left and right of the entrance, neat lines of sturdy huts, on stilts, windowless, rising on a squarish incline. Further up the slope, the huts seem flimsy, of more recent construction. Indeed, the British built the camp originally as a barracks, for troops or workers. When war broke out, it became an internment camp for some 200–250 Japanese locals, hence the newer huts – a point clear to the Kempei-tai. Somehow, this compound must now accommodate all 1500 Australians.

Their new quarters number some 40 huts, measuring about 43 by 20 feet, with three cubicles in each, arranged around an open parade ground. On a knoll near the centre of the parade ground stands a huge, apparently dead, mengaris tree, rising 230 feet into the sky. Curiously, the tree lacks leaves – perhaps as a result of repeated lightning strikes. Supported by flailing buttress roots, the 'Big Tree' becomes a natural meeting point, 'like a mediaeval commons',[4] where the prisoners hold small church services, singalongs and smokos. 'See you at the Big Tree' becomes a common refrain.[5] Lieutenant Russ Ewin admires the stark beauty of its 'vivid blue' trunk during storms; for him, the tree stands for 'permanence and survival'.[6] Lieutenant Hugh Waring calls it 'the one we loved so much'. The crevices in the buttress offer perfect hiding places: Lieutenant Tony White later hides a pistol in its roots, and rumours circulate of cash and treasure left there. In time, the Big Tree will exert a strange hold on the prisoners' minds: as a towering symbol, of hope or oppression.

Hope of what? Escape? Evenly spaced electric lights and sentry boxes guard the inner, barbed-wire fence, stretched taut between wooden pylons. The wire can easily be dug under. Beyond the wire, the prisoners glimpse clumps of cinnamon, coffee and rubber trees, and, to the west and east, dense jungle – more intimidating than any human barrier. To the north, the fence spans a foul-smelling swamp; above the fetid water, Japanese guards patrol a wooden walkway. The only gate, the one through which they entered, stands in the sights of a machine gun.

The afternoon rain pours down as the men file into their new accommodation; their morning cheer has deserted them. The Australian officers – lieutenants, captains and above – are allocated the stronger, wooden huts near the gates; the other ranks are dispersed through the rest. The captains sleep eight to a cubicle, the lieutenants 10 and the men 15 – making about 24 officers and 45 men to a hut. The officers' huts have shelves and electric lights. The men sleep in smaller, damaged huts made of atap – the woven leaves of the nipa palm – with leaking roofs and thatched walls riddled with holes. Richard Braithwaite recalls, 'a couple of them collapsed just after we arrived there. The rats played havoc with them and they were anything but weather-proof.'[7] Rats, bedbugs, lice and mosquitoes are to be their constant companions through the hot, wet nights. The lavatories are filthy drops, near or underneath the huts, without doors, on which the men sit four to a thunderbox. Water is pumped from the nearby Sibuga River, boiled in a large tank and then piped to the kitchen and showers.

'Breakfast we have rice and green stew, black tea,' notes Private Tom Burns in his diary. 'Lunch stinkin fish the smell of which could knock you down . . . There are Japanese guards inside and outside the compound. They are all armed with rifles and fixed bayonets.' Then he cheers up: 'We are allowed one packet of fags per week. They have started a canteen for the whole camp.'[8] The food improves, for a while.

Within two days, Burns and other younger, fitter men receive their first instructions: to slash a rough track through the jungle, from the camp to a construction site. On the first day, a storm howls around them as they hack away with their machetes. After a few miles, they reach an expanse of white, volcanic rock – 'tuff' – stretching away like a solidified lava flow under the wet and scraggy regrowth. The RAF intended to build an airfield on this partly cleared site; the Japanese will now complete what the British began – using Australian slave labour.

◆

A few days later, during roll call – *tenko* – the prisoners learn the use to which they will be put. Above them, on a small platform by the Big Tree, overlooking the parade ground, stands the camp commandant, Captain Hoshijima Susumi – a tall, thinly built engineer, who addresses them in faltering English. Hoshijima is, by accounts, fond of parades and protocol, and is attired for the occasion in a neatly pressed uniform, his Italian pistol on one hip and long katana sword on the other. He begins his 'welcoming address' through an interpreter but frequently interrupts in English. He regales the 'prisoners of the Japanese' with the wonders of the Greater East Asian Co-Prosperity Sphere and promises that Japan will be victorious, 'even if it takes a hundred years'.[9]

He ends with a death sentence:

> You have been brought here to Sandakan to have the honour
> to build for the Imperial Japanese Forces an aerodrome; you
> will work, you will build this aerodrome if it takes three years.
> I tell you, I have powers of life and death over you, and you
> will build this aerodrome if you stay here until your bones rot
> under the tropical sun.[10]

5

OFFICERS AND MEN

*Been [sic] a POW I have made several attempts to put into
writing my experiences as a prisoner of war but so far have
had little success mainly through lack of inspiration added to
the thought that perhaps it would make very dull reading.*
Private Tom Burns' first entry in his Sandakan diary

THE CIVILIANS IN SANDAKAN have been secretly active.
If most whites are interned on Berhala, those with critical jobs
remain in their posts in town. They have used their freedom to
great effect. Among them are the 'Europeans': Gerald Mavor,
chief engineer and manager of the Sandakan Light and Power
Company; A. E. Philips, general manager of the North Borneo
Trading Company; Dr J. F. Laband, a dental surgeon and refugee
from Nazi Germany; Dr Val Stookes, a local general practitioner;
and Dr James Taylor, the Australian-born surgeon-general and
principal medical officer. The local constabulary – mostly Dusun
and Malayans – are permitted to stay in their jobs too, under loose
Japanese control.

In early 1942, these two groups developed close links with
Chinese, Malayan and other native people who opposed the
occupation, and together sowed the seedlings of a larger resistance

movement. In time, the names of several families – Funk, Azcona, Lagan, Lai, Apostol, Cohen and others – will resound with the astonishing bravery and ingenuity of the Sandakan 'underground'.

At first, these 'free' men and women turn their minds to smuggling food and medical aid to their families and friends interned on Berhala Island. They rely on trusted members of the local constabulary, who share their hatred of the Japanese: police officers of Malayan, Chinese and tribal descent – a happy example of mixed-race cooperation bound by a common enemy. Prominent among these are Sergeant Major Yangsalang, a Dusun tribesman; Warrant Officer Jemadar Ujagar Singh, a Sikh; Inspector Samuel Guriaman and Sergeant Abin, of Dusun or other tribal origins; and the legendary future resistance fighter Corporal Koram bin Andaur, a Murut tribesman.[1]

Yangsalang and Ujagar, who control the police roster at Berhala's Quarantine Station, select trusted guards to make contact with civilian interns. They do so through a nightwatchman called Mohammed Salleh, who works for the leper settlement – has done for three years – and travels daily from the mainland with medicine and supplies for the lepers. The Japanese allow Salleh to continue in this role, and he makes great clandestine use of it – transmitting the internees' requests for food and aid, via the police guards, to the surgeon-general, Dr Taylor, in town.

Dr Taylor, whose calm, quiet demeanour disguises a soul of iron, responds with the same selfless courage. Heedless of the risks, this steady surgeon from Yass, in New South Wales, procures the medicines, food and clothing ordered, and sends it back to the island under cover of a carefully selected police guard. This isn't pure altruism, of course: money lubricates the process.

The Berhala civilians pay for the aid out of their savings.

Within weeks, a regular flow of vital supplies finds its way to the Berhala camp – thanks to the growing network of Europeans, Chinese, Malays, Indians and tribal people, who double as secret procurers, messengers, runners and passers of secret packages, all under the noses of the Japanese authority. Some Berhala civilians also donate funds for the greater good of the camp. Mrs Moselle Cohen, from a family of wealthy shop-owners, is the biggest financial backer of the operation. The native people, too, contribute generously.

In time, the Sandakan underground will penetrate the very fabric of the community and reach inside the prison camp. The willingness of its members to risk their lives in defiance of the new regime is a powerful indictment of Japanese pledges to 'liberate' them. The brutality of the new imperialists drives many followers to join the civilian resistance. Consider, for example, the police constable Tahir Matusin, who, disgusted at the sight of a Japanese sentry severely beating an old Hakka woman – who forgot to bow on her way to the marketplace – gives his loyalty to the fledgling network.[2]

◆

Eight miles inland, unaware of this furtive civilian activity in town, the prisoners orientate themselves to their new home. The men mentally resist the label 'prisoner of war'. In their minds, they strive to remain soldiers: officers, sergeants, corporals and privates. They struggle to maintain the dignity of the Australian Imperial Force and the spirit of their battalions, companies and platoons. But the arbitrary amalgamation of B Force has diminished these bonds; the old tribal lines are breaking. For now, the traditional demarcation between officers and men remains. In one sense, the wedge is driven more deeply, by the Japanese Army's preferential treatment towards enemy officers, who are initially exempt from the work detail. This provokes some bitterness in the ranks.

It is undeserved. Most officers are united in their genuine concern for the troops and hatred of the enemy. The better majors, captains and lieutenants serve as buffers between the Japanese and the troops. Some insist on working with the men. They play a protective role. Lieutenant Colonel Arthur Walsh, despite his being a stickler for form, finds it within himself to resist the Japanese, who brand him a troublemaker, a man to be watched. Within weeks of his arrival, Walsh finds ways to improve the men's morale and their food supply. He obtains permission, for example, to plant a vegetable garden in the Experimental Farm – giving his officers-cum-gardeners a chance to work unsupervised outside the wire. They are quick to exploit this opportunity, and during July the camp intelligence officer, Lieutenant Norman Sligo, a 42-year-old New Zealander, formerly of the Naval Reserve, contacts the members of the civilian resistance via this garden plot. He widens these connections through his new role as canteen officer.

Energetically on hand is Captain Lionel Matthews. Dubbed 'The Duke' after his likeness to the Duke of Gloucester, a future governor of Australia, Matthews is tall, fit, proud and unusually brave – to the point, some think, of recklessness. He seems, to some of his fellow officers, impervious to fear and physical pain. Born in Adelaide to a 'gruff, raw-boned plumber and iron-worker',[3] the boy grew up a powerful swimmer, lifesaver and amateur boxer. The army suited Matthews' competitive streak and satisfied his 'obsession for fine clothes'[4] – possibly a reaction to his humble origins. His trimmed moustache completes the likeness to the Duke. Sent to Singapore with Eight Division Signals, he served with distinction as signals officer of the 27 Brigade, maintaining the Australians' cable communications throughout the battle of Gemas and on the island.

His character is constructively rebellious; he is determined to succeed in whatever he sets his mind to, even if it involves unorthodox methods – surely the result of an aggressive father, who could 'fight like a threshing machine'.[5] But the gentleness of Matthews' mother imbues in him something else – an innate sense of what is just and decent, which his swashbuckling character tends to overshadow. He exudes 'mischief with a ready smile' and is likely at any time to explode into 'raucous infectious laughter', as an old friend later writes of him.[6] Matthews is one of life's practical-jokers, which can exasperate his colleagues. A superb signals officer, he uses Morse like a mother tongue – a skill that never deserts him in the ordeal ahead.

Matthews wastes no time in stamping his authority on the camp. His agile mind quickly comprehends the little circle of local resistance, chiefly through meeting civilians linked to Dr Taylor at their rendezvous point – a cowshed in the grounds of the Experimental Farm. When Sligo dies in August, of dysentery, Matthews replaces him as the prisoners' intelligence officer – giving him a window on the world outside the camp.

Comprehending the linkages to Sandakan and Berhala, he soon conceives of a deeper, more subversive plan: to establish an underground network involving the prisoners, the civilians and the native people – extending, ultimately, to Allied guerrillas then landing in Borneo. Perhaps even weapons could be smuggled in, he considers. Gradually, the vision of a prisoner uprising takes hold in Matthews' hyperactive brain.

◆

Matthews' ideas devolve upon his second-in-command, Lieutenant Rod Wells, whose patient, quiet temperament offsets the more buccaneering demeanour of his senior officer. Wells, possessed of a sharp intellect and a natural aptitude for maths and science, is determined to solve the most pressing needs of the camp. He displays an unusual skill at improvisation. For Wells, 'no problem was too difficult to solve, no situation so desperate that it could not be overcome', writes his wife, Pamela, whom Wells met after the war.[7]

Born in 1920 to dairy farmers, the young Wells showed a prodigious talent for electronics. He designed a crystal set out of a 'cat's whisker' (wire electrodes) at the age of eight; and a 12-volt lighting system for the farmhouse aged 15, which he also hitched up to powerful transmitters that sent radio signals, quite illegally, over a wide area, 'blotting out all other radio reception for miles around'.[8] His wife will later enumerate his many brushes with death during his boyhood: he almost drowned in a diving helmet made from a kerosene tin, narrowly escaped the explosion of a bottle full of gelignite he had manufactured and luckily avoided poisoning himself on the fumes of a batch of nitric acid he had produced in his bedroom, which corroded his bedstead.[9]

The lad quickly mastered Morse code with the help of the local telegraph office; but his biggest achievement, while a teenager, was to build from scratch a shortwave radio receiver, on which he tuned in to the chimes of Big Ben preceding the BBC news.

In 1939, Wells enlisted in the Australian Army, received his commission and sailed with 8th Division Signals – Matthews' unit – to Singapore. Arriving in Sandakan with B Force, he soon apprehended the loopholes in the prison system – the freedom of the gardening detail, for example. He takes charge of the wood-collecting party, offering him easy access to members of the local resistance. With the scarcest resources, Wells turns his mind to the possibility of building a secret radio.

◆

A few scraps – a notebook here, a logbook there – help to explain the officers' thoughts and actions in 1942, their first year of imprisonment. Captain Stan Woods, adjutant to Walsh, is a trove of information and a meticulous record-taker. A handwritten character assessment in April 1942 describes him as having a 'hasty temper and irritability', 'physical courage' and a 'practical nature'. He is 'generous', 'modest', with 'a high sense of duty', and 'decisive of opinion whether right or wrong' – in a word, stubborn.[10]

Woods keeps voluminous records of his fellow officers' daily activities, expenditure and salaries, which the Japanese Army pay to Walsh, who has power of attorney to receive wages on the officers' behalf. 'All officers have now signed for salary 5 1/2 months from 15 August 1942,' Woods writes at the time. 'A total of $12,863.25.' That amount is banked 'in Lt Hoshijima's name in the Yokohama Specie Bank Sandakan'.[11] The officers spend spare cash on medical supplies, tobacco and food and have good credit at the well-stocked canteen, which sells bananas, tomatoes, pawpaw, turtle eggs, coconuts and cigarettes: the seven majors get

$15 of credit each; 35 captains get $10 each; and 88 lieutenants and three padres get $5 each.[12] The other ranks also enjoy the use of a canteen and receive a small salary. No prisoners are obliged to work on Sundays, allowing them the freedom to indulge in a concert or boxing match on Saturday nights.

Later in 1942, Woods sets himself the dogged task of drawing up a monthly log of the officers' working parties, health, sick days, working hours, expenses and other particulars. It offers an extraordinary glimpse of the officers' conditions and daily life in the camp. We read of their diseases, stints in hospital and work details: wood-gathering, cleaning, camp duties, farming and, in time, building the aerodrome alongside the other ranks. Woods' fastidious eye for detail and precise hand makes his log a wonder of tidiness and efficiency in such dismal circumstances. As well, his book of 'Recipes' – surely wishful thinking – reveals an abiding sense of humour and lists such delicacies as 'Sour Cream Pie', 'Coconut Ice Cream' and 'Nasi Goreng'; Stan even feels obliged to explain how to make 'Toasted Cheese Sandwiches'.[13] In truth, a typical day's menu, he notes, lists rice with fish stew, dried fish stew or vegetable stew, plus, 'Tea with each meal. No bread. Salt very scarce.'[14]

Neither officers nor the other ranks are permitted to write letters home; they may, however, send the occasional postcard. On 20 June 1942, Woods sends the first of three cards that his future wife, Belinda, will receive in the next three years. She gets it on 13 September 1943:

DEAREST BELINDA,
I AM BEING WELL TREATED AS A PRISONER OF
WAR. PLEASE ASK JACK TO WRITE MY BROTHER

THAT I AM VERY FIT . . . HOPE YOU AND
HOMEFOLK ARE IN GOOD HEALTH. ALWAYS
YOURS LOVINGLY, STAN.[15]

Among the reinforcements sent to Singapore in 1941 was
Lieutenant Russ Ewin, 24, the product of a hard-working Labor-
voting family. His father was a government grader responsible for
the quality of rabbit meat, his mother a housewife, during the
worst of the Depression. An academically gifted lad, Ewin was
acutely class-conscious at a time when Australian society was
socially stratified along lines of income, education and religion.
Anxious to move up in the world, at 16 he won a scholarship to
a Sydney business college and studied accounting: 'I was a brash
young bloke, I had a few tickets on myself. I was very fastidious
about things' – especially dancing. He arranged local dances in
the grimly disapproving Methodist Church: 'the waltz, fox-trot,
quick-step'.[16]

He proposed to his sweetheart, Joyce, a few weeks before his
departure. It hadn't been an easy courtship. They were a bit on
and off, because, earlier in their relationship, she told Ewin, 'You
argue too much.' He eventually wooed her back: 'She asked about
marrying before I went; I said I might come back a wreck or not at
all. She organised the wedding in 3–4 days.' He embarked on 29
July 1941, a member of 8th Division Signals.

The 'other ranks' – non-commissioned officers (warrant
officers, sergeants and corporals) – include one of the most vibrant
figures in the camp, the raffish fixer and consummate wheeler-
dealer Warrant Officer 'Wild Bill' Sticpewich. Sticpewich is
an opportunist and adventurer, always scheming, irrepressible,
unstoppable, with the smarts of Milo Minderbinder, the memory

of an elephant and the survival instincts of Flashman. Unlike the fictional character, he is decisive and daring, with an odd gift for getting away with things that others would get a bashing for: such as the pet snake he keeps in his hut and brings out on parade, to the shock of the Japanese calling the roll. If some later accuse him of collaborating, Sticpewich's record suggests otherwise: he has chosen a different course to the rest because he sees that only by understanding the Japanese can the prisoners hope to exploit them, and survive. He learns a little Japanese. He keeps his eyes fixed on the camp activities. He remembers everything, even the location and amounts of rice storage at certain dates.

His work takes him outside the wire, to the Japanese stores and quarters. He sets up a 'Technical Group' of prison handymen, whose special treatment angers the other prisoners. It is true that he receives extra food – and is the only non-commissioned officer to acquire a mosquito net. Braithwaite describes him as unpopular and something of a bully: 'He fancied himself as a bit of a wrestler, and he was a very solidly built character and he used to pick on the young blokes and throw them around a bit.'[17] The lawyer Athol Moffitt sees another side, 'a rugged, survivor-type Aussie, an outstanding man. He had managed to get on the right side of the Japanese, and became invaluable to them. He was a carpenter and mechanic and could fix or make anything.'[18] In time, Sticpewich redeems himself in ways that would break a lesser man.

Then there are the ordinary privates. Some are extraordinary, in different ways – men such as the thoughtful Richard Braithwaite, the curiously unpopular entertainer Nelson Short, the sly, sharp-eyed, unbreakable Keith Botterill and the dissolute and conniving Bill Moxham.

'There were the odd characters, of course,' Braithwaite later recalls, 'the good, the bad and the indifferent . . . it was quite an amazing thing, the people who, from good family background and lived pretty well in their lives, some of them fell by the wayside; and others, the city rats you might say, you know – if you met them in the street you'd be very suspicious of them back home – came good'.

Bombardier Richard Braithwaite, 22, may be said to have 'come good'. The illegitimate son of a plumber, he grew up in Coorparoo, Brisbane, in bizarre circumstances. His mother had him when she was barely 17. To hide this shameful fact, her parents raised him while she, a single mother, pretended to be his sister. The teenage Braithwaite discovered his true provenance at school, when a teacher accidentally revealed it. The lad was compelled to adjust to his 'sister' being his mother.

The boy grew into a superb athlete, super fit and highly driven. His sporting prowess seemed to help him overcome – or shun – the disturbing revelation of his parentage: 'In his late teens he played all four football codes in one weekend,' his son later recalls.[19] Braithwaite left school at 16 to take up an apprenticeship as a 'wet plate photographer'. He became a dapper young man, well groomed, with dark-brown hair neatly cut over a serious, thoughtful face. Though academically disinclined, he was bright and adaptable, and gifted in a way that eluded his educators. His memory for detail was astonishing. Years later, Braithwaite will register an IQ of 140, the highest ever recorded by psychiatrists at Greenslopes repatriation hospital.

Braithwaite enlisted later than his peers – when Italy entered the war – and joined the 2/15th Field Regiment. 'My father was a sort of reluctant soldier,' his son later says. In photographs, Braithwaite's piercing eyes suggest a suspicious or defensive nature.

His family circumstances weigh heavily; he seems wholly concentrated on the moment, on his guard. He was occasionally prone to bursts of anger, his son recalls: 'My father didn't take shit from anyone. He was short-tempered in those days.'[20] In September 1941, he was demoted from lance bombardier to gunner as punishment for striking a sergeant soon after arriving in Singapore. (He was later reappointed bombardier.) Indeed, Braithwaite's troubled past, steely resolve and refusal to suffer fools mark him out as a survivor.

The privates generally hail from tough, hard-working backgrounds as labourers, drivers, salesmen, farmhands, cooks, butchers, blacksmiths, carpenters and stationhands. They range in age from teenagers – who lie about their birth dates – to fifty-year-olds. Private Tom Burns, aged 33, is an introspective storeman from Queensland and one of the few to commit his thoughts secretly to paper. He is an only child, single, and his next of kin are 'all deceased'. Perhaps he writes for an imaginary friend, or a future audience. Us? The memory of his parents? The result is the only diary to survive Sandakan, later exhumed battered and mouldering among his remains. Burns' broken words cry out from that silence like a message in a bottle. We have read his description of the cruelty at sea; yet in the prison camp he seems to lose faith in his ability to chronicle his life:

Been [*sic*] a POW I have made several attempts to put into writing my experiences as a prisoner of war but so far have had little success mainly through lack of inspiration added to the thought that perhaps it would make very dull reading. Having so far succeeded in evading the attempts of the Japanese inspections . . . to remove all writing materials

and pens and pencils it has occurred to me to make another
attempt even if only for the purpose of filling in time . . .[21]

The youngest soldiers, aged 17–21, occupy a hut at the end of
a row backing on to the swamp, literally at the dead end of the
camp, hence their name 'Dead End Kids'. As author Anthony Hill
later describes them, they are 'trouble-makers, mainly youthful
– indeed some under-age – . . . high-spirited, anti-authoritarian,
self-reliant young larrikins, forever on the scrounge and risking
much'.[22]

One is Bill Young – Billy the Kid, they call him. He enlisted
in the army at 15, claiming he was 19; a fictitious aunt, Martha
– the only woman's name he can spell – was his best witness.
Born in 1925, Young grew up in Sydney's inner west during the
Great Depression. His father, Bill Senior, was a communist, who
dragged the boy along to epic nights of sign-writing. They lived
in a boarding house in Ultimo, courtesy of a pair of old circus
performers turned fruit-stall-holders, who paid the two Bills' rent.
In 1937, Bill Senior stowed away on a ship bound for England,
then to Spain, to join the Spanish Civil War. The old man never
returned (one of 15 Australians to die fighting Franco's forces).
The boy, fatherless and homeless, left school at 14 and got a job
delivering telegrams. In 1940, he volunteered – first for the navy,
who discovered his age – and then for the army, who didn't. They
trained him quickly enough to join the 2/29th Battalion, which
was rushed up to Malaya.[23]

At Sandakan, the lad is up for anything. Escape? Young
is always the first to put his hand up. His greatest friend is Joey
Crome, just nine months older than Billy, whose father runs the
picture theatre at Bondi Junction. Anchored off Miri, on the

voyage to Sandakan, the pair contemplated swimming for it: 'In you go then . . .' said Crome.

'You're the kid from Bondi! You go first,' said Young.

Another Dead End Kid is Wally Ford, whom everyone calls Henry, from Hobart, much younger than the 21 he claims to be, and 'always with his rather lop-sided, boyish grin'. There is also Harry Longley, a farmer's son from Yass, in New South Wales, again only 17 when he enlisted, while claiming to be 21. 'Harry was the leader of these younger blokes,' writes Hill. '[H]e had a countryman's experience of knowing what to do in an emergency.' And there is Jimmy Finn of the 2/30th Battalion, small, nuggety and muscular, and a champion boxer: 'a bantamweight, with a steam-hammer fist', and one of the stars of the occasional boxing matches the Japanese allow. Another boxing star is John 'Snowy' Bryant, who fought his way out of the poverty of the Depression. He will soon perform in a sensational bout with Jimmy 'Punchy' Donohue, which even a few Japanese guards attend.

Of the older men, there are two Private Keatings, both lorry drivers with working-class Irish origins, who in other respects are opposites. Michael Keating, 49, from Oldtown, Kilkenny, of the 2/3rd Motor Ambulance Company, Australian Army Service Corps, is one of the oldest men in B Force. He is a heavy drinking, tattooed rabble-rouser, court-martialled for 'neglecting to obey orders' and demoted to private on 21 September 1941.[24] And there is William Matthew Keating, 32, of Annandale, in Sydney's inner west – a tough young man who served with selfless duty in the 8th Division Postal Unit, Australian Army Postal Service, before finding himself captured and shipped to Sandakan. Something else distinguishes Bill Keating, unknown to him at the time:

he is about to become the uncle of a future prime minister of Australia.[25]

These men are among the 1500 or so Australian prisoners for whom the squat atap barracks in the jungle eight miles west of Sandakan is now 'home'. The severity of the prison camps of Imperial Japan tends to follow the example of the local officers and guards, but no prisoner of Sandakan realises what lies in store for him in this wretched place. For now, with the war still in the balance, the guards' treatment of the prisoners is relatively lenient. With every passing month, with each Japanese military setback, the prospects for the prisoners here will grow increasingly bleak, but nothing – not their worst nightmares – could prepare these men for the ordeal that is yet to come.

PART

2

THE CAMP

6

FIRST ESCAPES

If you are to handle [the prisoners] successfully, you must enter into their state of mind. They are also human, and if we treat them compassionately, they will respond by placing their confidence in us.
Lieutenant Colonel Suga Tatsuji, commanding officer of
Borneo Prisoner of War Internment Area, to his prison staff

THE SUN RISES ON SMUDGES of life, restrained by wire and jungle, and casts scrawny shadows of a dog, a monkey, a man. The light glances over a dirt clearing, a huge tree, some bent figures, a rigid guard and into a row of little stilted huts. In the distance, a stray dog whines, somehow conscious of its place in the food chain; soon, the dogs will compete with men for food. No cock crows: the birds have all been eaten.

Few people – rubber sappers and residual coolie labour – live near this place, segregated by forest and plantations, as if its inhabitants are a community of untouchables, set apart from the rest of the human race.

Inside the huts, the men stir; the Dead End Kids inhale the swamp breath. Dawn heralds another unreal day, as the soldiers wake with jolting reminders of their abject fate, before fading back into submission. Blindingly real in the glare of the morning light is the evidence everywhere of their captivity: the wire, the guards. Many of the men keeping watch are Formosan. With their rough khaki fatigues and dirty appearance, they cut unimpressive figures alongside the Japanese, who are typically dressed in clean shirts and breeches with long puttees. On their heads, the Japanese wear cloth caps or steel helmets, which are slung over their right shoulders when not required. The officers are resplendently turned out in olive twill tunics and cavalry breeches and field boots; their swords, the cherished symbol of samurai power, always at their sides. A white cloth patch and symbol, pinned over the left breast, designates the soldier's unit.[1]

The Formosans answer to the Japanese guards, many of whom, aged 30–35, are line soldiers of some years' service. Some claim to have fought in New Guinea – possibly on the Kokoda Track – but owing to ill-health or wounds have been withdrawn for guard duty. The Japanese guards in turn answer to the camp commandant, Captain Hoshijima Susumi, who is himself answerable to the headquarters of the Japanese prison network in Borneo, based in Kuching, under the command of the 'Westernised' Lieutenant Colonel Suga Tatsuji. Far beyond Suga stands the real power in the South-West Pacific, in the scowling Japanese strongholds of Rabaul, Singapore and Manila.

Lowest in the pecking order of imperial authority, the Formosans are regular recipients of Japanese wrath, beatings and poor rations. The first batch are uncertain of their authority – shy, even frightened, of the white soldiers in their charge. Many are young – mere boys, aged 16–20, some of them products of the Bushido Youth Corps. In a dismal trick of fate, they hail originally from China. Their ancestors have lived for generations in Japanese-occupied Formosa, and these young men think of themselves as thoroughly inducted into the Japanese Empire. 'Most of them have never fired a rifle,' observes one witness, Sergeant Walter Wallace. 'The fighting qualities of these boys are nil. They are frightened of the darkness and very nervous when moving among the POWs.'[2] They speak a little English and some Malay.

They are slapped, or beaten, routinely, for any lapse in discipline – an extension of the ferocious corporal punishment that applies in Japanese boys' schools of the day and treats grown men rather like animals who must be taught a lesson. This thinking is predicated on the idea that men are more likely to respond to a slap or a kick than a carrot or a mature order. Thus, the senior officers slap the junior ones; the junior officers beat the sergeants; the sergeants beat the corporals; the corporals punch the privates; the privates punch the guards. And on it goes, an unimpeded wave of violence, stupid, dull, incoherent – until something snaps in the mind of the mute recipient and a savage is formed. In time, terrified of their Japanese masters and contemptuous of their Anglo-Saxon captives, many lowly guards tend to lash out with blind fury at anything that upsets them.

The white prisoner persists at the fag end of this system. His peculiar state as the captive of the yellow man has hitherto distanced him from the most brutal reprisals, which the Japanese routinely inflict on what they regard as Asia's 'lesser' races, chiefly the Chinese and Koreans. But, as conditions deteriorate and labour demands increase, the status of the Australian (and later British) soldiers in Sandakan is made emphatically clear: they are the slaves at the base of this crushing hierarchy, the nethermost recipients of all the pent-up rage of a regime that is slowly, inexorably losing.

◆

One morning, in early August 1942, something is palpably wrong in the camp. As the Australians gather for *tenko*, they notice a new tension, hair-trigger aggressive. Until now, the food at No. 1 Prisoner of War Camp has been tolerable, the stores full. Breakfast is usually rice slop, vegetables, occasionally fish. This morning, nothing. The young Formosans are more than usually agitated, and the Japanese guards furious. The unspoken cause is alive in the minds of everyone present: over the past week, as many as 15 prisoners have escaped. The Japanese officers appear personally affronted, as if the prisoners have committed a crime against the authority of the empire – an insult to the Imperial will.

The Australians have no truck with this superstition, of course; it amuses them to think that their mates have offended the descendant of a sun goddess. The sun is their enemy. They love the night, and their duty as soldiers is to break out under cover of darkness. Queenslanders Matt Carr and Herb Trackson, ammunition drivers in the Australian Army Service Corps, have made the first attempt, on the night of 29 July.

Trackson is a tough young butcher, lover of rugby; Carr an itinerant bushman, quiet, unassuming. During the Battle of Muar, in Malaya, the pair delivered ammunition to the 2/15 Field Regiment under heavy fire. In the embrace of a swept monsoonal sky, they wriggled under the wire, carrying a haversack with matches, a knife, groundsheet, two mess tins of cooked rice and some rice cakes. They reached the coast after days of thrashing through forest and sprinting across rubber fields. A Chinese woman fed them, and a native boy guided them to a waterfront kampong, west of Sandakan, where they found a canoe. They paddled to Pulau Bai, an uninhabited island in Sandakan Harbour, where they rested among the mangroves, feeding on coconuts, melons and oysters; and then to the eastern shore of the island, where they staggered on, Trackson sick with malaria. They met a group of Chinese salt-makers, who informed them of the price on their heads.

On 25 August, a month after their escape, a Malay leads them to a deserted plantation, promising to return with food. He betrays them to the Japanese. Back at Sandakan, they are turned over to the Kempei-tai and initially treated well, permitted a shower, fed milk, cake and bananas. A Japanese medical officer nurses the delirious Trackson back to health. 'I wouldn't be here but for the good treatment I got,' Trackson later says.[3]

In late July and early August, a further nine Australians have broken out of Sandakan Prison Camp. The first group – Edward Allen, Murray Jacka, Jeff Shelley and Tom Harrington – also of the Australian Army Service Corps, carried a small supply of food, a compass and anti-malarial medication, courtesy of the resourceful Warrant Officer Bill Sticpewich. They headed 19 miles north-west, through rubber and forest, then doubled back towards the town area, moving perilously close to the local Kempei-tai office. They lasted a week before the secretary of the British North Borneo Timber Company, in fear of reprisals, betrayed them to the Japanese.

The six recaptured prisoners, resigned to severe punishment, are shipped to Kuching, where the local Kempei-tai confines them to wire-mesh cages for a few months, after which they are perfunctorily tried and sentenced to death. They win a reprieve. Harrington will thereafter die of illness in Kuching, while the rest will be sent back to Singapore, to spend years in the dreaded Outram Road Gaol.

Another five made a break in July 1942, led by the

remarkable 21-year-old bushman Alan Minty, raised on a sheep and cattle station in Bairnsdale, Victoria. All were from the 2/29th Battalion, including the old soldier and Englishman Fred New, and the young bandsman and stretcher-bearer Bruce McWilliams. They crawled under the wire on the night of 31 July and headed west, with 'no particular plan other than to get away from the Japanese'.[4] They hid near a Chinese tobacco farm, seven miles inland – a lucky choice, as it happened: the farm manager, Foo Seng Chow, is linked to the Chinese resistance and, in turn, connected with Dr Taylor's operation. The escapees received food through the redoubtable Sergeant Abin, who, like many of the young constabulary, seemed to be everywhere at once – channelling food, running messages, delivering parcels – at great personal risk. The five built a squat humpy in the jungle and survive for five months on food sent through the Chinese network and funded by local people. Then, caught in a muddy mangrove swamp, they will endure the soul-rupturing experience of recapture, dispatch to Kuching and thence to Outram Road.

◆

Back in Sandakan that August, few prisoners hold out any hope for the escapees' survival. 'I'm afraid they won't get too far in this class of country,' Tom Burns writes gloomily in his diary.[5] And now he and his fellow inmates learn the price of their mates' defiance: the prisoners are ordered to line up on the parade ground and are left for hours in the morning sun. There is a body count, a recount, a lecture by a senior guard on good behaviour and patience and 'a lot of other bull after which they dismissed us', Burns writes. The men return to their huts; there is no work that day. In coming days, the Japanese impose a more concerted punishment: the food ration is cut, the cigarette issue ceases and the canteen closes. 'The tucker gets very rough from now on,' Burns records: just watery stew, little rice.

The camp regime more closely monitors the men. Each prisoner receives a number, which he must wear on his hat at all times. The double wire fencing is strengthened and an extra guard detail applied morning and night. Arbitrary beatings increase. 'One has to keep a pretty cool head and just take it from them as it will make it bad for everybody if we strike them back,' Burns writes. 'But we will get our chance someday . . . They won't get any mercy from any of our chaps as we all have a score to settle with these yellow Bs.' He refers, in part, to the Japanese massacre of wounded soldiers at Alexandra Hospital in Singapore.

The punishments worsen, Burns writes, as the year progresses, and the 'Japs keep telling us that they heavily bombed Darwin [it happened seven months earlier] and the city of Sydney [a lie]'. Burns is not taken in. '[A]ll lies and a big bluff,' he concludes. He accurately connects Japanese military failure with the prisoners' worsening treatment, linking rumours that the Allies have retaken Burma (untrue, at this point) with harder work on the aerodrome and 'beltings every day'.

On his discharge from the camp hospital, after six weeks, Burns witnesses the Japanese guards beat up a boy who is 'just getting over an attack of malaria'. The capture of Trackson, Carr, Shelley, Allen, Jacka and Harrington bears out his fears: each is sentenced to four to five years in Outram Road Gaol. A punitive mood hangs over the camp. One young soldier, caught laughing on parade, is kicked in his shins until they're a bloody mess, then forced to stand on parade for hours with his eyes to the sun and his arms outstretched.

This regime of brute force is deaf to the relatively moderate authority then issuing from Kuching. On 15 August, Lieutenant Colonel Suga addresses the officers and senior guards of the newly established Borneo Prisoner Internment Area. Outlining the aims of the prison system, Suga ascribes to the camps the noble role of a 'gymnasium', in which the prisoners 'are to be trained to appreciate and subscribe to the Japanese spirit, their fundamental misconceptions of Japan corrected, and the doctrine of white superiority thoroughly rooted out'.[6]

In fulfilling their august charter, the prison staff are expected to show unusual powers of self-control. They must, in their dealings with the prisoners, eradicate 'the slightest trace of adulation of Americans and Englishmen'. Suga goes on to declare:

> Conduct yourself in the spirit of, and in a manner befitting a citizen of the first of nations . . . strike the happy mean between harshness and leniency. To show maudlin sympathy or to lapse into sentimental indulgence, thus creating the impression that you can be influenced like a little child, is extremely reprehensible. But at the same time it is equally unpardonable . . . to vent your private spite in excessive harshness . . .

The one essential in handling prisoners of war is 'not to be capricious', Suga prescribes. 'Rewards must be uniform and punishment relentless. Let there be no half-measures.'

For their part, the prisoners must be made to feel 'the realities of their position' and 'to understand that they hardly can expect to be better fed and clothed than our own soldiers'. Nonetheless, Suga continues, prisoners must be treated kindly if sick or 'afflicted with any other misfortune which calls for sympathy': 'If you are to handle them successfully, you must enter into their state of mind. They are also human, and if we treat them compassionately, they will respond by placing their confidence in us.'

He orders the prison guards not to interfere with the prisoners' 'usages, customs, religious practices [and] musical proclivities', as if they were a strange new species. '[T]hey are so different from us in language, customs and habits, they frequently misinterpret our intentions and are inclined to become uneasy. Thus arise unrest and disorder of all kinds . . .' He exhorts his officials to get acquainted with the prisoners and 'understand their psychology', the better for 'using them on labour projects', which is the aim of his speech.

Top of the list of prisoners' crimes against Japan, Suga adds, is that of escape, and to counteract it he insists – as did Japanese commandants throughout the empire – that all prisoners be called upon to sign 'an undertaking renouncing all intention to attempt a getaway'.

7

THE COMMANDANT

I personally will not sign this document!
Lieutenant Colonel Walsh refusing to cooperate
with Hoshijima's no-escape rule

THE FIRST YEAR OF CAPTIVITY is tolerable, with a variety of small liberties and even a few comforts. The food supply, though poor, is more or less consistent, and the leniency returns after most of the escapees have been recaptured. The canteen resumes operation, offering tobacco at 15 cents a tahil (2/3 of an ounce), fruit at seven cents a pound, turtle eggs at one or two cents each, and fish at 20 cents a pound.[1] In their rigidly prescriptive fashion, the Japanese authorise an 'Amusing Hour' on Saturday nights, during which the prisoners may sing, play games and so on, but 'No War song nor Martial Air is allowed – not only in amusing hour, but always,' a stern poster warns.[2] Nelson Short, with his banjo or ukelele, and his friend Jack Stanley stage a vaudeville act, singing 'Walking My Baby Back Home' and other popular songs.[3] Sunday is to be 'a holiday' under camp rules issued in the name of Captain George Cook, a voyage-only officer (promoted only for the voyage over) who becomes the prisoners' liaison. His earnest application to the role, which includes issuing instructions on how to salute and show respect to the Japanese – such as bowing if they lack hats – earns Cook the hatred of the soldiers and a deserved reputation as a collaborator.[4]

In their off days and 'amusing hours', the fitter prisoners organise light sporting events. The Japanese guards, never having seen a game of Aussie Rules, take a curious interest in the sight. The prisoners fashion a shallow swimming pool out of water draining from the swamp. In the evenings, the prisoners are allowed to read – some have copies of Shakespeare or the Bible; others prefer chess or two-up. There are few electric lights, mainly kerosene lamps.

Tradesmen are encouraged to apply their skills, and the Japanese order the carpenters among them to make furniture. They also build a small chapel out of atap. A few services are held there. The officers make a tentative attempt to introduce educational courses in agriculture, accountancy, shorthand, arts and crafts. These begin with the best intentions – to discipline the mind and body – but the prisoners' enthusiasm fades in the oppressive atmosphere. Nonetheless, the wood-carving lessons yield a few hand-carved utensils and a chess set. Two courses, on navigation and geography, prove popular among those with an eye on escape. And there is some interest in the local flora and fauna, given their possible aid in survival: which animals and vegetation are edible? The risk of being poisoned by a spitting cobra, red-headed krait or diamond-headed viper diminish their appeal even to hungry men; but pythons and monitor lizards are prized, and their numbers around the camp rapidly decline.

The officers are allowed to erect a small stage and perform concerts, involving singing, comedy, musicals and burlesques. Betting – on anything – is the favourite pastime, and many prisoners have a punt, with savings retained from Singapore and their forced-labour pay from the Japanese of ten to 25 cents a day.

Gambling riotously proceeds in a secret dugout under the hut of 'Gunboat Simpson', where up to a dozen men assemble nightly for pontoon or poker.[5] They sit 'in a ring round a depression in the earth where a big tree had once stood, screened from view by a curtain of old blankets and atap, and lit by a globe let down through the hut floor'.[6] Minimum entry is a ten-cents stake, with Gunboat parked at the entrance to check it. The Dead End Kids pool their resources. The first to enter shows Gunboat the money, sits by the outer blanket then passes the cash underneath into the hands of a waiting Kid, who repeats the process until all gain admission.

The Japanese initially turn a blind eye to the hugely popular night-time boxing matches, with heavy betting on prizefighters such as Punchy Donohue, Snowy Bryant, Jimmy Finn and the part-Aboriginal Jimmy Darlington. At one bout, 'as hot and thick with the smell of blood as any evening in the Tin Shed at Sydney Rushcutters Bay',[7] the firm favourite Snowy Bryant dances rings around Punchy Donohue, who, with his eyebrows split, seems 'to walk on the back of his heels' for most of the fight, much slower than the nimble-footed Bryant. When all seems lost, Punchy lands a massive uppercut on Snowy's jaw. Bryant goes down, out for the count. The crowd leaps to its feet, and the bankrupted chief bookie is able to pay only a cent in the dollar.

The prisoners' cash savings are hidden or buried. Suspicions are rife. One 'young kid' accused of stealing cash, Braithwaite recalls, is hauled before a prisoners' kangaroo court and pronounced guilty. Punched, shunned, sent to Coventry, the lad pleads his innocence with tears streaming down his face.

Sometime later, his accusers discover a rat's nest made of cash in the atap rafters: 'Now that made everyone feel badly; we certainly apologised to this kid, but he never recovered from that . . . he became more or less a real introvert and, er, he sort of deteriorated in his health and, er, I often thought about this young kid and I thought, well, we probably killed him.'[8]

Cash not spent on the canteen or gambling goes to a general hospital fund, to help care for the sick and wounded – in spite of which, the soldiers' health continues to decline. In August and September 1942, dysentery is rife, and the first severe cases of beriberi emerge. Malaria, mercifully, is yet to appear in great numbers, despite the prevalence of mosquitoes. The chief problem is the scarcity of salt and vitamin B, which accelerates the slow withdrawal of the human body from the task of sustaining itself. Tom Burns has lost three stone; bigger men feel the loss more severely. The unhygienic conditions are the chief breeder of disease. The camp has two cans of disinfectant, no more, throughout the year, and the guards refuse to replace the bucket latrines (eventually, the men are allowed to dig pit latrines). The result is a spectrum of tropical conditions, from dysentery to severe tinea, Singapore Ear, jungle sores, hookworm and other ailments. These confine the sick to the camp 'hospital' – a cramped hut alive with rats, bugs, lice and other insects, so repellent that the lesser afflicted prefer to convalesce on the outside.

Their deteriorating health is relieved, if not retarded, by the occasional freak appearance of better food – the slaughter of a pig or other animal, even a yak or dugong, according to some accounts.[9] The offal and remains of these creatures are tossed to the prisoners after the Japanese have consumed the better parts. But what actually sustains the men is the near-magical appearance of medical supplies and nutrients through the workings of Dr James Taylor's underground network, whose local tentacles have now infiltrated the prison camp. It is this supply, above all, that keeps the death rate in the camp at three per month in the last six months of 1942.[10]

◆

The prisoners are cruelly disabused of their hopes of further lenience in early September. 'What a day,' Tom Burns writes in his diary on the night of 2 September, one that will 'probably go down as the most eventful since we have been prisoners of war'.[11] It begins ordinarily enough: the prisoners assemble on the parade ground for roll call – the slow or reluctant are 'chased' from their huts by Japanese guards – under the Big Tree in anticipation of the arrival of Hoshijima, who has been instructed to crack down on camp security in the wake of the breakouts. Specifically, he is to enact Lieutenant Colonel Suga's orders that all prisoners sign a non-escape clause.

Lieutenant Colonel Walsh later recalls:

> The whole force was massed facing the guardroom. Tables had been placed . . . at the end of the line of troops on the western side. Extra troops had been brought in by the IJA [Imperial Japanese Army] from Sandakan. Machine guns were mounted on the guardroom overlooking the parade. There were about 150 fully armed Japanese soldiers about, there were hand grenades, etc, and we were absolutely corralled like a mob of sheep.[12]

Hoshijima shortly appears on the platform in his well-pressed uniform, sporting, as usual, his pistols and sword. He seems attired to address a departing army, not to berate a group of prisoners of war. An engineering graduate of Osaka University, Hoshijima is a tall, slim man, who comports himself with the prim accomplishment of a school prefect. He carries himself with erect self-importance and tends to ride his horse – an old racehorse – around the compound and out to the airfield. '[Y]ou'd be working on a working party and next thing you'd look up and there he'd be sitting on his horse, just up above you, watching you,' Braithwaite recalls.[13]

Hoshijima seems to regard himself as a pure example of Japanese 'spirit', demonstrated by an unthinking obedience to any Japanese power greater than himself. Appointed by Lieutenant General Maeda Toshitame, the then commandant of the Borneo Defence Forces, Hoshijima has two responsibilities in Sandakan: to build an airfield and to command the prison camp. The engineer's pride makes the construction of the airfield his chief concern, demoting his role as camp commandant to an ancillary duty, the fulfilment of which he leaves mainly to subordinates. He considers the prisoners only insofar as they represent a labour force; their welfare is not his concern.

'He was a man who didn't seem to have any human compassion at all,' Braithwaite later says.[14] So it surprises the Australian officers when Hoshijima listens to their protest, that the construction of the airfield contravenes the clause of the Geneva Convention forbidding the use of prisoners as slave labour. Japan has signed but not ratified the Convention, and Hoshijima, for once, is compelled to think for himself. Indeed, he decides to exempt the officers from drome labour duties – sowing further discontent in the ranks.

Normally, Hoshijima would not dream of questioning imperial orders, laws or regulations, regardless of how unreasonable, cruel or plain stupid they might be. Like many of his fellow officers, he considers this unthinking reflex a virtue. 'During my school years and the years I have spent in the Army,' he later pleads before his trial, 'I have never been once punished for breaking any regulations.'[15] He clings to his degrees and paper qualifications, as though they give him the substance he otherwise lacks. This typical Japanese 'organisation man' is 'arrogant in his treatment of those under his command, yet sycophantic and deferential to his superiors'.[16] Those superiors include the recently arrived Kempei-tai, whose powers extend to the security of the Japanese prison network.

And so, mindful of his recent orders from Suga, and anxious not to upset the Kempei-tai, Hoshijima now acts firmly to prevent any further attempts to escape. He announces to the parade, through his interpreter Osawa, that all prisoners of war must sign a 'No Escape Declaration', which stipulates that any prisoner caught defying the order will be summarily executed. The contract contains three clauses:

— We will attempt to accomplish any order given by
  the Japanese.
— We will not attempt to escape.
— We are aware that we will be shot if we attempt
  to escape.[17]

The oath is roughly translated as 'I promise not to escape and if any of us should attempt to do so we request that you shoot them to death'.[18] It thereby appears to impose a collective obligation on the prisoners to approve the execution of a fellow soldier – a grave breach of the Geneva Convention and affront to the spirit of mateship that has animated the Australian Army since Gallipoli. The idea of an Australian soldier nodding compliantly to the execution of a friend – 'Yes, sir, he deserved it, sir' – for trying to escape the Japanese runs counter to the most basic understanding of the psychology of the Australians. But the Japanese commandant is in earnest; in his world, the Australians ought to feel *grateful* for the opportunity to obey an order of the Imperial Army, whose ultimate provenance is the emperor himself.

Hoshijima orders Walsh, as the prisoners' commanding officer, to read the oath aloud and instruct the prisoners to sign it. Walsh steps forward. Defiant murmurs ripple down the lines. The diggers do not like the diminutive colonel. A graduate of Duntroon, he formerly commanded the 2/10th Field Regiment. He was selected as Sandakan camp commander in Singapore as a last-minute replacement for Brigadier Harold Taylor, nicknamed the 'Chancellor of Changi' for his work on running educational courses in the prison before being shipped to China along with other officers above the rank of colonel.[19] Walsh is a gunner, to boot, which little enhances his status in the eyes of infantrymen; he seems aloof, cut off from the men, and shares a hut with the medical officers. He has so far shown little sign of leadership – delegating most of the camp administration to junior officers, chiefly Majors John Workman and Monty Blanksby. The ensuing events, however, briefly cast Walsh as a man of rare courage, whom his many detractors appear to have misjudged.

Walsh reads the contract. The clause that forces the prisoners to accede to the Japanese killing anyone who tries to escape disgusts him. Walsh refuses to sign. The oath is in breach of the Geneva Convention, he insists. He abruptly explains to Hoshijima that it is an Allied prisoner's duty to attempt to escape. 'I personally will not sign this document!' he announces and throws the paper to the ground.

Machine guns swivel; Japanese guards raise their rifles. Four seize Walsh, slap him and stand ready to shoot – on Hoshijima's nod. The prisoners rally to Walsh's side. They realise that the contract is not binding. Some shout 'We will sign!' in order to save his life – and possibly theirs.[20] Walsh refuses. Nests of machine-gunners train their weapons on the crowd; some soldiers clutch grenades. In fury, the prisoners seem about to rush the Japanese, or break out; it seems at any moment the parade ground will be awash in blood. '[W]e would have been massacred, no doubt,' Braithwaite later recalls.[21]

The guards bind Walsh's hands and march him out of the gate, flanked by a firing squad. 'There was dead silence,' Braithwaite says, 'a feeling of menace, that something was going to explode.' The prisoners are 'ready to make a break for it. The guards knew it. Some of them were trembling.' The prisoners urge Hoshijima to reconsider; the interpreter passes on their pleas.

Hoshijima orders a stay of execution. He asks Major John Workman why the Australian commander won't sign. Workman replies, according to Hoshijima's account, 'Europeans do not use "we" in making such declarations.' To which Hoshijima replies, 'That is our mistake, so we will correct it.' After brief negotiations, the commandant agrees to replace the phrase 'we request that you shoot them' with, 'I understand that any prisoner attempting to escape will be shot' – thus shifting the collective responsibility from the group to the individual. 'Everybody agreed to sign.'[22]

The compromise saves Japanese face – and Walsh's life.

Workman eases the task of signing the hated document by making it clear to the men that they are doing so under duress. In the event, many troops make a mockery of the whole undertaking, by signing as 'Errol Flynn', 'Donald Duck', 'Ned Kelly' or other comic-book characters or popular heroes.[23] The act scarcely dims the prisoners' hopes of escape. A core group of officers – Captains Matthews, Ken Mosher, Rod Jeffrey and Jim Heaslop – continues to study the possibility of a mass breakout.[24]

For their insubordination, the prisoners are forced to stand in the sun for several hours while the guards search the huts for incriminating papers, letters or diaries. All writing materials are confiscated. The Australians return to their beds at twilight, amid rigorous analysis of the day's events. Granted, Walsh may be a 'Duntroon wanker' and a stickler for form and rank, the diggers reckon, but the bloke has guts. Burns' well-concealed pen and diary survive the search and convey the mood: 'The whole camp is very proud of Col. Walsh. The guts he showed was fair dinkum Aussie spirit and I know if ever the time comes we will be with him to the last man.'[25]

The colonel's new-found respect turns out to be short-lived. In October 1942, Walsh and several other officers, including the popular senior medical officer Lieutenant Colonel E. M. Sheppard, are sent to Kuching – the headquarters of the Japanese prison network in Borneo. In the coming months, Walsh's nerves fray and break. He retreats into himself and seems to lose his grip. He jumps when summoned by the Japanese, so nervous that he runs at their beck and call. He 'scampered', recalls Hugh Waring, 'like a boy in a half-skip'.[26] A small man, Walsh seems further diminished by his habit of eagerly saluting his Japanese masters two or three times, often taking a backward step 'into a gutter'.[27]

In time, the colonel becomes a source of embarrassment to his fellow officers. And yet, the transformation of Walsh from a brave and resolute soldier to a nervous wreck surely calls for sympathy, not condemnation. Few men have stared down an execution and then lived among their executioners.

8

THE DROME

*The Japanese government very good treat you well, so you
must have impatience while we get inconveniences for you . . .
You work hard, finish airfield, you be fine . . . This is fact.*
Lieutenant Colonel Suga to the prisoners

VICTORY IN THE PACIFIC depends on air power: no
army, or ship, can survive without air protection, as the fate of
HMS *Repulse* and *Prince of Wales* demonstrated in December
1941. Helpless under relentless Japanese air bombardment, the
battleships were destroyed within three hours, with the loss of
1000 sailors. For most of 1942, the Japanese Zero has been the
reigning steel bird in the Pacific sky, but bombers and supply
planes have also been critical in securing the southerly advance of
the Imperial forces and in nourishing the distant garrisons. The
planes rely upon launch pads – fixed or floating – from which to
guard the extremities of the empire.

Following the Japanese conquest of the Philippines in early
1942, Manila has served as the main supply base for troops
advancing south. Aircraft leaving the Philippines, however, en
route to Singapore, Java, Celebes, Rabaul and Timor, must refuel
somewhere – and Sandakan in Borneo is perfectly positioned

as a midway refuelling point. An aerodrome is earmarked for construction, and Japanese commanders in Borneo are ordered to build one long enough to accommodate fighters and supply planes. Its construction will require 'an enormous amount of forced labor',[1] drawn from the prison camps of Changi. In late 1942, 1500 Australians are available in Sandakan to start the job, but the Japanese reckon more will be needed in the coming months. Large groups of civilians are also forced to work on the airfield; in addition, some 4000 Javanese are shipped into Borneo to swell the labour force.

The sight of 'white coolies' taking up the pick and shovel is a profound inversion of the settled order of things. It is the starkest expression of Japan's propaganda and psychological offensive, which aims to overturn assumptions of Western supremacy and embrace the notion of 'Asia for the Asians'. The message initially finds favour among indigenous groups in Burma, India, Thailand and Indochina, long exploited by their white colonial masters. But their faith in Japanese promises of 'liberty' rapidly disappears when millions find themselves enslaved to Tokyo's master plan, yoked to the Thai–Burma Railway, underground mines, airfields and other projects, along with having their food and resources appropriated wholesale to the 'Greater East Asian Co-Prosperity Sphere', a rapidly emerging euphemism for Imperial Japan.

◆

Every morning, a bugler, Paddy Maguire, rallies the camp from its fitful sleep. 'Tired and hungry men stir, curse the bugler, curse the Japs and curse themselves for not taking notice of their mates when they queued up for Enlistment – "You'll be sorry," they warned them – and then tell Paddy what to do with the bugle.'[2]

The prisoners, drafted into batches of 40 men, follow a strict daily work schedule: breakfast – plain rice – at 7 am; parade and roll call at 7.45 am; move out at 8 am, marching along three miles of jungle track to the aerodrome site, often singing 'They'll Be Dropping One Hundred Pounders When They Come' to the tune of 'She'll Be Coming 'Round the Mountain'; hard labour – land-clearing, digging, rock-breaking – until noon, with a smoko at around 11 am, and a ten-minute break each hour; lunch – rice and watery stew (no salt) – until 1 pm; hard labour until 6 pm; return to camp for dinner (the same as lunch); and roll call.[3] Lights out at 10 pm.

Under the watchful eye of high bamboo towers positioned around the building site, the prisoners begin clearing and grading the bleached landscape. Speed is critical, they are constantly told. The finished airfield must comprise a long runway, aircraft bays and taxi lanes capable of accepting bombers and large supply planes. The stronger men chop down coconut and rubber trees; others clear the undergrowth – roots, scrub, the forest detritus – and break the ground. Several skip lines run from the high ground to the low, bearing the waste. The skips, to Japanese satisfaction, have been imported from Burma, where the British used them to build the Burma Road. It is sweltering, back-breaking work under the Borneo sun, and it goes on hour after hour, day after day, hundreds of salt-deprived bodies sweating it out, bending, straightening, bending, carrying on.

The severity of the labour regime varies according to the character of the commander of prison labour. This man may be lenient or brutal. At one point early in the construction, Australian officers are ordered to oversee the work, with a very spartan guard presence. 'There was a period of approximately six weeks when the work on the aerodrome was placed entirely under control of our own officers,' recalls Lieutenant Rod Wells. '[T]hey did not interfere with us.' That benign regimen is a one-off; and working conditions worsen in general.

Some guards are unbearably harsh. The Australian slaves can expect no restraint, for example, from Lieutenant Okahara, commander of drome labour, who bears an unfortunate likeness to the Japanese cliché on wartime propaganda posters of a squat, bespectacled fanatic. Okahara has a peculiar talent for cruelty, which escalates with every bit of bad news about the Japanese war effort. He is like a barometer of his nation's failing, intensifying the beatings and humiliation as news arrives of another reversal on the front.

When the Australians hear a rumour, unfounded, that 'our forces' have retaken Burma and Singapore, the 'Jap guards' avenge the loss by beating up the Australian officers – setting an ominous pattern for the months and years ahead. 'They are handing out beltings every day,' Tom Burns hears, from his sickbed. 'They lined up our officers and belted them across the backs with a thick cane. Gee it makes one's blood boil to see them get away with it.'[4] The slightest provocation – smiling on parade, eating while passing a sentry, failing to bow or salute – elicits a slap or punch or kick in the shins. A minor infringement leads to the punishment of a whole working party. The most common method is to stand the prisoners in noonday sun, with their arms outstretched, for hours on end; any relaxation provokes a thrashing.

The bashings at the drome grow harsher and more frequent as the Japanese fret over Allied incursions. The food ration deteriorates, and the prisoners' hopes of survival fade. Complaints to Okahara go unheeded. 'I cannot help what happens to Australian soldiers,' he insists.[5] So it continues. Burns recoils from this hateful little world; but there is no escape from the thudding presence of the guards.

◆

At first, the men resist their enslavement to the Japanese war effort. Go-slows, wilful blindness, laziness, incompetence: the Australians apply every possible means of delaying, or sabotaging, the construction of the airfield. Missing tools, broken equipment, dodgy assembly – Denny Garland and his mates pretend to saw through a log with the blunt side of a saw – all alert the Japanese to a pattern of obstruction, culminating in a crackdown.

One day, an unusually large number of picks, steel rails and shovels disappear. The Japanese foreman orders the senior Australian officer present to find them – or the prisoners will be severely punished. The officer, Captain Ken Mosher, a tough, battle-hardened soldier, threatens to deny the men their next rice meal unless the equipment is returned. Twice he shouts his demand, to silence. In reply, one digger, Private Eric 'Mo' Davis, lands a punch on Mosher's jaw. 'Now give us the bloody rice!' Davis shouts. Mosher threatens to court-martial him on their release, to which Davis imperturbably answers, 'And if you do, I'll tell every newspaper in the country that you aided and abetted the Japanese while we were trying to sabotage them.' Mosher yields, and the men surge forward for their rice.[6]

Mosher's aims are protective, in the interests of survival – hardly treasonable. Yet the incident rankles, and it sets a troubling precedent for what in future is felt to constitute collaboration. The smarter officers and other ranks realise, however, that survival, individually and as a group, will depend to some degree on cooperation with the Japanese. Knee-jerk resistance and hotheadedness are, they soon find, the quickest paths to self-destruction.

◆

In October 1942, Hoshijima receives fresh orders from Kuching to complete the airfield and connecting roads as soon as possible. The order passes down the ranks: more labour is needed – at least another 400–600 prisoners. But they cannot be found, owing to sickness; dysentery is rife in the prison camp. In reply, the guards storm through the hospital hut, upending the sick and wounded from their beds. The doctors and padres are pressed into work details, and the officers – hitherto exempt from hard labour – join the men at the drome.

An incident early that month spurs the work to a furious pace: Lieutenant Colonel Suga visits the Sandakan No. 1 and Berhala Island prison camps. The commandant of the Borneo prison network seems a courteous, open-minded man – a former schoolteacher from Hiroshima, who curiously sports a row of First World War British service ribbons, the legacy of his participation in the Great War, when Japan was a British ally. Suga is thought not to tolerate the abuse of the prisoners, and he remonstrates with his officers to ensure the guards show restraint. He is a rarity, whose concern only goes so far; his senior commanders routinely overrule him. When Australian officers complain that enforcing prisoners to work on airfields of military importance is against the

Geneva Convention, Suga replies that Premier Tojo 'had explicitly ordered that POWs be used on military projects'.[7]

Suga insists on appearing before the prisoners wearing a pith helmet and long katana sword, which provokes mirth in the Australian ranks. His speech, in broken English, promises that he 'would feed, clothe and protect us and look after our sick', recalls Sticpewich. His last words provoke laughter, as transcribed in one account: 'The Japanese government very good treat you well, so you must have impatience while we get inconveniences for you,' concluding with, 'This is fact' – or 'This is fucked', to Australian ears. As the muffled hilarity subsides, the prisoners realise that the message is a pointed threat: 'All Japanese officers – Samurai. All Japanese officers – honourable. You work hard, finish airfield, you be fine.'[8]

Indeed, up to Suga's visit, 'things were not too bad', Sticpewich later recalls. 'After Suga's visit we were made to count in Japanese on the parades and if we made a mistake in the counting we would be . . . slapped in the face with hands, thumped in the back with rifle butts and kicked in the shins.' Failing to stand at attention elicits the same response. At the time, beatings are administered by Japanese guards – 'old soldiers' and 'not so bad', Sticpewich notes. 'The beatings were apparently part of Japanese ordinary Army discipline and were not brutally administered.'[9] That relative 'restraint' lasts until April 1943, when younger, more vicious Formosan guards, the so-called 'Kichi' – a nickname meaning 'small soldiers' – take over.

◆

The pressure on the prisoners hardens as the months pass. Any hint of sabotage or go-slow is met with crushing violence. A darker pattern starts to emerge: the prisoners are clearly being punished for no appreciable reason. The whip hand of the overseer aims to break down the Australian assumption of fairness, of basic justice. In time, the 'punishments' are administered arbitrarily, with no connection to any perceived transgression. The Formosan guards are used as Japanese tools to crush the Australian spirit. This is a daily bodily assault, engineered to strike fear and submission in the recipients. Armed with pick-handles and heavy mangrove and teak sticks, the guards roam the lines of white coolies, looking for the next target. They lash out at random, leaving some prisoners temporarily crippled and unable to work.

In this atmosphere, actual infringement of the rules provokes a rain of blows on the miscreant. If the men look sideways while they work, they are beaten; if the men rest, or talk, they are beaten. The Japanese and Formosan guards devise new kinds of punishments. 'We would have to stand to attention [holding] a piece of heavy timber above our heads. On the slightest movement the Japanese guards would beat you again. Men getting this punishment were kept there about two hours and longer,' Richard Braithwaite later recalls.[10] Or they force the Australians to beat each other. Prisoners in charge of work parties are compelled to line up their men and strike them: 'If they are not striking hard enough in the Japanese guard's opinion, he demonstrated, often with disastrous results.' Broken jaws, bloody shins are common; later, one man's eye is gouged out, Braithwaite states. 'I would rather you hit me than have [the Japanese] hit me,' a soldier tells Braithwaite, a sentiment shared throughout the camp. The soldiers try to appear to hit each other harder to avoid a Japanese or Formosan stepping in.

◆

December brings the rainy season, plus some cheer. Near Christmas, the Japanese permit the prisoners to stage a concert, with a hearty meal. It may seem a bizarre anomaly, but sudden lenience and indulgences are symptomatic of the inexplicable character of the Japanese leadership, buffeted about on news from afar or the mood of the moment: today they are lenient; tomorrow they are brutal. It hasn't escaped notice, either, that 8 December is the first anniversary of the Battle of Pearl Harbor – a cause for celebration in the Japanese barracks.

And so the Christmas concert is allowed to proceed. Captain Hoshijima and all the Japanese guards attend. Fifty patients are carried out on stretchers to watch. Even the Japanese governor of North Borneo, Kumabe Tanuke, shows up, dressed 'like a character out of Gilbert and Sullivan', in shorts and long johns, short socks, sword, medals and decorations.[11]

The officers' choir performs, along with a variety show called 'Radio Rubbish', with songs and sketches, which receives a tumultuous reception.[12] 'The Finale,' recalls Captain Claude Pickford years later, 'will remain with me and all those who were there for the rest of our lives.' On cue, everyone on stage begins to sing 'There'll Always Be an England', followed by 'God Save the Queen'. All the troops join in: 'It caught everybody so much that all the Jap guards stood up, even Hoshijima . . . the whole atmosphere was electric.'

Then Major Frank Fleming, acting force commander, stands to address the crowd. Before raising with the men 'one or two ideas which may be of some help in the future', Fleming thanks Hoshijima:

for allowing us to meet together this evening. I have been very happy today to see and to feel the splendid spirit of comradeship, helpfulness and quiet enjoyment of the good food we have been so fortunate to obtain. I feel that our morale has been steadily rising since the beginning of the Christmas Season and tonight will long remain in our memories as a high water mark.

On February 15 last we surrendered at Singapore and became PW. To most of us it seemed unbelievable. Our faculties were numbed and we were unable to think clearly. We moved as sleep-walkers, as men in a dream. It seemed the end of all things.

Then gradually we realised that we were still soldiers and members of the AIF, still wore the uniform our fathers had made famous and still had a duty to ourselves and our Country. Let us resolve tonight, to go on with our heads up and our eyes straight to meet whatever may be our lot in the same spirit as the old AIF fought and won an undying tradition . . .

. . . Let us be ever-ready to help the weaker amongst us . . . whose footsteps may stumble and whose will may falter as the road becomes rougher . . .

Tonight I dedicate myself anew to this force. I pledge myself to continue to serve you to the end, to the limit of my powers and in the interests of you all . . .

Finally on this Christmas night our thoughts naturally turn towards our homes, to those who love, whose thought and prayers will be with us and who wait lovingly for us. We owe it to them to see that we return to them as good men . . . and that we do nothing that would disgrace them or the names we and they bear.

And finally, gentlemen, when the going is tough and the way is rough, if conditions become more difficult, as indeed they may, when the burden seems well nigh unbearable, let us hear a voice saying 'Even these things shall pass'.

Yes, gentlemen – 'Even these things shall pass', and in the Almighty's own good time we shall return to Australia . . . I wish you all a good Christmas and the best for the coming year.[13]

9

FLESH AND BONE

He would go along the lines of sick and 'no duty'
PWs . . . beating them up and telling them they
were not sick, and sending them to work.
Warrant Officer Bill Sticpewich on how
one guard forced the sick to work

NEWS OF THE FIRST Japanese land defeat arrives, in late 1942, from Papua, where the Australian militia and regular forces, having delayed the invaders in a bloody stand at Isurava on the Kokoda Track and steadily driven them over the Owen Stanley Range, are now pounding their positions at Gona and Buna on the Papuan north coast.[1] The Americans, meanwhile, have landed on the Solomon Islands and will not leave until the Japanese are dislodged. The war is turning against Nippon – and the Allied prisoners are to be punished for the losses.

In Borneo, local resistance deepens. There are rumours of a native revolt in Sandakan and signs of rebellion in the mountainous interior. The Japanese respond with savagery. The Chinese, the usual suspects, are the first to be targeted. Soon, the Malays and the indigenous tribes feel the steel-capped boot of Japanese wrath. Accounts of random Japanese brutality permeate and appal local communities, such as these, heard by an Australian prisoner, Sergeant Walter Wallace: a pregnant Chinese woman is tied up and forced to kneel, on the airfield, in the sun for half a day, while being beaten about the head, back and breasts; and a Chinese man trying to sell food to the camp canteen is stripped to the waist and tied to a post for the day, during which Japanese guards frequently ash lit cigarettes on his bare body.[2]

And yet willing collaborators are never far from the surface. Hungry men may do anything for a dollar, and the Japanese soon establish a network of locals prepared to hunt down and expose escaped prisoners. A fissure runs through this once peaceful community, which splits the people. Citizens, families, tribes are forced to choose: to collaborate, or to resist and face the terrible consequences.

◆

For the prisoners, the worst punishment – worse than beatings or forced labour – is the deterioration or denial of rations. Hunger is their greatest fear. The days of meat when Japan celebrated 'victory' – served at Changi after the pyrrhic victory at the Battle of the Coral Sea – are long gone. There are no victories to celebrate in the second half of 1942. In June, the Battle of Midway destroyed the myth of Japanese naval supremacy when, in a surprise attack, the US fleet sank four enemy aircraft carriers in a sea battle that historian John Keegan calls 'the most stunning and decisive blow in the history of naval warfare'.[3] These events, so gratifying to the Allied forces and families back home, intensify the punishment regime in the prison camps: the rice ration is progressively cut and tapioca, a poor substitute, gradually replaces it.[4] It is just the start.

Longer hours and more punitive methods apply at the drome. Nature claims the soldiers' uniforms. They work shirtless, shortless and, finally, in simple loincloths – the fundoshi, or 'lap lap' – which become, for many, their only items of clothing. Braithwaite receives an issue of 'two fundoshis' during almost three years in captivity. Their boots rapidly wear out, and their bare feet complete the reversion of men from proud units of the Australian Imperial Force to a kind of primitive, nomadic tribe.[5] They resort to wearing whatever they can make, pilfer or substitute. Some tailor shorts from old kitbags or discarded rice bags, and fashion footwear out of canvas strips or carve wooden clogs, which click about the drome in a grim reminder of the prisoners' subservient status. In time, the men resemble – on parade and at the drome – 'a fancy dress show', as Braithwaite later describes the motley assortment of lap laps, hand-sewn shorts, clogs and rags on display.[6]

The prisoners try to retain a semblance of health and hygiene. To obtain food and medicine – chiefly quinine – they bribe the guards with whatever they can rustle up: Braithwaite's watch fetches 30 quinine tablets. In the wet season, malaria begins to spread through the camp – there being no nets or repellents to protect human skin from the *Anopheles* mosquito, the parasite's carrier – and the onset of the shakes, the hot and cold sweats, is routine by 1943. Quinine in plentiful supply sits in Japanese storage, but the guards share little with the prisoners. The disease – chiefly the cerebral variant – starts to kill, and the prisoners store whatever quinine they can trade or secrete for the most desperate cases.[7]

Other conditions steadily claim the weaker or more vulnerable. Tropical ulcers – grotesque sores that eat the flesh away and expose the bone – are treated with 'very weak aquaflavin', supplied sparingly, while copper sulphate cuts away the rotting flesh. The wounds are wrapped in old clothes and rags; the Japanese medical officers supply no gauze or dressings.

In its acute form, beriberi, caused by a lack of vitamin B and other deprivations, provokes swelling in the joints, muscles and testicles, and a collapse of kidney functioning, for which there is no treatment. Massive swelling occurs in the most acute cases. Many prisoners contract the disease, in various intensities. Braithwaite has beriberi and (unknown to him) hookworm, but the medics have no medicines with which to treat him.

Hygiene rapidly deteriorates in the fading months of 1942: a couple of cans of disinfectant is the only germ-killer available. Once exhausted, it is not replaced. The Japanese pay no attention to sanitation: excrement is tossed into the swamp. Later, observes Braithwaite, the prisoners are 'forced to use human excrement for manure for the gardens, regardless of where it came from' – often from prisoners with dysentery, thereby spreading the disease.[8] And working in bare feet amid the muck hastens the epidemic.

◆

Spurred on by burgeoning evidence of their nation's failed adventure in empire, the Japanese in Borneo continue to take their frustrations out on the only enemy target available, the prisoners. This exaction of revenge seems to manifest a puerile, playground brutality, in which the bully kicks the man on the ground. In this case, however, the bully is armed and fed and answers on pain of a beating to a system that expects, indeed demands, his complete rejection of the notion of compassion. The 'ideals' of bushido have no purchase on the ranks of these recomposed 'samurai', in the dull equation of master and slave.

The Formosans are not inducted into this cult of the warrior, the 'higher calling' of Japanese military culture. They are treated as irredeemable outcasts, and express their frustration and spite in pitiless displays of fury, usually directed at the prisoners. Thus the Australians – and later the British prisoners who join them – are on the receiving end of two sources of fury: Japanese anger over the fading hopes of the war, and Formosan humiliation at being treated as the lowest rung in Japanese authority.

These men seem unknowable from this great distance; their inhumanity is a kind of freakish event, the dark origins of which we struggle to fathom. We can see the guards better through the eyes of the prisoners, who 'humanise' their tormentors in the time-honoured Australian fashion: by giving them nicknames. Among the most brutal are: Kiyoshima Tadeo – whom the prisoners call 'Panther Tooth' or the 'Black Panther' – known for standing over and kicking men when on the ground trying to exercise; Kawakami Koyashi– the 'Gold-Toothed Runt' or the 'Gold-Toothed Shin-Kicking Bastard' – whose shortness forces him to jump to the prisoners' height in order to punch them, or to knock them down to his level with his rifle butt, whereupon he invariably kicks them in the shins; and Kunizowa – 'Euclid' – reviled for jumping on prisoners' backs or kicking them in the ribs when too weak to raise their bodies. There is also Kitamura Kotaro, a ju-jitsu expert whose first kick invariably lands on the prisoners' testicles. When the English medical officer Captain Frank Daniels protests at the serious damage this does to a young English soldier, Kitamura lays a boot between Daniels' legs, and the medic has to be helped back to camp.

Especially hated is Fukishima Masao – the 'Black Bastard' – for his attacks on the sick and wounded. His job is to generate working parties and send them out of the camp. Those unable to work stay behind and face the wrath of Fukishima, who kicks and bashes them to get them to work. When the Australian medical officers – Captains John Oakeshott and Domenic Picone – later object to the treatment, they are slapped and punched, and nothing changes. The sick and wounded continue to be sent to work, barefoot, chiefly in the vegetable gardens, spreading manure from small tins.

Some of these captors, and later arrivals, comprise a monstrous regiment that the Australians dub the 'basher gang', a roaming tribe of younger guards composed almost entirely of Formosans, under the command of a brute called Lieutenant Moritake, whose talent for cruelty lies in delegating the job of bashing the prisoners to the worst characters under his command.

One is called Kada, whom the diggers nickname Mad Mick or Black Mick. Kada's gang, armed with sword-shaped pick-handles, select groups of prisoners to receive punishment in rotation, regardless of whether they have infringed the rules or worked hard. This is naked sadism, a spectator sport. The basher gangs practise ju-jitsu on the prisoners, where a kind of tag team bounces them around, punching and kicking them. One intelligence report documents a man thrown among the guards then hurled on the ground and kicked in the stomach and face. The attacks turn the men 'into nervous wrecks, always fearing a bashing for no reason'. The most common group punishment is 'flying practice', with which everyone is familiar. The men are forced to stand with their arms outstretched and stare into the sun for hours at a time; anyone whose arms sag or face turns promptly receives a rain of blows, driving him to his knees.[9]

And yet the Formosans, and indeed some of the Japanese, are not all the monsters of popular description, as the prisoners gradually discover. Even the worst can be surprisingly lenient, when the mood takes them. Okahara, on better days, allows locals to sell food to the prisoners, at a cordoned-off section of the drome. Hoshijima allows the prisoners to tune in to Radio Tokyo. A few guards exhibit genuine signs of a vestigial humanity; they sense, and sometimes practise, a duty of care towards the prisoners. One is Toyoda Kokishi, a Formosan guard who demonstrates exceptional concern for the prisoners of war in his care at the drome, serving them proper food at lunchtime, allowing them rest breaks and to work at their own pace. He shares his whisky with the men he befriends and helps to cover one digger's gambling losses, according to reports.[10] Toyoda is an exception – one of several in the coming months who attempt to make this little corner of hell tolerable.

◆

In early 1943, in spite of the harsher work regime, the prisoners' conditions curiously improve. Their health declines less rapidly as their bodies adjust to the circumstances, and they become better organised. The death rate, in fact, averages about one per month in the first half of this new year – a third of the rate during the latter stages of 1942, when their bodies buckled under the sudden imposition of a poor diet, brutal treatment and unsanitary conditions. Another factor is the smoother operation of the underground – the band of loyal local people – through their links with Dr Taylor and, in recent months, Captain Lionel Matthews.

The men adapt to their environment. Furtive contacts with

native people yield valuable medical tips: finely ground charcoal apparently assists patients with dysentery; the tongkat shrub helps to ease fever and flu; wood ash from the kitchens seems to aid ulcers and jungle sores;[11] and yeast is suggested as a palliative for 'kurap' – a common scaly skin condition like pellagra characterised by cracked lips, a dry tongue, suppurating palms, weeping, bloodshot eyes and an intolerably itchy scrotum. The medics are also kept busy by a cluster of hernia and appendix operations, and through having to straighten fractures sustained by bashings. Lucky patients receive a local anaesthetic.

From May 1943, these medical aids are of little use to sick men who suddenly find themselves being forced to work. The Japanese need more workers: an additional 300 on the drome, 200–300 to build roads, 40 on woodcutting parties and 12 drivers. To meet the total required, a new policy is introduced: henceforth, no medical complaint will exempt a prisoner from work. All working parties must be full, regardless of the state of the men. The policy is announced in a memo of 26 May, distributed to all ranks, in the names of the Australian medical officers Majors Frank Fleming and Hugh Rayson, and signed by Captain George Cook, the prisoners' liaison officer. Headed 'WORKING PARTIES', the memo states:

> The Imperial Japanese Army Authorities have stated that Working Parties will be filled, even if there are insufficiently medically fit men available. The responsibility of demanding these parties is entirely in the hands of the IJA. We have been informed that whilst full parties are insisted on, the IJA wish to minimise the sending out of men who are marked unfit by our Medical Officers . . .
>
> Every endeavour has been made by us to avoid the sending

out of men marked unfit by the MOs [Medical Officers]. In this we have failed, and it must be clearly understood that when a man is marked unfit by an MO it does not necessarily mean that he will not be sent out on a work party demanded by the IJA.[12]

Captain Cook's is the only signature; earlier, he signed a set of rules, issued by Hoshijima, that obliged all sick prisoners to work, when ordered, in the garden plots.[13]

The question is how to enact such a decree. Some guards recoil from the order and face serious disciplining. Most simply tell the sick to get up and work. The guards responsible are the Kichi. This 'bad lot', writes Burns, make up the basher gangs and are not squeamish about forcing sick men to work. They force men suffering from malaria, beriberi and tropical ulcers to get up and hobble to the aerodrome or gardens – on pain of a reduced ration if they refuse. That prospect compels the very sick to rise from their beds. 'More than half of these men are unfit for work but the Japs hand them all a pick and shovel and then stand over them and make them work hard,' Burns writes.[14]

Sergeant Wallace recalls, 'Guards went through the camp and turned men out of hospital, also doctors and padres.'[15] Some relish the task, using hideous methods to force the sick out of bed. The worst is Fukishima, the Black Bastard. Sticpewich relates that:

His job was to produce working parties from the camp and he did so at all costs, in the following manner. He would have a full roll call; after all those who could go to work had left camp. This meant only sick remained in camp. He would go along the lines of sick and 'no duty' PWs and pick them out to work, beating them up and telling them they were not sick, and sending them to work. One of his methods of picking out a PW was to kick the PW on a bandaged leg to see if it really was an ulcer. It might be mentioned that this is the most cruel thing anyone could witness, as anyone who has had an ulcer knows the severe pain one has to endure without having an animal kick it. Some of those he picked out were in such a bad condition that the Doctors would appeal and raise objections to the general manner in obtaining these work parties. All these sick would be sent to work in the garden spreading manure, human excreta mixed with water . . . [causing] the marked increase in dysentery and secondary infections in ulcers.[16]

In due course, any man who can walk, regardless of his health, is sent to the gardens or the drome. None of the senior Japanese officers – and certainly not Hoshijima – intervenes to stop this barbarity.

10

THE CAGE

The first seven days got no food. No water for the first three days . . . Every evening would be – a bashing. Hit with sticks and fists and kicking . . . no wash in that forty days.
Keith Botterill, on his 40 days in the cage

PRIVATE JIMMY DARLINGTON, 27, of Barraba, a small mining town in New England, New South Wales, described himself as a 'concrete worker' on his enlistment papers and entered the name 'Molly May Madigan', whom he called his 'unmarried wife', as 'next of kin'. His photo depicts a hard man, with a high, jutting brow, dark complexion, broad shoulders and piercing, suspicious eyes. He is deeply proud of his part-Aboriginal heritage. His army record lists fines for 'drunkenness' and 'indecent language', but he serves as an effective and reliable batman to Captain Ken Mosher. Darlington is, in short, a fairly normal example of the great larrikin tradition of the Australian digger: lazy, drunk and irreverent off duty; brave, sober and hard-working on.

He was sent to Singapore as part of the 2/18th Battalion and performed as well as any soldier. But it was in the ring where Darlington excelled, as the pride of the 8th Division's boxing line-up. At five foot eight, he made up for his size with sudden well-aimed flourishes of his fists that decked men twice as big. At home, he was a boxer of regional repute; in Singapore, before the fall, he fought in a series of exhibition matches, earning his backers a lot of money.

After the fall, Darlington's military record reports him, on 1 April 1942, as 'MISSING – PRISONER OF WAR – BORNEO'. His record then goes silent. More than three years later, on 8 September 1945, Private Darlington's name reappears on the official record, as 'recovered from Japanese at Changi PW camp'. In the intervening 1245 days of active service, a Mr Darlington, J. – presumably Jimmy's father – of Henry Street, Barraba, has received a single postcard from his son.[1] In Australia, on 7 January 1946, the young man is discharged 'on compassionate grounds': he has deep scars on both arms, his right leg and right thumb; and his right arm, horribly misshapen, has suffered a terrible break, according to the medical report on his discharge papers. His brain is numb and incommunicative. Nobody who has seen what happened to Jimmy Darlington in the intervening years will live to forget it.

On 17 February 1943, Darlington is working in the cookhouse at the airfield, helping to prepare the prisoners' rations. A little after lunch, the guard nicknamed Mad Mick barges in and drops his dirty underwear into the 44-gallon rice drum, used to boil the prisoners' rice. (An alternative account describes the guard shoving the cooks aside and demanding a large quantity of rice.) Darlington, disgusted, objects to the presence of the guard's underpants in the prisoners' pot. Mad Mick lashes out with his sword stick. Darlington dodges it, sees red and throws a whiplash uppercut that knocks the guard out – along with several of Mad Mick's teeth.

Immediately, several Japanese and Formosans set upon the

Australian with sticks, rifle butts and boots. Darlington is beaten unconscious. In full view of the prisoners at the drome, his inert body is bound with wet rope, his arms trussed behind his back and tied to his legs.

It is the pain in his right arm, drawn back at an agonising angle behind his waist, that brings him back to consciousness. Darlington wakes to find himself being dragged to a place near a skip and forced to kneel on sharpened splinters. A long piece of wood is rammed behind his knees and the guards jump on either end, using the wooden beam like a see-saw. 'Whenever he fainted or fell off the wood he was revived with a bucket of water and again set upright,' a witness recalls.[2] The guards, Formosan and Japanese, continue this torture, off and on, for half a day. As the ropes dry, they bite into Darlington's flesh, cutting off the circulation. His hands and feet turn purple then black. Seeing he must surely die, his fellow soldiers distract the guards' attention by yelling and throwing down their tools, while the ambulanceman Sergeant W. 'Mac' McDonough rushes to Darlington's aid, cuts the rope that binds him and releases the pressure.

Darlington lives, but only just. Covered in blood and wounds, his arm badly broken, his face puffed up, his eyes shut, he is taken back to camp and thrown into the small 'cage', out of sight of the men. In this small wood and bamboo box, he curls up alone, quivering. 'I saw him when he was brought into camp,' recalls Braithwaite. 'He was insane with rage. He was tied with his arms behind his back and his legs tied to his arms.'[3] Medical officers plead to help him, but the Japanese refuse. He is refused any food for two days. Darlington is set apart by this new horror – among the prisoners, but somehow not of them. He is removed from their temporal concerns, but his pain is omnipresent and so extreme that he howls without end. His cries, like a wailing dog's, are heard throughout the camp, but no one is permitted to go to his aid. The Japanese continue to refuse to allow medical help. It is their intention to leave him howling as a warning to the rest. He passes out; he regains consciousness later in the night. His cries resume and wake the prisoners, who hear him begging the guards to kill him.[4]

Unable to bear the sound, the guards send for an Australian medic, who administers morphine – the prisoners' reserve supply – which puts Darlington to sleep. After a night in the cage, Darlington's ruined body is dragged out, past the shocked faces of his fellow prisoners, and dumped in a truck bound for an unknown destination. At the sight, Captain Ken Mosher falls out, strides across the parade ground and shakes the near-lifeless hand of his faithful adjutant.

◆

The severity of Darlington's torture draws a line between the prisoners' past treatment and their future expectations. Until now, none has witnessed such prolonged and merciless cruelty. Indeed, Darlington's ordeal has forced the prisoners to contemplate several novel forms of torture. One is omnipresent in the camp: the cage – called 'esau' by the Japanese.

There are two cages in the camp in 1943. Each is 'something like a circus proprietor would keep a baboon in', Sticpewich later recalls.[5] They are both squat wooden boxes, with thick wooden slats, originally built by the Japanese to humiliate their own troops (for which they are never used). The small cage stands behind the Japanese barracks, out of sight of the men, 'for all intents and purposes a large dog kennel'.[6] It is about six feet long, five deep and four high. Two or three prisoners are interned at a time. Soon, a larger cage is built in front of the guardhouse, big enough to hold several men. Made of wooden bars two inches wide by one inch thick, the Japanese cages are larger than the little bamboo 'Tiger Cages' that the South Vietnamese will use in the Vietnam War, but they serve the same function: to isolate, torment and humiliate the occupant. A third cage is built in town, used to punish locals and exhibit Allied prisoners to the civilians. The cage is a feature of all Japanese prison camps: the one in Kuching is constructed out of barbed wire on a wooden frame and rumoured to have a partially barbed-wire floor. Later, to punish growing resistance, the Japanese order the prisoners to construct two larger cages in the prison camp – the biggest, built in October 1944, is 15 feet by nine by nine and intended to facilitate 'group punishments'. Dick Braithwaite later recalls that 'as many men as possible' were crammed into it.[7]

Inside the cage, the men are forced to sit cross-legged for days. The maximum sentence is 30 days, but some men will spend five or six weeks in the cage, or longer. Denied beds or blankets, and dressed only in loincloths and perhaps a loose shirt, they are exposed nightly to swarms of mosquitoes, against which protective nets are forbidden. Typically, they receive no food for the first week and thereafter just one serve of rice per day. As all are permitted just two visits to the toilet a day, those with dysentery and bowel problems are obliged to urinate and defecate through the bamboo slats that comprise the floor, within full view of the passing guards and prisoners.

Any minor infringement can result in being thrown in the cage, but typical 'crimes' leading to incarceration are stealing food, 'going slow' at the drome, failing to stand to attention in the presence of the guards, and leaving work parties. Scores of prisoners will be locked inside in the coming years, with little food, just water. Many will die as a result of their incarceration.

Private Keith Botterill is put in the cage on three separate occasions, for stealing food. His longest sentence lasts 40 days, he later claims, surpassing the supposed 30-day maximum. He later testifies:

> The first seven days got no food. No water for the first three days. And then they forced you to drink until you were sick on the third night . . . Every evening would be – a bashing. Hit with sticks and fists and kicking . . . no wash in that forty days.

He shares the cage with 17 others, in the constant company of lice, mosquitoes and skin diseases. 'Not allowed to talk, we used to whisper. We had to kneel down all day, there wasn't room to lay down of a night, we'd all lay side by side, squashed up . . .'[8]

Every morning, the inmates of the cage are taken out for exercise: 'PT'. 'This consisted of a severe bashing,' recalls Botterill. Guards are commonly seen jumping on the backs of prisoners doing push-ups. 'Men had to be carried back into the cage crying; some collapsed but a bucket of water was thrown over them to bring them to again.'[9] There are exceptions to this reign of violence: some guards try to help the men in the cage. One, nicknamed Sparkles, for his easy-going nature, smuggles food, by night, to them through the wooden slats. (He also smuggles food into the camp from the outside.) Ordered to bash the prisoners on the slightest pretext, Sparkles often restrains himself, to the anger of his superiors. Or he attempts a perfunctory bashing, then smiles and apologises to the victim afterwards.[10] Sparkles, and a few others, offer only temporary relief. Most of those condemned to the cage contract malaria and suffer severe malnutrition. Their psychological state also deteriorates, engendering chronic fear and depression. A sullen death wish lingers over those of a weaker mental disposition, which is precisely the Japanese intention.

The cage reduces its prisoners to a kind of zoo animal, except that here the exhibits are constant reminders to the observers that they might be next. The cage thus serves several purposes: an especially painful prison cell; a constant warning to the prisoners on the outside; and a form of round-the-clock humiliation. It is, of course, another clear breach of the Geneva Convention, which permits the punishment of prisoners but prescribes basic care at all times: at a minimum, two hours' exercise per day, an adequate diet and access to medical care. Such international protocols are mere scraps of paper here; they are strange laws, descended from another world. Hoshijima is aware of his obligations under international law but feels no compunction to act on them. Yet Japan's own laws stipulate that proper food, medical care and bedding (with mosquito nets, if needed) are to be provided to prisoners at all times.[11] Hoshijima's failure to enact them gives the lie to his claim of 'never having broken any regulations'; but he feels no moral obligation, and the terrible cries issuing from the cage scarcely distract him from the task ahead: to build the airfield as quickly as possible.

◆
◇

The sight of Darlington's ordeal appears to spur, rather than dull, the soldiers' dreams of escape. Within days, two of the Dead End

Kids dare to break out. The young privates Billy Young (just 17 in 1943; he enlisted aged 15) and Miles Pierce Brown (known to all as MP) seem to prepare well. On several previous nights, they left camp through a hole cut in the wire fence beneath the swamp that abuts the back of their hut, to scavenge tapioca, yams, coconuts, fruit and 'cigarette weed' made from banana or pawpaw. On those occasions, they wriggled back through the hole 'like eels', their packs full of food, eluding any guards on the boardwalk above and on the sentry towers nearby, guided through the brackish water by a line connected from the boardwalk's pylons to the hut. One tug on the line signalled 'all-clear'; two tugs signalled 'danger'.

It is the privilege of youth to care little for the consequences of their actions, however rash, and the Dead End Kids constantly push the boundaries in spite of the remonstrations of older men that their nightly excursions endanger the rest. But 'full bellies were always worth the risks of being caught', Young notes, and the older soldiers do not let their disapproval of the means affect their appetite for the spoils: all share in the results of the Kids' successful foraging expeditions.[12]

Billy Young has been caught four times in seven months ducking off to find food and has spent several days in the cage. It is thought that his extreme youth protects him from more severe punishment – torture, a longer stint in the bamboo box – and he grows bolder. On one occasion, he and Private Joey Crome leave a 'dunny party' – emptying toilet buckets into the swamp – and return with chickens in their buckets. A guard catches them re-entering the camp; they are severely beaten and flung into the cage for two days. On another, Young, Crome and Punchy Donohue encounter a party of guards in the jungle and flee. Donohue is caught; Young and Crome return via the swamp, swimming beneath the guards sitting on the boardwalk above. Donohue is threatened with death unless the pair declare themselves. They do so, and the three are let off because the guards, embarrassed at how the kids escaped and got back into camp, decide not to report the incident.

And so, just days after Darlington's ordeal, equipped with an old map and some food stashed in a nearby cave, Billy Young and MP Brown attempt to break out again, this time for good. Returning after roll call to the airfield one lunchtime, they run for it rather than show up late. After just a couple of hours on the track, they are caught, roped together, pressed back to camp and beaten. The guards take turns. MP's head is so badly lacerated that he seems to have been scalped. Both lie unconscious outside the boilerhouse when the prisoners return.

On recovering, Young is taken before Hoshijima, who, heavily drunk, screams and punches the dazed teenager, who collapses at the foot of the commandant's stairs. Young's last memory of the camp is being driven away in the back of a truck tied to his friend; their destination, Sandakan and the Kempei-tai, for further interrogation and torture, and then to Kuching, where they encounter the wreckage of Jimmy Darlington. Eventually, the Australians are sentenced, along with other prisoners and natives, in a 'mass trial', to Outram Road Gaol in Singapore. Young gets four years; Darlington six months.

The diggers learn that the cage is not the worst punishment the Japanese are capable of inflicting. Outram Road, reputed to be the most brutal prison in the Japanese Empire, is reserved only for those deemed to have committed 'serious' crimes, such as escape. Here, Young, MP, Darlington and others are individually confined to very small stone cells, 'too small to stretch out or stand upright in, and with no bedding or fittings other than a bucket'.[13] They are naked but for their lap laps. The food is rice and water, twice daily. The Japanese and Sikh guards impose complete silence. In these conditions, the prisoners quickly contract beriberi, scabies and other diseases; none can hope to survive their sentences, usually from two to ten years.

No one back in Sandakan knows what has become of them; most assume they have been executed. The sight of the torture and summary removal – presumably to a killing ground – of three of the youngest soldiers in Sandakan casts a pall of fear and loathing over the camp, and firms the resolve of a few to resist, and possibly organise a rising against, the Japanese.

RESISTANCE

11

THE RADIO

To our absolute dismay on the first night . . . all the perimeter
lights just about took off, almost blew the globes out.
Lieutenant Rod Wells, on diverting the camp's
electricity supply to power the secret radio

BY EARLY 1943, the civilian resistance is an intricate web of
secret assignations, nimble couriers and stealthy 'drop offs' – in
palm trees, by roadsides, in caches – the detection of which
would mean torture, prolonged caging and probable death for
the organisers. Valuable supplies of medicine and food flow to
the internees on Berhala and to the prisoners, thanks to dozens
of local people – European, Malayan, Chinese and native – all
of whom assume extraordinary risks in keeping the lines of
communication open.

Several prisoners are not only intimately involved but also play
leading roles – notably Captain Lionel Matthews, Lieutenant Rod
Wells and Lieutenant Gordon Weynton. Fellow officers critical
to the operation include Captain Stan Woods (who doubles with
Wells as Matthews' second-in-command) and Lieutenant Russ
Ewin. But it is the courage and skill of Matthews and Wells
that drive the network from inside the camp. Their links with

Dr Taylor and the Berhala Island civilians, established via contacts with Sandakan residents such as Dick Majinal and Sergeant Abin, whom they meet on the gardening detail, set in motion Matthews' ideas of broadening the network into an underground resistance movement. He not only aims to ensure the continuing flow of supplies and information to the prisoners; he hopes to connect with Allied guerrillas then believed to be in Borneo. His fount of communication is the officers' wood-gathering party, which, mysteriously, continues to be poorly guarded. (Until recently, there was also the palm-nut-foraging party, which procured vital supplies of vitamin B through notes left in palm trees for Dr Taylor's couriers, until the Japanese curbed its operations.)

From these fragile beginnings, Matthews and Wells have built a communication network that feeds the supply chain to the camp. But it has much greater ambitions: to develop contacts with Allied units outside Borneo and even organise a prisoner uprising and breakout. Consider, for example, the underground's amazing achievements in one month, September 1942. In those four weeks, Matthews and Wells managed to procure the following items:

- a crystal detector and a set of headphones from Dick Majinal;
- two radio tubes from Lamberto Apostol, the Filipino in charge of the Experimental Farm (and originally employed by the Department of Forestry);
- route plans of the electrical and telephone service lines from Ah Ping, the Chinese manager of the camp's power supply;
- useful forestry and agricultural information relating to the island's interior, as well as survey maps of British

North Borneo, from Apostol and others;

- a constant flow of reports from civilian working parties detailing Japanese activities in Sandakan and the surrounding area – a source of vital information that will fertilise Matthews' plan for a prison uprising to coincide with a guerrilla attack;
- a weekly letter service, between the prison camp, the former governor on Berhala Island and Dr Taylor in Sandakan Hospital; and
- via Alex Funk, a .38 revolver (smuggled into the camp) and details of the activities of a number of Chinese people in the Sandakan area who, according to Wells, 'were in contact with Filipino guerrillas on Batu Batu', in the Sulus.[1]

This extraordinary network is perilously vulnerable to compromise downstream, through bribes and espionage. The risks of discovery heighten with the presence in the camp of several known collaborators and suspected spies, one of whom is revealed as the pro-Japanese spook Ah Fok Lo, known as Jackie Lo, a Malay-Chinese who speaks fluent English and is appointed to monitor the prisoners. The wood-collection party is soon aware of Lo's true identity and is almost caught exchanging messages on several occasions. It survives Lo's scrutiny, for now.

◆

Everyone in the underground – whether a courier, clerk, donor or smuggler – does so in full knowledge of the terrible risks. Dr Taylor, Matthews and their local comrades occupy the centre of this spreading web, which continues to deliver a stream of medical and food supplies to the prisoners. The system, at the start, operates like this: working from his surgery in Sandakan Hospital, Taylor routinely buys drugs with his own money and then, in his Drug Stores Book, records the purchases as designated for the native people. (He is authorised by the Japanese to dispense medicines to the locals.) It is through this device that regular, if small, supplies of medicines and food eventually reach the prison camp, via various subterfuges and exchanges set up between Matthews and Wells and local people, chiefly Sergeant Abin, Peter Raymond Lai and Lamberto Apostol. Lai, a civilian hospital dresser, is in fact the first to inform Matthews of Dr Taylor's smuggling operation, and other civilian activities; and the first to deliver a parcel of medicines from the hospital for the use of the prisoners.

Matthews, as always, puts his own neck on the line: he eagerly takes a job carting cow dung from a nearby cattle shed to the prisoners' gardens. The dung run provides an excellent cover for his deepening contacts with locals. The cowshed itself becomes a hive of exchange and 'many a deep-hatched plot',[2] quietly orchestrated through its manager, Matusup bin Gungau, and his formidable wife, Halima, who often acts as a go-between with Matthews. It is on these dung-carrying excursions that Matthews deals with a myriad of contacts – Apostol, Lai, and Wong Yun Siew, also known as 'Pop' Wong, to name a few – who pass him food and other supplies, forming close bonds and friendships.

The medical supplies are never enough, of course, because Dr Taylor's network is the only source and this cannot meet the demand. The Japanese deny all medicines to the prisoners, stockpiling most for themselves. And yet, for almost ten months, the network smuggles into camp weekly supplies of: Atebrin, quinine, ether, sterilised bandages, iodine and other disinfectants, some surgical instruments, food for the seriously ill, and other chemicals needed for the primary batteries that will power a radio.[3]

In the first few months of 1943, the resistance deepens into a secret labyrinth of connections, reaching into the local community and financed in part by the 'emergency fund' – initially intended to provide financial assistance to escapees – set up by Dr Taylor and Ernesto Lagan, with the connivance of the Sandakan governor. Dr Taylor even establishes a money market and currency-exchange system. The fund grows. The donors include many local people, notably Mrs Moselle Cohen, who owns a department store in Sandakan. Dr Taylor's wife, Celia, is intimately involved, doing most of the fund's clerical work; as is Maggie, the wife of Alex, of the redoubtable Funk family.

◆

The radio is the finest, and most dangerous, achievement of the resistance: a daring joint venture between civilians and prisoners, who together manage to smuggle into the camp the parts necessary to build a receiver powerful enough to tune in to British, Australian and American broadcasts. The process of building the radio, undetected, has taken several months, starting in late 1942. It has involved an extraordinary confluence of courage, skill and luck, which pivots on the willingness of locals – European, Malayan, Chinese and native Sabah – to risk their lives in the common aim of defeating the Japanese.

First, they had to find parts that met the radio's

specifications. In late 1942, Lieutenant Gordon Weynton, Corporal J. Rickards and others constructed a crystal set using primitive materials. But it could only pick up local stations. More sophisticated components were needed. The breakthrough came from an unexpected accessory, the Chinese businessman Heng Joo Ming, who was not at that point a member of the resistance. Ming, as overseer ('mandor', or head slave) of the coolie workforce, readily undertook to steal components from a storage shed located near the airfield, close to his home. He passed them to Wallace, who in turn sold them to Corporal Rickards, who, flush with cash that he had saved in Singapore, was more than happy to buy the valuable contraband. Rickards then set his mind to the task of assembling the radio, for which he needed expert help. News of the parts reached Matthews and his superior, Major Frank Fleming, who, at first, wanted nothing to do with this perilous clandestine activity.

Ming soon becomes one of the most loyal attendants of the resistance. He befriends several Australians, to whom he smuggles food after the latter's severe bashing, and the wheeler-dealer, Sergeant Walter Wallace, who is itching to escape. These life-and-death relationships form not because local people sympathise with the Australians. While many do, few are willing to risk their lives solely for the prisoners' relief. More precisely, it is because, furious at the way the Japanese have treated their families and country, they see the Allies as the only hope of ridding Borneo of the hated occupiers. And, of course, there is money involved: every step is financially lubricated.

The Chinese, such as Ming and Ah Ping, are special cases, constantly aware of Japan's ongoing racial war against their people, expressed in posters hung around town: '[T]he Chinese must always remember that the Japanese commander holds power of life and death over them and at the word of the Japanese commander, they can be killed instantly.[4] Opposing this malign presence means forming links with Allied guerrillas and the prisoners, in order to foment some kind of organised resistance.

Matthews threw himself at the radio project with scarcely a thought for the consequences. He immediately involved the technical prodigy Rod Wells, as well as Weynton, Rickards and Corporals Arnold Small and Cyril Mills – exposing them to terrible punishment if caught. Weynton had the distinction of having successfully built the earlier crystal set. He also fixed a Japanese radio soon after his arrival, allowing the enemy to tune into Radio Tokyo's report of the death of the Duke of Kent, King George VI's younger brother. Now, he was given overall responsibility for supervising construction of the receiver.

Night after night, in various darkened huts, the signalmen gathered to build the radio receiver. As always, Matthews' radical ideas – *Perhaps we can radio Allied guerrilla units? Organise an uprising? Or a rescue?* – outpaced his capacity to fulfil them. But he never wearied of the pursuit. Obstacles that would appear insurmountable to lesser men seem mere hurdles in the path of this dauntless spirit.

The radio party worked with feverish intent. By November 1942, they had everything required to switch it on, except a power supply. They needed batteries; none were procurable. Wells solved the problem with his usual inventiveness. He and Weynton converted the alternating current into direct current by means of a chemical rectifier that tapped into the camp's electricity supply. They used test tubes secretly supplied by Sergeant W. 'Mac' McDonough; metal foil pilfered from the lining of a rice chest;

and a chemical solution, drawn from the medicines slipped into the camp via Dr Taylor's couriers.

The powerhouse, a hundred yards or so outside the prison camp, which provides its electricity, was the final link in the chain. The existing voltage was not strong enough to power the radio, so Wells and Matthews conspired to raise it – with the help of the Chinese manager Ah Ping, ably assisted by an Australian engineer, Sergeant Alf Stevens, of the 2/4th Machine Gun Battalion, and his three assistants. In an extraordinary concession, the Japanese, in response to a request by Stevens' senior officer (who happens to be Matthews), have allowed the engineer to live at the powerhouse and work with Ping, ostensibly to improve the operation of the electricity grid.

It was another masterstroke of foresight by Matthews. From his new home, Stevens has been able to collect and dispatch messages – he sent at least 40 to various addresses in the first few months – harvest news from natives and, most critically, control the power supply.[5] Stevens persuaded Ping to deliver a power surge timed to coincide with the nightly operation of the radio. Ping agreed, in return for news from China, should the radio work. The extra fuel required to fire up the boiler room arrived courtesy of the prisoners' wood party – completing the circle of espionage, enemy penetration and technical brilliance that characterises the resistance.

On his first attempt, Ping delivered the extra voltage so powerfully that the camp lights flared up. 'To our absolute dismay on the first night,' Wells later writes, 'all the perimeter lights just about took off, almost blew the globes out.' Visibly shaken, Wells instructed Ping and Stevens to raise the power gradually, 'one volt at a time'.[6]

Next day I explained to Ah Ping 'Gently, gently catchee monkey', you know, a little bit of wood on at nine o'clock, a little bit more at 10 and gradually work it up to about 300 rpm on the main fly wheel. Leave it there for about half an hour then gradually bring it down.[7]

Henceforth, from about 9 pm each night, the perimeter lights blazed gradually brighter, with incremental surges in the voltage. Around midnight, the radio tapped into this surplus power, undetected, before the lights started to fade again. The Japanese suspected nothing; one guard was overheard saying, 'Ah Ping very loyal citizen, because when sun go down and get dark we want lot of light to watch prisoners.'[8]

It worked. On the night of 4 November, the chimes of Big Ben and an English accent announcing 'This is the BBC' crackled over the receiver – the first news of the outside world the men had received in almost a year. The next program, as it happened, was about hop-growing in Kent.[9] In the following days, Wells tuned in to the BBC World News, Radio Australia and Voice of America, to the delight of the few signallers sitting in the darkened hut.

The Australians have imposed a tight security cordon around the radio and limit reception to bursts of five to ten minutes, only at night. A Radio Watch has been established; the receiver is hidden in a false drawer in the carpenter's shop. In darkness, the radio operators – usually Wells, Weynton or Rickards – tune in to foreign reports detailing the progress of the war: the collapse of Germany, Japan's defeat at sea after the Battle of Midway, the start of the Solomons campaign, and many other items.

Captain Stan Woods takes down the news in shorthand, transcribes it and produces copies for distribution. Some are single-paged news summaries, titled *Sandakan Ausso* – in sly imitation of the Japanese propaganda sheets *Sandakan Nippo*.[10] Others are longer, hidden in Wells' socks and all sorts of places, before distribution to officers and key contacts in Sandakan town and Berhala Island – via the indefatigable local policeman Sergeant Abin. Abin, the official courier to Berhala, who also serves as police sentry outside camp, receives the notes literally off the back of the truck carrying the wood party as it passes through the gates. Ewin, a regular messenger, and Abin complete this transaction behind the guards' backs. It is extremely dangerous, but the dissemination of news is repayment to the members of the network; without them, the radio would never have existed. And that is how the Chinese community in Sandakan receives news of the events in its homeland and Manchuria.

In May 1943, Rickards falls seriously ill, and Weynton and Woods assume full responsibility for reception and dissemination of the news. In the meantime, however, the quality of the set deteriorates. Weynton is assigned the job of partially rebuilding it. He relies on condensers, valves and other parts, supplied again by Ming and other members of the underground. Every transaction, every scrap of paper issuing out of camp, runs the risk of discovery. Their success breeds complacency, and the officers and men grow lax.

◆

In early 1943, with the radio crackling in the background, valuable printed intelligence reaches the prison camp via the well-worn route of the wood-collection party. It involves Allied and Japanese troop movements in Borneo – information that hardens

Matthews' hopes of contacting guerrillas and fomenting a prisoner uprising. The source is Alex Funk, whose family's commitment to the resistance is unbreakable. Funk has managed to procure, to Matthews' and Wells' amazement, two detailed maps of the Sandakan area showing the dispositions of the Japanese barracks, machine-gun posts and communications facilities, including the British Government's former radio station three miles out of town. More intelligence follows, via the police, powerhouse staff and truck drivers then working in and near Sandakan (the key couriers are Apostol, Wong, Abin, the Sikh policeman Ujagar Singh and a reliable Malayan called Matusup bin Gungau). They receive government forestry maps, details of jungle tracks into the interior and, most preciously, an old British North Borneo map marking the location of Japanese barracks and buildings. Matthews incorporates this fresh information onto his 'master' maps. To avoid discovery, he keeps half the material, which he buries in the camp, and Wells keeps the other half, which he buries outside Abin's police station.

Matthews and Wells are in the van of a movement threatened daily with discovery. They seem utterly unfazed and persist in taking inordinate risks. Matthews, for example, assumes responsibility for the .38 revolver, which he elects to carry back into camp (from the wood party) in his haversack. Russ Ewin later recalls Matthews' intimate role in the smuggling operation and his opening of many notes and letters that would, if found, incriminate him: correspondence, for example, from the governor of British North Borneo, on Berhala Island, thanking him for the news bulletins; advice from the Berhala internees in relation to cash advances to pay for medical supplies for the prisoners' hospital; a letter from Major Rice-Oxley instructing Matthews to succeed him as commander of the Borneo Volunteer Corps; sealed tins containing Borneo currency, which Matthews exchanges for Australian currency with the assistance of Dr Taylor; and many letters from Dr Taylor in relation to food and medical supplies to the prisoners, using the codenames Geebung (Taylor) and Roslyn (Matthews, derived from Rosslyn, the name of a park near his home after which his youngest brother, Ross, was named).[11]

In February, Wells and Matthews step deeper into perilous terrain: they establish contact with an American-led Filipino guerrilla force, through messages sent by the resistance. They determine to build a radio transmitter, in order to send, as well as receive, information, in the expectation of making contact with more Allied guerrillas then rumoured to be landing in Borneo. The necessary transmitter parts arrive through the usual channels, concealed in a false-bottomed onion box. This is mysteriously stolen, and an ominous sense of being watched intrudes on the operation. The Australian officers institute a 'court of enquiry', which fails to find the culprit. Meanwhile, Wells sends word out for duplicate parts, but, as he later grimly records, '[I] designed and commenced construction of the transmitter which was never completed.'[12]

12

THE UNDERGROUND

With the full knowledge of the risks involved Mrs Celia
Taylor actively assisted her husband in his endeavours to
lighten the burden of the POWs. Mrs Taylor did most of
the clerical work connected with the organisation.
Report on the Sandakan resistance, by Lieutenant Rod Wells

'I REMEMBER,' Ernesto Lagan's son Alban later writes, 'that many people used to come to the house in various disguises, sometimes their faces were deliberately dirtied so that they could not be easily recognised. They met in one room, the windows and doors were closed.'[1] The boy recalls being told never to interrupt 'his father's friends'.

The house in question is Lagan's modest bungalow. Dr Taylor, Koram, Abin and at least one of the Funk brothers are usually present, but many others pass through. Dr Val Stookes and his colleague Dr Wands and nurse Phoebe Lai – pivotal in smuggling medicines from Sandakan Hospital – and Gerald Mavor, the works manager – crucial to finding the parts for the radio – occasionally attend or are aware of the nightly meetings. The members come in darkness and leave before dawn, red-eyed, tense and constantly aware of the peril.

In early 1943, the members of this core resistance hold these nocturnal meetings in 'safe houses' in town, usually two or three times a week. They sometimes meet at Dr Taylor's bungalow, or the Funks' palatial 11-room estate. Their chief topics are the activities of the prisoners, the intelligence flow and the state of the Berhala civilian interns. They learn in January, for example, that the Japanese are to move all women and children on Berhala to an unknown destination, rumoured (correctly) to be Kuching. It is also rumoured (incorrectly) that adult females will be used as 'comfort women' and the men left behind to be executed. Neither fear eventuates when, on 12 January, Berhala's 47 women and 15 children are safely shipped to Kuching and interned – in better conditions – in the Lintang Barracks, Suga's headquarters in Borneo. The prisoner-officers in Sandakan will later join them.[2]

In March and April, these midnight conversations tend in a more dangerous direction: there is talk of a plan, originated by Matthews, for a mass prison breakout timed to coincide with a local uprising against the Japanese.

The 'little organisation' – as Dr Taylor later calls the resistance – has come a long way in a year. It is now a fully fledged underground movement, with astonishing reach. It delivers regular supplies of food and medicines to the prisoners in Sandakan and Berhala; raises cash to pay for supplies and arms; provides parts for the radio and planned transmitter; actively sabotages Japanese facilities and machinery; and circulates intelligence reports on Japanese activities and transcripts of the BBC World Service to key agents, selected officers in the prison camp, and – until January 1943 – the civilian internees at Berhala. Lieutenant Tony White first hears of the secret operation while working in the vegetable garden: 'One of the locals walked by and threw a package at my feet: "That's for Captain Matthews!" he said. I hid it in a pile of wood, and later gave it to Matthews.'[3]

At the heart of this little empire is the Taylor–Matthews relationship. Outside the prison camp, Dr Taylor is indisputably the key figure of the underground; inside it, Matthews is. The doctor and the army captain forge a bond of trust. They have not met, yet know each other through secret correspondence.

◆

Tokyo's policy of neo-imperialism plays itself out in microcosm in North Borneo. The occupying forces sequester the food and property they require, with little, if any, compensation to the locals. They shoot the farmers' livestock, occupy the farms, dragoon the natives as coolie labour and beat up anyone who resists. In consequence, many native townsfolk flee to their old homes in the interior and join forces with the villagers, themselves forced into the forest, where, armed with blowpipes and machetes, they turn their minds to fighting and sabotage. In these circumstances, the only path for disaffected native people left in Sandakan is the burgeoning underground. And the Malays, Chinese and natives of Sabah now take up the baton of resistance and run with it.

Indeed, what began as the brainchild of senior officers in the Sandakan constabulary now involves the lives of many different tribes and ethnic groups, whose relationships extend well into the Borneo interior and to the west coast. Remarkable examples are the former members of the Borneo Volunteers and local constabulary who have chosen to work with the Japanese-controlled civilian police, expressly to spy on the enemy. They include Koram, Lagan, Abin, Apostol and many others. They, along with the three Funk brothers, Alex, Johnny and Patrick – who have worked, at various times, for the Public Works Department – serve as the eyes and ears of the underground. They act in the name of, and with the aid of, whole community groups bound not only through friendship and often marriage but also by their shared hatred of the occupier.

Lagan's involvement, like that of many senior members of the police force, is rooted in loyalty to his former European bosses, notably Major Rice-Oxley, now interned in Kuching. But he is also appalled by the Japanese treatment of his people and the Australian prisoners, which spurs his personal mission to fight the enemy from within. He turns to Dr Taylor as an outlet for this spirit. 'Ernest Lagan,' a report by the appointed Death March investigator Lieutenant Colonel Harry Jackson later notes, 'was in fact Taylor's first lieutenant in the underground movement. As soon as the Australians arrived at Sandakan he began to interest himself in their welfare.'[4]

Corporal Koram bin Andaur is a formidable agent, master of elusion and an effective spy. Brave to the point of recklessness, his exploits soon acquire legendary status in the villages of the interior. A fellow police officer describes him thus:

Korom [sic] . . . was a Murut from Pensiangan district, deep in the Interior and the most remote place, which took two to three weeks walk on foot from the nearest district of Keningau, at that time. Being so remote the people were well known for practising Black Magic and Korom was best known for that. When he joined the police, he was well known among the police force through out Sabah and became the talk of the people in the Interior. Even to this day his name still lingers on the younger generations. Korom was a Guru Silat (martial arts instructor) and a boxer. He used to join boxing competitions before the coming of the Japanese.[5]

No family gives so much to the cause, in blood and money, as the Funks, chiefly the brothers – Paddy, Alex and Johnny. At the outbreak of war, the Funks served in various prominent local roles – their father was the first non-white to become a magistrate – and the family is one of the most distinguished and richest in Sandakan. Of Eurasian descent, the three brothers are strikingly handsome, with beautiful wives, all of whom are highly educated and fearlessly dedicated to the resistance. It is Alex Funk, for example, who supplies critical maps of the Sandakan area, pinpointing the Japanese barracks, machine-gun posts and communications posts.[6] And the Funks are behind the extremely dangerous job of hiding smuggled arms in a cache outside town.

Other key figures are the Azconas, Felix senior and Felix junior, who own a radio shop in Sandakan. Felix senior has delivered parts to Wells' men and volunteered for several acts of sabotage of Japanese machinery. And there are the brave couriers Dick Majinal and his friend 'Pop' Wong (so called because, at 43, Pop was deemed old by the younger prisoners), and younger agents such as Peter Raymond Lai and Matusup bin Gungau – all of whom are well known to Matthews, who has met them all, at the cowshed, or on the wood- and dung-collecting parties. On one occasion, Wong, hearing of the prisoners' severe salt shortage, delivers a much-needed sack of salt, which Matthews smuggles into camp on his dung cart. Of course, there are many others, too numerous to name here (see Appendix 3).

◆

Talk of a prisoner breakout, and an uprising, shifts the underground's priorities from the preservation of local lives to the taking of Japanese ones. Guns and money must be procured; links with Allied forces somehow established. At a stroke, the underground's operations move beyond the comparatively modest goals of distributing food, medicines and radio news (extraordinary though these achievements are). The hushed talk is of smuggling in weapons and forging a relationship between the Sandakan underground and a unit of Filipino guerrillas working undercover for the United States submarine forces then stationed in the Philippines (USFIP). This connection lends substance to Matthews' dream – which some of his fellow officers deem suicidal – of occupying the prison camp and holding on until the Allies invade. Henceforth, the resistance pours its efforts into buying weapons and planning the uprising.

The pivotal figure is a Chinese–Filipino former sandalwood trader called Wong Mu Sing, who serves as a lieutenant in USFIP – and whom Lagan had the prescience to recruit in early 1942. Since then, Mu Sing, ably assisted by Felix Azcona and other key resistance leaders, has distinguished himself many times, smuggling arms and ammunition from Tawi-Tawi and other islands to Sandakan in the holds of his ocean-going kompits (small native boats) and powerboats, and relaying news of the prison camp and Japanese strength in Borneo to his American and Filipino superiors. His most valuable piece of information is a map of Sandakan town, pinpointing the residences of top Japanese people – commanders, Kempei-tai and others.[7] The map proves critical in planning Allied bombing missions.

By February 1943, Mu Sing's Tawi-Tawi smuggling ring, co-led by another Filipino guerrilla, Corporal Alberto Quadra, has brought ashore an arms cache containing two machine guns, 27 rifles and 2500 rounds of ammunition. The Funk brothers hide the cache 15 miles west of town. It is now a matter of choosing the right time to distribute the weapons, which must coincide with the arrival of a guerrilla force on the Borneo mainland.

◆

As these plans develop, threats and opportunities arrive. In April and May, a series of events strains the underground and risks exposing it through the sudden dissemination of information to a much wider circle of people. A source of immediate pressure on security is the huge influx of new prisoners who arrive in Borneo in April.

During April, more than 750 British prisoners, after a ghastly ordeal at sea and several months in prison camps in Kuching and Jesselton, disembark at Sandakan. Exhausted, sick, malnourished and ill-treated, they are an amalgam of several British regiments, including a large proportion of Royal Air Force personnel – mostly ground staff taken prisoner at Singapore and Java. On arrival, under the authority of the Japanese officer Captain Nagai Hirawa, they move into 'Compound Number 2', a line of atap huts separated from the Australian compound.

From the start, the Commonwealth forces are kept firmly

apart. The Japanese impose a strict cordon around each prison compound, and the rank and file, on either side, see little of one another. The arrangement is a red rag to Matthews' bullish instinct to expand the resistance, and he leaps at the opportunity to contact the 'Poms'. Indeed, within a week of the British appearance, 'the [BBC] news sheets were finding their way into the British compound', notes the Jackson report.[8] His method of communicating with the British is, however, extremely dangerous. Australian truck drivers – prisoner volunteers – are instructed to throw screwed up balls of paper containing news and information among the British workers while driving past their working parties. A single sheet, if found by the guards, risks blowing the secret of the entire radio operation.

On 21 April, 500 Australians, making up 'E Force', disembark at Sandakan. The unit had originally contained 1000 men, half of whom were British, bound for Kuching's Lintang Barracks. The all-Australian remainder – comprising 18 officers and 482 other ranks – lands at Berhala Island. E Force has spent two weeks at sea in the hold of the hell ship *Taka Maru* and a few days in Kuching, where their commanding officer, Major John Fairley, was replaced by Captain Rod Richardson. The voyage, like that of B Force nine months earlier, has been unforgettably awful, endured in suffocating, disease-ridden conditions – with just four feet between the floor and the ceiling in one section of the hold.[9]

Several battle-hardened Australians and one Scot passed this nightmare voyage deep in talk. Lieutenant Rex Blow, Captain Ray Steele and Private Robert Kerr ('Jock') McLaren are no ordinary soldiers; they are fit and very tough, and psychologically programmed never to surrender. The Japanese have unwittingly chosen the wrong men to mistreat. Intelligent, experienced and utterly ruthless, Blow, McLaren, Steele and others are the last people you want as enemies. Their captivity has bred a cold and restless fury in their minds, guided by an unquenchable urge to escape and resume the war with the Japanese. As the hell ship neared Berhala, its explosive human cargo knew one thing: as Japan retreated, the prisoners would bear the brunt of a loser's vengeance, which could only mean slaughter or slow death through sickness or starvation. Escape is the only option.

◆

For now, these men and the rest of E Force must remain on Berhala, pending the extension of the Sandakan Prison Camp to accommodate them. The 500 prisoners are crammed into three huts, each originally built for 50, in the Quarantine Station, adjacent to the lepers' home. The compound covers about a quarter of an acre. Hygiene rapidly deteriorates. Trench latrines have to be dug daily, but the swampy ground makes it impossible to dig more than two feet before striking water. Soon, the whole area is befouled with human waste. The guards offer relief from these disgusting conditions by letting the prisoners move around and bathe in the sea. Unknown to the Japanese, the Berhala guards, handpicked by Sergeant Major Yangsalang among former members of the North Borneo Constabulary, are loyal to the Sandakan underground, which now spreads its vines to the officers of E Force.

Particularly impressed – and responsive – are Blow and his colleagues, who immediately familiarise themselves with the extraordinary network. Their first contact is with Mohammed Salleh, the ubiquitous Berhala watchman who delivered Dr

Taylor's first supplies to the island's civilians the previous year. Within a few days, Blow has the measure of Salleh's role. Others in the know take great pleasure in the sight of his little runabout drawing alongside the Quarantine Station's jetty, laden with supplies of medicine, courtesy of Dr Taylor. The Japanese authorities oddly tolerate Salleh's deliveries but warn him not to speak to the Australians, who are 'very bad men'. Salleh readily agrees, putting on a show of contempt for the prisoners, which satisfies the Japanese that he can be trusted. Little do they realise, according to the later report by Lieutenant Colonel Harry Jackson, 'the cunning that exists within the skull of the diminutive Salleh'.[10]

The result is that, within weeks of E Force's arrival, its second-in-command, Captain Steele, as well as Blow and McLaren, are in regular contact with Matthews and know the extent of the underground's operation – thanks to the efforts of the local police and, of course, everyone's favourite middleman Dr James Taylor. To Blow and McLaren, these connections are godsends, and they plan their escape in full knowledge that the cash and local support is available to help them. If they can pull it off, they have every intention of taking the fight back to the Japanese and are determined to apply the destructive power that a few well-trained, covert soldiers can unleash in a sustained guerrilla war.

13

THE BERHALA EIGHT

It struck me at the time that we might have a bit of difficulty sinking a destroyer with a .38 revolver.

Lieutenant Rex Blow, on evading a Japanese
ship during his escape from Berhala

LIEUTENANT REX BLOW is a young artilleryman of the 2/10th Field Regiment. Compact, ruddy and tough, Blow epitomises the sort of dashing young officer who appears in the pages of Buchan and Waugh. He is highly intelligent, a strong athlete, a powerful swimmer – and seemingly indifferent to danger. It is just as well, because Blow always seems to be finding new challenges to inflict on his battered body. Indeed, it is impossible to picture this future guerrilla leader in his pre-war role: working for the Commonwealth Bank in Australia. During the voyage from Changi to Sandakan, he has befriended another soldier destined to share his reputation as 'the most outstanding guerrilla commander of the southern Philippines', according to one historian.[1]

At the grand old age of 42, Private (later Captain) Jock McLaren, a resilient Scot, seems to function, like Blow, in a state of nerveless anticipation of his next death-defying act. He is five foot eleven inches tall, lean and sharp-featured, with fair hair and blue eyes. The wiry McLaren takes naturally 'to the terrible risks involved in clandestine operations', as one observer remarked.[2] A veteran of the Great War, where he was wounded and decorated, McLaren emigrated to Australia in 1922 and established a veterinary clinic with his wife in Queensland. Soon after Hitler invaded Poland, McLaren volunteered for the Australian Citizens Military Force, transferred to the Australian Imperial Force and was sent to Malaya in 1941 with the 2/10th Ordnance Field Workshop.

Weeks after the fall of Singapore, McLaren and two mates wormed 'their way under Changi's barbed wire'[3], swam to the mainland and joined a band of Chinese guerrillas fighting the Japanese on the Johore Peninsula. After five months in the jungle, a treacherous Malayan policeman sold him back to the Japanese, for $25. On six successive mornings, he was led out of his cell to face Japanese firing squads. On each occasion, the guards – wounded old soldiers who respected the Scotsman's courage – refrained from firing. This stroke of luck saved McLaren's and his mates' lives – thought at the time to be the only Allied troops to avoid execution after recapture.[4] The Japanese will rue the day they failed to pull the trigger.

The experience fortified McLaren for another escape attempt, spurred on by his hatred of the enemy. He once witnessed by a Malayan roadside the bodies of hundreds of Chinese women and children, massacred by the Japanese. He saw Chinese 'branded with a Rising Sun on their forehead and arms', he later recalls. 'I saw a British brigadier lashed every morning for about three weeks but they couldn't break his spirit.'[5] McLaren is that rare thing: a man of high principle, sharp intelligence and courage. According to one biography, 'A natural leader and a man of driving energy.'[6]

◆

In late May 1943, we find Blow and McLaren on Berhala Island, still with E Force, like wolves prowling the periphery of a pen. In such characters, the desire for revenge, the longing for freedom, is a force of nature. Nightly, they develop their escape plan; daily, they reconnoitre the island, looking for hideouts. They swim to strengthen their bodies, fill their minds with local intelligence and cultivate the police guards – through whom they maintain regular contact with Matthews.

The two soldiers examine the escape plan from every angle. How many men should assist? How will they get off the island and divert the attention of the Japanese search patrols? How on earth will they reach the Filipino guerrillas on Tawi-Tawi – a journey that, to any normal person, seems nigh impossible? They draw up a checklist of what they need, from where and from whom. Food and cash? Assured through the underground, courtesy of Koram and Dr Taylor. Directions? Blow has buried a compass on the beach. Weapons? Blow has smuggled in a .38 revolver – which he hid in a corner of his groundsheet when ordered to shake it free during inspection. Local intelligence? McLaren and Sapper Jim Kennedy, a fellow veteran of the Great War, study the island while on timber-gathering excursions, noting the bays, cliffs, streams and ridges. And, most of all, transport? McLaren has seen anchored in the bay where the lepers live, on the seaward side of the island, a small, seagoing dugout canoe.

These ingredients form a recipe for a plan of simple, daring ingenuity. By May, another five Berhala prisoners, itching to break out, have decided to join them. As well as Kennedy, they are: Captain Ray Steele, the quick-thinking second-in-command of E Force, who considered escaping Changi and twice backed proposals to mount prisoner uprisings on the hell ships that carried the force from Singapore to Berhala (plans that British officers, who accompanied E Force as far as Kuching, rejected as too dangerous); the pugnacious Lieutenant Charlie Wagner of the 2/18th Battalion, recipient of the Distinguished Conduct Medal in Malaya, for returning through Japanese lines on a motorbike to locate fellow troops lost after a contact with the enemy; Lieutenant Leslie Miles Gillon of the 2/10th Field Regiment; and Private Rex Butler, of the 8th Division Australian Army Service Corps.

The plan meets unexpected opposition, however, from the officer commanding E Force, Captain Richardson. An officer's responsibility is to stay with his men, Richardson insists. The Japanese will severely punish those who stay behind, he argues. To this, Steele and Blow reply that the risk of reprisals is unlikely; and that it is an officer's, and indeed every soldier's, duty to attempt to escape and rejoin the war effort. In any case, the officers, kept in separate huts from the men, have no authority and are merely administrative pawns for the Japanese. Richardson reluctantly gives the mission his imprimatur.

The decisive factor is a stream of mesmerising intelligence from Captain Matthews, sent to Berhala via Corporal Koram. As well as the radio transcripts that arrive throughout May, Koram verbally informs Wagner, who is reasonably fluent in Malay, about the state of the prisoners and Matthews' plans for a breakout. He also confirms that Sandakan resistance leaders are in regular contact with Colonel Alexandrajo Suarez, commander of the Filipino guerrillas. Indeed, throughout June 1943, Suarez informs his American superiors of Blow's escape plan. Every cog in the underground is on high alert: the guards in Berhala; Dr

Taylor's civilian agents; and Matthews' prison network. That seals the decision: they must escape, to join the guerrillas and assist the underground. And they must attempt to do so now. It will be far more difficult at the inland camp.

Meanwhile, far away in the Batu Batu and Sanga Sanga areas of the Sulu Islands, a thousand-strong force of Filipino guerrillas awaits orders to go into action. Their destination is not yet decided, and it is not necessarily North Borneo. They are a combat force, at war; not a prisoner-rescue unit. Their leader, Colonel Suarez, formerly of the Philippines Constabulary, was wounded in action fighting the Japanese in late 1941 when in command of the US 125th Regiment. A master of local geography and an experienced guerrilla fighter, Suarez keeps his American liaison officer well informed of developments in Borneo; American submarines are made fully aware.

◆

In May, Blow and McLaren reluctantly agreed to accept an eighth member of the escape party: Sergeant Walter Wallace, of the 2/15th Field Regiment, who has been hiding out on the other side of Berhala. Wallace fits uneasily into their plan; he has reached the island with the help of underground agents after his initial attempt to escape with two 8th Division signallers ended in disaster.

The story reflects poorly on Wallace as a single-minded maverick who chose to defy his officers' instructions and take risks that imperilled himself and others. In Sandakan, his friendship with Heng Joo Ming, the overseer at the airfield, yielded vital information about the existence and whereabouts of a boat. Wallace hastily dispatched letters, delivered in the shoes of a young runner called Sini (Chin Piang Sinn) to Suarez and the Filipino guerrillas, then on an operation in Borneo. In an extremely hazardous mission, Sini delivered Wallace's mail, returned and advised the Australian to wait. When Wallace informed Major Fleming, his superior officer, of this unauthorised correspondence, the latter grew extremely agitated and roundly rebuked the sergeant. Wallace's response was to plan his escape without involving Fleming or indeed any other officer. In fact, Wallace had provoked a camp inquiry over allegations that he stole malaria tablets and radio parts – the vital transmitter components – which, according to the accusation, he intended to trade to raise funds for his escape. The allegations are unproven; but Wallace's single-minded actions reflect a callous, if correct, judgement that survival, now, is probably a case of every man for himself.

Wallace persuaded two fellow prisoners, the thickset Howard Harvey, 21, of Townsville, and Theodore Mackay, 32, of Thursday Island, to join his plan. Theodore Mackay is a pseudonym for Daniel MacKenzie, wanted for going absent without leave under his real name. Both are 8th Division signalmen.

After lights out in late April, the three wriggled under the wire and headed in a vaguely south-westerly direction. Their goal was to find the rumoured boat, sail downriver to the sea and head for Tawi-Tawi. They bungled it from the start, by taking the wrong direction. After a fraught journey of four days, through swamp, jungle and mangrove, they doubled back, thoroughly lost, hoping to avoid the prison camp. They entered country heavily patrolled by search parties. Friendly natives offered food, but after a week every village was aware of the price on the heads of the three Australians – and the terrible risks of sheltering them. Desperate, hungry and lost – and frustrated by Wallace's insistence on staying in the shelter of the forest – Harvey and McKenzie struck out alone, in an easterly direction towards the coast.

The pair travelled downriver – probably on the Sungei Sibuga – on a makeshift raft. (At one point, they passed Wallace, who lingered in the jungle, watching.) They reached the river's mouth, where a few local Malays, eager for the bounty, informed the Japanese. Two truckloads of guards, under the command of Moritake, apprehended the fugitives and took them straight to a killing ground. Harvey died instantly of gunshots to the head; McKenzie struggled and was killed with rifle butt and bayonet. The guards dumped the bodies on the side of the airfield. Later, Australian prisoners buried them in a cemetery near the Eight Mile Police Post, the first victims of the new 'no-escape' clause, which treats any attempt as a capital offence.

Wallace trudged on, over tangled roots, through mud and swampland. 'The trees were more dense than ever,' he later writes. 'I felt terribly sick and tired. Life was almost unbearable but my will to live was still there.'[7] On 11 May – after almost two weeks in the wild – Wallace found the home of Heng Joo Ming and hid in his friend's chicken coop. He survived for another few days – long enough for Dr Taylor and Matthews to decide what to do with him. Since he could not be smuggled back into the prison camp, they determined that he should be taken to Berhala to join McLaren and Blow's group. Hence his presence, camping by a river on one side of the island, when Blow's men arrived.

◆

Events bring forward the escape to early June. On the 4th, a Japanese barge arrives at Berhala; its purpose is to start shipping

E Force prisoners to the mainland, for transfer by truck to the prison camp. A rumour, borne out by a doubling in the number of guards, warns that the barge will be leaving with its first batch of prisoners at dawn the next day. Blow and McLaren resolve to put their plan in motion that night.

Blow's plan is to find their way to the leper compound and steal the lepers' canoe. In this little craft, three of his party are to paddle 46 miles across open ocean, to Suarez's meeting point – at Tawi-Tawi. Nobody challenges this proposition, however unlikely its chances of success. The rest, meanwhile, are to hide out in the Berhala jungle on the ridge near the leper colony and await a rendezvous with the Suarez guerrillas once the canoe has made contact. In the event, the execution of the plan is more complicated . . . with a few ingenious ruses thrown in to confuse the Japanese.

At first, it seems easy: just before curfew, the seven prisoners walk past the Japanese guard, saluting smartly. It is their last opportunity to use the latrines before lock-up, at 7 pm. They carry small parcels of food in their pockets. Friendly guards – former local police constables – keep a close eye on the Japanese. The latrines are a few dung holes overhanging the beach. The seven men drop through the holes, scramble up the tidal scum of rubbish and excrement to the mangroves and then creep along a steep path to the ridge above the leper colony. Meanwhile, Koram picks up Wallace from his hideout on the banks of a stream a few hundred yards from the compound.

Blow and Wagner pass the lepers' huts to the beach, swim out to the canoe moored offshore, raise the anchor and paddle in. The clanking of the anchor awakens the lepers, several of whom, alarmed at the loss of their only means of catching fish, rush off to report the theft. At the same time, McLaren, Blow, Wagner, Kennedy and Butler take to sea in the little craft. Though heavily weighed down, they paddle around the point, while Steele, Gillon and Wallace keep watch in the jungle above the ridge. At the base of Berhala's soaring red cliffs, Blow and Wagner slip off the canoe and swim to a cave set in the walls. They spend the night climbing the cliff with the help of overhanging vines and rendezvous with Steele's group the next day. At the same time, McLaren, Kennedy and Butler set off on the long paddle to Tawi-Tawi. All night, they paddle in a south-easterly direction across Sandakan Harbour. They plan to travel by night and hide in mangrove swamps by day, feeding off the land, or on whatever they can scrounge from native villages.

Meanwhile, Koram unties and promptly sinks three boats on the northern side of the island. He then puts on a pair of Australian Army boots and stomps around in the mud near the point from which the boats would have embarked – and returns undetected to the mainland late that night.[8]

◆

The next morning, there is uproar: the three boat-owners discover their loss and join the lepers in complaining to the Japanese, who immediately set out to investigate. The 'clue' works: the boot-prints 'prove' the escaped Australians have stolen the boats, and the Japanese instantly launch a sea and air search. The escapees' absence from the morning roll call reveals their identities, and the hunt is on.

All day, McLaren, Kennedy and Butler hide with their canoe in the swamps; all night, they hug the east coast of Borneo, moving steadily south. By the second morning, they reach the mouth of the Segama River and drag the canoe among the mangroves. Nearby, friendly native fishermen offer them raw fish and coconuts. Upon hearing McLaren's name, one fisherman says he knows a fellow by the same name, working at the North Borneo Timber Company. 'My cousin!' McLaren replies, without hesitation, and the natives grow more helpful, cooking up a fish feast that evening.[9]

After dark, the fugitives resume the voyage, reaching Tambisan Island on 7 June, and then, on the 10th, the point at which they must leave the coast and ply the rougher seas due east, across the Sibutu Passage: open ocean for 46 miles to Tawi-Tawi. On the first attempt, storms force them back. They set out again on the 12th, 'in calm seas, travelling by moonlight'.[10] They paddle for 29 hours without a proper rest.[11] In two days, they reach their destination: the azure waters over the reefs of Sanga Sanga, where the exhausted soldiers collapse on the sand.

A young Filipino, Quizon Usman, leads them across the channel in his outrigger, to his parents' home, where they enjoy cakes, fruit and coffee. After ten days of paddling, they reach Tawi-Tawi on 14 June. 'They were free,' writes historian Kevin Smith, 'the first POWs of the Japanese taken at Singapore to have escaped successfully from Borneo.'[12] The next day, after another 19 miles of canoeing, they round the coastline and alight upon the town of Batu Batu, headquarters of Colonel Suarez and the Filipino guerrillas. Solid meals in a safe house are served, while Suarez's radio operator sends a message to Australia: three men have successfully escaped British North Borneo.

Melbourne abruptly replies: 'Glad to have you in the area. Here are your orders.' They are to cooperate with the American and

Filipino officers in every way that seems 'helpful and reasonable'. As well, they are to report Japanese sea and air movements.[13]

◆

Back at Berhala, Blow, Steele, Wagner, Gillon and Wallace wait in a crevice in the red cliffs, wrapped in groundsheets against the driving rain, with no possibility of fires. Occasionally, they steal out at night to forage for food. They wait for about ten days in this condition, speaking at a whisper, tensing when the birdsong stops, hoping their proximity to the sea will cover their smell and confuse the Japanese patrol dogs. Their luck lasts; the Japanese search parties rarely leave the bush tracks and prefer to avoid the leper colony, whose misshapen members, furious at the loss of their canoe, continue to demand reparations.

In time, fewer patrols appear, and the five men move inland to a hideout near Wallace's old refuge, shrouded in forest by a stream in the hills. 'It was a space in the middle of waving trees,' Wallace later writes, 'a first class position.'[14] They drink from a pool of fresh water, dry their clothes on the branches and sleep on beds made of saplings. For several days, they live here, awaiting news from Koram of any sign of the guerrillas. But the Japanese constantly survey the island, blocking any attempt at a landing. One day – almost a fortnight since they escaped – Koram appears, laden with fish, prawns, rice and some bananas. Henceforth, he visits regularly by night, bringing food and information from Dr Taylor and Salleh – all largely financed by the ever-reliable Mrs Cohen.

On 22 June, the Japanese patrols cease and the enemy guards depart. Berhala Island is empty: the Australian component of

E Force has left, to join B Force and, soon, the British prisoners of war. Shortly, a total of about 2400 prisoners will be enslaved at the prison camp and airfield. It is time to go. That night, the five soldiers pay a warm farewell to Koram and Salleh in the deserted guardhouse. At twilight on the 26th, sitting on the seaward beach smoking native cheroots – the signal in the darkness – they hear the gentle dipping of oars and the flap of a sail. Deliverance arrives in the form of an ocean-going, twenty-six-foot native craft with a single mast bearing a square-rigged sail. The redoubtable Quadra, commanding a crew of three, welcomes them aboard.

The boat looks like any other small fishing vessel plying the Sulu Sea, except for the addition of removable decking that disguises a false bottom. They leave the island, by wind and oar, and follow the rough route of Steele's canoe. By night, they head south towards Hog Point, from where they take an easterly course due north of Sibutu Island. The next day, the winds drop and they languish becalmed in the Sibutu Channel. In the distance, they see a Japanese destroyer bearing down on their position. In an instant, the deck is torn up, the five Australians jump into the boat's false bottom and cover themselves in heavy bags of rice.

As the enemy vessel approaches, Blow whispers a sharp, final instruction to the crew: 'Wave, be friendly!'[15] The Filipinos oblige by breaking into delighted grins, waving briskly as the Japanese destroyer pulls alongside. After a brief exchange, the enemy departs. 'It struck me at the time that we might have a bit of difficulty sinking a destroyer with a .38 revolver,' Blow later recalls.[16] 'We were glad when they went off. The bags of rice . . . each weighed 220 lbs and we could scarcely move our cramped limbs when they were lifted from us.'[17]

14

GUERRILLAS

*Lovely sight. Sinking Jap boats. Dead bodies all along the
jetty and a bit of disorganised firing from their defences.*
Captain Jock McLaren, after another successful guerrilla raid

---

FOR A FEW DAYS, the men rest and enjoy the fruits of freedom.
Steele, Blow, Wagner, Wallace and Gillon are happily reunited
with McLaren, Butler and Kennedy. The Muslim Moro people
who live on the main island of Tawi-Tawi throw a great party for
the Australians. '[E]verybody got full on coconut, tuba, dancing,
singing, eating, drinking,' Steele later remembers.[1]

If some of the Berhala Eight expect to return home and
resume the war within the Australian Army, the American-led
Filipino guerrillas have other plans, which have been approved by
Melbourne. Suarez needs good soldiers: instructors and leaders
who understand tactics. Men of the calibre of Blow and McLaren
fit the bill.

Their swift immersion in the Filipino guerrilla movement
follows. It is a well-armed network of soldiers and civilian
survivors of the Japanese invasion, embedded throughout the
islands of the Philippines and its southern province of Mindanao,
and gradually infiltrating the villages. 'Guerrillas were virtually

running both the civil and military administration of many towns on Mindanao,' observes Kevin Smith.[2] Catholic and Muslim Filipinos are prevailed upon to set aside their animosity and serve in the same combat units.

Ultimately, the Mindanao guerrillas rely on the American forces to arm and supply them. USFIP incorporates six divisions of the 10th Military District, under the command of men such as Colonels Wendell Fertig and Charlie Hedges, both of whom are destined to play a central role in the Filipino resistance. The whole operation proceeds under the watchful eye of the supreme commander in the Pacific, General Douglas MacArthur, who, after his controversial escape from the Bataan Peninsula, will stop at nothing to fulfil his vow to the Filipino people: 'I shall return'.

Henceforth, the Berhala men and their Filipino – or native Moro – comrades embark on a series of spectacular hit-and-run operations that would dumbfound the most hardened military observer. In Tawi-Tawi, the eight are immediately promoted, to endow their new responsibilities with authority: Steele is made Suarez's second-in-command; Blow appointed commander of the 1st Battalion on Tawi-Tawi, with Gillon as his second-in-command (later promoted to regimental adjutant); Wallace is elevated to warrant officer and chief recruits instructor; while McLaren, Kennedy and Butler are promoted to sergeants and assistant recruit instructors. The eight excel in their new roles. Steele, given unlimited resources for planning and supplies, arranges to buy the island's entire rice crop to feed the 1000-strong guerrilla force.[3] Blow's 70-man company acquires a reputation for extraordinary aggression and courage.

McLaren, later described as 'a natural leader' in Steele's report of the events, leads or participates in the ambush of an enemy sub-chaser, a fighting patrol against a large band of 'pro-Jap Moros' and the removal of two unexploded 250-pound aerial bombs.[4] Kennedy commands an engineering unit with astonishing verve: his men construct small bridges and viaducts, pontoons for river crossings, a new officers' barracks and lookout platforms. He joins bush patrols and ambush operations, and is 'highly respected by all ranks', notes Steele. Blow quickly appreciates McLaren's leadership qualities and gives the Scot the authority to raise a battalion of Moro warriors. His men go into action 'joyfully beating big brass gongs, dancing, shouting and cutting at the air with their deadly bolos'.[5] Under McLaren's tutelage, they specialise in sudden, blood-curdling night attacks and ambushes on much larger Japanese units. Sometimes, after a successful raid, his Moro fighters are seen to toss a Japanese head into the cooking pot, or take the heart out of a freshly killed enemy and 'drink the blood and eat the liver'.[6]

Butler performs his job with similar courage and efficiency, applying Australian bushcraft to great effect in clearing emergency trails, food dumps and troop concentration areas. A buffalo hunter and superb shot, Butler manages to hit low-flying Japanese bombers several times as they pass overhead and is credited with killing at least one Japanese pilot (or gunner) and wounding another. He shortly meets his end – shot during the fighting with pro-enemy Moros, who decapitate his body and sell his head to the Japanese, who mount it on a pike on the island of Jolo to warn the locals of the cost of supporting the American-led resistance. The Australian's record is held in such high esteem that Colonel Suarez recommends that his Batu Batu headquarters be renamed 'Camp Butler'.[7]

After five months on Tawi-Tawi, the Berhala seven (minus Butler) receive orders to proceed to Mindanao. The Australians, two sick Americans and a native crew take a small boat a few hundred miles across open sea. Keeping well concealed below deck, they survive close encounters with several Japanese patrol boats. 'One day they sailed right into a Jap convoy,' an officer later reports, 'but got away by keeping serenely to their course and refusing to run.'[8] They reach Sindagan, on the west coast of Zamboanga Province, in late 1943. There follows a 70-mile, five-day march over the mountains to the east coast, a small sea crossing and a 34-mile truck ride to Liangan, in the province of Lanao, where they present themselves to the American Corps Commander of the Filipino guerrillas, Colonel Fertig. Throughout this epic journey, sickness – malaria, a double hernia and other tropical diseases – harasses the little party. And there are casualties. In one Japanese raid, a sniper shoots Wagner above the right eye; he dies instantly. But nothing diminishes their determination to take the war to the Japanese. When Blow and McLaren are later temporarily repatriated to Australia, their commander-in-chief, General Sir Thomas Blamey, orders them on leave. 'We only want a fortnight,' the two soldiers will reply. 'We still have a score to settle with the Japanese. We remember Lt Wagner.'[9]

In the following months, Blow's and McLaren's men achieve a series of ever-more-daring tactical victories from their Philippine base. Nimble-footed strike teams attack and destroy Japanese patrols – even forcing 300 enemy soldiers off Mindanao. They dispatch radio reports of Japanese shipping movements to Australia, capture the Japanese-held Malanang airfield and other facilities, and commandeer an old 26-foot whaleboat with which to attack Japanese ports. McLaren christens it *The Bastard*. Often, his crew bedecks *The Bastard* in the Rising Sun flag, dresses up in stolen Japanese uniforms and sails cheerfully into enemy-held harbours, to a rousing reception. Recalling his departure from one corpse-strewn pier, McLaren, the self-styled 'admiral' of this little guerrilla navy, notes, 'Lovely sight. Sinking Jap boats. Dead bodies all along the jetty and a bit of disorganised firing from their defences.'[10]

McLaren's whaleboat incursions are soon the scourge of the Moro Gulf and lethally demonstrate his theory that 'the closer you are to the Japanese the safer you are'. In 1944, the Australian Army will duly reward him with a promotion – to captain – and the Military Cross. But the Japanese bestow the most lavish recognition of his success: a 70,000-peso bounty on his head, dead or alive – a price McLaren regards as 'reasonable'.[11]

McLaren is acting, technically, on the orders of Blow, as his superior officer; but in practice the men regard each other as equals. Rex Blow has unfailing faith in the older man's ability to inflict terrible harm on the enemy. For his own part, Blow is similarly recognised by the Americans and Australians as one of the most formidable guerrilla leaders of the Pacific War, always organising and often leading attacks on Japanese positions in the Philippines and elsewhere. In time, Blow and McLaren and their men achieve one of the most sustained and effective covert actions against Japanese interests in the Pacific, earning Blow a Distinguished Service Order and McLaren a bar to his Military Cross. The Australian Government refuses to permit their acceptance of high American decorations – McLaren is recommended for the Silver Star – in line with an absurd Commonwealth ruling that disallows foreign honours.

◆

The guerrilla war operates at the sharp end of a new direction in military thinking: the creation of special undercover units – hit and run, deep-penetration squads whose job is to collect intelligence, sabotage, and inflict death and disruption deep inside enemy lines. The pioneering example is that of the unconventional British officer Orde Wingate, recipient of a Distinguished Service Order and two bars for his operations in Palestine and Burma. Wingate is best known for his creation of the Chindits, airborne deep-penetration units drawn mostly from the 77th Indian Brigade, who are fighting the Japanese in Burma and India.

In 1943–44, these 'Special Forces' proliferate. All over the South-West Pacific, small units of fearless men, their faces blackened, parachute into remote jungle clearings, land on silent bays by moonlight, or slip into hostile seas in small submarines or 'Sleeping Beauties' (motorised submersible canoes), with explicit instructions to penetrate Japanese lines, gather intelligence and generally wreak havoc in the rear. The first Australian Special Forces tend to be drawn from independent 'commando' units, such as the 2/2nd and 2/4th Independent Companies, who wage a remarkably successful guerrilla campaign in Timor. In 1943, similar operations are under way in New Guinea, New Britain, Bougainville and Borneo. Many are small-scale raiding parties specialising in reconnaissance and sabotage.

Their existence comes under the control of a complex jurisdiction, modelled on the British Special Operations Executive (SOE) formed to promote underground movements and covert activities in the European war – notably in the Balkans, the French underground and Poland, and within the German Reich itself. From the outset, SOE receives a virtual carte blanche to act outside the rules that normally govern regular army services. SOE is directly responsible to the British War Cabinet – and not the usual army lines of command. This unprecedented freedom confers on special units great powers of movement and engagement, and access to immense resources. Whether the units are supplying civilian resistance movements or bombing neutral territory, they necessarily contravene the strict rules governing 'regular' warfare, and are 'illegal' insofar as any pedantic scrutiny of the rulebook goes. But fighting a total war on two vast fronts determines the 'rules' of war. As the official history of the SOE's Australian counterpart, Special Operations Australia, makes clear:

SOE was considered by the [UK] War Cabinet as a separate service, a service able to carry out tasks which could not be undertaken by the other services. For example, the employment of civilians, foreign national and native peoples for subversive activities is a breach of the Laws and Usages of War imposed on the regular services . . . Similarly, the carrying out of operations in neutral countries, despite technicalities of neutrality, is a breach of International Law. For these and other similar reasons, the regular services could not participate in such work without involving the Government.[12]

◆

In 1942, Australia joined this secret war with the creation of SOE Australia, part of the Inter-Allied Service Department (IASD), itself a component of the Allied Intelligence Bureau, the highest military intelligence authority answerable to Canberra and London. The intricacies and stress points of this complex organisation were not conducive to its smooth operation, and a shake-up was inevitable. For one thing, SOE Australia did not fit comfortably within the existing context of the Australian Armed Forces: what was needed was an all-Australian outfit severed from the encumbrances of its British parent. The man who directed the impetus for change was that deeply patriotic, if widely disliked, Australian General Sir Thomas Blamey, commander-in-chief of Allied Landforces in the South-West Pacific.

Blamey is credited with the idea of creating, in early 1943, Special Operations Australia (SOA) or the Services Reconnaissance Department (SRD) – the two names are used interchangeably. The new outfit includes a smattering of highly experienced British members, whose training and guidance prove indispensable. The creation of SOA opens a new episode in Australian warfare, a story of extraordinary men bound to wage war, like their British and American counterparts, 'in small bands hundreds of miles in advance of their fellows in the regular services'.[13]

The Z Special Unit – known as 'Z Force' – raised in June 1942, is one of SOA's proudest achievements. So effective is Z Force that it becomes the model for the future Special Air Service, or SAS. Its 'originals' are regarded as the toughest, most ruthless and most resourceful men in the Australian Army. This is a close, and closed, world, and such soldiers are aware of the exploits of their counterparts in Britain and America. Blow, McLaren and Wagner et al., for example, are recognised well beyond the confines of Canberra's need to know. They, Wingate, their British counterparts, and American guerrilla leaders such as Captain John Hamner are the pioneers of covert operations. Henceforth, their example is to be extended with the full backing of Allied military intelligence, logistics and the three Allied governments.

In the ensuing two years, Z Force will mount 81 covert operations behind enemy lines, in Singapore, New Guinea, New Caledonia, Borneo and elsewhere, inflicting great damage on the Japanese war effort. One of the most famous is the *Krait* raid on Singapore Harbour in September 1943. Less spectacular, but no less daring, are operations in Ambon and Timor. Some operations are successful; others racked by misfortune. Their missions are broadly the same: to study, sabotage and slaughter the enemy. These men, carefully trained in secret locations – in hidden inlets, for example, in Middle Harbour, Sydney – will spend months, even years, in the most dangerous situations conceivable, living off the land, risking death day and night, nurturing difficult relationships with the native people, whose loyalties are often unclear.

◆

At no time, however, is their brief explicitly directed at rescuing Allied prisoners. That is not their job; they lack the manpower to undertake operations on that scale. Rescue missions drain resources and do little to assist the prosecution of the war, according to the priorities in MacArthur's headquarters in Brisbane. The men who comprise Special Operations Australia are combat soldiers sent to fight a war, not rescue teams sent to relieve weak and dispirited POWs and local people. Recovered prisoners need care and hospitalisation before they are fit enough to return to the lines. The brutal truth, as the plans and actions of Generals MacArthur and Blamey show, is that the war must be fought, and won, before precious resources may be spared to save prisoners and civilians.

To this end, Blamey is determined to impress MacArthur, his fierce rival during the Papuan campaign of 1942, with some Commonwealth flag-waving behind enemy lines.[14] His new unit is trained to do a lot more than waving flags, of course. Malaya and Borneo are considered primary targets for the first sallies of a British–Australian covert unit. In early 1943, Allied Special Forces earmark British North Borneo as a priority for intelligence-gathering. The British are anxious not to lose their former colony and the oil and timber riches it contains, and the Australians are keen to eradicate the enemy presence along the Malayan barrier, so near to home. The fact that some 2500 Australian and British prisoners of war languish in Sandakan is a misfortune, incidental to their core mission. The harsh equation of war is how to destroy the enemy's means of waging it. In this context, the Special Forces are not sent to Borneo on an express mission to liberate the prison camp – that may, at some point, be a by-product of their core purpose, as the Americans soon demonstrate in the Philippines. The SOA is not, and never will be, a compassionate crusade.

The Australian graduates – or, more accurately, the survivors – of the first SOA courses in special operations know this. They are hungry for action, under the tutelage and leadership of two inspiring Englishmen, Lieutenant Colonel Egerton Mott (director) and Major Ambrose Trappes-Lomax (training and supplies). Mott, who has a difficult tenure, is relieved by Colonel P. J. E. Chapman-Walker. The first mission, sent in January 1943 to sabotage oil facilities in Singapore, is a dispiriting failure: their ship experiences engine trouble soon after leaving Sydney.

Confidence and momentum are strong, however, and the political and military will is there, to press ahead with a series of sustained operations behind Japanese lines. Borneo, however,

poses an exceptional challenge to SOA's remit. While topographi-
cal and ethnic information is easily obtainable, thanks to British
colonial records, the island's immense size, rough terrain and
impenetrable interior, as well as the lack of verifiable intelligence
on the Japanese, seem to conspire against early attempts to embed
a special force in the mountains above Jesselton, or in the jungles
along the rivers west of Sandakan.

Here, guerrilla units can expect to encounter one of the
toughest environments of any in the South-West Pacific. And
incoming intelligence early that year – before the underground
starts making regular contact with the Philippines – is ropy at
best. Where, exactly, does the enemy's strength lie? In Kuching?
Jesselton? Sandakan? Or in the interior? Who among the locals
can be trusted? Even when the Matthews–Taylor network starts
cooking with gas, the flow of information, of letters and notebooks, is but a forlorn crackle in the deadly silence emanating
from the world's third-biggest island. Had Matthews and Wells
succeeded in building a radio transmitter, the prosecution of
the war in Borneo would have been transformed in the Allies'
favour, facilitating the smooth coordination of Special Forces in
the area.

Undaunted by these obstacles – and determined to overcome them – SOA sets in motion the first attempt to penetrate
British North Borneo. It is called, wishfully enough, Operation
PYTHON, led by a British import with exceptional credentials:
an SOE-trained English Army officer who speaks Malay and local
dialects, who has managed a plantation in British North Borneo
for 20 years and who knows the local people, native and Chinese.
His name is Major Francis George Leach Chester, nicknamed
'Gort', because his thick moustache, receding hairline and large

round head remind his fellow officers of Field Marshal Viscount Gort, then Governor of Malta.

Major 'Gort' Chester is something of a Cincinnatus – the Roman centurion who laid down his plough to take up the sword – plucked from his plantation, which he so lovingly tends, to conduct war in Asia, hoping one day to return to the sleepy embrace of the British colony and his farm. Gort has a more intriguing résumé than this pastoral fable suggests: he doubles as a spy on His Majesty's service and has long been involved in clandestine operations as part of MI6, Britain's overseas intelligence service, to which he was recruited before the war.

Operation PYTHON's first mission to British North Borneo ('PYTHON I'), planned for late 1943, is to infiltrate friendly tribes, establish an intelligence-gathering operation and 'prepare the ground work for a campaign of sabotage and underground resistance'.[15] Rescuing the prisoners is not, and never will be, an official part of its brief. In any case, even if the aim of Gort's mission were to smash open the prison camp, one cold fact militates against it: the underground network serves the interests of his covert operation. Taylor, Matthews, Wells and their men have made themselves indispensable. Their superb intelligence on Japanese movements in Borneo is precisely what Gort is here to obtain. Leave them in captivity, the better to gather information on the Japanese, runs the thinking. Matthews, by his actions, agrees: the captain has had many chances to escape, through his excellent contacts. On one occasion, according to research by his son,[16] he personally declined an audacious offer by Suarez to rescue him and all the prisoners – surely a presumptuous decision to make on behalf of hundreds of sick and dying men? At another time, Matthews shuns a local proposal that he should escape and join the Filipino guerrillas. Instead, he elects to stay and run one of the most dangerous 'behind enemy lines' operations of the war. His duty, he says at the time, is to 'stand by with my boys' and 'go through thick and thin with them under any circumstances'.[17] The remarkable thing about Matthews, Taylor, Wells and their network – which surely commends them for the highest award for bravery – is what they do not do, as much as what they do.

Right now, the underground's priority is to contact the PYTHON mission reported to be landing later that year in Borneo. Matthews' cherished uprising will depend on Special Forces' support, supplies and men. First, he will have to make contact with the little band of commandos.

15

ARRIVALS

[T]he thing was important enough for us to risk our own
personal upsets . . . I appease my conscience when it pricks
me, with the knowledge that none of us could wave a flag
when armistice is signed if I hadn't had a finger in the pie.

Captain John Oakeshott, Australian medical officer

My Dear Cath,
Just a few lines to let you know all is well. I am trusting that you
and the two boys are keeping in the best of health . . . Well Dear,
we are just about on the point of landing, were [sic] it is, God only
knows . . . Well Dear, how's your cold feet now that winter's there.
I wish I had them here, they would be all right down my back.

Gunner Ernie Hazzard, Royal Artillery

TENSIONS RISE AS THE PRISON CAMP expands. The new
arrivals – the British and Australians of E Force – are kept strictly
segregated; B Force is also off-limits to the arrivals. The guards
shave the heads of E Force men to distinguish them from the rest.
The Australians and British receive separate compounds; each

man is given a new number, allocated alphabetically in groups determined by rank, and inscribed on a wooden tag. The regime tightens in all respects: food is scarce; medical supplies severely limited. Hoshijima, the commandant, instructs his men to be extra vigilant after the breakout from Berhala.

Despite these conditions, the Australians seem remarkably resilient – no doubt due to their adaptability, the underground smuggling ring and the resourcefulness of the medics. Near the end of June 1943, only a few men have died of illnesses. The British prisoners have succumbed at a more rapid rate, with nine dead since their arrival about ten weeks earlier.[1] Perhaps the British constitution is less adaptable to extreme tropical conditions, the Australians think. The truth, however, appears to be the severity of their terrible journey to the prison camp, via Kuching and Jesselton.

Among the E Force Australians are the medical officers Captains John Oakeshott and Domenic Picone, who form a strong bond, drawn together by the soldiers' constant demands on their meagre resources. Oakeshott is the model of the stoic medic, quiet and calm under pressure, resolute in his duty to the men. A graduate of Sydney University, he worked as a general practitioner in Lismore between 1928 and 1941. He and his wife Enid have two children, Robert and Elizabeth (Robert's son is the independent MP Rob Oakeshott). In 1941, John Oakeshott enlisted as a medical officer in the Australian Army Medical Corps, having reconciled his decision with his conscience and family. Writing to his sister Kathleen at the time, he explained that he and Enid had 'worked it out' and 'that the thing was important enough for us to risk our own personal upsets . . . I appease my conscience when it pricks me, with the knowledge that none of us could wave a flag when armistice is signed if I hadn't had a finger in the pie.'[2]

Oakeshott found his whole body on the line in the last days of Singapore, during which he tended the wounded with the same calm resolution and, as one of his medical orderlies later recalls, 'earned the respect of all, especially as his quiet manner had led inexperienced men to think he might be timid in action: this was not the case'.[3]

Less is known of Captain Picone, as he never married and most of his close family have passed away. He is similarly erudite and rather swottish in appearance, with an engaging, intelligent face beaming out from behind black-rimmed spectacles. Initially a pharmacist, he graduated in medicine from Melbourne University in 1936 and enlisted with the 2/10th Field Regiment at Enoggera in Brisbane. He was a GP at Cooroy at the time.

At Sandakan, the two doctors throw themselves at their 'stupendous task' with the spirit of 'true medical gentlemen', in the phrase of Major John Fairley, the commander of E Force.[4] Neither Oakeshott's nor Picone's families are aware of their true circumstances at this stage of the war, only that they are 'prisoners of the Japanese'. The most insuperable problem facing the medics is the soldiers' loss of strength due to vitamin deficiency. Wounds from bashings may heal, but the prisoners' general health begins to suffer symptoms of chronic decline: exhaustion and an extreme listlessness set in. By August, an increasing number of cases of night-blindness due to an acute lack of vitamin A prompts the medical officers to apply to the Japanese for permission to gather palm nuts, to supply the prisoners with palm oil. Permission is granted and a small party join the woodcutters outside the wire, adding to Matthews' and Wells' resources of subversion.[5]

◆

The arrival in April 1943 of about 800 British prisoners, after their horrendous voyage from Singapore via Jesselton, fundamentally alters the tenor of the camp. It seems that several guards display a higher regard for Englishmen than for Australians, sparking talk of preferential treatment. Matthews and his men care little for these spurious distinctions; they hanker only to get in touch with their British allies and spread the word of the underground – and they take extreme risks to do so.

Who are these British units? Some 400 are members of the Royal Artillery, representing four regiments and 13 batteries. Most are 'Java Gunners', transferred from Batavia, after the island fell, to Changi and thence to Sandakan. The rest are Royal Air Force, also transported from Java, and diverse infantry regiments shipped from Singapore: the Worcestershire Regiment, Argyll and Sutherland Highlanders, Royal Corps of Signals, Royal Army Medical Corps, Royal Army Service Corps, Royal Electrical and Mechanical Engineers and Pioneer Corps.[6]

The British infuse the prison with nostalgia for a place vastly different from the warm, peaceable, southern land of their Australian allies. Britain is a world of doodlebugs, freezing winters, music halls, great silver barrage balloons, sirens in the daylight, darkness, howling warnings and the all clear, boarded-up shop windows and the familiar English insouciance of 'BUSINESS AS USUAL' written outside. Typical of the men is Gunner Joe Stephens, of the Royal Artillery.

Before he went to war, Joey Stephens used to play the accordion in bomb shelters – 'Silent Night' and other carols. During the first Christmas Eve in Sandakan, when conditions were not so harsh, an Australian remembers 'a Tommy' sitting on a mound at the drome playing 'Silent Night' on the accordion.[7] His sister, Teresa, who was ten at the time, later felt sure it was her brother, Joey. He had been stationed in Java until the island swiftly folded under Japanese bombing in February 1942 and he was shipped to Borneo.

That month, Gunner Ernest Hazzard, a gas-meter reader from London, also found himself in East Java, after his ship was diverted from Persia to garrison the island. Hazzard was a member of 48 Battery, under the command of Major P. P. Andrews. A tall, lean, good-looking man, Hazzard is a brilliant fixer of things – skills he later puts to good use in Borneo. He is calm, methodical and warmly considerate of his friends. 'My father was a gentleman who wouldn't hurt anyone,' says his son, Tony. He wrote his last letter to his wife, Cath, on arrival in Batavia on 4 February:

> My Dear Cath,
> Just a few lines to let you know all is well. I am trusting that you and the two boys are keeping in the best of health . . . Well Dear, we are just about on the point of landing, were [sic] it is, God only knows . . . Well Dear, how's your cold feet now that winter's there. I wish I had them here, they would be all right down my back. Just now I feel as if I've just come out of a bath its so hot . . . Well Darling, how is everything at home. I bet the garden will be looking lovely by the time you get this letter . . . Well dear, remember me to all at home and round about . . . Will close now. Just waiting for the end to come & get on our way home again.
> So Cheerio Darling, keep your chin up & keep smiling, All my love & kisses to you and the boys,

Ernie xxxxxxx
John xxxxxx
Tony xxxxxx

PS I often think of Tony the last time I came home –
My Daddy

Four weeks later, on 9 March, the island fell, with the unconditional surrender of all British personnel to the Japanese. Hazzard's unit, formed a matter of weeks ago, had experienced no 'close fighting'. The humiliating Order of Capitulation to the British gunners resulted in 'white flags' being raised over the island and all guards wearing 'white armbands'. Major Sitwell 'deeply regrets the necessity and orders us to comply', the note concludes.[8]

The Japanese divided the surviving units and transferred some to Changi. As Hazzard prepared to leave, his commanding officer wrote to all ranks: 'I do not know where you are going but situations will arise which call for patience and hard work and I know that you will buckle to and help as you have here. The course of the War is long but the end is sure.'[9]

Les Mockridge was not the first prisoner of war in the Mockridge family: two brothers were captured during the Monmouth Rebellion of 1685. The notorious Judge Jeffreys found both guilty of treason, sent one to the gallows and had the other transported to Barbados. 'Sold to a reverend he was never heard of again,' Les's son Steve wistfully writes.[10] Les was born in a village near Taunton, Somerset, in October 1918 and grew up a determined, possibly obstinate young man with a strong idea of right and wrong and a sharp sense of humour. An electrician by trade, he joined the Royal Air Force in 1939 and trained as an instrument repairer. Leading Aircraftman Mockridge arrived in Malaya in 1941 and was transferred to Java shortly before the fall of Singapore. He ended up in Sandakan via a painfully convoluted route: several months in Batavian prison camps, then Changi, then shipped with 800 other British prisoners to Jesselton, as slave labour on the airstrip and, finally, to Sandakan in April 1943, with E Force.

Another man sent to Java was David Glyn Phillips, of Neath, South Wales. Born in 1911, he was expected to take charge of the family's successful drapery business. Instead, he enlisted in the RAF, partly as a result of feelings of resentment towards his domineering self-made father, who refused to allow him to choose a different future. As a result, Phillips grew closer to his mother, who sympathised with his dream of doing something other than drapery. Another motive encouraged him to enlist: a strong sense of duty to join the war effort, for which he enthusiastically volunteered. 'He apparently told my mother he could no longer just sit around the local Conservative Club endlessly discussing events,' his son, Jeffrey Phillips, says. 'He felt he could not stand idly by and see other men fight and die for their country.'[11] David Phillips sailed for Java on 4 December 1941. Within two months, he was taken prisoner and sent to Singapore. Hazzard, Stephens, Mockridge and Phillips were among about 800 British servicemen who departed Changi in April 1943 as part of E Force, aboard the hell ship *De Klerk*, bound for Sandakan.

16

BETRAYAL

Lagan was a brave man and the information extracted
from him was not given willingly; he felt ashamed
that he had been forced to divulge anything . . .
Australian report on the torture of Ernesto
Lagan by the Japanese Kempei-tai

TIME SEEMS TO PASS SLOWLY when you most want
to quicken it: to speed the hands with a swirl of your finger, or
smash the device in fury at its indifferent pace. The prisoners have
surrendered to the slow grind of time. The sun and rain clock
the seasons: there is no spring, no winter, just heat and wet. The
heat clutches at the throat and chest; the monsoon beats, like tiny
hammer-blows, on the head; the humidity drains the body. The
men are used to it.

The cloak of vegetation that once seemed impenetrable,
hysterical, is now accepted as part of their normality. Perhaps it
is their saviour. The tangled green mess beyond the wire beckons
the dreamers to come and hide in its gorgon-like embrace: surely
hope exists somewhere out there? Surely the guards wouldn't
search for them *there*? But the holes in the vines and the shadows
under the vaulting canopy deceive. They lead nowhere, or to the

sea. They are the mad alleyways of nature's dead ends.

As the months pass, the prisoners grow weary of dreams of escape and resign themselves to conditions as they are. This is their life now; their only hope is to survive. But their 'normality' is a slow death sentence. Is it normal to perform hard labour all day without an adequate meal? To be beaten on a whim? To be forced to stand for hours in the sun? Is it normal to see a man dragged to the cage and confined there for days? Such experiences occur daily in the lives of some 1800 Australian and 640 British prisoners held in Sandakan Prisoner of War Camp during 1943 and 1944.

The heroic efforts of the medical officers provide some relief. They somehow scavenge, with Dr Taylor's help, the necessary equipment – a scalpel, needles, morphine – to conduct basic surgery (mostly appendectomies), reset broken limbs and tend to the worst cases of tropical sickness. They make syringes out of wood. Braithwaite witnesses one operation:

> The tropical ulcers were extremely painful . . . I'd see fellows with the shin bone bared from knee to ankle, the bone, the entire bone. And the blokes in the Medical Corps, they used to get in there with scissors and they'd snip the rotten flesh away, which of course sickened them and was extremely painful . . . And these fellows would be white and the sweat would be pouring but they wouldn't make a sound, you know. But after they'd gone you'd hear little whimpers . . . I'm sure I couldn't have taken it.[1]

And not all the Japanese, or their Formosan guards, are mindlessly brutal all the time. Even Hoshijima conducts experiments in comfort, with his ludicrous 'Friendship Garden Parties' for the Australian and British officers – an awkward attempt at fraternising with his counterparts in rank. A fair number of Allied officers gladly accept his invitation, bringing with it the prospect of better food – and drawing snarls of 'collaborator' from the uninvited other ranks.

◆

The Japanese battle demons of their own: the whisper of defeat ripples through their lines as the Imperial bases in the South-West Pacific are steadily overthrown. The most rigidly indoctrinated soldiers refuse to accept reality: for them, 'spirit' and the sun goddess will overcome every obstacle. They seek reassurance in superstition: the empire will never die, because the emperor is divinely sent, immortal and so on. Surrender is, of course, unthinkable. And yet an unspoken sense of doom preys on the minds of the more rational officers and men, who dimly accept the encroaching signs of defeat.

The fall of the Solomons and Papua have forced the Japanese to retreat, or 'advance in a different direction', as they euphemistically put it, for the first time. Japan's mounting losses at sea and in the air are harbingers of the utter collapse of the imperial adventure, the failure of the crusade to occupy the British, French and Dutch colonies, which began with outpourings of triumphalism in China in 1931. The less self-deceiving commanders – chiefly Yamashita, the Tiger of Malaya – read something worse in the terrible losses at Papua (a near 95 per cent casualty rate) and Guadalcanal (where 20,748 out of 31,400 Japanese troops perish); the annihilation of the Japanese forces on Attu Island; the death of Admiral Yamamoto Isoroku, commander of the Japanese fleet, on 18 April 1943; and the near-complete destruction of the Japanese Navy. They are haunted by the prospect of unconditional surrender.

On land and in the air, the Allies are firmly on the offensive. Throughout 1943 and 1944, American aircraft spearhead MacArthur's great island-by-island northward advance, the purpose of which is to sweep past the bulk of the Japanese Army, then stationed in China and Manchuria, and reach the shores of Japan. A string of Pacific atolls – stinking outposts of doomed men – fall to the Allied offensive. The islands are vital: they represent airfields. Any island within aerial reach of Japanese positions is slated for reconquest. But not all: some, of limited strategic value, or containing large concentrations of Japanese, such as Rabaul and Formosa, are bombed and bypassed; others – Tarawa, for example – are invaded, with heavy American losses. But the fate of Borneo, among others, remains uncertain. MacArthur commissions urgent studies of the feasibility of invasion.

◆

Encircled by intimations of defeat, the Japanese commanders in Borneo develop a siege mentality, a defiant stand, overlaying a mood of grim foreboding. Yet, if Suga and Hoshijima privately sense the prospect of surrender in the Allied offensive hurtling towards them, they outwardly deny what their 'stomach art' – the ancient Japanese idea of divining the truth literally in 'gut feel' – tells them. Japanese spirit will prevail! Japan will never surrender! Japan will be victorious! And why should this not be true? Less than two years ago, their men were shouting *'Banzai!'* on Singapore island.

The Japanese try to dignify the brutal treatment of the prisoners as a kind of losers' justice: if we die, you die. In this hair-trigger climate, the slightest offence sets off unbridled savagery. Thus, Sergeant John Codlin, one of the prisoners' paymasters, is beaten about the head with a pick-handle and hospitalised for weeks after witnessing, and being asked to identify, two guards who attempt to embezzle the prisoners' funds. There are many similar cases. On one occasion, an Australian is beaten so badly he loses an eye. Broken limbs, severe bruising and deep lacerations are almost daily occurrences.

◆

Meanwhile, those at the heart of the underground can scarcely believe the apparent ease with which they have circumvented Japanese authority – manifested in the play-dumb faces of loyal police officers, the steady, subversive routine of the civilians and in the guarded stoicism of the ringleaders.

But the risks are deepening. The network has widened beyond the capacity of the ringleaders to control it. The arrival of the new prisoners encourages a more daring approach to intelligence-gathering and delivery. Adding further complexity is the underground's reach into the interior and to the west coast, where rebellion is brewing. The local people see the planned Kinabalu uprising as part of a much wider revolt against the Japanese, cornered in Jesselton, where a Chinese-led guerrilla movement is gathering strength.

For their part, Matthews and Wells remain wedded to the plan to build a radio transmitter, enabling them to send outgoing messages to the guerrillas. This closes the circle of vital interests crucial to the success of a prison breakout and uprising. The ringleaders' waking hours are dominated by the hope of an uprising. Hatred and the thirst for revenge sustains them. Every act of Japanese barbarity is noted in the slow accretion of evidence of war crimes. A bloody insurrection and summary justice must surely follow, if there is any grace on earth.

Matthews isn't dreaming; as always, he is acting. He has formed an escape committee, crystallising his brazen plan for a prison breakout. His conception is simple, and unrealistic. The stronger prisoners and loyal local police, armed with weapons smuggled in from the Philippines, are to overpower the guards. The prisoners will then move the sick and wounded to a ridge above the camp, which they will defend until the American-led reinforcements arrive – hopefully in the brief window of time before some 1400 Japanese troops in Borneo launch their counter-attack. The point of the plan is to save everyone – to take *all* prisoners, including the sick and wounded – and inflict a counter-blow that will destroy the Japanese on the island. Is it madness? Can it be done? In a world without any conventional measure of sanity, the plan is no madder than Blow's epic escape.

None of the resistance leaders is aware of an event in June 1943 that might have counselled caution: the Japanese apprehended and brutally suppressed an uprising at Banjarmasin, in the formerly Dutch-controlled province of South Borneo. More than 200 people were arrested and jailed, and 26 publicly shot, including the leader, Dr B. J. Haga, the former governor of the province. In Sandakan, the underground carries on seemingly oblivious to the dangers. We have got this far: why not press on? Indeed, the resistance leaders have forced events to the point at which a grand plan of immense audacity[2] may just work

– at the very moment when they are, in fact, most vulnerable to interception and betrayal.

◆

The motive is banal. Neither fear of nor loyalty to the Japanese inspires the betrayal, just money. It is a tawdry act of extortion. A 'business venture' – the sale of rice on the black market – between Heng Joo Ming and a sweeper at the airfield called Dominic Koh fails after an argument over illegal dealing. In anger, Koh informs an Indian friend, Bah Chik, of Heng Joo Ming's involvement in Wallace's escape. Koh and Bah Chik see an opportunity to extort a little cash. Bah Chik, a close associate of the spy for the Japanese Jackie Ah Fok Lo, threatens to betray Heng to the Japanese unless he pays him a protection fee (to be secretly shared with Koh). Heng, a proud, loyal man, scornfully calls Bah Chik's bluff and pays nothing. The two blackmailers act on their threat and inform Jackie Lo.

The agent Lo is nothing if not thorough: the Kempei-tai is soon aware of the plot. Heng and his father, Jakariah, are arrested before dawn on 18 July 1943 and taken to a spacious bungalow on Tanahmerah Road, formerly the home of the general manager of Bakau and Kenya Extract Company and now notorious as the 'house of torture'. The Kempei-tai wastes no time: a guard skilled at ju-jitsu throws the two men about the room. When this fails to elicit names, son and father are subjected to water-torture. Large amounts of liquid are forced down Heng's throat, after which an interrogator jumps from a chair onto his painfully distended stomach. The sound of his elderly father enduring the same treatment adds psychological torment to Heng's physical agony.

He yields, as any human would, admitting his involvement with the underground. Names spill forth: Dr Taylor, Matthews, Mu Sing, Lagan, the Funks.[3]

The secret police arrest dozens in the coming weeks. They start with members of Heng's family (his de facto wife and her mother), his assistant Sini (who is severely tortured), Lamberto Apostol and several others. The scale of the operation astonishes the Kempei-tai and humiliates Hoshijima. Clearly, there will be no mercy. On 19 July, two of the biggest names in the resistance are apprehended at Kempei-tai headquarters: Ernesto Lagan and Dr Taylor. The manner of their arrest is designed to inflict the maximum humiliation on Lagan, the brave police detective who has done so much for the prisoners. Kempei-tai men pick him up at his home at 7 am on 18 July 1943 and drive him to the Sandakan Civil Hospital, where Dr Taylor works. Lagan, mystified, is ordered to arrest Dr Taylor (and medical assistant Dr Wands). Lagan initially refuses but, under the threat of violence to his family, obeys. And so the local policeman is forced to 'arrest' his old friend, the local doctor. The Kempei-tai then charges both men and takes them to its headquarters.

Several key underground figures follow. In the coming days, Mu Sing, Paddy Funk, Dick Majinal, Gerald Mavor, the watchman Salleh and Corporal Koram are arrested, the latter variously informed upon by those aware of his involvement with the Berhala escapees. The lepers have been busy.

A truckload of troops arrives to arrest Paddy Funk: perhaps his prominent local family, and their substantial estate, next door to the prison camp, warrant such attention. No deference is shown to the son of the former magistrate: Funk is slapped and kicked and thrown into the truck. His brothers will soon follow.

◆

And now they come for Matthews. While Heng has mentioned Matthews under torture, Lagan yields the crucial confirmation, signing a statement of admission after the infliction of long and terrible pain. Lagan's name is destined never to be forgotten in post-war Sabah. 'Lagan,' one report later says, 'was a brave man and the information extracted from him was not given willingly; he felt ashamed that he had been forced to divulge anything, but nevertheless his thoughts were still for the welfare of the Australians.'[4]

Matthews is tending the garden with fellow officers when the Japanese, led by Hoshijima, arrive on the morning of 22 July 1943. The guards search the prison compound. The record of what they find varies according to the source. Clearly, however, they fail to find the wireless transmitter parts and letters (several written to Governor Smith), which have been hastily hidden by Captain John Rowell, then ill in bed. Later, they find two revolvers and nominal rolls of the prisoners, which another officer, Russ Ewin, has removed from the cupboard in Matthews' hut and hidden inside a chimney stack at the eight-mile police station. Hoshijima personally inspects the spoils and finds in Matthews' wallet a card from one of the Berhala internees. Two days later, another search yields more incriminating evidence: a list of radio parts secreted into the camp; three maps, of Sandakan town, Japanese troop positions and their accommodation; and a small black notebook – Wells' BBC news transcripts, which the Japanese describe as a 'diary'.

17

THE KEMPEI-TAI

Matthews communicated using Morse. He would come back from interrogation, sit down, cross his legs as we were instructed to, and tap his fingers . . . He would go through the topic of which he'd been interrogated that morning and the answers he'd delivered.

Lieutenant Gordon Weynton describing the finger-

tapping code Matthews used to communicate

with inmates in the Kempei-tai cells

THE ROUND-UP IS THOROUGH, and the repercussions immense. The prisoners face the consequences with stoic calm and show great presence of mind during the arrests. Wells, after taking the Japanese investigators on a futile riffle through the camp, repeatedly denies the existence, or any knowledge, of a radio – despite the BBC transcripts found in his notebook.

Eventually, Wells abandons this charade – the transcripts are clear evidence of the radio's existence – but he has bought time for others to secrete the evidence. He surrenders the half-built transmitter in order to save the functioning receiver (which Sticpewich has earlier removed from its secret compartment, stuffing the compartment with fish and fruit). Hoshijima personally beats Wells, tightening a handkerchief around his neck, 'screwing it up tight . . . as he was punching him'.[1] At 6 pm on 24 July 1943, the commandant parades Wells before the prisoners. 'Look at this man,' Hoshijima yells. 'You will not see him again!' Wells is hauled away to a black limousine and driven to Kempei-tai headquarters in Sandakan.

At the same time, several prisoners suspected of being involved in the radio, or the wider underground, are interrogated, beaten and caged. They include Sticpewich, who protests his innocence without effect, as do several fellow officers and sergeants. Their treatment is lenient compared with the punishment that awaits the core suspects: Matthews, Wells, Dr Taylor, Weynton, Lagan, the Funk brothers, Heng Joo Ming, Ah Ping, Azcona and scores of others. Some of the lesser accused, against whom the evidence is weak, are interred in Sandakan Gaol, under the authority of sympathetic local police. The jail is seen as a 'holiday camp' alongside the Kempei-tai's house of torture, where the key underground figures are now sent.[2]

◆

Formed in 1881 under a decree called the Kempei Ordnance, the Kempei-tai's functions are defined by a special charter, the *Kempei Rei* of 1898, amended twenty-six times before the Second World War, to incorporate the unit's larger role in Japan's rapidly expanding empire. By 1943, the force has at least 36,000 regular members, excluding tens of thousands of civilian agents in overseas territories, such as Jackie Lo in Borneo.

Originally modelled on the French gendarmerie, the Kempei-tai has evolved into a secret service comparable with Germany's SS. Its agents are not military police in the British or Australian sense – i.e. internal law-enforcers, whom the diggers tend to mock. Kempei-tai agents have an explicitly political as well as military role. Ferreting out subversive elements in Tojo's Japan is one of their most serious and dreaded occupations. A totalitarian regime is defined by the rule of the state through force. In this sense, the secret police are the eyes and ears – and baton-wielders and steel-capped-boot kickers – of the government. Attesting to the organisation's political influence is the fact that Premier Tojo commanded the Kempei-tai before his accession to the leadership. At home, the Kempei-tai is directly responsible to the interior minister and enforces domestic controls, such as the Peace Preservation Law, through a secret unit called the Tokko, or 'Special Higher Police'. In Japanese-occupied territories, Kempei-tai agents answer to the war minister and control the security of the empire. They are universally feared, by everyone from privates to commanders.

Kempei-tai agents in Borneo acquire a more sinister role. Being self-regulated, and operating in such remote conditions, they endow themselves with virtually unlimited powers, unanswerable to any authority. The officers become a law unto themselves, drunk on their godlike freedom to arbitrate between life and death. They are notoriously cruel – but the word 'cruel' is inapt, as it presupposes a moral context, or the idea that the perpetrators are conscious of the crime. It implies the existence of a restraining conscience. On the contrary, these men have been trained to delight in brutality. Kempei-tai officers typically demonstrate, and appear proud of, the compassionless execution of their duties. Some of the worst take a sadistic delight in inflicting pain. Those of a more clinical stamp regard torture as simply part of their 'duty'; for them, it is a badge of honour to extract the information and dispatch the victim as efficiently as possible.

From Korea, through Manchuria and China, to Indochina, the men of the Kempei-tai have cut a swathe of blood and terror. Their job is to instil dread in the people. And, like their counterparts in other totalitarian regimes, they prefer to dress up for the part. Officers appear at formal occasions in high, black leather boots, a red *kepi* (a cap with flat, round top), a sash, and a cavalry uniform adorned with a red chrysanthemum under the lapel, black chevrons on their collars, and a white armband bearing the characters *ken* (憲, 'law') and *hei* (兵, 'soldier'). The officers may wear a sabre; the NCOs a bayonet. All Kempei-tai agents carry a pistol. The junior NCOs – sergeants and corporals – are deputed to carry out the punishments, for which they use a *shinai*, or bamboo kendo sword, among other implements.

◆

There are four cells beneath the bungalow on Tanahmerah Road: two large rectangular ones, to accommodate male and female prisoners, an interrogation room and the office of the senior officer 'supervising' the interrogations. Upstairs, with a lavish view of the bay, is the office of the commander of the local Kempei-tai, Murakami Seisaku. Japanese guards surround the bungalow with bayonets fixed.

The prisoners crammed into the big cell are forbidden to talk, smile or look at each other. 'All were made to sit crossed legged Japanese style and to look at the floor. Any one found disobeying was brutally beaten up by three or four guards,' recalls Melvyn Funk, son of Johnny Funk.[3] Twelve guards stand over the prisoners at all times. The redoubtable Koram, after enduring 'a severe form of the water torture', has already managed to escape, by climbing out of the lavatory window. Six follow his attempt, are caught and executed.

The main interrogators are Sergeant Major 'Bulldog' Ehara Kesao, Sergeant Watazumi and Corporal Motoki Hiroshi. (Others include Sergeants Kobara Toshio and Tsuji Toyoji, and Corporal Kono Kinzaburo.)[4] When a prisoner's name is called, he is brought into the interrogation room, asked a few perfunctory questions and beaten with slaps, kicks and wooden swords. If this fails to elicit the correct answers, harsher measures are applied. The Kempei-tai specialises in several hideous forms of torture. The most commonly applied in Borneo are:

- The Darlington punishment: the prisoner is forced to kneel on a plank, specially carved with spikes. The interrogator places a long piece of wood behind the victim's knees. Two Japanese guards stand on each end of it, like a see-saw, severely lacerating the prisoner's knees. The torture usually lasts an hour.
- A ju-jitsu expert throws the prisoner all around the cell, bashing his body against the walls and floor. 'They would badly twist all limbs and used their boots freely,' writes Melvyn Funk.[5] Several guards would sometimes apply the punishment, working like a tag team.
- The prisoner is jammed into a specially constructed chair and whipped across the head. This would usually last for about half a day, again with guards working in relay.

- Water-torture, infamous throughout the Japanese
  Empire, in which the victim is forced to consume
  large amounts of water. 'When the victim's stomach
  was full to bursting, a Kempei-tai officer would jump
  on him from the top of a chair,' according to Japanese
  historian Tanaka Yuki.[6]
- Rice torture, in which the victim is starved for several
  days then force-fed a large quantity of rice. A hose
  would then be inserted in the prisoner's throat and
  water pumped in. The rice would expand, causing
  excruciating pain 'as the stomach stretched to its limit',
  resulting in internal and rectal bleeding, according
  to Tanaka.[7]

The Japanese apply many other forms of extreme rendition throughout the Pacific. Suffice to say, after a few days at the hands of the Kempei-tai, the victim tends to say whatever he's told to. Many beg to be killed. For this reason, the interrogators are never sure of the reliability of the information extracted under extreme duress. Their solution in Sandakan is to torture as many suspects for as long as possible to validate the 'story' of the underground, the unfolding scale of which enrages the Japanese commanders in Kuching.

◆

The experience of Matthews, Wells, Taylor, the Funk brothers, Heng Joo Ming and several others defies comprehension. Tens of thousands of civilians and prisoners of war are tortured throughout the Japanese Empire, but the Borneo case is exceptional for its extreme, sustained inhumanity. According to several accounts, this is sheer sadism. As Wells relates, one guard, Motoki Hiroshi, laughs and shouts while flogging him and Matthews 'until we were so bruised . . . that we could not walk'.[8] No Japanese government since the war has acknowledged – far less compensated the victims' families for – the shocking catalogue of atrocities inflicted in Sandakan.

Before their 'interrogation' begins, Matthews and Wells are kept in solitary confinement under the police station. Within 24 hours, Matthews is moved to the main cell; Wells is kept in isolation. Thus far, Lagan, Heng Joo Ming, his father and their loyal retainer, Sini, have endured the worst of the Kempei-tai. Sini, a young lad the Japanese think breakable, heroically resists and is thrown back into the cell, where Captain Matthews sits with his comrades in the resistance.

The prisoners live under constant observation, day and night. The male prisoners must sit cross-legged, without talking, from dawn until 9.30 at night. The ration is about five ounces of rice a day; the human body requires 65 ounces (2000 calories) of rice to survive.[9] The two meals per day consist of half a small cup of rice and a piece of rock salt, 'such as is used for animals in Australia', or a dried fish head. 'It would be a small fish head,' Wells later recalls. 'The volume of either the rock salt or the fish head would not exceed half a cubic inch.'[10] Washing is permitted only at the discretion of the guard; meals are eaten with hands; no toilet paper, bedding or clothing, other than a pair of shorts, is issued; no footwear is permitted.

In these circumstances, Matthews meets the man he has addressed so often as 'Geebung'. One morning in late July, Dr Taylor is led into the cell. 'That's when I first met Matthews,'

Dr Taylor later says. 'I had a strong feeling about Matthews, you know. He looked like Jesus Christ; he was a big tall man and a kind man.' If Matthews looks faintly Christ-like in his long hair, beard and wretched condition, he is the first to admit that he is human, all too human. And yet – like Taylor, Wells and Weynton – he has something few possess: an astonishing capacity to resist pain.

Matthews endures the full spectrum of physical agony: he is water-tortured, whipped, thrashed by ju-jitsu experts and racked. Dr Taylor similarly is dragged off to the interrogation cells and flogged to within an inch of his life. According to one account:

> The Japanese practice of slashing a wooden sandal, previously rubbed in wet sand, across the face soon had Dr Taylor's face looking like a raw piece of meat. A middle-aged man of small stature, it seems impossible that Dr Taylor was able to survive the terrific floggings that were meted out to him.[11]

Yet, despite this 'gravel rash', as he later calls it, Dr Taylor refuses to divulge or admit a thing.[12] Another of the Kempei-tai's 'favourite tricks', he later says, is 'to give me this beefsteak face, blacken both my eyes and then conduct me to a small room in which my wife was held under arrest . . . She would then be invited to inspect me and instructed to tell me to speak the truth or otherwise they would repeat the dose.' Celia Taylor, though shocked by her husband's state, resists 'with the greatest fortitude'.[13]

Wells' treatment is extreme even by Kempei-tai standards. The historical record is incomplete without a brief description of this man's ordeal, however disturbing. Seen as the mastermind of the radio, Wells is kept in solitary confinement for three weeks, while others are plied for information. During that time, he is thrashed daily with a whip and a wooden sword. Then they rack him – a mediaeval form of torture also applied to Matthews and Weynton. His hands are cuffed and tied to a rafter; his legs stretched out on another rafter. A piece of wood, six feet long and four inches square, is placed across the ankles. The rafter to which his legs are strapped is drawn taut; the guards stand at either end of the wood over the ankles. The effect is to stretch Wells' arms and legs, strip all the flesh away from his ankles and almost break the ankle bones. Wells survives this for two minutes then falls unconscious. The guards throw water over his face and resume. This time, they strike him repeatedly with a wooden sword and a small hammer. 'They would hit on the one place on the head continually with the hammer,' he later says.[14] And they drive a nail into one ear, puncturing his eardrum. Wells never recovers his hearing in that ear.

The process continues: on 16 August Wells is forced to consume a large quantity of rice. The guards then thrust a hose into his mouth and pump water into the residual cavity in his stomach. After about four hours, the rice swells up. Wells later describes the appalling aftermath:

> I had not had a motion for 26 days after I had been arrested, mainly because of nervous re-action, the light rations and the floggings. After the administration of this rice I tried for about three hours to bring it up again . . . I was successful in bringing up quite a bit of the soaked raw rice, the remainder of which went through the other way and pulled quite a large amount of my bowel out through the anus. I had to work that

in with my own hands. I asked for medical attention, but was ignored. After about a week I managed to work it all back.[15]

None of this extracts a word from the man. Matthews, Taylor and Weynton similarly refuse to yield a single name that has not already been given or a single piece of useful information. Wells is later confined to an observation room, where 'no communication, writing or anything of that nature' is allowed.[16] He remains in this state for three months.

◆
◇

The Australians are defiant to the last. During the hours between their 'interrogation', Matthews develops a means of communicating with his fellow inmates using Morse code. He transmits words in Morse by tapping the short-long code on his knee – thus informing his fellow inmates of the questions asked during his interrogation. It is a miracle of ingenuity, mental toughness and physical resilience. After each round with the Kempei-tai, Matthews would appear bloody and bruised before his friends and resume tapping out the latest from the interrogation room.

Weynton, recently released from the cage on a separate charge, and now in custody for his involvement with the radio, describes the scene:

We were placed in a triangular formation, all facing the sentry whose instructions were to watch and make sure there was no talking. Matthews communicated using Morse. He would come back from interrogation, sit down, cross his legs as we were instructed to, and tap his fingers . . . He would go through the topic of which he'd been interrogated that morning and the answers he'd delivered.[17]

The messages, observes another witness, 'not only enabled prisoners to avoid accidental incrimination, but they boosted confidence'.[18]

Matthews' signallers are well trained. Weynton is able to reply in code. Soon, Wells joins them. Their ensuing Morse 'conversations' conjure the extraordinary picture of three skinny Australians, thrashed to within an inch of their lives, tapping away on their knees while awaiting their next torture session. A sentry who observes the persistent finger movements indicates to the relieving guard that Matthews may have gone a little crazy – and might turn dangerous.[19]

Johnny Funk, who shares Matthews' cell for a time, recalls reading the code: '"I have not said a word," Matthews taps, and appeals to the others not to break. Try not to divulge a thing, he urges his comrades, and concludes with a plea: "If anything happens to me, Johnny, and if you ever happen to meet my wife or any Australians, tell them that I have died for my country."'[20]

◆

The families of the accused, too, are harassed. Lagan's wife, Katherine, and their four children are singled out. A week after Kempei-tai officers break her husband, they return his blood-stained clothes to this poor woman, who is left to wonder what else remains of him. They then grill her about her husband's activities. She says she knows nothing. They push her violently around the room. She holds firm, denying any knowledge of Lagan's diary (which she has burnt, on his instructions).

The Japanese return to her house day after day, ransacking it and harassing the family. On one occasion, they order Katherine and the children into a room upstairs and draw the blinds. 'This is your last chance,' they tell her. 'Either you tell all you know or else you will suffer.' She replies, 'Honestly I know nothing about his affairs, even if you have to kill me.'[21] They choose softer methods: they send Katherine and three of her children downstairs, and detain her ten-year-old son, to whom they promise chocolates and presents if he talks about his father. His mother has already warned him of Japanese ruses, and the boy replies that he cannot recall anything.

For a fortnight, a Kempei-tai officer stays in Katherine Lagan's home, waking her in the middle of night to fire questions at her. She says nothing. At length, they give up; and she and two of her children are permitted to take food to Ernesto. She finds him thin and pale and 'devoid of any strength'.[22] On a later visit, she brings a change of clothes. Helping him to remove his soiled shirt, she finds a huge blue bruise running down one side of his body and a large cut, now a railroad of stitches, deep in his back. She cries at the sight: how did he receive these injuries? He lies that he fell down.

She whispers, 'Is there anything you want to tell me?'

'Yes,' he says, 'please send me extra food, as I want to give some to the five Australians who are imprisoned here with me.'

'But there is not enough money,' she replies.

Lagan tells his wife to 'sell my clothes and shoes and buy more food with the money'.[23]

The Kempei-tai continue to harass her, demanding that she

report to Kempei-tai headquarters every morning. Hoshijima intervenes, offering freedom to her husband in return for information. 'This is your last chance to talk,' he tells her. 'There is nothing I can say.'[24] They turn on her ten-year-old son again: he is ordered to attend Hoshijima's office each night, where he is showered with sweets, toys and soap. '[H]e obtained no information from him,' Jackson writes. 'The little boy was carried home asleep in the arms of a Jap at 2 am every morning.'[25]

Other families are similarly hounded. Heng Joo Ming's wife, Siti, is beaten up and separated from her husband, who pleads for the Kempei-tai men to release her. They do so a fortnight later. Heng's last words to her when they part are, 'This has all been due to one man, Dominic Koh. If I am ever free again I will know how to deal with him, but if I do not return my friends will know how to deal with him.' (After the war, Koh is sentenced to 18 months' prison.)

In sum, the Japanese beat, whip, rack and/or water-torture 200 prisoners – mostly civilians. The three Funk brothers are shockingly dealt with: Paddy Funk twice receives the water treatment. Salleh, Ah Ping, Yangsalang, Apostol and several police officers are arrested in late July and brutally treated. After prolonged beatings, Pop Wong, the 'old' underground hand, feigns madness and is removed to Buli Sim Sim Mental Asylum.

Throughout August and September 1943, the arrests continue, and the house of torture continues its grisly business. More Australian soldiers are brought in: Private Frank Martin is so severely mutilated he cannot move; Sergeants Alf Stevens, Joe Weston, Colin Lander and Macalister Blain, Sappers Carl Jensen, Don Marshall and Ted Keating, and Private Tom Rumble are hauled in and beaten senseless or given the log treatment or other fiendish devices. Marshall, deemed a 'hard case', is burnt with cigarettes.[26] Mrs Cohen, Mrs Mavor and Mrs Taylor are arrested and confined to cells. Back at the prison camp, everyone is held collectively responsible and punished. The guards' viciousness is widely dispensed, the rations severely cut and workloads made heavier. The Formosans are panicky, quick to accuse. The crackdown spreads inland, from where the artillery bursts sound like distant thunder.

18

MOUNTAIN REVOLT

The hunt for Japanese heads had begun.
Maxwell Hall, historian of the Double Tenth
Uprising by the Kinabalu Guerrillas

FRESH RESISTANCE BURGEONS on the west coast of Borneo throughout 1943 and connects with tribes in the interior. The uprising is led by a group of volunteers known as the Kinabalu Guerrillas – mostly Chinese, native farmers and small traders, from Jesselton and in the villages around Mount Kinabalu. Independent of, but in touch with, the Sandakan underground, their aims are broadly the same: to overthrow the occupying Japanese forces, in alliance with – so they hope – Allied units, including the covert PYTHON I and II operations, which plan to land in the area.

The rebellion has deep roots linked directly to the 'policies' of the occupying power. The Japanese tyranny over the native people operates through humiliation, violence and economic subjugation. The general population is routinely debased and abused. Native women receive no protection, and the Imperial forces rape and molest many. Church buildings in Jesselton are turned into brothels, where the soldiers force young girls – many brought from Java – into prostitution.

Fear and slavish subservience accompany the people's daily routine. Anyone who fails to bow to and salute the Japanese is slapped and beaten; anyone suspected of disloyalty or allegiance with Western allies is tortured – often to death. Public slapping is no 'kindergarten affair', notes the historian Maxwell Hall:

> The culprit was expected to stand patiently while his assailant slapped him with the full force of his outstretched arm and hand. It may have begun gently, just to warm up, but soon each blow, right or left, would knock the culprit sideways and at each blow he was expected to come up straight ready for the next.[1]

In tandem with physical cruelty, the Japanese wipe out the people's livelihoods. They requisition food – usually 50 per cent of the harvested crop – to feed their regiments. Grasping middlemen often drive the total take to 80 per cent. Local farmers respond by hiding any produce they can, in false partitions in their homes, between bed mattresses or buried out of sight. If the Japanese deign to buy food, they usually offer less than half the market value, to be paid for in worthless paper currency. One note has a bunch of bananas printed on it, and such 'banana currency' is the subject of ridicule and contempt.

Farmers are conscripted into labour gangs, to build roads and airstrips at Jesselton, Keningau and Kudat. This stupidly denies the country the labour to produce much-needed food. Villagers' farms lie fallow and food grows scarce in the invaders' parasitic grip. To meet a food emergency, the Japanese order the clearing of most rubber plantations and the planting of rice, cassava and other foods. The harvest is completely controlled to serve Japanese needs.

Other forms of economic harassment chip away at the people's productive capacity. The Japanese confiscate the hunting weapons of Murut warriors; chop down the coconut trees of the gentler Dusun, who traditionally climb them to retrieve the fruit; and confiscate the livestock of the interior tribes.

As in the east, the Chinese are set aside for special treatment. Chinese women are used to 'comfort' the soldiers. The community is forced to endure all sorts of threats and punishments simply because they are Chinese – as revealed by propaganda distributed in pamphlets and posters throughout Borneo in 1942–45:

> A warning to oversea Chinese,
> . . . Since the outbreak of the war in east Asia, the Chinese
> . . . have behaved as an enemy, by helping the enemy. When
> Japanese troops repulsed Great Britain, America and the
> Dutch East Indies and then occupied Borneo, the Chinese
> changed their attitude and pretended that they knew nothing.
> Let not the Chinese forget that the power of seizing and putting
> them all to death rests with one decision of the Japanese High
> Command. Although the Chinese are now allowed their
> freedom, it is only temporary to enable the Japanese to watch
> their movements. Now let the Chinese reflect deeply and
> come to their senses before another notice.

◆

The Japanese try to suppress any signs of resistance by recruiting teams of local collaborators. They use the crudest kinds of persuasion: bribery and threats. Offers of cash, clothing and rations, as well as warnings of retaliation against their families, persuade young men to join the Japanese police force. These agents, nominally loyal to the conquerors, are ordered to penetrate the interior tribes, who are thought to be more amenable to diktat, bearing gifts of food and cash.

The meetings between the Japanese and the tribes are a ritual of lies, which proceed throughout the island in 1943–44. A Japanese unit, accompanied by their local interlocutors, arrives in a village and calls a meeting with the chiefs, from whom they demand detailed information – of their village's productive capacity, land use, occupation and so on. None openly defies the Japanese, of course. According to a Japanese account, 'These people were always amenable and replied to the questions without a note of distrust. At the end of the meeting each man was paid one yen as expenses to cover his attendance.'[2] To refuse would ensure the destruction of their villages and livelihood. So most tribal elders cooperate, at least publicly, in return for $3–$10 a month in 'loyalty' fees – a paltry sum, but it buys the people a little protection, at least for now. Any failure to meet the terms of the agreement leads to swift and terrible repercussions. In time, many villages are ransacked, their leaders executed and their inhabitants forced into the jungle.

Turning the weak into informers and spies; pitching tribe against tribe, village against village; crushing native farms and infrastructure; rupturing the local economy: all spark a deep and abiding hatred for the Japanese, and a yearning for revenge. As the Imperial Army moves inland, rumours of its approach drive many villagers into the jungle. The Japanese usually torch the deserted kampongs out of spite; and the forest-dwellers prepare to take their revenge, with ancient weapons such as the machete and blowpipe.

Conditions in the villages worsen as the Japanese supply lines fail. In 1943, the occupying forces strip the country of whatever they need: tools, livestock, gold, clothing, building materials . . . whatever will sustain their increasingly isolated army. The argument that the Japanese in Borneo are also suffering has no traction on the minds of people whose food is routinely appropriated to Nippon. In fairness, some Japanese try to protect local interests, and, remarkably, about two-thirds of the island's livestock survives the war – mostly draught cattle used to plough the fields.[3]

But not in Ranau. During 1943, the Japanese Army occupies this pretty town at the base of Mount Kinabalu. Ranau straddles the east–west bridle paths and waterways, a transit point between the uppermost navigable reaches of the Labuk River – three days' march away, bearing supplies from Sandakan and the east – and the road down to Jesselton in the west. It has an airfield, and food at this time is plentiful, sequestered from the rich local paddy and vegetable gardens. Ranau soon contains the largest concentration of Japanese troops in the interior. They show no restraint and the local tribes, forced from their homes into the jungle, or pressed into labour teams, are filled with rage towards the occupying power, of an intensity that has few parallels in Borneo.

◆

The rebels rally around their charismatic, if reckless, leader. In late 1940, a Chinese herbalist returned to Jesselton from mainland China, where he had been working with the Red Cross and as an intelligence officer for the Chinese Government. Albert Kwok, the son of a Kuching dentist, came back carrying deep feelings of hostility towards the Japanese occupation. A well-built, handsome young man with a penetrating gaze, Kwok is an expert in herbal medicine, and indeed a specialist in easing the pains associated with piles. He swiftly became a popular figure around Jesselton, where he practised his 'healing' until the demand for the treatment exhausted his supply of herbs. His political interests, in any case, soon eclipsed his medical skills. Kwok, a zealous supporter of the Chinese Republican cause, unwisely makes no secret of the fact that he dreams of an uprising against the Japanese in Borneo. 'Probably every person in Jesselton . . . knew that he was planning to overthrow the Japanese. Though there were countless spies about, no-one betrayed him to the Japanese,' observes Maxwell Hall.[4]

Kwok's early attempts to generate pockets of resistance failed. The people's fear is the biggest obstacle. In February 1942, he tried to reach Long Nawan, on the Kayan River in Dutch Borneo, where the local people, a few Americans and about 50 Dutch marines staged a hopeless uprising, which the Japanese crushed, with the slaughter of everyone involved. In 1943, he tried again to channel the people's feelings towards armed rebellion. This time, he used the services of Imam Marajukim, a Muslim cleric, and Lim Keng Fatt, a 50-year-old Jesselton trader and active member of the Overseas Chinese Defence Association of Borneo, set up to prevent local Chinese from collaborating with the enemy. They put him in contact with the Filipino guerrillas and Lieutenant Colonel Suarez.

In early 1943, Kwok and Fatt sailed to Tawi-Tawi to meet Suarez in his guerrilla headquarters. Having satisfied himself as to the herbalist's bona fides – Kwok happened to cure his sick wife – Suarez inducted him into the guerrilla movement as 'one of my personal advisers'.[5]

Kwok returns to Jesselton at the end of May 1943, nominally as Suarez's 'representative on financial affairs'; in practice as the spearhead of a local uprising. Kwok's mission is to raise funds to spy on the Japanese and purchase military supplies 'that we badly need in order to destroy and exterminate our common enemy', as Suarez informs the US Army Forces, Philippines Headquarters, Sulu Sector.[6]

This unlikely guerrilla leader is made a military intelligence officer with the rank of third lieutenant. Kwok throws himself at the task. With Japanese attention diverted by the 'Sandakan Incident' – as the Japanese refer to the crushing of the underground – he raises a small band of loyal Chinese. They meet secretly in Jesselton to plan the uprising. Theirs are the dreams of political rebels and idealists, not the hard-headed assessment of serious military strategists. In any case, Allied support is not yet forthcoming: the Australian Special Forces are yet to make a successful landfall on the west coast.

Kwok's reserves of hope and courage always seem to outstrip his means. He resolves to make another visit to Tawi-Tawi, to plead with Suarez for help. (On the way, he delivers cash and supplies to the resistance on the Sulu Islands, whose fierce 'Bolo Battalion' engages in fighting with a Japanese expedition sent from Sandakan. The Sulu Islanders resist for three days and capture 31 Japanese prisoners, who are taken out to sea, beheaded and thrown overboard. Neither side is inclined to clemency.)

If some Australian and US special units regard Kwok as a maverick, a one-man revolutionary, and something of a romantic upstart, they underestimate his allure as a folk hero, inspirational leader and formidable fund-raiser. Suarez sees qualities in Kwok that elude the Allies and instructs him to take the war to the

Japanese in North Borneo by any means available. Kwok resolves to unleash havoc. By 10 September 1943, the Chinese leader has amassed a war chest of $550,000 – according to some sources – donated by the Filipino units, Sandakan civilians and various tribal groups. The fund is partly to pay the bounty on the lives of the enemy: Kwok values each Japanese head at between $200 and $400, depending on the victim's rank.

◆

Kwok's Kinabalu Guerrilla Defence Force, named after the sacred peak to the west of Jesselton, gathers notoriety and adherents. Despite Japanese efforts forcibly to conscript some 3000 Chinese into a reserve unit, the local Chinese secretly rally to Kwok's standard. New leaders emerge: Wong Tze An, a local landowner, who offers his Menggatal property as the guerrillas' secret headquarters; and two formidable behind-the-scenes operators, Dr Lau Lai, a short, plump medical officer in the North Borneo Government, and Cheah Loong Ghee, a rubber-plantation owner and casino operator. Both are thought to be collaborators – an elaborate front for their shadowy support for the Kinabalu Guerrillas. Kwok's field commanders include Charles Peter, a former chief police officer; Hiew Syn Yong, deputy assistant district officer; Kong Tze Phui, a former scoutmaster and troop leader of the Basel Mission Scout Troop; and several others.

In September, Kwok's men leave their bases at Inanam, Talibong and Tuaran, and spread along the roads and railway stations between Jesselton and Mount Kinabalu. What they lack in training and equipment, they make up for in guts and panache. Unfortunately, many local recruits do not share their physical courage or determination. When the Japanese start to conscript local men – thus removing Kwok's pool of manpower – the guerrilla leader decides to strike. He chooses the eve of 10 October 1943, the tenth day of the tenth moon, or the 'Double Tenth', celebrated in China as the start of the Wuchang Uprising in 1911, which led to the collapse of the Qing Dynasty on 1 January 1912. Similar uprisings are planned in Singapore and elsewhere in the Japanese Empire.

Despite having spies crawling all over Borneo, the Japanese are in the dark when the revolution starts: their troops have no inkling of the force about to erupt from the mountain fastness and fall upon the western towns. The guerrillas form up in darkness along the roadsides leading west from the foot of Mount Kinabalu. A Dusun gong sounds the start, and they board the trucks: 'The hunt for Japanese heads had begun.'[7] Armed with a few Lee-Enfield carbines, and 40 rounds a piece, knives, clubs, a few hand grenades and two machine guns, and dressed in dark work clothes, loincloths and soot or black paint, the first units of the Kinabalu Guerrillas speed off down the road towards Jesselton. One group attacks Tuaran, killing four Japanese guards at the local police station and seizing much-needed rifles, before joining the advance on the western capital.

◆
▽

In Jesselton that night, the Japanese host a presentation to prominent citizens at the Koa Club, the former Recreation Building. The themes are 'peace and prosperity' of the Co-Prosperity Sphere, and the happiness Chinese people can expect under Japanese rule. The meeting disperses at news of the attack. The guerrillas' convoy advances on the town across the sea wall, via Menggatal. Upon reaching the town centre, the fighters leap from the trucks and attack the police station and the military post office. Others ignite a bonfire at the end of the wharf, to signal the start of the uprising. In the ensuing confusion, the Japanese flee the town, pursued by gangs of screaming guerrillas who hunt them down in gardens, buildings and along the shore. Whenever Japanese troops are found, Kwok's men, with one eye on the reward, leave no head unbagged. Civilian Japanese, too, are decapitated – such is the need of the bounty – contrary to Kwok's orders to spare the civilian population.

To commemorate his victory, Kwok plasters a proclamation on the walls of Jesselton, appealing for the people's cooperation and declaring a state of war with the Japanese. He signs it 'Wong Fah Min', his alias, and gives his rank as commander of the North Borneo Oversea Chinese Defence Force. The notice accuses the Japanese of impoverishing the population, stealing farmers' food and dishonouring local women. It claims, somewhat wishfully, the full support of the Allies.

By midnight, the guerrillas control the town. Fifty Japanese lie dead, in Jesselton and nearby towns. Buglers sound the retreat. The guerrilla leaders are appointed to local administrative jobs as news of the revolt spreads. The next morning, the Chinese national flag, the Union Jack, the Stars and Stripes and the Sabah flag fly over Jesselton.

◆

It is short-lived. Haste, naivety and a conspicuous lack of Allied support imperil the uprising. The Kinabalu Guerrillas have moved too fast, without adequate, or even confirmed, backing. Their peremptory occupation of the western capital lasts a matter of days. The appearance of Japanese fighters swiftly disabuses the locals of the belief, put about by Kwok, that the Americans are coming. Allied aircraft are painfully absent. A rumoured covert Allied mission – in fact, a PYTHON team – supposed to be delivering arms, ammunition and medicine, never arrives; through an administrative cock-up, the shipment – to Gort Chester's fury – is left on the wharf in Fremantle.

Had the supplies arrived, they would have been too late. As Japanese reinforcements descend on Jesselton, Kwok's little army weakens: snipers, a lack of food, collaborators and spies drain the early elation of the Double Tenth. The Japanese put a high price on the rebels' heads, offering (in Japanese wartime currency) $1000 to $5000 to anyone who captures the leaders. It is a compliment of sorts. The dragnet offers to pardon 'Whoever was guilty and participated in the revolt and who ran away' if any answering to that description agree to assist the Japanese.

Kwok's men are soon isolated and forlorn. Fathers, anxious to see their wives and children again, are offered an early discharge from the rebel army. Terror crowds in on Kwok's residual force, as the people abandon them. 'The lack of reinforcements depresses them. Their women watch them with mingled feelings. The headmen of villages eye them with disfavour,' writes Hall.[8] The remnant of Kwok's army is driven into hiding, near a village outside the capital, whose inhabitants the Japanese threaten to kill unless they surrender him and his remaining force. To avoid a massacre, Kwok agrees to surrender. On 19 December, a terrified collaborator leads Kwok and his men to a road outside the village, where they lay down their weapons at the feet of the Japanese commanders.

They are taken to the Jesselton Sports Club, the western headquarters of the Kempei-tai, with other accused, in readiness for trial. The defeat of the Kinabalu Guerrillas, the failure of the Double Tenth, ends the revolt in the west. Chinese suspects flee to the interior, where hatred of the Japanese festers around Ranau and Mount Kinabalu. The jungles seethe with evicted villagers. Fleeting acts of resistance ensue. And yet, with the leaders of the Double Tenth and the Sandakan underground in Japanese prisons, the people of Borneo have nothing left to hope for.

19

KUCHING

Doctor Yamamoto never attended to . . . sick or
diseased men in that filthy germ-ridden hole.
Sapper Lionel E. Morris of the Royal
Engineers on Kuching prison hospital

THE REVOLT IN THE WEST further enrages the Japanese
authorities in Borneo and exposes huge holes in their security.
Harsh measures are necessary to crush the spirit of resistance
altogether. The reprisals are thorough and merciless. Japanese
search parties scour the west coast of Borneo for rebels. Pamphlets
fall from planes, warning:

> The Japanese forces have surrounded you and you are now
> like a fish in a pan . . . those who resist will be destroyed.
> All good people must hoist Japanese flags . . . Although you
> may escape to the jungles and hills for a time, the Japanese
> military forces will capture you just the same.[1]

A notice emblazons the streets and buildings of Jesselton and
surrounding towns:

Whoever fails to return to his home by the evening of 20 October 1943 will be deemed to be implicated in the revolt or in communication with the rebels. Therefore everyone must return home immediately. Heavy punishment will follow.[2]

Village chiefs are compelled to order their tribes to return and to punish those who fail – placing tribal elders in the invidious position of being forced to betray their own people. To the east, Japanese landing parties attack the islanders between Borneo and Tawi-Tawi – thought to harbour rebels. Hundreds are rounded up and slaughtered.

On 14 October, Imperial aircraft bomb Jesselton and neighbouring villages. At Tuaran and other hotbeds of resistance, low-flying Zeros strafe villagers trying to escape by boat. Survivors are herded into the district offices. The men, many of them old and sick, are forced to stand for hours in the sun; the women and children are kept in pens beneath the buildings.

Interrogations begin. 'Guilty' Murut, Dusun, Bajaus, Chinese and Indian locals reflect the great ethnic mix in Borneo, united against the enemy – and a clear sign of Japan's failure to win over the region's inhabitants. Hundreds are rounded up. Most are grilled and beaten, and their homes burnt. At Tuaran, any Chinese inhabitant who cannot prove his or her innocence is bound, herded along the riverbank and decapitated; their bodies thrown in the water. Those able to prove their innocence, and willing to pledge their allegiance to Japan, receive 'good citizen' badges – a piece of square cloth bearing the words, in Chinese characters, 'West Coast Civil Administrators Seal'. The villagers are quick to forge and distribute the badges to the vulnerable, or weak, or those in hiding. In the ensuing months, many rebels continue fighting the Japanese under the guise of 'good citizens'.

The arrests and interrogations last four months. Whole communities are uprooted, divided, tortured and shot or put to the sword. Terrified native people, ordered to punish the perpetrators, start killing Chinese as the latter return to their villages. Families are arrested and threatened with death unless they find the rebels in their midst. The Kempei-tai tends not to harm the wives and children, however, who are allowed to visit their husbands, fathers and sons in jail.

The officers of the Kempei-tai work day and night extracting confessions. The Chinese, as usual, get special treatment. One rebel leader is crushed under hundreds of pounds of stones; another laid in a coffin and threatened with being buried alive; others beaten to death in broad daylight; dozens hung between joists by ropes tied to their hands and feet and left there to wilt like 'salted fish'; several Christians are nailed to boards 'with spikes driven through the palms of their hands'.[3]

Kwok's surrender hardly satiates the beast: the Japanese hunt continues well into January 1944. That month, they massacre the perpetrators. Of 400 prisoners held at Batu Tiga Prison, 176 receive death sentences. On 21 January, a convoy of closed trucks takes the condemned men to an open trench near Petagas Railway Bridge, between Tanjong Aru and Putatan. Here, the five rebel leaders – Kwok, Charles Peter, Chan Chau Kong, Kong Tze Phui and Lee Tek Phui – are decapitated, one by one, with a single swipe of a double-handed sword. Peter's head is only partially severed as he slides to the ground. The executioners kick the heads and bodies into the trench. The rest are machine-gunned. The men condemned to prison are sent to Labuan, where, sick and starving, they slowly perish in captivity: nine of 131 will survive the war.

When they hear of the debacle, Allied operatives are disdainful of Kwok's activities. Kwok is seen in Brisbane and Morotai as a hopeless romantic with little or no military skill. One Special Forces report describes his uprising as singularly 'disastrous', with Kwok dead and his men, 'scattered to the four winds'. Kwok 'apparently roped in the local native police, who are dispersed into the jungle . . . Many villages from KHOTA, BELUD to BEAFORT [sic] have been razed to the ground', with 2000 dead in Jesselton.[4] A separate, 'MOST SECRET' report damns Kwok's 'foolishness' in launching the uprising.[5]

Two resistance leaders, Dr Lau Lai and Cheah Loong Ghee, who helped to finance the uprising, escape suspicion under the guise of collaboration. In April 1944, they try to mount a second attack. They are detected, arrested and tortured beyond the bounds of the imagination: burnt, hung from their thumbs, pumped with water . . . Dr Lau, unable to bear any more, succumbs and tells all he knows; Cheah Loong Ghee superhumanly resists. 'Not one single name or secret was ever dragged from his lips,' writes Maxwell Hall. 'Though pieces of his flesh were sliced from him and held before his eyes under threat of more to be cut, he still refused to speak.'[6] Dr Lau Lai is hanged on 15 August 1944; Cheah Loong Ghee dies in prison.

To the Japanese, it seems, the uprising is defeated: the rebels dead or captured; the revolt thoroughly crushed. They are wrong. Word of the atrocities spreads like bushfire to the mountain villages and beyond, to the riverside communities stretching away to the east. Revulsion fills the people of Ranau and the surrounding hamlets. Utter hatred of the Japanese permeates the forests and foothills of Mount Kinabalu, where the tribes long for the day of vengeance. Many villagers flee their homes and live in the jungle, on tapioca, fruit and whatever animals – birds, wild boar – they can catch. With their superb bush skills, the pygmy tribes around Paginatan can live indefinitely in the forest. They can kill a monkey at 55 yards with their blowpipes.

◆

Meanwhile, in Sandakan, the Japanese apply a new policy designed to crush the prisoners' spirits: the officers are to be separated from the other ranks and sent to Kuching. At a stroke, the policy breaks that rare bond between the leaders and the led. If some officers are loathed, most remain symbols of authority and strength in the eyes of the men. The younger privates rely on the officers as father-figures and sources of reassurance. That relationship is now to be cut. No longer will the soldiers feel the life-affirming sense of mutual respect between them and their commanders; no longer will the ordinary soldier sense the presence, however damaged, of the spirit that has directed his actions since the days of recruitment.

The move is carried out with great haste. Early on 16 October 1943, while the soldiers are out at the drome, the Australian and British officers are ordered on parade. The majors, captains and lieutenants emerge from their huts, to find a ring of bayonet-wielding guards on the parade ground. All officers, with a few exceptions, are ordered to pack and prepare to move to Kuching. A list of names, signed by Captain George Cook, the camp liaison officer, is read. No contact with the men is permitted; no officer is allowed to send letters, exchange possessions or say goodbye. Close friendships are rent apart; brothers separated. Lieutenant Ron Olliss is refused any contact with his brother, John; the pair have shared the same unit throughout the war. Most officers protest that they cannot leave the men – but are overruled by the Japanese, and placed on two-hour notice to depart. They gather up their scant belongings and march out. Within hours, they find themselves on a small river steamer bound for Kuching.

Eight Australian officers, with critical duties, are listed to remain in Sandakan: Captain Cook, the new prisoners' leader; Captain Jim Heaslop, in charge of canteen/rations; Lieutenant Gordon Good, the quartermaster; the chaplains Harold Wardale-Greenwood and Albert Thompson; and medical officers Captains John Oakeshott, Domenic Picone and Rod Jeffrey.

The medical officers and chaplains are determined to stay, regardless of their presence on Cook's list. Their duty, they make clear, is with the men. Lieutenant Bill Bowden has never forgotten the sight of Oakeshott walking resolutely off the parade ground and back to his hut, ready to assist his soldiers on their return from the airfield.

The remaining chaplains, Thompson and Wardale-Greenwood, of the Church of England, are protestant (Alan Garland, a chaplain and corporal in E Force, is too). Yet the two Catholic officers, Captains Austin O'Donovan and John Rogers, despite their protests, are ordered to move to Kuching, well aware that their departure leaves no one to administer last rites to Catholic prisoners.

All British officers are also moved to Kuching, with the exception of: Captains Jim Mills, appointed the British prisoners' commanding officer, and Frank Daniels, a medic; Lieutenant Ian Rolfe, camp administrator; and the Royal Air Force officers Flight Lieutenant Raymond Blackledge, a medic, Squadron Leader John Wanless, a chaplain, and three of the oldest servicemen, Flying

Officers Humphrey ('Harry') Burgess, 40, and Alf Linge, 51, and the hospital administrator Stan Cressey, 45.

The remaining British prisoners, anxious to know why Matthews' news bulletins no longer arrive, draw straws to decide who should feign illness in order to be transferred – so they hope – to the Australian prison hospital to find the reason. Leading Aircraftman Les Mockridge draws the short straw – with extraordinary consequences – as his son later recounts: 'My father . . . held back all bodily waste functions for some days until he became ill enough to be removed from the British camp. Unfortunately for him, appendicitis was diagnosed. He was taken to the camp hospital. Unsure of the consequences of owning up to the situation, he went through with the ordeal.' On 16 October 1943, a Japanese doctor removed Mockridge's perfectly healthy appendix under local anaesthetic.

But the ruse works. Mockridge meets the Australian prisoners then under arrest – solving the mystery of the shortage of news – and strikes up a friendship with Matthews, who inducts the Englishman into his elaborate plans for escape. 'They both had a love of scouting and earned each other's trust. So close, my father became part of Captain Matthews' incredible escape plan' – in which Mockridge and the Australians would somehow 'escape from their prison, make their way to the airfield, steal a plane (flown by my father) and fly to freedom. When my father pointed out to Matthews that he was an RAF electrician and not a pilot, Matthews responded that he was in the RAF and that was good enough for him. My father believed that Matthews and Wells knew they were to face execution, and therefore were prepared to take a last chance.'[7] (Mockridge's mock illness saves his life: 'contaminated' by his contact with the Australians, he is ordered to depart for Kuching with the officers, where he is confined in the officers' compound.)

Stripped of their commanders, the Australian and British rank and file are amalgamated into a single unit: 1750 of the original 2400 remain. Sickness, malnutrition and Japanese brutality have killed the rest, apart from the few who are incarcerated in Outram Gaol.[8] The composite unit moves into No. 1 Compound (the former B Force huts). E Force gladly vacates No. 3 Compound, which lacks electricity and an adequate water supply. To this dreadful place, the Japanese now shift the sick and wounded, whose long, dark nights of uncared-for pain, relying only on muddy, well-drawn water, can scarcely be imagined.

◆

The officers' voyage to Kuching is relatively comfortable: the river steamer is not a hell ship. Food is always scarce, of course. Down the coast, they encounter a gale that tosses the little vessel about, causing panic among the Formosan guards. They land at Kuching, a dusty little town 22 miles up the Sarawak River, on 22 October and proceed by truck to a new prison, about five miles south-east, called Lintang Barracks, originally a British Indian Army barracks. The Japanese have expanded it to accommodate up to 3000 prisoners – military and civilian – in palm-thatched buildings, 98 feet long, set in neat rows on low stilts, surrounded by rolls of barbed wire. Each hut contains 30–100 people.

Lintang, the headquarters of the Japanese prison system in Borneo, is more bearable than Sandakan – which isn't saying much. The camp commandant, Lieutenant Colonel Suga Tatsuji, is regarded as lenient, even kind – a reputation his second-in-command, Lieutenant (later Captain) Nagata pointedly does not share. Neither is aware that, under their noses, the British have built a radio and tune in regularly to home news on the progress of war, their chief form of clandestine entertainment. Unlike Matthews, Wells and Weynton, they are never discovered.

Like Changi, Lintang contains prisoners of many nationalities – British, Dutch, Indian, Chinese and Indonesian – captured in Java or Singapore, as well as civilian internees, many of them women and children. All prisoners are answerable to their appointed camp master or mistress, who liaises in turn with the Japanese commandant, Suga. The British officers' barracks is 'perhaps the most commodious',[9] under the command of Lieutenant Colonel M. C. Russell, until his death on 5 June 1943, when he is replaced by Lieutenant Colonel T. C. Whimster.

The civilian barracks are certainly less 'commodious': each prisoner is allowed a space six feet by four feet in which to live and store their few possessions. Among the 280 female internees are 160 nuns, 85 lay women – including the author Agnes Newton Keith – and 34 children under ten. (All boys aged ten and over are deemed adults and sent to the male prison.) The civilian internees try to self-police, to boost morale and deter the attention of the guards. In any case, a little hierarchy applies, which treats civilians less harshly than prisoners, among whom the officers fare better than the other ranks, who endure the same gradations of hardship that applied at Sandakan: those who fail to abide by the rules are beaten or caged; those who try to escape can expect to be shot.

The prisoners are allowed to send the occasional postcard, which must conform to rigid specifications – and wording. The Japanese authorities offer a choice of 'sample' wording – for example:

'Nothing is lacking in this camp and we are satisfied with our lives here.'

'All officials in the camp are kind and generous, so there is no need for you to worry about me.'

'The Japanese Military Authorities provide us with sufficient food and medicines . . . we are grateful from the bottom of our hearts.'

'This camp is a natural flower garden, and how happy I should be if only you were here.'[10]

The purpleness of the prose seems to correlate with the deterioration in the conditions; if so, that would explain the new wording on offer in 1945, when conditions in Kuching are at their worst:

'Borneo is a suitable place for living, a dreamland where the scenery is beautiful, little birds sing and very delicious fruits grow.'

'How happy I am when, smoking a cigarette in the shade of the coconut leaves in this comfortable dreamland, which is full of beautiful flower gardens and delicious fruits, I imagine your smiling face.'[11]

◆
◇

The reality makes a black joke of these glad tidings, of course. In

1943–44, the daily rice ration in Lintang is about 11 ounces per person, falling to about four ounces by the end of the war. The inmates resort to collecting snakes, snails and frogs – and, if they can be found, rats, cats and dogs. A single Red Cross parcel arrives between March 1942 and September 1945. Disease spreads. The mortality rate among the British soldiers is devastating: two-thirds of the 2000 POWs will die here.[12] Scabies, dysentery, dengue, malaria, beriberi and tropical ulcers are widespread: 600 men were unfit for work in January 1943.[13] 'Men wasted away from their normal weight of over ten stone to three or four stones,' British Corporal E. R. Pepler later notes. 'As the time passed on to 1945, the deaths in our camp were taking place at two or three every day.'[14]

One reason is the shocking state of the camp's hospital, 'a filthy germ-ridden hole' under the command of 'Doctor' Yamamoto, whose few medical staff 'never attended to . . . sick or diseased men', according to Sapper Lionel E. Morris of the Royal Engineers.[15] Yamamoto is, in fact, the antithesis of a doctor, a living insult to the Hippocratic Oath. His job is to kill not to cure the sick, and he goes about his business without the slightest duty of care. He refuses to issue rations to the severely ill – consigning them to a hasty death – and beats sick prisoners and medical officers who appeal to him for medicine. If it were not for the British prisoners pooling their food and giving it to those in need, the death rate would be far higher. The British medics – Colonel King and Captain Bailey in the male compound, and Dr Gibson in the women's – contend with these appalling circumstances in the hope of saving lives. It has not yet dawned on them that the Kuching Barracks is in the grip of a policy of slow starvation.

The prisoners grow their own food, of course, but much of

the camp work – including stock-breeding, for example – serves to feed the Japanese. The civilians adopt strict rules to overcome this. One of the civilian internees' rules states: 'Any persons who are not performing some useful work in war-time are failing in their moral obligation. Internees should therefore do their best to do such work as . . . agriculture, farming, and stock-breeding, in order to increase the supply of foodstuffs to the camp.'[16]

By day, the men are put to hard labour on the airfields at Batu Tujoh, south of Kuching – another flagrant breach of the Hague Convention (which outlaws the use of prisoners on military projects). Ignoring this, the Kuching commanders warn that anyone who refuses to work will be executed. The few hundred fit enough to work manage, nonetheless, to inflict a few small acts of sabotage, such as adding urine and water to fuel designated for Zero fighters.[17]

Throughout, some Japanese guards reveal a vestigial kindness; yet such moments are incongruous and tokenistic, rather like the sight of a tinpot dictator trying to prove he's human by clutching babies. The guards are, nonetheless, willing to turn a blind eye to a little school established by the British Lieutenant Frank 'Tinker' Bell, called the 'Kuching University', with classes in modern languages, navigation and public-speaking. He and his teaching staff even award diplomas. At Christmas, the guards donate toys, biscuits and sweets to the children; the women prisoners make toys out of barbed wire, wood and debris. There is something desperately heroic about these homely gestures – at a time when the 1943 Christmas concert is called off and the performers forced to 'disband due to the illness and death of its members'.[18]

The Australian officers join this new world on 22 October 1943 and are consigned to their own barracks in line with the policy of segregating the nationalities. Complete segregation in a racial menagerie of British, Chinese, Indonesian, Indian and Dutch is, of course, impossible. Cards is the most popular form of recreation, then the hope of a concert. Captain John Rowell decides to dust down a musical comedy – 'PC Swing' – he wrote, and hoped to perform, in Sandakan. Rehearsals begin in November and prove a great distraction: 'the play meant ninety minutes of transportation from their miserable existence into another world'.[19] The musical is a hit with the 'laughing, chattering crowd', who wildly applaud when the curtain, fashioned out of old rags and blankets, rises on a makeshift stage in a vacant hut.

Its success excites huge demand for entertainment, so much so that on 14 January 1944 the Australian officers arrange a writing competition – 'Are You a Playwright?' – to find the best prison talent. The entrants' ten-minute sketches are performed over two consecutive Sunday nights. There follows a series of musicals, comedies, dramas and radio plays – staged with the simulated effects of a radio – written, directed and performed by half-starved men, many of whom do not survive the rehearsals. The costumes and sets are scrounged from bits and pieces lying around the camp or donated from Kuching. Yet the humour, richness and variety of the productions do wonders for morale: Gilbert and Sullivan's *HMS Pinafore*; 'Harem Scarem', a musical comedy; 'The Jury Retires', a murder trial; 'Wreckage', a drama of three men who survive a shipwreck on a south-sea island; 'Murder Manor', a mystery thriller; 'Sinbad the Sailor', a full-length pantomime; and many more.

Some have a tragic gestation. 'Love on the Double Cross', a musical romance set on an American ranch, written by Lieutenant

Bunny Glover, is postponed several times due to the sickness or death of the performers and crew, and a torrential downpour upsets the opening night. 'Fundosi Follies' is performed by – and staged exclusively for – men with contagious skin diseases, such as scabies, who are confined to a special hut. The name refers to the fundoses, or lap laps, they're obliged to wear during treatment. It is, in every sense of the billing, 'a strictly diseased-only show', featuring the 'lap lap lads and other scabs', accompanied by a choral sextet, with music arranged by Lieutenant John Pool, a former band-leader, and the camp choir, led by Captain Claude Pickford (which finds several ruses to get around Japanese attempts to ban it).[20] A singular pleasure ends these Sunday-night shows: a rice bun and cup of tea, served just before lights out, as Lieutenant George K. Forbes (author of the comedy 'Murder Manor') later writes: 'Over this sumptuous repast the night's performance would be discussed and criticised, much as any home-going theatre crowd would discuss a play back home.'[21]

The Japanese tend to overlook, or relax, the racial boundaries on theatre nights, and other nationalities are permitted to cross the wire to attend the Aussie entertainment. At first, the British seem disinclined to join in. Little organised entertainment issues from their compound, where a grim fixation on their wretched circumstances seems to explain the pall of silence. The British have been here longer, and the English constitution seems more vulnerable to the tropical climate. On other occasions, however, the English perk up, delighting in their small orchestra, with handmade instruments, and occasionally even deigning to join the Aussies. The Dutch have no such colonial reservations, and a great fraternal spirit briefly unites the Dutch and Australians, for whom laughter is the elixir of hope and the stage their only escape.

Forbes captures this mood:

A man, not fully aware that he was the victim of an incipient lack of faith would congregate with his fellows one Sunday evening to watch other men portray the lives of fictional beings. These beings would live in a happy world where privations were non-existent and pleasant interests predominated. At the fall of the curtain he would find that he had been transported for ninety minutes to another world, which in some degree he had shared. Hope would spring anew from the play's suggestion that such things were possible, and for a varying period would combat his mental condition.[22]

His words appear in 'Borneo Burlesque', a booklet Forbes produces after the war with fellow officers Don Johnston, Jock Britz and Bill Clayton. Its reissue in 2011 is exquisite recognition of the timelessness of this transcendent spirit.

The concerts cease on New Year's Eve 1943–44, when the Japanese cut the electricity. The prisoners are too ill to continue anyway. The officers rally to fill the void. Members of their 'Education Committee' resume lectures – frowned upon in Sandakan – on a great range of topics, including history, law, biology, bookkeeping, philosophy, languages, coffee-making in Java, timber cutting, fishing, marriage and sex.[23] The lecturers are gifted specialists, and some men reach 'university level' in their chosen subjects. So, too, do the British – though with a limited syllabus – where several officers attain a standard of French and Spanish equivalent to Cambridge BA Honours. The Japanese even, inexplicably, permit and supply a prison library – surely a gesture of Lieutenant Colonel Suga's – a luxury rarely seen in other prisons. An exception is Changi, incidentally, where the Australian Lieutenant Colonel 'Black Jack' Galleghan convinces the Japanese that books would 'reduce thoughts of escape'. By the end of the war, Changi library contains 20,000 books.[24] After two years in Kuching, Captain Frank Mills feels moved to remark upon 'how cultured everyone was'.[25]

▲
▽

Another ship arrives at Kuching on 2 November 1943, bearing a terrible human cargo: 53 civilians and 28 Australian prisoners of war disembark and move slowly along the wharf, dishevelled, bandaged and broken-limbed, barely alive. For the past week, they have been 'handcuffed' and 'roped to the deck' of a small boat. 'We were exposed to the waves . . . coming over the railings,' Wells recalls. 'We had no cover during that journey day or night.' The 53 locals were the backbone of the civilian underground – doctors, traders, policemen, clerks, forest rangers, overseers, watchmen, boat men and labourers – representing the great ethnic mix of Sabah: Europeans, Eurasians, Chinese, Dusun/Kadazan, Indians, Murut, Filipinos, Javanese and one Jewish woman.[26] The 28 Australians formed the nucleus of the prisoners' underground. All are now the walking wounded of a war crime.

Torture has extracted these 80 'guilty' men and one woman from a line-up of 200 suspects in Sandakan. They are charged with crimes relating to the Sandakan Incident. Their forthcoming trial is perfunctory; their guilt assumed. All that remains is their sentencing. Mindful of his likely fate, Matthews' comrades have urged him to escape. Jump overboard and swim ashore, they suggested during the voyage – to a man scarcely able to walk. Had he the strength, he would have declined the chance, he has told them: 'You'd collect it if I did . . . anyway, there is nowhere to escape to.'[27]

In Kuching, nowhere indeed: the Australians are doubly condemned, as prisoners of war and 'criminals'. Their cells are tiny, filled with bugs and vermin, in which they 'sit cross-legged all day facing the wall'.[28] Mrs Cohen is kept in solitary confinement – a nod at her gender – and beaten up on occasions for failing to sit at attention. The rations are not too foul for the first two months: half a pint of rice, beans, vegetable soup and occasionally fish. In time, the prisoners do rudimentary jobs: they garden, empty latrine buckets, polish bottles and clean Japanese military boots.

Dr Taylor is permitted to administer limited medical care, but none of the sick may enter the hospital (with the exception of Gerald Mavor, who has a double hernia). Malnutrition hastens the spread of scabies – 'Some of the prisoners had literally hardly a square inch of their bodies not covered with sores,' observes Wells – until a new Japanese guard takes rare preventative action, boiling the blankets and spraying the infected with sulphur, which halts the epidemic. Other diseases continue their fatal ministry. Sapper Ted Keating, sustained by little gifts of food from his comrades' rations, succumbs to beriberi on 5 February 1945. With 'a little attention by the Japanese', Keating's death would have been easily prevented, according to Dr Taylor.[29] The good doctor labours under the misapprehension that medics have a duty to do no harm, regardless of their location or circumstances. His benevolence has no place in this upside-down world: most Japanese medics are here not to sustain human life but to terminate it.

20

EXECUTION

Keep your chin up boys. What the Japs do to
me doesn't matter. They can't win.
Captain Lionel Matthews, after being sentenced
to death by a Japanese court martial

ASKED BY FELLOW OFFICERS to choose the lines he most admires from the *Rubaiyat* of Omar Khayyam, Captain Lionel Matthews chooses these:

So when at last the Angel of the drink
Of Darkness finds you by the riverbrink,
And, proffering his Cup, invites your Soul
Forth to your lips to quaff it – do not shrink.

Perhaps the spirit of the verse has helped sustain the man who, in Kuching, continues to maintain his silence, refuses to name his accomplices or confess. If so, it is a great compliment to the poet, given that Matthews and his comrades have borne the worst agony the human body is able to bear.

They sit in the Kempei-tai prisons in Kuching, in bamboo cages 20 feet square and six and a half feet high, 25 crammed into each.

Matthews weighs six stone; he was about 15 stone when he left Australia. Wells is in a similar state. Communication is forbidden, but the Australian signallers continue their finger-tapping code.

Torture of the ringleaders resumes but is less harsh – a form of continuing punishment rather than a means of extracting information: the Japanese have what they need. The trouble is, Matthews, Wells and Dr Taylor refuse to confess to any 'crimes', and their resistance infuriates the Kempei-tai. Nor do they demonstrate any respect for – or fear of – the secret police. On one occasion, while tied face down in the dirt under the roasting sun, Matthews nods to the guards as if needing to tell them something. When they bend down to listen, he spits in their faces – provoking a frenzy of kicking and beating with rifle butts. This is one of several examples of Matthews' defiance, according to his son.[1]

◆

The trial of the leaders of the Sandakan underground opens at 9 am on 3 February 1944 in St Teresa's School – a Catholic convent commandeered by the Kempei-tai – in Kuching. To the Japanese, it is a show-trial, a lesson to Borneo; to Borneo, it is a travesty of the most primitive notions of justice. Three 'judges' from Singapore are flown in, such is the publicity attached to the case: chief judge Lieutenant Colonel Egami Sobei; acting chief judge Major Nishihara Shuji; and junior judge Captain Tsutsui Yoichi. The prosecuting officer, Captain Watanabe Haruo, is held in low regard; Nishihara at one point describes him as 'an old fool' who knows nothing about the law.[2] There are no lawyers for the defence, and no jury. A prominent observer is Lieutenant Colonel Suga Tatsuji, chief commandant of the Japanese prisoner-of-war camps in Borneo.[3]

The judges and prosecutor sit on a raised dais behind a long table. Nishihara is the dominant influence and bosses the others about. 'The president and judges were only puppets and decorations of the court,' says Sumaga Yoshiro, the court interpreter (in later sworn testimony before the Allied War Crimes Tribunal, set up after the war). 'They were told what to do and how to do it by Major Nishihara.'[4] Commandant Suga places himself at the back of the court.

The court martial – *gunritsu kaigi* – of civilians and prisoners of war proceeds without any semblance of justice. 'It was designed to enforce discipline in occupied areas and to minimize the possibility and spread of resistance and sabotage,' according to Professor Tanaka Yuki. 'The principles of natural justice were of no consideration in its application. It was used to make an example of those civilians who had engaged in anti-Japanese activity – even those who were remotely suspected of having done so.'[5]

Nonetheless, the trials have received the imprimatur of the highest officials in the South-West Pacific. The Sandakan Kempei-tai's 'evidence' against the Australians and civilians has been sent to Colonel Machiguchi, head of the Kempei-tai in Kuching, who in turn has passed it to Major General Managi Keishi, chief of staff of the army. From there, it has progressed to Lieutenant General Yamawaki Masataka, general officer commanding the Japanese forces in North Borneo, who has given the order to proceed.

The 'guilt' of the civilians is a foregone conclusion, though Dr Taylor has admitted nothing. The doctor and other Europeans are tried on 3 February 1944. Deliberate mistranslations of the evidence condemn them. Dr Taylor and Mavor receive 15 years' imprisonment with hard labour at Outram Road Gaol; the rest get various prison terms. Mrs Moselle Cohen is fined and sent back to Sandakan, where she later dies – drowned at sea, claims one Japanese report. Another story alleges that she is placed inside a barrel and rolled until dead. The trial of the native resistance leaders is delayed until 2 March.

On 29 February, Matthews, Wells and three other Australian prisoners of war – Stevens, Corporals Charles Roffey and McMillan (Weynton was tried ten days earlier) – are led into the courtroom, handcuffed. They stand behind the interpreter, Sumaga, who describes the presentation of 'evidence' to the courthouse and the sentencing process.

The two-month investigation of the Sandakan Incident has revealed parts of a radio in the prison camp and links between the accused and Filipino guerrillas – according to the prosecution's statement, translated by Sumaga. The prosecution, he says, will find that Matthews received written confirmation from Colonel Suarez of 10,000 Filipinos preparing to invade Borneo, destroy the Japanese and rescue the prisoners:

> Capt Matthews believed this information and started to organize the armed group assisted mainly by the native and Indian policemen at Sandakan and ordered them to pool arms and equipment at secret places . . . His plan was carried out very cleverly and smoothly. He sent, by a native boy, a letter to Colonel Suarez to make sure of the date of his attack on Sandakan, but he could not get his answer. He was disappointed, a little . . .[6]

Major Nishihara then reads the case for the prosecution – in Japanese. None of the defendants is given a copy of what he has been accused of. Matthews objects and asks for legal representation for all defendants, which is refused. Japanese courts martial in occupied areas never allow the accused a defence counsel; the rule also applies to the trial of Japanese soldiers, according to Watanabe Haruo. No witnesses for the defence are allowed. (Interestingly, Watanabe later claims at his own trial that had the Australians requested witnesses, 'they would have been made available'.[7])

The prisoners give their names, units, ranks and places of birth. The charges are read: Stevens, Roffey and McMillan are accused of breaching regulations, spreading Allied radio news of the progress of the war that is unfavourable to Japan and harbouring hostile feelings towards Japan. Wells and Weynton are charged with the same crimes. Matthews is accused of the far more serious crimes of espionage and planning a rebellion, the evidence for which is the revolver, ammunition, maps and the 'diary' found during the prison search.

Captain Watanabe asks the accused if they have anything to say. 'No, we have nothing to say,' Matthews and Wells reply, 'but we believe that we have done what we have been required to do in the circumstances as soldiers.' The court interprets this statement as a plea of guilt. The interpreter claims that the prisoners have said, 'We accept punishment according to the law which is fair and just.' Wells and others later firmly deny this, arguing that they did not admit guilt: 'We had to admit a few minor things, because of the evidence given by the natives, but the statement written by the Military Police was in most instances a deliberate misinterpretation of facts.'[8] Wells adds that he, Matthews and Weynton were forced to sign admission statements written in Japanese characters, in their names, without any prior translation.

The three accused are not told what the charges are; they do not know 'what they were guilty of'.[9]

Their spoken statements to the court are also deliberately misinterpreted. 'I was asked the question in English by the interpreter,' Wells later says, citing one example. 'I said, "No, that is not so." I heard him reply to the Court President in Japanese, "Yes, that is so."'[10] Wells has enough knowledge of Japanese to conclude, 'it was obvious that they just ignored any denials of fact that we made. They just glossed over them and went to the next question. Our denials were not taken into consideration.'[11]

Not every Japanese official is complicit in this legal farce. At one point, Lieutenant Colonel Suga rises from his chair at the back of the courtroom and asks that the trial be held in line with international standards, and that the accused receive lenient sentences – an uncommon act even during the trial of Japanese. '[I]n a trial of enemy prisoners it was extremely unusual and courageous,' notes Professor Tanaka.[12] Suga is aware that the trial is, to say the least, utterly at odds with the precepts of international law. He is ignored.

◆

The judges retire for the evening, and deliver their verdicts to the civilian and military defendants over the following days. On 2 March, the civilian defendants appear before the judges in chains. Eight are condemned to death: Ernesto Lagan, Heng Joo Ming, Sergeant Abin, Alex Funk, Felix Azcona, Jemadar Ujagar Singh, Wong Mu Sing and Matusup bin Gungau. The rest receive prison sentences ranging from six months to 15 years (see Appendix 2).

'When the judge announced that they were to be executed,' according to the Jackson report, 'a pitiful scene ensued. Some of the sentenced men, weakened by their months of imprisonment and torture, began to weep loudly and beg for mercy. The group was dragged out of court by a length of rope.'[13]

The sentencing of the Australian soldiers is delayed. The details of their cases and reasons for their punishment are described in a court document, which Japanese interpreters have attempted to translate in the phonetic: 'Defendant Rional Collin Matthews, who had a hostile feeling for the Japanese troops even after the surrender and dislike for the life of a prisoner, was watching for a chance to escape.'

The radio, arms cache, diaries, maps, intelligence on the Japanese in Sandakan and the prisoners' contacts with the Filipino guerrillas constitute evidence of a planned prisoner uprising and rebellion – which Wells and Matthews refuse to accept without legal representation. Their most heinous crime – given its predominance in the sentencing notes – appears to be their repeated attempt to 'spread rumours' of Japan's failing war effort and to present Nippon 'in an unfavourable light'. On more than ten occasions, between November 1942 and February 1943, Matthews sent 'news' to the governor of North Borneo and Berhala civilians, 'unfavorable to the Japanese troops'; and passed on information about Japan's heavy losses in sea battles with the American fleet and land battles with Allied troops in New Guinea.[14] Matthews, in addition:

transmitted more than 20 times (between December 1942 and July 1943) to Mr Teller (sic – Taylor) . . . news unfavorable to the Japanese troops that the US Air Force attacked the Japanese transport ships and sunk 32 warships . . . and brought down many aircrafts in the area near the Bismark Islands.[15]

Other prisoners are similarly indicted on the 'crime' of disseminating information critical of the Japanese war. Clearly, the judges consider this worse than an insult. The Australians have dared to mock the Japanese, no less, causing them to 'lose face' – an unforgivable act in the minds of these pseudo-samurai.

◆

The night before their sentencing, Wells and Matthews receive a visit from Suga in their cells: he offers each man a banana and a copy of *Tokyo Ichinichi*, a Japanese daily newspaper. Their photographs appear on the front page. The story reports that two days earlier Weynton had been sentenced to ten years in prison for 'the violation of prisoner of war regulations' – i.e. building a radio – and 'spreading rumours'.[16]

The next morning, the two Australians are led handcuffed back into the courtroom. Lieutenant Colonel Egami, a 50-year-old father of seven, in his ceremonial role as chief judge, summarises the charges and reads the sentences, to which no right of appeal is allowed. Wells, for 'violating prisoner of war regulations and spreading rumours', gets 12 years' solitary confinement with hard labour; Sergeant Alfred Stevens six years' penal servitude; Corporals McMillan and Roffey eighteen months' penal servitude; Matthews, for 'violating prison of war regulations, spreading rumours, espionage and planning a rebellion', death by shooting.[17]

Wells and Matthews embrace. Wells expected death (it later

transpires that a bureaucratic mistake has spared him). Matthews is stoic as always: he has anticipated execution and is resigned to his fate. 'Please tell my wife,' he asks his friend, 'that I will always love her, and tell my sons to fight until we have our victory.' He is allowed to write a last letter to Lorna, which he takes an hour to compose. She never receives it.

Lieutenant General Yamawaki upholds the court's decision and orders the executions to proceed immediately. The condemned men are taken from the courthouse – trussed up like animals, observes Dr Taylor.[18] Matthews slices a finger across his throat as he passes the prisoners waiting outside.

The killing field is a forest clearing near the Kuching airfield. Some Japanese accounts describe Matthews as travelling there in a passenger car and the civilians in closed prison vans.[19] In fact, all are pressed into the back of a truck. As they drive off, Matthews shouts through the grille, 'Keep your chin up boys. What the Japs do to me doesn't matter. They can't win.'[20]

Major Nishihara – in charge of the executions – Lieutenant Colonel Suga and Captain Watanabe are among several witnesses. A guard from the Kuching Army Detention camp, Sugiyama Tadachi, leads the five-man firing squad. Each of the condemned men – eight locals and one Australian officer – is blindfolded with white cloth and bound to a stake with a cross-beam, along a deep trench. A guard later claims that Matthews refused to wear the blindfold. Fortified by friendship and common cause, they await death in silence. None flinches.

The firing squad stands on the opposite side of the grave and is told to aim at 'a mark near the centre of the forehead of the victim'.[21] One witness, Kurata Kizo, observes the firing squad standing 'two or three metres away from the prisoners'. Nishihara gives the order. 'I think most only fired one shot but others fired twice,' Kurata recalls. Watanabe concurs: 'Most of the prisoners were killed instantly.'[22]

There are various accounts of Matthews' death. Some claim, without evidence, that he tore off his blindfold on the point of death and shouted 'My God and King Forever' at the Japanese, before being riddled. Another story is that the Japanese beheaded him, because one end of his coffin is reportedly found drenched in blood. But Japanese witnesses state under oath that he died by firing squad. 'Captain Matthews was shot between the eyes and killed with the first shot,' Watanabe says. The Australian Army has accepted that conclusion: the man who resisted the worst the Japanese could hurl at him died calmly, bravely and probably blindfolded before a firing squad. Whatever happened in the forest that afternoon, his executioners later recall that Captain Lionel Matthews died 'a very brave man'.[23]

◆

One day in 1944, an Australian gravedigging party sits under a tree in a cemetery near St Catherine's Church in Kuching and wonders whose body is destined for the hole they have just dug. The answer soon arrives in a Japanese panel-van, which pulls up beside them. The guards order the gravediggers to drag out a coffin. They do so with great difficulty, as the base is 'extremely slippery with congealed blood'.[24] They have no idea whose corpse they are lowering into the soil. Hot and exhausted, one of the gravediggers faints, but he avoids falling forward into the trench. A Japanese guard laughs. One gravedigger later describes the scene 'of us standing there, dressed only in loin cloths, barefoot and just skin and bone, having buried someone, not even knowing who it was – and that rotten Jap laughed'.[25]

The gravediggers learn some time later that the man they buried that day was 'a Captain Matthews . . . everyone who had known him in Sandakan said what a brave and fearless bloke he was. A terrible way to end your life.'[26]

After the funeral, Lieutenant Colonel Suga, who professes to be Christian, authorises the placement of a wooden cross on Matthews' grave. The Kuching commandant is reported as later telling a group of Australian officers, 'I have just executed the bravest man I have ever met.'[27]

Matthews is the only victim to receive a funeral, a coffin and a headstone. The rest of the dead are buried in a mass grave; the Japanese refuse appeals from the Sikh community that Ujagar Singh be cremated in line with Sikh funeral rites. None of the families is notified. Not until long after the war will they hear, sometimes by accident, that their husbands and fathers were executed; it will take them longer to find the grave. Lorna Matthews is informed in a glib official letter, in late 1944, that her husband was executed at Kuching. Katherine Lagan refuses to accept that Ernesto has been shot and spends the rest of her life obsessed by a belief that her husband is still alive.

21

RESCUE?

I am extremely disappointed with the lack of care taken in the choosing of personnel . . . in the future they should be chosen with special regard to being round pegs in round holes. Small parties having to live together for many months in great discomfort and NO little NERVE strain should know each other . . . it is imperative that future parties do their training and live together . . . This was promised to me before I left Australia and has NOT been done . . . [in the first operation] the last-minute selection of merely healthy bodies is ill-timed and useless.

Major Gort Chester, on one of the first, disastrous
commando missions into Borneo

THE PRISONERS OF SANDAKAN and Kuching hear rumours of the fate of Matthews, Wells and the resistance leaders, and the collapse of the Jesselton revolt. None is aware of the fate of Allied Special Forces on the island. News of the troubled incursions of the PYTHON teams, the existence of Gort Chester and his commandos, would have nurtured a tentative hope of rescue. Those connections appear severed forever now, with the collapse of the resistance.

The first PYTHON operation, for example, in September

1943, proceeds without a clear idea of the state of the underground and the execution of its leaders. The little unit of six men – two British and four Australians – embarks by submarine from Western Australia on 24 September 1943, equipped with enough supplies and arms to last four months. They reach the east coast of Borneo within a fortnight. Some 3507 pounds of stores are brought ashore by rubber boat at a deserted beach. Various recces proceed. Contact with the American-led guerrillas from Tawi-Tawi fails: Captain Hamner arrives in Borneo on 23 November, but they botch a planned rendezvous. Disease, exhaustion and mishap plague Gort Chester's men every step of the way. Inexperience leads to some terrible mistakes, which threaten to alert the Japanese to the whole enterprise. On 7 December, PYTHON I withdraws to Tawi-Tawi.

The mission ends with some nice-sounding official language about the establishment of an intelligence 'organisation' on the east coast of Borneo, as well as some desultory 'coast-watching' and monitoring of Japanese shipping movements. Australian Special Forces' PYTHON I is a poor start to covert operations in Borneo – Gort's fury at his men's errors is a sign of that – but it is a start.

As usual, the repercussions of the Sandakan Incident fall like a hammer-blow on the prisoners, the easiest target for vengeance for both the Incident and the Chinese revolt. In Kuching, any transgression is savagely put down. 'They took reprisals in thrashings and ill-treatment out of all proportion to the offences committed, and took every opportunity to demean us,' recalls J. L. Noakes, on the marked change in the Japanese in the latter half of 1944.[1]

On 5 June 1944, the British soldier Lionel Morris is arrested in the Kuching Barracks on the trumped-up charge of possession of a diary, which had been confiscated from him a year earlier without punishment. Now, he is subjected to three months of sustained torture by the Kempei-tai, who try to link him to the Sandakan Incident and the Double Tenth. They beat him to a pulp and threaten to behead him unless he confesses. On at least two occasions, he is led blindfolded to a grass quadrangle, made to kneel, with his hands bound and tied to his ankles, and forced to wait, expecting the blow of the sword at any moment:

> Once again there was the long wait on my knees . . . In my dark little world beneath the bandages I waited. A hand was placed on my forehead forcing it forward – this had not happened before, and I was more convinced than ever that this time it really was my lot. Another pause and the ice cold flat of a sword was laid on the nape of my neck and held there . . . Blackness descended, my world ceased to be. I had passed clean out.[2]

In Sandakan, similar reprisals are visited on any suspects. Here, the officers have departed, and a cold, hard silence intrudes. The privates and non-commissioned officers exist in a strange limbo state, in the confines of bamboo, wire and jungle, conscious of being isolated yet always in the sights of the Japanese.

The rice ration is progressively cut in 1944 and will virtually cease altogether near the end of this year, due in part to American submarine disruption of the sea lanes between Sandakan and Kuching. Tapioca soon replaces rice as the prisoners' staple. Hoshijima continues to authorise the slaughter of a pig on Japanese festive days, from which the offal and bones are thrown to the prisoners – and sometimes the dogs – to fight over.

The food crisis calls for a strict and fair policy of food distribution, which the stronger prisoners – warrant officers and sergeants – strive to institute. Their lean and hungry figures are seen poring over the food ration to ensure it is equally shared, and using their mugs and dixies as scooping tins to apportion the watery rice fairly. Deep mistrust eyes the hands that serve this slop; tempers flare at the faintest suspicion of favouritism – an early sign of the incipient breakdown of civil order. In some men, the animal longing for food overrides those qualities of fairness and restraint that depend for their expression on basic sustenance. The prisoners' fragile sense of order – their strict routine and food regime – starts to buckle and break. In some men, the collective will to resist yields to individual despair, and a Darwinian desperation takes hold, a sense that only the fed, the daring and the collaborative will survive.

The supply of medical aid – never strong – also ceases in mid-1944. As Japan's defeat looms, Hoshijima is in no mood to make concessions to the prisoners. Japanese privations compel the guards to impound the rice and medical supplies. They purloin Red Cross parcels, leaving only bandages and a few quinine tablets for the prisoners. Diseases proliferate, and the remaining medics – officers Picone and Oakeshott, and a few medical orderlies – tend the men's needs with the most primitive means available: they cut away rotting flesh around yaws, or tropical ulcers, with nail scissors or sharpened spoons; they dab wounds with an acidic solution that tends to devour the healthy and the dead tissue.

The maintenance of the camp deteriorates: the electricity and water supply to the prisoners' huts ceases. The men resort to catching the afternoon's deluge for their water. By night, darkness like treacle covers the camp and its forlorn inhabitants, broken only by a few flickering hurricane lamps. The helpless murmuring of the sick and wounded arises from the pestilential huts, the plague houses of a mediaeval village.

◆

At Allied Headquarters, South-West Pacific Area, in Brisbane, where MacArthur's and Blamey's tense duumvirate leads the counter-offensive, the prisoners' fate barely registers in the grand plans for the defeat of the enemy. Understandably, High Command has a total war to win – an immense conflict being fought on several vast fronts. Concern for prisoners is felt, but action on their behalf – beyond the Philippine action – is not part of MacArthur's military imperative. Prison camps are scattered through Asia; and Sandakan is just another. And if elements of the Armed Forces – chiefly in the newly created SRD and SOA – nurture ideas of rescuing prisoners, and even draw up plans to do so, the top brass regard the prospect as a maverick sideline to the chief priority, the prosecution of the war.

Indeed, the creation of Special Forces – and the raising of Australia's first parachute battalion in 1943–44 – encourages some to hope that such units will be dropped behind enemy lines to free the prisoners in tandem with the attack on the enemy. Certainly, the relief of prisoners has followed Allied operations on several Pacific atolls; but this is the happy by-product, not the chief goal, of strategic incursions, whose chief purpose is the destruction of the Japanese. If an island is of no strategic use, poses no threat, or is logistically difficult to invade, then Allied Landforces will most likely bypass it and bomb the Japanese positions from the air

– regardless of whether they contain prisoners of war.

The same argument applies to Borneo: an island is earmarked for invasion only where sound strategic reasons prevail. This condemns the Australians and British at Sandakan to captivity for the duration. Such are the brutal truths of fighting a total war with limited resources.

◆

Set against those imperatives are, however, Borneo's special circumstances. The Allies know a lot about the camp and the state of the prisoners. The island presents an alluring test case for a prisoner-rescue attempt. Allied intelligence – sent via Matthews to Colonel Suarez – has already seeded the idea in the minds of Special Forces. The escape of the Berhala Eight, and the statements of Blow and McLaren, have added tantalising detail to the portrait of a prison on the edge of breaking out: e.g. the numbers of men and their resources, and the size and precise location of the Japanese forces.

In tandem, Allied war plans have incorporated the intelligence gathered by the underground before its destruction. And the return to Australia of Steele, Wallace and Kennedy on 11 March 1944 has put flesh on the bones of Brisbane's understanding of the prison camp. Indeed, Gort Chester recommends, in a PYTHON report, that 'WALLACE (although very unreliable) . . . has details of this camp and its occupants, contacts, etc., and a plan to return. Although WALLACE is NOT the man to return, his [rescue] plan may be practicable. MOST of the prisoners would need building up morally before *any* contact is made with them.' (Gort's emphasis).[3]

All of this encourages SRD officers to continue what Matthews and Dr Taylor and the local people have begun: if not another rebellion, then possibly the liberation of the prison through the actual invasion of Borneo. The trouble is, with the collapse of the underground, and the loss of the stream of intelligence, the island is reverting to what it has always seemed in the Western mind: a dark mass of jungle and mountain, inscrutable and hostile, the haunt of headhunters and cannibals.

Nonetheless, Operation PYTHON's abortive early incursions into Borneo inspire several follow-up attempts. Their mission is not, and never will be, to free, or even relieve, the prisoners. From the outset, their role is clear: to harass, gather intelligence on, sabotage, attack and kill the enemy. Such are the instructions of the most senior American and Australian commanders, who directly oversee Z Force and others, for whom every air, land and sea resource is critical to the war effort.

It little helps their case that the newly formed Special Forces has got off to such a poor start. Operation PYTHON's original brief was to fix and maintain a radio contact with rebels in the Mount Kinabalu and Jesselton area – and plainly not to contact prisoners. But its actual achievements are a catalogue of mishaps and disasters. Consider the fate of the four PYTHON missions that penetrate Borneo during 1944. No doubt, these small groups of very brave men endure incredible privations and take terrible risks. But their operations fail to fulfil their basic aims. The first mission fails to deliver arms and supplies to Kwok and his men, and is forced to return. The second leads to the loss of three soldiers: Lieutenant Alfred Rudwick and Sergeants Bill Brandis and Donald McKenzie. Brandis strays into the jungle, loses his way and finds himself captured, near-naked and semi-starved, by the Japanese. Rudwick and McKenzie similarly end up in enemy hands. All three are allegedly tortured and executed as spies, despite pleading their right to be treated as prisoners of war in line with the Geneva Convention, as they were captured in uniform (just) and surrendered their weapons.[4]

A third mission, accompanied by intrepid American sailors, is sent to rescue the missing men. It engages in a fierce skirmish with the Japanese and is forced to retire.

A fourth mission slimly succeeds, but its goal is extraction, not incursion – a derivation of the previous mission's failure. Led by the great American submariner Sam Dealy, the mission's purpose is to rendezvous with and extract Gort and his fellow commandos. To reach the rendezvous at the southernmost point of Tangusu Bay, Gort's six-man team has to thrash through virgin jungle for two weeks. They emerge from the forest around 6 June, heavily bearded, dressed in torn and rotting clothes, and feasted on by families of leeches. They sit in a fetid swamp, awaiting the submarine USS *Harder* – which fails to appear on time – listening to 'the scuffling of large mud crabs in the mangroves'.[5]

In such circumstances, even the hardened Gort contemplates surrender or taking his suicide L-pill. On the second day, all join in the Lord's Prayer; their condition 'worse than being on the run'.[6] After two days, Dealy's submarine, which has made four attempts to find the rendezvous point, surfaces in the starlit bay and sends two folboats ashore; they run aground in the mud at about 165 yards from where the men sit in the swamp. The men wade out to meet their saviours. The journey home is fraught with attacks by Japanese depth charges, which jolt and puncture the sub, forcing it to dive to a perilous 66 fathoms. At one point, Gort asks Dealy, 'I say old man, would you mind taking me back to Borneo.' The USS *Harder* reaches Darwin on 21 June 1944, having survived a journey through Japanese-infested seas: at least 88 enemy shipping movements are detected in the area, according to Allied intelligence.

The lessons of PYTHON are clear: the Allies' lack of ongoing intelligence and Borneo's size and extremely difficult terrain pose severe challenges to covert operations, let alone a rescue plan. Incursions behind enemy lines require men with expert bush skills, superhuman endurance and nerves of steel – talents distinctly lacking in several sent on these haphazardly assembled teams. Less likely, in consequence, is the pursuit of any plan to invade the island or rescue the prisoners.

Gort Chester's report on the PYTHON operations captures the depth of this failure. He writes:

> I am extremely disappointed with the lack of care taken in the choosing of personnel . . . in the future they should be chosen with special regard to being round pegs in round holes. Small parties having to live together for many months in great discomfort and NO little NERVE strain should know each other, and be able to live in such circumstances without discord, and it is imperative that future parties do their training and live together . . . This was promised to me before I left Australia and has NOT been done . . . [in the first operation] the last-minute selection of merely healthy bodies is ill-timed and useless.[7]

The former MI6 agent is especially angry at the Australian Army for failing to send guerrillas with any working knowledge of the local language. Not a single member of the PYTHON teams

– with the exception of Gort – understands 'Coolie Malay', he complains. 'The arrival of men understanding nothing is of no use and NOT fair to the man or myself.' Worse, several of the 'commandos' sent to Borneo even lack the ability to apply the three 'golden rules of jungle lore':

1. If lost, stay until found.
2. Always know the direction of the coast from your position.
3. Be aware that most water in rivers runs to the sea.

'These may appear childish,' Gort writes, 'but are NOT, in view of the unfortunate loss of BRANDEIS [sic], who apparently did NOT know them.' He singles out Brandis' inexperience as 'proof of the necessity for the greatest care in the selection of personnel'.[8]

Future commandos should be: expert in the use of several small arms, including the rifle, Austen grenade and Bren gun; trained in how to handle small sailing boats; proficient with explosives, and their application to demolition and sabotage; sound at signalling, and able to send and receive at least 8–10 words per minute in Morse.[9] The fact that Gort has to stress the need for such skills is a measure of the woeful unpreparedness of the early SRD forces – and further hinders any hope of penetrating Borneo or helping the prisoners.

◆

The overarching truth is that the relief of Allied prisoners *anywhere* in the Japanese Empire – from Sandakan and Changi, to Korea and Nagasaki – is a very low priority, if it exists at all, in the planning by MacArthur and Blamey, who are loath to divert precious resources to prisoner and civilian relief. Undoubtedly the most precious of these resources is aircraft. A land invasion of Borneo would require large numbers of paratroopers – at least a company (100 men) and ideally a battalion (800 men) – to be dropped behind enemy lines. That would require many aircraft – but none is available for such a mission in 1943 or 1944. Consider this gloomy assessment, in late 1943:

28 October 1943

SUBJECT: *Training Operations – 1st Australian Parachute Battalion*

TO: *Commander, Allied Landforces [General Sir Thomas Blamey]*

FROM: *R. K. Sutherland, Major General U.S. Army, Chief of Staff*

The Commander, Allied Air Forces, has referred to this Headquarters your letter of 18 October 1943 . . . where it has been given the most careful consideration. The amount of air transport which now exists in the Southwest Pacific Area is not sufficient for the accomplishment of the missions assigned by the Joint Chiefs of Staff. In spite of continued efforts by this Headquarters to secure aircraft for projected operations and for training purposes, it has thus far been impossible to obtain a sufficient number to meet operational requirements and there is little prospect of relief within any predictable time in the future. The means that would be required for this training do not, therefore, now exist in the Southwest Pacific Area. This is regretted but it is a condition beyond the control of General Headquarters.[10]

Three Douglas DC-3s are somehow cobbled together for parachute training in Australia; but a request for a C-47 – the military version of the aircraft – lodged with the minister for air stalls in early 1944. The planes cannot be diverted from troop carrier and cargo commitments, which have 'increased out of all proportion to the availability of aircraft', Brigadier General Donald Wilson tells the chief of the air staff in Melbourne.[11] So much for the influence of the minister for air.

The lack of aircraft means that, by the end of 1944, 1 Australian Parachute Battalion has not in fact completed a single mass jump, of battalion size, critical to the success of an invasion of Borneo or prisoner rescue. Operation Apple Sauce – several company-size jumps – is thought a success despite several casualties: '. . . 1944 ended,' notes the Battalion history, 'it had been a year of unremitting physical training, marches and two parachute jumps that resulted in many casualties . . . The CO [commanding officer] was disturbed by the casualty rate.'[12] Indeed, the commanding officer, John Overall, reprimands elements of 'All Companies' for failing to know their duties prior to emplaning, 'a large percentage of bad exits', and such confusion during the descent in high winds that men 'forgot their parachute control'.[13]

Improvement awaits the delivery of more planes. Until a sufficient number can be found, 'the operational training of the unit cannot be completed', the Australian chief of the general staff informs the air chief in November 1944. Twelve C-47s are needed to complete four company-size parachute jumps; until their delivery, mass jumping will not proceed.[14] The situation is a classic example of SNAFU: 'situation normal all fucked up'. Indeed, RAAF HQ is surprised to learn of the demands of the Australian

Army, whose order for 12 aircraft is the 'first indication' that such cooperation between the two services will be necessary, according to an RAAF cable of 25 November – an astonishing admission after three years of war.[15] In the event, only half the planes are supplied at this time, severely limiting the Parachute Battalion's training capacity and shelving any practical hope of an invasion of Borneo or rescue of the prisoners.

◆

Notwithstanding these dire circumstances, the Services Reconnaissance Department perseveres with plans to succeed PYTHON with a new round of covert operations to North Borneo, called, suitably, AGAS, the Malayan word for sandfly (an *agas* inflicts a small, irritating bite). AGAS receives the imprimatur of Lieutenant General Richard Sutherland, MacArthur's chief of staff. The first is scheduled for late 1944 but is delayed until the end of the wet season, January 1945. Its official purpose is to establish an intelligence foothold on the west coast. The second operation – AGAS II – scheduled for February, is pushed back indefinitely. It has a special mission: to reconnoitre the prison camp near Sandakan. There is no great urgency, however, in the SRD's planning department, where the usually hard-working Major Charles Finlay, director of planning, seems 'almost lethargic', according to the department's documents – a sign of the priority he places on the mission.[16]

And yet, AGAS II is supposed to gather intelligence essential for the launch of a mooted rescue plan, conceived in 1944, called PROJECT KINGFISHER, whose mission is 'to ascertain what assistance can be given by Services Reconnaissance Department in a combat airborne/naval operation, the object of which is to rescue and evacuate all prisoners of war from the PW camps in the SANDAKAN area of BRITISH NORTH BORNEO'.[17]

KINGFISHER is more often referred to as a 'project' than a 'plan'; it is never referred to as an official 'Operation'. It envisages the following extraordinary confluence of events. Undercover agents would make contact with senior prisoners, who, tipped off about the rescue, would prepare the fittest to recover arms dropped from aircraft on drop day, D-Day. Meanwhile, a reconnaissance party on the ground would place homing devices on the drop zones to guide in the Australian paratroopers, and then lead them to the prison camp. The paratroopers would surround, attack and overwhelm the Japanese, and lead the prisoners to evacuation points and waiting submarines.

KINGFISHER reads, in short, as a recipe for disaster. A whiff of fantasy permeates the whole scenario. In any case, this is a speculative study, not a proper operational plan. Consider, for example, three 'unusual factors' – stark warnings of likely failure – identified as arising out of the 'special type of target', the Sandakan Prison Camp, 'to be attacked':

1. The poor physical condition of the prisoners, which is likely 'to make evacuation difficult'.
2. The timing of the attack, which must 'coincide with the concentration of the prisoners-of-war in the Camp'.
3. The Japanese reaction – the enemy must be allowed as little time as possible 'to remove or massacre' the prisoners.[18]

Added to these are the questions of which of five parachute drop zones – including the prison camp itself and the airfield – are the most suitable, and what the Japanese strength is likely to be. Six machine guns are believed to surround the camp and airfield (the Japanese are thought to have 'no artillery').

AGAS I and II are responsible for furnishing the SRD with the answers, chiefly: the best drop zones and the positions of enemy defences, searchlights, radar, patrols and troop concentrations, as well as the times when the prisoners are all inside the camp perimeter. Such information is 'essential' before KINGFISHER might be planned in detail.[19]

But the feasibility study stalls. While MacArthur provisionally approves the further drafting of KINGFISHER, in December 1944 the whole exercise is conditional upon there being the aircraft and the men available – and, of course, confidence in the Australian SRD to execute it. None of these conditions is close to being met by the end of 1944: the aircraft are not available at the time required; the paratroopers are inadequately trained; and the SRD's morale is reeling from successive disasters in Borneo.

On 20 December, a mission to send photo-reconnaissance planes to Sandakan is indefinitely postponed. Headquarters, Allied Forces, in a cable to the Allied Intelligence Bureau, explains, 'too late to execute the mission requested by 30 December'. Nor are low-altitude photos available of the prison camp and its surrounding region – a critical requirement. 'It is not considered feasible to send a low altitude photo mission into this area at the present time,' the cable warns.[20] For now, PROJECT KINGFISHER remains just that: a project, not an operation, to which the SRD attaches 'no great priority' – and yet there it sits on the relevant desks, gnawing away at the 'to do' list, gaining credibility simply by existing, and daring someone to attempt it.[21]

THEY MARCH

22

NEW YEAR 1945

*Men had to be carried back into the cage, crying; some
collapsed but a bucket of water was thrown over them.*
Keith Botterill

IN LATE 1944, ALLIED AIRCRAFT bomb Sandakan for the
first time. The first raid, on 14 October, destroys much of the
town unopposed by any serious ground fire. Frequent raids on
Sandakan and the airfield follow. On 22 October, American P-38
Lightnings bomb and strafe the drome – damaging dozens of
Japanese aircraft in the vicinity and killing three Australians. A
low strafing raid on 30 October kills another two prisoners.

As Allied air raids intensify, Hoshijima permits the erection
of a huge wooden sign bearing the letters 'P. O. W.' in the open
area between the prisoners' compound and the Japanese barracks.
When the sign fails to deter an attack – two of three subsequent
P-38s appear to miss it and strafe the camp – the commandant
orders it to be moved to higher ground. For a time, Allied aircraft
avoid the prison camp,[1] while the surrounding jungle and airfield
remain prime targets. In December, however, a bomb lands
on a wood-gathering party outside the wire, killing about 20
prisoners – British and Australian – and a few Formosan guards.

In time, friendly fire will be responsible for the deaths of about 30 Australian and British prisoners.² By Christmas, air raids render the airfield – the scene of so much blood and sweat – useless.

Despite their lethal presence, the planes are a welcome indication to the prisoners of which side now commands the Pacific air. On Christmas Day, Liberator aircraft inflict the 'heaviest bombing to date' on Sandakan. Sticpewich later recalls, 'To us prisoners it was a great Christmas box, although it upset our meal as it happened about 11 am.'³ The Christmas raid 'finishes' Sandakan: puts an end to the airfield and unearths evidence of the prisoners' attempts to sabotage its construction. The bombs exhume jettisoned shovels, picks, mallets and railway lines in the craters, to Japanese fury. The next day, 200 prisoners are ordered to fill the craters, so that the last two serviceable Japanese planes are able to escape. Three days later, the Allies bomb the strip again, and the prisoners are forced to fill in the holes by night. 'We knew this was labour in vain,' Sticpewich later says. The bombers return every few days.

◆

More distressing than bombardment or the Japanese is the prisoners' chronic anxiety over where they will get their next meal. Christmas dinner is the 'best meal' of 1944: pork soup, a tin of rice and dried fish. This is something of a miraculous aberration, served during the worsening food crisis. Indeed, the food supply has steadily diminished as the war comes to the Japanese. The lack of rice obsesses the prisoners. Are they being starved to death? Is this how they will die, as punishment for winning the war? The halving of the rice ration in the second half of 1944, and the near-complete loss of canteen supplies, ratchets up the death rate. About 425 Australian and British prisoners die between September 1944 and January 1945 – of beriberi and dysentery, exacerbated by malnutrition. Malaria, too, is an ever-present and growing danger. Desultory efforts to disinfect the swamp fail to curb the mosquitoes.[4]

Acute hunger pangs drive the prisoners to take extreme, potentially lethal, risks. The nightly blackouts tempt many under the wire on food-scavenging excursions, or to leave their work posts to attempt to trade with the locals. If caught, the punishment is severe: an automatic flogging, weeks in the cage and likely death. The threat fails to deter desperate men driven to extremes, such as Sapper William Hinchcliff, caught picking up coconuts – an illegal act. Before the war, Hinchcliff, a carpenter, was a lively young man and a great lover of dancing, so much so that he formed a jitterbug club in his home village of Coledale in New South Wales. Here, in Japanese captivity, sick and severely malnourished, his jitterbugging days seem glimpses of an alien world. Hinchcliff – the first prisoner caught 'stealing' food under the new regime – is one of those unfortunates of whom the Japanese choose to make an example. Their methods ensure he will never dance again. Like Jimmy Darlington, Hinchcliff is subject to the see-sawing torture – a beam inserted behind his knees and stamped on by the guards. Barely able to walk, he is then made to stand for hours in the sun with his arms outstretched, and beaten whenever he sinks – and finally caged for seven days without food, blanket, clothing or a mosquito net. Sticpewich witnesses the result:

> Hinchcliff was put in the cage and left there without food but
> he could get water when he went to the latrine, for which he

was let out twice a day. He was without a hat and dressed only in shorts, and had to sit up to attention all day. Every morning just before the guard went off, and again every afternoon between three and four o'clock, Hinchcliff would be taken out and the guards, often two and as many as four, would beat him with sticks, fists and kick him. Each beating would last about five minutes and after standing to attention for a while he would be put back in the cage.[5]

After this ordeal, a shadow of the man – broken, bloody and starving – is sent stumbling back to his hut. 'He never went out to work again,' Sticpewich later states, 'and died about two months later, his resistance completely broken by this punishment.'[6] The shocking treatment of Hinchcliff fails to deter others, such is their need of food. In late November, eight Australian prisoners break into the Japanese Q-Store in search of food, partly to feed a friend, Private Jack Betts, who is suffering from severe dysentery and beriberi. It takes the Japanese a month to discover the culprits. One is Private J. M. 'Bluey' Anderson, who tried to enlist in the army at the age of 14 and was accepted at 16. He is now 19. All of the offenders are caged for weeks.

A bigger cage, ten feet by 20 feet, is built to confine the rising numbers willing to defy the Japanese in order to survive. Three cages are now in use in the prison camp. One is reportedly built on the recommendation of Captain George Cook, who, according to several accounts – not all of them reliable – has now become an arch collaborator who will do anything to ingratiate himself with his Japanese masters.[7]

In January 1945, some 17 Australian prisoners are crammed inside the new cage, as punishment for trying to squirrel away a little extra food or for bartering with the locals. Most of these men are starving and in the grip of illness, but their dire condition has no bearing on the length or severity of the punishment. They are made to sit cross-legged on the bamboo floor all day. If they topple over, they are dragged out and beaten. They receive two outings per day: to go the toilet and for 'PT', physical exercise. 'This consisted of a severe bashing,' Botterill later testifies. 'Men had to be carried back into the cage, crying; some collapsed but a bucket of water was thrown over them.'[8] Two regularly caged prisoners and perennial larrikins – Privates Len Annear and James Bowe – receive three terms in the cage in 1944–45, lasting three weeks, 44 days and six weeks, for various misdemeanours. Neither lives long after this body-crushing marathon.

Keith Botterill is sentenced to three periods inside, lasting, he later claims, seven, 20 and 40 days, for three counts of stealing food. In the first instance, he is charged with taking food from the Australian officers' store, presided over by Captain Cook, who, Botterill claims, approves the punishment.[9] Botterill emerges from his third caging emaciated and black, his body covered in scabies, his hair and beard caked in dirt. It seems to have no deterrent effect: on the night of his release, he claims to have gone under the wire, again, to gather sweet potatoes with a mate, Private Allan Quailey. The timing of this seems incredible, given Botterill's condition – and later fans questions over the credibility of his testimony.

◆
▽

Accusations of 'collaboration' fly on the slightest suspicion of favouritism. In this climate, feelings against Cook, the 'voyage officer', harden – and with justification. Cook, as the prisoners' nominal leader and spokesman, ingratiates himself with the enemy at any opportunity. The Japanese use him as a buffer between them and the men, and he falls into line willingly. His signature often appears at the bottom of intolerable orders issued to the camp.

By 1945, Cook is clearly 'in' with the Japanese. A timid, unquestioning man, he seems to do their bidding: ordering the prisoners about, making lists, issuing commands and even, according to some claims, recommending punishments. And yet, as the prisoners' representative officer, Cook appears to be maligned for several things he has not done. No evidence suggests he ordered the construction of the cages, but he undoubtedly develops an unpalatably close relationship with the Japanese. Other officers are forgiving of the man. Lieutenant Tony White believes Cook 'had to get along with the Japs; he had to be realistic. Often what looked like collaboration was in fact an effort to get things done.'[10]

By this time, Botterill has become a tough, wiry, deeply suspicious young man, with an instinctive distrust of officers and all figures of authority. A born survivor, the product of a tough working-class boyhood in rural Australia and inner Sydney, he contemplates the world with the roving eye of a tout, with a knack for seeing the main chance. This is a trait he shares with Sticpewich, an even cannier operator – a talent Botterill recognises and seems envious and perhaps scared of. Botterill is quick to denounce men as collaborators, damning Cook repeatedly as a Jap-lover; but wisely withholding the allegation against Sticpewich until after the latter's death, long after the war ends.

The situation at the time is more complex: Botterill overlooks

Sticpewich's sincere attempts to use his influence to help the men. Even Cook has his moments, speaking out, for example, on behalf of Privates Gordon Barber, Arthur Clement and Fred Weeks, who are caged and bashed for going under the wire to find food. All three lose their lives as a result of the treatment. Barber expires in the cage. Clement, a hulking provost, succumbs a month or so after his release. Weeks, unable to walk due to paralysis and internal injuries, is taken out of the cage on a stretcher and dies seven days later.[11] Cook receives a slap from Hoshijima for his insubordination. Had Cook persisted, no doubt he too would have been caged and possibly killed.

Sticpewich is one of the few to sympathise with Cook, perhaps because he shares the man's motives, if not his methods. 'Wild Bill' Sticpewich is one of those wily operators who excels at infiltrating and exploiting the Japanese. As a master 'Mr Fixit', and the most senior non-commissioned officer, he has little trouble wangling a job as head of the 'Technical Party' of carpenters, engineers, plumbers, electricians and drivers, who enjoy enviable freedoms not available to other prisoners. They're allowed to work outside the wire, under the control and patronage of the Japanese quartermaster, who indulges 'his' prisoners with supplementary rations to such an extent that they receive 'an extra meal a day or as much as they could eat of sweet potatoes, tapioca, greens, sugar, salt and at times meat and fish'.[12]

Sticpewich's Technical Party also lands the plum job of camp slaughterer – a humiliation in Japanese eyes, as abattoirs in Japan are traditionally run by members of the untouchable 'burakumin' class. That social distinction matters little in Borneo: Sticpewich's team is thrown a share of the slaughtered animal – usually the offal, a few bones and the blood. 'This made a tasty stew for all and was a day to be looked forward to,' Sticpewich later recalls.[13]

His Technical Party does attempt to act in the prisoners' interests; for example, as the channel through which inward supplies – and contraband – enter the camp, including medical aid and extra food for the dangerously ill. It seems, however, that few of these luxuries reach the designated recipients after the Japanese, and Sticpewich's 'handlers', receive or take their share. The rising death rate of the men, and the stable girths of the Technical Party, attest to this conclusion.

◆

For the Australian and British prisoners, the New Year opens with sources of relief and despair. Relief because, from January 1945, work on the airfield has stopped – regular Allied bombing has ruled out any attempt to repair it. Despair because, during the first ten days of 1945, the prisoners receive the last of their rice rations – any available rice is hitherto stockpiled in Japanese stores.

On 27 January, there are 1135 Australian prisoners alive, down from 1560 on 1 September 1944 – and most of those 425 deaths are directly attributable to the poor diet and severe malnutrition. The gravedigging parties are active daily; though the days of Braithwaite's little engraving service – he used to carve the name of the deceased into a scrap of metal and place it on the grave – are long gone. The hunt is on for any scrap of food. Tapioca, swamp cabbage and yams, swamp snail and snake are collected and devoured; some even consider 'putrefied cow entrails laced with maggots' edible.[14] News of Cook and one or two other officers accepting invitations to dine with Hoshijima provoke hatred and disgust. With rising panic, the men turn to the forest. 'Used to watch the monkeys when we were out on working parties,' Owen Campbell later says. 'What they ate, we ate.'[15]

23

THE FIRST MARCH

Whether they are destroyed individually or in groups,
or however it is done, with mass bombing, poisonous
smoke, poisons, drowning, decapitations, or what,
dispose of the prisoners as the situation dictates.
Japanese military policy manual found at Taihoku
on Formosa, describing the measures to be taken
against prisoners in 'urgent situations'

ONE DAY IN LATE JANUARY 1945, 455 prisoners – 335 Australian and 120 British – are ordered to gather their few belongings, assemble on the parade ground and prepare to march. They are to march out of Sandakan Prison Camp in a westward direction. None knows where he is headed – simply a place with better food and medicine, the Japanese promise. None is fit for the ordeal ahead, as the Japanese know. Each man has lost at least three stone, suffers from the usual tropical afflictions and is severely malnourished – the result of three years of ill-treatment. Yet these are the healthiest men in the camp. Even the sick come forward when asked to volunteer for the journey, drawn by the hope of plentiful food at their undisclosed destination. The volunteers are culled to the 'fittest' available.

Three days before the prisoners' departure, rumours point to their destination: somewhere on the west coast, probably Jesselton. It baffles the prisoners and provokes a flurry of questions. Are they being sent to build Japanese defences there? Or to be used as shields for the Japanese Army, fleeing aerial bombardment? The more optimistic wonder whether they are going to a better place to enable the defeated Japanese to mitigate the charge of war crimes. Harder heads conclude they're being used as carriers, to help the Japs escape the Allied invasion. The truth is darker than any of them suspect.

In early January, Lieutenant General Yamawaki Masataka, the officer then commanding 37 Army, gives an official explanation for the march to Captain Yamamoto Shoichi, a battalion commander of the 25th Mixed Regiment in Sandakan, who is selected to lead it. Ordering Yamamoto to transfer 360 Japanese troops and a machine-gun company to Tuaran and Jesselton, Yamawaki instructs him to take 500 prisoners of war for use as carriers and a labour force on the west coast. Several Japanese battalions, he adds, will move west in the coming months, to protect the oilfields.

The order is sent to Hoshijima, who acts with his usual school-prefect efficiency. The prisoners will perform a critical job on the march, he believes. They will:

1. Act as carriers for troop movements to the west-coast
    garrisons of Tuaran and Jesselton, in the event of an
    Allied landing on Borneo soil. America's invasion
    of the Philippines, and the Australian landing on
    Tarakan and build-up on Morotai point to a likely
    attack, probably on the west coast. If from the east, the

Japanese will evacuate west. Either way, the journey must proceed.

2. Help the Sandakan garrison escape air strikes. The town has been bombed to rubble, with nothing left to defend and further raids imminent. The garrison is not big enough to defend the coastline and should be concentrated on the less vulnerable west coast.

Hoshijima claims, as a sweetener to the prisoners, that their destination has plentiful food and medical supplies. Privately, he muses, the prisoners would prove 'troublesome' if left behind.

The Japanese later argue, at their war-crimes trials, that the marches were partly intended to save the prisoners' lives. According to this self-serving nonsense, Hoshijima claims to have proposed to Major General Kuroda of 37 Army Headquarters that all prisoners be shipped to Kuching to escape air raids on Sandakan. Kuroda rejects the plan because the Allies' complete air supremacy would lead to the total destruction of the sea convoy – at this time, few ships leaving Sandakan reach their destinations. Kuroda claims that Ranau has been chosen as the prisoners' secret destination out of consideration for their safety: 'Ranau at that time was still safe from bombardment and comparatively abundant with more foodstuffs and medical materials, therefore seemed to be the most suitable place for PWs' refuge.'[1]

◆

Mass slaughter is the last act of the Japanese war. Throughout 1945, in remote places, with no strategic value, prisoners are herded together to build railroads, airfields, roads – all hopeless projects now, under Allied control of the air. The aim is to work the prisoners to death. This accords with the policy of Japanese High Command, which is not simply a case of 'kill the prisoners'. They must first be sapped of their strength in the cause of Imperial Japan. Their humiliation and drawn-out death has a disturbing psychological dimension. In Nippon's eyes, the prisoners should have destroyed themselves in captivity – the only honourable course open to Japanese prisoners. Since they failed to do so, according to Japanese thinking, they do not deserve to be treated with the dignity and respect of soldiers. They are no better than slave labour, to be worked like draught horses, until, when lame or too exhausted to continue, they must be disposed of. Such is the nihilistic mindset of a military regime for whom, as Japanese historian Kiyosawa Kiyoshi writes in January 1945, 'there is no philosophy of life, only a philosophy of death'.[2]

Another reason to kill the prisoners is to dispense with the witnesses of Japanese war crimes. As the Allied war closes in, the prisoners remain dangerous sources of evidence of Japanese atrocities. And so, in accordance with Japanese official policy, all prisoners must be got rid of; none must be allowed to fall back into the enemy's hands; none must be free to witness Japan's humiliation and defeat.

And yet, the order, 'kill the prisoners', is vague and inconsistent. Officially, at this stage of the war, it applies to any prisoner thought likely to fall into enemy hands, according to the most-cited source for the instruction: a headquarters log recovered from a prison camp in Formosa, dated 1 August 1944. 'When an uprising of large [prisoner] numbers cannot be suppressed without the use of firearms,' it states, or, 'When escapees from the camp may turn into a hostile fighting force', 'extreme measures' must be taken against them.

Whether they are destroyed individually or in groups, or however it is done, with mass bombing, poisonous smoke, poisons, drowning, decapitations, or what, dispose of them as the situation dictates. In any case, it is the aim not to allow the escape of a single one, to annihilate them all, and not to leave any traces.[3]

But this does not prescribe the destruction of *all* prisoners; it specifies those trying to escape or rebel against the prison. Nor does it mention the fate of prisoners about to be liberated. However, the loose wording and fury of Japanese officers at the fag ends of the war leads them to apply it, in practice, to all prisoners. The document also refers darkly to the 'final solution' for prisoners of war – and this, combined with ominous measures such as the separation of officers and other ranks throughout the empire, and the building of trenches, moats and tunnels, which look suspiciously like mass graves, sends the grimmest message to the prisoners.

Elsewhere in the Pacific, the 'kill the prisoners' policy is not universally applied. Not all Japanese commandants fulfil the grisly task assigned them, due to uncertainty about the order, ill-health, defeat and an intangible 'human factor', as the historian Gavan Daws shows in his excellent analysis.[4] The Philippines is the first test case. The commandant on the southern island of Palawan enacts the policy to the letter: 150 surviving American prisoners of war are herded into air-raid shelters, drenched with gasoline and set alight; those who come running out are machine-gunned or clubbed to death. At Davao, the last prisoners are just 'left for dead'. At Cabanatuan, where the Japanese are reduced to 'living skeletons' and unable to enact their orders, American and

Filipino Special Forces rescue all survivors. In Manila, the guards at Bilibid 'just left' the prison compound – fleeing for their lives. In the Japanese homeland, however, a more concerted picture emerges: there, the army is under instructions to slaughter all prisoners when and if the Allied forces invade, according to the Japanese researcher Toru Fukubayashi: 'Mr. Yamashita, who was the commander of Iruka Branch Camp (Nagoya No. 4) in Mie Prefecture, told me in 1998 that ideas about how to kill the POWs had been discussed among the principal members of the branch camp.'[5] The picture is, as Daws concludes, 'mixed'.

Nor are the 'methods' of the Japanese and their guards applied uniformly, or very efficiently – contrary to the Japanese Army's reputation for Prussian thoroughness. Human factors tend to intrude at the moment of their defeat and disgrace. 'In some of the camps,' writes Daws, 'the commandants were in a perpetual rage now, and some of the guards, too. Other guards acted depressed, almost stunned. Some turned pleasant and watchful without saying why.'[6] Some talk openly about the end of Japan and request letters of commendation from the prisoners in order to save their own necks when the Allies arrive. And a few honest guards, who do befriend the prisoners, warn them that they are all going to die: '*Oru* men die.'[7]

On the other hand, signs of this policy manifest a pattern, in varying degrees, all over the Pacific. In many camps, officers are separated from enlisted men, rendering both vulnerable; deep trenches, moats and tunnels are dug, ostensibly for self-defence, but also, conceivably, for a coming massacre (such as happened at Palawan); pillboxes and machine-gun nests are erected facing inward – towards the prisoners – as happened in the Philippines and other Japanese-occupied territories under Allied attack. And rumours spread through the camps that the Japanese intend to use them as shields, or slaughter them in the rear, when the Allies invade.

Prisoners are aware, to varying degrees, of the coming horror: sometimes a few 'good' guards – or guards turned 'good' at the prospect of defeat – tip them off. In camps from Manchuria to Burma, many captives try to prepare for the coming massacre, to scavenge anything they can use as a weapon. They secrete knives, stockpile rocks and make crude Molotov cocktails out of sake bottles. They draw up plans to rush the guards. 'At Miyata on Kyushu,' writes Daws, the prisoners hear they're going to be 'taken down a disused mine and killed'. At Fukuoka 17, the end will come during *tenko*, in a hail of machine-gun fire. At Tha Muang in Thailand, a Korean nicknamed 'Red Balls' warns that if the Allies invade, the prisoners will be 'killed in the big ditches around camp'.[8] Some camps 'went over the edge into madness, with the Japanese hounding the prisoners to death as if death *was* the point'.[9]

The policy of extermination is inconsistently applied across the empire. As defeat looms, mindful of their own necks, some prison commandants interpret the order to 'annihilate the prisoners' as they see fit. Not all are mindless automatons intent on committing war crimes to specification – Colonel Suga, for example, exerts some restraint – but most are. Gavan Daws again gives the best description of the policy in action. 'Some Japanese officers demanded the killing of prisoners,' he writes in relation to Bataan, but his points prevail universally:

> Some encouraged it. Some tolerated it. A few opposed it; but even they endured it. No doubt any number of Japanese, officers and enlisted men, were just following orders, doing

their job, whatever that might have meant to them in the
service of their emperor. But nothing and nobody stopped
the Japanese from doing whatever they felt like to their
surrendered prisoners. Bushido, the way of the warrior, meant
whatever officers wanted it to mean. Discipline likewise meant
whatever they wanted it to. The result was mass atrocity.[10]

In Sandakan, the policy means enslaving the prisoners as porters,
to be worked until they collapse, after which they should be
killed. There are several precedents for the forced march. The
Bataan Death March, in which 76,000 American and Filipino
soldiers were flogged 80 miles up the Bataan Peninsula, with
about 5000–10,000 dying of starvation, disease or execution in
1942, has set an atrocious example – the facts of which are known
to Allied planners in 1945. In 1944–45, in Batavia and Manchuria
and elsewhere, Japanese commanders plan to repeat the atrocity.
The 3000 prisoners of Bicycle Camp in Batavia are to be taken
on a 'long walk', until all are dead. Similarly, in Manchuria, any
prisoners falling out of a planned 40-mile march into the freezing
mountains will be shot. Allied intervention and other factors
mercifully prevent these marches from proceeding. In Sandakan,
no such intervening events prevent the decision to force-march
more than 1000 Australians and British into the heart of Borneo.

▲
▽

In late 1944, Lieutenant General Baba Masao succeeds Yamawaki
and inherits the decision to march troops and prisoners to the west
coast. Born in 1892, Baba has risen through the Japanese cavalry
to assume divisional and then army command. He is a short,

skinny man with a jutting jaw and a persistent expression of proud contempt. On assuming command, he launches a plan to crush the insurgents and guerrilla activities in the west and interior. To this end, Baba aims to strengthen the Japanese garrisons in the kampongs along the inland route.

If Baba inherits the order to march sick and hungry men over the world's least hospitable terrain, he prosecutes it with diabolic zeal and utter indifference to the prisoners' suffering. He later claims to be ignorant of the men's condition – a shameless lie. Baba is well aware of the state of the prisoners before they depart and has full knowledge – via his own reconnaissance and a report by Yamamoto, who will lead the First March – of the country through which the prisoners must pass.[11]

The commander of the Borneo prison camps, Colonel Suga, and the Sandakan commandant, Hoshijima, both report to Baba. It is they who enact Baba's orders, and they will later claim to have defended the prisoners against the harsh conditions. Indeed, Hoshijima later argues, at his war-crimes trial, that he held back 45 men from the original 500 sent on the First March because they were 'too sick'. Asked about the state of the rest, he answers, 'Not so good. Army HQ [Baba] issued orders to send 500 prisoners. About 200 were not fit for the march and I tried to keep 100 back. Army HQ said they must go. Even so I only sent 455 . . .'[12]

But how will they achieve it? There are no roads running east to west. The roads are confined to the coastal towns. Only rough native trails connect the villages in the interior. A few British bridle tracks – known as 'rentis' – run from the east coast to the nearby hinterland, such as Beluran in the Labuk area. Even so, before the war very few white men 'could claim to have been across this hazardous country by foot'.[13]

After invading Borneo, the Japanese were quick to realise the need for a transport route across the island, over which they could carry arms and supplies. At first, they relied on the shipping route around the island, but this was steadily closed as the Allies won control of the air. So they engaged the local people to cut a route. The prospect of building a road was clearly unrealistic, and they settled on a foot track, to connect Sandakan, through gradually ascending country, to Ranau, 160 miles west, and then down to the coast to Jesselton via the Mount Kinabalu foothills. The critical – and most difficult – Sandakan–Ranau leg was completed in three stages, during 1942. The first stage connects the existing British rentis at the 42-mile western marker (or 'peg') with the head waters of the Sapi River; the second stage connects Sapi to Tampias, a further 62 miles west; and the final stage follows an existing native foot track, from Tampias to Ranau. Thereafter, the track joins a British-built track linking Ranau to Tuaran and Jesselton, 76 miles west of Ranau.

The Japanese, however, mistook the loyalties of the 'coolie' labourers whom they ordered to cut the track. Indispensable to the job was a native called Orang Tuan Kulang, headman of the village of Maunad and the local Dusun chief. Kulang is an experienced hunter and reputedly deadly with local weapons, the blowpipe and parang (a curved machete-like knife).[14] He knows central Borneo extremely well, privately despises the Japanese and takes every opportunity to harass and terrorise them. In time, Lieutenant Colonel Jackson later writes, 'he alone holds the secret of many a Jap death in Borneo'.[15]

In their ignorance, the Japanese appointed Kulang as their pathfinder and surveyor of the track's crucial middle section. Assuming the track was for Japanese use, he ordered his machete-wielding tribesmen to cut the most difficult route they could find. According to one witness, 'Many was the time that he deliberately arranged for the track to be cut up the side of an impassable mountain range and then tell the Japs that it was no good and that they would have to find another way.'[16]

Many native people assisted him, notably Bede Soemole 'Sandshoe' Willie, the Eurasian district officer for Beluran, who worked with Gort Chester on the PYTHON operations; and the extraordinarily energetic Kanak, headman of the village of Tandu Batu and chief of the Orang Sungei, or River People, who was assigned to cut the critical 55-mile mid-section, from Celo to Tampias. None realised they were creating a ribbon of death for Australian and British men about to be driven across it.

The track does not of itself pose much challenge to fit, healthy individuals with plentiful food, clothing and medical supplies. It has none of the excruciating peaks and troughs of the Kokoda Track over the Owen Stanleys. And yet it tends along a perverse route, winding up mountainsides when it might have meandered along river valleys, crashing into prehistoric jungle when it might have stuck to airy plantations. It slices through thickets of scrub; emerges on brief plateaux of spiky grassland; plunges into any number of streams and swampy wetland; and spans or runs along the banks of several rivers (notably the Maunad, the Pandan Pandan, Celo, Bonkud and Telupid), before reaching the village of Telupid, on the banks of the Labuk River, at the base of the gradually rising Maitland Ranges. From here, the track traverses the jungle-capped ridges of the foothills – not especially high, or precipitous, but a formidable obstacle to heavily laden, sick and hungry men. Past Tampias, the fiendishly contrived route reaches the old, comparatively benign native rentis, which wind on to Paginatan, a little township on a hillside in a curve of the Labuk River, 128.5 miles west of Sandakan, before ascending the Crocker Ranges and arriving at Ranau, spread out on a plateau a further 26 miles west, in the shadow of Mount Kinabalu.

◆

The man responsible for leading the First March, Captain Yamamoto Shoichi, has recently arrived in Borneo via service in Labuan, Jesselton and Kudat. Aged 44, bespectacled, proud, an accomplished soldier – and veteran of Manchuria, where he served at the age of 21 – he received his commission in the Emperor's Army in 1938. Yamamoto sees himself as leading a Japanese infantry unit – the 1st Battalion, 25th Mixed Regiment – not a prison march; the prisoners are relevant to him only insofar as they perform the role of carriers. He has no interest in their fate beyond this duty. Even so, this is Yamamoto's first experience of dealing with the wretched white man. On 24 January, he confers with his fellow officers chosen to command the march and issues the following orders: the march will be completed as quickly as possible, within a schedule of 12 days to Ranau and 21 to Tuaran; the prisoners are to be treated with the minimum attention thought necessary to keep them moving; the officers and guards have no licence to kill the fit, but any prisoner 'who could not carry on or keep up' is to be disposed of.[17]

In January – the middle of the rainy season – the Sandakan Prison Camp is replete with talk of a move to another part of Borneo, rich with plentiful food, 'a veritable garden of Eden'.[18] Such are the Japanese entreaties to the fittest. And why shouldn't the men believe them? Hope is the prisoners' only recourse – the last gasp of men at their extremity. Nothing could be worse than Sandakan, just as nothing could be worse than Changi, so they accept the news of a transfer as 'something to look forward to'.

Many clamour to join the march, and the fittest are carefully selected. Those excluded – the sick, the weak, the morbid, the mad – lapse into a deeper malaise. Surely they are being kept behind to die, they fear. The fittest have no choice and are ordered to join the march regardless of whether they want to. Brothers, friends, are divided; young men who for months have sat beside their sick mates must abandon them and move out. Tom Burns, the only child, with his diary as his only companion, is too sick to walk, and stays. The malarial Gordon Dorizzi must remain, too, while his two brothers, Herbert and Thomas, are ordered to join the march.

Hoshijima realises that even the fitter prisoners, who have lived for weeks on tapioca and two and a half ounces of rice per day – the dregs of the last reserves – cannot shoulder heavy loads for more than 155 miles in tropical heat. They need fattening. So the 455 men on his list are to receive extra rations in the days before departure. A small pig is shared between the 55 men of the first detachment, and 40 pounds of dried fish is set aside to last the whole journey. Hoshijima orders the slaughter of his emaciated horse, of which the hooves and guts are added to the prisoners' pot, while the Japanese get the poor creature's flesh and organs. In addition, each man will receive six pounds of rice for the journey and a small quantity of salt. Food dumps are to be expected at regular intervals along the track. The men are to wear only the clothes on their backs. Those with nothing to wear but loincloths are given shorts and shirts. 'Jikatabi', latex-rubber slip-on shoes, are distributed to those without boots, who comprise 90 per cent of the total, their Australian boots having long since worn out.

The 455 prisoners are to march out in nine groups of about 50, one or two per day, each under the command of a Japanese officer and 30–40 guards, mostly Formosan. The first is to leave at dawn on 28 January, under the command of Captain Iino Shigero. Before their departure, Yamamoto gathers together the commanders of the first eight groups – pointedly not involving Lieutenant Abe Kazuo, who will lead the ninth and last group. He tells them that High Command – that is, General Baba in Kuching – expressly desires that no prisoner be left behind along the route. The order is made explicit to Lieutenant Abe, leader of the designated 'killing' platoon in the rear: all prisoners who fall behind are to be 'disposed of'.[19]

▲

As the hour of departure approaches, the prisoners farewell their friends – breaking a bond that began, for many, in Singapore. Nobody knows precisely where they're going, or for what purpose. If west, how far west? Will they ever see the men with whom they've spent every waking hour for the best part of three years of shared struggle and mutual dependence?

In the glancing light of dawn, a crowd – of prisoners, guards, Japanese – stand near the gates and watch the first detachment depart. At about 6 am, the first 55 Australians selected for the First March trudge out of the camp, escorted by more than 30 Formosans. Before they depart, each man is allocated three pounds of rice, two and a half pounds of dried fish and a little salt, which is supposed to last a few days before they reach the first of apparently several food dumps.[20]

Leading the prisoners out is Captain Rod Jeffrey, the 2/20th Battalion's much-loved medic, with the support of Warrant Officer Charles Watson and Sergeant Colin Smyth. They march up the path in crumbling boots or their rubber shoes and disappear into the jungle shadows. Over the next five days, eight groups follow. They include the exemplary Warrant Officer A. E. Johns (leading Group 5), a medic, who regards the lives of the men in his party as his personal responsibility, and the similarly upstanding Warrant Officer John Kinder of the Royal Australian Air Force (leading Group 7), who exhibits an extraordinary duty of care for his men. Bringing up the rear are some 55 British prisoners in Group 9, which departs on 6 February 1945, whose guards include the figures of Kitamura Kotaro and Hayashi Yoshinori, of chilling reputation in Sandakan, under the command of Lieutenant Abe. Later, dozens of guards will claim under oath that they 'do not know what happened' to the prisoners who fell into the hands of these 'men in the rear'.[21]

At the eight-mile peg, the first group is ordered to turn right and their spirits plunge. If some cling to the hope of heading east, into Sandakan, and to better conditions, they are abruptly disabused. The little file heads west, into darkness.

24

WHITE PORTERS

*I was left with a party of five. These five men were very
sick and suffering a great deal. Although my orders from
Lieutenant Abe were to kill them I did not have the heart to
do such a thing, and so left them behind, without food and
water, to die . . . Looking back now and remembering how
ill the POWs were I feel it might have been more humane
to have killed them and buried them before going on.*

Private Endo, a member of Lieutenant Abe's killing platoon

YAMAMOTO EXPECTS THE PRISONERS to reach Ranau within 12 days – a tough deadline even for healthy men. The question is whether they will make Ranau at all. And none, surely, will have the strength to carry on to Tuaran, the ultimate destination. The section between Ranau and Tuaran represents 'the most difficult and strenuous portion of the whole track'.[1] Yamamoto does not concern himself with the human cost of his policy. He measures his performance against the benchmarks set by the Imperial Army, whose soldiers are known to march 20–25 miles a day on a cup of rice. He ignores the fact that these men have spent three years enslaved to the Japanese war machine. In Yamamoto's eyes, his Australian and British captives are no longer soldiers; they are white porters, workhorses, coolies. He is determined to sweat the strongest for as long as they can stand it.

The Japanese commander's first glimpse of his new carriers bodes ill for the success of the journey: they shuffle forward along the bitumen beyond the eight-mile peg, a dismal file of sick, thin, bearded men, in tattered clothes, or just shorts or loincloths, with obscene ulcers on their legs. The dismaying sight elicits merely the self-interested enquiries of a slave driver. Are these the fittest available, Yamamoto insists. How much can they carry? How much food will they consume? Sitting beside his guard detail are great piles of hessian sacks containing ammunition, rice and anything else thought necessary. The prisoners are loaded up: an ammunition sack is slung across the front of each man; a rice sack over his back. The combined weight is about 55 pounds.

Yamamoto and his troops set off at a brisk pace at the head of the line of stronger prisoners. The rest of his men wait. After a day's delay, due to heavy rain, the tottering figures in the rear follow, goaded along by at least several Formosan guards taking up the rear.

After about seven miles of bitumen, they enter the 'green cage' along a jungle track about ten feet wide: 'Once you leave the road and . . . walk on this track you feel as if you have left the last shred of civilisation behind you,' writes one observer. '[I]t feels as if you are starting a journey into another world.'² Ration points and supply dumps are said to have been set up along the route, at Maunad (49.5 miles), Sapi (60 miles), Boto (103 miles), Papan (120 miles) and Paginatan (138 miles). These caches are primarily for the Japanese, with a residual amount set aside to sustain the prisoners. The thought alone helps to drive the men on, stumbling and sliding along the muddy path. They soon tear off, or wear out, their flimsy rubber shoes, which offer little grip, and continue in bare feet.

The jungle closes around this wretched file. Nature's better adapted species are raucously evident: the grunts of wild boar, the screams of monkey and orang-utan. The men press on, oblivious. Waving to and fro on leaves and stones, the Borneo brown leech attaches itself to the passing feast of bare flesh, injects an anti-coagulant and feeds. Only a burnt stick or prized cigarette or a sprinkle of vital salt easily removes the parasite, leaving streams of blood – a minor irritant in the spectrum of their concerns.

Mud flats between the swollen tributaries of the Labuk River delay progress. At one point, the file surmounts a crocodile-infested swamp along a bamboo boardwalk. The 'march' – it is never a march – henceforth degenerates into a plodding, silent trudge, and the men, driven by the sheer mental will to live, cling to thoughts beyond their immediate pain, somewhere *not here*.

◆

The going is flat, at first, with jungle-clad hills that suddenly rise out of the tangled lowlands and severely test the weak. Beyond the 15-mile marker, banana trees, bamboo and palms gather thickly by the track, interspersed with long, orderly lines of rubber. Here and there, set in small dirt clearings, are the stilted kampongs of farmers, bordered by coconut and tapioca. In the dirty yards, children stand and gawk at the passing white men, until their frightened parents usher them inside, behind the bamboo screens, to sit on the earthen floor, which they share with a goat and a few scrawny fowl.

At the end of the first day, the prisoners collapse on the

swampy forest floor, somewhere beyond the Gum Gum River. The stragglers come in, sucking lungfuls of air. These men endure the worst of it, because the guards refuse to let them rest when they reach the points where the stronger men wait. Forced to continue, they fall further back with every stage. Those first nights, in and above the swamps, the men search for the driest, leech-free spot, a tree to lean on. Some fashion a '*sulap*' or lean-to, out of a banana palm. Sometimes, a native hut is available for shelter. Most nights, they just lie on the ground. Mosquitoes are their nightly companions, and only the hacking coughs of the sick and the dismal rain on the forest canopy interrupt their constant whine.

After four days, the column reaches the Maunad River. The first group receives the first share of the food dumps. It lifts their spirits. But sickness kills several men, including the huge Bob Chipperfield and Herbert Dorizzi, youngest of three brothers, whose brother Gordon dies on the same day back in Sandakan.

The later groups are worse off, as the food dumps are rapidly exhausted. Some never existed. Often, the Formosans, or Japanese, move ahead and gorge themselves on the supplies. At Buta, the third supply point, little food is left for the upcoming third and fourth groups of prisoners, and virtually nothing for the seventh, eighth and ninth. And so the rations they carry, that were supposed to last four days, must stretch to eight.[3] But very little of the original ration is left, and the men are horrified to discover that their remaining food amounts to two meals a day, each consisting of 'a pint of watery rice garnished with whatever greens they could get . . . usually edible foliage from the jungle and nearly always fern tips'. A natural banquet exists in the jungle: wild ginger, bananas, snails, jungle crabs, figs, cumquats, limes, tapioca, betelnut, and an array of edible bugs and caterpillars. Wild boar and three species of deer roam the jungle floor, while monkeys cavort in the trees – routine targets for local hunters armed with blowpipes and knives.[4] None of it is available to the prisoners, who are not permitted to leave the track. As they pass through villages, some men implore the inhabitants to share their food supplies – but the locals risk severe punishment if caught.

◆

Men stumble and fall. A desultory effort is made to carry the sick and lame on makeshift stretchers, but exhaustion overwhelms the most determined efforts of the stretcher-bearers. Gradually, the stragglers succumb, lie down by the track, unable to move, and pass away. The mud, the weight, the lack of food, grind down the strongest constitutions, already suffering from either dysentery, malaria or beriberi. Not all of the men are so afflicted, yet most have some kind of tropical ailment or leg ulcer. Their friends press the stragglers to get up before the guards arrive to decide the issue.

If the combination of disease and hunger doesn't kill a man, the Japanese or Formosan guards finish the job. The shooting, bayoneting or clubbing to death of prisoners unable to walk is a settled policy, determined well before the prisoners leave Sandakan. The termination begins now, in hidden jungle clearings, or behind trees, by the side of the track. Men who drop out are 'immediately shot', Botterill later recalls. 'I saw four men shot . . . by the Japanese sergeant-major.'[5]

Not all the Japanese officers are trigger-happy brutes, but that does not mean they are humane. They are pragmatic, self-interested. Their own health is failing. They realise they need the prisoners to bear food and supplies. So they try to keep the men on their feet. Botterill later says that the commanding officer, Lieutenant Toyohara Kihaku, of Group 3, tries to help the men as much as possible.[6] He sends the sick and weak ahead each morning, to give them an hour's head start. Regardless, once a man cannot lift himself off the ground, he ceases to be of any use.

Nobody knows how many die of disease and how many are murdered. The willingness and brutality with which the Japanese and Formosans dispatch the prisoners varies according to the character of the executioner. All function under Abe's orders, but not all act accordingly: some seem to delight in blood and relish the job; others consider the slaughter a regrettable if necessary business.

A few shun the order to kill already dying men. When an Australian sergeant, for example, his legs severely bloated with beriberi, drops out, he seems to 'go off his head' and pleads with Warrant Officer Clive Warrington, the most senior-ranked prisoner in the group, to shoot him. Lieutenant Toyohara tries to encourage the sergeant. At this, the sick man goes berserk, 'shouting insults at the Japanese and pleading for someone to kill him', as the historian Lynette Silver records.[7] He then refuses to move. Sergeant Major Gotanda is deputed to shoot him, but only with the consent of Warrington. Warrington obliges and writes out an authority, but Gotanda cannot pull the trigger. The prisoner is now thrashing about on the ground, 'paralysed from the waist down', and 'completely mad', according to one witness.[8] So Gotanda hands Warrington his revolver and orders him to kill the sergeant. This Warrington does. 'He had to be shot; he was struggling against us when we were trying to help him, and then I shot him,' Warrington is later quoted as saying.[9]

In time, shooting the stragglers becomes a routine task, a perfunctory duty, for the Formosans and Japanese. The preliminary paperwork that logged the first casualties is soon dispensed with. No orders are given. Abe's killing platoon are fully briefed. A week out of Ranau, as they ascend a steep hill towards Telupid, two Australians, Private David Humphries and Corporal Donald Palmer, collapse, too sick to continue. Japanese soldiers shoot them where they lie. Three more Australian prisoners are shortly murdered on that forgotten hill.[10]

The dreadful reports in the rear spur on the upright and conjure scenes of their own bodies lying unclaimed in this savage world. The horror of dying here, in this dreadful place, on the whim of brutes, drives the stronger into a green hell. In some men, the qualities of fairness and duty fall away like a curtain over a caged beast. 'We turned into animals,' says Botterill later, 'and that's how we survived. If you tried to be human you were left behind and died.'[11]

Self-sacrifice and courage mean nothing without the ingredients necessary to sustain them, essentially food and health. And, with every passing day, the food supply declines. The guards devour the forward dumps, and the later groups, desperate for sustenance, find only a few scraps. Each group finds the food supply a little poorer than the group that preceded it, to the extent that the Japanese themselves are compelled to act. Lieutenant Toyohara of Group 3 sends a corporal forward to reconnoitre the food situation and, if necessary, barter for livestock with the surrounding villages, using blankets, clothes and any personal belongings confiscated from the prisoners. By the time the last groups reach Paginatan, 'even the local villages were running out of food available for barter', notes Professor Tanaka. 'The situation became so desperate that Japanese soldiers resorted to stealing rations from POWs.'[12]

And yet, at this stage of the journey, Botterill's bestial instincts do not apply to everyone. Most of the men have not yet yielded to the basest self-interest. Botterill underestimates the determination and resilience of those who share their fellow soldiers' burden, who encourage and reassure the younger, or sickest men. Some of these are tearful and inconsolable; others at the outer limits of sanity. Their helpers and mates retain an elemental goodness. They know they must not give in or fall behind. The doctors attend to those with broken limbs, infected wounds, shaking bodies and liquid bowels with a dedication that sublimates the spirit of the Hippocratic Oath. Consider Warrant Officer A. E. Johns, of the Royal Army Medical Corps, who has even 'impressed the Japanese immensely by the manner in which he attempts to protect the other PW members of his party'.[13]

The padres and chaplains, too, use their battered authority and reliance on gods and saints to aid and reassure the men. If such terrible circumstances test their faith, they dare not admit doubt to the searching eyes of dying men, with no other consolation in their last living moments than the promise of an afterlife.

◆

Soon, the rear groups stumble upon the casualties of the forward ones. They encounter men crawling along the rentis, barely alive, desperate to keep moving. The familiar sound of gunfire terminates these ghastly cases. 'We would go on and then shortly after hear shots and men squealing out,' records Botterill later. 'When this occurred there were always Japanese behind us, and it was they who did the shooting. Although I did not see the bodies of any men who had been shot in the parties that had gone before me, often I could smell them.'[14]

Private Bill Moxham, of Group 7, passes many bodies but cannot recognise them in the haste to move on, prodded and goaded by the guards. At one point, he sees a corpse 'sprawled right across the track' with a shovel in its hands – 'he had not been dead very long'; at another, he recognises the colour patch on the uniform of Gunner Williams, from his own regiment, the 2/10th, now dead. 'The guards kept us going at full pace all the time,' he later recalls. 'On the way, I suppose I saw or smelt between 20 and 30 bodies. There could have been a lot more.'[15]

Of his group, 44 out of 50 reach Paginatan, where many collapse and die. The six who have failed to make it perish either from sickness or gunfire. In one case, Moxham and four others receive permission from the Japanese to go back and retrieve a sick man. 'We brought him to camp, but he was dead next morning,' Moxham later recalls. In the case of Private Tom Coughlan, the Japanese 'refused to permit us to return for him. I suppose they shot him . . . In all my dealings with the Japanese, I have never seen anyone of our chaps after they have been left with the Japs. Once you stopped – you stopped for good.'[16]

The ninth group is the last in the long line of prisoners, guards and troops that snakes over the land, through swamps, up hills, down valleys, past jungle, across grassland and rubber, and finally up the long ascent via Paginatan to Ranau. The torn shorts or patches of Group 9 are the only signs that these men were once members of the Royal Army, Royal Artillery or Royal Air Force. Their bodies are scarified by the sun, their ribcages protruding through taut skin, their legs buckling under the weight of their burdens, their minds focused on their next meal, the man in front, the proximity of the guards. Every few places down the line, men drop out, fall to their knees and inch forward on all fours in anticipation of the bullet or blow to the head. For this group of British prisoners receives virtually no extra food: all the food dumps are near exhausted.

Some men wander, delirious, off the path and into the forest, pleading for relief, imploring the sky – anything to deliver them from the agony of starvation. Deliverance is not long coming up the track. The report of gunshot, the thudding blade announce the arrival of Abe's men, followed by a flutter of birds and resumption of the forest hum. No more the sound of human pleas or the shouts of futile defiance.

As their circumstances worsen and revulsion sets in, a few of Abe's hand-selected thugs refuse to obey orders to join in the daily round of horror. According to later testimony by one of Abe's guards, Private Endo:

> I was left with a party of five. These five men were very sick and suffering a great deal. Although my orders from Lieutenant Abe were to kill them I did not have the heart to do such a thing, and so left them behind, without food and water, to die. I believe that Private Sato [another member of the killing platoon] did the same thing. On these occasions there were no officers or NCOs present to see that we carried out our orders. Looking back now and remembering how ill the POWs were I feel it might have been more humane to have killed them and buried them before going on.[17]

◆

Some men dream of escape, but the Japanese have no need to worry, it seems. The prisoners, they conclude, have neither the strength to run for it nor the willpower to sustain themselves through days or weeks of jungle. That, however, underestimates a determined and resourceful few, who never lose an eye on the main chance should it present itself, despite their appalling circumstances.

Several prisoners, aware of their likely fate, conjure suicidal escape plans. Five members of Group 2 plunge into the jungle somewhere between the Mandorin and Sapi Rivers, and disappear without trace. Another five of Group 5 similarly flee the wretched line and reach Mumiang on the coast, are recaptured and suffer terrible beatings before being shot or dying of sickness.

Equally daring is the breakout attempt of four extremely sick men: two Australians, Corporal Ken Molde (also known as Leigh Dawson) and Gunner Eric Fuller; and two Britons, Gunner Bois Roberts and Leading Aircraftman Herbert Beardshaw. On 13 February, Dawson and Fuller fall back on Bauto, before the steep ascent to Telupid, where the British prisoners catch up with them. None is fit to continue the march; all face death at the hands of the guards, then moving up the track towards them. They decide to make a last desperate bid for life. Flailing through the forest, travelling only at night, the four men survive for several days, until their discovery on 17 February by Hussin bin Ulan, who cares for them in his village. Here, despite the brave charity of the native people, they gradually expire, one by one, between March and May, of dysentery, beriberi and general weakness.

Many prisoners give up and refuse to move. A mile past

Nelapak, Allan Quailey slumps against a tree. His friend Richard Murray urges him to get up and walk. Quailey refuses. Soon, the guards arrive; they order Murray to keep moving. The sound of gunshot confirms Quailey's end, as Murray later tells Botterill. Dozens are similarly dealt with, including the seriously ill Gunner Perc Carter and his friend Sapper Len Haye, a stretcher case, whose condition is reported by Kulang, the ubiquitous headman who now witnesses the unintended consequences of his attempt to make the track as difficult as possible. Kulang offers to care for the sick men in his hut, but the Japanese refuse. Instead, Carter and Haye are transferred to a spot 110 yards from the Maunad camp. Before they leave, Carter gives Kulang a photo of his family. A little while later, the headman hears two shots: Haye dies still lying in his stretcher.

Or they are literally beaten to death. When the Australian medic Private Rod Richards dares object to being prodded in the back with a rifle, the guard binds Richards' hands, beats him senseless and throws the bleeding body into a gully by the side of the track. Next morning, prisoners of war and guards coming up the track hear Richards' cries of agony and scramble down to find him partially paralysed. He later collapses before the column arrives at Tampias.[18]

Groups 6 to 9 comprise more than 100 British servicemen, many of whom are killed with similar relish or expediency, with the curious exception of two seriously ill prisoners, Private George Carter, of Group 6, and an unnamed British soldier, who are sent back to Sandakan with two sick Japanese guards. When he hears of this error, Yamamoto severely reprimands the group's commander, Lieutenant Tanaka Shojiro, who promises to apply a harsher regime in future. Indeed, Group 6 of the First

Death March appears to be the worst for cruelty. Tanaka insists, for example, on the prisoners carrying his luggage strung up on bamboo poles as well as their other loads, and he does not make any effort to control the rampaging Formosans (one of whom is responsible for Richards' fate).

At the village of Tampias, they feed on tapioca, ferns, sweet potatoes – anything growing and edible. Here, the Lubak River must be forded, and the prisoners line up to wade across at the shallowest point; the sickest are put in canoes. The Japanese cross by boat. Local tribesmen are pressed into service as boatmen. A native canoeist called Yumpil bin Yaron, now very old and weather-worn – just as one would imagine a Dusun 'ferryman' – later describes the scene: 'The canoes took four prisoners each. We took them across the river for two Japanese dollars per week.'[19] The prisoners point at fruit and then at their open mouths, hoping the local people will get some. 'They pointed at passionfruit, tapioca, anything they could eat,' Yumpil says. But it is forbidden to feed the white men.

Prisoners who do not have the energy to cross the river are shot, Yumpil recalls: 'The Japanese would ask the prisoner-of-war to move, but the prisoner-of-war very weak and couldn't move, so the Japanese just shot them.'[20] How did he feel, helping the Japanese to get these dreadfully sick young men over the river? 'Very sad. Sometimes I cried because I couldn't do anything to help them.' But he remembers also feeling 'very angry at the Japanese'. Indeed, his tribe has set traps in the jungle for Japanese stragglers and hunts them down with its blowpipes. Yumpil also recalls seeing many Japanese corpses scattered along the track, killed by disease and, later, strafing by Allied planes. 'The Japanese would chop the hands off the bodies' – Yumpil does a chopping action with one hand – 'and send the bones home'.[21]

Only the first group manages the requisite 11 miles a day. Eleven are dead by the time they reach Paginatan, a little village perched on an embankment above the Labuk River, some 28 miles from Ranau. Japanese troops have visited a scorched-earth policy on the local people here, which breeds intense hatred. Reports of tribal girls being carried off, never to be heard of again, are common, according to a woman living near Paginatan.[22] One tribal elder, Zudin, 15 at the time, claims that he and his friends so hated the occupying forces that they hunted down and killed 'about 100 Japanese stragglers' with their blowpipes: 'We only attacked the last ones in the line then ran away into the jungle.'[23] Zudin reckons he can kill a monkey with his blowpipe at 33 yards.

Near Paginatan, six prisoners stagger into the jungle in a desperate attempt to escape. A native girl, Domima, 12 years old, is feeding her family's pigs in the area when she encounters the men, who attract her attention by throwing small stones. She tells her father, who instructs her to take rice and fish to the men. Three times a day, for six days, she lays the food in the same place, but she only sees the wasted bodies of the men once – an unforgettable sight, she says. On the seventh day, the escapees have gone, leaving a little can: 'At first I was scared because I thought it was a bomb.' But she summons her courage. 'It made a rattling sound.' She opens the can and finds six gold wedding rings, the soldiers' last possessions. Her family hides them under their house. Domima, now about 80, still wears one of the rings. The soldiers never return – and are either shot or die of illness.[24]

Two more Australians expire on the gruelling final climb from Paginatan to the Ranau plateau. Of the 55 who set off in the first group, 42 reach Ranau on 12 February, 15 days after they left Sandakan. Of Group 9, just 22 of 50 British prisoners make it – most collapsed from hunger, after finding the food dumps exhausted, and were shot.[25] On 19 February, 189 of the 275 men in the first five groups, and about 120 of the 190 men in the last four, have survived the march. In total, 309 prisoners have reached Ranau and Paginatan, out of the 455 'fittest' prisoners who left Sandakan.[26]

25

THE GUARDS

One [Australian] was puffed up with beri beri in the
legs and face and was getting along all right on his own
and could have made it; but the Japs would not leave
him alone, they tried to force him along, and eventually
he collapsed. They kicked him on the ground . . .

Private Bill Moxham

RANAU IN 1945 IS A VILLAGE of earthen streets, bamboo
and palm-frond kampongs, and cinnamon-coloured atap shops
set on a river flat in the shadow of Mount Kinabalu. The tranquil
appearance is deceptive: a Japanese garrison occupies the town.
Most of the inhabitants have left, to join the fighters in the forests.
In the foothills of the sacred peak live the Dusun and other tribal
groups, still flush with the spirit of resistance after the collapse
of the Double Tenth. Stories of rape, murder, cannibalism and
torture by the Japanese foment fear and loathing of the occupying
forces. Japanese reprisals have been thorough after the terrible end
of Kwok's Kinabalu Guerrillas. The villages around Ranau have
been torched or occupied, forcing thousands into the forest to live
off the land, using their blowpipes to kill wild boar, monkeys,
birds – and Japanese stragglers. Locals tell grisly tales of tribesmen

being tied up and 'eaten slowly', kept alive to preserve the uneaten flesh – a practice also recorded by Papuan natives during the Japanese occupation in 1942.

At the village of Sinarut, near Ranau, the survivors of the First March are ordered to stop; here, they will camp temporarily. They are incapable of reaching Tuaran – even the guards can see this glaring fact. All have dysentery, beriberi and/or malaria. They are now corralled into a wired enclosure – 'No. 1 Prison Camp' – containing a few atap huts, close to the airstrip, under the command of Lieutenant Watanabe Genzo, who has recently arrived from Kuching.

Their severely depleted numbers, and broken condition, disturb Watanabe's estimations. How, he wonders, will these men complete their new duties? Specifically, how will they carry rice to the Japanese garrison back in Paginatan? His concern is a matter of military pragmatism. The war is rapidly coming to Borneo; even in Ranau, the threat of air bombardment is ever-present. A sense of being isolated, cut off in the South-West Pacific, gradually pervades the Japanese garrison, as the Allied armies swirl around this great green island.

The men no longer observe the exacting standards of fairness they did in Sandakan: '[W]hen they arrived at Ranau most of them developed the habit of keeping all they could get for themselves,' according to Jackson's account. 'Jealousy and suspicion was rife, and maltreatment and starvation had affected some of their minds to such a state that they acted like primitive people and animals . . . quarrelling over food.'[1] It is an accurate, if callously worded, description: what on earth are these men to do other than scrape and beg and fight for their next meal?

The natives witness the rapid rate of attrition with helpless dismay. Some try to give food to the passing lines. Encountering a few white men lingering on 'Tamu', or market day, who frantically indicate their hunger by pointing to their mouths, the locals slip them a little rice, tapioca and other morsels, which they squirrel away in their loincloths or torn shirts.

'I saw the Australian soldiers marching past near the Japanese rest house twelve kilometres from Ranau,' according to one Mrs Pelabiew, a girl at the time, whose family live in Ranau:

> The soldiers were staggering along, some leaning on sticks as they walked. They were very weak and in bad condition, some wearing shirts and many of them wearing big hats. Our people had great sympathy for them, but we could do nothing. I was a very little girl, and on one occasion I gave the prisoners some left-over scraps from Japanese meals. My mother let me give them rice and tapioca. They hid the food in the pockets of their shirts. They were very hungry and would eat any jungle foods they could find. The Japanese were well fed.[2]

◆

Their dire condition has no influence on Japanese orders that they keep working – *marching*. The Japanese supply lines are severely strained, yet their garrisons in Ranau and Paginatan require a steady resupply of food and equipment. To this gruelling task – the delivery of supplies between the two kampongs – the remnant of the First March is now assigned.

If the fitter prisoners in Groups 1 to 5 are in no state to do so, those in the last groups now spilling into Paginatan are utterly wretched. These 195 men – many of them British – have received the smallest share of the food dumps and only about 130 live to see Paginatan, according to one source. (The figure varies – other sources claim that 138 or 160 reach Paginatan.)[3] Within days of their arrival, many succumb to sickness and hunger. Within four weeks, about 70–80 die. By early March, only about 30–40 are alive.

They eke out an existence in deserted huts, or in the open, awaiting the move to Ranau. 'I was at Paginatan for a month,' Moxham later says. 'We were told the reason for being retained there was that the Ranau barracks were not finished; but that was a joke because they were never built.'[4]

The real reason, of course, is to keep them back to serve as carriers on the Paginatan–Ranau shuttle. Oblivious to the horrendous rate of attrition, the guards, under the command of Lieutenant Watanabe Genzo and Captain Nagai Hirawa, order the few dozen survivors at Paginatan to shoulder bags of rice weighing 44 pounds and other supplies and carry them to Ranau, reload, and return – a round trip of five days over the steepest sections of the track.

Paginatan sits on an embankment above the Labuk River, in a reasonably flat stretch of the track, comprising about eight village huts set in thick jungle that presses in on three sides. From here, the track rises and falls for some five miles to Segindai, where a small rest hut offers a brief reprieve, then twists around a steep mountainside for another four miles. This is the most severe section, causing many of the prisoners to collapse. From Segindai, those still alive and on their feet grunt and sweat for a further three miles, over mercifully flat terrain, to Nelapak. It is then another six miles to Muruk, where they rest overnight in the shade of a huge tree overhanging a natural swimming hole in the Kenanapan River. The day starts with another steep ascent, then the last eight-mile stretch to Ranau.

The journey kills about half the men who attempt it, according to Botterill, who survives the trip. Among those who perish is John Brinkman, the beloved son of a family of Dutch émigrés who came to Australia when the boy was eight. He grew up in Sydney and attended Sydney Boys High School. Alas, years later, his distraught mother will destroy his letters before she passes away, but one postcard from Borneo remains extant. 'Dear Relatives,' Brinkman writes, 'My health is GOOD' (he uses capitalised words in the spaces provided on the Japanese card). 'Please remember me to EVERYONE – POW Camp Borneo.'[5]

As usual, the sick are slaughtered in the rear as they fall out. The survivors are ordered to repeat the trip. They repeat it six times. Moxham remembers burying 'four to five bodies' a day during the month in Paginatan, and on the march. They eat ferns, snails, frogs. '[O]ne party caught some pythons,' he recalls. 'They got anything at all to make up for the food they should have got from the Japs.'[6] Anything to propel them forward, because 'once you stopped', Botterill adds, 'you stopped for good. The Japs had no time for the sick. They would not even feed them.'[7]

By 1 April 1945, 302 of the original 455 Australians and British who left Sandakan three months earlier are dead: 123 have died on the main journey; 89 at Ranau; and about 90 at the Paginatan camp and on the six rice journeys between Paginatan and Ranau.[8] By 25 April – Anzac Day – the death toll has soared to 90 per cent: just 46 members of the First March remain alive. On this day, when Australians at home stand in silent commemoration of previous wars, the Allies bomb Ranau for the first time and the Japanese retaliate, as usual, by punishing the few prisoners left.

◆

In such appalling circumstances, it is simple to present the Japanese commanders and guards as monsters. It is hard, and perhaps unconscionable, to attempt to examine them as normal human beings. But we must try to understand them if we are to comprehend why they behave as they do. Most are Formosan – the curious Sino-Japanese issue of the former Japanese colony – some 30–40 of whom are assigned to each prisoner group under the command of two Japanese officers.

The Formosans are young, unintelligent, brutalised and terrified of their masters. They find themselves hungry and sick in a strange land, guarding a line of white men whose dreadful state seems a shocking harbinger of their own. Unsurprising, then, that the Formosans tend to follow to the letter, or seek to outdo, the vicious example of their Japanese overlords. They hope to curry favour with their Japanese masters – and perhaps extract a little more food, or better conditions, for themselves. With a few extraordinary exceptions, they resort to any act of brutality that might enhance their chances of survival.

The Japanese and Formosans, for example, appropriate most of the food supply and confiscate the prisoners' blankets and any clothing, to trade for extra food with the native people. 'The Japs thus obtained some sweet potatoes and pigs,' Bill Moxham later recalls. 'We got only a few sweet potatoes.' The guards – Japanese and Formosan – consider sick or disabled prisoners as a burden and an inconvenience. Some derive sadistic pleasure from bashing and killing them, and forcing other prisoners to witness it. 'On the march from Paginatan to Ranau, I think 24 of our 36 died,' Moxham later says:

> One was puffed up with beri beri in the legs and face and was getting along all right on his own and could have made it; but the Japs would not leave him alone, they tried to force him along, and eventually he collapsed. They kicked him on the ground . . .

The man is called Noel Parker. A Formosan guard, Hayashi, nicknamed 'Ming the Merciless', continues bashing Parker in the head with a rifle butt. 'The soldier was left there. The party marched on,' Moxham later states.[9]

Warrant Officer Kinder returns to plead with Hayashi to stop, but, brandishing his rifle at Kinder, the Formosan continues beating Parker for another ten minutes. He dies soon afterwards. Botterill, coming up the track with a rice bag, encounters Parker's bloody corpse. The guards forced Kinder to watch him being killed, Botterill later claims.[10]

◆

What sort of men are capable of such acts? Questions of motive mean little to the prisoners at this point. Their daily struggle is to stay vertical, to move forward and to find food. But for as long as they have life in them, they will not forget the names and faces of their torturers.

Those names and faces are little-known to us. Few photographs are available. Their actual characters are elusive. We see them through the prisoners' eyes, as brutes, freaks of nature, animals with nicknames. A handful exhibit signs of recognisable humanity; most are simply indifferent to the prisoners' fate, concerned only with their survival. Some seem to swing between extremes: cruel and coarse one moment, docile and apologetic the next. Others are plain brutes and murderers, who will 'follow orders' if it drives everyone under their command into the maw of hell. Prominently represented among the latter species are the officers and higher ranks:

- Captain Yamamoto Shoichi, commander of the First March, who presses the men on when it is clear that most are on the verge of collapse. On his orders, the killing squad goes calmly about its business, killing stragglers. Yamamoto feels – if he can be said to feel – only for his fellow soldiers. Of Lieutenant Abe Kazuo, commander of the killing squad, for example, he later says, 'I felt sorry for him . . . as [Lieutenant] Abe's group was the last in the march, I thought that there may not be sufficient food and medical supplies.'[11]
- Lieutenant Abe Kazuo, an officer in the 20th Independent Machine Gun Battalion. He and his killing platoon are responsible for the slaughter of hundreds of sick men, which commences in earnest after Maunad.
- Captain Nagai Hirawa, a Japanese guard well known to British prisoners. He commanded the transfer of the British from Jesselton to Sandakan in 1942 and, in 1944, moved British officers to Labuan, where many would die, in shocking conditions. Nagai is

sometimes considerate, in small ways, such as lending his gramophone to the British officers' medical clinic in Jesselton and permitting the British to bury their dead with proper funeral services. He befriends Warrant Officer Sticpewich, whom he respects. Yet he can suddenly switch to extreme malice: for example, laughing when an Australian burial party in Ranau drops a corpse and furiously ordering Botterill and others to endure a sixth rice journey to Paginatan, when it is clear that several will die. Like many Japanese officers, he admires his counterparts in the Allied army and holds other ranks in contempt.

Every step of the journey is taken in fear of the Japanese and Formosan guards, of whom Kiyoshima, Kawakami, Kitamura, Fukishima, Hayashi, Beppu Yoichi and Okada Toshiharu are the most reviled. Several worked at the drome, and in the Sandakan camp, and are notorious for their brutality. Kunizowa (Euclid) is memorable for jumping on the prisoners' backs when they were too weak to raise their bodies. Beppu, Hayashi and Okada are of a similar mould: sullen, self-loathing young men, terrified of their superiors and contemptuous of the prisoners, whose very existence they blame for their own tribulations, for which they seek to destroy them.

◆

Back at Sandakan, in late April, a new commandant, Captain Takakuwa Takuo, is about to succeed Hoshijima, who receives notice that he is to be relieved of his duties. As Takakuwa prepares to leave for Sandakan, he receives fresh orders from Baba in Kuching: to clear the remaining prisoners of war, and force-march every last Australian and British prisoner to Ranau.

On assuming command, Takakuwa realises the prisoners cannot manage this. He then further reduces their chances of survival by refusing, or failing, to feed them:

> Rice supplies to Sandakan had been cut off during the time of Captain Hoshijima . . . The Japanese received their food rations through the Army but PWs only had what they grew themselves. I officially issued no rice to them while I was there and I consider that they did not have sufficient to live on. I tried to get rice for them but orders forbade it so I let them have the tapioca they were growing.[12]

In short, the Japanese are being fed and the prisoners starved. To Takakuwa, the message is palpably clear: 37 Army Headquarters has no further use for the prisoners. His job is to finish them off.

26

AN EXAMPLE

[H]e only attempted to escape in order to receive the
bullet that would release him from his misery.
Jackson report, on the cases of Cleary and Crease

THE MEN ARE NOT SUPINE in their extremity. A flicker of
hope appears at each turn. Is this the end? Have we reached a rest
point? Is there food in the next village? Perhaps we can survive on
frogs and snails, on fruit and leaves? The more resilient, resourceful
or conniving – men such as Botterill, Sticpewich and Moxham –
never lose sight of the chance of escape. Botterill devises shrewd
methods of accumulating rice, fruit and other forest nutrients on
his rice-carrying missions between Paginatan and Ranau – for
which he doggedly volunteers, despite the exhausting journey,
to avoid contact with sick prisoners then dying in the villages at
either end. The strength to keep moving helps save his life.

Hope, too, persists in the minds of the plainly hopeless
cases, who stagger along in a kind of suspended disbelief in
certain death. Their very movement proves they are alive, against
impossible odds. Many soon falter and slide to their knees. Inertia,
they know, is a death sentence; and they await the end with
resignation, or perhaps relief. For most, it is mercifully swift: by

gunshot. At least one soldier, however, is strangled, and many are killed with a blow to the head, mutilated or bayoneted to death.

Worse is about to descend on the Australian and British prisoners. Most of the young Formosan guards are now beyond the reach of any recognisable human constraint; several are plainly insane. Their own condition is dire. More than two dozen have already died and many are very sick or hungry. If they drop, they too can expect instant death. In this, the Japanese killing squads are at least consistent: they apply the same rules to their own as they apply to the guards and prisoners. In fact, of the 35 Japanese and Formosans who have perished so far on the march, most have been killed by Japanese death squads bringing up the rear, whose orders are to shoot *anyone* who cannot walk.

And the guards feel increasingly desperate – and isolated – especially after the Japanese soldiers then garrisoned at Ranau are ordered to continue to Tuaran. Their departure – without their 'white coolies' – signifies an unspoken fact: the prisoners have reached the end of their usefulness. In this atmosphere, death is only a matter of time. The Formosans and a few Japanese officers who remain behind – including Takakuwa, Nagai and Watanabe – tend to blame the surviving Australian and British prisoners for their every misfortune.

One constant source of acute concern are the frequent Allied bombing raids, which intensify over Ranau throughout March and April 1945. The prisoners are ordered to dig foxholes and bomb shelters outside the camp, for the use of the Japanese. Moxham later remembers Allied planes flying over and machine-gunning the Japanese positions and the prison camp itself, just a few atap huts surrounded by rolls of wire: '[W]e all ran out. The guards had their rifles up and were going to shoot anybody trying to get outside the wire.'[1] In such moments, the prisoners learn the meaning of the term 'human shields'.

◆

About this time, several guards are in disgrace for failing to prevent the escape of two young Australian gunners, Albert Cleary and his good friend Wally Crease, who dashed into the jungle on 1 March. Captain Nagai punishes the guards responsible – a new Japanese guard, Lieutenant Suzuki Taichi, whom the prisoners dub 'The Mongolian Monster', Kawakami and Kitamura – by sending them on a three-mile run followed by a public slapping. Their humiliation has an explicit aim: to see that this never happens again. The guards get the message, and intend to make an example of the escapees if and when caught. Suzuki later admits that he is seized by extreme 'hatred' for the errant Australians.[2]

Meanwhile, Crease and Cleary (also known as Gardner) are slogging through the forest in the hope of finding a few friendly Chinese, who earlier offered to help and guide them to the west coast. They last a week. On around 7 March, a Japanese patrol recaptures them and drags them back to Ranau. Keith Botterill, returning from his rice-carrying duties, witnesses the result as he passes the guardhouse. 'I saw Private Cleary kneeling down,' he later states, under oath, 'with a log behind his knees and between his legs. He only had a [loincloth] on, and had a lot of dried and fresh blood over his face and body. His arms were tied well up behind his back.'[3]

Kitamura, Kawakami, Suzuki and others 'kick viciously' all over Cleary's body, according to Botterill's account, 'the face and mouth and everywhere possible; holding his head up and hitting him in the throat with the bare knuckles. They were charging at him with a rifle and fixed bayonet, stopping about an inch from his face. I saw Kitamura spit at him . . .' Later, Botterill sees the same guards taking turns at jumping on each end of the log, 'making him scream'.[4] Botterill has, it seems wilfully, confused Suzuki Taichi with Suzuki Saburo. Though surely guilty of other war crimes, the evidence suggests that the latter is elsewhere during the torture of Cleary (see Chapter 40, The Trials).

Every half-hour, the guards drag the Australian to his feet. This takes several minutes, because his legs are virtually paralysed and crumple beneath the weight of his body. They prop him up and several guards – Japanese and Formosan – again rain blows on him, with their fists, sticks, rifle butts, 'anything that comes to hand'. The beatings and log treatment continue intermittently for five hours, until 7.30 that night, according to Botterill. All night, and especially during the changing of the guard, Cleary moans and screams. The next morning, they put Cleary back on the log and resume jumping on it, and beating him with their fists and rifle butts. Kawakami replaces Kitamura at 9 am – a tag team of torturers – and the pair continue thrashing Cleary. Then they turn to Crease, who is subjected to the same treatment. It goes on, intermittently, all day and into a third day, with three Japanese guards applying the torture.

Unable to bear any more, Crease makes a suicidal bid for freedom. While Kawakami's attention is diverted, Crease somehow raises himself and staggers out of the guardhouse, into the jungle – more a death wish than a serious effort to flee. '[H]e only attempted to escape in order to receive the bullet that would release him from his misery,' the Jackson report later concludes.[5]

At this point, Botterill's account must be read with great care. No doubt, these atrocities occurred – as the Jackson report and other sources aver (not least Lynette Silver's account and a 2012 report on The Global Mail website) – yet Botterill is an unreliable witness. After the war, he perjures himself at the War Crimes Tribunal, condemning at least two men against whom he has little evidence, as he confides to Lynette Silver years later. Yet it is clear from his witness statement that his testimony is deeply unreliable. The extraordinary detail about Cleary and Crease – the precise times, the measurements of the instruments of torture – suggests that he observes these events at very close range, over three days; indeed, he claims to have watched scenes of unimaginable horror for hours at a time. Yet why do the Japanese let him see such acts? Indeed, how is he able to? During the march, the Japanese were careful to kill the prisoners out of sight: in the jungle or off the track. Yet here, suddenly, Botterill is permitted to see the worst the Japanese guards can do. If he is present, as he claims, he dares not intervene or beg them to stop, as that might well mean a slow death sentence for him, too. But how can he look at all? He seems transfixed by the sight; he describes the men 'squealing' in agony, rather as one might describe a tormented animal.

In fairness, Botterill has himself endured the worst of Japanese punishment – some 40 days in the cage – and has good reason to embellish the horror of what he sees. Yet some of his facts are plainly dubious and his testimony exaggerated. He describes Crease, during his suicidal second escape attempt, as 'grabbing' an army work jacket and 'leaping' out of a window. A man who has endured two days of the log treatment cannot jump out of windows; he is scarcely able to walk. In a later interview, Botterill qualifies his account: '[Crease] was given the extra stamina to go by the thought that it was better to be shot in the back or anywhere.'[6]

◆

Yet other evidence – gleaned from the Jackson report and the later interrogation of the guards – supports Botterill's description of what happens next. The guards soon find Crease wandering the jungle and shoot him dead. Then, infuriated by Crease's second escape, they pile all their anger and humiliation onto Cleary. They chain this barely living creature to a tree ten yards from the guardhouse, fully exposed to the sun, wearing only a loincloth and in full view of everyone. Delirious with pain, Cleary howls like a wounded dog. 'Cleary was sitting down when I first saw him,' Botterill continues. 'He was very dirty and . . . had long blue blisters across his face and chest and legs; his body was covered with dried blood . . . There was excreta lying over the ground and over his legs.'

Each day, as they pass, the guards lay a perfunctory boot or fist into Cleary's inert form – they do this 'about 30 times a day', Botterill claims. How he is able to count the number of kicks remains a mystery. Sometimes, they spit or urinate on him. After three days, they dump the young man's body in a gutter between a dirt road and grass. Cleary lies there, almost unconscious.

The other prisoners seem dimly aware of something new in their midst – a kind of sustained sadism administered with an intensity they have hitherto not seen. '[The guards] were happy and enjoying it,' Botterill concludes.[7] The awful sight of Cleary prompts some to try to help. 'We continually asked [the Japanese],' Botterill later states, 'could we go to his assistance to give him some help to clean him up but it was refused so often it became useless.' Any prisoner seen trying to talk to, or feed, Cleary is severely beaten.

Cleary receives no medical attention; he hangs on to life on one meal a day, which flows straight through him. No doubt, he has acute dysentery, but to suggest this is his most critical ailment is like saying a baby seal torn apart by sharks died of influenza. The guards occasionally throw him some scraps of food. He endures this agony for four more days, during which Botterill manages to impart 'a few words of encouragement', to which Cleary replies, 'They are killing me,' or words to that effect. On the second-last day of his life, Cleary is forced to crawl back to the guardhouse ahead of a swinging Japanese boot. At last, his torturers dump him, a bag of blood and bones, at the feet of his fellow prisoners. 'If you escape the same thing will happen to you,' shouts Kawakami.

His friends carry Cleary to a stream, gently wash his body, feed and try to revive him. The appalled medics are unable to do anything other than 'let the poor bastard die'.[8]

On 20 March, after enduring almost 15 straight days of unimaginable torture, Cleary dies in a hut in the company of his fellow Australians. That day, a Japanese medical officer, Sergeant Okada, certifies that Cleary died of 'dysentery'.[9]

Bill Moxham: reckless, privately educated, insubordinate and a born survivor. He recalled burying 'four to five bodies' a day at Paginatan. (AWM 041486)

Bill Sticpewich: the consummate fixer, condemned by some as a 'friend' of the Japanese, who nonetheless proved a powerful witness at the war-crimes trials and vital in finding the relics of the dead. (AWM 122775)

Nelson Short: a cook and entertainer who feigned madness in Singapore in the hope of being sent home. On the Death Marches, he recalled shaking hands with men too weak to stand and saying goodbye. (AWM 041487)

Keith Botterill: the Nyngan-born Depression kid. He spent 40 days in the cage and later lied to the war-crimes trial in order to secure the execution of a Japanese prisoner. (AWM 041485)

Richard Braithwaite: thoughtful, highly intelligent, sustained by his unwavering anger at the enemy. After his escape, he came upon a Japanese soldier and, in a burst of vengeful fury, bashed him to death. (AWM 041488)

Owen Campbell: a farmer and a Christian, he escaped with three others and found himself wandering in delirium through the jungle after burying one of his friends. (AWM 041489)

Short, Sticpewich and Botterill (L to R): three of the six survivors (depicted on the previous two pages), who stayed alive through cunning, self-regard and sheer mental toughness. As Botterill later said, on the Death Marches, the selfless were as good as dead. (AWM OG3553)

The war-crimes trial in Tokyo summoned Bill Sticpewich to give evidence. Seen here in the dock, he gave vivid testimony about the Sandakan atrocities and was said to have fixed his eyes on Tojo as he spoke. (AWM P02289.002)

Gunner Albert Cleary, captured while trying to escape, was subjected for days to constant torture – tied up, kicked, beaten and urinated on – until he died of 'dysentery', according to the Japanese official records. (AWM P02468.516)

Wally Crease escaped with Cleary and was also captured and then tortured. Crease's and Cleary's story is one of the most barbaric acts of sustained cruelty imaginable. Crease managed to escape again and was shot. (AWM P02467.371)

Captain Lionel Matthews earned the George Cross for his astonishing courage as leader of the prisoners' resistance organisation and, when caught, for his refusal to break during weeks of hideous torture by the Kempei-tai. (AWM P02468.317)

Lieutenant Rod Wells' prodigious skills in electronics enabled him to design and help build an underground radio in the prison camp. Like Matthews, he never broke under torture.
(AWM P03863.001)

Chaplain Harold Wardale-Greenwood, who took up arms in Singapore and survived the Death Marches, died of disease in Ranau. Overwhelmed by scenes of Japanese cruelty to his men, he lost his religious faith.
(AWM P00102.014)

Dr James Taylor and his wife, Celia, were pivotal figures in the Sandakan underground, bravely defying the Japanese by helping to smuggle medicine and food to the prisoners and civilians.

Sergeant Dick Majinal, of the Borneo Police, who played an integral role in the Sandakan underground resistance – working with Matthews to smuggle food into the camp. (AWM P02494.038)

Halima binte Binting, the formidable wife of Matusup bin Gungau, who was executed by the Japanese for his central role in the underground. (AWM P02494.021)

Three children of Ernesto Lagan, one of the heroes of the resistance. Kempei-tai agents threatened them with torture to extract information from Ernesto's wife. (AWM P02494.025)

Katherine Lagan, Ernesto's wife, refused to accept that the Japanese had executed her husband and spent the rest of her life awaiting his return. (AWM P02494.026)

Kulang, the ubiquitous Dusun headman, hunted the enemy with his blowpipe and, according to Major Jackson, held the secret 'of many a Jap death in Borneo'. (AWM 042512)

Barigah, a Dusun farmer, proved crucial to saving the lives of Moxham, Botterill and Short. Defying the Japanese, he sheltered and fed the escapees, and delivered a rescue note to Allied commandos. (AWM 042561)

At the age of 12, Domima binte Akui – the 'ring lady' – gave food to Australian soldiers who had escaped the Japanese. They repaid her kindness by giving her their wedding rings. She still possesses one. (Mark Friezer)

Yumpil bin Yaron was forced to assist the Japanese in ferrying the Australian and British prisoners across a river in small native canoes. He remembers feeling very sad, 'because I could not do anything to help them'. (Mark Friezer)

Aged 15, Zudin and his native friends so hated the enemy that they hunted down and attacked Japanese stragglers with their blowpipes. He claims they shot and killed 'about 100'.
(Mark Friezer)

Proud, prickly, and contemptuous of his British superiors, Lieutenant General Gordon Bennett, the Australian commander in Malaya, is infamous for fleeing Singapore and leaving his men to Japanese captivity. (AWM P01461.002)

General Sir Thomas Blamey, the most senior Australian commander in the Pacific, was loth to divert scarce resources to a proposal to rescue the prisoners in Borneo. A sound administrator, he is credited with the creation of Special Operations Australia (SOA). (AWM P03014.017)

Blamey and the supreme commander in the Pacific, General Douglas MacArthur, had a difficult relationship. Blamey later blamed MacArthur for abandoning a 'plan' to rescue the prisoners, when in fact they had both opposed the idea. (State Library of Victoria H30887)

At the fall of Singapore, the Japanese Army threatened to enter the city and slaughter civilians unless the British surrendered the colony. Chaos reigned, and many Allied soldiers deserted as the Japanese bombed the island. (State Library of Victoria H99.200/732)

At the surrender of Singapore, 50,000 British and Australian troops entered Japanese captivity; about a third would die in dreadful conditions in prison camps throughout the Japanese Empire. Virtually all of those destined for Sandakan and the Death Marches would never come home. (Mondadori via Getty Images, 141556273)

The burnt-out frame of a prisoners' hut in the Sandakan Prisoner of War Camp. The Japanese torched the huts before they fled inland, to Ranau, driving more than a thousand sick and starving prisoners before them. Hundreds of bodies were later found in the vicinity. (AWM 120457)

Emaciated Chinese, Malay and Javanese men, women and children in a wrecked shed, used as a temporary hospital, in Sandakan, eight days after the Allies landed in Borneo. Desperately ill, the people lie on bare boards open to the weather, with no water and little food. Such was the legacy of the Japanese occupation. (AWM 121774)

Paginatan village was a Japanese food dump and garrison, 26 miles on the Sandakan side of Ranau. From here, the Australian and British prisoners were forced to carry heavy rice loads back and forth over the mountains to Ranau. (AWM 042511)

Near Paginatan, North Borneo, in October 1950. Members of the Australian–British Reward Mission retrace the route taken on the Sandakan–Ranau Death Marches in order to locate and reward those natives who had assisted the prisoners of war. (AWM P02494.012)

The grave of an Australian victim of the Japanese Forces, shot while trying to escape – one of hundreds along the route of the Sandakan–Ranau Death Marches. Most graves were unmarked. A native farmer buried the victim near the 16-mile peg; a Chinese local erected the cross. (AWM 042578)

Gunner G. Dooley, of the 2/3rd Australian Tank Attack Regiment, reads Australian identity discs recovered from a mass grave in Sandakan Prisoner of War Camp. The area was found to contain approximately 300 bodies of men left behind to die after the mobile prisoners were force-marched to Ranau. (AWM 120450)

At the end of 1945, the combined Australian–British Reward Mission first went to Borneo to compensate the native people for their help. Here, at Paginatan village, members of the Mission record the story of a widow called Bureh who witnessed Japanese treatment of prisoners of war on the Sandakan–Ranau Death Marches. (AWM 042514)

Lieutenant Colonel Harry Jackson presents a reward to a boy who aided the Sandakan underground. Jackson was sent to Borneo after the war to distribute cash and merit certificates to the local people who had helped the Allies. (AWM P02494.034)

Jackson spent months in Borneo after the war, listening to horrific stories told by local people under Japanese occupation. Here, he poses with locals from the village of Sapi. (AWM P02494.031)

Lieutenant Colonel Suga Tatsuji, commander of the Japanese prison network in Borneo, ordered his men to 'strike the happy mean between harshness and leniency'. In Sandakan, he presided over a near-100 per cent death rate. He took his own life after the armistice. (AWM 116922)

Captain Hoshijima Susumi (centre), Japanese commandant of the prisoner-of-war camp at Sandakan – seen here chatting with his defence lawyers – was confident he would escape punishment because he assumed there were no witnesses to his crimes. He was later executed as a war criminal. (AWM 133913)

Kono Kinzaburo (left), a member of the Kempei-tai, was among several guards responsible for torturing Captain Lionel Matthews, Lieutenant Rod Wells and other Australians. Their methods involved the 'rice torture' – filling the victim's stomach with raw rice and forcing water in through a hose. (AWM 121770)

Lieutenant General Baba Masao, who enacted orders to force-march the Australian and British prisoners into the Borneo interior. At his trial, he was found guilty of war crimes and executed. (AWM OG3496)

Kempei-tai officers, responsible for torturing, or ordering the torture of, Australian and British prisoners. The Kempei-tai officers include (second from right) Sergeant Major Ehara Kesao, nicknamed 'Bulldog', and (far right) Sergeant Major Matsui Shintaro. (AWM 121764)

An RAAF officer interrogates Hosotani Naoji, with the assistance of Sergeant Mamo, a US Army interpreter attached to the 9th Division. Hosotani confessed to shooting two Australian prisoners and five Chinese civilians. The Allies interrogated scores of suspected Japanese war criminals the year after the war ended. (AWM 121782)

27

SELF-SACRIFICED

Don't say anything. They can't shoot us all.
Botterill whispering to Murray, on punishment parade,
after the Japanese discover their stolen food

IN SOME MEN, the human impulse to care, to give a damn, persists, confounding Botterill's observation that the selfless – the good men – are as good as dead on the march. If so, not yet: even *in extremis*, some soldiers struggle to help, defend, even risk their lives for their friends.

A striking example is Richard Murray. Born in Scotland in 1914, he emigrated to Australia as a young man, then married and settled with his wife, Margaret, and their young son, in Hurstville, Sydney. He worked as a labourer and enlisted on 12 August 1940. His enlistment photo, as a private in the 22nd Brigade, portrays a thickset soldier with a tough, irreverent countenance – all the hallmarks of the typical Aussie larrikin – befitting the man who would become his unit's welterweight boxing champion.

Murray's service record reveals a brave, disorderly, rebellious soldier at odds with authority. His charge sheet in Australia and Malaya is a catalogue of crimes and misdemeanours. He is found guilty of: 'breaking ship' – fined, Pounds 3; failing to obey a lawful command – fined, Pounds 1; absent without leave – fined, Pounds 2; using insubordinate language to his superior – penalty, 14 days' confinement; and going AWOL on the Johore Peninsula, from 21–22 November 1941, probably for a drink.[1] Murray's charge sheet is no worse than that of many diggers and exceeds only slightly the record for insubordination of Keith Botterill, ten years younger, with whom he forms a close friendship.[2]

They remain best mates throughout the battle for Singapore – during which they prove themselves courageous soldiers, participating in a bayonet charge on Japanese positions at Bukit Timah village – and through all the months in Changi and the years in Sandakan. They share the same subversive spirit and tough, working-class roots. Murray, at 31, is something of a father figure, or elder brother, to the 21-year-old Botterill, the Nyngan lad raised in the toughest years of the Depression. Both are survivors in whom hard experience of poverty has bred a streetwise survival instinct. It serves them well in captivity: if they have been brave soldiers, they prove even tougher prisoners. The two men find themselves in Group 3 during the First March, during which Murray, who has become a kind of mentor to Botterill, scrounges food and medicines, and helps the younger man overcome the worst of the Ranau–Paginatan rice round.

Many prisoners cling to similar friendships. They find a friend and stick by him as though he were the last scrap of life on earth worth holding on to. These friendships transcend the idea of 'mateship'. Your friend in Japanese captivity is something much more: a nurse, guide, priest and gravedigger. Your friend will feed, clean and bury you – and be there hopefully to ensure your grave is properly marked. The duty is mutual. Trust in one another is felt in the full consciousness of imminent death.

◆

In early April 1945, on the last rice party from Paginatan, Botterill and Murray re-enter Ranau. They encounter scenes straight out of a mediaeval epidemic. No wire or guards are needed here; most prisoners cannot walk, let alone escape. To avoid infection, the Japanese have established their camp a few hundred yards away from the few flimsy atap huts where scores of Australians and British have been left to die, on the stilted floors, or on the earth underneath. The effects of dysentery and beriberi – the biggest killers – present a stark contrast between the gaunt, skull-like faces of the former and the ballooning, swollen limbs of the latter. The worst sufferers from dysentery crawl between the stilts below the floor and, in Silver's apt phrase, 'valiantly scratch a hole in the earth with their dixies'[3] to relieve themselves. Many are too weak to move and lie in their excrement in the huts. Clouds of flies settle on everything, spreading illness. Every night, more men expire; and every morning the living check those alongside them for signs of life.

Botterill, too, seems to give up hope: his muscles and testicles are swollen with beriberi. Others convulse with malaria. Ranau has become a village of the damned. The living seem an aberration here, freaks of nature. Surely the peace of death is preferable to this? But Murray will have none of his friend's defeatism and drags Botterill from his 'deathbed' at the back of a hut, shakes him down and encourages him to keep going – to choose life. Together, they will see this through, somehow; together, they may even escape. The words have a magical effect. Despite his pitiful state, Botterill is one of the fitter specimens in the camp: he can actually walk.

Murray urges him to volunteer for a small working party transferring atap to a site about five miles south of town – that of a new prison camp, set in jungle to avoid the strafing and bombing runs of Allied aircraft. Physical activity again seems to reinvigorate Botterill, and his health improves – thanks to Murray's stoic intervention. The pair begin further carrier duties over a relatively short distance, with lighter loads.

◆

By early May, there are less than 60 survivors of the First March. Several succumb to illness each day, leaving half that number within a week. On 6 May, the medic Rod Jeffrey dies. His last days are less than edifying, according to one account. He allegedly declines to administer to the needs of the men, preferring to tend the Japanese sick in exchange for food.[4] He claims that this is for the prisoners' good, presumably meaning to share the spoils. The memory of his better days, constantly caring for the sick and wounded, and leading Group 1 out on the First March, seems another world to the desperate men who frantically ransack his medical kit. Scalpels are purloined to lance boils; medicines and gauzes snatched away. Jeffrey is buried in one of several mass graves being dug by the survivors. Among the gravediggers are Murray and Botterill, two of just 30 Australians and British now alive at the camp in Sinarut, near Ranau.

At this time, the Japanese announce what the prisoners consider a death sentence: within 20 days, they will march to Kuching. The distance will surely kill them, if the guards don't, conclude Botterill and Murray. It is time to risk everything and flee. They and two others, Lance Corporal Norm Allie and Private

Norm Grist, devise a plan to escape west, to the coast.

The journey will require food, lots of it. Botterill has the answer, having discovered, a few days earlier, a Japanese rice dump, where he was taken by a guard to get 'a bag for the cookhouse'.[5] On the night of 15 May, the four men raid the store – which is left unlocked – and steal a 44-pound sack of rice, and several bags of biscuits and sweets. They divide the food up; some is given to the sick. All except Murray hide theirs in the jungle. Murray conceals his under a hut, where, on 20 May, a Japanese guard discovers the biscuit tin.

The usual storm breaks over the prisoners' heads. The 30 men are lined up – the sick propped up on sticks – as Lieutenant Suzuki walks furiously down the two lines, demanding to know who stole the food, the punishment for which is summary execution.

'Don't say anything,' Botterill whispers to Murray, in the front line. 'They can't shoot us all.'[6] Suzuki continues striding up and down, shouting threats. Sensing that everyone may be severely punished, or possibly killed, Murray steps forward and identifies himself as the sole culprit. Nobody else is involved, he insists. 'Everybody was paraded,' Moxham recalls, 'and Murray stepped forward and took the whole blame.'[7]

The guards march Murray at bayonet point to a tree near the Japanese huts, to which he is tied and severely beaten. Later that afternoon, Suzuki, Kawakami and two other guards lead him into the jungle and bayonet him to death. Afterward, according to Silver's account, 'Kawakami swaggered down to the Formosan hut and made a great show of wiping his bayonet on the grass, boasting to his fellows that he had "blooded his blade" on a prisoner.'[8]

'They took my mate,' Botterill later mourns, 'and they killed him with a bayonet . . . That just busted me. I thought, there goes my life. That was the chap that brought food to me when I was sick and vice-versa. He was the bloke I was going to escape with.'[9]

Sticpewich later recalls, 'a PW took the responsibility for a party who . . . stole biscuits and rice from the Jap store house. They were caught eating the biscuits and this particular brave lad took the blame for the theft and said he was only sharing the spoils with his friends. He was taken straight away, briefly questioned and was killed.'[10]

28

RESCUE?

To establish a party in the area of Sandakan BNB for the purpose
of obtaining and relaying to Australia the detailed intelligence
essential for the planning of a combined airborne naval operation
on the POW camps in the area, aimed at effecting a rescue and
withdrawal by sea of the prisoners therein, and such information
as is laid down under the project known as KINGFISHER.

Special Reconnaissance Department's outline of Project
KINGFISHER, the doomed rescue mission

IN ALLIED HEADQUARTERS, in Brisbane and Manila, the fate
of the prisoners of Sandakan warrants no more, or less, attention
than that of men in other rat-infested sinks of the crumbling
empire, in Burma, Korea, Manchuria and the Japanese homeland.
There is a striking exception, however, which, in the minds of
Australian planners in the Special Reconnaissance Department,
sets a powerful precedent: the spectacular rescue on 23 February
1945 of some 2147 Allied prisoners of war and civilians held in
Los Banos internment camp in the Philippines. No doubt, this is a
great military and humanitarian feat, which the American general
presents as one of the goals of his invasion of the Philippines.
In truth, the rescue is a by-product of MacArthur's strategic

reconquest of the Pacific islands, applied with peculiar intensity to the Philippines. His vow to 'return' and reclaim the land from which the Japanese ejected him has become, in the intervening years, a full-blown personal obsession.

In the realm of MacArthur's ego, it is not fanciful to suggest that he feels a personal debt to every American survivor of the Japanese conquest of Corregidor and Bataan; hence their rescue. Yet he does not feel the same about the Australians and British on Borneo. MacArthur feels no personal, military or political obligation to mount a prisoner-rescue effort elsewhere in the Pacific, least of all to islands lacking strategic value that would contribute little or nothing to his northward rush to Tokyo.

And yet, Borneo is a special case, for a simple reason: the Allies have hard intelligence on the state of the prisoners and their location – information not forthcoming from other, more distant, camps in the Japanese Empire. Indeed, by May 1945, the Allies *know* the Japanese are force-marching to death hundreds of sick and starving Australian and British soldiers – a form of torture as cruel as the Bataan Death March, the barbarity of which certainly resonates with MacArthur. And it disturbs them. The question is whether this information accelerates the fragile rescue 'project' that sits in the files of the Special Reconnaissance Department under the codename 'KINGFISHER'.

Since January, the Services Reconnaissance Department and organs of military intelligence have gleaned precise information about the state of the Borneo prisoners through the special operations of AGAS, or 'sandfly' – small teams (numbered I to IV) of phenomenally brave Australian and British commandos whose job is to penetrate the island's interior, harass the Japanese and gather intelligence. These operations need to be seen in context, as just one of many Special Forces' initiatives in the South-West Pacific – as part of the legendary Z Special Unit, popularly called Z Force – which include Operations RIMAU, JAYWICK and KRAIT; and, in Borneo, PYTHON and SEMUT. The dispatches of AGAS are graphically informative. Throughout 1945, they detail the dreadful state, and probable extermination, of hundreds of prisoners in Borneo. These reports land on Special Reconnaissance Department desks with a thud of reproach, given the failure, or inability, of the recipients to act.

That failure may be traced to the mysterious machinations of High Command – through the ultimate agency of Generals MacArthur and Blamey – who decide in early 1945 to shelve any further work on KINGFISHER. The project scarcely registers in MacArthur's grand purview, of course. Neither he nor Blamey issues direct orders to 'cancel' KINGFISHER, for the simple reason that, from their perspective, it has never really begun. The planes are simply not going to be spared; the resources, in men and materiel, being critical to the war effort. The commanders leave no trail to themselves for this decision – there are no generals' fingerprints on KINGFISHER – for the understandable reason that nobody in charge wishes to be seen by posterity, and the prisoners' families, as the terminators of a humane and compassionate idea. In fairness, the commanders are locked in a total war, against a bloody regime that refuses to surrender. They need every plane they can get.

◆

And yet, if the shelving of the 'rescue plan' at command level is treated as a regrettable consequence of strategic priorities, some middle-ranked officers in Special Forces see this as an act of callous indifference to the plight of thousands of soldiers. The termination of KINGFISHER is executed with the bureaucratic equivalent of a magician's disappearing trick – a sleight of hand that heightens hopes even as it snatches them away.

This is what happens: on 12 February 1945, AGAS commando units are ordered to assume a new and apparently critical role. According to this swiftly 'altered plan', AGAS II – the unit provisionally earmarked for the rescue later in 1945 – is cancelled and its mission rolled into AGAS I, then preparing for dispatch to Borneo. Under this new arrangement, AGAS I, under Major Gort Chester, is to absorb the designated KINGFISHER personnel, led by Captain Derek (Jock) Sutcliffe. It will incorporate its meagre resources – it still lacks the much-needed planes – and a new brief, which is:

> To establish a party in the area of Sandakan BNB for the purpose of obtaining and relaying to Australia the detailed intelligence essential for the planning of a combined airborne naval operation on the POW camps in the area, aimed at effecting a rescue and withdrawal by sea of the prisoners therein, and such information as is laid down under the project known as KINGFISHER.[1]

On paper, this reads as if KINGFISHER is being brought forward and endowed with a new and pressing urgency. The 'reassignment' of the 'rescue' mission has fed the wishful thinking of those who, since the war, have imagined that KINGFISHER was poised to go ahead. In fact, it is being digested by a very different operation, Major Chester's intelligence-gathering mission. Chester, of course, has never had any involvement with KINGFISHER or a mooted rescue effort. Nor does he get along with Captain Sutcliffe, in whom he has 'no confidence'.[2] When he hears of the plan, he immediately sees the futility of the project and, according to Jack Wong Sue, 'ranted and raved about the idiocy of AGAS I being given the KINGFISHER role'.[3]

In truth, the new plan skewers any hope of KINGFISHER taking effect at all, for the simple reason that the aircraft and paratroopers essential for the mission are not yet ready; indeed, they are never expected to be available. Any spare aircraft are deployed in support of MacArthur's operations. Warwick Johnstone, who volunteered for the 1st Australian Independent Parachute Company in November 1943, later recalls, 'The rescue was never planned; it was not going to go ahead.'[4]

By lumping KINGFISHER together with a separate operation that cannot possibly fulfil the task proposed in the time available, the new 'plan' amounts to the dissolution of the whole project. The passage of time soon renders the mission impossible. 'It is clear,' Athol Moffitt later concludes, 'that, by early March, from outside AGAS I, a decision must have been made not to pursue the paratroop rescue operation.'[5] More accurately, he continues, KINGFISHER 'never commenced': 'there is not the slightest indication anywhere in the record of any attempt to get any, much less "detailed", information of the prison camp, about the drop zones or any of the other information which the KINGFISHER plan required'.[6]

◆

The result on the ground is confusion. On 3 March 1945,

members of AGAS I leave Darwin by submarine, bound for Borneo. Their exact role is unclear: are they expected to reconnoitre a rescue operation? To identify drop zones for Allied paratroopers? Or to do what they have previously done: train locals and gather intelligence? And, if so, for what purpose? As it happens, they're expected to do a bit of everything and adapt to fast-changing circumstances. AGAS I is led by Major Gort Chester – accompanied by Captain Sutcliffe, nominally in charge of KINGFISHER, and the redoubtable Sergeant Jack Wong Sue. Together, this little band of British and Australian commandos lands at Labuk Bay in early March and makes contact with natives on Jembongan Island. The team establishes a base here and, throughout March and April, recruits and trains some 70 natives for covert operations. The locals' anti-Japanese credentials are irreproachable.

'The attitude of the natives on the whole,' concludes a Special Reconnaissance Department report from Morotai on 29 May 1945, 'has been most friendly, and everywhere a keen desire to help the Allied forces is shown. Generally speaking, forced labour, taking of crops, rape and general maltreatment by the Japanese, have increased the natural disposition of these natives to remain loyal to the previous [i.e. British] administration . . .'[7]

That month, Sutcliffe's men produce a 'General Report on Ranau' (Sandakan, now under frequent Allied bombardment, being of little use), which reveals the town's road grid, building layout, population (7500), land use, surrounding tracks, rivers and weather. The report identifies possible airfields – 'landing grounds' – but warns, 'On 30 May 11 x 1000 lb bombs were dropped, cratering runways and rendering it unserviceable.' The destruction by Allied bombers of the Ranau airfield, along with those in

Sandakan and Jesselton, renders impossible the evacuation of prisoners by air (helicopters, of course, are not yet available). KINGFISHER, however, has envisaged the prisoners' overland flight to the coast – where submarines would be waiting. Clearly, such a flight is impossible from Ranau, with the drome destroyed – as AGAS I discovers. Even if it were feasible, the commandos soon discover the terrible condition of the men and the extreme difficulty of moving them. The scales fall from the eyes of the most diehard exponents of the proposed rescue mission.

AGAS I nonetheless carries on – for several months – examining the Japanese ground-strength and the various routes from Ranau to the coast. As usual, progress is slow, and the unit grows restive. In May, aware that the Japanese are alert to their presence, Sutcliffe and Chester introduce a 'new policy' of aggressive intervention – based on the old truism that offence is the best form of defence. Their goal is, according to a mission report, 'to strike vigorously at the Japs, inflicting as much damage and casualties as possible'.[8]

And so, on 29 May, they advance inland to Sungei Sungei and establish a base on the Sugut River, where the men are divided. One group moves into the vicinity of Telupid, on the Death March route, to monitor any passing prisoners. The second has the same role but in the area of Meridi. On 7 June, the first group attacks, with 'complete success', a small enemy garrison in the village of Aling, killing 11 of 30 Japanese soldiers, with only one loss.[9] But their first combat experience terrifies the native guerrillas, who desert en masse, forcing Sutcliffe to abandon the 'search and destroy' tactics.

AGAS I then reverts to its original plan – whatever this may be – and sets up 'a more or less permanent base' in the high hills above Ranau, from where the team aims to 'cut Japanese communications NORTH, SOUTH, EAST of RANAU'.[10] Here, native agents loyal to the Allies defy the 'shoot on sight' policy of the Japanese and transmit accurate information on the prisoners' movements and condition as far as Ranau. 'My agents,' Chester writes, in June 1945, 'previously working SAPI, MAUNAD area can no longer visit these places. The Japs are shooting natives on sight and it is too much to ask a man to go there when he is aware of this, and even if I sent him he would probably invent news.' But he has already received an extraordinary piece of intelligence: AGAS I knows 'definitely' that 'a week ago' upward of '300 prisoners' passed through the vicinity of Boto. These men are the survivors of the Second Death March.

'I am naturally most anxious to assist them,' Chester writes, 'but I think if any precipitate action were undertaken to effect rescue and should be only partly successful it would mean immediate slaughter of remainder. (Your advice and policy on this matter is urgently requested).'[11]

No advice or policy is sent, and AGAS I has just shown why: one of KINGFISHER's core inhibitors is that, if attacked, the Japanese are likely to annihilate every last prisoner. That fear is no longer theoretical – the cruel truth is that every prisoner in Borneo is now the target of a Japanese policy of slow murder. Their extermination is well advanced, according to native eyewitnesses of the Second Death March in June and July. The facts of this pitiable epic reach Australia via AGAS agents, through the witness of local farmers and coolie labourers working near the Sandakan Prison Camp and along the track. Their accounts conjure the impression of a descent into the darkest circles of hell:

On approx 1 Jun[e], approx 600 PW left SANDAKAN and proceeded beyond SAPI towards RANAU. They have NOT been heard of since. Those who were too sick to walk were shot. A further 100 (approx), who were too sick to travel, were left in an open field near the PW camp [in Sandakan] after the camp had been burnt.

Further into the same report, AGAS I concludes – wrongly – that there are 'NO' prisoners left in the Sandakan camp vicinity, 'and a great percentage of those previously here have died of sickness or have been callously shot'.[12] The truth is rather more complex and tragic.

As for the Japanese and Formosans, they've been reduced to a mob of desperate men being driven to collapse by the constant torment of Allied air strikes. The walking carcass of the Imperial Army occasionally shakes a defiant fist at this dismal fate. In June, Japanese soldiers launch a reign of terror in the interior, 'constantly robbing civilians and shooting up native villages and boats'. The 'Japs are continually moving around' to escape Allied air bombardment. 'They seldom remain in houses by day, and wherever possible enter the jungle. Enemy morale is quite low.'[13]

◆

Hard intelligence on the state of Allied prisoners in Borneo disturbs morning tea on the parliamentary terraces in Canberra and London, and furrows brows in top military meetings in Singapore, Manila and Brisbane – chiefly because it confirms the worst reports of the Services Reconnaissance Department, whose proposal to rescue the men remains on the drawing board. The trouble is that news of the Death Marches across Borneo is 'not what AGAS (KINGFISHER) was originally sent to find out', as Athol Moffitt later writes. 'This is what KINGFISHER intended to prevent, but tragically did not.' This overstates the actual progress of the rescue mission. In later years, many people – soldiers, historians, commentators – convince themselves that KINGFISHER was tragically dashed at the point of consummation, by old generals with little or no concern for the prisoners. This is unfair (see Chapter 42, Home). The commanders later duck questions about why they were unable to procure supply planes and paratroopers. Understandably, none wishes to be seen to have failed to avert a massacre. And at the time they were fighting a total war. KINGFISHER was a sideline and only acquired the status of a palpable prospect years later, through the lens of what might have been.

A bigger picture rolls along in tandem with the Death Marches, and tends to sideline KINGFISHER and the possibility of a prisoner rescue. It is worth reminding ourselves that military bureaucrats run the war machine, with little professional concern for the fate of about 1000 soldiers in central Borneo. And so it happened that in late 1944, in Washington, the US chiefs of staff approved the execution of conventional military operations against Borneo, partly in order to establish a base for the British fleet in Brunei Bay. Such operations might have implied the possibility of the rescue of the prisoners in tandem with an overall invasion of the island, following the example of the Philippines. That was never on the agenda. The British chiefs of staff promptly scratched the plan to establish a naval base on Borneo in early 1945: 'British Chiefs of Staff have taken note of operations against Borneo approved by US Chiefs of Staff . . . but they must point out that main object of these operations . . . does not in their view justify initial and continuing expenditure of effort.'[14]

The British chiefs deem Brunei Bay unsuitable as a base because: it is too far from the main theatre of operations against Japan; its development would take too long; it is also too far from the navy's main bases in Australia. So much for that idea, which had been scheduled to begin on 23 May, in conjunction with the landings at Tarakan and Balikpapan – on 1 May and 28 June respectively. Instead, the British pressed for a naval base in the Philippines.[15]

◆

What of the Australian diggers? Are they available to rescue their countrymen? Somewhere in the South-West Pacific, in late 1944 and early 1945, the Australian soldiers are fighting. But where? Few know, precisely. The defence force and the government are silent on the matter. The media are kept ignorant. A question that appears on no serious agenda is this: will the so-called 'mopping up' operations by the Australian Imperial Force in the South-West Pacific involve Borneo – and, if so, will those operations include the rescue of prisoners of war in the region? The short answer is no. The long answer is intricate.

In late 1944, MacArthur demanded that Blamey provide the full complement of the Australian Army to replace US forces in Papua New Guinea, Bougainville and New Britain. Borneo was not listed among those priorities. The American general's insistence on twice as many Australians as Blamey deemed necessary was designed to avoid, it appears, the embarrassment of a smaller Australian contingent seen doing the job of a much bigger American one. 'It could not be shown that Australian troops were capable of the same job as the Americans, but with only a third of the numbers,' writes the historian Karl James of the Australian War Memorial.[16]

And while Blamey seems personally 'at ease with the idea that an Australian brigade was the equivalent of an American division' – given his experience of their performance at Buna and Sanananda – he had no choice other than to obey his superior. In the event, however, Blamey has decided to deploy fewer Australian troops in the region, in deference to the overriding concern of Canberra: to limit casualties. The result has been a slow, grinding war of containment, of small, deadly patrols through jungle and swampland, over mountains and into valleys. And it is has been lethal. The reoccupation of Bougainville alone will eventually kill 516 Australian soldiers and wound 1572; the recapture of Borneo is considered merely a political gesture of little strategic consequence.

Meanwhile, in November 1944, MacArthur moved his advance headquarters to the Philippines. No Australian soldiers participated in the liberation. On 4 February 1945, Lieutenant General Frank Berryman, commander of the First Australian Corps and close to MacArthur, wrote in his diary that MacArthur was 'now busy staging his triumphant entry and to date no senior Australian officer has been invited to participate – one would think the [Australian forces] are not part of SWPA or that we did not do the bulk of the fighting in the critical stages of the campaign when our resources were so limited'.

The exclusion of the Australians is frustrating, and bewildering, to a nation raised on the assumption that they will fight their allies' wars, wherever they may erupt, from Gallipoli to Pozières. But this is South East Asia, Australia's neighbour – and up until January 1945 there has barely been a word of the Australian Imperial Force's activities in the region. MacArthur's headquarters has not released any information concerning Australian offensive operations in New Guinea and Bougainville. 'There were only vague statements that the AIF would be deployed in the "future",' concludes Karl James.[17] While the people digest stories of spectacular Allied actions in Europe, the Australian diggers in the Pacific appear to have been 'removed from the picture'.[18] *The Sydney Morning Herald* describes the Australian Imperial Force as a 'fighting army held in leash'; nor did the Australian people like their forces 'relegated to a secondary role or left indefinitely in reserve while the Pacific war marches to its climax'.[19] At the time, a *Canberra Times* editorial appealed to the public's irreverent sense of humour: 'Will anyone knowing the whereabouts of Australian soldiers in action in the South-West Pacific please communicate at once with the Australian Government.'[20]

◆

In January 1945, MacArthur bowed to pressure from Canberra and deigned to give the Australians a stronger role in victory in the Pacific: to liberate Borneo and the Dutch East Indies. But the Borneo operations, dubbed OBOE, have been cut to half the scale envisaged by MacArthur. Just three of a proposed six amphibious operations have proceeded down the east coast of the island and to Labuan, beginning in April 1945. Only two-thirds of the available troops have been used. The Australian Government refuses to release the 6th Division, then in New Guinea, and the job is left to the 7th and 9th. Aircraft are indeed available, but the Americans refuse to release any, and the RAAF's 1st Tactical Air Force's fighters and bombers are earmarked for air operations south of the Philippines. The idea of releasing these to accompany a high-risk prisoner-rescue mission in the centre of Borneo is seen as fanciful.

The landings concentrate on the coastal strongholds of Tarakan, Brunei, Labuan and Balikpapan. Sandakan (already bombed) and the overland route to Ranau are not on the list of desirable objectives; the prisoners are not even mentioned. At the time, most senior Australian officers condemn the OBOE operations as 'lacking any real object' – a view the US chiefs of staff share. Admiral Ernest King, commander-in-chief, United States Fleet, dismisses the Balikpapan operation of 1 July 1945 (OBOE 2) as 'unnecessary'.[21] But MacArthur insists on OBOE's prosecution and threatens to disrupt the Australian Army's involvement if the 7th Division is withdrawn and it fails to proceed – a bluff that works, as James shows:

> [T]he OBOE operations themselves were spectacular and more lavishly supported than any other Australian operation of the war. The AIF was at the peak of its efficiency. The 7th and 9th Divisions were experienced, its soldiers well trained and drilled in their tasks, and its young leaders battle hardened. The RAN and RAAF were also prominent in each operation, with minesweepers through to heavy cruisers participating in the invasion while Australian fighters and bombers, including four-engine heavy bombers, were constantly overhead. Each operation was conducted successfully with skill and bravery.[22]

Several hundred Australians are killed and thousands wounded in OBOE operations between April and July 1945. They succeed, however, in their core goal of securing the coastal strongholds and protecting some 70,000 civilians. In strategic terms, the operations are seen as unnecessary. Even if the Japanese forces still held Borneo's vast oilfields, not a barrel would have penetrated the US naval blockade then flung around the Japanese homeland.

All this boils down to a stark truth: Borneo has little or no strategic role in mid-1945, at the time when the prisoners are enduring the worst of the Death Marches. The American and British joint planning staff are bluntly clear on this point, in a report tabled on 10 April 1945, which concludes that 'the military and economic advantages to be gained by the occupation of Borneo would be small, and unlikely materially to assist [the] operations in Malaya'.[23]

By this stage, with Japan's defeat inevitable, the British and American joint planners are more interested in the island's natural wealth than in the people who control or are stationed in Borneo. The monthly oil and rubber tonnage exercises their minds more than the fate of a few hundred sick and broken men. But not even this constitutes a compelling reason to invade. In Brunei, for example, 'the amount of oil and rubber which could be obtained . . . does not constitute a very weighty argument in favour of undertaking operations in that area in the near future'.[24] The same dismal assessment applies to the whole island, the joint planners point out, in April 1945: 'We conclude that, if the proposed occupation of Borneo is carried out, the military and economic advantages would be small.'[25] And a later report concludes, 'The development of any area in Borneo would require resources which could probably only be provided at the expense of our other requirements in the Pacific.'

Little wonder that the Australian Army is slated for what MacArthur calls 'mopping up' operations; and less wonder that the prisoners are given little or no consideration. Soldiers first and foremost, they understand this harsh reality: that the war must be won before they can be rescued. '[F]rom the overall picture, did we count?' wonders Braithwaite later. 'Um, see, we were expendable, we weren't much use, we were only a nuisance as far as, er, diverting any forces to save our hides . . . See, we, if it's us, our own life is important to us, it's the only thing we have, but when you take nations at war, on a world war, we just don't count.'[26]

29

THE SECOND MARCH

*I killed two PWs on the march on Tsuji's orders. In
both cases, the PWs were so sick that they begged to be
killed. I asked Tsuji about it and he said OK.*

Shoji Shinsuke, nicknamed 'Sparkles', a guard
who participated in the killing platoon

HOSHIJIMA IS OFFICIALLY RELIEVED of his duties as
camp commandant on 17 May 1945. His decision to permit
the display of the huge 33-by-33-foot POW sign has displeased
his superiors, it appears, and the engineer's skills are no longer
required. According to one account, Hoshijima marks his
departure by holding a fishing competition and a farewell
banquet for the remaining Allied officers, at which Captains
Cook and Mills, as 'guests of honour', deliver speeches of thanks.[1]
The commandant has little trouble serving up a feast. Amassed
under his bungalow at the time is 90 tons of rice, and there is
another 54 tons at the bombproof store. Nor will he or his guests
go sick. Hoshijima leaves behind medical stocks containing about
950,000 quinine tablets, 160,000 of them under his house, and
vast quantities of vitamins A, B, C and D, Red Cross parcels and
surgical equipment. None of it, not even a bandage, is given to the

prisoners. When the medic Captain Picone is caught borrowing a light bulb, with which to light his surgical hut in order to perform an emergency operation on a patient with a ruptured ulcer, he is beaten up and made to stand at attention for two hours while the patient lies bleeding in darkness on the operating table.

Hoshijima's successor, Captain Takakuwa Takuo, thus inherits substantial supplies, ensuring the health and fitness of himself and his men for some time. Like Hoshijima, he has no intention of improving the prisoners' lot. He is by several accounts a vile-spirited man, whose methods make Hoshijima's seem almost tolerant. Takakuwa is not an engineer, with priorities above the prison camp; he is a line commander, with direct instructions to deal with the problem of the prison camp. As such, he is fully conscious of what he is about to do and realises that compelling these men to walk to Ranau will surely kill them all. Even relatively healthy Japanese soldiers are, by this stage, unable to make the journey. Takakuwa has, for example, recently heard that only 200 of 800 Japanese infantrymen survived a march between Tawao and Jesselton in January 1945; and 40 of 150 cavalry troops made the journey from Sandakan to Ranau in the past month. Most died of disease, exacerbated by malnutrition and exhaustion.[2] Yet those men were fit-and-fed Japanese soldiers. What hope, then, for these men, prisoners of several years and physically spent?

In the third week of May, 824 prisoners remain alive at the eight-mile camp at Sandakan. Of these, Takakuwa reckons 439 Australians and 97 British are fit to walk – a total of 536.[3] The remaining 288 are hospital or stretcher cases, dying at the rate of ten a day. They know little of the fate of their comrades – except scant news from two sick prisoners who have returned. None is aware of what is in store for them, the sheer deadly impossibility of what lies ahead.

The stretcher cases cannot move; and stretcher parties would be unlikely to endure more than three days bearing such weight. Not even Takakuwa is blind to the impossibility of taking them. Having inherited the decision to move the men, he asks for urgent advice from 37 Army HQ in Kuching. Takakuwa's problem is: how? How is he expected to get these men on their feet? His concerns are practical, not humanitarian. His predecessor Hoshijima dispensed with the alternative plan of marching them to the town of Kemansi – due to the lack of food there. Ranau is the only other option, an 'other Eden', with plentiful supplies, according to Japanese mythology. In fact, since the arrival of the First March, Ranau has degenerated into a disease-ridden ghost town. The natives have fled. Just a dozen or so survivors of the First March cling to life, hiding in a second jungle camp to escape Allied air raids.

In the east, during May, airborne bombardment and shore attacks on Sandakan and surrounds are a near-daily occurrence. The Allied invasion of British North Borneo is believed imminent. On 23 May, air raids target the prison camp for the first time. The pilots apparently believe the prisoners have perished or departed (partly due to the removal of the POW sign). The raids kill a number of prisoners. In total, between 20 and 30 eventually die of friendly air bombardment. Richard Braithwaite survives two near-misses that kill, or badly injure, a few mates. Four days later, on 27 May, American PT boats penetrate Sandakan Harbour, and a huge joint sea and air bombardment of the town and the area erupts, sending the Japanese scurrying into the jungle.[4] Takakuwa draws the obvious conclusions: the Allies will surely recapture

Sandakan within days and the prison camp must soon follow.

In response, the Second March is swiftly brought forward: chiefly to prevent the prisoners from falling into Allied hands, which is now very likely if they stay put. Indeed, under Japanese policy, only in extreme circumstances are prisoners to be 'freed' – a euphemism for left to die – as laid out in the instructions Takakuwa inherits from Hoshijima (who received them from 37 Army Headquarters in Kuching):

PRISONERS OF WAR MUST BE PREVENTED BY ALL MEANS AVAILABLE FROM FALLING INTO ENEMY HANDS. THEY SHOULD EITHER BE RELOCATED AWAY FROM THE FRONT OR COLLECTED AT SUITABLE POINTS AND TIMES WITH AN EYE TO ENEMY AIR RAIDS, SHORE BOMBARDMENTS ETC. THEY SHOULD BE KEPT ALIVE TO THE LAST WHEREVER THEIR LABOUR IS NEEDED. IN DESPERATE CIRCUMSTANCES, WHERE THERE IS NO TIME TO MOVE THEM, THEY MAY, AS A LAST RESORT, BE SET FREE.[5]

According to this prescription, the Sandakan prisoners should be moved from the coast, worked as porters for as long as they can stand and, when their ability to work expires, 'disposed of'. None must live to bear witness to Japanese humiliation or war crimes. 'Saving face' appears to be the chief psychological underpinning of the Imperial Army's policy to 'kill the prisoners'. 'Desperate circumstances' are not specified but refer presumably to the threat of complete annihilation, when moving the prisoners is not possible.

This overlooks the fact that Japanese prisoner-of-war camps

have, in effect, applied the order 'kill the prisoners' for years, by enslaving sick and underfed men, grinding them under a regime of violence and torture, and, as in Bataan, force-marching them to death. The Japanese in charge at Sandakan Prisoner No. 1 Camp have adopted the same 'method' as Bataan – and are now well into the second phase of extermination. They intend to complete what they have begun – with a measure of thoroughness hitherto unprecedented in the Pacific War. Force-marching the surviving prisoners to Ranau has, in this light, a twofold intent: to crush the spirit of the living and hasten the death of the dying. Those too sick to depart Sandakan are to be 'freed' – left on a hillside, naked to the elements, until they die of 'natural causes'.

◆

And so, hurried by air raids and the looming threat of an Allied invasion, Takakuwa calls an urgent meeting with his officers the next day, 28 May 1945. His instructions are clear: all prisoners able to walk must be ready to go the following evening. Those unable to rise are 'to be taken to the gardens in No. 2 Compound and left there in the open'.[6] Sergeant Major Murozumi Hisao and 15 guards will remain with these 'lying cases' until the latter are dead and then join the rest of the Japanese Army in Ranau. In the meantime, the camp, the huts, all stores – every last trace of what happened here – are to be destroyed.

Panic grips the camp. Rumours fly that the Allies have landed. Guards rush about packing, storing, ordering. Prisoners salvage whatever they can of any belongings, in readiness for the move. On 29 May, the 536 walking cases – only a fifth of whom could be deemed 'fit' – are paraded and organised into three 'clusters'

– each containing four groups of about 50 men – led respectively by Lieutenants Suzuki Saburo and Watanabe Genzo (second-in-command to Takakuwa) and Sergeant Tsuji. Groups 1–8 are virtually all Australian; Group 9 a mix of British and Australian; and Groups 10 and 11 all British. The groups are to take turns leading their clusters, in a kind of leapfrogging action, so that the leading prisoners are regularly being moved to the end. As with the First March, stragglers or the incapacitated are to be killed by death squads bringing up the rear.

Each group's leader is chosen from among the remaining Allied officers or senior non-commissioned officers. They come from a variety of battalions and regiments. Leading Group 1 is Captain Jim Heaslop (2/10th Field Regiment), a married former accountant and exemplary officer, educated at Brisbane Boys' Grammar, where he became head prefect. At the head of Group 2 is Warrant Officer Sticpewich, the jack of all trades and 'friend' of the Japanese. Leading Group 3 is the chaplain Harold Wardale-Greenwood, a man outwardly determined to uphold his faith, for the sake of the men, but inwardly shaken by the worm of doubt that moves in his heart. As they prepare to move out, Wardale-Greenwood wonders, not for the first time, where God is in all this. The two dedicated medics, Captains Oakeshott and Picone, lead Groups 4 and 5 respectively with a duty of unflagging care, which, given their lack of medical supplies, is a mix of wishful thinking and astonishing resilience. Warrant Officer Jonathan Dixon leads Group 6. Captain Cook, at the head of Group 7, issues instructions to his fellow leaders that 'no officer should drop out at any point for they had a duty of care to look after the prisoners' best interests at all times'.[7] Perhaps this contradicts the man's reputation as a cowardly collaborator. It seems more likely, however, that it reflects the extent to which Cook mouths, in the language of 'care', Japanese interests. Truth, as always, is a multi-headed Hydra, constantly eluding our settled ideas with a different face. Lieutenant Gordon Good leads Group 8, and the British officers Flying Officer Harry Burgess, Captain Frank Daniels and Lieutenant Geoffrey Chopping lead Groups 9, 10 and 11.

As these 'healthy' men prepare to depart, the 288 remaining sick cases, most of whom cannot move, are carried or stagger from their huts, to be laid in a wired paddock, in rows, in the open. No cooks or medics are left behind to help them.[8] Among them is the young diarist Tom Burns, too sick to move. So too are five of the eight surviving British officers: Captain James Mills (who is believed to have attended Hoshijima's departure party, just a few weeks ago, with Cook and others), Flying Officers Alfred Linge and Stan Cressey and Lieutenants Philip Young and Ian Rolfe. These men have nothing but the rags they wear and, if lucky, a groundsheet. There is no medicine and little food. A few die during the transfer and are rolled into slit trenches dug nearby. It is clear to anyone who witnesses the scene that these skeletal forms, barely living, are being left behind to die.

The guards destroy the camp. They blow up the ammunition depots – except for as much ammunition as the prisoners can carry – torch the second and third prison compounds and burn down all but a few buildings used by the remaining Japanese staff. Flames consume the prisoners' atap huts within minutes. The stores that cannot be carried turn rapidly to ash. The prisoners' home for the past three years is soon a smouldering wreck. 'It was a strange, sad sort of feeling to see those huts going up in flames,' Richard Braithwaite later recalls. '[T]hings that we'd made and cherished, the little bits of wood that had become more or less like the family jewels, they were going up in smoke.'[9] He is forced to leave behind his wooden chess set, which he carved himself. 'When we were ordered out of the camp it was something of a shock, because we were settled into it . . .' Despite the fact that the prisoners have always dreamt of escaping from it, 'this sudden uprooting from an ordered existence, out to this open field . . . it was a very depressing thing'.[10]

Rumours flare of an end of the war, as low-flying Catalinas appear in the sky, drawn to the smoke. Nearby explosions announce the destruction of Sandakan and raise the prospect in every prisoner's head of liberation, amid intimations of doom. The sight of Allied planes is both a blessing and an awful warning: do the pilots consider us dead or departed? And the stricken thought rises from the smoking remains: we have nowhere to go except where the Japanese order us; no hut, no bed, no shelter – just the loincloth around our waist, the ragged shirt on our backs and the great expanse of jungle to the west.

Some men still hold a candle for the idea that the Japanese have seen sense, at last, and intend to march them down to the waterfront to surrender with goodwill. The slaughter of five pigs that afternoon – an extraordinary feast for both the guards and the prisoners in readiness for the march – fuels the rumour. Perhaps we're being fattened up for presentation to the Allies, runs one wistful dream; perhaps the Japs are trying to destroy evidence of their bestiality before the Allies arrive, runs another.[11] It is a sustaining hope. The air raids further panic the Japanese officers and guards, who hasten the approach of the start of the Second March.

◆

At 1700 hours, Takakuwa orders every prisoner fit to walk to move out within two hours. Before they set off, the commandant inspects his little legion of cripples. Many are wearing calipers – sticks strapped to their legs – to support their weight, which their muscles, infected by tropical ulcers, cannot. Very few have footwear and the majority 'just hobbled around the camp as best as their joints, stiffened by beri beri, would permit'.[12] Some groups are ordered to carry Japanese bed rolls as well as their loads.

Some of the very sick, under the misapprehension of being taken to Sandakan to be handed over to the Allies, struggle to their feet. The 288 sick – or rather fewer, now – are left behind and condemned as hopeless cases. Jackson later records:

> The pitiful column moved off from the camp gate and marched as best they could down the road . . . Any hopes they had of going to Sandakan were dashed to the ground when they received the order to turn to the right when they reached the bitumen road . . . Many of them knew that they would probably not see another day out and the disappointment of not turning to the left sapped up any reserve morale that they may have had remaining.[13]

There follows an atrocity the facts of which enter the realm of inexpressible horror. The long file of men staggers, trips and slides all night, through swamp and jungle and plantation, by the light of swinging lamps under a blanket of indifferent darkness. They move along the muddy banks of the Labuk's tributaries in a sort of muffled silence, broken by the crunch of leaves under bare feet or worn rubber, the wheeze and moans of the sick, the shrieking orders of the guards and the prisoners' mumbled response.

The diminishing line advances about eight miles a day. Each man lives on a single riceball – less than four ounces – daily, scooped from the four pounds that has been allotted him on departure, meant to last ten days. Ration points supply a little sugar and salt, which are swiftly shared out to avoid requisitioning by the guards. And there is the jungle complement of fruit, ferns and berries, and, on the mud flats at least, a scatter of tiny crabs, which some men try to catch. Allied aircraft occasionally fly overheard, sending the line of guards and prisoners scrambling into the jungle.

They start dropping out within 12–15 miles: staggering about the forest and then sliding to their knees. Volleys of rifle butts, sticks and bayonets force them back on their feet. 'I have seen many a man,' recalls Nelson Short, 'belted along and butted with the rifle in the back, with the Japanese saying, "Faster", "Faster" all the time.'[14] Those who cannot move are dealt with – some beaten and eye-gouged before the inevitable bullet or bayonet. Every so often, the forest jolts and birds flutter into the sky at the sound of gunshot, heralding the arrival of Tsuji's killing platoon.

Following Abe's example on the First Death March, Tsuji's death squad brings up the rear like a silent fury, the very sight of which means death to the prostrate victim. Among his official 'killers' are Fukishima, well known to the prisoners as the Black Bastard, and the sadistic Corporal Katayama. 'Each morning,' Fukishima later testifies, 'there were many PWs who could not continue the march. On the orders of S/M Tsuji we grouped these together. I recorded the numbers and the balance were shot by Formosan guards . . .'[15]

At 5.30 pm on the second day, seven crippled men, unable to walk without the aid of a crutch, refuse to go on. Katayama and his thugs rain blows on these fallen prisoners, who manage another 20–30 yards before collapsing. Katayama then kicks them off the track. Soon, from the jungle fastness, comes the sound of gunfire. Four are shot in the back, dead, and two lie wounded, according to a Chinese witness, Chin Kin Choi, who later investigates. One prisoner escapes into the jungle but is soon shot and later found 'doubled up with a wound in the stomach', dead. The Japanese hunting party returns to shoot through the head the two wounded men.[16]

Dozens, soon scores, perish; most are murdered after collapsing from illness or hunger. 'Those that dropped out during the day's march were killed,' confirms Shoji Shinsuke ('Sparkles'), who participates in the slaughter. 'I killed two PWs on the march on Tsuji's orders. In both cases, the PWs were so sick that they begged to be killed. I asked Tsuji about it and he said OK.'[17] Sparkles, a relatively humane man, is one of a few guards who seem torn between obeying orders and revulsion at what he is ordered to do. At Sandakan, he often smuggled food to caged prisoners, warned the men of imminent 'acts of bastardry' and 'restrained himself from many beatings', according to Sticpewich.[18]

As the march advances, and the casualties mount, the slaughter goes on and on. The guards are ordered to 'take turns' in Tsuji's death squad. 'On the way to Ranau,' recalls one member of the killing platoon, Nagahiro Masao, 'I took my turn in Tsuji's party four times; I had to kill in two of the four times. All the Formosans had to take their turn . . . Takakuwa ordered this.'[19] One guard, Nakayama Tamao, nicknamed 'The Grub', later remembers his part in Tsuji's murderous carousel: 'I had to shoot one [Australian prisoner]. Takakuwa was present and said, "Shoot that man". We then went on, leaving the bodies behind. Tsuji and

Fukushima took the names of the men. I do not think they were buried.'[20]

Fukishima tries to hide the evidence of a systematic extermination from the prisoners: 'It was not wise to let the PWs know that this was going on, so we used to give the other PWs about two hours start . . . There were about 90 killed outright.' His figure considerably understates the final tally.

The equation 'walking = life' goads the stronger ones up the track towards Telupid. Every morning, fewer men set off; and those unable to lift themselves at dawn await with silent resignation the blow to the head, or the bullet. For many, the prospect of death offers a sense of relief. The little ritual repeats itself every morning: the doomed man shakes hands with his friends, shares out the last of his rations (to prevent the guards taking it) and passes on messages to his loved ones. 'In the morning,' Nelson Short later recollects, 'when the men were too weak to stand, we used to shake hands with them and say goodbye as they more or less knew what was going to happen.'[21] Then the spent man sits by a tree, or on a log, and awaits his fate, coming up the track. Some men are seen sitting quietly, stoically, as their executioners arrive; others tearfully cling to a memory – of their parents, wife or child – as they await death; some leave this life hurling curses at the Japanese and defiantly goading them to 'let me have it'.[22] Others, such as Gunboat Simpson, famous for his gambling nights, simply walk off into the jungle, never to be seen again. Tsuji's men are rotated every day, so that every guard on the march participates in, or witnesses, the slaughter – an unseen war crime committed in the depths of the last great wilderness on earth.

On 4 June 1945, the weary line encounters signs of the First

March in the form of a bleached skeleton propped against a tree. Nearby lies a mouldy Australian hat and the badge of the Australian Army.

TWO

A native . . . picked me up and then I collapsed. They
gave me food and they treated me well and they told me
the Japs were still in Sandakan and offered to look after
me. They were very very good people and they said they
would keep me there until the Americans came.
Richard Braithwaite, on being found
alive by the people of Sabah

BLEACHED SKELETONS, BONES, bits of clothing, blankets, kitbags, identity discs and other items fleetingly identifiable as Australian or British litter the forest. The living pass in silence through the relics of the First March. Every object sends a warning: to flee, to hide, to escape this place. A few fitter men, fortified by the strange belief that they can, they must, survive, hear the call.

Near the village of Maunad, the guards announce that each group faces another ten days' march. It is, in effect, a death sentence, the prisoners now fully realise. Most have no hope of completing such a journey. Each man has half a tin of sugar and the same of salt – to last the whole trip – and a dwindling rice ration of three ounces per day. By 6 June 1945, the Second

March has killed 118 Australian and British soldiers.

The survivors spill into the deserted village – merely a few huts and three large sheds. Their eyes strain for something to eat in the dusty clearing and empty dwellings. The Japanese have been here first and ransacked the place. Despair fills the men. Dozens decide they cannot go on; some just lie down and await death.

At the Tangkual River crossing, near Maunad, Japanese and Formosan guards – according to two native eyewitnesses – arrange in a circle 35 Australian and British prisoners who are unable to proceed, tie them together with cords attached to their genitals, and shoot them, by rifle and machine gun. All die. 'The last party heard the distant shots as they struggled along the track,' Jackson observes.[1] An AGAS agent later records, 'Natives report that PW at Telupid when on the march were naked and tied together by the penis . . . 35 PW in good health were shot while so tied.'[2] 'Good health' in this context means they are not dead yet. One Australian, pretending to be dead, escapes wearing only a hat and a singlet, and finds refuge in the home of Hee Choi and his family. Although afraid of the Japanese, they offer him food and a hiding place – an act of great courage at a time when the Kempei-tai threatens natives who harbour escapees with new and hideous forms of torture. According to one source, the victim is bound to a rubber tree suspended above the ground. One end of a wire is tied around his testicles, the other around a brick, which is balanced on his head. The Japanese then slash the trunk and ignite the flammable rubber sap dripping onto the brick and the victim's skin, causing him to flinch. As the brick falls, he is castrated.[3]

▲
▽

Owen Campbell decides he cannot go on. British by birth, Campbell is 29 years old at the time of the march. Before the war, he lived with his wife, Evelyn, on their farm at Toowong, in Queensland. His army photo presents a wild-looking soldier with unkempt hair and a strange, demonic gaze; it misrepresents a fundamentally decent man, who led a simple Christian life on the family's small farm. Small and compact, at the time of his escape he wears the marks of three years in prison: a cheekbone smashed in by a gun butt; an eye socket scarred.

On 6 June, Campbell and four others – Privates Sid Webber and Ted Skinner, Lance Corporal Ted Emmett, and a fourth who was likely to have been Private Keith Costin (not Jack Austen, as has been mistakenly recorded) – decide the time is right to flee.

Webber – 'Siddy' to his family – is a dapper young man, aged 24, with shining brown eyes, dark curly hair and olive skin. 'Siddy was a great catch,' his loving niece June Fowler-Smith remembers many years later. 'He loved ballroom dancing. He was a beautiful dancer, and in great demand.'[4] Skinner, from Tenterfield, is remembered as a brave and gentle soul, of strong religious faith, who always carried his Bible with him.[5] Emmett, of the 2/10th Field Ambulance, is an idealistic young man, from a loving family, given to trying his hand at poetry. A few weeks before the fall of Singapore, *The Australian Women's Weekly* published his poem 'Thoughts of Youth'. It was the last memory his family received before his captivity and dispatch to Sandakan:

> Who can see the dream youth sees,
> Or probe the secret mind,
> As youth sails o'er the troubled seas
> And leaves his home behind?[6]

The five men have spent the previous few months gathering whatever items they can find, should the chance arise, to help them escape: a compass (which Emmett has kept since Singapore), fishing lines, some quinine tablets (which Campbell has traded for his watch) and extra clothing.

Their plan is simple – and initially works. On 7 June, Allied aircraft appear overhead, forcing, as usual, the Japanese and Formosan guards to scatter into the bush. They leave their packs on the side of the track. Campbell and his mates seize the chance. They hobble over to the packs, grab several tins of rice, six tins of salmon and some dried fish, and plunge into the jungle.

They move as fast as their illness and hunger will allow, travelling inland, away from the track and coast. They manage only a mile that day, wait to avoid patrols, then advance for a further four days under cover of the forest. Skinner contracts dysentery, and his health rapidly deteriorates. Campbell is swollen with beriberi and shows the symptoms of malaria; he swallows a couple of quinine tablets. The others fare a little better. They decide to rest on 11 June, for two days. On the 13th, Skinner appears too sick to move and tries to persuade the others to abandon him: 'I can go no further.' The rest decide to split up. Campbell elects to stay with Skinner while the other three set off to seek help.

For four days, Campbell and Skinner sit in the forest, eating their share of the remaining food. Skinner's condition deteriorates further and, rather than burden the escape party with his condition, he decides to take his own life. According to Campbell's later account, 'About the 16th I went down to get some water and fish and on my return found Skinner had cut his throat. I buried Skinner.'[7]

Campbell's story, later told to an amazed Major Dick Noone, offers no details about Skinner's last hours alive, or whether the dead man left a verbal or written message, which seems likely given his religious faith. They remain shrouded in mystery.[8] Campbell later tells the ABC journalist Fred Simpson, '[Skinner] had tried to persuade me that I should go on and that there was no hope for him. There have been other men who would have done the same thing that my mate did, but there have been none braver. I buried him and then pushed on.'[9] Later, Campbell explains that, lacking the time to bury the body, he covered it in branches and leaves.

Campbell pushes on to join the others. During the night, he catches crabs and some kind of animal, which he eats raw.[10] He travels downstream and soon encounters a Malayan lean-to – a mere blanket on sticks – about 60 yards from the shore. Inside is Costin, then very ill. The other two, Webber and Emmett, are fishing. Campbell joins them, and the three men hail a passing prahu, a native fishing craft, with Malays on board. As it approaches the bank, a Japanese concealed beneath the gunwale stands and fires, killing Webber and Emmett instantly. 'It was so quick they had no chance and fell into the river,' Campbell later says.[11] Alive and shielded by a rise in the bank, Campbell runs back to the lean-to. He and Costin hurry away but the latter is too sick to survive longer than a few nights. On the night of 21 June, Campbell later recalls, 'I buried him as best I could and pushed on next morning alone.'[12]

Campbell travels alone for another 11 hot days and teeming nights, through forest, along rivers, up ridges. Between about 25 June and 3 July – his delirious state blurs the precise times and dates – he roams the jungle 'like something wild'.[13] He discards his gear and, at one point, semi-naked under a tree, awakes to find a wild boar nuzzling him and seemingly about to take a bite out of his leg. He thrusts a stick at the animal and drives it off. Somehow, he summons the energy to move, but he suffers from morning blindness, a symptom of beriberi. He scrabbles together a diet of jungle fungus and crabs. Severely malnourished, he grows delusional and experiences hallucinations. He chats with his dead mates as though they're still walking along beside him – ghostly visitations in the play of a sick man's mind.[14] He reaches a river, a few hundred feet wide, and tries to cross it on a log. A passing Japanese sees him and fires, wounding him in the wrist. Campbell dives underwater and somehow manages to swim to the safety of mangroves on the other bank. He passes the night there, in the cover of the forest on the shore, and next morning resumes his journey in a state of heightened delirium.

On what seems the last day of his life, he crawls to the banks of the Maunad River, where Japanese and Malayan boats ply the waterway. 'I could hardly stand on my feet.'[15] Too sick to care for the consequences, he hails a prahu, which appears to be avoiding the main traffic. The boat draws near the bank, and two Malayans appear. They give their names as Galuting and Lap. They prove friendly and take him to their village near Maunad, where the people give him clothes and feed him soup, rice and prawns. Shortly, he is moved to a more remote village, where, on two occasions in the ensuing days, the friendly local police hide him in the back of a hut.

Of all the local people who try to help Campbell – and there are many – none is as crucial to his survival than Orang Tuan Kulang, the hunter and Dusun chief who helped build the track from Sandakan and whose ubiquitous presence seems to hover

over Borneo like a sort of benign spirit. By an extraordinary stroke of good fortune, Kulang finds Campbell's refuge. The tribal leader later says:

> When we got near, we found that the women were panicky, thinking that we were Japanese . . . as we approached we were recognised and Ambiau [who had been hiding Campbell] came forward and told me that he had an escaped Australian PW in hiding. When I approached the white man he was trembling and I was startled to see his condition. He looked like an orang-utan, he was thin and covered with hair and scabies.[16]

At first, this close inspection by a native chief, who seems faintly amused by the sight of a dishevelled, bearded white man, makes Campbell nervous. Then Kulang smiles – 'I assured him that I was his friend and not a Jap' – and addresses him in Malay. Campbell cannot understand, and 'we both laughed at this fact'. To prove his friendship, Kulang shows Campbell a letter from the Services Reconnaissance Department, revealing that he is an agent for the Allies. On reading it, Campbell falls into Kulang's arms – the meeting answers his most fervent prayers – and vows to follow the Dusun to the ends of the earth if need be. In the ensuing days, Kulang and the villagers feed and shave him, and move him to a safer hiding place. Campbell gradually regains his strength. A few days later, on 19 July, Campbell is deemed fit enough to attempt the journey to rejoin the Allies.

Four prahus carrying a party of 47 men accompany the Australian down a Labuk tributary, to the mouth of the Bongaya River – a journey of some six nights' paddling. Kulang gives

the Australian an Owen gun; the others are armed with .303s –
courtesy of the Services Reconnaissance Department. On 20
July, Campbell progresses upriver for seven hours, to the Special
Forces hideout. During the journey, he passes out. 'I obtained
some hot coconut oil and massaged him,' Kulang recalls.[17] Here,
Lieutenant Jock Hollingworth, an AGAS officer then running a
team of guerrillas on the coast, awaits Campbell's arrival, having
been tipped off by local agents. Their astonished meeting is brief.
In line with instructions from Sutcliffe, prahu and seaplane carry
Campbell to the safety of the USS *Pokomoke*, a US aircraft carrier
anchored a safe distance offshore.

The ship's hospital receives in silent shock this barely human
form, rent with tropical diseases, covered in sores and scaly skin,
acutely malnourished, severely deficient in vitamins, and weighing
seven stone, less than half his normal weight. Campbell's
extraordinary escape prompts a cipher cable, sent on 24 July, to
Allied Headquarters. Note the importance placed on immediate
press censorship:

> SECRET. for GS int from FINLAY. QX14380 gnr
> CAMPBELL Owen Colin 2/10 fd regt aust PW recovered ex
> BORNEO by SRD now at TAWI TAWI too ill for on movt.
> interrogating offr cannot arrive before PM 25 jul thus will
> not have been cautioned against press interviews. request you
> contact DGPR and if necessary Adjutant General Branch
> ensure no infm passed to press.[18]

Campbell's debriefing starts that day. The whole terrible story
tumbles forth, slowly at first, from cracked lips, to the astonished
interviewers: his miraculous flight, the Death March, the prison

camp, his memory of burying Skinner, Hoshijima's practice of 'king hitting' prisoners, Nagai's threat to starve the prisoners to death as 'the best punishment for us'.[19] His account of the Death Marches – 'We saw a lot of skeletons on the track and the graves . . . I saw three PWs with their skulls bashed in . . . and plenty of others alive lying by the road . . . The killers were coming along the lines to finish off those who could not go on'[20] – confirms the Services Reconnaissance Department's worst fears: surely little hope remains for the few hundred men then approaching Ranau? Of one group – probably Group 2 of the Second March – Campbell recalls that just 17 out of 50 men were alive at the 48-mile peg, adding, 'We were too tired and hungry to take much notice . . .'[21]

Nonetheless, AGAS decides to proceed with the insertion of two commandos at Pitas, near the northern tip of Borneo: Flying Officer Geoffrey Ripley and Corporal Amos Hywood, accompanied by several local police constables. Their mission is to reach Ranau and gather intelligence on – and, if possible, make contact with – the prisoners, in the hope of affording some kind of swift relief if and when the Japanese capitulate. The landings at Tarakan, Balikpapan and Sandakan are now well advanced – and the end is surely only a matter of time. The route chosen by the AGAS agents, however, will take them down the Bengkoka River and overland, through some of the most impenetrable terrain on earth. Even if they reach the men, there is little they will be able to do without aircraft and paratroopers.

Meanwhile, Campbell improves and takes to pottering about the ship's deck. He cannot help noticing the daily arrival of native prahus bumping the side of the ship, offering fruit and vegetables – and promptly warns the American officers of Japs lying in the canoes' bottoms.

◆

Back on the march, the guards ignore, or seem unaware of, the missing men. Their exhausted condition has induced listlessness; their attention span wanes and discipline lapses. The roll call is haphazard. Other prisoners see their chance coming: men such as Bill Sticpewich, who bides his time, for now. No doubt, his 'technical team' has done well out of fraternising, procuring extra rations and better conditions. But such favouritism is levelling off, in what has become survival of the fittest. Sticpewich is certainly among the fittest, but those who accuse him of indulging at the prisoners' expense overlook his manifest courage. This courage is evident on several occasions, not least during the crossing of the Mandorin River, on 8 June – the day after Campbell's escape. A mud-covered log with a wire handrail, the bridge is set high over the torrent. Halfway across, a prisoner freezes, and would surely have been shot had Sticpewich not gone back over the bridge to assist the petrified man and shoulder his gear. The man's terror is well founded: at least three Australians, including Jack West, of the 2/30th Battalion, too weak to balance themselves, slip off the bridge and drown.

Another man with a keen eye on escape is Richard Braithwaite, who is in a dreadful state. If Sticpewich is fit enough to choose his moment, Braithwaite, like Campbell, literally has no choice: he must flee now or he will die. Every morning, he suffers malarial blackouts. One day, he feels so awful he considers killing himself. A spur in his side to stay alive is the action of his friends, who prop him up at roll call. One morning, six others, including two of Braithwaite's closest mates, cannot stand up and are 'disposed of'. Also shot, with the same indifference as shown to any prisoner, is the Japanese interpreter Ozawa, found 'wandering around in a most disoriented state', according to Silver.[22] The sick are treated exactly the same – killed, when too weak to work – regardless of whether they are Japanese, Formosan, Australian or British.

Braithwaite's terrible condition draws the attention of the guards, who attempt to hasten his demise with daily beatings. It happens to several other weak cases. 'Every morning I was being kicked, bashed,' he later recalls.[23] One day, he slips down a slope and receives a beating so severe the guard responsible leaves him for dead. Amazingly, Braithwaite manages to lift himself up and rejoin his group.

The secret to his resilience lies in his physique and character. A strong, athletic teenager before the war, Braithwaite retains something of that residual strength in his 27-year-old frame. His mental agility also equips him for the epic ahead. A perceptive observer, he carries many painful memories with him: for example, of his close friends and fellow prisoners, the twins Cecil and Fred Glover of Mosman, Sydney. After Cec dies in an air raid on Sandakan, in early 1945, Braithwaite is allotted the job of telling Fred: 'And Fred cried for a week. He didn't, didn't stop crying . . . you know twins, they're so close aren't they.' Fred died on the First March. The memory of his mates – he assumes both are dead – hardens and infuriates Braithwaite. His anger is not blind; rather, it seems to switch on something inside the man, something unrelenting and indestructible. 'Yes, it's quite amazing how, when anger does things,' he later says. 'I had an experience when I was in [a youth club] and I lifted a five-hundredweight case with one hand to get a fellow's leg out of it . . . But in the prison camp something would make you suddenly angry. It may be a thought, may be something someone said, may be something the

Japs did, but you were suddenly angry, and you'd feel the strength surge back through you. And it was quite incredible.'[24] This inner rage will soon save his life.

In early June, Braithwaite decides his only hope of survival is to walk off the track and hide in the jungle until the Japanese are gone, then wait until he is strong enough to reach the coast: 'I became aware it was a one-way trip when we started to hear shots . . . and there was no hope for anyone who fell out.'[25] The sound of machine-gun fire during the massacre at Tangkual Crossing makes up his mind. Eschewing an offer by Gunner Wal Blatch to accompany him – because Braithwaite fears his comparative weakness will delay Blatch – he decides to strike out alone. His plan is simple: at the crossing of a small creek – while the Japanese guards are out of sight – Braithwaite tumbles into the unknown world a few yards off the track and lies for hours in the seclusion of the forest. Weeks later, he tells his story to an AGAS commando:

> I don't know if it was the blazed track as it was all swamps and very, very hard going. I don't think the Japs were in much better condition to carry on. At the Lubak River the chances had dropped down considerably and the next morning when I got up I carried on for about a mile and I just about collapsed and I thought about committing suicide. I don't know how but I got down into the jungle and I waited there . . .[26]

While sitting there, Braithwaite hears two gunshots, which he presumes to be the murder of his friends Jake Mildenhall and Rex Hodges. (He later returns to the site to find their bodies hidden under leaves.) Moving further into the forest, nestling in among an ants' nest – 'I've never seen ants like them, about an inch and a half long . . . kept running over me'[27] – Braithwaite waits all afternoon, 'thinking, thinking out and I decided that I had nothing to lose and would try and make the end of the river for I knew the PT boats were near the Lubak River'. After the last Japanese appear to leave, he heads back down the track in the direction of Mandoring:

'I started down the river and it was very hard going and I spent the night on the bank of the river. I kept going the next day but I could only go about 1/4 mile . . .' For five racked days, he stumbles through the scrub, along riverbanks and animal tracks, passing three deserted Japanese outposts, tormented by jungle ants, scorpions and snake-infested swamps, which would sound like Boys' Own embellishments anywhere but here. He eventually reaches the river and continues his journey along the edge of the bank, swimming with the current: 'I forgot about crocodiles.'

And then, suddenly, coming around a sharp bend, is a Japanese soldier: 'He must have been pretty sick too, because he was just hobbling, getting along. He didn't have a rifle or bayonet . . . and we more or less just ran into each other on the track . . .'[28]

Before the Japanese could say a word, Braithwaite grabbed a branch, and 'clobbered him and killed him'.[29] A sudden, almost reflexive act to destroy the cause of so much misery and pent-up fury, or, as Braithwaite suggests in another account, a calculated ambush? 'A branch lay handy and I picked it up and waited. I don't think he ever knew what hit him. I seemed to go berserk then. I hit him and hit him and smashed him as he lay there dead. I was crying and saying as I did it: "That's for Cec. That's for Reg. That's for murdering my mates."'[30] His inner fury, felt on behalf of so many, seems to fortify him for this act; it seems astonishing that a terribly weak man could kill a soldier. While we only have his word that it happened, Braithwaite was a sincere and remarkably driven individual; nor do we know the state of the Japanese victim.

◆

One morning, finding himself off the track, near a river and apparently lost, Braithwaite attempts to build a raft. Seeing an old fisherman out checking his fish traps, he calls for help, gently in Malayan. The old man paddles over and invites the Australian aboard. They float downstream to the fisherman's home, at Sapi Village, where Braithwaite, like Campbell, is in luck. His rescuer is Abing bin Luma, headman of Sapi, whose inhabitants loathe the Japanese. His arrival here, to feel a warm hand on his shoulder, to taste good food and experience human kindness, quite overwhelms him:

> A native . . . picked me up and then I collapsed. They gave me food and they treated me well and they told me the Japs were still in Sandakan and offered to look after me. They were very very good people and they said they would keep me there until the Americans came.[31]

The villagers hide him in a compartment behind a false wall in Abing's house. That night, he enjoys hot food and a bath, and hears news of white guerrillas in the area. Within days, several villagers, including Abing and a Filipino fugitive, Loreto Padua (also known as Abdul Raschid), accompany Braithwaite on the perilous journey to Libaran Island. Two canoes, each containing eight men, paddle through the night of 13 June and arrive safely late on the 14th. Here, he enjoys 'a beautiful innerspring mattress', and spends his evenings on the verandah of a little hut by the sea, eating green mangoes with soy sauce. The next day, an American PT boat appears in the bay. Braithwaite and his native friends paddle furiously out to it, waving a white flag. On pulling alongside, an incredulous Lieutenant James, commander of US PT Boat 112, exclaims, 'Good Christ, it's an Aussie. What would you like, Aussie?' Braithwaite replies, 'A pint of beer.'

His story tumbles forth again, in fits and starts, during several interviews, interspersed with close medical care and all the comforts of the US Navy. On 17 June, the Australian Military Forces sends a cipher message to Landops HQ: 'BRAITHWAITE UNFIT FOR MOV [*sic*] FOR ONE WEEK MALNUTRITION AND MALARIA. GHQ HAS CONCURRED RETENTION HOSP TILL FIT TO MOVE THEN REQUEST MOV MOROTAI . . .'[32]

In early July, an American hospital ship transfers Braithwaite to Morotai. He receives bully beef, vitamin pills, liver injections – 'they really filled me up with everything'.[33] His story so appals Allied Command that, as with Campbell's account, they immediately take every action to suppress it – issuing a cable on 29 June 1945 (in response, it seems, to a small newspaper item on the 27th about his rescue) to the effect that Braithwaite's experience and condition 'should not be made known to the next of kin'; and that if the family enquire further, they should be told only that 'he is receiving careful medical attention in Allied territory . . . but his exact location cannot be divulged at present'.[34] After his interrogation, an American officer says, 'We're going in now to look for your friends' – at which Braithwaite rolls to the side of his bunk, turns his face to the wall and cries, 'You'll be too late.'[35]

31

THE CHAPLAIN

There cannot be a God, there just cannot be a God
for men to suffer and be treated like this.
Chaplain Harold Wardale-Greenwood, at
the end of the Second Death March

HIS PHOTO SHOWS an intelligent, compassionate man with
gentle eyes, an aquiline nose and an expression of benign concern
on the brink of a smile. It is the picture of a young army chaplain
who, before the war, believed in a hopeful world guided by our
better angels, where all that is good and honest eventually
triumphs. Chaplain Harold Wardale-Greenwood is a patient
man. In June 1945, he reaches Ranau and survives the Second
March – just. His story is a bellwether of the spiritual degradation
of men subjected to such cruelty.

Wardale-Greenwood has never worn rose-tinted spectacles;
he understands human nature and the depths to which it
can sink. Born in Durham, England, on 20 March 1909, he
emigrated to Australia and found himself enlisting in the 2/19th
Battalion, Australian Imperial Force, at the outbreak of the
Second World War. 'Minister of Religion' is the occupation given
on his enlistment form.[1] A reverend of the Church of England,

Wardale-Greenwood and his wife, Marjory, settled in 'The Manse', Rainbow, in the state of Victoria. Their son, Ian, was born in October 1941, three months before Harold was taken prisoner in Singapore, making him nine months old when his father was shipped to Sandakan, as a member of B Force.

An Australian military bureaucrat will later cite the date, place and cause of Chaplain Wardale-Greenwood's death: 18.7.45, in Borneo, of malaria. In fact, he dies on 12 July, near Ranau, of far more complex causes. He is 36. The official record contains a list of his medals – the 1939/45 Star, Pacific Star, Defence Medal and War Medal – granted to all who served in the Pacific Theatre and posted to the families after the war. Wardale-Greenwood's widow is to receive her late husband's medals in September 1951.[2]

These mute military facts barely touch on the life of Chaplain Wardale-Greenwood. Most witnesses die with him. But the fellow officers who remember him attest that he was always more than a chaplain. During the fierce fighting in Malaya, for example, he grabbed control of a machine gun after the gunner died and continued fighting.[3] In Singapore, he earned a recommendation for the Military Cross, for courage in tending wounded soldiers under heavy fire. As waves of Japanese troops tore into the Australian positions, the chaplain, with little regard for his personal safety, crawled up and down the lines of the wounded and dying, tending to their medical and spiritual needs.

The chaplain's selfless duty continued in captivity. He arrived in Sandakan already a familiar and cherished presence among the soldiers, constantly at the bedsides of the sick and by the graves of the dead, where he regularly delivered short, moving sermons that summoned hope of an afterlife for the deceased. Within weeks of his arrival, Wardale-Greenwood laid to rest the Gloucester-born blacksmith Sapper Bill Redman, who had died of dysentery aged 31, leaving a widow and three infant sons.

Wardale-Greenwood, however, went further than his spiritual remit and proved, as Silver rightly concludes, 'as heroic in captivity as he had been in battle'.[4] Aware of the brutality of the guards at the airfield, he secretly offered to work in place of the sick and wounded, giving them much-needed 'rest days'. When the Japanese discovered the ruse, they caged the chaplain for 36 hours, which he spent in quiet contemplation of the Bible – in fact, he became so engrossed in reading that the Japanese decided he could not be suffering enough and confiscated the book.

Wardale-Greenwood was not alone in his heroic ministrations: several Anglican chaplains and Catholic padres offered comfort to stricken men and raised morale in the early years of captivity. The prisoners – mostly Catholic, Protestant or agnostic – grew to depend on these stoic earthly spirits. In 1943, Wardale-Greenwood declined the chance to go to Kuching with other officers, electing instead to stay with the men in Sandakan. His duty, as he saw it, was to attend to the spiritual hopes of the sick and dying. Two other Protestant chaplains remained as well: Albert Thompson and Corporal Alan Garland. Two padres, Captains John Rogers and Austin O'Donovan, despite their vehement protests, were ordered to leave for Kuching, thus denying absolution to Catholic soldiers.

'Brave' and 'tough' Wardale-Greenwood certainly is; but such banal adjectives fall well short of the man who, on entering the green hell through which he is forced to walk, at the head of 50 prisoners, shows an unceasing duty of care for the young men strung out behind him, concealing from them the shredded vestiges of a faith soon to be subjected to the most profound tests that God, if he exists – though the very idea here seems absurd – may contrive to throw at a mortal being.

◆

By mid-1945, Wardale-Greenwood is the longest surviving chaplain in Borneo. Having outlived his Catholic and Protestant colleagues, he finds himself in June 1945 leading Group 3 on the Second March to Ranau. He departs in a state of deep distress at the thought of having to leave the sick behind, on the muddy earth at Sandakan. His mood darkens as the march progresses and its purpose becomes clear. Conscious of being flayed to death on this dismal track, he summons all his remaining Christian strength in a desperate effort to reassure his fellow soldiers: he urges his group to pray; he leads little services to the memory of dead friends; he dares to believe in a vision of heavenly grace.

In private moments of despair, he appeals beyond the forest to the empty sky, for some message of hope, some note, or light, of divine intervention. None comes; nobody is listening. All around him, the chaplain sees only cruelty, wretchedness and suffering. If God exists, He continues mysteriously to refrain from making his presence felt to this lonely appellant, who trudges on with all the embattled constancy and searching doubt of a twentieth-century Job.

Illness and exhaustion render Wardale-Greenwood vulnerable to the counsel of despair. His stomach is empty; his ulcered feet are bare; his limbs are swollen with beriberi. He leads his men on, through mud and rain. They reach the high country near Ranau. More of his group fall beside the track, shortly followed by the crack of gunfire, and the chaplain succumbs to deep depression and something of an eclipse of the spirit. Unable to reconcile such appalling cruelty with the existence of a benevolent god, he yields to the slow creep of disillusionment. By the time he reaches Ranau, with a fraction of his men left, the chaplain apprehends an utterly godless world, in which any last fragments of faith are plunged in the blackest psychological shade.

At a rest area near Ranau in early July, Private Nelson Short is out gathering firewood. On his way back, he passes Wardale-Greenwood and hears the chaplain muttering, over and over again, 'There cannot be a God, there just cannot be a God for men to suffer and be treated like this.'5 Within a few days, Harold Wardale-Greenwood is dead – of sickness, exhaustion and, it appears, a broken spirit. His friends bury him with fitting reverence. If he dies having lost his faith in God, the men never lose their faith in him.

The full story of Harold Wardale-Greenwood's brief life exists in his soul and mind, a realm beyond our comprehension. The bare story related here describes the cruel disabusing of a man who, borne down by the extremity of the pain he sees and feels around him, and the silence of the god to whom he hopes and prays, ceases to believe. His journey is the very antithesis of Paul's on the road to Damascus: God is dead in the jungles of Borneo, along with His kindly, once-fervent disciple.

32

THE LAST JUNGLE CAMP

'What has happened to the rest of you?' Sticpewich asked.
Sergeant Stacey replied, 'They just systematically exterminated us.'
Sergeant Stacey on meeting Sticpewich at
the last jungle camp in Ranau

IT IS A GREEN DEPRESSION about five miles south of
Ranau. In another world, at another time, this little ditch might
be thought tranquil. Here, the jungle gives onto palm plantations
that cling to the hillsides down to the valley floor, where a loamy,
silt-laden stream ripples by. The hollow offers protection from air
raids: the reason the Japanese select it as the site for the third –
and last – jungle camp.

Gazing now over this wretched dent in the earth, and knowing
what happened here from May 1945, the mind's eye conjures
another scene, of perfect hell: a damp melange of jungle exudes
the stench of rotting vegetation; rows of abandoned palms, like
skeletal forms, seem to move up the valley sides; huge droplets of
monsoonal rain harden with repeated bursts on bare skin; squat,
vermin-ridden huts and lean-tos materialise as the last pathetic
homes of the damned; and crazed Formosan guards shriek
intermittently at a dwindling group of silent, uncomprehending

white men. Such are the salient features of the prisoners' final days and nights.

During May, the few mobile men – held at the second (temporary) jungle camp near Ranau – deliver atap and other supplies here, and set to work building three huts for the Japanese. They work under the forest canopy by the creek bed, invisible from the air. The porters include the tireless Keith Botterill and Bill Moxham.

On 10 June, the 19 survivors of the First March are ordered to get up and march from their temporary jungle camp at Sinarut to this sheltered valley. Just ten men rise from their beds; the other nine are on the verge of death. They sit or lie amid the corpses of 36 recently deceased. The relatively healthy Norm Allie volunteers to stay and look after the nine sick. Six are stretcher cases. They have hours to live.

That night, Lieutenant Suzuki Taichi, Sergeant Iwabe Shigaru and seven guards carry the stretcher cases to a burial ground a short distance away and shoot them where they lie. Suzuki shoots the first three, according to Sticpewich; the remainder are lined up side by side on the ground and shot by the seven-guard firing squad.[1] The last pair to die, according to Silver, are believed to have pleaded with their executioners to hurry up and 'finish them off'.[2] Allie and one other prisoner still standing by are then gunned down. The guards haul the bodies into a shallow ditch, where they join the remains of 21 Australian and British soldiers previously buried there. Nearby is the fresh grave of the deeply humane Warrant Officer John Kinder, who succumbed to recurrent illness. Moxham, who nursed and comforted him through his final days, buried him that morning beneath a small white cross – the only prisoner at Ranau to receive a marked gravestone.

Of the 455 men who left Sandakan on the First March five months earlier, just six scrawny humans remain alive on 20 June. Five are Australian – Botterill, Moxham, Sergeant Richard Stacey, Private Norm Grist and Sapper Arthur Bird – and one is English, Gunner Norm Frost. Four of the last ten – Colin Wright, Rolf Newling, Evan Davies and Stan Roberts – expired between 13 and 19 June.

The six survivors await their fate exposed to the sun and rain. They have no shelter except the forest. They sit on the riverbank. The river sluices by the grey strip of sediment. On 26 June, something stirs on the hill: a line of half-naked, hollow-eyed men coming down in single file. A few appear in rude good health: Captain Cook and Warrant Officer Sticpewich and his fellow technicians. The rest are walking cadavers. To their horror, Moxham and Botterill recognise these men as the first survivors of the Second Death March. The final count reveals that 142 Australians and 42 British men have reached Ranau, of the original 536 – fewer than the First March, many of whom subsequently died in the disease sinks of Ranau and Paginatan.

Takakuwa and his senior officers, Watanabe and Suzuki, order the guards to keep the six survivors of the First March apart from the new arrivals. The two groups are cordoned off, like the carriers of some contagious disease. The ever-resourceful Botterill and Moxham, however, manage to make contact with Captain Picone, from the Second March. The shock is mutual: Picone's at this pitiful remnant of the 455 men on the First March; Botterill's and Moxham's at news that behind Picone, strewn over the hills and valleys, lie the remains of 351 prisoners: 295 Australians and 56 British. A few – Braithwaite and Campbell – have escaped, presumed dead.

The experience of the Second March has exceeded in pathos and sheer agony that of the first. Botterill hears stories of men reduced by the lack of food to propelling themselves up the track on their hands and knees, driving themselves over ridges at a crawl, and sliding down the other sides on their backsides – only to be shot when they could not drag themselves further.[3] The guards have found any pretext to kill. Prisoners still wearing their watches or wedding rings have been ordered to fall out regardless of their fitness to continue. Later, the guards would reappear, wearing the watch or ring and carrying the victim's clothes, blanket or haversack to sell to the natives.

Sticpewich soon finds a way of talking to the six survivors of the First March: 'When we went down to the river to cook that night we saw the Jap quarters and the six personnel in question. Two of them were very sick and we were not allowed to talk to any of them.' He recognises five as Australians on the First March and within two days gets a chance to talk to them.

'What has happened to the rest of you?' Sticpewich asks.

Sergeant Stacey replies, 'They just systematically exterminated us.'[4]

Sticpewich enquires after his friends: yes, all dead; yes, mostly shot. Some, such as Private Richards, were beaten and thrown into gullies. Others starved to death.

Sticpewich has seen their webbing, boots, shoes and bodies. And, near Ranau, 'the bodies' bones were scattered around as though they had been mauled by pigs and there were five skulls . . .'[5] He recalls witnessing the death of Warrant Officer Dixon, 'bashed to insensibility by a guard whose nickname was Top Hat' (or 'Gentleman Jim' to the British prisoners). Jonathan Dixon and Jimmy Barlow, another Australian soldier too weak to move, regained consciousness but Top Hat refused to allow them to rejoin the line. 'I never saw either of them again,' Sticpewich relates. 'Later during the march I saw Top Hat wearing Dixon's gold ring.'[6]

◆

The 184 survivors of the second atrocity crowd into 'death valley', as it is called, in late June. There is no shelter: the Japanese and Formosans occupy the three huts on the riverbank. The prisoners' only protection from the sun and rain is 'to crawl into the scrub'.[7] Within three days, 20 of the new arrivals are dead. The remaining men continue to expire at this rate. The food ration amounts to two ounces of rice per man per day; and 'we were made to take the water from below the Jap camp', 500 yards downriver of the spot where the Japanese urinate, wash and bathe.[8]

Some 18 prisoners are deputed to water-carrying duties, which involve hauling about a hundred buckets a day a half-mile back to camp. The job eventually kills all except one, Driver Owen Evans. He only survives because he cannot continue due to internal injuries sustained by a beating for his 'failure' to stop a fellow prisoner from stealing a potato from the guards' cookhouse.[9] Added to this are the prisoners' incessant duties: gathering wood and vegetables, collecting bags of rice from Ranau. Throughout June, lines of 'thin, weary, bent, bearded and barefooted white men' are a painfully familiar sight passing through the village.[10]

They work on a cup of watery rice a day. On 30 June, Sticpewich receives permission to build a hut for the prisoners. The stronger men, under his direction, gather whatever materials they can scrounge: bamboo, palm fronds and bits of atap. Sticpewich and his relatively fit four-man technical team take the lead in the construction. Until its completion, the prisoners continue to sleep under flimsy lean-tos, camouflaged with palm fronds.

On 13 July, the hut is finished. The effort reduces their number to 'about 100'.[11] Twenty by 16 feet, it offers a welcome shelter from the sun and rain. About 40 men occupy the stilted floor, and those with severe dysentery, unable to control their bowels, lie splayed on the mud below. All are 'covered in lice and scabies'.[12]

Before its completion, a handful of survivors – Botterill and Moxham from the First March, Nelson Short and Frank 'Andy' Anderson from the second – enact a strange, effulgent dream and their only source of hope: they escape.

THREE

ONE NIGHT IN POURING RAIN, these four young Australians
decide the time is right. On 7 July, Keith Botterill, Bill Moxham,
Nelson Short and Andy Anderson set in motion a plan of which
they have been talking for months. It is perhaps a melancholy
judgement on humanity that the most insubordinate and
irresponsible of men, self-interested chancers, distinctly lacking
in a sense of deference or duty, also appear to make the best
survivors, and escapees. It bleakly bears out Botterill's rather
self-aware observation that in Borneo the good and selfless and
dutiful are as good as dead. We've met Botterill: the Nyngan-
born Depression kid with the somewhat loaded charge sheet. Yet
alongside Moxham, Short and Anderson, Botterill's service record
looks exemplary. Moxham, the dysfunctional son of a wealthy
Sydney family, was born with 'a wild, almost reckless streak which
had never been tamed despite his having attended expensive
Sydney private schools', as Lynette Silver observes.[1] After leaving
school at 17, the lad was sent to manage one of his family's rural

estates, which he did for 11 years before enlisting, in 1940, along with his two 'equally wild' brothers, Tom and Harry. Moxham promptly displayed a chronic incapacity to take orders and adhere to basic military discipline, absenting himself without leave on several occasions. Perhaps his connections, or good performance as a soldier, mitigated the charges, for he never lost the single stripe of a lance bombardier.

Nelson Short's character seems to leap straight out of a low-budget travelling-circus act. An 'entertainer', of sorts, this curiously unpopular balladeer comes across as one of those ingratiating people who rely on bad jokes and unfunny pranks to get along. He appears to be a man of marked selfishness, as later witnesses attest, and carries a list of petty misdemeanours against his name, such as failing to clean dixie lids, going absent without leave and failing to appear on parade. Born in 1917, fair-haired, five feet six inches high, and raised in Enfield, Sydney, he enlisted in the army expecting to be a cook (his trade) but found himself a private infantryman in the 2/18th Battalion. In Singapore, he promptly tried to get out of active service by feigning madness. He invented a 'dog', and took the imaginary animal everywhere, patting it and talking to it, and sharing it with an equally hallucinatory 'wife'. (Short married the day before his departure.) On 21 July 1941, a medical officer diagnosed a form of neurasthenia and consigned the man to hospital. Hopes of being sent home were dashed when his ruse was discovered, and he received a long stint on kitchen duties – an ironic demotion from his hopes of being an army cook. But his example impressed others, and soon other privates in his battalion were found leading imaginary dogs, horses and even sheep around the barracks, hoping to be sent home, persuading journalists that the Australian Army had gone mad and leading to one successful repatriation. Bluey Haydon, detained after punching a major for kicking his 'dog', found himself declared unfit for service and on a boat to Australia, for which he thanked Short. 'You invented the dog Shorty,' he later wrote, 'but I am riding the bastard home.'[2]

The military-service record of Andy Anderson, 24, single, of Kelvin Grove, Brisbane, is a familiar catalogue of misdemeanours, only considerably worse. Since 1940, he's been variously fined, charged and detained for a range of offences: 'disobeying a lawful command', 'failing to carry out duties', 'absenting himself from a place of parade', 'conduct to the prejudice of good order'. On 5 June 1941, he received 28 days' detention for stealing a military vehicle, drunk. He enjoyed a beer and the local women, and was hospitalised for venereal disease on several occasions in Singapore. He left Changi for Sandakan on 23 March 1943, as part of E Force, and survived through sheer willpower and cunning, to reach this dreadful impasse in the heart of Borneo, the last post of his sad, brief life.

These are the men who propose to risk everything in one of the most daring escape attempts of the march. Several events bring forward the plan. Moxham has heard from a prison guard called Memora – who claims to be Christian – that every prisoner still alive will soon be shot.[3] 'I told Captain Heaslop what was going to happen,' Moxham later says, '. . . that it was wise for anyone who was able, to escape – that it was just as good being shot in the jungle as waiting for it in the camp.'[4]

◆

Another powerful motivator is the renewed fury of the guards. In late June and early July, tempers flare over the slightest provocation. A murderous, hair-trigger aggression permeates every moment. The death rate accelerates; the beatings increase in number and intensity. With bad news about the war arriving daily, the Japanese officers find a mute target for their vengeance in these few prostrate Commonwealth soldiers.

An event raises Formosan rage to fever pitch. On 1 July, a deeply troubled Formosan guard, Nakamura Koji, perhaps with one eye on the armistice, confides in Sticpewich – the prisoners' spokesman, with Cook sick – that he regrets his cruelty towards the prisoners and wishes to extend the hand of friendship. Nakamura warns the Australian that the Japanese are going to kill all the prisoners – echoing Memora. Nakamura seems sincere and his motives understandable: he has recently been beaten up by two Japanese officers.

The two men walk quietly towards the cattle pen, where Sticpewich's team oversees the slaughter of cows for the Japanese. They stop and talk. Nakamura rails against the superiors, angrily berating the Japanese officers as 'no good'. 'I will kill myself before surrendering to the Allies,' Nakamura tells Sticpewich, who slyly replies that if an Australian were in a similar position he would shoot the Japanese before shooting himself. Nakamura listens carefully and agrees. '*Beso sia mati* – tomorrow I die,' he says. And so too will 'all the Japanese officers who have treated me badly and killed Australians'.[5] Sticpewich believes him and informs other prisoners of a coming 'coup'.

The next day, Nakamura fulfils his promise. He bursts into the commander's hut, where Suzuki confers with Takakuwa. He shoots Suzuki dead, wounds Takakuwa and slightly injures three others: Takakuwa's batman, the medical orderly Fugita and Captain Cook, who has been told of the 'coup'. Nakamura then blows his brains out. The consequences of this killing spree are dire, both for the guards and the prisoners.

Medical officers Oakeshott and Picone are immediately ordered to treat the wounded; the rest are sent to gather firewood for Suzuki's funeral pyre. The next day, Lieutenant Watanabe, the acting commander, orders the guards on parade and gives them a severe dressing down. As usual, they respond to personal humiliation by blaming, and punishing, the prisoners.

Some receive severe beatings 'for leaving the area to defecate'.[6] As Botterill says later, 'The sick men were actually beaten more than the others because the Japanese hated them and considered them to be a nuisance.'[7] Others die of drawn-out illness, harsh treatment and malnutrition: Captain Heaslop, Chaplain Wardale-Greenwood, Warrant Officer Laurie Maddock, Sergeant Richard Stacey, Private Keith Wrigley and the tireless medical orderly Private Jim Bowe, later described as 'always cheerful in caring for the sick and wounded' and 'the best morale builder in the camp'.[8] In this spirit, Bowe declines an invitation to join Botterill and others in an escape plan. He chooses to stay with the sick – and shortly dies of 'enteritis', according to Japanese records, though the actual cause is the cumulative effect of disease and malnutrition.

Two cases – Sergeant Robert Horder and Sapper Arthur Bird – serve to illustrate the outer limits of savagery into which this world has plunged. Finding two Japanese rifling through his last possessions, which include a watch and a ring, Horder furiously denounces them as 'thieves and mongrels'.[9] They set upon him with kicks and punches, in full view of the camp. 'No part of his body was spared,' according to the Jackson report, 'and after 10 minutes of this treatment he lapsed into unconsciousness from which he never emerged, and died that night.'[10]

Arthur 'Dicky' Bird's horrific end demonstrates what the sick can expect. Ordered to make up the numbers on a cane-cutting detail, Bird, suffering from beriberi, malaria and leg ulcers, protests that he cannot work. 'I am crook, I cannot come,' he cries, through the prisoners' interpreter Corporal Lance Maskey.[11] Moxham and Botterill implore the guards to leave Bird alone; their pleas are ignored. Maskey also tries to intervene. He, too, is shoved aside and slapped.

The Australians then witness the dreadful result. An especially bitter guard, Fukishima Masao, descends on Bird with a frenzied burst of bashing and kicking. 'My friend,' recalls Moxham, a close friend of Bird's, 'collapsed to the ground and immediately Fukishima kicked him repeatedly around the face and head.' The attack damages Bird's head so badly that he still lies unconscious in his blood when the work detail returns, hours later that afternoon. Botterill and others try to carry him back to their hut, but his pain is too great. Bird pleads to be left, still. The medics Oakeshott and Picone come but are helpless without drugs or surgical instruments. Bird falls into a coma and dies a day later, the victim of another act of mindless sadism. For Moxham and Botterill, it is the last straw, the final entry in a monstrous catalogue of crimes. The appalled Oakeshott pleads with the escaping party to do one thing if they survive: to tell his story and get justice for Arthur Bird.

◆

The escape attempt is the last resort of desperate men. Like Crease, hoping for a bullet in the back on his pitch into the jungle, Moxham, Botterill, Short and Anderson know the action is probably suicidal. But they also know this: they will die if they stay in this pit of disease, where the Japanese have clearly determined that no prisoners will survive. It is now a fact, not a rumour, as Sticpewich and Moxham know: both have received tip-offs that the Japanese commanders plan to destroy every last prisoner. Most do not need this confirmation: the evidence of their eyes announces that none of them will walk out of this valley alive.

And yet, despite their growing awareness, none opts to join the escape when the four invite the others. Some nurse a faint hope of mercy or rescue; others rightly conclude that the journey will kill them. Few are strong enough, or willing. Some, remembering the ghastly end of Cleary and Crease, refuse with a shudder: capture means a slow and excruciating death.

The four men even approach Cook (according to Jackson's account, disputed by others), the officer Botterill most despises. Cook declines the offer to join them, writes Jackson, 'possibly because he was on friendly terms with the Japanese administration' and does not wish to endanger his life.[12] Cook has another reason, it seems: he retains the camp records, which he jealously guards and hopes to use as leverage with the Japanese when the war ends. And yet, the fact that he is invited to join the escape attempt – as Jackson asserts – suggests a degree of trust in him at odds with the reputation, heaped on him after the war, as a 'Jap lover'.

Two men refuse out of a sense of duty: Captains Oakeshott and Picone decline chiefly because, as senior medical officers, they feel they must stay with the sick. In the same spirit of goodwill, these men donate their remaining cash – they actually have some – to the escapees. Oakeshott also parts with his boots, which he decides are of no further use and are soon seen on the feet of Moxham.

◆

They prepare as well as can be expected. Food is the priority. With their usual ingenuity, Moxham and Botterill locate a rice dump a few miles along the track to Ranau. At about 9 pm that night, under cover of heavy rain, the four men creep past a Japanese sentry sheltering from the downpour in a lean-to. They move along the track to the rice cache, seize about ten pounds each and continue past Ranau, where they strike off on a new path, towards Kundarson and their ultimate destination, Jesselton, 62 miles to the west, on the coast.

The next day, Anderson's sickness halts their advance. In a valley, the party find a cave, where they rest to let him recover. They cook rice mixed with green bananas over a bamboo fire. After six days, Anderson rallies, and they resume their journey, winding through the mountainous country past Mount Kinabalu. Anderson's foot ulcer worsens in the difficult terrain, making progress extremely slow. About five miles west of Ranau, he is unable to move. They rest in a deserted hut – indefinitely, it seems; the terrain is simply too exhausting. A nearby vegetable garden yields tapioca and sweet potato – a brief reprieve from the onset of starvation.

The four men are lucky in one crucial respect. They are walking through the heart of Dusun country, and most natives feel deep hostility towards the Japanese; they have not forgotten the wholesale slaughter and burning of their villages following the Kinabalu uprising. The Japanese maintain a few small, disease-ridden garrisons, containing dwindling numbers of men. Few of them dare venture alone into the jungle: any enemy who strays into this region can expect to be peppered with poison darts or decapitated and dismembered. The escapees are thus fairly safe from Japanese patrols, for now; and far more so than Campbell and Braithwaite to the east.

And so, when a Dusun farmer called Barigah Katus discovers four skinny, half-naked white men, he is disposed to help them. Barigah is the headman of Batu Lima village and commands great respect in the area. Jackson later describes him as 'a typical Dusun', 'small in stature' and 'no mental genius', but possessing that 'slow, steady temperament' that enables him to endure the toughest conditions 'without excessive worry'.[13] Barigah is on his way to sell some bananas when he hears voices issuing from the abandoned hut. 'Api Api,' the Australians nervously reply – Malay for 'Jesselton' – when Barigah asks their destination. He warns of concentrations of Japanese at Jesselton and urges them to stay put.

The Australians trust no one and fear everyone. They have seen how the Japanese reward natives who inform on white prisoners, and punish those who collaborate. 'We were trying to keep away from the natives as much as possible,' Moxham later says, 'because they . . . seemed to be on whichever side seemed to them to be winning.'[14] Right now, their only interest is finding food – and hunger offers them no choice other than to accept Barigah's help: 'We decided to trust this native – whether he proved trustworthy or not had to take care of itself.'[15] And so they stay, and await Barigah's return.

One afternoon, to the occupants' shock, an unarmed Japanese soldier walks up to the hut and looks in. 'His eyes nearly popped out of his head' at the sight of us, Moxham recalls.[16] The reaction is mutual. The Japanese demands to know if they are the four prisoners who are reported missing. The Australians disavow all knowledge and manage to persuade him that the hut is a sickroom for their working party, and their guard is not far away. According to Moxham's account, the soldier accepts this story, offers to return later that day with quinine and walks away. The three men draw the conclusion that the Japanese will return, lift Anderson up and scramble off into the scrub.[17]

Barigah proves trustworthy. He catches up with them the next day, drawn by smoke from their fire. The Kempei-tai has put a price on their heads, he warns: $1000 in Japanese currency and several bags of rice. He insists they find a better place to hide. Together, they move into the jungle, and Barigah brings food – rice and sweet potatoes, a great improvement on tapioca – and shelter. He, his family and friends – including fellow natives known as Gundi, Ladooma, Magador, Kantong and Sumping – build two sulaps, which they slash out of the jungle with their machetes. In the ensuing week, Barigah and his comrades move the prisoners to a more substantial hut near a stream on his farm. It is one of many examples of the exceptional risks the native people of Borneo are willing to take to help Allied prisoners. All four would be dead by now without their help. When Japanese patrols, for example, search Barigah's kampong in the coming days, he directs the patrols to other villages further away – at great risk to his family and village.[18]

No amount of food or care will save Anderson, whose illness is too advanced. He dies on 28 July. Barigah buries him. The three surviving Australians feel a sense of relief: Anderson's condition has delayed their escape and drained resources. Their feelings are appreciable: these men exist, now, at the outer limits of endurance.

Their every action is pared to the exigencies of survival. They behave more like scavenging animals than men, as Jackson later writes:

> At the time of Anderson's death . . . they were rapidly approaching the stage where they would have done physical violence to each other if they were able. The division of every little piece of food was jealously supervised and they were apt to suspect each other of trying to get more than their share of the spoils.[19]

According to Lynette Silver, 'it was now a case of every man for himself. Each watched every move the others made, lest someone take more than his fair share of the food. They were beginning to hate the sight of each other . . .'[20]

Then, a break at last. In early August, Barigah's cousin, a 17-year-old known as Kaingal, arrives at the hut with the astonishing news of 'some English soldiers' about 30 miles away, in the Lansat region of Ranau. The amazed Australians await confirmation, which Barigah soon provides. Yes, the white soldiers are near, he reports a day or so later; and he requests a written note to take to them. Moxham joyfully obliges and pencils a hasty letter for immediate dispatch, signed also by Botterill and Short:

> To O.C. in charge of English and American Forces,
> We are three Australian prisoners of war. We escaped from camp early in July as Nippon was starving all men. They were dying six and seven a day. After a few days out this Dusun O.T. [Orang Tua] found us and has looked after us ever since, building a little hut in the jungle.

We are still in very weak condition but quite OK . . .

Hope it will not be long before I see you as there are to my knowledge about ten or twenty men (prisoners) left out of 3000 or more.

Do all you can for Baragh pronunced Baruga [*sic*].

We are five mile from Ranau.[21]

Two weeks later, Barigah delivers a second note (heavy rain prevents him taking this first one) to the commandos. Days later, to their astonishment, the escapees receive a reply borne, like winged angels, by Barigah and his friend Andong Ajak. One Lieutenant Ripley of Z Unit writes that the war is almost over and urges the prisoners to stay where they are: a rescue party is on its way.[22] If the kiss of life had a verbal equivalent, this is surely it. The men rally and fire up. Ripley, who leads the AGAS III detachment, has moved heaven and hell to get there – cutting through some of the world's most treacherous terrain. He dispatches food, a bottle of vitamin B tablets, matches and a packet of Lifesavers. He signals for more food drops and men – two medics, a signaller and several AIF commandos are flown in – and sends a rescue party led by Private John 'Lofty' Hodges, a tall, rugged Aussie straight out of Hollywood casting, guided by friendly natives.

The escaped prisoners feel hope – and gratitude for their Dusun friends and guides. Such is their craving for life that, eschewing the rattan and bamboo stretchers provided by helpful villagers, they make themselves get up and walk towards Ripley's camp. Their last 'march', some 12 miles through thick jungle, to Silad – the new base of the AGAS team, ten miles from Ranau – is expected to take three days. They set off after dark in the third week of August but halt at 5 am the next day, unable to proceed any further: 'Their legs were so swollen with beri beri that the natives had to assist in lifting their feet over the logs.'[23] They stagger on for another day and night, often reduced to advancing on their hands and knees. Finally, they collapse, utterly spent, by the side of the track.

On 24 August 1945, 'Lofty' Hodges encounters three living skeletons on the ground, their hair and beards matted with dirt, their lips cracked and bleeding, their legs bloated, their eyes shining.

'How ya goin' boys?' he yells in a heavy Australian accent.

Botterill weeps with happiness and relief; Hodges is speechless. 'Botterill, Moxham and Short were in a terrible condition,' Norm Wallace, one of Hodges' team, later recalls. 'They were a shocking sight, the memory has remained with me all these years. It did not seem possible that human beings could be in such a condition and remain conscious and mentally alert.'[24]

Botterill and Moxham are carried into camp on stretchers; Short is able to walk. Botterill weighs six stone, some of which is fluid caused by beriberi, which has inflated his scrotum to a diameter of nine inches: 'you couldn't put his testicles in a hat', Moxham later jokes.[25] Moxham himself weighs four stone ten pounds; and Short just four and a half stone – down from his original 11 stone. The survivors spend the next few weeks under intensive observation and care. Botterill, the closest to death, needs careful and gradual nourishment, in small increments, which Hodges personally administers. Slowly, the three men recover, aided by the arrival of regular food drops and medical supplies, and are able to contemplate the enormity of what they have survived. And somewhere in Botterill's head resounds

Oakeshott's parting command: if they come through, their first duty is to get justice for Arthur Bird and the men they have left behind.

34

ONE

You go now. Go jungle. If you stay you will be
mati. *All men very short time* mati mati.
A guard, Takahara, warning Bill Sticpewich to escape or die

WARRANT OFFICER BILL STICPEWICH has never been
of more use to the Japanese than in these last awful months. As
jack of all trades, slaughterer (of livestock) and prisoners' leader
– since Cook's illness and fall from grace – Sticpewich succeeds
in ingratiating himself with several senior guards. His technical
skills, rough-hewn charm and command of basic Japanese and
Malayan further recommend him. His robust presence and 'can-
do' demeanour works: the guards respect and confide in him.
He is the first prisoner to know what is happening in the camp
and along the track. The evidence suggests that he shares this
intelligence, and part of his largesse, with other survivors. Take,
for example, his ability to procure medical supplies – atebrin and
quinine – and extra food at the jungle camp, items he shares with
the medical officers and the men.[1]

Despite his friendly relations with the Japanese, Sticpewich
has been unfairly branded a collaborator. He uses his influence, for
example, on several occasions to help his fellow men. He routinely

shares inside information with Captains Cook, Oakeshott and Picone – the last Australian officers alive in the camp. He proves a brave, if helpless, leader on the Second March, saving at least one soldier from certain death, despite his own exhaustion and the terrible rate of attrition. 'I, being one of the fittest to leave the camp . . . don't think I could have lasted another two days after reaching Ranau,' he later says. His group left Sandakan with 50 men; by midday the following day, after several rests, 'we had 36'. His party 'eventually got to Ranau 13 strong and four days after arriving at Ranau it was 5 strong'.[2] Throughout this ordeal, Sticpewich resists the opportunity to escape – which often presented itself – choosing to stay with his men.

On the downside, his special relationship with his captors confers advantages clearly not enjoyed by other prisoners. He and his technical group are better supplied with food and quinine, and when the going gets rough they take more than their fair share. 'I was never really starving,' Sticpewich later says.[3] In the last days, he appears in rude good health, relatively speaking, in a camp full of skeletons. If he may be accused of anything, it is of being human, all too human; of advancing his own chances of survival when he knows all is lost; of using his special situation to aid, most of the time, his fellow men – and then himself.

As the author Kevin Smith rightly concludes, Sticpewich 'kept his eyes and ears open, courageously remembering with resourceful duplicity very many of the enemy's deeds. He was driven by his conscience, quite aware of the critics among his comrades.'[4] Sticpewich later writes to his sister, 'somebody had to do this unpleasing task . . .'[5]

◆

For weeks, Sticpewich has been aware of the plan to massacre the prisoners. He first heard of it in Sandakan, when a Japanese guard called Yoshikoa – nicknamed 'Masturbation' – informed him that every prisoner is 'to be killed'; the guard added, smiling, that 'it would be a good thing'.[6] Other guards are similarly, dangerously candid: the vengeful Nakamura, too, chose Sticpewich as his confidante before shooting several Japanese guards and himself.

A third warning persuades the Australian. It arises from the friendship between Sticpewich and a former Japanese soldier, Takahara Nisu, the guard then in charge of the Australian's Technical Party. Takahara is 'friendly' and treats the party 'very decently', Sticpewich later recalls.[7] Indeed, Takahara, who calls himself a Christian, seems sincere in his concern for the prisoners. In Sandakan, he supplied Sticpewich's men with medicines and food and delivered their messages to the natives. Now, at the jungle camp, Takahara slips bottles of quinine and bananas to Sticpewich and his friends. 'This happened regularly throughout our stay at Ranau camp,' the Australian warrant officer later recalls.[8]

On the night of 27 July, making his way back to the hut after extinguishing the fire on the creek bed, Sticpewich feels a hand on his shoulder. He stops and sees Takahara in the darkness.

'You go now,' says the guard, in a sharp whisper. 'Go jungle. If you stay you will be *mati*. All men very short time *mati mati*.'[9]

'How do you know this – that we're all going to be killed?' Sticpewich asks.

'I saw Takakuwa's papers which say you all be *mati* . . .' The guard adds, 'You no speak to other soldiers!' – and seems to think this 'a great joke'.[10]

It reinforces a graver warning, by a Japanese medical orderly, that Takakuwa possesses an order – 'the Paper' – that states that all prisoners must die. Added to this are fresh rumours of Japanese guards injecting prisoners with petrol 'to cause immediate death', and talk of 'gasoline and syringes'.[11] Sticpewich needs no further convincing and decides 'it was time I got out' and 'anybody else out who was willing to come and take the risk'.[12]

◆

Before his flight, Sticpewich puts his extraordinary memory to work, collating the names of the dead and how they died: a treasure trove of evidence. He also asks Oakeshott, Picone and Cook to join him. Picone feels persuaded to go but decides to stay with his fellow officers. The same applies to Oakeshott, who, owing to his lack of boots and a big ulcer on one foot, 'said he would be too much of an encumbrance', Sticpewich recalls. Their duty to the sick never seems to desert these courageous medical officers; and yet, both surely realise their services are now redundant. They are themselves seriously in need of medical attention.

As for Cook, who is relatively healthy – even, by some accounts, indecently fat – he declines the chance to escape, due to his slight gunshot wound and expectation of being spared. Cook remains the gatekeeper of the prisoners' records, including the numbering system that identifies the unmarked graves at Sandakan Prison Camp and along the track. Cook believes these records may be useful – perhaps a lifesaver – and refuses Sticpewich's request for them. He promises, however, to put the records in a tin under a prominent tree, for reclamation later, should his life be in danger – a risky proposition and dereliction of his duty to the recovery of the remains of the dead.[13]

Of the other ranks, only Private Herman Reither, though very sick, is willing to have a shot. 'The other personnel,' Sticpewich later recalls, are 'too sick or incompetent to make the attempt.' Indeed, they cannot bury the dead. The current gravedigging detail – a job rotated daily among the prisoners – is too weak to perform the job. It involves fastening rattan to the body and dragging it 30 yards or so to the new cemetery. Each corpse demands the remaining strength of about half a dozen men. In consequence, several of the dead are left naked in the sun in the camp clearing, drawing scavengers – wild animals and the guards who 'vie with each other' to claim the gear of the sick and the soon-to-die.[14] They order the removal, for example, of the clothes of the deceased. These pitiful rags are washed and hung up to dry, whereupon the Japanese hasten to possess them – unless, as Sticpewich later claims, the prisoners get there first.[15]

◆

Sticpewich and Reither spend the evening of 28 July feigning illness – thus condemning themselves to lie among the sick and wounded. Who are these men, he wonders, looking around at the prostrate forms on their rattan beds. He is determined to remember their names, and tallies 32 Australian 'other ranks' still alive. He overlooks another ten, including six British prisoners (three officers and three other ranks). The exact number is elusive, because men are dying hourly; any sum fixes on the number alive at a single point in time. A day later, the figure falls below 30. Indeed, of the 32 very sick with whom Sticpewich and Reither spend their last hours in the camp, eight are on the verge of death.

Six of these have already lapsed into unconsciousness and will die that night or the next.

That evening, Sticpewich serves up a meal of boiled tapioca. Then, in the smoking lull after the dousing of the fires, when the prisoners crawl into bed for another night of sweat and struggle, Sticpewich and Reither creep into the forest and past the guardhouse. They hide by the side of the track on the ridge above the camp, close enough to witness the hornets' nest stirred up by their escape next morning: the eruption of confusion and anger among the Japanese; the usual slapping and king-hitting of the guards deemed responsible; and the inevitable scapegoating of the prisoners.

The details of what happens next are vague; the only sources are Jackson's and Sticpewich's statements. Sticpewich and Reither stay hidden for a day and a night, until the search patrols return to camp, then move towards Ranau through dense forest. A kindly native called Ginssas bin Gangass shelters them in his hut. When a Japanese soldier happens to visit, he hides them under a grass mat. A few days later, on 2 August, Gangass transfers them to the care of the resistance fighter and Kadazan Christian Adihil bin Ambilid (also known as Godohil), who hides them for a week in his home near the village of Sumaang, of which he is headman. It is a testament to their staunch loyalty that none of Ambilid's villagers is tempted by the 2000-Borneo-dollar bounty – a small fortune – that the Japanese place on the Australians' heads. Reither arrives in Sumaang with mysterious wounds to his stomach, arms and legs, consistent with the blows of a bayonet. The cause is never explained; the villagers who treat him ask no questions.

Sticpewich, meanwhile, in his usual energetic form, sets the wheels of survival in motion. A runner, Ambilid's brother-in-law, known as Zimban, is dispatched with a message to Allied forces then thought to be landing at Jesselton. In fact, they have been redirected to Lansat after news of the whereabouts of Ripley's AGAS unit – of whose epic journey from Pitas to Ranau the area is thick with rumours. Ambilid, on Sticpewich's instructions, sends another runner to the jungle camp to assess the state of the prisoners. The runner later returns to say that only about 20 men remain alive.

On 8 August, Reither dies of sickness and causes possibly related to his unexplained wounds. The next day, Sticpewich travels by horse to Lansat, to find the AGAS men. He arrives – a limp, hungry and slightly incoherent bundle, swaying with every step of the exhausted animal – a few days before Moxham, Botterill and Short. The three younger men are stunned to find, on their recovery, Sticpewich in their midst – but none feels any warmth towards the warrant officer. Moxham and Botterill accuse him, along with Cook and other officers, of being 'white Japs' and collaborators.

They greet him sullenly, but the mood, in Moxham's case, soon turns dark. According to one account, Moxham promises to tear Sticpewich apart when he recovers. Indeed, Moxham's fury is so intense that Sticpewich is laid in a separate tent,[16] where he quickly recovers. His relative fitness reinforces their claim of his being 'close' to the enemy. But fury alone does not make the allegation fact; any conclusion awaits later, closer scrutiny.

The escape of Sticpewich provokes the usual Japanese histrionics and Formosan tantrums, yet with greater intensity than previously. Superstitious guards who befriended Sticpewich despair at the void left by the absence of this peculiarly robust character, who has given them, and many prisoners, some hope in hell. To them, losing this swaggering spirit is rather like losing a good-luck charm, the last talisman of their dreadful existence. They might as well have killed the albatross. In their misery, they turn on the last few prisoners alive – and master and slave, torturer and tortured, yellow and white man face the final act of the Pacific War locked together in a sort of Darwinian *danse macabre*.

35

MATI MATI

There is no rice, so I am killing the lot of you
today. Is there anything you have to say?
Sergeant Tsuji Toyoji to the last few prisoners alive

CAPTAINS PICONE AND OAKESHOTT know that death awaits them and all who remain here. Yet they stay. All around them lie the sick and dying, whom they are incapable of helping now. 'They had no medical supplies,' the mother of Owen Evans later writes to the family of another victim, 'and they were treated no better than the men, starved and beaten just the same, but . . . when these boys who escaped asked the doctors to escape with them, they refused to leave the sick men at Ranau . . .'[1]

The dead pass away conscious of having survived years of imprisonment and hundreds of miles on foot across Borneo. By any measure, theirs is a supreme testament to the will to live – and a complete negation of the spirit of Imperial Japan, which stands merely for death and destruction. In this sense, every man's struggle is the very antithesis of the nihilistic regime under which they perish. In such circumstances, the will to live is surely the highest form of courage and defiance.

Their faces are unknown to us, but their names persist as

haunting reminders of one of the darkest chapters in our history. On 28 July 1945, 42 Australian and seven British prisoners cling to life. A rescue attempt, even now, might save them; but Ripley and his AGAS men, camped nearby, decide not to attempt it. A rush on the camp might lead to a massacre. A fortnight later, Morotai headquarters echoes their concerns. 'STOP ALL FURTHER ACTIVITIES,' Gort Chester warns, in a signal sent on 12 August. 'DO NOT WANT TO AGGRAVATE DANGER OF POWS BEING KILLED.'[2] By then, it is too late.

The list of the remaining men, according to Sticpewich's reckoning and later calculations, includes the following:

Australian
(mostly members of the 22nd Brigade, 8th Division)

Officers
Captain George Cook, 39, of Failford, New South Wales
Captain John Oakeshott, 44, of Lismore, New South Wales
Captain Domenic Picone, 36, of Perth

Other Ranks
Private George A. Bolton, 33, of Leichhardt, New South Wales
Private Jim Burgess, 39, of Mackay, Queensland
Lance Corporal John E. Burke, 38, of Millaa Millaa,
      Queensland
Private Colin K. Chapman, 30, of Paddington,
      New South Wales
Sergeant John Codlin, 36, of Narellan, New South Wales
Corporal Thomas Connolly, 36, of Sydney, New South Wales
Private Albert Doyle, 27, of Kogarah, New South Wales

Sergeant Len Doyle, 37, of Carlton, New South Wales

Private Owen Evans, 24, of Wyalong, New South Wales

Lance Corporal Anthony Fahey, 35, of Bowral,
New South Wales

Sergeant Andrew Ferguson, 38, of Cootamundra, New South
Wales

Private Jimmy Finn, 24, of Sydney, New South Wales

Private Frank Fitzpatrick, 45, of Loch, Victoria

Private Len A. Gagan, 24, of Enfield, New South Wales

Lance Corporal John Kealey, 36, of Kelvin Grove, Queensland
(born Lancaster, England)

Private Joe Kopanica, 25, of Royal Park, Victoria (born
Czechoslovakia)

Staff Sergeant Bill McDonald, 44, of Armidale,
New South Wales

Corporal Lance Maskey, 27, of Sydney, New South Wales

Private Douglas May, 28, of Carlton, Victoria

Signalman Jack McMartin, 23, of Thornton, Victoria

Sergeant Ernest Munro, 34, of St Marys, New South Wales

Private Edmund Noonan, 28, of Kyogle, New South Wales
(whose brother Bill died in the jungle camp a week earlier)

Private (Edward) Johnny O'Donohue, 24, of Grafton,
New South Wales

Sergeant Lawrence Paulett, 33, of Chillagoe, Queensland

Sergeant Lyall Powell, 25, of Townsville, Queensland

Private Thomas Reading, 33, of Barraba, New South Wales

Lance Corporal George Shepherd, 25, of Newcastle,
New South Wales

Private Edward Terrett, 25, of Sydney, New South Wales

Private Arthur Thorns, 27, of Trafalgar, Western Australia

Sergeant William Vaughan, 26, of Deniliquin,
New South Wales
Corporal Don L. Wilkinson, 25 (address unknown)
Private Ray Wiseman, 25 (address unknown)

British

Officers
Flying Officer Harry Burgess, 41, of Stamford, Lincolnshire
Lieutenant Geoffrey Chopping, 26, of Colchester, Essex
Captain Frank Daniels, 39 (address unknown)

Other Ranks
Roy Hodgson, 24 (address unknown)
Aircraftman Joe McCandless, 28, of County Down, Northern
Ireland
Albert Sands (RAF, details unknown)
Samuel Smith, 38 (RAF, details unknown)

More than half the Australians are from rural families. Others
are from hardened working-class backgrounds. The officers tend
to have genteel, middle-class upbringings. Eighteen are older
men – over 30 or in their early 40s – whose survival confounds
expectations. At 44, Staff Sergeant Bill McDonald, of the 2/18th
Battalion, is a veteran of the Great War and Malaya, and one
of the oldest non-commissioned officers in the Australian forces.
A tailor's son from Armidale in north-west New South Wales,
McDonald ran away from home aged 14 to join the AIF at the
outbreak of the Great War. His father retrieved the lad, but

McDonald's determination proved unshakeable. He enlisted – successfully – at 17 and found himself bound for Europe just before the armistice. Nicknamed 'The Brigadier', the burly McDonald is a keen sportsman and happily married family man, with a wife and three children at home. His skill at his father's trade made him the obvious choice for the battalion's tailor. At Sandakan and along the march, he fashioned a veritable wardrobe out of whatever scraps of material he could find, repairing several men's shorts with 'patches from a kitbag'.[3] His proudest exhibit was Bill Moxham's kitbag trousers.

Among the younger men, Private Johnny O'Donohue, 24, from the dairy country in northern New South Wales, left Australia in 1941 with two other locals – John Barnier, 21, and John Jackson, one of five soldiers of Aboriginal descent who served in Borneo. The three attended the same school. Their childhood had echoes of Huckleberry Finn's, Australian-style: hand-milking cows, riding their bikes to local dances, swimming and fishing in the creek, and singing around the piano on Sunday nights. O'Donohue 'was a young man who liked his beer and was full of life'.[4] He enlisted at 19 and joined the 2/20th Battalion. Barnier's younger sister, Maureen, on seeing her brother and his friends off on the platform of the old North Coast mail train, turned her face to the station's picket fence and recalls sobbing 'as if her heart would break', as she later told Silver.[5] Barnier and Jackson both died of malaria, back in Sandakan camp; O'Donohue just survived. During the Malayan campaign, he carried his uncle's prayer book in his breast pocket. Nothing is left of it now.

Here, too, is Corporal Lance Maskey, the prisoners' interpreter, thanks to a smattering of Japanese. His job upset some of the younger privates, including Botterill and Moxham, who lumped Maskey in with Sticpewich and others they accused of collaborating. They naively laid the accusation at any Australian or British serviceman who tried to improve the prisoners' lot by cooperating with the enemy. It is wholly unwarranted. Maskey is, in fact, a brave young man who has done his best to use his position to aid his friends, most memorably when he tried to intervene to stop Bird's murder.

Some men are not supposed to have got this far. Consider Sergeant John 'Mort' Codlin, the Sandakan camp paymaster, whose survival amazes his comrades. In June 1943, Codlin suffered severe wounds and was hospitalised for a week after being smashed about the head with a pick-handle – punishment for identifying two guards as the embezzlers of funds from the camp canteen. Born in 1909, Codlin is a quiet man, 'tall, slender and athletic', and an expert horseman and tennis player.[6] Before the war, he commuted daily from his home in the Blue Mountains west of Sydney to his job at a bank in the city. He embarked for Malaya in May 1941 with the 8th Division's Command Pay Office, and in Singapore represented the AIF in cricket. A wife and young daughter await his return.

And here is Private Josef Kopanica, a Czech-born pastry chef who emigrated with his family to Australia in 1932, aged 12. His father, a railwayman, worked long hours to build a life in their adopted country. Josef, the eldest of four boys, grew up a staunch patriot and enthusiastically volunteered for the AIF in time for the Malayan campaign. He arrived in Singapore in May 1941. The lad has come a long way from his Czechoslovakian roots: a defender of Australian interests in Singapore and a captive of the Imperial Japanese Army.

Sticpewich's intelligence proves accurate. Soon after Bill's escape, Captain Takakuwa brings forward his plan to kill the surviving prisoners. On 31 July, Sergeant Major Beppu Yoichi returns after four days fruitlessly hunting down the two latest escapees. Despite his acute malaria, he dutifully obeys a summons to present himself, along with other senior non-commissioned officers, in Takakuwa's office the next day. The others include Tsuji, Okada Toshiharu and Watanabe.

Takakuwa gets straight to the point: 'Owing to certain regrettable incidents of PWs escaping during the last fortnight, it is necessary for the rest of them to be disposed of.'[7] Takakuwa is in fact enacting orders that have been sitting on his desk for some time, and which have little to do with Sticpewich. Nonetheless, the escape, and the prisoners' inability to work, hastens the inevitable.

Takakuwa briefly examines the methods of 'disposal' and issues the following instructions, according to Beppu's recollection: 'Sgt Okada was to take all the PWs who were too sick to walk; S/M Tsuji would take the walking PWs and I was to take the five officers. In vain I protested that I was ill and unable to do it.'[8]

The executions are to proceed that day, by firing squad. The three Japanese sergeants receive lists of the condemned and maps showing the chosen killing grounds. In the event, however, 25 of the 42 murders are delayed. Seventeen – the 'stretcher cases' – go ahead on 1 August, under Okada's command.

Okada dutifully appoints a firing squad comprising nine Formosans, to conduct the executions, and four Japanese soldiers, to guard the area. He enters the prisoners' hut and chases – 'hunts out', says one witness – the 17 men, who are barely able to walk.

'They were just able to struggle out,' recalls Matsuda Nobunaga, appointed to Okada's party.[9] Fifteen must be carried in their stretchers to the killing field; the other two are forced to crawl, beaten as they go. At the site, 'the prisoners were lying or sitting down' in their stretchers, another witness later says.[10]

Soon after 11 am, the firing squad raise their rifles and shoot the 17 men where they lie. Okada later describes the massacre:

> As I had no interpreter with me the PWs were not told what was going to happen to them, but they probably realised their fate when they got to the cemetery. The PWs were put down on the ground, the guards lined up and I ordered them to open fire. The Formosans did not want to shoot, and neither did I, but I had my orders and so had to fire first to set an example to them. We then kept on firing until they were all dead.[11]

In fact, Okada sets an example of how to kill: he shoots the first through the head at close range, according to a Japanese witness, the soldier Yoshikawa Tatsuhiko: 'Sgt Okada demonstrated how to kill the PWs with a rifle; he shot one.' Among the victims are Maskey and Evans. That afternoon, the Formosans dig two large graves and roll the bodies in. Another witness, Morioka Teikichi, later recalls, 'The PWs who were killed up at the grave site . . . were so ill that there was no possible chance for them to escape.'[12] Two Formosans, one of whom is Takahara, Sticpewich's informant, are so disgusted by their actions they will try to escape the jungle camp.[13]

The members of the firing squad later try to exonerate themselves before the War Crimes Tribunal. 'I fired two shots but do not know if I killed anyone,' remarks one, Yasuyama Eikichi.[14] 'I was detailed to shoot Maskey but I did not,' claims another, Morioka Teikichi.

◆

Contrary to the Jackson report and other records at the time, the final massacres at Ranau occur not on 1 August, as widely reported – but almost a month later, and two weeks after the Japanese surrender, on the 15th. Natives observe the last few prisoners alive as late as 27 August, when Edmundo Jaimi, a resident of Ranau, witnesses '10 European prisoners pass 112-mile camp . . . They were very thin and dressed in rags. They were carrying something in bags. Prior to me seeing these prisoners I knew that two lots of pamphlets were dropped. The first one the Japanese thought was propaganda.'[15]

Indeed, that day, knowing full well the war is over – having read Allied pamphlets confirming Japan's surrender – Takakuwa issues his final orders to Tsuji: kill the ten 'walking cases'. To this end, Tsuji summons the psychopathic tendencies for which he was so hated as leader of the killing platoon during the Second March and which he now means to deploy in a final act of pointless inhumanity. The victims are led some 440 yards along the Tambunan Road towards Ranau – each man carries a sack, thinking he is off on a foraging exercise. Tsuji stops by a tree in a jungle clearing and distributes tobacco and tea. It is a calculated act of cruelty: the prisoners do not realise this smoko is their last. Tsuji then orders the guards to form a circle around the doomed men and announces, almost casually, 'There is no rice, so I am killing the lot of you today. Is there anything you have to say?'

Only one man speaks: he reportedly requests another cigarette.[16] None attempts to escape: 'They were in such a poor physical state they could not escape even if they had tried to.'[17]

Tsuji means to execute them one by one. He leaves the circle and goes to a place behind a small hill some 30 yards away. Each man is brought before him, alone, and then summarily shot by the accompanying guard – at near-point-blank range. Tsuji seems to relish the performance, yet the 'relay' and close range of the killing appears to revolt several Formosans, who later claim to have refused to shoot when ordered.

Their sudden squeamishness is hardly credible, especially in the case of Fukishima Masao, the man who bashed Bird to death and inflicted so much misery on the men at Sandakan. 'One at a time,' Fukishima later tells the War Crimes Tribunal, 'we were ordered by Tsuji to bring a PW about 20 m into the jungle . . . Tsuji told me to kill the first PW, but being a Formosan I refused to kill any.'[18] Tsuji then 'scolds' Fukishima, snatches the rifle, shouting, 'This is the way,' and shoots the first man through the head.

Other guards similarly claim – at their trials – that they refused to kill the men in such circumstances. Toyoka Eijiro protests that he is 'afraid' to shoot; twice Tsuji orders him to pull the trigger: 'I could not refuse this command and killed the PW about three yards away.'[19] Another, Matsuba Shokichi, a basher nicknamed 'Wooden Head', also claims to have refused to fire, to which Tsuji scolds and screams at him to pull the trigger: 'I then fired but missed', so 'Tsuji took the rifle and killed the prisoner himself'.[20] Another guard, Takeuchi Yoshimitsu, nicknamed 'Lisps', who mistreats the prisoners – 'only when ordered', he later claims – brings the eighth victim before Tsuji. The Japanese sergeant asks the condemned man if he has anything to say. 'Yes, shoot me in the forehead,' the prisoner is said to have replied.[21]

▲

On the same day, the malarial Beppu is detailed to murder the officers. The Australians Oakeshott, Picone, Cook, and the Britons Chopping and Daniels, are brought to a clearing on the right-hand side of the road to Ranau, near the 111-mile peg. The five men have been led to believe they are being taken to the Kempei-tai for questioning, in the hope they are being processed for release. Beppu goes on ahead, 'as I was feeling so ill and feverish', and rests in the shade of a tree near the killing ground. Two Japanese soldiers stand guard, with orders to shoot the officers if they try to run and to ensure 'that no natives should happen by and see what was going on'.[22]

Conflicting accounts describe what happens next. The five men are rested and allowed to smoke. They relax, loosen their belts. One removes his shirt in the sunshine. Beppu later claims to have been sleeping at the time of the killing, woken by gunshot. 'In accordance with my instructions' the guards 'killed the five PWs'. The men die neither bound nor blindfolded, he states, 'nor did I hear any screams from them'.

Beppu's story is full of holes. He lies under oath and changes his statement before the War Crimes Tribunal (see Chapter 40, The Trials) from, 'I did not kill any but the guards were acting under my instructions, and I feel that I am equally responsible with them for the deaths,' to, 'I only passed these instructions on from Captain Takakuwa; [the massacre] is not my responsibility.'[23]

The members of the Formosan firing squad roundly contradict

him. Yamamoto Jiro, nicknamed 'Happy', tells the Tribunal:

> Beppu was with us all the time and when we reached [the
> killing ground], Beppu said 'Shoot'; Kawakami, Hashimoto,
> Nagahiro and myself fired . . . I do not think the officers knew
> of their impending fate . . . I fired but I do not know whether
> I hit anyone.[24]

Another, Nagahiro Masao, similarly testifies that Beppu was not
only awake during the murders but also participated in the killing.
While the Australian and British officers rested on the side of the
road, 'Sgt Beppu took out his pistol . . . We then all fired together
at the officers, who were about 20 yards away . . . I was very upset
at the time.'[25] A fourth gunman, Hashimoto Masao, nicknamed
'Smiler', and hitherto a considerate guard, similarly remembers
Beppu's involvement: 'the five of us fired at the PWs; Beppu used
his pistol. I had to shoot Captain Daniels.'[26]

The first officer to die seems to have been the unfortunate
Cook, for whom the devastating moment of realisation, that his
efforts at pleasing the Japanese have come to this, can only be
imagined. Half an hour later, two Japanese guards arrive with
shovels and the firing squad buries the bodies.[27] On his return to
camp, Beppu feels so ill 'that I went straight to bed and did not
speak to the others'.[28]

36

THE LAST

[W]hen British American come – all men die!
Orders to Lieutenant Moritake, the last commandant
of Sandakan Prisoner of War Camp

ALL THAT IS LEFT of Sandakan Prison Camp, in July 1945, are smouldering hut stumps, the smell of charcoal and rot, and some 280 dying men, sitting or lying in the open, nursing their illnesses and wounds. They have been, literally, left for dead. The exact number is difficult to fix on, given the rapid death rate. These are the immoveable sick, shoved out of their huts after the Second March departed and herded onto the hillside above No. 2 Prison Compound. Their 'skin-covered frames' lie on patches of grass inside double rolls of barbed wire.[1] Some have managed to scrape together a few humpies beneath a nearby line of rubber trees. Their food consists of a little rice, tapioca, wild kang kong (a leafy green vegetable) and whatever a few friendly Chinese are able to smuggle through the wire. A small dam provides water. If the stronger still try to care for the weak, these last acts of mateship are but gestures of dying support, a handshake on the journey to the undiscovered country.

They stare at the sun. They drink the rain. Night and day

merge in the general delirium of their experience: time has no measure. If some see a glimmer of hope – say, in Allied planes overhead – the guards perceive the obvious: these living forms have days, at most a week, to live. The man who will decide how and when they die is Lieutenant Moritake, who succeeded Sergeant Major Murozumi Hisao on 1 June, as the last commandant of Sandakan Prison Camp.

Moritake has a large oval face, of very dark complexion, and stands just five feet three inches high. One witness describes him as having a very round head, pointed chin, small nose, broadly set eyes and low brow, with 'fierce-looking, bushy eyebrows' and 'close cropped hair'.[2] He has a well-earned reputation for extreme cruelty allied with a ferocious temper. When he arrives back in Sandakan, from Kemansi, he is severely ill with malaria. The cadavers on the hill irritate him. His orders are to shift these remaining prisoners to Ranau or otherwise get rid of them; whatever he does, it amounts to a general death sentence. Hot with impatience, Moritake hastens to complete the duties allotted him, after which he is free to leave for Ranau.

Moritake is loathed not only by the prisoners but also by his own guards, as Jackson later asserts. The guards well remember him, when he served as one of Hoshijima's underlings. It was Moritake who ordered them to strike the prisoners, on no pretext, with large pieces of jagged wood. His preferred method of torture was to force the prisoners to hold small barrels of water on their heads; the guards were ordered to bash – preferably in the armpits, crutch and chest – any man who failed to maintain this position for the appointed time. Under Moritake's regime, any guard who shirked his 'duty' to inflict maximum pain on the men was himself severely punished.

The grim task ahead suits Moritake's psychological state, which chimes with his superiors' interests. Moritake nurses a morbid fear that the prisoners may outlive him and testify against him. He thus has a personal stake in fully executing his orders: to ensure the elimination of any future eyewitnesses to his, and Japanese, war crimes. Another fear gnaws at Moritake: at this moment, Japanese commanders in Kuching anticipate a large Allied landing – perhaps 20,000 troops or a division – either at Sandakan or somewhere on the east coast. If so, the prison – or what is left of it – stands in the eye of the coming storm. From the Allied point of view, of course, the invasion of Borneo is just one thrust in the great theatre of the Pacific. At this moment, the Allies are swiftly dismembering the Japanese Empire. American Superfortresses pound the enemy's homeland daily. The US Navy blockade squeezes the Japanese economy and blocks reinforcements from Manchuria. Admiral Halsey's carrier aircraft unleash fresh attacks on Japanese military targets – kamikaze airfields, coal ferries, munitions plants (which General Curtis LeMay's five-month firebombing campaign against Japanese civilians has largely ignored). By July 1945, Japan is, in every sense, an utterly defeated nation.

And yet, like thousands of other sick soldiers of Nippon, forsaken on lonely atolls, Moritake peers at the dreadful place he has made of his scrap of earth and prepares to fight to the last. He knows nothing of the firebombing of Japanese cities; the Emperor's intervention in the war; and the secret, if futile, attempts by his government to send 'peace' feelers to Russia. He acts as if in a bubble, sealed off from the counsel of despair and reason. He thinks only in terms of the banal mantras of his official orders, which he continues to believe issue directly from the Imperial will, the voice of the Sacred Crane: Hirohito, no less.

◆

Some 150 Australians and British are still breathing on the drenched hillside above the prison camp – with little food or shelter and no medical care. Moritake gets it in his head that these men are malingerers, deliberately feigning illness to avoid the march to Ranau, as Jackson later writes: 'Any normal person in their right senses would have known that there wasn't a man in the camp who was not in a very bad way, but Moritake was not a normal person nor was he in his right senses.'[3] This may extend a defence of madness to Moritake for what follows, but the Japanese officer is clearly in the grip of sanity – as measured according to his ability to act within the confines allotted to him by his superiors. Most of the time, he acts only in order to fulfil his instructions: had he been told to destroy every last ant or spider in the vicinity, he would surely have done so, without questioning the merit or otherwise of the order. In a similar vein, he takes the command 'kill the prisoners' to be eminently just, on the sole grounds that any such order issuing from his superiors is ultimately the word of Hirohito, hence self-evidently correct. This, indeed, is the very command Takakuwa leaves with Moritake before his departure with the Second March, as handed down by Lieutenant General Baba in Kuching: 'when British American come – all men die!'[4]

And so Moritake acts on his suspicions. He plans the annihilation of the remaining men, using a few dozen soldiers and guards under his command – including Hinata 'Sourpuss' Genzo, the murderer of Private Jack Orr, shot when he attempted to escape in March. First, he burns what remains of the prison camp – removing any last shelter other than his and the guards' huts; and then, on 9 June 1945, he orders 75 of the 'fittest' prisoners to get up and walk. They limp away on crutches to the trucks, which take them to the 15-mile peg. Leaving behind about 90 men who lack the strength to move, the 75 members of the Last March set off on their doomed journey to Ranau, in the charge of Second Lieutenant Iwashita, several Formosan guards and 37 Japanese soldiers, most of whom are also very ill. Their condition scarcely compares with the state of the prisoners, of course, for whom death comes mercifully fast. All except four men die within a day or so, collapsing of disease and hunger, and murdered by Corporal Katayama's killing unit bringing up the rear, or the Kempei-tai sergeant Hosotani Naoji (who is well known for having recently killed five Chinese).

Mercifully for the relatives, we do not know the names of the last four wretched men who stagger beyond the 40-mile mark; but witnesses to their condition confirm the worst. One AGAS agent, a 23-year-old Javanese labourer called Aman bin Daras, recalls seeing '100-plus white prisoners' on the march between Mile 17 to Mile 42, who seem 'very weak and sick'. By Mile 42, he observes 'only four' left, and 'these were most probably also shot as several reports stated four white prisoners were seen at that time in the vicinity but NO further news was heard of them'.[5]

Other witnesses lurk in the jungle near the Beluran turn-off, some 40 miles up the track, where AGAS insurgents Gort Chester and Jack Wong Sue – a formidable Malayan-Australian commando with a talent for assuming the guise of a local – and their few men lie in wait for the Japanese. In all their experience of the horrors of war, nothing prepares them for what they are about to see. 'Into their line of vision,' writes Silver, 'came a contingent of Japanese guards, followed by four skeletal creatures, so starved and emaciated they looked more like mummified corpses than human beings.'[6]

The Japanese murder the four men before they reach the Tangkual Crossing. Of the killers, one, Ichigawa Takegoro, survives the war but dies before the Allies are able to interrogate him. Thus ends the third of the Sandakan Death Marches. (Native people claim the Japanese attempted to force the rest on a Fourth March, via a northern route through Beluran, Klagan and Lingkabau, but there is little evidence for this; and it strains credulity that any of the remaining prisoners could stand up, far less walk this distance.) Of the approximately 150 prisoners alive when the Last March left, by 12 July fewer than 90 remain breathing – the last gasp of life out of nearly 2500 Australians and British sent here in 1942–43.[7]

37

CRUCIFIED

*He had his arms outstretched; one nail was driven through his
left hand, another through his right hand and two through
his feet . . . The other PWs avoided this horror spot.*
Wong Hiong, Chinese witness to the alleged crucifixion of an
English officer, in a statement to his Australian interrogators

---

THE LAST DAYS OF SANDAKAN seem to exist beyond
mortal or animal experience. What happens here is the ultimate
expression of Japan's death cult, coming at the fag ends of the
worst conflict the world has known. After six years of war, more
than fifty million people lie dead. The few Commonwealth
prisoners still alive in Sandakan have not yet joined that statistic.

The Japanese in Borneo know the war is almost over; they
know they will be caught and tried for war crimes if they survive.
So why not preserve what they have not yet killed – and plead
'mitigating circumstances' to their future judges? That might
have been sensible, or at least 'pragmatic'. Even men who have not
shown a trace of humanity might see the expediency of belatedly
pretending to. Yet this is to impose a Western framework, the
motive of self-preservation, even guilt, on psyches indoctrinated
to ascribe 'honour' to the least honourable and most despicable of

acts. The last Japanese authorities in Borneo consider no option other than to kill everything that is emblematic of their defeat and disgrace. In this sense, to describe the Japanese officers and guards as 'beasts' – as many have since done – is to debase the animal kingdom. No animal torments its opponent for pleasure; no animal destroys its own species.

The end of days confounds any conventional Western appreciation of 'motive'. The horror that now descends on the remaining Australian and British prisoners is near impossible to put down. But we must persevere, for the sake of history and the truths we profess to hold dear, in order to enter in the record the story of one of the grisliest atrocities of the twentieth century.

◆

At the eight-mile prison camp, Moritake scans the last prisoners alive: about 90 in number, all stretcher cases. Somehow, they must be removed, got rid of, his orders tell him. This suits Moritake: for his part, he refuses to allow any prisoner to outlive him, lest they should judge him and the regime he represents. But how to get rid of them? Few can walk, so marching them to death is impossible. They will eventually pass away of illness or hunger, he concludes, but when? Will the Allies liberate the camp before then? As Moritake broods on these questions, the remaining British prisoners have found a source of food, and hope, in the courage of an officer.

The tall English officer who administers the British compound is fit enough to 'steal'. In early June, soon after the Third March has left, the Englishman finds himself being dragged to the cage – punishment for stealing a pig and sharing it with his starving soldiers. On this individual, Moritake decides to inflict his final abomination, as an example to the rest and a last gesture of contempt for the white man and what he represents. Moritake orders, according to the sworn testimony of a young Chinese witness, that the Englishman be crucified.

The witness's name is Wong Hiong, aged 16 at the time of the alleged crime, and 19 during his interrogation. Hiong is an intelligent, observant young man and a past favourite of the prisoners. The Japanese employ him as a cook and kitchen-hand, and treat him as a sort of mascot. He has the run of the camp grounds, and is a familiar face around the prisoners' huts and the guards' quarters.

Nobody really troubles to question Hiong's bright-eyed presence. As such, he sees things nobody else sees, as his unbearably vivid testimony demonstrates. Hiong is considered by the Allies, when they interrogate him, as a 'reliable eyewitness', a judgement that later investigations reinforce:

I was employed by the Japanese for a period of 9 and a half months, from about October 1944 to August 1945. I worked as a cook and cut swamp cabbage just outside the Mile 8 Camp, near the boiler house. The PWs at this time were very thin, their ribs were showing, and the flesh was going from their faces leaving only a frame of bones. The officers had shirts, but most of the others only had 'G' strings protecting their private parts. The Japs said, 'Don't give them clothes, clothing helps them to stay healthy.' The Japs too were getting weaker and were frightened that the PW would last longer than they would.

The PWs were getting . . . mainly the outside leaves of the

swamp water cabbage and Ubi Kayu (yam). The hearts of the cabbages were kept by the Japanese for themselves. I saw rice given only once [while] I was there. They had no salt, oil or meat. Sometimes the PW got fish which had gone bad and which the Japs had rejected. The PW cooked them without oil and ate them ravenously. Their drinking water came from a buffalo [hole] now being used as a dam. They were without towels, and owing to the confiscation of razors had long hair and beards.[1]

Hiong remembers a tall, friendly English officer – believed to be Captain James Mills, of the Royal Artillery[2] – sitting in the small cage, wearing a white cap made out of a piece of singlet. The Englishman 'used to wink at me' and 'make signs with his fingers' when the guards passed, Hiong later tells his interrogators. 'He was the biggest man I had ever seen' – about 'six foot six inches high'. In better times, this English officer – a leader of the British compound – was often seen carrying around a book listing the prison roll, a job that conferred better rations; hence his present comparative health. He has light ginger hair, balding in front, a broad face and a slightly hooked nose. Hiong recalls in particular the man's broad chest and long arms and fingers, and 'a watch with a large winding piece'. The eagle-eyed witness also notices a signet ring 'on the middle finger of his right hand'.[3]

A few days later, on his way to the latrine, Hiong notices a large wooden cross – 'about seven feet high' – erected in the compound, some 30 yards from the guardhouse and 90 yards from the cookhouse. The cage is empty; and the Englishman sits smoking in front of the Japanese guardhouse.

Shortly, two guards – believed to be Hinata Genzo and

Fukuda Nobuo – drag the Englishman to his feet and lead him to the cross. He wears only a loincloth. He seems faintly Christ-like in other ways. His theft of a pig to feed his friends is, in such circumstances, deserving of the highest praise and something of a miracle. There the likeness ends. His journey to this tropical Calvary has no 'stations' – it is but a brief trudge across a dusty camp ground. There is no one called 'Mary' to pray and care for him – his mother is thousands of miles away and the prostitutes are native comfort women. There are no repentant thieves, or baying mobs, or crown of thorns, or any prospect of resurrection. This, if Hiong's account is true, is the real thing, stripped of the miracles that make the Roman punishment of Christ redemptive, or at least bearable.

The cross's beam is 'large enough to take a man's outstretched arms', Hiong recalls. The guards bind the Englishman's body against it: 'He had his arms outstretched; one nail was driven through his left hand, another through his right hand and two through his feet.' The Englishman screams and sags forward. A guard takes a piece of cloth and 'stuffs it into his mouth'.[4] Hiong attests, 'I cried as I saw the blood flowing from his hands and feet.'

Moritake then allegedly hammers a long nail through the prisoner's forehead and into the wood. 'The Jap lieutenant stood on a chair and drove the nail in with a hammer,' Hiong says. 'He took a butcher's knife about ten inches long and made a gash in the man's left thigh. He carved a slice of flesh off it and placed it on a plank in front of the cross. He did the same to the right thigh. Although the nail had been through the man's forehead his body still moved as if with breathing.'

Moritake slits the victim's stomach open as far as the navel and draws out his intestines:

He then put on rubber gloves and again using the knife cut away the heart and the liver, which he also placed on the plank with the other flesh. The flesh was then carried away on the plank to Number 2 Camp. I do not know what the Japs did with it.

It is most likely that the Japanese consumed it: the Imperial Army routinely cannibalised prisoners and native people when supplies ran out, according to many documents. Starving Japanese soldiers in New Guinea referred to the flesh of white men as 'white pork'. In Papua and other islands, the Japanese forces were known to slice parts off living captives, who were kept alive to preserve the remaining flesh.[5] Several commanders – notably an officer called Tsuji, the butcher of Singapore – are known to have boasted of eating human organs. And in Paginatan, one of the four Australian survivors of the Last March 'after being shot was immediately cut up, cooked and eaten by Jap troops', according to an AGAS report.[6]

The Japanese exhibit the Englishman's mutilated corpse – still on the cross – in front of the remaining prisoners, according to Hiong. Within days, the body is 'putrefied with flies and maggots', and Moritake orders the guards to burn the evidence. They drench the body and crucifix in kerosene and ignite it, leaving a pile of ash and bones. 'The other PWs avoided this horror spot,' recalls Hiong.[7]

◆

Two years after the war, Allied investigators will reveal flaws in Wong's accounts (he gives two, slightly variant, descriptions), suggesting that the Englishman may have been wired, rather than nailed, to a cross or board. The victim's grave – to which Hiong accurately leads the investigators – contains wire, four nails six inches long and four of three inches, but no ten-inch nail. 'The human remains,' concludes Professor Tanaka, 'were too decomposed to provide any evidence of crucifixion, so only the existence of the nails provides substantial verification of Hiong's testimony.'[8]

The Japanese and Formosans flatly deny all knowledge of the alleged crucifixion, according to statements given to Allied interrogators in July–August 1947. But their statements are flawed and sometimes contradictory. Most clearly remember the Englishman, leader of the British compound, yet claim not to know what happened to him. Some remember a man answering to his description sitting in the cage. All acknowledge the existence of a 'small cross' in the compound. The responses of Yanagawa Hideo, a guard in Compound Two at the time, are typical:

What became of the sick prisoners of war?
75 who became able to walk were sent to RANAU, this was in about the middle of June 1945; they were controlled by 20–30 Japanese and two Formosans . . .

What do you know about a crucifixion that took place in No. 2 Compound [the British compound]?
No such thing happened.

Some of the Chinese employed by the compound witnessed the crucifixion.
The Chinese are mistaken.

The Chinese witnessed the crucifixion, YANAGAWA, and besides,
they mention you as being present at the time the crucifixion occurred.
That is not so, I am concealing nothing.

There are many Japanese at present in the condemned cells at the
Compound who are now trying to put the responsibility onto others.
If you do not tell the truth, YANAGAWA, you may be doing the
same thing.
I cannot be afraid, because no such thing happened.

It happened alright, YANAGAWA, so why persist in denying it?
It did not happen.

What do you know about a large wooden cross at the camp?
There was a small cross in No. 2 Compound.

What was it used for?
All the time I was there it was above a grave . . .

Where was the cross situated in relation to the gate of the compound?
About 30 metres from the gate to the cross . . .

Do you still persist in denying that you know nothing about a Prisoner
of War being crucified in No. 2 Compound?
I know nothing about it . . .[9]

Other Japanese and Formosans accurately describe the British
leader as a 'heavily built' man, 'inclined to be bald', with a 'ginger
moustache' and 'three stars on each shoulder',[10] whose name they
cannot recall, or pronounce. Some refer to him simply as Honcho

(leader), or Hancho – confirming, at least, their knowledge of the Englishman's status. Many remember this officer calling the roll every morning at No. 2 Compound. Driven to exasperation, Allied interrogators demand to know the name 'of the Japanese officer who nailed a PW to a large cross inside the Compound'.[11] All the guards under examination deny any knowledge; yet all remember the existence of the 'small white cross'. Conscious of the likely repercussions if found guilty, they seem to have pre-agreed their answers to any questions relating to the death of the English officer.

Wong may have been tempted by the Allies' financial reward to embellish his story. And yet, this seems out of character in the young man. And his eyewitness descriptions of other atrocities are accurate in all respects. And there is, as Tanaka observes, the evidence of the nails. One is left to conclude that the Englishman probably died a terrible death, mutilated while nailed or wired to a cross or wooden board.

◆

By the end of June 1945, 65 Australian and 22 British prisoners remain on the slope above the burnt-out camp. A fortnight later, 50 persist, of whom 23 are regarded by the Japanese as being able to walk.

In the Japanese hut below the hill, Moritake lies dying of malaria and other complications. On 13 July, the commandant receives a fresh order to move to Ranau. First, he must deal with the prisoners. He orders the guards to massacre the 'walking cases' in situ. These 23 men include Private Tom Burns, the diarist who wrote so vividly of the prisoners' early years of confinement and who seems to have had stark premonitions of their collective fate.

Late that afternoon, these men are forced to limp out of camp and are driven to the bomb-cratered airfield that they spent so much blood and sweat trying to build. Beneath a revetment near a shelter, beside a trench 33 feet long, three feet wide and five feet deep, the 23 men are arranged – with some standing and some sitting. A firing squad murders them all.

The guards responsible bear the names Murozumi, Nishikawa Yoshinori, Nagata, Goto, Yanagawa, Ikeda, Ishimaru, Matsuda, Fukuda, Hirota, Toyoda and Sawata.[12] Javanese coolies roll the bodies into the slit trench. Diligent Japanese paperwork claims the 23 men perished of disease – 'natural causes' – over two days, 13–15 July. When Hiong asks a guard about the sound of gunshots, he replies that they have been out shooting ducks. 'How many did you shoot?' Hiong asks. 'Twenty-three,' the guard replies.[13]

The remaining stretcher cases are left to die in the open. The only food they get is a small rice ration; they drink whatever happens to fall on their faces. Some are barely able to open their mouths. The stronger ones manage to keep a few scant belongings by their sides: a dixie, a blanket, a razor. Moritake's death on 18 July offers little reprieve: the guards feel no compunction, and have no orders, to act in the prisoners' interests. The 'ration' disappears and a small bucket of rice is dumped in their vicinity. Most prisoners can't reach it.

Appalled, Hiong tries to help. He steals a little coarse salt from the camp kitchen, which he wraps up for the prisoners. Caught and beaten, he sustains severe damage to his left eye: 'The Japs said if I did that again they would cut my head off . . .'[14] A friendly native, Ali Asa, brings some tapioca and kang kong, which the men nibble uncooked. It merely prolongs the inevitable. An English officer, Lieutenant Philip Young, dies on 26 July, and the rest fade away. In the first week of August, five survivors remain: the Australians John Davis, 34, Walter Hancock, 42, Ivan Sinclair, 36, and John Skinner, 31; and one British soldier, Harold Rooker, 31. They beg for more food, but Ali Asa refuses: the Japanese threaten to shoot anyone caught helping the prisoners.

All except one man – believed to be John Skinner – die in the coming days. On the morning of 15 August – the day Emperor Hirohito broadcasts his message of surrender to the Japanese people – Murozumi, Moritake's successor, leads the guards into the prison compound. Hiong climbs a rubber tree to get a better view. He recognises the prisoner as a tall, thin, dark-haired man to whom he once gave salt in return for a pair of ragged shorts. Murozumi forces the Australian to his feet. The guards push him up the slope, to a trench drain. Some carry shovels. The prisoner is blindfolded with a black cloth and made to kneel. Then, with a swipe of his sword, Murozumi beheads the last prisoner of Sandakan and kicks the remains into the trench.[15] Later, Hiong guides investigators to the grave, from where the victim's torso and skull are unearthed. Under later examination, Murozumi completely denies any knowledge of it. 'This never occurred,' he lies. He reads from the same script when asked about 'a prisoner who was nailed to a cross': 'I have never heard of or seen such a thing . . .'[16]

REVELATION

38

SURRENDER

[C]ontact the local Japanese commander in the Sandakan
area and negotiate with him for the handover of
the Australian prisoners of war in that area.
Orders from Lieutenant General Frank Berryman to the
commander of units preparing to land in Borneo

THAT DAY, 15 AUGUST 1945, Japan's leaders accept the terms of the Potsdam Proclamation: the US ultimatum to Japan to surrender or face 'prompt and utter destruction'. 'We declared war on America and Britain,' Emperor Hirohito announces in a radio broadcast to the nation, 'out of Our sincere desire to ensure Japan's self-preservation and the stabilization of East Asia, it being far from Our thought either to infringe upon the sovereignty of other nations or to embark upon territorial aggrandizement.' But, 'despite the best that has been done by everyone . . . and the devoted service of our one hundred million people, the war situation has developed not necessarily to Japan's advantage, while the general trends of the world have all turned against her interest'.[1]

Japan has not, in fact, technically 'surrendered' according to this broadcast; Hirohito never uses the word. His speech is intended chiefly to calm the army and navy malcontents who remain wedded to insurrection, and to project the image of a nation that has decided, of its own volition, to submit to Allied demands. He conveys the impression that Japan itself – and not the millions of victims of Japanese imperialism – has suffered a grievous loss, and therein lies the genesis for the staggering idea, still pedalled by some elements in Japan today, of the nation as 'victim' of the Pacific War.

There is another reason why Tokyo has 'decided' to end the war, the Emperor continues: '. . . the enemy had begun to employ a new and most cruel bomb, the power of which to do damage is indeed incalculable, taking the toll of many innocent lives'. Here is another trump card in Hirohito's propaganda offensive. Until now, the atomic bombs that destroyed Hiroshima on 6 August and Nagasaki on 9 August, with the immediate deaths of more than 100,000 people – mostly women, children and the elderly – have barely figured in any calculation by the nation's leaders in Tokyo about if and when Japan would surrender. Sixty-six Japanese cities already lay in smouldering ruins as a result of 'conventional' firebombing; the deaths of two more cities do not 'shock Japan into submission', as Washington later claims.

And yet, in his surrender speech, Hirohito not only cites the atomic bombs as factors in Japan's decision to surrender, he also casts Japan as the saviour of the world. Without the surrender of Nippon, he continues, the world faces the threat of atomic war, which would possibly 'lead to the total extinction of human civilization'. Japan's capitulation, he infers, has heroically delivered the human race from nuclear annihilation – a grotesque travesty that debauches the history of the Hirohito regime's responsibility for the outbreak of war, the slaughter of millions of Asian civilians and the subjection of tens of thousands of Allied soldiers to torture, starvation and death.

In fact, the atomic bombs have had no meaningful impact on Japan's decision to lay down its weapons. On the contrary, since Hiroshima's destruction, state propaganda has girded the people to prepare themselves to continue fighting a nuclear-armed America. The Big Six warlords who rule Japan refused to surrender unless America met Japan's sole condition: that Hirohito and the Imperial dynasty be spared. Otherwise, the old men in Tokyo were hell-bent on continuing the war even if it meant sacrificing every last Japanese man, woman and child.

In the end, America met the Japanese condition. The evidence clearly shows that the Soviet invasion of Japanese-occupied Manchuria on 8 August; the complete US naval blockade of the Japanese homeland, which throttled her economy; the destruction of Japan's navy; and Washington's offer to preserve Hirohito's life and dynasty together brought about the end of the war. Those who claim the atomic bombs 'shocked Japan into submission' are deluded by post-war propaganda designed to ease America's conscience over the use of a weapon that had no meaningful military significance. Indeed, the atomic bombs were militarily unnecessary, as Generals Eisenhower and MacArthur and Admirals Halsey and Leahy remark after the war.[2] The tipping point that has sealed Japan's surrender is the gift of Hirohito's life, implicit in the 'Byrnes Note' sent to Tokyo on 11 August.

Despite these naked facts, many in the West continue to praise the atomic bombs as the saviour of the prisoners' lives and the sole harbingers of peace. In thrall to the mushroom clouds, few today mention the other, far more influential factors cited above. In truth, and of little comfort to the families of Allied prisoners, the men who died at Sandakan and other prison camps would have died regardless of whether the atomic bombs were used. Yet, in their grief, these families might direct their feelings elsewhere. They might wonder why American air forces spent six months bombing Japanese civilians, which did nothing to force Japan's surrender. In fact, the firebombing campaign against Japanese cities rather prolonged the war, by diverting valuable air and ground resources to a futile exercise in the annihilation of non-combatants. Why, prisoners' families may ask, were hundreds of Allied bombers wasted on destroying old men, women and children, and not used to complete the destruction of Japan's war machine? Many of the country's coal ferries, arsenals and kamikaze airfields were still operating in late June 1945 – when Admiral Halsey's aircraft carriers arrived to do the job General Curtis LeMay's incendiary campaign had manifestly failed to do. Indeed, for five months American conventional aircraft were destroying 'unprofitable targets' – i.e. civilians – in the grim euphemism of Commander Fred Ashworth, weaponeer on the atomic-bomb mission to Nagasaki, when they might have been attacking 'profitable' targets, or indeed used to assist in the rescue of prisoners.

◆

Two days after Hirohito's broadcast, RAAF aircraft drop thousands of flyers over Sandakan, Kuching and other parts of Borneo. Written in Japanese and Malay, they announce the 'unconditional surrender' of Japan and warn Japanese ground forces of their duty to preserve the lives of surviving prisoners. Many leaflets – bearing the signatures of General Sir Thomas

Blamey, or Major General George Wootten – fall on or near the bones of hundreds of young men who died along the Sandakan–Ranau trail: a sad self-indictment of the Allies' failure to avert the tragedy.

At Sandakan, the flyers fall on mass graves and burnt huts and a few miserable Japanese guards who linger at the camp. On that day, 17 August, the Australian Army, with its curiously macabre sense of timing, proposes another prisoner-rescue plan. Colonel John Wilton at General Staff Headquarters envisages a commando raid on the prison camp and Ranau track, with the aim of saving some 200 men thought still to be alive. Planes, ships and supplies are somehow found, but his plan receives the same mute reply as Blamey's flyers and is cancelled on 20 August, after intelligence reports that not a single prisoner is alive in eastern Borneo. This is a week before the last five officers are gunned down and the very day that Murozumi torches the last of the prisoners' personal effects before fleeing to Ranau.

Murozumi flees into a death trap of Nippon's own making. The Japanese and Formosans here are in a wretched state. The Japanese 'hospital' contains 34 immovable creatures, the last stretcher cases of the enemy forces in the region. 'The hospital,' observes Ripley, when he finds it, 'was in a disgracefully filthy condition, all patients appeared very ill and unlikely to be able to walk for a very considerable time if ever.'[3] They do have considerable medical supplies, however, all withheld from the prisoners – just one more disgraceful legacy of the Japanese in Borneo.

Ripley's AGAS III commandos prepare to enter the town in mid-August, with instructions 'to release all PWs in the Ranau area' received from Advanced Headquarters, Allied Landforces.[4] Clearly, everyone expects to find a few prisoners alive. Indeed, in Sandakan, the commander of the Allied landing forces arrives with orders 'to contact the local Japanese commander in the Sandakan area and negotiate with him for the handover of the Australian prisoners of war in that area'. The order is signed 'Lieutenant General F. Berryman, Chief of MacArthur's Staff, Allied Landforces'.[5]

Ripley's men carry a list of good intentions: the preservation of lives; the delivery of medicines; the searching of the Sandakan–Ranau track; and the construction of a field hospital to help any survivors. Their orders are explicit: 'You will take no offensive action except in self-defence.'[6] In short, they must not attack the Japanese, or attempt to rescue through offensive action any remaining prisoners. Ripley and his men are, however, permitted to place a large white arrow on the hillside, pointing to the prison camp, in case paratroopers are able to land. (They never attempt to.)[7]

They pass through Ranau and enter the last jungle camp in a state of stunned disbelief. 'It is regretted,' AGAS III notes, with the Army's inimitable understatement, 'that the party was unable to rescue the remaining 20 odd PWs. They were all known to be in a very weak condition, many were actually dying and all were entirely dependent on each other for food, sanitation etc.'[8]

In late August, AGAS III is aware of just four survivors: Botterill, Short, Moxham and Sticpewich. Soon, they hear of Braithwaite and Campbell. Six survivors, so far. The dreadful truth begins to emerge. By September, they are able to draw up the first list of casualties. It is remarkably accurate:

Died at Sandakan prior to movement to Ranau:
  Australian: 700
  British: 480

Left at Sandakan: 250 (Japanese report no survivors)
Died en route to Ranau: 398
Died at Ranau: 680
Total: 2508

Six survivors out of 2508: a 99.8 per cent casualty rate – the worst of any prisoner-of-war camp in the Pacific or European theatres during the Second World War.

◆

The Allies impose a tentative order on the anarchy of Sabah. Lists are made, names given, supplies delivered and casualties tallied. Suspected native collaborators are rounded up. Some are killed or mutilated, the early victims of vigilante justice. Local people who have rendered 'excellent service' to the prisoners are thanked and promised a reward. The first Japanese war criminals are identified.

Ripley's commandos log this melancholy job in terse statements. It is the first draft of the revelation of these appalling events:

12 Aug. 45 Ripley listed 8 Jap War Criminals. Ripley instructed by Gort STOP FURTHER ACTIVITIES do not want to aggravate danger of POW's being killed.

14 Aug. 45 109 3/4 Miles; 110 1/4 Miles – Nil PWs seen either location. No Guards.

18 Aug. 45 Following escapees in contact with us: NX58617

Pte SHORT N; Pte BOTTERILL, K; Cpl MOXHAM . . .
Uncertain Japs know of surrender.

20 Aug. 45 . . . probably no prisoners left at RANAU.

25 Aug. 45 . . . Bulk strength [of Japanese] at RANAU 200 of
which 40% are sick. Consider this low estimate.

26 Aug. 45 All rumours tend to show that Japs may move
to SAPONG ESTATE to surrender. RANAU strength 300.
Strong guard 114 mile possibly in anticipation arrival Aust.
Army. No further information PWs.

28 Aug. 45 Confirmed that RANAU [surviving] PWs left for
TAMBUNAN 27 Aug.

1 Sept 45 Following information reliable. Native policeman
from TAMBUNAN did not meet PWs on his way to
RANAU. Native reports finding near mile 110 3/4 a number
of discarded Aust Hats bearing Prisoners number on Wooden
Tags. Graves nearby. No estimate capacity but not there 20
days ago. Hat does not mark location of grave . . .

PWs that moved from RANAU 27 Aug have all been
murdered and buried at MENGAWA 30 Aug . . .

660 known to have died RANAU . . . 700 Aust and 480
British died at SANDAKAN, prior to movement June 45.
250 mixed Aust and British left at SANDAKAN due to
inability to walk . . . Of 2612 PWs reported by Ripley in

SANDAKAN from Oct 43 to date only four are known to be alive. 150 Aust Officers and 50 Aust O/Rs [other ranks] marched to KUCHING and 100? British to LABUAN. Their fate unknown. 250 sick remained at SANDAKAN and were probably killed in Aug massacre. The remaining 2258 PWs are reported to have died.[10]

◆

From the bridges of battleships and the operations rooms of generals, to mid-west American towns and the Home Counties of England, the world celebrates peace after so many years of stubborn fighting. On the morning of 2 September, General Douglas MacArthur receives the Japanese surrender in Tokyo Bay, aboard the battleship *Missouri*. Admirals, generals and officials converge on the mother ship at anchor amid 260 vessels representing America, Britain, China, Australia and other Allies. After last-minute wrangling over who should sign the surrender document, Hirohito authorises his new foreign minister, the one-legged Mamoru Shigemitsu, First Class of the Imperial Order of the Rising Sun, and General Umezu Yoshijiro, First Class of the Imperial Order of the Rising Sun and Second Class of the Imperial Military Order of the Golden Kite.

MacArthur's few words befit the nobler aspirations of the moment:

. . . Nor is it for us here to meet, representing as we do the majority of the people of the earth, in a spirit of distrust, malice or hatred. But rather it is for us, both victors and vanquished, to rise to that higher dignity which alone befits the sacred purposes we are about to serve, committing all our people unreservedly to faithful compliance.[11]

The Japanese signatures proclaim their 'unconditional' surrender of all Japanese forces 'wherever situated' and the immediate liberation of Allied prisoners of war and civilian internees. The emperor, the government of Japan 'and their successors' – the Imperial dynasty already duly recognised – having signed the surrender, must carry out the provisions of the Potsdam Declaration 'in good faith'.[12]

The news ripples through the Empire and silences most of the diehard Japanese units of the South-West Pacific. On 10 September, Major General George Wootten, commander of the Australian 9th Division, receives the surrender of all of Borneo from Lieutenant General Baba Masao. The message is transmitted to outlying Japanese posts, who are ordered to lay down their weapons. The next day, relief forces flow into Kuching, to find dreadful scenes. Ten days earlier, Lieutenant Colonel Suga officially informed the Kuching prisoners of the Japanese surrender. In the intervening period, before the camp's liberation, a nurse, Hilda Bates, visited the sick prisoners of war:

I was horrified to see the condition of some of the men. I was pretty well hardened to sickness, dirt and disease, but never had I seen anything like this in all my years of nursing. Pictures of hospitals during the Crimean War showed terrible conditions, but even those could not compare with the dreadful sights I met on this visit. Shells of men lay on the floor sunken-eyed and helpless; some were swollen with hunger, oedema and beri-beri, others in the last stages of dysentery, lay unconscious and dying. They had no pillows or clothes, few cups, fewer bowls, or even medical supplies . . . There were three hundred desperately sick men, many unable to help themselves, or to carry food to their mouths. Throughout our internment, we women had begged to be allowed to nurse the soldiers, but the Japanese refused our offer, saying this would be indecent.[13]

Sapper Lionel Morris, regarded as one of the 'healthy' prisoners, weighs five stone three pounds on his release.[14] Sacks of undelivered mail both to and from the prisoners are discovered in the camp on liberation.[15]

In total, 1740 men, 243 women and 38 children are incarcerated in Kuching's Lintang Barracks. Many are British and Australian officers transferred here from Sandakan in 1943. None of the officers is aware of the Death Marches or what has happened to their men. 'We didn't know what happened; no-one told us,' Russ Ewin later recalls.[16] After the war, some officers will attempt to contact the families of the deceased, but they have very little information with which to comfort relatives.

Alive among the 178 Australians is Lieutenant Colonel Arthur Walsh, the man who stood up to Hoshijima in 1943. Aglow with alcohol and somehow in possession of a bottle of Scotch, he seems to have suffered a nervous breakdown, according to one account.[17] Perhaps Walsh has had special access to Japanese stores. He is flown to Labuan for 'discussions' with his superiors. In a letter dated 14 September 1945, an Australian officer with the liberating force describes the conditions he confronted at Kuching:

Judging by the quantity of food available in Kuching when

the Relief Force arrived and by the adequate supplies which were then in stock in the Japanese storehouses, it is considered that the PW food ration could easily have been maintained at a level which would have kept the PW alive and reasonably healthy. However, a policy of slow starvation was carried out instead.[18]

◆

Colonel Suga Tatsuji, commander of Borneo prison camps, promptly submits to Allied interrogation. He claims to have had no association with the Sandakan–Ranau Death Marches or the transfer of 300 British servicemen to Miri – where most starved, were killed or died of illness – despite the fact that he was closely involved in both decisions. The record shows that Suga visited Sandakan in February 1945, with the 'doctor' of Kuching, Yamamoto Katsuji, and observed the state of the men at close quarters before they set off. He knew they were unfit to march but did nothing to intervene. And yet, it is true that he did not originate the order to march the prisoners. That came from 37 Army Headquarters in Kuching, in the form of General Yamawaki and his successor General Baba. Suga conveyed, but he did not formulate, the orders.[19] Nonetheless, he knew that his blind obedience in the hierarchy of a criminal military regime would 'have earned him the death sentence', concludes Professor Tanaka.[20]

Suga is sent to Labuan, where American sailors taunt and denounce him for the rumoured atrocities in Borneo. During further interrogation, Suga labours under a curious delusion: he seems to believe that, if Japan had invaded Australia – which was not, in fact, planned – he would have been appointed commander of prisoner-of-war camps there.[21] Suga is a complex case. He is in essence a kind man in the swim of brutishness. He must have found his orders abhorrent. He is the only Japanese commander to have shown any concern for the prisoners – intervening, for example, in Matthews' trial. He cannot be held directly responsible for ordering the Death Marches. That disgrace hangs around the necks of those further up the pecking order. In such circumstances, Suga's life becomes intolerable. One night in the month after the armistice, he slits his throat and bleeds to death – an 'honourable' suicide, in the Japanese military tradition, committed in a cloud of mosquito repellent, according to one source: 'He had asked his batman to burn incense for him but as the man did not have any he lit a mosquito bomb.'[22]

◆

During August and September, the Allies steadily 'mop up' Japanese units throughout the South-West Pacific. It is a bloody, dangerous business. Many troops refuse to believe the surrender order. Some delude themselves that it is false propaganda and vow to resist. Little pockets keep fighting for weeks – 30 soldiers, for example, armed with machine guns at Napong, just north of Ranau, intend to 'stay put'. Most are killed or brought in by the end of that month. On 21 September, five AGAS commandos occupy the Japanese headquarters at Ranau, disarm 220 military and civil officers, and seize four machine guns, one tree mortar, 60 rifles and 12 pistols.[23]

A few thousand Japanese around Ranau and Mount Kinabalu are rounded up and searched. Allied troops confiscate watches, wallets, rings, clothes and blankets previously belonging to the prisoners. 'A considerable number of watches and other valuables were found to have been destroyed by fire by the enemy prior to our arrival,' Ripley writes. '. . . [T]he reason for this is obvious though no markings were found. The enemy also distributed a large quantity of clothing, blankets etc . . .'[24]

The Japanese and Formosans – themselves now prisoners – are paraded, forced to salute the Union Jack and marched off to prison in Jesselton. Before they depart, their interpreter publicly thanks Allied soldiers for their 'very kind and considerate treatment'.[25] The long file of Japanese prisoners shuffles off in the direction of Mount Kinabalu and down the western slopes towards the sea. Hundreds are massacred en route, picked off with blowpipes, guns or machetes by vengeful Dusun tribes who have not forgotten the atrocities inflicted on their people. The carnage is a turkey shoot. No one makes any special effort to protect the Japanese captives, who are easy prey for mass revenge, and for a few savage days the practice of headhunting is thoroughly revived.

Ross McCowan is a member of the liberating forces, drawn from the Australian 9th Division. His unit, the 2/3 Tank Attack Regiment, is given the task of landing at Sandakan, rounding up the Japanese garrison and shipping the survivors to prison in Jesselton. 'About 200 of us crowded into corvettes and set out,' he writes. On the deck, he strikes up a conversation with 'a lonely figure at the rail'. It is Johnny Funk, dressed in brand-new jungle greens and boots, with whom McCowan starts a long friendship. Jailed and tortured by the Kempei-tai, along with his brothers, Alex and Paddy – all of whom were crucial to the Sandakan resistance – Johnny tells McCowan that he is returning home to Sandakan to find his wife and son, Melvyn.

The corvettes steam into Sandakan Bay and put out paravanes

in case of mines. The decks are covered in tripod-mounted machine guns. McCowan and every other man levels his rifle, safety catch off, at the sea wall. 'There was a suspicion they weren't going to surrender,' he writes. 'That suited us. As we drew near the wharf we saw the entire Japanese garrison lined up on it. As we came alongside, they all bowed – deeply.'[26] The Australians are dismayed, at first, to see Funk shaking hands with two Japanese – but it later transpires that these two managed to transmute his death sentence to 15 years' jail: 'he was thanking them for saving him from having his head chopped off', McCowan recalls.

Sandakan town has been 'bombed out of existence', McCowan observes. The only structures standing are parts of the wharf and treasury. The landing force smashes the treasury open and 'the troops were throwing millions of Japanese invasion dollars out of the shambles'. Many of the local people are sick and wounded; most are homeless. Among their desperate faces, Johnny Funk finds his wife and son. (In later years, the family settles in Caloundra, in a little beach house not far from McCowan's.)

A tent is erected on the beach near the town to process the Japanese. 'We searched all the prisoners and their gear,' McCowan recalls. 'They all had Australian watches. They were hung by a length of wire or string inside their trousers . . .' A week later, they load the Japanese onto barges, for the journey to Jesselton. A mishap leads to several Japanese drowning:

The barges couldn't get in too close because it was high tide. We were pushing the prisoners off the ramps and into the water. It was over their heads. A lot of them just started to float out to sea. Suddenly someone shouted – 'We should save those bastards, so they can be tried and then executed'.

McCowan, a good surfer, saves two drowning Japanese soldiers, 'as did nearly everyone else'.[27]

◆

Meanwhile, the six survivors of the Death Marches are repatriated to Australia, for prolonged interrogation and rehabilitation. Braithwaite arrives in Sydney on 7 August, aboard the 2/2 Australian Hospital Ship, and is detained in Advanced Headquarters for four weeks. His next of kin are informed and advised of the 'undesirability [that] any publicity be given to [his] return to avoid being inundated with inquiries'.[28] In the ensuing weeks, Braithwaite is 'interrogated as much as possible', notes one rather insensitive staff officer. 'The process was at times a considerable mental strain and he was finally evacuated upon medical advice.'[29] Nonetheless, Braithwaite's formidable memory ably assists his interrogators in furnishing a comprehensive, and fairly accurate, list of those believed to have died.

'It was a terrible strain,' Braithwaite later says. 'Just lying there in that bed going through all those names, and then when I'd get to a name I'd lie back and close my eyes, visualise him, and then go through everything I knew about him. And when you're doing that, and this fellow [the interviewing colonel] saying "Colour of eyes? Next of kin?", you know, I got really mad. It's quite incredible, isn't it . . . but still, that's the Army. You go by numbers, don't you.'[30]

39

RELICS

*Keep your reason free from passion . . . Organise your
thoughts in regular order, from the simplest to the most
complete . . . The art of thinking is the art of believing.*
Entry in Private Tom Burns' diary, found buried
with other personal effects in a mass grave
in Sandakan Prisoner of War Camp

BETWEEN 7 SEPTEMBER and 25 November 1945, Captain
Leonard Darling, the prisoner-of-war liaison officer of the
9th Australian Division, leads the first investigation into the
whereabouts of prisoners in Borneo. His 20 or so 'Contact and
Inquiry Teams' are ordered to identify any surviving prisoners of
war and civilians; locate the graves of all deceased prisoners and
civilians; and instruct any witnesses to complete a war-crimes
questionnaire, in order to identify alleged 'A', 'B' and 'C' war
criminals.

Darling's investigators fan out across this broken land, on one
of the grimmest missions of the peace. They know something
of what has happened here: a few of his men participated in the
Special Forces missions; all have heard the terrible rumours.
Yet the scale of what they are about to discover is beyond any

preconception. It proves so shocking that the governments in Canberra and London decide to close the book on Borneo, to inform neither the press nor the public. The families are to be told the barest minimum of what has become of their sons, brothers and husbands. Henceforth, the raiment of official secrecy falls over Sabah, sealed off from the world like a contagious community.

◆

One of Darling's main sources of information is Warrant Officer Sticpewich, as well as native informants, AGAS files, Japanese prisoners and records, and other sources. His team reveals a picture of enforced starvation, deliberate medical neglect and murder that, from February 1945, was killing 200 prisoners a month, according to figures uncovered from Japanese death certificates:[1]

Month	Number of prisoners who died of starvation and related illness:
Nov 44	22
Dec 44	52
Jan 45	16
Feb 45	174
Mar 45	333 (after First Death March)
Apr 45	221
May 45	195
Jun–July 45	479 (after Second Death March)

The Japanese figures in fact overstate the true casualty rate for June–July, because they represent false death certificates for prisoners the Japanese knew to be in the Ranau area but for whom they had no definite information. Nor do Japanese death notices record the true cause of death; they tend to list 'malaria' and 'dysentery' where they should have entered 'bashing', 'torture' and 'murder'.

Allied investigators swiftly build a fairly accurate picture of the enormity of the tragedy, thanks largely to Sticpewich's testimony, a chilling aspect of which is his recollection of the relics encountered along the track during the Second March. On 19 October 1945, Sticpewich states in sworn testimony before Mr Justice Mansfield:

I saw during the march to Ranau decomposed bodies and skeletons on the side of the track . . . and articles of Australian equipment, such as water bottles, haversacks and packs and general articles of Australian clothing. All along the track there was evidence of previous marches having gone over the same route because there were empty wallets and personal photographs and Australian and English army pay books . . .[2]

One of Darling's field teams (3 PW Contact and Inquiry Team) reaches Ranau on 12 November 1945. Led by Captain Thomas Mort, the team is instructed to investigate the fate of the 30–35 prisoners said by Sticpewich to be alive on 28 July. A week of searching ensues. Mort's men discover evidence of the 52-mile forced rice-carrying march, to Paginatan and back – and the appalling conditions of the three Ranau prison camps. Of the last jungle camp, Mort writes:

210 PW at this stage had no accommodation and lived for the first 10 days in the open whilst the compound was being built . . . A thorough search . . . for personal effects revealed that NO equipment or clothing remained [except] a few trinkets. A search for Capt COOK's records, presumed buried, was unsuccessful.[3]

In the Japanese guards' hut, they find a few Allied surrender pamphlets and an empty American Red Cross box, intended for, but never delivered to, the prisoners. Sworn statements from locals indicate that a few prisoners were alive at the end of August – a reference to the five officers murdered on 27 August, almost a fortnight after Tokyo surrendered:

One native swears that the last week in AUG he saw what he thought to be a killing area by the amount of blood on the ground. He also found two fresh graves which turned out to contain three certain identified Officers' bodies . . . one skull had been cleft in half.[4]

A representative of the War Graves Unit uncovers used rounds beside the graves.

From Sandakan to Ranau, the investigators find hasty attempts to burn, destroy or hide the evidence. The prisoners' hut built by Sticpewich's men at the last jungle camp is half-demolished. The Japanese 'wanted to cover up as much evidence as they could', notes Mort. Shortly, his field unit uncovers burial areas in and around Ranau containing 541 bodies – in mass graves, a bomb crater and several isolated graves, all unmarked.[5]

◆

A sadder trawl of war relics can scarcely be imagined than that gathered by the investigators, under the category of 'identity information'. At No. 1 Camp in Sandakan, they unearth the identity discs of Warrant Officer Charles Watson, Bombardier Bill McGee, Gunners Bill Leadbeatter and John Madeley, Privates Ted Skinner, Herb Dorizzi, W. J. Smith and Arthur Attenborough, and the metal plates of Privates Percy Addison and V. Jones. Nobody else is yet identifiable among the few items initially recovered; this in an area where hundreds died.

Found beside – or in – two isolated graves at the 111-mile peg, scene of the murder of the last living officers, are: a Sam Browne belt, owner 'indecipherable'; one shirt 'with holes in epaulettes to fit badges for rank of captain' and with a thermometer in the pocket (presumably belonging to one of the medical officers); three British Army pattern web belts; two expended .25 Japanese cartridges; and one RAF officer's cap and badge.[6] A witness to the atrocity, Kabirau, tells the investigators:

> At about the middle of September I was walking along an animal track just off the main road . . . when I came upon two large graves only about a week to 10 days old – there were no sticks or crosses on the graves and I thought they might have been Japanese.

Mass graves near Ranau's No. 2 Camp yield solid evidence of who died here: a page from a Commonwealth Bank pass book; a pay-book photo of Robert Twiss; the identity discs of members of the Suffolk Regiment, Gordon Highlanders and the RAF; and a motley array of personal items, including a groundsheet, sweatband, kitbags, haversacks, greatcoat, towel, spoons, pay books, part of a draft roll and a Perspex ring, and teeth (presumably false). And there is the haunting scribble, found in a notebook: 'Will – QX 22054 John William SEELEY LAST – Allotted Wife – Patricia Evelyn Mary LAST, Summerhill.'[7]

Perhaps the most melancholy harvest is the great assortment of clothing and personal effects handed in by native people, who would trade it for food with the prisoners or guards. The list readily identifies the original owners of working jackets, dixies and a lonely 'Wallet with photo – woman and child', the property of Private L. F. Buckley. Investigators find an exotic array of badges, belonging to the Northamptonshire Gordons, Singapore Royal Engineers, Royal Army Medical Corps, Royal Corps of Signals, Royal Army Service Corps, Royal Engineers and the Malay States Volunteer Rifles.[8]

All along the track from Sandakan to Ranau, through November and December, the Allied field teams continue their grisly work. A plan to search the track to Tampias on foot is unaccountably withdrawn and replaced with a pointless journey upriver, undertaken by Captain G. Cocks and members of AGAS, and downgraded to an intelligence-gathering mission. Their guide is the headman Kulang, and the mission futile. According to Silver, 'At no time were they permitted to move any further than one mile from the river.'[9]

Stray encounters with village headmen yield a trove of material attesting to the vibrant spirits of the prisoners in the earlier years of incarceration: the Radio Rubbish Concert Programme, for example, bearing the names of Sergeant Les Hales and seven privates, handed in by the village headman at Telupid, Orang Tuan Gundi. Gundi also possesses a statement, signed by four prisoners – two Australians (Fuller and Dawson) and two British

(Roberts and Beardshaw) – promising to pay him $400 if their escape attempt succeeded. It failed: they died of sickness and were buried in the jungle. Some members of Allied field units treat the search, in part, as a souvenir-gathering exercise and pocket the trinkets of the enemy: Japanese badges, artefacts and the medals of Governor Kumabe Tanuke.

◆

At the eight-mile camp near Sandakan, all is found burnt, desolate and drenched. The smell of smoke and something acrid, sickly, awaits the members of the 23 Australian War Graves Unit, who enter the camp in September. Their job is to interview native witnesses, and identify the graves and remains of prisoners. The unit's commander, Captain Robert Houghton, and his team identify about 145 graves marked by wooden crosses with metal plates – many inscribed by Braithwaite – bearing the soldier's number, rank, name, unit and date of death. This was a time, about 1942–43, when the dead were afforded a decent burial.

On 17 October 1945, No. 3 Australian Prisoner of War Contact and Inquiry Team, under the command of Captain G. Cocks, arrives at the eight-mile camp. Cocks' men – under the daily supervision of Lieutenant Eric Robertson – build on the War Graves Unit's initial work and gather evidence for the forthcoming war-crimes trials. As anticipated, they find no surviving prisoners. They unearth graves and examine the contents. They easily identify some 23 bodies, marked by rotting wooden crosses, buried in the Civil Cemetery in town in 1942.

In the last week of October, their work gets more difficult – and harrowing. At the No. 1 Prison Compound cemetery,

Cocks calculates that the remains of 660 men, including the 145 identified by Houghton, are buried here, many in mass graves. At No. 2 Compound, they find the bones of an estimated 253 British and Australian prisoners buried around the site and in slit trenches. Eighty are marked; the rest scattered or in mass graves, often stacked on top of each other. In most cases, the prisoners' leather dog tags are decomposed – making identification extremely difficult.[10] By 30 October, the War Graves Unit has identified 1200 graves of Allied prisoners in the Sandakan area.[11] The Japanese cooperate, supplying Allied translators with hundreds of death certificates giving the location and cause of death of prisoners in Sandakan and along the Sandakan–Ranau track. These are of dubious merit, however, in ascertaining the cause of death. Robertson's men are instructed not to exhume the bodies, pending a decision on where the Commonwealth dead will finally be laid to rest.

The investigators uncover a great variety of personal effects in the Sandakan camp, which help to identify the owners. Here, for example, is Dick Braithwaite's wool jacket (taken from him by the Japanese); Ron Moran's pay book; a hand-drawn 1943 Christmas menu signed by Tom Burns and others; and a baby's silver Christening mug inscribed 'Bridget Catherine from her Godmother, September 1940'. Items they have taken with them from Changi include a Christmas menu bearing the signatures of Nelson Short, Tom Burns and 16 other men.

Inside a wrecked hut – possibly Moritake's last office – the investigators find Japanese medical stores, rusty surgical instruments, dirty field dressings and vials of vaccines, unused. Scattered about the whole camp are pay books – revealing several dozen identities – boxes of Red Cross 'comfort' items, military badges, web packs (one of which is filled with five watches, two cigarette cases and some identity discs) and other paraphernalia.[12] Many Red Cross items are found in the Japanese huts, proving they confiscated aid meant for the prisoners.

Unearthed military badges convey the sheer diversity of the regiments incarcerated here. As well as the Australian Imperial Force and Royal Army are the 54 Lachlan Macquarie Regiment, 16 Cameron Highlanders, Gordon Highlanders, Singapore Volunteer Force, Black Watch, Penang and Province of Wellesley Volunteers, as well as the East Surrey, Cambridgeshire, Suffolk, Argyle and Sutherland, Border, Bedfordshire, Hertfordshire and Sherwood Foresters (Nottinghamshire and Derbyshire) regiments. Three miscellaneous badges represent the Malaya Automobile Association, Singapore Airport Hotel and a Malayan Revenue Officer.[13]

The discovery on the hill above the compound of forlorn personal effects beside rows of empty stretchers appals the investigating team. Shaving gear, dixies, blankets and a bucket of prepared rice are found beside improvised stretchers, hastily abandoned, which 'indicate that the occupants were taken away without warning', Robertson concludes. 'The mass graves and number of bodies of 4 to 5 months decomposition suggests a final massacre of the remaining sick prisoners.'[14]

Hampering the efforts to identify the dead is the lack of a list of their names and causes of death. Investigators at Ranau, for example, are unable to locate the tin with Captain Cook's registry of prisoners, severely limiting efforts to identify the remains of prisoners buried back at Sandakan and along the track. They dig around the tree where Cook was supposed to have buried it, with no luck. It appears the Japanese have destroyed this particularly useful piece of evidence. Japanese death certificates tend to be unreliable, and self-serving, and invariably fail to identify the chief cause of death: murder or forced starvation. Nor do they find any documents, such as diaries or lists, in the Sandakan camp. Rumours of prisoner rolls, or even hidden treasure, buried at the base of the Big Tree prove false.

◆

The search spreads inland. Earlier, in the west of the island, it embraced Jesselton, Kinabalu, Kuching, Labuan and the dreadful scenes at Miri, the west-coast oil town where 44 British prisoners were found massacred and some 5000 Chinese and Javanese starved to death after the Japanese plundered their crops and slaughtered their livestock. (Many were seen 'dragging themselves on their bellies through the streets. Too weak to get shelter they died like flies on the roadside.')[15] It envelops Ripley's investigations around Ranau and penetrates the regions around the Sandakan–Ranau track, and the villages of Paginatan, Telupid, Maunad and others along the rentis. Evidence of massacres, of isolated killings, and of more gradual extermination, through disease and starvation, in dismal jungle clearings or near villages adds to the emerging portrait of a sustained crime against humanity involving the whole of Sabah and other parts of Borneo. The death toll includes prisoners, civilians, native people and slave labour, chiefly workers imported from Java and other islands. Indeed, the Javanese coolies are treated no better than the prisoners: just a handful of the 4000 Javanese brought to Borneo are alive at the end of the war.

Small search parties unearth evidence of cold-blooded murder:

skulls bashed in, bearing single bullet holes or decapitated. A party of Cocks, two AGAS commandos and a member of 23 War Graves Unit, for example, locates a 'skull and Aust hat' at the 17.5-mile peg in mid-November. At the 27-mile peg near Tindok, they find the remains of four prisoners: 'One unburied skeleton covered by Aust. Working Jacket' – a few of the hundreds of corpses that are impossible to identify.[16]

Numerous statements from local people are gathered to check and corroborate the findings. Ghastly reports of cannibalism emerge. Kulang passes on his brother's eyewitness account of the fate of two prisoners who, suffering from scabies and beriberi, were shot at Maunad on 4 August and dismembered, 'the infected parts [legs and arms] cut off, and the trunks placed in a boat . . . My brother did not see the bodies eaten but assumed this was the intention of the Japanese as they were very short of food at the time.'[17] Gundi's men report witnessing sick prisoners being shot dead, dismembered and eaten. From Paginatan, similar reports arrive.

By 4 December 1945, the names of 700 Japanese and Formosans are linked to war crimes, on a growing list drawn up for Major R. Stewart, 9th Australian Division war-crimes officer. At this stage, they comprise all Japanese guards and staff at Kuching, and other areas. A separate list contains the alleged war criminals in and around Sandakan, and on the Death March route.

◆

The recovery of bodies, identification of the dead and reconstruction of the whole sickening story proceeds for months, indeed years. It is continuing to this day. For the families – Australian, British and those in Borneo – who have not located the remains of their sons or husbands, it will never end. The local people – the indigenous tribes, Malayan, Chinese, European – lend their knowledge and jungle skills to this immense task. They start enthusiastically, but it takes Commonwealth cash to elicit the thoroughness required to search the island. Some locals have spent years in Japanese prisons, in Kuching, Outram Gaol, Sandakan and elsewhere; others have resisted the Japanese from the forest, and emerge from their jungle redoubts wide-eyed, relieved and astonished to be alive. Surveying the wreckage of their homeland, they set their chins to the task of restoration and rehabilitation. But first they must make peace with the spirits of the dead and help exhume the bodies from the 'land below the wind', the title of Kuching prisoner Agnes Keith's beautiful memoir. Swathes of Borneo have become a huge cemetery.

In June 1946, a renewed search gets under way, this time on a bigger scale, spurred by the families' anxiety and the significant shortfall between the identification of the recovered remains and the total number of missing men. Three Australian Army War Graves Units (AAWGU) carve up the country into areas of responsibility: 8 AAWGU will cover the area around Sandakan and west along the track to Paginatan; 31 AAWGU the area around Jesselton and east along the track to Paginatan; and 23 AAWGU the Kuching area and Labuan.[18]

The first swiftly recovers further bodies in Sandakan Prison Camp, following the clearance and mass excavation of the burial grounds located the previous year. Most of the corpses are identifiable – through personal effects – with the exception of 52 'unknown Australian' and 108 'unknown British' soldiers' remains. Private Ray Battram, working on an exhumation team, finds to his shock that many bodies buried in rough wooden coffins in 1942–43 are remarkably intact – some of the flesh remains on the faces and limbs, and the hair and beards have survived in the airless boxes – but not sufficiently to allow identification, and they quickly rot on exposure.[19] Bodies buried later in the war are found wrapped in banana leaves or simply left in the open, where they quickly putrefy. In time, all will be transferred to a Commonwealth war grave in Labuan.

The search along the track towards Ranau is far more difficult. The scrutinising eye of Sticpewich, who accompanies part of the mission, detects many oversights and failings of command. His dismay at the shoddy progress of the search sets him in fierce dispute with his unit commanders, who threaten to relieve him. Sticpewich is made of sterner stuff and persuades them to agree to re-search the track between Paginatan and Tampias. Accompanied by 22 local gravediggers and 28 carriers, Sticpewich extends the search more deeply into the jungle on either side of the track and recovers 14 missed corpses – before he is relieved of his job and sent back to Sandakan.

In late 1946, the Tokyo War Crimes Tribunal summons Sticpewich to appear as a witness in trials of 12 Class A war criminals, including ex-premier General Tojo Hideki. According to newspaper accounts, Sticpewich turns in a memorable performance. Describing his work with a Commonwealth War Graves Unit, he tells the court that of 280 bodies recovered along part of the Death March route, 80 per cent had their skulls broken, jaws broken and faces kicked in. As he speaks, Sticpewich glares at Tojo and other high-ranking defendants.[20]

He returns to Borneo in late 1946, hoping to resume his work with the War Graves Units, which have recently made a horrific discovery: the contents of the mass grave at the airstrip, where 23 sick prisoners were mown down. One is Tom Burns, whose body they exhume along with his haversack and diary. The diary, damp, crumbling but generally readable, is the only written account of the Sandakan prison to survive the tragedy. Through Burns' eyes, we have seen the conditions on the hell ship and the early years of the prison camp. He was too sick to march. His calm reflections on himself, the art of thinking and how best to punt on a racehorse reach out to us at this great distance and summon a quiet sense of pity for this young man, whom we can readily see scribbling his thoughts in his forsaken world:

Art of thinking.

Keep your reason free from passion . . . Organise your thoughts in regular order, from the simplest to the most complete. Divide problems into as many parts as possible . . . The art of thinking is the art of believing. Thinking is easy, acting is difficult and to put one's thought into action is the most difficult . . . In order to act correctly we must make an effort to think correctly . . .

[advice to a Punter]:

It is better to learn a few things perfectly than many things indifferently . . . A Punter should have a quick intelligence it is an excellent idea to say nothing impose silence on talkative men. Silence is golden think of the three wise monkeys always on the racecourse (all information false as almost everything is exaggerated distorted or suppressed he must use his own imagination).[21]

◆

On his arrival back in Borneo, after giving testimony in Japan, Sticpewich is coldly informed that his services are not required. He returns in frustration to Australia. Yet again, he is not so easily deterred. Anxious letters from families, the stirrings of conscience and the power of memory compel him to return to Borneo. In order to get there, he proves a constant thorn in the side of the military authorities. In a strongly worded letter to Lieutenant Colonel Chapman, director of War Graves Services, dated March 1947, he persuades the authorities to extend the search for bodies. At the heart of his complaint is his belief that previous searches – in which Sticpewich had participated – failed to do a thorough job in finding them:

> On several occasions I expressed to Capt Johnston [the leader of an earlier search] the fact he was not giving me a fair go, and not treating me right as I came up here to help and search and he was placing every obstacle in my way. I gave him my reasons why I state a proper search had not been conducted . . .
>
> There was no personal supervision over the native searchers by a European, natives have to be strictly supervised, or else they will take the line of least resistance meaning, instead of a strict pattern search they will go where it is easy travelling.
>
> . . . a further check of all areas should be again made. For instance, when I was enroute to Ranau as a PW it was, as

far as I can remember, between Sai and Monyad [Maunad] where I placed 5 skulls in a big clay jar, at a PW Camp rest site, this was on about 11 June 45, this location has not been discovered, to date that I know of.

Sticpewich complains of being treated like 'an interloper', 'of no consequence' and contemptuously dismissed as a 'WO1' (warrant officer first class). To which he responds:

I deemed it my duty to take a personal interest in the whole of the Borneo area as I am the senior of 2396 PW who were left at Sandakan after the majority of officers were transferred to Muching [Kuching] in September 1943.

Its [*sic*] our duty to those who were not as fortunate as I to leave no stone unturned to do everything possible.

The way I feel is that some one has been responsible for wasting some of my time and taxpayers [*sic*] money, in the face of so many next of kin demanding to know what is being done . . .

Indeed, Sticpewich has referred many families' inquiries to the army. He cites one in particular: a Mr W. J. Simpson, of Richmond, who has received a photo of his son from a native, retrieved along the track by a previous reconnaissance party. The father sent the photo to Sticpewich, who wrote back promising to investigate, which the father patiently accepts. His son's photo is but a small glimpse of the tragedy, the scale of which not a single family yet comprehends. Sticpewich appreciates this, in his letter to the War Graves Services: 'If some next of kin had been given this much information unofficially they may not have been as considerate as Simpson. But they all must be considered.' He warns of 300 prisoners still missing along the rentis, and 37 missing at Ranau, concluding, 'in my own mind . . . I have endeavoured to do my utmost to lessen the anxiety and sorrow of the next of kin of the still missing members in [Borneo]'.[22]

The letter has the desired effect, persuading Lieutenant Colonel Chapman that 'more remains may be recovered if the track is again gone over', and the War Graves Department 'is strongly of the opinion that a further search should be undertaken'. In short, Sticpewich is to be unleashed again on the rentis; this time with the acting rank of captain, 'in order that he may be equipped with greater authority' and the right resources.[23]

◆

And so the extraordinary man sets off, in May 1947, on a six-week, bone-gathering marathon, at the head of an immense expedition dubbed the Australian Research Party, comprising several military personnel and scores of native people from kampongs all along the Death March route.

By 1 July 1947, this great procession of investigators, guides and diggers unearths the remains of another 109 bodies – of which 42 are found in Paginatan and 31 near the Sandakan Prison Camp – by the end of which the whole party is sick with sunstroke, pneumonia, staked feet, yaws and measles.[24] Sticpewich personally supervises the exhumations and recoveries. The expedition's success is due to its penetrating deeper into the jungle on either side of the track (300 yards compared with 22 yards previously) and gathering a trove of information from local police and natives.[25]

Sticpewich's laudable efforts go unthanked and unrecognised, largely because of his continuing withering assessments of the performance of 8 and 31 War Grave Units.[26] Of a previous search near the last jungle camp at Ranau, for example, he writes:

> I am of the opinion that there could have been much more care taken in this area by 8 AAWGU as the area was one unsitely [sic] mess with human remains scattered about the ground surface. The Research Party bagged all these scattered portions of skeletons and reburied them in each respective site at cemetery.[27]

Never one for diplomatic niceties, Sticpewich fails to recognise that without War Graves' resources – not least in paying for and supplying his expedition – the whole exercise would not have been possible. At one point on the journey, for example, 180 natives pound the track in his wake, in the pay of the Australian Government.

The 109 recovered corpses are given a mass-burial service by Reverend Sparrow of Sandakan. Some 270 bodies are still unaccounted for, which Sticpewich explains with his customary bluntness:

> Owing to laps [sic] of time, weather conditions and the fact that those who perished along the rentis were not buried, the animals strewed their bones about, water washed many away, besides evidence of cannibalism this will account for some or most of the missing . . .[28]

By the end of the two-year search, 2163 bodies are recovered

out of 2428 (1787 Australians and 641 British) then known to
have died at Sandakan prison, Ranau or on the Death Marches.
In 1949, the corpses of these, as well as others from Kuching and
elsewhere in Borneo, are moved to a dedicated Commonwealth
cemetery in Labuan. 'Unknown' marks the headstones of the
unknown or missing soldiers; the name of every victim of these
atrocities is inscribed on the nearby walls.

40

THE TRIALS

I knew that I would have to move in the near future
and rather than be encumbered and hampered
with sick PWs thought it best to kill them.
Captain Takakuwa, testifying before the War Crimes Tribunal

ON 16 OCTOBER 1945, Warrant Officer Bill Sticpewich is
brought before Allied officers for formal questioning. Earlier, in
Labuan, he gave an extensive statement about the condition of
the last 32 prisoners he saw alive before his escape. At the time,
however, Sticpewich found it 'difficult to distinguish' whether
some of the men 'were dead or unconscious'.[1] Sticpewich now
seeks to correct any errors he may have made in that initial
interview.

In advance of this meeting – and in light of the forthcoming
war-crimes trials – the Allied Recovery Unit takes a close interest
in the reliability of the escapees' testimonies. The six survivors
have been through hell and, while everyone sympathises,
the accuracy of their testimony is critical – to the severity of
punishment and the historical record. As the Allied Recovery
Unit notes:

RELIABILITY OF INFORMANTS:

STICPEWICH is considered to be a most reliable informant. He displayed an earnest desire to assist in the clarification of the fate of missing members, and applied himself to the task in an intelligent manner. There was a complete absence of any attempt at exaggeration or supposition on his part, and where he was uncertain of a casualty he refrained from expressing an opinion.

Pte BOTTERILL is considered unreliable as an informant. He showed a disinclination to give information and tactful persuasion is necessary to induce him to fulfil his duty in this regard. The possibility of his making hasty and possibly exaggerated statements to shorten his interrogation should not be overlooked. He is a type who is both uncooperative and devoid of a sense of responsibility.[2]

In fairness, at the time of this remark, Botterill is being evacuated with serious medical complaints. Botterill, like Short, Moxham, Campbell and Braithwaite, has endured a more gruelling ordeal than Sticpewich, whose friendship with the Japanese guards has left him in comparatively good health. Nor is Botterill disposed under interrogation to give the Japanese or Formosans the benefit of the doubt, in those few cases where doubt exists. The sheer horror of his experience, absolute hatred of the Japanese and primal ache for revenge lead him wilfully to distort the accuracy of his testimony.

Sticpewich is deemed the safer authority, because of his obvious maturity, grasp of the bigger picture and formidable memory. His evidence, both factual and anecdotal, is of great value to the war-crimes investigators. Not only is he able to name those responsible for the worst excesses; he can also recall their characters, nicknames and appearance and quote their most callous orders. Soon, his appearance at the war-crimes trials will shock the Japanese defendants – who believed him dead – and demolish their defence under a catalogue of lacerating evidence. His statutory declaration is a model of well-informed candour, which he delivers with an acute eye for devastating detail. For example:

> During the 2 1/2 years or thereabouts in which I was a PW at Sandakan, I became familiar with the habits and conduct of practically all the Formosan guards who numbered about 110 at first . . . With few exceptions, all . . . were very cruel in their treatment of PWs and of their own initiative frequently carried out cruel beatings and assaults on PWs to an excessive degree.

Sticpewich cites three of the worst: Hayashi Yoshinori, Kitamura Kotaro and Kiyoshima Tadeo, all of whom are tried in early 1946. Hayashi, he states, is nicknamed 'Ming the Merciless', 'because of the frequency and severity of his assaults and beatings of PWs'. After his discharge from the Quartermaster's Department, and relegation to guard duties, Hayashi's 'treatment of PWs can only be described as cruel in the extreme':

> He was on guard duty over a period of about 18 months and there was hardly a day when . . . I did not see him beating, in one form or another, some one or more prisoners. Hayashi's main weapons were his rifle butt and heavy stick . . . On parades, if a PW relaxed in the slightest [he] would deliver a

heavy blow with his rifle butt in the kidneys and small of the back.

Sticpewich alleges that Hayashi regularly smashed up prisoners with a stick during their 'breaks' from the cage, when already weakened by starvation rations.[3]

Kitamura, one of the worst of the Formosans:

excelled in cruelty on the slightest pretext. He was a flash, show-off type who prided himself on his ju-jitsu prowess and never lost an opportunity to practise his art. For the most trivial offences, such as smoking or gambling, wandering around the camp after lights out, a PW if caught by Kitamura would be made to stand to attention and thereupon Kitamura would practise his ju-jitsu on the prisoner. He would continue throwing the PW to the ground until he himself became tired . . .[4]

Kiyoshima the prisoners called 'Panther Tooth', because he had two gold teeth and would sneak up on his prey at night: 'His favourite weapon was a broomstick handle with which he used to beat the PW over the head and about the body.' Sticpewich witnessed him break two handles, refit new ones, and resume a bashing.[5]

Asked to comment on the accuracy of statements supplied by Japanese and Formosans, Sticpewich appends short 'notes' at the end of each, which check the guards' special pleading and often devastate their credibility. Under Captain Nagai Hirawa's statement, Sticpewich writes that he 'definitely did NOT like the Aussie manner and spirit, which he tried to break' and had a 'better feeling' for the British. His 'beatings of Australians was much more intense'. Nagai insisted on cremations, banned burials and refused to allow padres at funerals.[6]

Of Yanai Kenji, who tries to pass himself off as restrained, Sticpewich says that he carried out many beatings and flogged one prisoner, caught stealing at Ranau, so badly that the victim couldn't work: 'Doctors diagnosed internal injuries, contused liver and kidneys as a result.'[7]

Miyajima Hikozaburo – nicknamed the 'English-Speaking Bastard' – 'used [English] in a disgusting manner to prisoners, calling them "fucking bastards" and [threatening] to "fuck your mother and sister when I get to Australia"'. All Australian men would be his 'slaves', and eventually the Japanese would 'kill us all'. Examples of this guard's ill-treatment of prisoners are 'too numerous to recall'.[8]

Sticpewich takes care to acknowledge the few acts of restraint. Several – perhaps half a dozen – guards refused to ill-treat the men, such as Takata Kunio. In charge of a 20-man wood party in Sandakan, Takata 'stole extra foodstuffs for them . . . I know of one instance when he was beaten by his officers for not obeying orders to ill-treat PWs.'[9] Several guards mistreated the prisoners 'only on orders' and were severely reprimanded or beaten themselves if they failed to exact sufficient punishment. A guard named 'Happy' earned his nickname by disobeying orders to bash and being cheerfully disposed towards the prisoners.[10] Some guards would murder on orders and then, when out of sight of the Japanese officers, gave the prisoners food. Yokota Kinzo, for example, beat and killed when told to, then later 'misappropriated foodstuffs and vegetables and gave them to the PWs'.[11]

Sticpewich lays the blame for the worst atrocities upon

Moritake and Murozumi, who 'got as many prisoners on their feet as possible' for the Second Death March 'by tipping them off their beds; others were on crutches and walking sticks; all were forced out of the gate to participate in the march to Ranau'. And Fukishima Masao, also known as the 'Black Bastard', is similarly condemned for forcing sick men to work, picking them out of the lines regardless of their condition and 'kicking them on their ulcers'. This guard admitted to 'watching' – with pleasure, Sticpewich suggests – the gradual deterioration of prisoners in the cage.

The surviving prisoners at Kuching similarly indict their former guards and torturers. The officer-in-charge of the British compound, Lieutenant S. T. Sunderland, for example, cites one horrific example: one 'Hideo' – full name not given – who 'struck prisoners whenever he could'. This guard affords an excellent example of how closely allied are stupidity and cruelty, as revealed during his interrogation:

Why did you beat prisoners?
Because they stole food and other things.

Did you boast about being the worst basher in the camp . . .?
Yes.

How many prisoners died at Labuan?
About 200 . . .

What did they die of?
Malaria and beri beri.

What happened to the remainder?
We took them to the mainland where some more died of
malnutrition. The prisoners left were killed . . .

Why were they killed?
S/M [Sergeant Major] Sugino ordered us to kill them.

Why?
He told us to kill them.

Did any try to escape?
No. After they were shot some of the wounded tried to crawl
away and S/M Sugino ordered us to kill them with our
bayonets.

How many did you kill yourself?
2 or 3 of the British and about 4 of the Indians.

Why?
S/M Sugino ordered it . . .

What happened to Captain Campbell?
The top of his head was shot off.[12]

On New Year's Day 1946, a hastily convened military court in
Labuan prepares to try the Japanese and Formosans in Borneo for
war crimes. Captain Gregor Barr, the 9th Division legal officer,
summarises the position in a letter at the time to HQ: 'there are

approximately 130 Japs awaiting trial for offences in category B. There are no cases in category A.'[13] In other words, those on trial are neither senior, nor their crimes important, enough to be grouped as Class A war criminals of the stature of, say, Premier Tojo Hideki or General Yamashita, the Tiger of Malaya. Most are common soldiers or guards.

The 130 are divided into the following cases – to be tried individually or in groups:

- Captain Hoshijima, the officer commanding Sandakan Prisoner of War Camp: 'He is being charged on four separate charges of ill-treatment [of prisoners].'
- Captain Takakuwa and Lieutenant Watanabe: the officer commanding and second-in-command respectively during the Second March from Sandakan to Ranau, and subsequently at Ranau prison camp. They are jointly charged with 'causing the murders on the march' and 'three later massacres [of prisoners]'.
- 21 guards are charged with 'murder' during the Second Sandakan–Ranau March.
- 20–30 guards are charged with 'three separate massacres' of prisoners at Ranau.
- 40–60 guards are charged with 'ill-treatment' at the prison camp in Kuching.[14]

Many Japanese and Formosans suspected of war crimes – chiefly in relation to the 'ill-treatment' of prisoners on the First March and in Sandakan and Ranau prison camps – have not yet been fully investigated. This will take time, and the British Government is impatient for the return of its colony. Hankering to resume its position as the mercantile power in Borneo, London is breathing down the necks of the military authorities to get on with it. An unseemly haste drives the military tribunals – an expedience denied the Allied prisoners during three years of injustice and utter misery. The war-crimes trials are to start as soon as possible, on 3 January 1946.

◆

The Allied prosecutor is a smart young barrister from Sydney called Athol Moffitt, flown into Labuan on 29 December 1945 from Brunei, where he had been conducting civilian cases. The lawyer is an officer of the 9th Division and combines a forensic legal brain and mastery of the English language with a profound appreciation of the ethical quagmire into which he is about to step. Destined to be a New South Wales Supreme Court judge, Moffitt instinctively grasps the historic importance of these trials of 'a crime without parallel in Australian history'. He is determined not to rely on the rough military justice of those baying for revenge. His memoirs contain his guiding principles, and they are laudable:

> The duty of a prosecutor [of war crimes] was greater than merely to produce evidence sufficient to support some finding of guilt . . . The occasion of the trial, as I saw it, afforded me the opportunity of establishing the full extent of the responsibility Hoshijima in fact had for the deaths of the prisoners in his charge and later. The principal, or at least initiating cause of those deaths appeared to be the starvation

of the prisoners, leading to their physical collapse and the contracting of diseases . . .

Moffitt eschews the 'special provisions' in the Australian War Crimes Act, which facilitate proof of guilt during wartime conditions (such as in cases where all witnesses are dead): '. . . but it seemed to me, as a lawyer that, at the end of the case, the determination of guilt and the imposition of any penalty, particularly the death penalty, ought to be solidly based on proof of matters of substance by clear direct evidence'.[15]

The trials are conducted in two courtrooms inside a large tent in the shade of a coconut grove on Timabalai Beach, Labuan, giving onto the China Sea. Moffitt's file contains 50 sworn statements, including those by the six escapees: Sticpewich, Braithwaite, Short, Nelson, Campbell and Botterill. Only Sticpewich, however, will be called as a key military witness to most of the hearings; and Moffitt awaits the warrant officer's arrival like a man on the threshold of an epiphany. He regards Sticpewich, whose interrogation report he has read, as the ace in the pack of the prosecution. The amazing fact of his survival, his intimate involvement in the prisoners' ordeal and his incendiary evidence mark him out as Moffitt's most crucial witness.

◆

If the war-crimes trials are 'victors' justice', as some later decide, then the victors at Labuan are fair-minded to a fault. Takakuwa, Watanabe, Baba, Hoshijima and other defendants are granted every dignity and right of a proper court martial. Four Japanese lawyers, led by Colonel Yamada – a charming, bilingual graduate of Cambridge University – are on hand to plead the defendants' cases. These men are highly intelligent, Tokyo-trained advocates, determined to defend their countrymen, who, Moffitt must prove beyond doubt, were responsible for the torture, beating, starvation, denial of medical aid and/or force-marching to death of some 2500 Australian and British prisoners, and the massacre of the survivors.

The commanders of the Second Death March, Captain Takakuwa Takuo and Lieutenant Watanabe Genzo, are the first to be tried, from 3–5 January, on one charge of mass murder – in that they 'caused to be killed numerous unknown PW' – and three charges of massacre, of 33 prisoners, at or near Ranau, in August 1945.

Takakuwa opens his testimony with the diehard soldier's defence: he was only acting under orders. He soon adjusts this tactic. Stating that he was ordered by 37 Army HQ – that is, commanding officer General Baba Masao – to move all prisoners to Ranau 'regardless of their condition', Takakuwa claims he protested that 'there were 400 stretcher cases and 200 could not walk and only about a fifth would reach their destination'. This is a clear admission that he knew the precise state of the men, and their chances of survival, well in advance of the march. He states that he made these facts known to the staff officer at 37 Army HQ in Kuching. But, 'I received no reply to this signal and interpreted this as confirmation to carry out the previous order. On my own responsibility I left 288 prisoners behind and later was reprimanded for this.'[16]

In other words, Takakuwa claims that he disobeyed explicit instructions – to move all the prisoners – but, having decided to move most of them, he then accepts responsibility for their fate.

He argues that he set up ration points on the track but concedes that they were inadequate, or swiftly exhausted, or non-existent. 'There were no medical posts along the route,' he says, implying that this somehow justified his bloody remedy:

My initial plan was to leave those that became too sick to travel behind with someone to look after them, but the numbers were so great that this scheme proved impracticable. I therefore instructed S/M Tsuji [leader of the killing party] to bring along whatever PWs that he could and as a last resource [sic] to shoot the PWs rather than leave them behind to die.

He thus attempts to present mass murder as an act of 'humane killing'.

He then departs from the 'I was acting under orders' defence and accepts the decision as his alone:

These orders were issued on my own responsibility and were not issued on any higher authority. When I arrived at Ranau I reported to Major Watanabe Yoshio. When I told him that I had been forced to kill many of the PWs on the way over he said it was a very difficult march and could not be helped.[17]

In the same vein of self-condemnation, Takakuwa states that he instructed his staff to kill the remaining prisoners at Ranau rather than waste precious rations on sick and hungry men. With the Allied bombers closing in, as he states in pre-trial evidence (and later, in another version, to the court):

I knew that I would have to move in the near future and rather than be encumbered and hampered with sick PWs thought it best to kill them. My other reasons were that there was no food, and I feared that they would all escape. When the order to move finally arrived all the PWs were dead.

He thought of sending some prisoners to a machine-gun unit, to carry their ammunition to Beaufort: 'it did not matter if they died while employed on this task'.[18] In the event, he decided, as he tells the court, that 'it was best to dispose of them as they had become very cumbersome'. 'Criminally insane' or 'sociopathic' or any other modern label seems to fall short of describing this individual, whose testimony must surely rank as one of the most banal confessions of mass slaughter ever presented at a trial.

Watanabe's testimony echoes Takakuwa's. It was this officer who ordered the lower ranks to be the executioners. He expected the utmost brutality from his men, thus creating many witnesses against him. His defence of obedience to orders fails under cross-examination. As second-in-command, Watanabe 'acted on his own discretion in many respects and did so enthusiastically, and that he efficiently planned schemes to dispose of the maximum number of prisoners', Moffitt concludes.[19]

Probing further into the brains of these men offers no further insight into their motives. Like so many junior field officers, they come across as ignorant automatons of the Japanese Empire. Needless to say, their guilt is clearly established, and Moffitt – drawing also on the evidence of witnesses Sticpewich, Nelson Short and Formosan guards – easily dismantles their defence that the prisoners were 'humanely killed':

the circumstances of the march from start to finish and what occurred at Ranau made any defence based on humanity and killing as a last resort, quite ridiculous. At every stage of the march and of the imprisonment of the POWs at Ranau, there was unimaginable barbarity, cruelty and acts of deprivation . . .[20]

Takakuwa Takuo and Watanabe Genzo (and several guards) are condemned by their admission of, and direct involvement in, the atrocities committed on the Second Death March. Both men are found guilty and sentenced to death: Takakuwa by hanging, at Rabaul on 6 April 1946; Watanabe by firing squad, at Morotai on 16 March 1946.

◆

Moffitt faces a tougher quarry in Captain Hoshijima Susumi. The first commandant of the Sandakan Prison Camp is accused of four charges of war crimes alleged to have occurred between September 1942 and May 1945. He is held responsible for allowing sick and ill-fed prisoners to be:

- closely confined under inhuman conditions and cruelly beaten while confined, 'as a result whereof certain PWs died';
- tortured and cruelly beaten by soldiers under his command;
- employed on manual and heavy labour;
- refused adequate food and proper medical care.[21]

Moffitt boils down these clauses to: cruelty, cruelty by

confinement in a cage resulting in POW deaths, starvation and denial of medical attention causing deaths, and forcing sick men to do heavy work.[22] In his legal arsenal against Hoshijima, Moffitt plans to deploy two powerful weapons: the detailed testimony of Sticpewich and a statement from the Japanese Lieutenant Arai, a quartermaster at Sandakan Prison Camp. He needs both, as Hoshijima proves a wily adversary.

Under pre-trial interrogation, the engineer defends himself on the grounds that he acted on the orders of Japanese HQ in Kuching; that the prisoners' deaths were due to the shortage of rice, or lack of medical supplies; and that 'he had done his best to provide substitutes' and tried always to treat the prisoners 'with kindness'.[23] Hoshijima, at this point, has no idea that an Australian survivor of the Death Marches is about to stride into court and tear apart his testimony.

Indeed, Sticpewich's arrival in Labuan is the 'answer to my prosecutor's prayers', writes Moffitt. This 'typical Aussie – fairly rough, but hail fellow well met with a ton of resource and personality' enters the courtroom on 8 January 1946, to the astonishment of the Japanese defendants.

The case proceeds for two weeks, from 8 to 20 January 1946. Few journalists attend (and only one politician, Frank Forde, Australian Minister for the Army, makes an appearance, fleetingly, at the hearings). Hoshijima is led in by Gurkha guards on the first day. The tall Japanese engineer clicks the heels of his well-polished boots, salutes the court and gazes 'intently, even defiantly, at those who were to try him'.[24] He strikes Moffitt as 'an impressive man with a domineering personality', and hardly the monster portrayed by rumour. The Australian lawyer closely observes Hoshijima throughout the trial. The defendant, he notices, never relaxes his 'steely look': 'At times he wore a sinister set type of smile.'[25] The smile disappears when Sticpewich enters the courtroom, and Hoshijima visibly pales. Here, all of a sudden, is the living antidote to the commandant's poison; here is a man who saw everything. Hoshijima and his henchmen had presumed the prisoners were all dead – especially this one, who has witnessed their atrocities first-hand and knows, literally, where the bodies are hidden.

Proving that Hoshijima deliberately starved the prisoners to death is critical to the success of Moffitt's case. The evidence of Arai and Sticpewich amply supports that contention. Arai testifies that, 'The POWs in January 1945, in my opinion, were not getting enough rice, taken with other things, to keep them alive.' He confirms to the court's satisfaction that the Japanese failed to supply any rice to the prisoners after February 1945. The inmates were then left to live off the meagre foodstuffs they had saved, most of which was later confiscated and/or used to supply the First March. In consequence, they had only 11 ounces of rice per prisoner per day from January 1945.

Sticpewich follows up with a searing indictment of Japanese neglect of the prisoners' food and medical needs. The man best equipped to observe the Japanese at close quarters – and Sticpewich, who speaks a smattering of Japanese, often worked outside the wire with the guards – testifies that his captors kept large amounts of rice in storage, at various times in the first half of 1945, including 1000 bags under Hoshijima's bungalow and 1200 bags in other locations. His evidence shows that the Japanese were well supplied with food at all times because, as Moffitt later adjudges, they 'were eating the food of the starving prisoners!'.[26]

Hoshijima's testimony is self-incriminating. He cannot

reconcile the discrepancy between the deaths of some 800 prisoners (a figure he revises upwards during the trial) that occurred, as he admits, at Sandakan prison while he was commandant, and the death of just one Japanese in that period. He tries to argue that the lack of medical care killed the prisoners. In fact, as becomes plain, Hoshijima's refusal to feed the prisoners coincided with the stoppage of work on the airfield in January 1945, after it was destroyed by Allied bombers. As slave labourers, they were useful and so required feeding; as idle captives, they were deemed useless and henceforth disposable. Certainly, he decided, they would not share his precious food or medical stores.

The court hears that Hoshijima personally ended the prisoners' rice ration three months before Japanese HQ in the South-West Pacific issued the same order. Moffitt expertly draws out the point that most of those who died in the camp died of illnesses linked to severe malnutrition that began in the three-month period after Hoshijima's order. The Japanese commander's degree in chemistry further damages his defence: he well knew the link between beriberi and vitamin deficiency and concedes that, at the time of their deaths, many soldiers weighed as little as five stone.

As for Hoshijima's claim that a lack of medicines killed the prisoners, a reliable witness is available to soundly refute it: Dr James Taylor. The stoic doctor has survived Outram Gaol and, though weakened by years of imprisonment and torture, testifies that in 1943 he set aside enough quinine to supply British North Borneo for two years. Most, however, was subsequently confiscated by the Japanese. Red Cross parcels were similarly denied the prisoners, as Sticpewich recalls, and routinely appropriated by the Japanese. The warrant officer should know:

he translated the parcels' labels for the Japanese. Many prisoners – including the escapee Braithwaite – were reduced to trading their watches and other items for quinine tablets.

Finally, Moffitt turns to the charge of cruelty, and Sticpewich spares no one the grisly details. For days, the court hears in grim-faced silence the stories of severe flogging and bashing, of Darlington's horrible torture, of men crammed for weeks in the cage, of the sick being kicked out of bed and forced to work, of eye-gouging, king-hitting, smashed jaws and limbs . . . the long, gradual dismemberment of body and spirit. Hoshijima cannot deny that he presided over much of this. He admits that he personally beat prisoners, ordered the building of the cage and sentenced some prisoners to periods inside, without trial, for minor 'offences' such as stealing vegetables.

Nonetheless, he and his defence team fight doggedly every step of the way. Hoshijima claims in general terms to have been 'kind' to the prisoners; he only beat them occasionally. 'If they would not work I hit them,' he tells the court; he would do the same to any Japanese soldier who failed to perform.[27] As an example of his 'kindness', he cites a decision to slaughter his fine white stallion – 'Hossie's Horse', the Australians nickname it – to help feed them. But Sticpewich corrects this: the horse had been abandoned, and the prisoners received only the head, hooves and intestines; the Japanese consumed the heart and liver along with the horse's flesh. 'He treated the horse the same as he did us . . . he killed it. We only got the entrails.'[28] Yet Hoshijima's most self-defeating testimony relates to Jimmy Darlington. After first denying all knowledge of, and his presence at, the prolonged torture of this part-Aboriginal soldier, Hoshijima admits to being a witness to it. He then protests that 'when I saw it I returned to my office and put out an order to stop the punishment'.[29] His threefold lie fails to impress the court.

On 16 January 1946, Hoshijima's lawyers call an adjournment; their client appears to be suffering a malarial attack. '[S]urely irony,' Moffitt writes with disgust, 'when this is the man who denied medicines to POWs dying of malaria at 6 to 7 a day'.[30] The court resumes, for four more days of examination and cross-examination, during which Hoshijima's guilt is proven beyond doubt. Before sentencing, he is invited to address the court. In a desperate last flourish, he invokes the grandeur of the Japanese Empire, its defeat of Russia and other irrelevancies. He blames Lieutenant Colonel Suga, now conveniently dead, for any excesses that may have occurred at Sandakan. His tone is that of a grievously wronged schoolboy. Unable to accept blame, he clings pathetically to his past 'good character', as though this should exonerate him. He cites his ten years at Osaka University: 'I was the leader and representative of my class. I was also chairman of the Students' Committee. I would like you to take this into consideration when you judge my character.' In the army, 'I have never been once punished for breaking any regulations. Instead I have always been rewarded and praised for my work.'[31]

He implores his accusers to recognise his kindly thoughts for the men: 'When I did these things I was thinking all the time [of] the happiness and protection of the prisoners.'[32] He begs them to 'understand all the difficulties that were in my path and to show mercy in your judgement'. He bemoans the absence of his 'friends', Captains Mills and Cook, respectively the British and Australian prisoners' leaders, both slaughtered by Hoshijima's successors. Had they been available as witnesses, surely they would have vouched for his good character, he pleads. After all, had they not attended his farewell dinner after he was sacked as camp commandant?

In despair, he claims that he has been misinterpreted; he blames his superiors, his orders, his lack of supplies; he even attempts to woo the court's sympathy with past examples of his decency to the Chinese, surely the least-favoured recipients of Hoshijima's 'kindness'. And then, having exhausted his quiver of appeals and excuses, Hoshijima falls on Allied mercy – as father and husband:

> my first son was born just four days before my being pulled into the Army on 16th September 1941. On that day I visited my wife in hospital . . . When I think of the future of my wife and children I cannot help feeling the hardest pains in my heart . . .[33]

His sincerity is as worthless as the quality of Japanese mercy: no Australian or British father and husband received the compassion this man now demands of his Allied judges. But this is not an eye-for-an-eye case. The vengeful Old Testament equation is neither the determinant, nor the justification, for Hoshijima's punishment, which is properly decided according to the law of the day. He is found guilty on all charges. After hearing his sentence – 'death by hanging' – he salutes, clicks his heels as he did on arrival, about-turns and marches out.

From his prison cell, Hoshijima continues fitfully issuing statements declaring his innocence, appealing for clemency, to no avail. His request to send a lock of hair and toenail parings to his family is refused, but he is allowed to write farewell letters. He sends ten home – many more than the prisoners were allowed to send home in three years. Hoshijima is hanged on 6 April 1946. Defiant to the last, he shouts, 'Long live the Emperor' as he mounts the gallows, and reportedly bites the hand of the provost who tries to silence him. The provost states calmly, 'This is for the Aussies you killed at Sandakan,' and releases the trap.[34]

◆

In late January, Moffitt turns to the most difficult case, as virtually all the witnesses are dead: the trials of those accused of atrocities committed on the First Death March. Captain Yamamoto heads the list of 11 Japanese defendants – four captains, five lieutenants, a warrant officer and a sergeant. They are to be tried together on two charges: the murder of numerous unknown prisoners of war, and the forcing of sick and underfed men on long forced marches 'as a result whereof many died'.[35]

Moffitt has just two key witnesses, Keith Botterill and Bill Moxham – who were on the march – and precious little evidence. Sticpewich was on the Second March. The witnesses can only speak for what happened on their legs of the journey, and this amounts to recollections of men falling behind, the sounds of gunshots and the same men never being seen again. It is insufficient evidence to prove the charge of murder. Botterill, however, claims to have seen a guard shoot four prisoners, but his testimony as to the identity of the guard is dubious.

Moffitt finds the missing link he needs in the pre-trial statement of one Lieutenant Abe, who led the last group – some 50 British prisoners, none of whom survived – and commanded the killing platoon that brought up the rear. Abe is an anomaly. While other officers on the march, having served Yamamoto for years, parrot a pre-agreed line that no prisoners were killed and all died of illness, Abe is not in on their lie. He tells the court that Yamamoto ordered him to kill any prisoners who were too ill to move or when 'there was no other course available'. Yamamoto further told Abe, according to the latter's statement, that he expected many to die and he would take responsibility for the killings. In essence, then, Abe testifies that Yamamoto appointed him to command the First March's killing squad.

Confronted with Abe's testimony, the astonished Yamamoto is forced to admit that he gave the orders but denies that he gave them to 'my men'; on the contrary, 'his' men were ordered not to kill or leave any POW behind. Moffitt's fine nose for a legal discrepancy picks up the stench of perjury. Further testimony from guards in Abe's unit, as well as Botterill's and Moxham's statements, gave the lie to Yamamoto's defence that his men helped the prisoners until they died of illness.

This 'conspiratorial lie' is further exposed by Sticpewich's evidence of Australian and British remains – bones, bits of uniform, personal effects – scattered along the track, which 'could only have been from the first march'. Taking all the evidence together, Moffitt rightly concludes that 'the general pattern of the march was that if men could not go on, they were shot along the trail', as it was 'hardly likely' that Abe acted alone. And most men were forced to march when they manifestly could not: certain death stalked them, whether by gunshot, forced starvation or disease resulting from gross neglect.

Moffitt neatly proves this by asking the Japanese officers commanding each of the prisoners' groups to draw charts of their progress to Ranau. 'The charts were a cross-examiner's dream,' Moffitt writes, because they show conclusively that sick and starving men were forced, regardless of their condition or Japanese 'kindness' – another universal lie – to get up each morning and march another 10–12 miles.[36] The guards unwittingly press the case against their officers. 'All I required of [the prisoners],' said one, in a typical statement, 'was that they should reach the night staging area . . . POWs had to travel regardless of how sick they were.'[37]

All the accused are found guilty. Their defence of military necessity, that they were acting on orders, holds no substance, because it is irrelevant to the charges. The prosecution finds them guilty of criminal conduct *during* the march – of forcing sick men to walk until they dropped, then shooting them where they fell. Their lawyer Yamada's argument, that the Death Marches were necessary to escape Allied landings and 'a tragic product of this war', for which the 'wild jungle land of Borneo' was to blame, holds little sway over the court.[38]

Before sentencing, the accused are permitted to address the tribunal. Yamamoto praises his young officers, who stand awkwardly in a line, and Moffitt is even moved to sympathise with these young men, 'pleasant, fresh-faced . . . in contrast to the evil-faced Hoshijima'. The young officers speak of their 'love' and sympathy for the prisoners, and recall acts of kindness towards them: sharing food, having special meals. No doubt, some were occasionally kind, but these are brittle reeds in the swim of barbarity. All receive death sentences except one, who is jailed for life.

Conflicting evidence relating to the identity of one of the accused prompts a retrial, in May 1946, in Rabaul. Judge Advocate General William Simpson returns a verdict of guilt to all except two defendants, who are acquitted of murder. The judge also commutes the death sentences to ten years' imprisonment in every case except for those of Yamamoto and Abe, who are condemned to die, by hanging, on 19 October 1946. One of those acquitted is Sergeant Major Gotanda, who, it transpires, Botterill has mistakenly identified as the murderer of four soldiers. It is one of several errors – wilful or accidental – committed by Botterill during the trials. Moffitt accepts part of the blame, for endeavouring to establish the identity of Gotanda 'without Botterill seeing the accused man'.

◆

Despite these successes, the War Crimes Tribunal has not yet arraigned the chief culprit, the man who ordered the Death Marches. Thus far, only soldiers and guards have been found guilty and sentenced. The court has punished the brutal executors, not the architects. Responsibility for the overall crime lies elsewhere.

Time distils the truth; two years pass before the reality emerges, and a man is brought before the court in Rabaul. From 28 May to 2 June 1946, an all-Australian tribunal presided over by Major General John Whitelaw tries the Japanese general alleged to have ordered the Death Marches. He is, of course, Lieutenant General Baba Masao, commanding officer of the 37th Imperial Army Corps based in Kuching during the occupation of Borneo.

The court hears evidence of the 'positive criminality' of the defendant, in that Baba issued direct orders to move the prisoners from Sandakan to Ranau, which he knew would result in their deaths. Baba gave these orders, which he had inherited, in January

1945, regardless of the prisoners' condition. One of his staff officers, Yamada Masaharu, will later claim that the order to move the prisoners from east to west issued from Imperial Headquarters in Tokyo in 1944. If so, Baba enacted them to the letter. He well knew, through his subordinate Colonel Takayama, who had visited the Sandakan compound before the First March left, that the prisoners were very weak, sick and hungry. Baba did nothing to alleviate their suffering; on the contrary, he forced through the orders he received. Many who died on the First March may have survived had they not been compelled to carry rice bags between Paginatan and Ranau, which contributed to the deaths of the last 250. Baba knew this through his agents. He also knew the condition of the 288 sick and dying men back in Sandakan, of whom 75 were forced on the Last March while the prison camp burnt. Baba drove this decision. None survived.

Baba's special pleading, apologies and explanations wear thin in the roasting courtroom. This is the man who, in early 1946, intervened on behalf of Japanese prisoners awaiting death. Their acts, he wrote to the Australian 9th Division HQ, 'done under the extraordinary circumstances and military discipline of Japan were actually irresistible and inevitable for them'.[39] According to this logic, the Japanese regime is responsible and not the troops (or, implicitly, the generals), who were helpless, forgivable pawns of Tokyo. The staggering irony here – apparently lost on Baba – is that the general himself personifies the very 'military discipline' he blames for driving these young men to commit atrocities.

His circular argument returns to condemn him. Baba saves neither his subordinates nor himself. He is sentenced to die for unlawfully disregarding and failing to discharge his duty as commander, and failing 'to control the operations of the members of his command, permitting them to commit brutal atrocities and other high crimes against people of the Commonwealth of Australia and its Allies'.[40] He is hanged by Australian Army authorities on 7 August 1947.

Sticpewich satisfies himself that justice has been done. After the trials, he writes to a friend:

> I have got to the bottom of all the war crimes here, especially the main ones. Where Australians, English and Indians were implicated, I have not let one go out of the whole bunch . . . I went to no end of trouble to round them all up but they are all in the bag now.[41]

Moffitt offers a more fitting summary of 'this grim and terrible story' of Australian and British prisoners, who:

> sick and weak, underfed and dying, [driven] through jungle swamps and over precipitous mountain passes, [were] . . . driven on and on at terrific speed by the guards at the rear who abused and beat them to keep them going – driven on and on by the knowledge that if they stopped they would be left to die or be shot.[42]

◆

Some of those responsible for these atrocities are never found, or tried, due to the lack of evidence or witnesses, most of whom were killed or died. Or they run away. Jimmy Darlington's chief torturer, for example, disappears. But two prominent cases do reach court: those accused of the ghastly murder of Gunner Albert

Cleary, and the murder and torture of Captain Lionel Matthews and his colleagues in the Sandakan underground.

The two key witnesses in Cleary's case are Botterill and Moxham, over whose credibility grave question marks remain. One can understand the emotional impulse to 'get' (Lynette Silver's word) the Japanese, who have inflicted so much misery on him; but Botterill's mistaken evidence against a defendant in a separate case, Gotanda, almost condemns to death a man Botterill elsewhere praised as being unusually kind to the prisoners.[43]

Botterill and Moxham are suspected of perjuring themselves in the trial and retrial of Fukishima, the 'Black Bastard', who is accused of the murder of Arthur Bird. In the retrial, Botterill and Moxham enlist the help of Sticpewich, their inveterate enemy, to exaggerate the evidence and ensure Fukishima pays the ultimate price. Botterill regards Sticpewich as 'the best liar'[44] he has ever met; he means this as a compliment. It is hard to see how the evidence could be exaggerated: the truth is surely enough to convict the accused. Fukishima may not have technically killed Bird, but he inflicted so much damage that, if the man did not die of his wounds, he came perilously close. In fact, he died a few hours after the bashing.

While Botterill has no compunctions about lying under oath, Sticpewich on the contrary has deeply impressed Moffitt and his legal staff with his accurate testimony. In the event, the court accepts the three witnesses' accounts against Fukishima, but a later review of the 'evidence' fails to confirm the sentence, apparently due to problems with some of it. It is deeply regrettable that some witness statements pervert the case against the man responsible for some of the most heinous crimes in Borneo.

Cleary's case is more complex, involving three guards, or

more, over some 15 days. Surely few human beings in history have suffered so dreadfully at the hands of his fellow species. Cleary was tortured until his life literally drained out of him. Botterill, understandably envenomed against the three accused, gives the court a detailed account of the slow and terrible destruction of this young man. Again, he has no need to exaggerate or embellish: the facts of Cleary's death exceed the limits of hyperbole. And much of what Botterill says actually happened, as others confirm.

And yet, his testimony is deeply suspect. There are clear doubts about whether Suzuki Saburo was, in fact, present during the days of torture; other witnesses claim he was in Paginatan at the time. Questions arise over which 'Suzuki' is on trial. At least two Suzukis were on the Death Marches and/or in Ranau: Suzuki Saburo and Suzuki Taichi. Botterill and Moxham appear to act on the assumption that it matters little which one is on trial, or which crimes the Japanese guard is being tried for, as long as he is found guilty of a war crime – any war crime – and punished. But that is not how the law works in civilised countries.

Botterill and Moxham assure the court that the Suzuki standing before them – Saburo – participated in the torture and murder of Cleary. They are lying. He and Moxham framed Saburo for the murder. They did it to 'stitch up the guards', Botterill confesses to Lynette Silver, reportedly on his death bed.[45] The court believes them. So does the Review Board, which upholds the verdict after a long appeal against inconsistencies in the prosecution's evidence. Kawakami, Kitamura and Suzuki Saburo are hanged at Rabaul on 18 October 1946. As Lynette Silver concludes:

> While some may argue that, in the end, justice, in a rough
> sort of way had prevailed, my reaction was one of great

disappointment. Apart from the moral question of sending someone, no matter how evil, to the gallows for a crime he did not commit, how could Botterill possibly expect me to believe any of his evidence when he and Moxham had lied under oath?[46]

In a separate case, Moxham may not have perjured himself when describing Noel Parker's awful death – securing a death sentence for the accused, Hayashi Yoshinori, also known as Ming the Merciless – but it seems likely. Once unleashed on their former tormentors, Botterill and Moxham set out to secure as many capital punishments as possible – so much so that Botterill feels compelled to withdraw his evidence against two Formosans, Gotanda and Toyoda Kokishi, whom he bore false witness against. Far from being a war criminal, Toyoda 'always acted kindly towards the PWs', Botterill writes, on 1 June 1946. Toyoda gave the men extra food and medical supplies, and warned them of imminent 'hate sessions', when bashings were more frequent. He even kept the prisoners abreast of world news.[47]

It is perhaps comforting to the families to know that at least two of the guards who tortured, bashed and – in effect – murdered Cleary and Crease were found guilty and put to death. Their execution has not, however, allayed the families' – and Australia's – horror at this terrible act of sustained brutality. A monument to Cleary, Crease, and other victims of the Death Marches stands in Ranau and attracts growing numbers of visitors. In 2012, Cleary's name appeared on a list of 13 Australians proposed for a posthumous Victoria Cross, the strict terms of which do not encompass victims of war crimes. In any case, Botterill's and Moxham's perjury is unlikely to impress the adjudicators. Their false witness was 'premeditated and deliberate', Lynette Silver argues. '[T]hey did it,' she told *The Sydney Morning Herald* on 13 March 2012, 'to secure a guilty verdict against the guards, one of whom was 40 kilometres away at the time of Cleary's capture. As a result, all three guards were hanged.'[48] Yet their lies about one guard take nothing away from the fact that at least two others bashed, kicked and knee-tortured this young man to death.

◆

Not until June 1949 are those accused of the torture of Matthews, Wells, Taylor and the members of the Sandakan underground summoned to trial. They are: Ehara Kesao, Kobara Toshio, Kono Kinzaburo, Yokota Hideo, Umeda Tomashige, Seki Yoichiro, Misaka Tatsuo, Mukai Mitsutaro and Matsui Shintaro. Most are sergeants and warrant officers with the Kempei-tai: unspeakable brutes trained to extract confessions under the most hideous forms of torture. Four further guards are charged with the murder of Matthews and others, and the violation of the laws of war: Yamawaki Masataka, Egami Sobei, Watanabe Haruo and Tsutsui Yoichi. In bringing the case, the Australian War Crimes authorities argue that the Japanese 'trial' of Matthews, Wells, Weynton, Taylor and the local people in March 1944 was unlawful and failed to adhere to rules on the treatment of prisoners; hence, 'the persons who carried out the execution of Matthews and the imprisonment of the others may be charged with a war crime'.[49]

Perhaps the worst was Ehara, of whom Dr Taylor, the target of many of his attacks, wrote to Lieutenant Colonel Jackson on 21 April 1947, 'I have no hesitation in labelling him a perfect fiend, and one who deserves to die, if he is not already dead, for his inhuman treatment of both Australians and Asiatics. This man was the worst . . .'[50] Ehara, however, is among those many Japanese who disappeared after the armistice and are never accountable for their actions.

The defendants' pre-trial statements are exercises in denial: the rack, water and rice tortures 'may have happened' but the defendants deny using them. Most admit to beating or slapping the prisoners, some of whom were 'severely dealt with', says one. A few guards recall 'hearing screams' and 'bitter cries' from the interrogation rooms.

None expresses any contrition or regret for what he is accused of having done, nor any sense of comprehending the scale of their abomination. The closest any come is Kono Kinzaburo, who says, 'I feel very sorry for these prisoners that were brought into Sandakan Kempei-tai and the treatment given these people was a very poor standard compared to what I received as a prisoner.'[51]

One defendant kicks a legal own goal, conceding that the Kempei-tai did apply the forms of torture reportedly used in Borneo:

> I heard that prisoners at Jesselton were, at times, handcuffed across an overhead beam so that their knees were just clear of the floor and then a beam put across the back of their legs and pressure applied, but did not hear or know of this happening at Sandakan. I did not at any time hear of prisoners being forced to swallow raw rice and then drink large quantities of water, but it may have happened. I do know that at times Malay and Chinese prisoners were forced to drink large quantities of water . . .[52]

In October 1950, two of the accused, Yamawaki and Watanabe, are tried by an Australian Military Court at Manus Island on charges of murder (of Matthews and others) and the violation of the laws of war (unlawful imprisonment of Matthews, Wells and others). The Japanese defendants are found not guilty on both charges – on the arguable legal point that:

> international law [the Geneva Convention] recognize[s] that prisoners of war should submit to the laws and orders of the country by which they are captured . . . Australian prisoners of war were punished by Japanese Court Martial because they violated the Japanese laws. The accused Watanabe merely carried out his duty as a prosecutor [in the Matthews trial, for example].[53]

The Australian prosecutors' precis of the verdict scarcely disguises their disgust:

> The PWs [Matthews, Wells and others] did not have a Defending Officer nor an interpreter. The[ir] trial [by the Japanese] was a sham, the execution [of Matthews] was murder and all the proceedings contrary to International Law. The Defence contended that the PW had been given a fair trial, in accordance with Japanese Military Law, before a properly convened court . . . The action complied with the Geneva Convention and therefore there was no case to answer.[54]

◆

The war-crimes hearings continue until the end of 1950. Of 898 Japanese and Formosans on Borneo's 'wanted' list, 444 are arrested and charged. Of the rest, 238 are released after interrogation (including some known war criminals, such as Captain Nagai, who is inexplicably freed), 36 are recorded dead and the remainder cannot be found. Throughout the Pacific, convictions are successfully brought against just 25 Class A criminals, of whom seven are executed, and 3000 Class B and C criminals, of whom 920 are executed.

The broader picture reveals the sheer brutality of Japanese wartime prisons and internment camps. Of 132,134 prisoners of war held by the Japanese during the Second World War, 27 per cent died, according to evidence given at the Tokyo war-crimes trials – compared with a four-per-cent death rate in German and Italian prisoner-of-war camps (i.e. 9348 out of 235,473). A greater proportion of Australian prisoners died in the Pacific than any other Allied nation: 8031 out of 22,376, a 36-per-cent death rate. The sheer inhumanity represented by this figure explains why the vast majority – some 73 per cent – of Japanese Class B and C war criminals were tried for crimes committed against prisoners of war: their murder, torture, ill-treatment and forced starvation.[55]

41

THE PEOPLE

No town in the world wears the wounds of war more terribly
and more honourably than does Sandakan . . . where 230
civilians were slaughtered because of their loyalty to the Allied
cause . . . it was courage of the rarest and finest quality . . .
the courage that survives defeat, that continues to strive when
there seems no chance of reward, and refuses to be conquered
even after the enemy has been victorious. It was what we
in England call 'two o'clock in the morning courage'.

His Excellency the new governor general of Malaya
and British Borneo, Malcolm MacDonald

LOCAL PEOPLE ARE INDISPENSABLE to the recovery
mission, for theirs has been an intimate sacrifice to the Allied
cause. When the Australian recovery teams arrive, the natives
emerge with delight from their villages and forest redoubts,
brandishing letters given to them by Australian and British
prisoners, in recognition of their help. Many smuggled food or
clothing to the prisoners on the march and in the camps; others
protected escapees – at great risk to their and their families' lives.
They naturally seek a reward, or recognition, for their courage.

The matter progresses to the desk of Colonel Edgar Griffin,

director, Prisoners of War and Internees, in Australia, who recommends to Minister for the Army Frank Forde that an officer be sent to investigate the claims, with the power to pay compensation 'not exceeding five pounds' per claimant. Any more would have to be cleared by the directorate of Prisoners of War and Internees. The officer chosen is Lieutenant Colonel Harry Jackson, 35, who works on Griffin's staff – 'a friendly little chap, of medium height, unimpressive build and looks like a small businessman from any suburb', in the sniffy assessment of *People* magazine, which somewhat callously adds that Jackson 'is the only son of a salesman'.[1] 'In spite of a beaked nose and jutting jaw,' it continues, 'his face is friendly.' Jackson is 'distinctly an extrovert' and apparently a disciple of Pelmanism, the trick of memorising things through their association, which contributes to his excellent memory for places, names and dates. He is, in short, a wise, compassionate man, clear-headed and fair. The Australian Government authorises him to draw on a fund of no more than £300.

Jackson arrives in Borneo in November 1946. On 11 November, he meets the tireless Sticpewich, who offers 'invaluable' information, Jackson later writes, 'which would assure the maximum success of the mission'.[2] Posterity seems to have understated, or overlooked, Sticpewich's Herculean efforts. Every ounce of his knowledge is placed at the disposal of Jackson's mission, which shortly draws the colonel into the blackest depths of the island's miserable war. In late November, his plan is to walk the whole length of the 'death track' to interview deserving recipients of his largesse. Poor weather and swollen rivers force an alternative. He decides to search three areas: Sandakan camp; Maunad to Sapi, where Campbell and Braithwaite escaped; and

Telupid to Ranau, where another four escaped. As he prepares to depart, stockpiling food, machetes and clothes, local authorities prevail upon him to offer war pensions to the widows of local resistance fighters, who died for the Allied cause.

Jackson soon learns of the extraordinary heroism of the local people involved in the underground and the radio, and those who aided Dr Taylor, Captain Matthews and the Berhala Eight. Slowly, the astonishing story unfolds of native assistance to the long line of exhausted and hungry prisoners on the track. Jackson resolves to write a fuller report – indeed, a short history – of what he hears.

In the following days, he interviews dozens of claimants, and their experiences furnish him and his team with a deep understanding of the cost of the war to this benighted country: of whole villages destroyed, families shattered and native people coerced into slavery or brutally eliminated. One after another, downcast and tearful, in possession of their terrible memories, the people tentatively come forward and quietly disburden themselves in the presence of this strange man. Jackson meets Orang Tuan Gundi and Barigah, who hid Moxham, Short, Botterill and Anderson; Ginssas bin Gangass, who protected Sticpewich and Reither, and who arrives at the jungle hearing perched upon a buffalo, with a bad case of beriberi, led by his little son. Dozens of others who offered food and aid along the death track hobble up to meet the Australian investigator (see list, Appendix 3).

Jackson hears harrowing accounts of those who tried to help the long line of prisoners, 'very thin, weak and sick-looking' as one woman relates, passing her village 'without boots, some without shirts, all had long beards, long hair and walked with bowed heads that swayed from side to side. Whenever they passed they made signs with the fingers and mouths that they were hungry and wanted food.'[3]

Another woman, Burih, describes how she gave the prisoners food at a time when her own husband was sick and ill-fed, and later died of malnutrition. Some natives hand over mementos the prisoners have given them: a wallet, belonging to Wally Read, for example; and a gold locket with a photo of a woman, presumably the wife or mother of the soldier. To this day, trekkers along the track encounter Domima binte Akui, the dignified and soft-spoken woman who, as a girl, gave food to escaped prisoners, who rewarded her with their wedding rings. Today, she is dubbed the 'ring lady' by local guides.

◆

Jackson learns of a darker side to the local war, of collaborators and informants and coercion. Borneo has been rent asunder, and the people split between those accused of joining the enemy and those who resisted, or who aided the Allies and the prisoners. Some have kept to themselves, hiding in the forest until the war menace retreated.

Ghastly accounts of collaboration circulate after the war. AGAS agents compile lists for the War Crimes Department, which is usually slower than native lynch mobs in finding, and punishing, the culprits. One Chinese collaborator, for example, procured the arrest of a woman and her three children; torture by the Japanese compelled the woman to commit suicide with her children 'by jumping in a river'.[4] And Habib Omar, a Bugis tribesman, 'at all times a conscientious pro-Jap', was responsible for the betrayal – and ultimate death – of Mr and Mrs Cohen, the Sandakan traders, who were severely harassed on their return to Sandakan. And three men are accused of betraying members of the PYTHON team, for which they were subsequently shot in Sandakan. And Amat Bin Yusop, a Bajau native and very active collaborator, whose actions caused many arrests of civilians and native leaders, the torture of whom led in at least one case to the suicide of the victim.[5]

The native people also yield evidence of indiscriminate Japanese savagery. Gundi, for example, tells of witnessing in June 1945 'approx 75 PWs [presumably the members of the Last March] unable to march ruthlessly shot in cold blood' and 'a case of cannibalism in which the Jap troops cut up, cooked and ate one of these dead PWs'.[6] Amat and Panjam of Sapi, both local AGAS recruits, report seeing villagers ordered to the end of a jetty and 'promptly shot' and 'babies thrown in the air, caught on bayonets and tossed in the water'. Whenever pregnant women were seen, 'they were shot outright'.[7] One must treat some of these stories with suspicion in the vengeful and often hysterical aftermath of war.

◆

In the second stage of his investigation, Jackson rewards civilians who resisted the Japanese in and around Sandakan, who joined the underground, harboured escapees and helped Wallace and the Berhala Eight escape. The testimonies are deeply distressing, offered by individuals 'scarcely able to comprehend that Jackson and his team had come so far to honour the promises of dead men', as Lynette Silver aptly writes.[8] Samuel Aruliah smuggled radio parts and passed messages to Berhala interns before being caught. His two children died as a result of his imprisonment.

For this sacrifice, a cash sum seems a kind of insult.[9]

By his actions, Jackson acknowledges that cash alone is not enough. He distributes food and medicine to genuine claimants, with a promise of cash later, to be transferred through the local, usually British, district officer. Many people also request a 'letter of good name', as such testimonials are 'highly treasured', Jackson notes, rather like an heirloom in a society that places great value on family honour. He obliges by instructing Army Headquarters to design a suitable certificate, approved by the Minister for the Army and published in English and Malayan.

The final count is 58 cash payments and 22 Certificates of Appreciation. Payments range from £5 for basic assistance to £823 for Mrs Katherine Lagan – Jackson is able to exceed his limit in 'special circumstances'. Katherine's husband, Ernesto, a leader of the underground, was executed, leaving her with four children to support. Indeed, the wives of the deceased present an especially harrowing case, and the widows of the victims of the Matthews–Taylor ring – including the wife of Alex Funk – receive special attention.

Katherine Lagan's story profoundly moves the Australian major. He finds her 'cowering in the darkened corner of a tumbledown hut in Sandakan, her hair over her face, her clothes dirty, her feet bare'.[10] At first, she responds to Jackson's enquiries with a nervous sigh or an astonished giggle. Gradually, she feels sufficiently reassured to talk. She tells of how the Kempei-tai ransacked her house, threatened to harm her children, dumped her husband's bloody clothes on her doorstep . . . and invited her to see her husband's tortured body. 'Have you anything else you would like to say to me?' Jackson gently asks, when she finishes speaking. 'My health is not good,' she replies. 'I am suffering from heart trouble and I ask you to give every consideration to helping me and my children, and their education.'[11] Hers is the largest cash dispensation.

Chang Siew Ha, widow of Soh Kem Seng, who was tortured to death by the Kempei-tai in Kuching, is similarly destitute. She is left with no money, the burnt wreckage of the family home and two children, aged six and seven. Asked to comment on her predicament, she tells Jackson, 'I have nothing more to say except that life is very difficult for me now and on behalf of my two small children I implore you or your government to assist us so that we can live.'[12] He recommends she receives a monthly pension of 20 Straits dollars.

Felix Azcona's widow, Taciana, has remarried by the time her case comes up, in January 1947, but Jackson deems her eligible nonetheless for compensation for the period after the war, when she relied on her mother to support her and her little boy, aged three. She receives 78 pounds and 15 shillings.[13]

Jackson is curiously precise in his financial allocations. Wong Yun Siew, for example, who smuggled radio parts to the prisoners, suffered water-torture, then escaped prison by feigning madness, receives 'Twenty Six Pounds Ten Shillings and Tenpence' for his efforts.[14] Johnny and Paddy Funk, though tortured and imprisoned, ask for no compensation but accept a donation to their medical costs. Payments of 'Eighty Seven Pounds, Fifteen Shillings and Tenpence' go to underground agents such as Lamberto Apostol, Peter Lai and Mohammed Salleh; while those who sheltered escapees such as Botterill, Short, Moxham and Sticpewich receive about £30, give or take a few shillings.

Adihil bin Ambilid, who harboured Sticpewich and Reither at great risk, modestly recalls, 'I fed and housed them . . . Pte Reither died at my house. I helped to bury him.'[15] Ginssas bin Gangass, who helped to save Sticpewich's life, is equally humble: 'I met two white men and took them to my house. I hid them under mats when the Japanese came. I told them that the white men had gone another way.'[16]

The more dangerous the task, it seems, the greater the 'risk bonus'. Gunner Owen Campbell's rescuers, including Lap, the man who canoed him downriver, receive about £15. The boatmen who ferried Braithwaite to Libaran Island, on the other hand, get about £7. Or, due to the rapid exhaustion of Jackson's funds, some locals receive very little. Amit, who helped to rehabilitate Braithwaite, sees just around £2.[17]

These are just a sample – and not all claims withstand scrutiny. Among Jackson's first claimants, Andu bin Patrick, who gave the prisoners some chops, protests that he also gave an Australian officer $100 and wants it back. Jackson quickly detects the rort: Patrick has written the 'IOU' himself.[18] The promise of a cash reward provokes a rush of bogus or inflated claims, from boatmen, farmers, guides and others in the pay of the Allies. Rex Blow's boatman, for example, demands 150 Straits dollars. '[I]f I may give you a little advice,' one district officer writes to Jackson, 'I would say don't pay much attention to these claims, else you will have hundreds.'[19]

The payments may seem paltry recognition for the risks and sacrifices involved, but the pound went a long way in those days, and cash is rather more useful than a piece of metal to impoverished civilians. And yet, Jackson's mission is, in fact, the Australian Government's cheap – and secretive – solution to the problem of how to reward the natives. Prime Minister Ben Chifley makes the point clear, in a confidential letter sent on 9 May 1947 to the MP Macalister Blain, a prisoner of war in Sandakan and Kuching, who shared a cell with Ernesto Lagan. Blain has been urging the government to donate public money to a proposed Sandakan Memorial Fund, an endeavour the prime minister firmly blocks. Chifley writes:

> The principle of creating a fund to provide assistance to destitute dependants of the murdered citizens of Sandakan is commendable, but the inhumane actions of the enemy during the war were so widespread that if a grant were made in the present case an embarrassing precedent would be created to the extent that the Commonwealth would be faced with the problem of contributing to other funds established to commemorate the sacrifices of civilians in other areas and countries, in which Australian troops operated.[20]

◆

If time heals, time takes a long time to work its soothing ministry in Sabah. Families in Borneo learn the truth about their shared history gradually and painfully. The experience of war filters through to the children and grandchildren; often years intervene before the truth is revealed. Not until March 1986 will Christopher Lagan know the full story of what became of his father, Ernesto, tortured and executed, via a letter from Jackson. Jackson explains to Lagan on 2 April 1986:

> I had a long think before I typed out the long story for you as I did not want to distress you with some of the stark details. However, after discussing it with my wife it was decided that you

should be given all the details without any attempt to soften the shocks. It is after all part of the history of your country.[21]

The Funk family's experience is the subject of numerous books and articles; but the truth takes many years to filter through to the children. One such, Doreen Hurst, daughter of Johnny Funk, becomes a tireless campaigner for historical clarity in relation to her family's monstrous ordeal. The Funks are exemplars of the observation that the Eurasian gene pool produces the most attractive people on earth. The family are products of the ancestral fusion of a Tasmanian surveyor, a native Sabah woman and their daughter's marriage to a Chinese rubber planter, who became British North Borneo's first local magistrate.

The four surviving sons mourn the loss of Alex, murdered by the Japanese, along with Matthews and eight fellow leaders of the underground. Johnny, having miraculously survived the rice torture and other hideous attempts to break him, arrives in Sandakan in late 1945 aboard a corvette to find his wife. His wife, Lillian, herself half-American, half-Filipino (her father was Colonel Guy Stratton, governor of the most southern archipelago), has survived years in the forest as one of the 'jungle wives', forced into hiding when the Japanese ransacked the family home. Hers has been an especially difficult ordeal, since the Japanese decreed that anyone caught helping the Funks – a well-known family throughout Borneo – would be shot. Soon after landing, Johnny sets out in a jeep with a mob of Australians to find her. In a coconut plantation, he sets eyes on a pitiably thin wraith of a woman, his wife. 'He could scarcely recognise her,' according to one report. 'She looked at him incredulously for a while, then broke into hysterical cries and sobs. The Australians had to calm her and assure her that Johnny was truly alive and allright.'[22] And yet, he would suffer the medical repercussions of torture for years: a broken jaw, a damaged eye, weak knees and chronic stomach problems. He undergoes a long stay in Singapore General Hospital, after which the family take a tour of Australia and decide to settle there.

Before they emigrate, Johnny tries – without success – to interest the returned British authorities in erecting a memorial to the eight underground leaders executed in Kuching. The price of British gratitude is expensive. So he personally raises, through friends, $2180, enough for a large marble tablet, on which he inscribes the words: 'In memory of the eight gallant men of all races who, loyal to the cause of freedom, rendered assistance to Allied prisoners of war at Sandakan camp, and were executed in Kuching on 2 March 1944, and also the five who died in prison.' With the approval of a special federal-government dispensation, he and Lillian and their three children – Melvyn, then 13, Doreen, 9, and Gilbert, 2 – settle in Melbourne, where he starts a career as a civil engineer.

◆

The new power in the land is the old one: Britain. The British Empire returns to Borneo with all the pomp and circumstance of a dowager empress reappearing at her own party to which she has been temporarily denied entry. That, at least, is how the English seem to portray their return: rounding off the natural order of things with a big pink smile, as if nothing has transpired in the interim. She returns to enjoy the fruits of peace: rubber, palm oil, tin and petroleum. The people appear to slip back into a state of supine, orderly, underpaid subjection.

Yet a sense of grievance is in the air, a yearning for a different world. The locals quaffed from the cup of freedom after the Japanese surrender, and many are dismayed at the easy resumption of the old order. The white man has been shown up as a dismal protector of their interests, and the colonial bond looks frayed and haggard. English pomp and ceremony masquerading as 'liberty' fools none of Sabah's hardened freedom fighters. They have not risked everything helping to kick out the Japanese imperialists only to see the old guard return. The Malayans, Chinese and locals endure the transition for now, biting hard on the slate of patience.

Meanwhile, the return of the British Empire is marked by an act of formal wreath-laying and a show of austere gratitude by those who, having stooped to conquer South East Asia, failed to protect her. The little ceremony is repeated throughout Asia. In Sandakan, His Excellency the new governor general of Malaya and British Borneo, Malcolm MacDonald, is on hand to unveil a temporary memorial to the local dead of the 'Colony of North Borneo'. 'No town in the world,' MacDonald solemnly declares on 17 September 1946, 'wears the wounds of war more terribly and more honourably than does Sandakan.' Promising to rebuild the town, he speaks eloquently of the courage of 230 civilians who were 'slaughtered because of their loyalty to the Allied cause':

> it was courage of the rarest and finest quality . . . the courage that survives defeat, that continues to strive when there seems no chance of reward, and refuses to be conquered even after the enemy has been victorious. It was what we in England call 'two o'clock in the morning courage'.[23]

42

HOME

Sandakan should be remembered because it was more than a battle between nations and more than a battle between conflicting ideologies; it was a war between human decency and human depravity. [The victims of the Death Marches] were as much casualties of evil as those who died in the Nazi death camps in Europe.

Prime Minister Paul Keating to a Sydney memorial service

THE OFFICERS WROTE THEIR first letters to loved ones from Kuching, and aboard the hospital ships bearing them home to Australia and Britain:

21 September 1945

Darling Joan,
I am the happiest man in the world. Two letters arrived from you with those wonderful words 'Liberated P.O.W.' on the envelopes . . .[1]

A week earlier, Lieutenant Tony White, a survivor of Kuching, sent his first letter to his wife since the fall of Singapore:

My dearest Joan,

This is difficult for me to write. I don't know how to begin. Often in the nights during the last few years – lying awake I've composed my first letter to you – but now the time has come I'm all at a loss. So if I ramble a bit – oh well, I guess you'll understand . . .

I just can't tell you how often thoughts of you have helped me in situations which have been not so pleasant . . .

I am writing this in bed – that has a mattress and sheets and a pillow – and it's grand. I had my first one hundred per cent civilised meal at breakfast this morning . . . (porridge, rolled oats, not rice) with milk & sugar, scrambled egg – tea . . . and I lost count of the number of pieces of bread and butter and marmalade I had – and it was grand – my old cobber malaria got jealous when he heard I was to leave Kuching three days ago so he decided to come with me . . .

Well darling I am sorry to say I've got to end – but as soon as this fever clears up I shall write a real letter . . . All the love in the world to you my dearest.[2]

Captain Stan Woods sails home aboard the hospital ship *Wanganella*. His first letters to his fiancée, Belinda – 'Blin' – conjure all the tenderness of a man in thrall to his dream of conjugal happiness:

POW Camp, Kuching, 11 September 1945

Belinda Beloved,

This is the first official letter I have been able to write you . . . Dear One, it is a great day to be able to say 'Hullo' after such a long, long time. After two years waiting your 3rd letter came, it was marvellous to receive it, to learn of your safety – what a tremendous relief it was to me . . .

Wanganella, 14 September 1945

Belinda Beloved,

Yes it's true we are really on the way home & free . . . it's a dream I think – perhaps I'll wake up soon & find I am in someone's arms – yours, darling one. Last night I felt like a boy let out of school – Put myself to bed at 9.30, awoke at 6 when the engine started up for we are on the way to Labuan. It is simply marvellous to sleep on a soft bed, clean sheets and pillows. Clean pyjamas . . . Angel . . . it's hard to write as I would wish . . . My love is yours – all of it & forever. Your Stan

Wanganella, 30 September 1945

My Wife Beloved,

. . . Thank you, Blin darling, for your wonderful letters and the beautiful thoughts they contain – they are simply heaven to me and make me very happy. What is the song, 'Love Is a Wonderful Thing' – it is to us dear & the future, the near future has lots of joy & happiness for us. Oh how I am longing to be with you . . . In your letter you said you would give me your bed, truly, my loved one, it will be marvellous when we can share a bed . . . Thank you for the pyjamas you have bought for me.[3]

He steps off the ship and into her arms. Within weeks, they are married.

◆

The army's formal communication with families is clinical, piecemeal and uncertain:

PRO FORMA

Dear . . .

It is with deep regret that I have to inform you that on interrogation of a former Australian Prisoner of War recovered from Borneo, uncorroborated information was obtained to the effect that your [son, husband, brother] died of illness (or as the case may be) about [date] whilst a Prisoner of War in Japanese hands in Borneo.

The reliability of the information is not questioned but pending confirmation of such information no action has been taken to alter your [son's, husband's, brother's] existing classification of 'Prisoner of War', and efforts are being made to obtain confirmation through the International Red Cross Committee, Geneva.

The distress which will be occasioned through receipt of this notification is fully appreciated, but it is considered that although the Department of Army is not prepared to amend the casualty classification on the uncorroborated statement of one informant, it is the Department's duty to tell you of the information which it has acquired . . .

Yours faithfully (etc.) . . .[4]

Many families of Australian victims receive this official letter in the last months of 1945. Whitehall sends a similar missive to British families, who also receive Royal condolences. The 'enclosed Scroll' sent 'by Command of the King' from 'Buckingham Palace' reads, 'The Queen and I offer you our heartfelt sympathy in your great sorrow. We pray that your country's gratitude for a life so nobly given in its service may bring you some measure of consolation.'[5] It joins the little cache of correspondence that families have gathered during the war years: a few scrawled letters from their son, brother or husband sent from Changi or Java before the capitulation, perhaps a prescribed postcard or two dictated by the Japanese – hints of an unfolding tragedy the scale of which families will take decades to comprehend.

The Commonwealth Governments and military authorities justify their official silence on various grounds: the truth is too shocking to release; the families must be spared the horror; the information is classified; transparency is detrimental to the national interest. In truth, the screen of secrecy conveniently serves to mask the authorities' neglect of the prisoners – of whose dire circumstances they had considerable knowledge through AGAS agents and escapees such as Blow, McLaren and, later, Braithwaite and Sticpewich. No argument justifies their refusal to reveal the facts to families desperate for information. In time, however, the truth is forced upon the governments, through the revelations of private researchers and maverick soldiers. It takes the bloody-minded persistence of Sticpewich, in 1946–47, to find the remaining bodies. And not until the pioneering investigative work of historians and investigators Athol Moffitt, Lynette Silver, Kevin Smith and Don Wall in the 1980s and 1990s are the facts revealed.

Meanwhile, parents and widows patiently await updates. Months later, their son's or husband's personal effects arrive. In January 1946, for example, Mrs D. L. Anderson takes delivery of the army badge belonging to her son, Gunner Francis Anderson. She has learnt of his death in Borneo in November 1945. 'Enclosed please find abovementioned badge,' the covering letter says. 'Will you please acknowledge receipt of same by signing this receipt and returning same to this office, at your earliest convenience.'[6] Years later, families receive the dead soldiers' awards and service medals – in the post.

◆

The army's bureaucratic efficiency is impeccable; its accuracy and sensitivity leave a lot to be desired. A flood of questions persist. Where are the soldiers buried? Where and how did they die? Did they really die of illness? The press fans speculation that darker truths lie beneath the Borneo canopy. The consolations of kings and prime ministers sound hollow without the facts of how, and in what circumstances, their loved ones perished.

For years, the truth eludes detection. The horror lurks in dusty files, interrogation reports, classified lists. True, the media reports the executions of the Japanese, and other sensational details, but little on the Death Marches. Sir William Webb's 'Report on the War Crimes Tribunal' is suppressed. Survivors are compelled to sign gagging orders. Dick Braithwaite is 'sworn to secrecy . . . under the Official Secrets Act . . . not to talk about it, to anyone', he later recalls. When *The Sydney Morning Herald* approaches him on the hospital ship, he complains to the ship's captain, who 'put the clamp on that'.[7] Only a single small item appears in the paper at the time. Keith Botterill and Bill Moxham are similarly silenced; both men know exactly how Richard Murray died – a case of self-sacrifice that saved Botterill's life – but his wife, Margaret, remains ignorant of this for years after the war.

British ex-prisoners are compelled to sign the same order; most do so on the ship taking them home. The order states:

> All ranks are hereby warned that they are forbidden to publish in any form whatsoever or communicate, either directly or indirectly, to the Press or to other unauthorised persons any accounts of escapes or experiences in P.O.W. camps . . . They will be held responsible for statements contained in communication to friends which may be . . . published in the Press or elsewhere . . .[8]

Nor are they permitted to speak to the Red Cross or other welfare organisations about their experiences.

Canberra and London prefer to shield the facts from the families. This is not a 'conspiracy', in the Machiavellian sense, as some attest; rather, simply an official policy of public denial. Families wait and wait, and hear nothing. As Jeffrey Phillips, the son of a British victim of Sandakan, says today, 'The British authorities were so ashamed of the mess they made of Singapore that they buried it under a big stone.'[9] And Rose Barry, sister of Corporal Bill Lake, who died at Sandakan, writes:

> Although our Government knew of the existence of 'Sandakan' we, the families, were never told . . . of the atrocities inflicted upon these lovely boys (most of whom never reached

manhood). Not a day passes when I [don't] look at Bill's photo on our wall and remember him.[10]

Brian Hales' uncle Les, a giant of a man, six foot four, nicknamed Lofty and adored by his family, died in Borneo on 5 April 1945. To this day, Brian never tires of gathering and disseminating information about the atrocity that consumed his uncle. Maureen Devereaux, similarly indefatigable in her pursuit of the truth, whose elder brother, John Barnier, died at Sandakan, possesses every letter he wrote from Singapore. By December 1941, her family had sent 60 letters and parcels, in reply to which he pleaded with them not to send any more socks. After the island fell, the mail ceased. 'He was my hero,' Maureen says. On Victory in the Pacific Day, she recalls, 'There was so much joy, hope and excitement. People were saying, "John will be home soon." We waited and waited, sitting round the wireless listening for news.' None came. 'I'm so happy for those who came home but I don't forgive the Japanese, although John had such a deep Christian faith he might want me to forgive.'[11]

Words cannot convey the suffering of families who lost all their sons. Several sets of brothers died in Borneo. How does one console the Dorizzi family, of Toodyay, Western Australia, whose sons – Gordon, 28, and Herbert, 26, died in Borneo on 11 February 1945, and a third, the eldest brother, Tom, a month later? Or the family of the Bexton brothers, Sid and Tom, aged 24 and 25, killed in June and July 1945? Or the parents of the Frost brothers, Edmund and Henry, of Stawell, Victoria, who died two weeks before the war ended; and of Henry and Joe Connor, of Victoria, both married with children and both dead within three weeks of each other? And there are the very young, who lied about their ages, such as Charles 'Baby' Mainstone, 15 or 16 on enlistment, who pretended to shave to pass for a man, dead in March 1945 while his father, a First World War digger, languished in a German prison camp.[12]

◆

In their search for answers, families experience a Kafkaesque sense of alienation, of standing at the gates of a labyrinth, whose secret lies somewhere inside but will never see the light of day. The British and Australian Governments' standard response is a few terse sentences: Private XXXX died of natural causes, of diseases or causes unknown, somewhere in the South-West Pacific or Borneo. They cite Japanese death certificates. 'Close the book', the families are effectively told. It is all wretchedly inadequate.

Official reticence arouses deep concerns and elicits further enquiries. Relatives in Australia and Britain probe the seams of officialdom in search of answers. In August 1945, the Oakeshott family anxiously awaits news of Captain John Oakeshott. On 27 October – two months after the Japanese murdered him – his wife, Enid, receives a telegram from the minister of the army. The postman hands the envelope to John's son, Bob, who had turned 15 that day. 'I gave it to my mother anticipating good news,' Bob later recalls.[13] The brief message informs the family that Oakeshott died in Borneo while a prisoner of war; the minister conveys his profound sympathy. It says nothing of how or where he died, or whether his body has been recovered.

Thus begins Enid Oakeshott's long, slow pursuit of truth. In 1945 and 1946, she places several requests in *POW News* seeking information. She receives four letters, from: her husband's medical orderly, Barton Wagner; Mollie Sticpewich, mother of Bill Sticpewich; Major John Fairley, commander of E Force when it left Singapore; and Marie Cole, who encloses a letter from one Mrs Evans, who, during the course of her own enquiries about her husband – bashed to death, she learns, for helping to steal a potato – yields a few scraps of information about Dr Oakeshott.

Wagner writes, on 5 January 1946, that Oakeshott:

> earned the respect of all, especially as his quiet manner had led
> inexperienced men to think he might be timid in action: this
> was not the case – during the greatest pressure of the last days
> of Singapore our Captain carried on in the same, quiet efficient
> manner which marked him in normal times . . . We trust that
> you and your little ones will be strengthened and comforted to
> carry on as your dear husband would have you do.[14]

But Wagner, who was captured and sent to Burma, has only half the story. Others vouch for his decency and courage but have no idea what became of him.

Clinging to these scraps, Enid re-approaches the military authorities. On 22 January 1946, the office of the minister for the army informs her that 'a careful examination of Japanese Death Certificates . . . of deceased personnel recently obtained by the Military Authorities establishes that his death was due to Acute Enteritis'.[15]

Enid refuses to accept the 'evidence' of Japanese death certificates. On 18 October 1947, she writes to the Department of Echelon and Records. A month later, on 13 November, the Department replies: 'there are strong grounds for belief [sic] that he, together with others, was in fact executed by the Japanese'

– on 1 August 1945, at a place called Ranau. The devastated family consults its atlas.

It has taken two years for Enid Oakeshott to be told that her husband was murdered. But she will never know how he died, or hear of his devotion to duty to the end or the whereabouts of his body. She dies in 1983. Fifteen years pass. On 5 May 1998, the Office of Australian War Graves alerts the family that Dr Oakeshott's grave has been identified at Labuan War Cemetery. Not until 7 October 2003 does it amend his 'cause of death' from illness to 'executed', with 15 others, on the revised date of 27 August 1945.

Five years later, in 2008, a plausible account of John's last moments emerges. Equipped with a metal detector, the tireless historian Lynette Silver and her husband make an astonishing discovery: they unearth on the riverbank at the jungle camp near Ranau a small stack of kitbag buckles, with an army tunic button bearing the words Australian Military Forces placed on top. A circle with a central dot is an internationally recognised sign of the Boy Scouts, signifying 'Gone Home' or 'Finished'. Dr Oakeshott had been a keen Boy Scout – indeed, he was vice president of the 3rd Lismore Scouting Group in 1941. Silver reasonably surmises that he and his fellow officers buried the buckles and button (as well as kitbag fitters, nearby) in the soil shortly before they were led away to be shot.[16] The discovery is the first confirmation of the location of the last jungle camp.

In 2011, I contacted Oakeshott's family. His son, Bob (father of the independent MP Rob Oakeshott), and daughter, Betty, remember him as a gentle, loving family man, a 'quiet Anglican', who loved camping in the countryside around Lismore. 'I remember he would come and kiss me goodnight, and say,

"Look after yourself, son,'" Bob recalls.[17] Betty wrote to me:

> One of my greatest disappointments was that my mother
> . . . never knew what my father endured and where his final
> resting place lies . . . He wrote beautiful letters to us which
> unfortunately my mother burnt just before she died. My
> mother was very loyal to his memory as they loved each other
> very much . . . When he went away I was told to pray for
> his return, I did and he did not return. When we received
> the telegram I believed he could not have died, so I tore up
> the telegram much to the consternation of my mother, as
> she needed it as proof of his death, and all she had were the
> tiny pieces. Actually I firmly believed he would walk out of
> the jungle and it was years later (3 in fact) that I realised this
> would not happen. I lost my faith . . . I know I was much
> loved by him . . . and I feel he would have been a gentle,
> calming, caring influence on the men he shared the end of
> his life with.[18]

As indeed he was.

Others also rely on the work of investigators and historians to
find the truth. I spoke to June Fowler-Smith, the beloved niece of
Sidney Webber – 'Siddy' – shot while trying to escape, with four
others, one of whom was Owen Campbell. June adored her young
uncle, whom she followed everywhere. 'I was Siddy's shadow,' she
recalls. Her grandmother – Siddy's mother – never knew what
happened to her son. The army said only that he was missing,
presumed dead. June discovers the truth decades later, through
the efforts of historian Don Wall, at whose book launch in the
early 1980s she meets Campbell, who witnessed Webber's death:

'He threw his arms around me and burst into tears . . . Owen remembered Siddy talking about me when they were roaming in the bush.' According to her account of their conversation, 'Owen wept, saying that he couldn't bury him, he was too sick.'[19]

Officers whose men died in the Death Marches send respectful notes to grieving wives and parents, a gracious attempt to console the inconsolable. Gwen Whitehead, wife of Lance Sergeant Barrie Whitehead, receives the dreaded telegram on 27 October 1945, informing her 'with deep regret' that her husband 'died whilst a prisoner of war on 13 July 1945 and desire to convey to you the profound sympathy of the Minister for the Army'. Barrie's death notice – claiming he died of malaria in Borneo (in fact, he had tried to escape and died of starvation at Ranau) – prompts a series of deeply felt letters to Gwen from men who knew her husband. He was 'one of the best NCOs of the battalion' and 'a first class soldier', writes one officer under whom he served.[20] While imprisoned at Sandakan, Whitehead's 'constant cheerfulness made him the friend of all', states another officer.[21] Captain Ken Mosher remembers Whitehead as 'my closest and most trusted friend' and an 'outstanding' soldier during the battle for Singapore, adding, 'This may help you in your sorrow.'[22] And Dick Braithwaite similarly urges her to 'be brave, dear lady, as all those lads were'.[23]

In the months and years after the war, Stan Woods similarly tries to help families find news of their sons. 'Fathers, wives would appear at Stan's home,' recalls his daughter Claire, 'asking, "Do you know about my son, my father, what about our men?" They were devastated.'[24] Stan knows only of the officers and little about the men sent on the Death Marches, as he told Belinda on his return home:

22 October 1945

My Belovedest Blin,

. . . Each day I sit down to write – then there is a call by
someone – 'Can I tell him anything about his son etc who was
in Borneo' – Well the hours go just trying to tell them gently
that there (is) almost no hope. It's awfully hard on them . . .[25]

◆

The truth takes longer to reach British families. Soon after the
war, the British Government promises an 'inquiry' by a War
Crimes Commission into excesses in Malaya. It hopes this will
close the door on family concerns. Christopher Elliott is having
none of it. The story foisted on him by the RAF about his brother,
Donald – who died on the Death Marches – that he perished of
unknown causes, like 'countless servicemen apparently lost forever
in the cruelty and vegetation of Malaya',[26] will not rest in peace.
The telegram, a model of officialdom, angers Christopher: 'LAC
Donald V Elliott . . . died while a POW in Japanese hands on 17
March, 1945.'[27] A follow-up on 5 November 1945 from the Air
Ministry informs Elliott's parents that their son died in 'Ramau,
Sumatra [sic] . . . No details, nor any information, regarding the
place of burial, are yet available.' The trouble is, the family cannot
find Ramau on the map of Sumatra. Then, on 18 December: 'it is
now known that your son died at Ranau'.[28]

Christopher worshipped Donald, whose love of aircraft led the
two boys bicycling to plane-crash sites in the English countryside
– and the older lad to Java, as an aircraftman. When he heard
the news of Donald's disappearance, Christopher 'got up from

the chair, and as I made a cup of tea, I stood on the exact spot where, three years before, I had said goodbye to my brother for the last time'.[29] Over the next ten years, he sets out to find the truth. He sends a stream of letters to the Air Ministry and to villages along the Death March routes: 'had the sawmills at Sandakan and Jesselton noticed unusual carvings on some of the trees? Donald liked leaving his mark on tree trunks and old barns in Suffolk.'[30] He visits Borneo, walks the Death March route and eventually, with local help, is guided to a grave near Paginatan that contained the remains of five men, including Donald's aircraftman's cap and name inside.

Other British families stubbornly contend with military bureaucracy, such as Gunner Joe Stephens' parents and sisters. Six months after the armistice, the Stephens family still has no news of him. On 24 January 1946, the Prisoners of War Department reply to his elder sister with a curt 'no information regarding your brother has reached this Department since we last wrote to you . . .'[31]

The family persists. On 15 April 1946, the Royal Artillery Records Office in London confirms that its enquiries about Gunner Stephens have been forwarded to the War Office, 'as it is very much regretted than no further information has been received in this office'.[32] Time passes; no news arrives. One day in 1948, the British Government officially confirms what the family has sadly accepted: Joe Stephens is not coming home. 'I was 16,' recalls Teresa Stephens, Joe's youngest sister. 'I came home from work, and my elder sister told me that Joey was dead.' He died somewhere in Borneo 'of beri beri' on 5 April 1945, according to a Japanese Death Notice.

Thirteen years pass before they confirm the location of his

body. On 21 March 1961, the Commonwealth War Graves Commission informs Teresa that her brother is buried in Labuan War Cemetery, North Borneo, Plot T, Row AA, Grave 4. The letter adds, helpfully, 'Labuan is a small island off the north-west coast of North Borneo . . .'[33] She writes to request a photo of the grave stone, but the Commission's work 'does not include providing photographs of individual graves', and she is directed to the British Legion. The letter encloses a photo of the cemetery ('as this is a spare print there is no charge') and a 'specimen drawing' of the kind of headstone on her brother's grave, showing the bronze plaque 'typical of war cemeteries in tropical climes'.[34]

The Phillips family, of Neath, South Wales, is still trying to come to terms with the death of David Glyn Phillips, a leading aircraftman, in Sandakan on 13 March 1945. Back then, the family was prominent in Neath's local business community. During the war, David's father, a self-made man with a domineering character, ran the Phillips Brothers department store – in which young David, a bookish boy, found himself reluctantly working. 'David read widely and seriously,' recalls his son, Jeffrey. 'I think the resentment against his father was a major factor which contributed to his decision to join the RAF . . .' The lad was, at the time, 'very close to his mother'.

In 1941, David sailed for Singapore, thence to Java – and into Japanese captivity. The family received one card before the island fell to the Japanese, 'and then silence'.[35] One day, a postcard arrived through the International Red Cross, confirming that he was a prisoner of war in Borneo. To be a prisoner of the Japanese was seen as somehow shameful; Jeffrey was mocked at school. Yet the family had hope; Germany and then Japan surrendered. But still no news.

One afternoon in September 1945, Jeffrey was called out of class and sent home; he was seven years old. 'The house was full of relatives,' he recalls, years later. 'Mother was huddled in a corner. It was very traumatic.' The adults talked quietly. The boy later learnt that his father had died in captivity, in a place called Sandakan, on 13 March 1945, of a strange disease called beriberi. He later discovers the truth – that brutality and malnutrition were the chief causes.

The news devastated the family. 'One felt as if the whole drive and impetus of the family had gone,' Jeffrey says.[36] David's father felt the loss bitterly: 'He had worked immensely hard during the war years to keep the family business running and no doubt was looking forward to handing over a flourishing concern to his son . . . His health collapsed, he sold the business and by December 1947 he had died.'[37]

The family buried the tragedy and rarely spoke of it. That David Phillips died at the hands of the Japanese was seen as not only tragic but also somehow unacceptable, even shameful, in the conservative Welsh town. Jeffrey and his sister were sent away to boarding school, and in 1951 David's widow remarried. 'It was a very upsetting experience for me,' Jeffrey recalls. 'My sister and I were away at school and when we came home dad's photos were gone. They had been like shrines in the house.'[38] The Phillips left Neath.

There is no known grave for David Glyn Phillips. But a plaque in his memory, on the local youth club in Neath, survived the building's demolition in 1995 and now stands in a quiet corner of his son's garden. His name appears on a memorial in Singapore and a gravestone on Labuan. Looking back, Jeffrey Phillips, now a successful lawyer, is more open. At a recent meeting of Children of

Far East Prisoners of War (COFEPOW), he refers to his father, in public, for the first time. 'I stood up and cried. I wasn't ashamed. It was very helpful.'[39] Like thousands who lost loved ones in the Pacific War, he has great difficulty reconciling his Christian belief in forgiveness with his enduring hatred towards the Japanese.

The York family, of Kettering, United Kingdom, experiences a grimly similar pattern of events. They receive a telegram in November 1945 informing them of the death of their son Reg, in Sandakan, while in Japanese captivity: 'No details, nor any information regarding the place of his burial, are yet available,' it states.[40] Then, on 4 July 1946, an official sentence from the Air Ministry relates that Aircraftman 1st Class Reginald York, of the Royal Air Force Volunteer Reserve, died in Sandakan on 5 April 1945 'of malaria'.[41] His mother secretes the notes with her little pile of memories: several letters, received en route to Malaya. One ends 'Let's hope this war is over quick'; and another 'Cheerio', or 'I remain, Your loving son, Reg xxxxx'.

His story gradually emerges: captured in Java, sent to Changi, sent to Borneo, died in Borneo. In the ensuing years, a few answers arrive. A fellow airman, Squadron Leader Ted Hardie, writes to Reg's brother: 'I remember him quite well now and must apologise for my bad memory when I began this letter . . .' And this, to Reg's nephew, Rod York, in June 2005, from Peter Lee, an RAF officer who survived Kuching: 'I cannot recall your uncle . . . although we must have met in Sandakan before my departure from there in August 1943, when all officers except 10 . . . were suddenly "ordered out".'[42]

The officers incarcerated in Kuching in 1943 owe their lives to the Allied landing on the west coast, which thwarted Japanese plans to massacre the surviving prisoners 'and not leave any trace'. Many came home unable to bear to speak of their captivity; some will carry the secret like a mark of shame. Several fine officers became sad, rather pathetic figures as prisoners; others stoically upheld their example as leaders.

Years later, several resolve to set down the truth. Flight Lieutenant Charlie Johnstone, of Mackay, Queensland, who spent three months in Sandakan then moved to Kuching, publishes his memoirs in 1995, at the request of his son, Doug. He writes:

> I have never been able to sit down and tell him or anyone much else of what occurred. Yes, at times when I have been in the mood, I have talked of odd incidents and sometimes regretted it later. Of course, I will never forget this episode in my life and even now, so many years later, I sometimes dream I am still in a Jap prisoner of war camp and will never get out. It is a terrifying experience.[43]

One officer who knows a great deal about his fellow men is Captain Stan Woods, who possesses a trove of notebooks and letters (now in the Australian War Memorial), which includes a stained, richly detailed notebook listing each officer's rank, religion, occupation, health, duties, activities and movement during the years of captivity in Sandakan. Hence, Captain Alec Bathgate suffered 'tinea in legs' and was 'in charge of parties at drome'; Captain Jock Britz had 'leg ulcers', worked on the airport and was a member of the 'Officers' Choir'; Captain George Cook 'became chief liaison officer' and is listed as deceased, 8 August

1945 (he was murdered on the 27th); Lieutenant Russ Ewin 'worked on airport, farm, road, playground' and was appointed 'Honorary Auditor – Canteen, Mess Funds'; Captain Jim Heaslop, though 'laid up for many weeks' by sickness, was 'Manager – Camp Canteen'; Captain Lionel Matthews, in command of 'Camp Agricultural Gardens', is listed as 'Deceased 2.3.44' with 'Memorial Service 5.3.44'; Captain Frank Mills, the medical officer (and father of the musician Jonathan Mills, who composed *Sandakan Threnody* in honour of the victims of the Death Marches), was seconded to the British prison camp; Captain Ken Mosher commanded the 'Drome Parties' from 11 June 1943 to 15 October 1943 and, in Kuching, the 'Hut Rep. Mess Finance Committee' (Mosher suffered from dengue fever, dysentery and other ailments).[44]

Woods' papers contain a 'Geebung' note, one of several sent between Captain Lionel Matthews (also known as 'Roslyn') and Dr James Taylor ('Geebung'), which monitored the prison smuggling operation and passed on BBC news picked up on the prison radio. 'Dear Geebung,' Matthews writes on 17 July 1943, '. . . Have some good news in bulletins this week. Should develop into something big. Have heard "messenger" may go to Kuching. Will endeavour to arrange substitute with him if this happens. Cheerio and thanks a lot for everything. Roslyn.'[45]

The 'good news' was a series of decisive Allied actions in the Pacific and Europe. For example: 'Australian and American forces are fighting a decisive action . . . 12 miles from SALAMUA [*sic*]' (16 July 1943); 'US bombers raided Jap. positions in Central and Southern Burma with no loss. Premier Tojo's hurried tour of the occupied territory did not include Burma probably because of heavy allied aerial activity over the area' (date not given); and

'In all 15 Jap. warships have been sunk in Kula Gulf in the past 14 days. The Jap. propagandists . . . said yesterday that the war in the SW Pacific had reached an extremely critical stage' (15 July 1943). The radio summaries even include transcripts of speeches in the House of Commons, Japanese ship movements and the detailed results of air battles in the Pacific.[46] It is easy to see why the discovery of the underground radio – and these transcripts – prompted such a ferocious crackdown.

Les Mockridge, the gentle, fair-haired, English aircraftman who drew the short straw in Sandakan and feigned appendicitis in order to contact the Australian prisoners, is another survivor of Kuching – and the only non-commissioned British serviceman to survive the Sandakan Prisoner of War Camp. He got home, to Trull, Somerset, on Armistice Day. The church bells pealed, and the whole village turned out to celebrate his safe return.

Mockridge's son, Steve, vividly recalls his father's account of meeting Captain Matthews in the Australian prisoners' hospital in Sandakan:

My father had pretended to have terrible stomach pains. They sent him to the Australian hospital [where the Japanese removed his perfectly healthy appendix]. One day, they brought in the terribly tortured figure of Captain Matthews. What drew my father and Matthews together was that they had both been senior scouts. Within days, Matthews came up with an escape plan.[47]

Matthews persisted with the plan until both he and Mockridge were removed to Kuching, a few days later. He would later describe Matthews as the bravest of men.

Survivors of Kuching remember Mockridge as the kindest. 'He looked after me after I got a severe beating,' a New Zealand Army officer told his son.[48] And he bore the watch and some personal effects of a fellow airman, Les Barnes, who, very sick and knowing he would die, asked Mockridge to convey the stuff to his mother in Hounslow. 'You are going to survive; I will die,' the lad had said. 'Take this to my mother.'[49] Les Barnes was murdered at Ranau; his heartbroken mother died five years later. And Mockridge tried to comfort families desperate for news of their sons. One father wrote:

> Dear Mr Mockridge, I do not suppose you knew my son [Ernest Peter Beale] . . . but . . . I wonder if you would drop me a line letting me know what you can about . . . the conditions you were under . . . Our great worry is that our son might have been done to death in a brutal fashion . . .[50]

Beale apparently died of malaria, in Sandakan, on 4 April 1945.

After the war Mockridge, like many ex-prisoners, experiences a troubled life. 'As a child,' his son recalls, 'I used to wake up hearing dad crying and screaming. I used to rush into his bedroom.' On the anniversaries of Armistice Day, 'dad used to cry his eyes out'. He tells his son that the marks on his body are scars from chickenpox; in fact, the Japanese stubbed out cigarettes on his flesh.[51] He takes a string of jobs and has difficulty making friends, because, his son says, 'he couldn't guarantee they'd be there'. It seems he fears they would die. He shuns physical contact. In time, he mellows, and marries Betty, whom he met 'on a train from Weymouth to Taunton'.[52] Mockridge dies in 2000 after a long struggle with motor neurone disease.

Of the 824 British prisoners of war transferred from Singapore to Borneo (641 of whom went to Sandakan), only 31 were alive at the armistice – all of whom had been moved to Kuching in 1943. Many relatives learn the truth not through official military or government channels but thanks to the investigations of an Australian soldier and ex-prisoner, Don Wall, in his books *Sandakan: The Last March* (1988) and *Kill the Prisoners* (1996).[53]

◆

Some survivors enjoy fulfilling lives. The story of Rod Wells, the electronics wizard who helped build the camp radio, and who survived the Kempei-tai and the horrors of Singapore's Outram Road Gaol, seems touched by the miraculous. After weeks of torture and the commutation of his death sentence – due to a Japanese 'clerical error' – to 12 years' penal servitude, Wells spent more than a year in solitary confinement, sick, hungry and periodically bashed. On his release, he weighed three stone.

He rebuilds his strength and proves fit enough to testify at the War Crimes Tribunal. He subsequently pursues a brilliant career in science. After enlisting for the Korean War, he attends the Royal Military College of Science at Wiltshire in England, where he completes postgraduate studies leading to a degree in nuclear physics at Cambridge University. He then works with the United Kingdom Ministry of Supply in their signals and radar research departments and the United Kingdom Atomic Weapons Research Establishment at Aldermaston. In 1956, he returns to Australia as one of two Australian Army officers on the scientific-response team at the Maralinga atomic tests. He subsequently serves in various top scientific roles with the British and Australian Governments, achieving, in 1964, the post of chief scientific/telecommunications officer to the Australian Departments of Defence and Foreign Affairs. An international expert on radio communications, aerials and surveillance techniques, Wells later works with ASIS in South East Asia and helps train Special Branch Police in covert counter-surveillance operations during the communist insurgency in Malaysia and Indonesia.

He and his wife, Pamela, a pharmacist, whom he married in 1974, retire in the 1980s and build a 'self-sufficient' home using sun- and wind-power to provide light and heating – a concept decades ahead of its time. In 1997, Wells is named an Odyssey Foundation Australian Achiever. With the onset of dementia and Parkinson's disease, he dies in 2003, a deeply mourned 'soldier, philanthropist, electronic genius, loyal monarchist and staunch nationalist'.[54] His close friend David Cornwell, better known as the writer John le Carré, says of him, 'Rod was a man among boys and I always felt inadequate in his presence: so much suffering, so much guts, get-up-and-go, so thoroughly decent and true. I'll never forget Rod Wells. Bless him.'[55]

Another lifelong friend, Barry Tinkler, remembers Wells thus: 'I haven't met a fellow as gentle and as positive in his attitude, and love of his country . . . He was one of the best teachers I've ever had in electronics.' Tinkler is one of the few people to whom Wells confides: 'Rod told me about his torture, and the most excruciating pain of the log treatment. He was sensitive about his deafness, the result of the Japanese driving a skewer into his head. He hated the Japanese – or more particularly the Kempei-tai – to the day he died.'[56]

Another survivor of Outram Road, Bill Young – a Dead End Kid – returns home to resume a boisterous and fulfilling life. Largely self-educated, he teaches himself to draw. He reads widely and writes poetry, appearing regularly at reunions and memorials, a much-loved speaker and willing sharer of his experiences. His broad smile, infectious sense of humour and absence of bitterness belie the memory of an experience that should have killed him. How has he dealt with the aftermath? 'Don't bullshit yourself, talk to yourself straight,' he explains. 'It doesn't matter how much bullshit is out there, as long as you talk to yourself straight.'[57]

Another three (of the 14) Dead End Kids survive: 'Mo' Davis, Terry Risely and Sid Outram, who were lucky enough to be taken with the officers to Kuching. The others were not so fortunate. Joey Crome and Wally Ford volunteered to join 300 mainly British prisoners of war sent to the island of Labuan to build another Japanese airfield. There, along with two-thirds of the prisoners, Crome and Ford died of disease, malnutrition and overwork. In March 1945, the survivors were shipped to the mainland; and in June the Japanese massacred the 44 survivors near Miri – all shot and buried in a mass grave.

Of the civilians who return, Dr James Taylor resumes his career as a doctor, working as a medical officer in the Commonwealth Repatriation Department in Turramurra, Sydney. He actively pursues justice on behalf of the native people in Borneo. On 30 January 1947, he writes to the Military Board, Victoria Barracks, offering to identify native members of the resistance and families of those executed by the Japanese:

I am particularly anxious to see justice done to the unfortunate people to whom it is due. I know, and am well-known to, the people of North Borneo . . . and am prepared to go back to Borneo and to assist the Commission in investigating these claims.[58]

Dr Taylor never recovers from his torture; but the Australian Government barely compensates him for his medical care. In 1952, he and his wife, Celia, apply to Canberra for compensation. On 20 March, they receive this reply – quoting recent remarks by the prime minister (which have appeared in the press):

> The Commonwealth Government has decided that the bulk of Japanese assets available for distribution in Australia shall be divided equally among former Australian prisoners of war in Japanese hands. Latest estimates put the value of these assets at Stg730,000. An amount of Stg25,000 will be appropriated from the proceeds of these assets for distribution among Australian civilians who suffered personal hardship at the Japanese hands. The remainder of the money will go to ex-prisoners.[59]

Taylor was tortured within an inch of his life. His medical records reveal several serious ongoing health complications. He suffers from 'chronic colitis [intestinal inflammation] resulting from untreated amoebic dysentery while a prisoner of war' (Dr N. A. Walker, 16 May 1952)[60] and 'Bilateral Conduction Deafness with an associated Cochlear Nerve degeneration . . . precipitated by the stresses and strains to which he could have been subjected whilst a Prisoner of War' (Dr T. H. O'Donnell, 13 March 1953).[61] In lodging a claim, on 13 February 1953, for compensation from the Civilian Internees' Trust Fund, Taylor confirms that his progressive deafness has been 'a grave handicap in the practice of my profession'.[62] He receives a few thousand pounds.

◆

Some receive ribbons attached to pieces of metal. In 1947, Captain Lionel Matthews is honoured with a posthumous George Cross. 'He steadfastly refused,' the citation states, 'to make admissions under brutal torture, beatings and starvation to implicate or endanger the lives of his associates. His conduct at all times was that of a very brave and courageous gentleman . . .' Even before his execution on 2 March 1944, Matthews 'defied the Japanese'. A witness to the citation, Rod Wells, says of Matthews in 1947:

> Capt. Matthews showed courage that was . . . an inspiration to all to remain silent under the most severe torture. [S]tretched on an improvised rack and severely beaten he still denied facts, the admission of which would probably have involved Senior Officers of the Force in the same fate as himself . . . When the death sentence was passed, Matthews . . . shook me by the hand, wished me good luck and stated that he was pleased to be going with such loyal friends – the natives who had worked with us. Later Japanese guards stated that he was shot after refusing to be blindfolded.[63]

Another eyewitness, Alan Weston, states:

> Captain Matthews in circumstances of the gravest danger to himself organised the North Borneo Armed Constabulary in readiness for a rising against the Japanese . . . Capt. Matthews

could have escaped on numerous occasions [with local help]
. . . but he declined to do so . . . For this devotion to duty,
unselfishness and extreme gallantry he paid the supreme
sacrifice.[64]

Dr Taylor adds, 'His sole care at all times was for those around
him . . . I consider him a most courageous man and in my opinion
he upheld the highest traditions of an Australian officer.'[65]

Few deserve higher recognition than now-Captain Robert
'Jock' McLaren, the lanky Scottish-born Australian who
twice escaped the Japanese, twice parachuted into Borneo on
intelligence-gathering missions, as part of the Z Special Unit,
and receives a bar to his Military Cross. Reading the citation,
Lieutenant General Sir John Lavarack remarks, 'It looks as if you
earned the VC.'[66] Recognised as one of the most effective Allied
soldiers of the Pacific campaign, McLaren's war record testifies to
astonishing fortitude during three years of guerrilla warfare. This
is the man who, while working behind enemy lines on Mindanao,
removed his appendix with a pocketknife and mirror and then
stitched up the wound.[67] After the war, McLaren retires to Papua
New Guinea, where he establishes a veterinary clinic. He dies in a
car crash in Wau in 1956.

Rex Blow, with whom McLaren escaped Berhala, receives
a Distinguished Service Order, the citation of which describes
him as 'the most outstanding guerrilla commander of the Pacific
War'.[68] Blow offered to join the proposed parachute rescue of
the Sandakan prisoners, which never eventuated. Instead, he
was posted to command various Z Force intelligence-gathering
operations. At the Japanese surrender, he assumed an active role
in 'mopping up' pockets of resistance. One operation, in Sarawak,

lasted more than two months, against an enemy force dug in with machine guns and mortars. 'I witnessed the end of this surrender,' writes Athol Moffitt, in Blow's obituary. 'I was on other duties [in Sarawak] in early November 1945, when a Murut runner arrived with a message on toilet paper. "Arriving tomorrow with 327 Japs many sick no food Blow sorry for the notepaper, but I have no other."'[69] The next day, the last of the Japanese forces in Borneo were marched out of the jungle in single file, with Blow at the head.

After the war, Blow joined the rejuvenated British Administration in Borneo. 'Among his duties, Blow, in a fast boat, pursued pirates, again active in the seas east of Borneo, well known to him,' concludes his obituary.[70] In 1987, Blow and his third wife are found happily growing pistachios in Victoria, with 'our great little son', aged two and a half, as Blow writes to Moffitt. He dreams of one day retiring to Queensland's Sunshine Coast.[71] On 11 July, he tells Moffitt, 'It must have been a great pleasure, being responsible for the conviction and hanging of Hoshijima. As soon as we saw that bastard we . . . agreed unanimously that there would not be a great future for us under that guy. He just looked evil.'[72] They are among his last words on the war.

◆

The six survivors have passed away now. Since the war, they lived hard, melancholy lives interspersed with fleeting moments of happiness and fraught with terrible memories and serious health complications. They responded variously to the label of 'hero' pinned on to them by an impressionable, hero-hungry nation. On the surface, some seemed to tough it out and live reasonably normal lives, as the wife of one victim told a meeting of Sandakan Family members in Canberra recently. His faith in God 'got Owen Campbell through', she says; his partying and dancing helped Nelson Short, 'a real Bojangles'; Keith Botterill's abusive father taught him to cope. Curiously, nobody mentions Sticpewich.

The truth is more painful. Braithwaite and Campbell shunned their unwanted fame and immersed themselves in their work – a newsagency and farm, respectively. They suffered profound psychological trauma. At the other extreme, Nelson Short appeared to revel in and exploit his new-found status, which seemed to fill a void in his unhappy life. In time, he took to drink. Years later, at memorial services, his drink-fuelled stories of the Death Marches sounded distinctly unedifying to the ears of at least one widow whose husband never came home, and who became the target of his unwanted attentions. A reliable source claims that Short, at his nadir, even offered news about the death of a prisoner to the latter's bereaved family in exchange for money. He died of a heart attack in 1995.

As degrading as this sounds, we judge anyone who has suffered so awfully at our peril. In this context, perhaps Bill Moxham's extreme reaction to his traumatic experiences seems the more 'normal' – or explicable. Unable to bear the life he had snatched from the teeth of death, this reckless young man, of privileged background, committed suicide in 1961. Moxham's hellish last days may be compared with those of the quiet Owen Campbell, who found a kind of solace with his Christian faith, his farm and his family. He died in peace in 2003.

Yet Bill Sticpewich seemed to enjoy the most robust return to 'normal' life. He stayed in the army, reached the rank of major, resumed an active life and was duly honoured with an MBE for his efforts during the War Graves investigations. Some still regarded him as a selfish opportunist – even a collaborator – according to the verdict of Botterill, who delivered it after Sticpewich's death. That judgement must be set against the citation to his MBE, which states that the year after the war Sticpewich 'identified about one hundred [Japanese] who had been concerned with the brutalities in the camp and the deaths . . . on various death marches. He returned to Labuan and rendered invaluable service in the interrogation of the Japanese,' without which many war criminals 'would not have been brought to justice'.[73]

In March 1966, Dr John O'Rourke, a Melbourne practitioner, examined Sticpewich's health: 'gun shot wounds left leg and thigh with retained shrapnel'; 'old tropical ulcer right leg'; and 'irritable colon'. Sticpewich also complained of gross arthritic disability in both shoulders. While a prisoner, according to O'Rourke, Sticpewich suffered many malarial attacks ('at least 8–10'); chronic dysentery 'for over 2½ years'; and hookworm, beriberi, pellagra and jungle fever. Sticpewich also endured pneumonia and cerebral malaria in Sandakan.[74] He died in a freak car accident in 1977; in fact, two cars were involved in the accident. On hearing the news, Dick Braithwaite reflected, 'how typical of Sticpewich, one car wouldn't have been enough'.[75]

Braithwaite is perhaps the most complex, and candid, case. In 1983, he agreed to an extensive interview with the Australian radio documentary maker Tim Bowden, during which he was honest enough to admit that he, too, would have obtained extra food had he 'been fortunate enough' to have been in Sticpewich's privileged position, which 'created an element of jealousy'.[76]

Braithwaite's is an uplifting story of a man who reached the edge of the abyss and pulled back from the brink. In 1947, he married Joyce Blatch, who had been married to his close friend, Gunner Wal Blatch. Blatch and Braithwaite had fought side by side in Singapore, working the same 25-pounder cannon. Blatch died on the Death March. On his return to Australia, Braithwaite consoled and then fell in love with Wal's widow. On their first date, to a theatre in Sydney's Kings Cross, Braithwaite almost passed out from an attack of malaria. When he later proposed, in August 1946, Joyce laughed, 'You haven't even kissed me yet.' Dick replied, 'That wouldn't have been right because you were my best friend's wife.'[77]

These anecdotes reveal none of the torment within this highly intelligent, sensitive man. Had the experience changed him as a person, Bowden asks.

'We can't see ourselves as others see us,' Braithwaite says. 'Er, I have no idea whether I'm a different person . . . I would say this, that I'm a more emotional person than I was. I find things upset me very easily. I have a lot to thank my wife for, because I gave her such a bad time after the war, er, that why she stayed with me I don't know, I wouldn't have . . . I knew I was hurting her, but she, she still stood by me . . .'[78]

Minor irritations, or daily routines, appear to be unassailably obstructive, he explains: 'it was a major, major task to have a shave, you know, everything seemed of mountainous proportions'. His dreams and memories seem to have possessed a hallucinatory power. One summer's day, near Newcastle in New South Wales, long after the war, Braithwaite recalls dozing off on the top deck of a bus: 'all of a sudden I could smell all the jungle smells of Borneo. It just came from nowhere, it was just oppressive. And I opened my eyes and as I opened my eyes I looked out and there's

Sticpewich walking along the street. Now, be [*sic*] no explanation for that. Because I hadn't seen him . . . And I, that's the last and only time I ever saw him'.[79]

Joyce has a vivid recollection of his mood and what she calls 'the nightmares'. 'Dick slept badly,' she says, 'and we had many disturbed nights . . . they were pretty terrible, some of them.' Half-awake, he would thrash around or attack her 'in self-defence more or less'.

'And then there was this recurrent thing we had,' she continues, 'about lice in the bed. He was quite sure that the bed was alive, and we would get up, fairly regularly, strip everything off and examine the mattress minutely. I got used to this routine and just accepted it as something we had to live with because he was convinced in his mind. And then he said to me, "I know you don't think the bed is alive or there's vermin in the bed, but," he said, "look at my arms," and he had, literally, bite marks and raised lumps . . . I suppose this was psychosomatic, I don't know, but he did actually have the marks on his body . . . and one was filled with great sadness that this should have happened and wonder how long this would have to last for him . . .'[80]

The condition lasted for about three years. Their marriage survived; his torments became less severe. For Joyce, the toughest thing was her husband's chronic bitterness and self-reproach. 'War brings out the best and the worst,' she later says, 'but the worst was far more horrible than he could ever have imagined, and this had an effect . . . he had this feeling "why me?"; he hated, in a way, to be the one to be saved when so many were lost. As he said, "Better men than I should have come back. I was the one, but why?" And I was inclined to say, "Well, there must be something very special for you to do," and he never liked that idea, that was the wrong thing to say I think now, and looking back I was young and enthusiastic and wanting to be a rather Pollyanna, and this seemed to irk him . . . he felt it was all so unjust and hadn't worked out at all as it should have . . .'[81] Dick Braithwaite died of cancer in 1986.

Keith Botterill passed away with acute emphysema in 1997. His troubled life found glimmers of happiness in his later years, when he rose to the expectations of his status as a Death March survivor. He helpfully offered interviews, attended memorials, educated the young. The revelation that he and Moxham perjured themselves at the war-crimes trials makes headlines in 2012, when Lynette Silver repeats her allegation (which appeared in a revised edition of her book in 2007)[82] that Botterill made a 'death bed' confession to her: Botterill confided that he lied under oath about how Gunner Albert Cleary died, in order to secure the death penalty for a Formosan guard who committed other heinous crimes but had not been involved in Cleary's death. 'Their perjury was premeditated and deliberate,' Silver says in an interview with *The Sydney Morning Herald*. 'They did it to secure a guilty verdict against the guards, one of whom was 40 kms away at the time of Cleary's capture. As a result, all three guards were hanged.'[83] Yet, one does not need Botterill's confession to see that he lied to the court: it is clear from any close reading of his court statements, and the conclusions of the military authorities, who regarded him as an unreliable witness. The more important point is that Botterill's perjury does not change the fact that poor Cleary died after a prolonged period of vicious torture.

◆

Today, families of the victims gather in Australia and Britain to remember and mourn. The younger generation have caught the baton. Heather Harrison-Lawrence, of Reading, Berkshire, has gathered a great file on her great-uncle, Gunner Henry John Lawrence, who died in Borneo. Her spirit never rests in pursuit of news of how and why. COFEPOW represents the victims' families' interests and offers a consoling forum after years of official and national indifference. In Australia, Maureen Devereaux, Brian Hales and other relatives have established the Sandakan Family of prisoners' relatives; it meets twice a year to keep the flame alive. Today, Australian councils in every major city commemorate the Death March and memorials have spread through country towns.

Modern Sabah, too, has been warmly receptive to commemoration ideas. The site of the former prison camp hosts a memorial and small museum in carefully maintained grounds. The beautiful, privately financed Kundasang War Memorial, established in 1962, offers tranquil gardens dedicated to the victims' different nationalities. And, at Ranau, small memorials – modest yet awe-inspiring – honour the civilians and prisoners.

On 1 August 1993, Prime Minister Paul Keating, whose uncle Bill died in Sandakan on 3 February 1945 (and whose family, as late as September 1974, had not received his official death certificate from Central Army Records)[84] unveils a memorial at Burwood Park in Sydney dedicated to 1800 Australians who died in Borneo. Keating chooses his words carefully: the Death Marches were acts of human depravity, he states – implying they cannot be glossed over as 'excesses of war', as the Japanese are wont to do. 'Sandakan should be remembered,' Keating continues, 'because it was more than a battle between nations and more than a battle between conflicting ideologies; it was a war between human decency and human depravity.'[85] The victims of the Death Marches 'were as much casualties of evil as those who died in the Nazi death camps in Europe'.[86]

◆

Controversy swirls around the Sandakan Death Marches. Why was the rescue 'plan' abandoned? Who killed it? Did the government conspire to conceal the truth about the Death Marches? What was the correct route of the Death Marches? Was there a Fourth March, in a north-westerly direction? Were AGAS agents in particular places at times they later claimed to be? The minutiae are pored over, squabbled over. Historians, families, armchair generals never tire of their pursuit of that most elusive prey, the truth. No doubt, this is a good thing, but we enter the ring with a sense of weary obligation, born of the reflection that all this squabbling forgets the fundamental point: that these men died as a result of acts of incomprehensible barbarity and should be quietly mourned in perpetuity as symbols of resistance to a repulsive regime. The rest seems tangential.

A long debate, for example, hovers over PROJECT KINGFISHER. Since 1947, some have argued that it was cancelled, or abandoned, on the cusp of execution. All the evidence suggests otherwise: that KINGFISHER was not even close to being properly planned or realised.

General Sir Thomas Blamey lights the powder. His special pleading, to the Second Annual Conference of the Australian Armoured Corps on 19 November 1947, is a model of self-exculpation in which he states that he dearly hoped the rescue would proceed, implying that MacArthur was responsible for killing it. 'We had high hopes of being able to use Australian parachute troops,' Blamey declared. 'We had complete plans for them. Our spies were in Japanese-held territory. We had established the necessary contacts with prisoners at Sandakan, and our parachute troops were going to relieve them. The parachute regiment didn't know what was planned, of course. But at the moment we wanted to act, we couldn't get the necessary aircraft to take them in. The operation would certainly have saved that death march of Sandakan. Destiny didn't permit us to carry it out.'[87]

His remark causes uproar in parliament and the press. The RSL demands an inquiry. Blamey's statement is false, or meretricious, on several levels. Questions are raised in parliament about how much the government knew of the rescue plan, and why planes weren't made available. The prime minister's reply is crystal clear: he knew nothing of a rescue plan, adding that 'there were many instances in which sufficient planes were not available for the conduct of particular operations'.[88] 'No Blamey Plan to Save POWs, Chifley Declares' and '"Destiny" Stopped POW Rescue' run the headlines on 4 December 1947.[89]

In fact, Blamey has not, at any time, recommended to Prime Minister Chifley, the defence minister or the Army Advisory Council that KINGFISHER should proceed. They have been completely in the dark. A memo to the prime minister on 3 December 1947 confirms that KINGFISHER 'did not receive consideration on a government level, *nor was there any request for representation by the Government to the Commander-in-Chief, SWPA, in support of any plan*'[90] (my emphasis). Blamey is the only man in a position to have pressed the government to make such representations to MacArthur. If, as he now claims, he held 'high hopes' for the rescue, then he might at least have alerted Canberra and the military authorities to the 'plan'. Blamey counter-argues that 'Most people know that Allied High Command operational plans were not submitted to the Australian Government.'[91] Utter nonsense. According to the government's memo, Canberra always expects to be informed of operational plans.

In fact, Blamey's belatedly vaunted rescue attempt never got beyond the drawing board, as Athol Moffitt informs the 1987 National Conference of the Veterans' Review Board. Rescuing the prisoners 'would have required a major offensive and it probably would have only resulted in the prisoners being shot anyhow . . . it was decided nothing could be done'.[92]

Nor is Sir John Overall, former commander of the 1st Australian Parachute Battalion, correct in later claiming the rescue 'was planned but covered up when not prosecuted'[93] – a classic case of projecting a desirable outcome on the past. KINGFISHER was not within an ace of being prosecuted, argues his fellow officer, Warwick Johnstone, because 'you needed constant air cover, a field hospital and ships in Sandakan Bay to care for these men so near to death. We alone were not sufficient.'[94] In his excellent analysis, Christopher Dawson reminds us that in late 1945 Australia landed 75,000 men in Borneo – at Tarakan, Balikpapan, Miri and Beaufort – but not a single soldier at Sandakan.[95]

Indeed, former defence minister Sir Frederick Shedden advises Chifley after the war that Advanced Land Headquarters (Landops) examined the rescue possibility 'and found it impractical'.[96] Lieutenant General Frank Berryman, Blamey's representative at MacArthur's headquarters, similarly dismissed the rescue proposal as 'unacceptable'. It would require carrier-borne combat aircraft (no carriers were operating south of the Philippines in 1945), a 600-bed hospital ship and a large amphibious task force, concluded Berryman and the American officers.[97] All this shows that MacArthur was not the only commander dismissive of the rescue proposal. Perhaps it is consoling to feed families the myth that KINGFISHER was close to being realised; the hard truth is that top brass had no intention of approving the project.

◆

Years after the war, a father and son convey the extremes of emotion that most families touched by these events share to some degree. When Tim Bowden asks Richard Braithwaite in his lengthy 1983 interview, 'What do you feel about the Japanese today?' Braithwaite replies, 'Well, put it this way: if you'd come here today and brought a Jap with you, I would not have reacted in any way; he'd have been entertained the same as you were. But he wouldn't have been invited back and neither would you . . . Um, no . . . I hold a certain hate for them because, and this came to the surface when . . . I [visited] the American war cemetery in Manila, and we lined up to give a short service and lay a wreath. And a busload of Japanese tourists came charging out of the bus . . . into the crypt, acting, jumping up and down and chattering away, taking photographs, and we obviously were standing there, about to do something, but they just completely ignored that . . . To give our fellows credit . . . no one moved or said anything, we just waited. But I, I was so burned up I had to walk off. Because I just, well, I had no idea what I might have done if I'd stayed there. I just had to walk away, a hundred yards away, and have a cigarette. But, but the people of Japan, I just can't blame the present generation for what happened. But I can never forget what Hoshijima said to us one day: "Even if we lose this war, a hundred years from now we will come back." And I feel that we still can't trust them. I hope I'm wrong.'[98]

His son, Professor Richard Braithwaite, understands his father's feelings. The Australian academic also makes an effort to understand the Japanese – so much so that in 2011 he takes the extraordinary decision to edit the memoirs of a Japanese soldier who served in the Imperial Army in Borneo. *An End to a War: A Japanese Soldier's Experience of the 1945 Death Marches of North Borneo* by Ueno Itsuyoshi is a well-written attempt by a reluctant Japanese draftee to convey the suffering of the Japanese Army, of whom 8500 died during their 370-mile march from Tawao to Jesselton. This march proceeded concurrently with the prisoners' Death Marches.

Braithwaite's decision to edit the memoir appears to be an expression of empathy born of a wish for reconciliation. Yet something else is at work here: had things turned out differently – as Braithwaite himself states – the Japanese author might easily have been his father's torturer or murderer. After his escape, Braithwaite senior killed a lone Japanese soldier 'in the jungle in a fit of hateful rage. He lay in wait and beat him to death.' Ueno Itsuyoshi was himself wandering the jungle at various times. 'They were both,' the son writes in the introduction, 'ordinary men who found themselves in extraordinarily tough circumstances through no fault of their own.' In this light, it is not fanciful to suggest that the son is, by editing this book, trying to lay to rest the ghosts of his father's life.

Both were brave soldiers; both suffered great hardship. Yet moral relativists who eschew absolute judgements and qualify atrocities by claiming that 'every side commits war crimes' utterly miss the point. The book's misleading subtitle unwittingly draws attention to the Japanese crime: this memoir focuses on the Japanese, not the prisoners', 'death marches'. The author encounters the Australians and British only once, referring to them as 'noble-looking, educated, blank, smiling and angry . . . They must have left their wives, children and parents in their home towns. I thought the war was cruel to all of us.'[99] But the Japanese were not *forcibly marched to death*. They died of disease. They were not the victims of brutality; they were its perpetrators. Unlike the prisoners, the Japanese had medicines, sporadic supplies of food, and slept in huts en route. They weren't systematically slaughtered. Most Japanese survived Allied prisons. And therein lies the great flaw in this book – and in the Japanese nation's memory of the war: a failure to distinguish between the terrible *experiences* of the Japanese Army and their premeditated destruction of prisoners of war and civilians.

Yet Ueno is capable of expressing his moral disgust elsewhere; towards his commanders, for example. Only after the armistice does he, now a prisoner, seemingly glimpse the enormity of what his countrymen have done. When an Australian sergeant tells a line of Japanese prisoners – who expect to be beaten and executed – 'The war has finished. You and I are not enemies anymore . . .' Ueno reflects, in a flash of self-recognition, 'While our army was winning, what sort of behaviour did we show towards the loser? We had imagined and prepared for the worst situations before lining up here, but the sergeant's first speech made us so happy.'[100]

It is the happiness of a Japanese prisoner who is suddenly

aware that he is not going to be thrashed, clubbed, racked, water-tortured, rice-tortured, starved, force-marched or shot. It is the elation of a soldier who knows he is going home. Not once were the Australian and British prisoners free to enjoy this sense of liberation; never were they able to contemplate the possibility of hope in this Japanese hell. Yet those who did not come home died in the knowledge that they had endured, and struggled to resist, the most odious of regimes. Their story will not satiate the public longing for battlefield heroes; nor will they adorn the Honour Rolls with decorations, or march in the bemedalled lines of memorial parades. They persist in our collective memory as men of a different order: their courage was not in the line of fire; their struggle was to live, to stay upright, to walk one step at a time, into the heart of a Japanese hell.

Postscript

As I wrote this book, I found myself turning away from the page and seeking solace in brief 'Notes to Self'. They served as a sort of mental sustenance along this terrible journey. I offer one here, which may help the reader to assimilate the meaning of what he or she has just read:

Human history is the last depository of the truth, or truths, about the end of days. It's all we have left when the last human trace disappears from our age, or era. Thus we must persevere . . . And yet, what happened here in Borneo seems at times beyond the imagination of humankind, outside the acceptable remit even of the realm of fiction. For who among our novelists would dare subject the world to a story that ends with the image of sick and starving men being clubbed, shot or bayoneted to death where they lie, amid the naked corpses of their friends? The measurelessly awful reality that descends on these poor men is near-impossible to write down. But I must persevere, for the sake of historic truth, and in the hope of conferring some sense of justice on behalf of the victims of one of the worst atrocities of the twentieth century.

APPENDIX 1

HONOUR ROLL OF AUSTRALIAN AND BRITISH SOLDIERS WHO DIED AT SANDAKAN OR ON THE SANDAKAN–RANAU DEATH MARCHES

AUSTRALIAN (1780 MEN)

Name	Date of death
Abbott, E. A.	21.1.43
Abfalter, P. J.	26.3.45
Adair, J.	22.2.45
Adam J. C.	26.5.45
Adams, A. M.	26.1.45
(served as White, A. M.)	
Adams, H.	14.6.45
Adams, T.	19.6.45
Addison, P. R.	15.5.45
Adlington, N. C.	12.2.45
Ainsworth, T. L.	9.6.45
Alberts, W.	31.3.45
Albress, A. S.	19.6.45
Alexander, E. C.	7.4.45
Allan, L. B.	21.2.45
Allen, J. M. E.	23.7.45
Allen, S. J.	7.6.45
Allie, N. R.	12.6.45
Allingham, M. A. G.	8.4.45
Allnutt, S. G.	20.5.45
Ambrose, G.	28.4.45
Anderson, A.	28.07.45
Anderson, C. W. M.	
See entry for Jubelski, C. W. M.	
Anderson, E. R.	9.2.45
Anderson, F. D.	1.3.45
Anderson, James F.	10.6.45
Anderson, J. M.	
See entry for Bowe, J. M.	
Anderson, P. A.	25.2.45
Anderson, W. O.	25.12.44

Name	Date of death
Andrews, S.	
See entry for Smith, E. W.	
Annand, D.	14.4.45
Annear, L. J.	20.2.45
Archard, C.	14.7.45
Archibald, G. R.	31.3.45
Argo, D. M.	25.5.45
Armstrong, F.	30.7.45
Armstrong, J. W.	12.7.45
Armstrong, R. W.	7.5.45
Armstrong, T. E.	13.5.45
Arnold, J. H.	5.4.45
Arnold, L. R.	4.6.45
Arthur, H. A.	11.6.45
Arthur, R. G.	5.6.45
Asgill, C. C.	17.7.45
Ashby, F. R.	15.3.45
Attenborough, A. R.	12.4.45
Auld, R. J.	5.6.45
Avice, S.	21.1.45
Aylett, R.	
See entry for Columbine, R. E.	
Ayres, C. H.	10.4.45
Ayton, A. C. J.	15.2.45
Baccus, A. A.	23.5.45
Bacon, S. T.	20.6.45
Badgery, B. L.	30.3.45
Bagnall, N. W.	5.5.45
Bagust, R. H.	18.7.45
Bailey, E. G.	5.6.45
Bailey, I. S.	4.12.44

Name	Date of death
Bailey, N. E.	10.6.45
Baird, J.	
See entry for Barrie, J.	
Balding, H. M.	3.4.45
Balgue, D. N.	4.6.45
Ball, C. G.	4.6.45
Ballard, G. M.	23.3.45
Bancroft, E. D.	10.6.45
Baragwanath, W.	19.3.45
Barber, G. K.	8.12.44
Barker, D. T.	7.6.45
Barker, G. J.	3.3.45
Barker, J. H.	15.2.45
Barkla, E. A.	7.6.45
Barlow, W. J.	7.6.45
Barnard, L. G.	18.3.45
Barnes, K. G.	1.5.45
Barnes, Reginald G.	7.3.45
Barnes, Ronald G.	14.2.45
Barnier, J. N.	12.6.45
Barratt, R. H.	10.12.44
Barrie, J.	14.6.45
(served as Baird, J.)	
Bartils, G. H.	21.6.45
Bastin, J. C.	17.3.45
Bates, A. E. R.	26.3.45
Bateson, D. F.	26.12.44
(served as Chandler, R. W.)	
Baxter, M. P.	8.6.45
Bayley, A. E.	10.2.45
Beard, W. H.	10.7.45
Beasley, H. C. J.	22.3.45

Beaumont, F. J.	10.3.45	Bott, J. E.	2.7.45	Bruce, R. C.	31.3.45
Beazley, J. D.	7.7.45	Bougoure, O. W.	21.5.45	Bryant, F. L.	8.6.45
Bedford, R. D. E.	10.6.45	Bourne, P. J.	27.5.45	Bryant, J. C.	29.3.45
Beer, N. P.	9.6.45	Bousie, G.	26.1.45	Buckley, H. W.	4.8.45
Beer, Walter H.	21.3.45	Boustead, M. G.	21.2.45	(served previously as Buckley,
Beer, William J.	14.6.45	Bovey, A. R.	24.4.45	N. J.)
Beetson, G. J.	1.11.44	Bow, W. N.	13.6.45	Buckley, J. J.	8.6.45
Behrendorff, C. S.	17.5.45	Bowe, J. M.	12.5.45	Buckley, L. F.	11.2.45
Belford, N.	23.5.45	(served as Anderson, J. M.)		Bullen, E. F.	25.4.45
Bell, M. C.	5.6.45	Bowe, W. J.	26.7.45	Bunch, N. H.	17.6.45
Bell, R. M.	29.4.45	Bowerman, H. F.	17.6.45	Bundey, G. W.	29.4.45
Bendall, B. A.	12.2.45	Bowman, H. R.	27.12.44	Burchnall, F. A.	4.6.45
Bennett, A. D.	22.3.45	Boxhorn, K.	17.5.45	Burchnall, F. R.	19.5.43
Bennett, Henry P.	15.2.45	Boyce, A. R.	6.3.45	Burgess, J.	30.7.45
Bennett, Horatio C.	17.2.45	Boyd, James William	16.5.45	Burgess, L.	19.9.44
Bennett, W. D.	14.7.45	Boyd, James William	23.6.45	Burgun, G.	6.3.45
Bennison, R. J.	14.3.45	Boyd, Robert	23.5.45	Burke, F. J.	7.6.45
Benson, G. E.	9.4.45	Boyd, Robert Thomas	22.3.45	Burke, J. E.	31.7.45
Betts, Jack	15.2.45	Boyes, W. E.	13.7.45	Burke, W. J.	12.6.45
Betts, James M.	12.4.45	Boyle, C. R.	7.2.45	Burley, K. B.	18.5.45
Beves, E. N.	13.7.45	Boyley, W. A.	17.6.45	Burling, J. H.	2.4.45
Bexton, S.	14.6.45	Brabham, V. G.	26.5.45	Burnell, A. D.	17.7.45
Bexton, T.	25.7.45	Brack, D. N.	17.5.45	Burnes, F. C.	23.5.45
Bice, C. J. S.	28.1.45	Bracken, C. N.	13.4.45	Burnett, E. R.	30.3.45
Biggs, F.	23.3.45	Brady, C.	22.2.45	Burns, C. E.	4.2.45
Bignell, K. W.	11.6.45	Brady, W. P.	8.2.45	Burns, R. N. B.	5.6.45
Bills, L.	14.2.45	Bray, E. W.	2.6.45	Burns, S. A. N.	31.1.45
Binstead, A. H.	28.5.45	Bray, J.	7.6.45	Burns, T.	13.7.45
Bird, A. W.	9.7.45	Bredbury, I.	23.5.45	Burridge, F. R.	21.8.44
Bird, B. S.	22.6.45	Brett, N. F.	1.1.45	Burrows, J.	25.4.45
Bird, C. R.	26.7.45	Brien, D. H.	24.2.45	Burton, E. G.	21.2.45
Bird, James E.	10.10.42	Brinkman, J. H.	7.3.45	Burton, G.	7.5.45
Bird, John K.	16.4.45	Brody, L.	4.6.45	Burzacott, M.	3.5.45
Black, J.	24.3.45	Brooker, W.	27.5.45	Bushell, R. F.	7.6.45
Blackie, J. W.	2.6.45	Broomham, C. F.	27.5.45	Butherway, J. H.	8.7.45
Blackwood, L. C.	7.6.45	Broughton, W. E.	3.12.44	Butler, T. L.	17.4.45
Blair, W. F.	14.5.45	Brown, A. A.	2.6.45	Bycroft, A. B.	7.3.45
Blatch, W. G.	1.6.45	Brown, C.	3.1.45	Byrne, B.	9.3.45
Blewett, C. B.	23.3.45	Brown, E. G.	4.2.45	Byrne, N. B. G.	12.1.45
Bloom, E.	8.2.45	Brown, F.	10.3.45	Cadwgan, A. D.	2.6.45
Bluford, E. H.	2.6.45	Brown, J. E.	7.2.45	Cain, C. J.	17.5.45
Blunden, A. J.	6.6.45	Brown, M.	20.6.45	Callander, H. M.	5.6.45
Board, W. E.	11.9.42	Brown, N. N.	31.3.45	Cameron, C. M.	31.1.45
Bobbin, R. J.	27.7.45	Brown, R. G.	11.7.45	Cameron, D. T.	11.4.45
Bock, H. J.	7.3.45	Brown, Samuel	15.7.45	Cameron, F.	7.6.45
Boese, R. J.	29.3.45	Brown, Sydney Walter	15.7.45	Cameron, J. K.	13.5.45
Bollard, J. T.	27.3.45	Brown, V. M. W.	21.5.45	Campbell, C.	19.6.45
Bolton, E. D.	22.6.45	Brown, William	19.3.45	Campbell, D. A.	11.5.45
Bolton, G. A.	29.7.45	Brown, William		Campbell, D. S.	23.3.45
Bond, F. T.	7.12.43	Frederick	15.5.45	Campbell, G. N. S.	2.9.45
Bonis, R. T.	3.5.45	Browning, J. H.	16.7.45	Campbell, J.	8.6.45
Booth, C. L.	24.11.44	Brownlee, G. F.	11.7.45	Campbell, M. L.	3.6.45

Campbell, R.	5.7.45	Clark, R. P.	24.2.45	Cook, A. J.	10.4.45
Campbell, W. R. E.	2.6.45	Clark, W. B.	2.8.45	Cook, G. R.	27.8.45
Candish, G. A.	4.12.42	Clarke, A.	4.6.45	Cook, J. T.	19.4.45
Canning, B. C.	8.4.45	Clarke, Leonard B.	5.6.45	Cook, L. C.	22.3.45
Canterbury, L. C.	7.5.45	Clarke, Leslie A.	14.6.45	Cooke, W.	10.6.45
Capon, W. A.	3.3.45	Clarkson, J. M.	14.2.45	Cooling, M. W.	8.6.45
Capper, G. H.	21.3.45	Clayton, J. H. V.	7.2.45	Coombe, R. J.	16.3.45
Carleton, R. V.	9.6.45	Clear, J. A.	24.5.45	Cooney, J.	15.4.45
Carley, F. A.	13.6.45	Cleary, A. N.	20.3.45	Cooper, J. A.	5.4.45
Carlson, A. R.	23.5.45	Clement, A.	9.3.45	Cooper, T. S.	16.2.45
Carlson, R. D.	22.6.45	Clements, T.	16.4.45	Cope, W. G.	27.3.45
Carnie, R. M.	17.3.45	Clifford, E. T.	8.2.45	Copelin, H. V.	27.5.45
Carr, B.	6.6.45	Clissold, J. J.	14.7.45	Copp, E. F.	12.5.45
Carroll, M.	10.5.45	Clucas, J. B.	19.5.45	Corbett, J. W. F.	4.3.45
Carson, W. J.	28.2.45	Clydsdale, T. J.	28.3.45	Corcoran, F. L.	10.7.45
Carter, G. C. D.	13.4.45	Clyne, E. F.	27.3.45	Cordy, F.	15.3.45
Carter, P. W. F.	2.3.45	Clyne, P. J.	10.9.45	Core, S. R.	20.6.45
Carthew, J. A. L.	12.2.45	Cochrane, E. A.	6.10.44	Corney, L. C.	25.2.45
Carveth, A. J.	5.6.45	Code, L. J.	2.2.45	Cornish, F.	21.5.45
Cassidy, L. A.	26.4.45	Codlin, J. M.	6.8.45	Costello, J.	21.6.45
Caterson, K. R.	13.6.45	Coffey, M. J.	18.4.45	Costello, K.	1.7.45
Cavenagh, C. R.	25.6.45	Coggins, P. R. N.	7.6.45	Costin, K. H.	21.6.45
Chamberlain, J. P.	8.10.44	Coghlan, R. V.	3.4.45	Coughlan, T.	14.2.45
Chandler, M. A.	28.3.45	Coker, R. H.	7.5.45	Coughlin, C. J.	16.4.45
Chandler, Roland K.	22.3.45	Cole, E. H.	18.5.45	Coulter, W. J. R.	3.6.45
Chandler, Robert W.		Cole, T. W. T.	7.6.45	Coulton, G. L.	14.4.45
See entry for Bateson, D. F.		Coleman, W. J.	2.3.45	Cousins, S. J.	20.6.45
Chant, J. R. A.	2.6.45	Collins, A. C.	12.6.45	Cowley, M. C.	17.5.45
Chapman, A. W.	9.2.45	(served as Smith, A. C.)		Cox, A. H.	7.5.45
Chapman, B. B.	25.4.45	Collins, C. R.	8.6.45	Cox, G. K.	5.4.45
Chapman, C. K.	28.7.45	Collins, H. W.	15.2.45	Cox, L.	20.4.45
Chapman, E. F.	29.3.45	Collins, R. B.	26.4.45	Cox, R. C.	13.4.45
Chapman, J. J.	5.7.45	Collins, S. G.	13.2.45	Coy, F. T.	20.6.45
Chapman, S. H.	3.5.45	Colls, L. W.	16.4.45	Crago, G.	29.11.44
Chapman, W. P.	10.2.45	Columbine, R. E.	7.2.45	Craig, A. C.	26.3.45
Charles, G. F.	7.6.45	(served as Aylett, R.)		Craig, R. F.	8.6.45
Charlton, R. J.	18.7.45	Colville, J. H.		Crane, A. B. E.	9.6.45
Chenhall, N. J.	7.4.45	See entry for Hamilton, J.		Cranney, R. T.	21.4.45
Child, F. T.	19.10.44	Colyer, G. W.	12.2.45	Crapp, H. S.	23.4.45
Chilvers, H. A. T.	31.3.45	Comber, C. O.	28.3.45	Crawford, J. O.	11.7.45
Chipperfield, R. W.	11.2.45	(served as Dempsey, P.)		Crawford, V. O.	7.6.45
Chisholm, H. F.	9.2.45	Commerford, G. F.	9.2.45	Craze, R.	2.4.45
Chisholm, R. S.	7.6.45	Commins, J. S. H.	8.5.45	Crease, W.	14.3.44
Christensen, H. G.	28.2.45	Condon, L. J.	16.5.45	Crees, R. J.	8.2.45
Christiansen, W.	7.6.45	Conley, H. S.	6.4.45	Crewdson, A. J.	27.4.45
Christie, N. M.	5.6.45	Connell, F.	8.4.45	Cribb, T. B.	19.2.45
Clack, J. P.	1.6.45	Connell, J. F.	28.4.45	Crighton, R. S.	20.5.45
Clair, T. E.	1.6.45	Connolly, T. W. J.	9.8.45	Crilly, R. J.	6.4.45
Clark, D. S.	29.12.44	Connor, H. F.	15.3.45	Cripps, W. G.	4.7.45
Clark, F. H.	5.3.45	Connor, J. C.	25.2.45	Crockett, E. R.	7.6.45
Clark, G. W.	8.6.45	Conquit, G. D.	2.6.45	Cross, A. H. W.	23.3.45
Clark, J. C.	15.4.45	Constable, W. A. J.	18.5.45	Cross, J. R.	12.6.45

Crossman, E. R.	4.6.45	Deshon, F. H.	24.4.45	Edwards, George	
Crouch, A. G.	24.4.45	Dezius, F. C.	29.5.45	Everard	25.7.45
Crowther, G. G.	8.3.45	Dickie, G. O.	12.4.45	Edwards, George	
Crumpton, R. F.	5.6.45	Dickman, F. H.	21.5.45	Henry	20.3.45
Cull, A.	17.6.45	Dickson, L. H.	26.5.45	Edwards, H. J.	27.4.45
Cumming, D. A.	21.1.45	Digby, G. H.	30.3.45	Egel, R. C.	6.2.45
Cummings, A. L.	7.6.45	Dixon, J.	9.6.45	Elderton, W. J.	25.3.45
Cummings, N. G.	24.6.45	Dixon, K. A. F.	6.3.45	Elliott, Stanley W.	15.6.45
Cundy, M. H.	4.10.42	Dixon, T. F. U.	24.1.45	Elliott, Sydney	21.2.45
Cunningham, J. M.	22.2.45	Dobson, T. R.	10.6.45	Elliott, T. A.	8.3.45
Currey, J. E.	18.12.44	Docwra, G. A.	26.2.45	Elliott, W. G.	13.1.45
Currey, W. J.	4.7.45	Doherty, L. L.	13.4.45	Ellis, A. G.	15.2.45
Currow, R. W.	28.3.45	Donohue, J. A.	30.5.45	Ellis, K. E.	21.1.45
Dale, A.	14.2.45	Dooley, F. E.	30.1.45	Elsley, G.	1.4.45
Dalton, W. J.	16.11.44	Doran, P. M.	13.2.45	Ely, T. H.	13.2.45
Dalton-Goodwin,		Dorizzi, G.	11.2.45	Emmett, E. V.	31.3.45
C. R.	1.5.43	Dorizzi, H.	11.2.45	Emmett, G.	31.3.45
Darragh, L. A.	20.6.45	Dorizzi, T. H.	11.3.45	Engelhart, N.	2.6.45
Daughters, J. S.	11.2.45	Douglas, W. E.	20.6.45	Ernst, J. A.	8.6.45
Davey, B. A.	9.2.45	Dowling, E.	6.3.45	Erwin, L. R.	2.6.45
Davey, C. W.	4.3.45	Down, T. H.	5.1.45	(served as Irwin, L. R.)	
Davidson, F. G.	4.7.45	Downes, I. G.	12.4.45	Essex, R. F.	14.3.45
Davidson, G. L. H.	10.6.45	Downey, H. A.	8.2.45	Etchell, A. E.	16.2.45
Davidson, R. R.	6.3.45	Downward, N. L.	23.5.45	Etheridge, J. O.	19.7.45
Davies, D. T.	4.1.45	Doyle, A. G.	9.8.45	Evans, B. H.	20.6.45
Davies, E. D.	16.6.45	Doyle, E. A.	15.2.45	Evans, E. C.	11.6.45
Davis, H. R. W. P.	23.2.45	Doyle, L. H.	2.8.45	Evans, G. J.	21.7.45
Davis, J. A.	9.8.45	Doyle, P. J.	12.6.45	Evans, J. W.	16.6.45
Davis, J. T.	5.1.45	Drinkwater, J. R.	10.6.45	Evans, L. M.	14.2.45
Davis, R. J.	13.7.45	Duckworth, S.	10.3.45	Evans, O. R.	12.8.45
Davis, R. V.	7.6.45	Duddington, H.	28.3.45	Evans, R. B.	14.3.45
Davison, E.	13.7.45	Duffy, L. J.	3.4.45	Evans, W. R.	28.8.42
Davison, J.	30.3.45	Duffy, S. D.	19.3.45	Evans, Walter C.	14.6.45
Dawes, L. A.	13.1.45	Duggan, S. J.	26.3.45	Evans, William G.	6.11.42
Dawson, A. B. G.	4.12.44	Duncalf, V. A.	20.1.45	Ewers, C. E.	17.5.45
Dawson, L. K.		Duncan, J. W. H.	15.3.45	Ewing, H.	11.2.45
See entry for Molde, K. C.		Dundas, R. C.	21.3.45	Ezzy, A. J. C.	5.3.45
Dawson, T.	29.4.45	Dunhill, E. G.	4.6.45	Fahey, A. M.	10.8.45
Day, A. T.	26.3.45	Dunhill, M. R.	22.3.45	Falco, J.	26.2.45
Day, G.	8.7.45	Dunkinson, J. L.	12.6.45	Farrell, A. R.	26.1.45
De Faye, C. L.	4.2.45	Dunn, C. H.	21.3.45	Farrell, V. H.	19.7.45
De Faye, J.	3.1.45	Dunne, J. J.	16.4.45	Farrey, L. W.	20.6.45
Deagan, M.	27.5.45	Durand, G. P.	4.2.45	Farrow, H.	30.5.45
DeCosta, G. F.	4.6.45	Dwyer, J.	17.4.45	Feldbauer, T. A.	27.3.45
Delahant, C. W.	21.4.45	Dyer, W.	24.6.45	Ferguson, A. J.	30.7.45
Dell, W. C.	4.3.45	Dyson, F. A.	9.4.45	Ferguson, J.	17.2.45
Demas, H. J.	28.4.45	Dyson, R. R.	19.3.45	Ferguson, K. D.	14.7.45
Dempsey, P.		Earle, L. H.	12.6.45	Ferguson, N. J.	20.6.45
See entry for Comber, C. O.		Earnshaw, W. H.	15.3.45	Ferguson, R. P.	23.3.45
Dempster, C.	6.2.45	Easton, H.	20.4.45	Fergusson, N. W.	14.6.45
Dengate, A. J.	17.6.45	Eastwood, G. E.	21.2.45	Ferris, G. R.	22.3.45
Dennehy, A. C.	24.4.45	Ebzery, T.	5.6.45	Fewer, J. R.	22.3.45

Field, G. L. C.	1.6.45	Fuller, E. J.	14.2.45	Good, G.	13.7.45
Field, S. A.	31.1.45	Fullgrabe, A. C.	20.4.45	Goodear, N. F.	7.6.45
Filewood, A.	1.8.45	Fuss, C. R.	17.3.45	Gooud, L.	18.6.45
Finch, W. H.	7.6.45	Gagan, L. A.	30.7.45	Gordon, T.	15.7.45
Findlay, J. G.	12.6.45	Gale, P. R.	16.4.45	Gould, A. R.	16.3.45
Fingher, E. A.	21.3.45	Gallard, R. F.	30.5.45	Gould, R. G.	3.3.45
(served as Fingher, R. until		Galton, D.	12.7.45	Gow, A. W.	25.6.45
13.10.42)		Gannon, W. J.	17.6.45	Gower, E. H.	15.9.42
Fingher, R.		Garde, H. G.	12.3.45	Graf, P. F.	1.7.45
See entry for Fingher, E. A.		Gardner, I. L. G.	28.3.43	Graham, G. A.	21.2.45
Finn, A. H.	20.7.45	Gardner, C. A.	6.4.45	Graham, J. L.	24.4.45
Finn, J. A.	1.8.45	Gardner, A. W.	5.6.45	Graham, Robert J.	5.6.45
Finn, W. M. G.	6.4.45	Gardner, E. J.	9.7.45	Graham, Ronald	4.6.45
Fisher, P. L.	10.4.45	Garland, A. W.	18.3.45	Graham, W. H.	9.4.45
Fisher, R. J.	16.4.45	Garner, G. C.	5.4.45	Grant, E. T.	21.6.45
Fitzgerald, G. S.	1.6.45	Garrard, J. H.	7.6.45	Grant, F. M.	14.2.45
Fitzgerald, H. R.	7.3.45	Garvin, J. T.	4.6.45	Grant, J. J.	7.6.45
Fitzgerald, J. D.	22.3.45	Gaskin, J.	20.7.45	Grave, R. L.	7.6.45
Fitzgerald, L. N.	15.7.45	Gauld, G. T.	10.2.45	Gray, R. S.	12.3.45
Fitzpatrick, D. A.	10.6.45	Gault, H. R.	27.4.45	Green, A. A.	13.6.45
Fitzpatrick, F. J.	5.8.45	Gaven, J.	11.3.45	Green, E. A.	12.4.45
Flanagan, W. J.	9.6.45	Gay, A. P. R.	14.6.45	Green, T. W.	22.1.45
Flavell, R. R.	17.2.45	Gaynor, B. G.	9.3.45	Greenfeld, F. R.	24.4.45
Flemming, A. C.	17.3.45	Geelan, W.	4.1.45	Greenup, C. R.	12.3.43
Fletcher, B. A.	11.6.45	Gellatly, R. A.	9.7.45	Greenway, A. C.	5.6.45
Fletcher, F. G. W.	11.10.42	Gemmill, S. C.	2.6.45	Greenwood, R. J.	24.6.45
Fletcher, J. S.	10.6.45	Gentle, T. R.	1.6.45	Gregory, G. E. H.	6.5.45
Flett, F. J.	18.8.45	Ghananburgh,		Griffin, K. C.	7.6.45
Flint, A. E.	10.6.45	C. M. M.	7.6.45	Griffin, T. M.	6.2.45
Flood, L. A.	3.7.45	(served as Maurice, C. M.)		Griffiths, E. R.	20.3.45
Floyed, A. E.	12.3.45	Gibbs, S. H.	24.2.45	Grigson, A. G.	9.6.45
Fogarty, J. M. H.	3.3.45	Gibson, J. B.	28.2.45	Grills, V. E.	3.7.45
Fogarty, M. J.	15.11.44	Gibson, N. A.	24.6.45	Grimwood, H.	17.7.45
Folkard, S. B.	10.6.45	Gill, H. M.	23.2.45	Grimwood, J. R.	2.7.45
Foote, P. N.	5.2.45	Gillen, P. P. M.	8.1.45	Grinter, C. A.	28.3.45
Ford, W. D.	3.12.44	Gillespie, W. G.	1.7.45	Grist, N. S.	10.7.45
Forrester, C. H.	15.6.45	Gillett, K.	14.3.45	Grono, P. R.	1.5.45
Forster, W. C. O.	8.3.45	Gilham, A. J. C.	13.3.45	Grosvenor, L. L.	6.3.45
Fosbury, B. J. A.	14.2.45	Gillies, A. J.	20.6.45	Grosvenor, R. J.	30.4.45
Foster, D.	7.6.45	Gilligan, C. A.	22.5.45	Grubb, D.	2.4.45
Fotheringham, T. R.	7.6.45	Gladwin, F. J.	22.1.45	Guinea, J. D.	9.4.45
Fox, E. H.	10.2.45	Glennie, J. T.	15.3.45	Gullidge, H. E.	28.5.45
Foxwell, C. A.	8.5.45	Gloag, D.	1.3.45	Hack, A. M.	4.2.45
Frame, C. W.	19.5.45	Glover, C. R.	24.5.45	Hackland, E. C. C.	27.1.45
Francis, F. C.	24.4.45	Glover, F. M.	18.6.45	(served as Toohey, C. J.)	
Franklin, F. G.	14.2.45	Glover, S.	5.6.45	Haddon, T.	13.7.45
Fraser, T. W.	25.2.45	Gode, H.	24.12.44	Hagston, G.	30.6.45
Frazier, J. W.	3.6.45	Godson, C. H.	6.6.45	Halden, W. J.	23.6.45
French, R. F.	19.7.45	Goldfinch, S. C.	13.7.45	Hales, L. J.	5.4.45
Frost, E. I.	2.8.45	Goldie, J. M.	4.6.45	Hales, R. A.	4.12.44
Frost, H. T.	24.7.45	Golding, R. S.	10.3.45	Hall, R. W.	10.7.45
Fry, V. J.	1.7.45	Goldsworthy, T. W.	20.4.45	Hall, T. B.	12.4.45

Halford, M. E.	29.3.45	Hedley, G. W.	28.4.45	How, V. K.	3.6.45
Haligan, J.	4.2.45	Helliwell, K. J.	19.5.45	Howard, E.	18.11.44
Halls, R. S.	14.10.43	Henley, J. B.	6.6.45	Howell, D. W.	11.6.45
Haly, S. O.	15.6.45	Henley, K. H.	24.4.45	Howson, H. R.	18.3.45
Hamalainen, F. E.	17.3.45	Hensby, H.	27.3.45	Hubbard, E. A. F.	24.6.45
Hamilton, H.	29.5.45	Henwood, E. J.	20.3.45	Huckle, R. A.	24.3.44
Hamilton, J.	30.3.45	Herd, B.	12.7.45	Hughes, A. P.	11.5.45
(served as Colville, J. H.)		Hewitt, H.	4.6.45	Hughes, K. G.	15.7.45
Hams, N. T.	25.3.45	Hewitt, N. L.	5.3.45	Hughes, Robert	4.6.45
Hancock, M. J.	23.4.45	Heyworth, W.	19.4.45	Hughes, Robert Reid	20.3.45
Hancock, W. J.	15.8.45	Hibbert, S. E.	21.11.44	Humbler, B. P.	5.12.44
Hankin, P. E.	15.6.45	Hickman, C.	20.4.45	Humfery, P. C. C.	23.5.45
Hankinson, R. F.	7.6.45	Hicks, H. R.	1.7.45	Humphreys, P. G.	26.5.45
Hannan, M. E.	5.2.45	Hicks, V. O.	11.2.45	Humphries, D.	13.2.45
Hansell, H. N.	27.2.45	Higgison, F. M. H.	12.6.45	Hunt, R. P.	13.2.45
Hanson, K. D.	15.2.45	Higgs, J. A.	12.4.45	Hunt, N. F.	29.5.45
Harcourt, R. B.	3.5.45	Higham, G. E. S.	2.2.45	Hunter, A. C. A.	12.7.45
Harding, L. C.	28.2.45	Hill, C. S.	2.6.45	Hunter, H. D.	4.12.44
Hardstaff, R. A.	14.4.45	Hill, E. T.	28.5.45	Hurley, E. T.	10.12.44
Hardy, A. A.	18.4.45	Hill, W.	4.4.45	Hurst, R. E.	2.4.45
Hardy, G. R.	31.5.45	Hinchcliff, W. H. W.	10.4.45	Hustler, F. E.	5.6.45
Hardy, L. E.	19.5.45	Hine, M.	10.2.45	Hutchinson, J. N.	4.2.45
Hargrave, C. H.	3.3.45	Hitchens, R.	19.4.45	Hutchinson, V.	2.6.45
Hargraves, J. V.	6.6.45	Hobbs, J. S.	4.3.45	Hutchison, C. E.	19.4.45
Harper, B. G.	30.3.45	Hodder, W. J.	31.1.45	Hutchison, G. E.	25.4.45
Harper, H. C.	13.5.45	Hodges, D.	7.6.45	Hutton, A. C.	30.3.45
Harpley, J. C.	20.7.45	Hodges, G.		Hutton, J. K.	22.4.45
Harrington, R. E.	29.5.45	See entry for McIntosh, G. H.		Hyett, R. G.	10.4.45
Harris, Charles	27.5.45	Hodges, J. D. G.	1.7.45	I'Anson, W. L.	1.5.45
Harris, Charles Henry	18.6.45	Hodges, R. E. C.	9.6.45	Iles, C.	21.5.45
Harris, Cyril M.	20.4.45	Hogan, D.	17.10.42	Ince, J. W. J.	4.6.45
Harris, J. O.	2.6.45	Hogbin, C. W.	24.3.45	Ingham, A. E.	29.4.45
Harris, L. A.	4.6.45	Hogg, W.	3.3.45	Ingram, C. E.	5.6.45
Harris, R. C.	19.6.45	Holdaway, L. J.	1.1.44	Ings, E. H.	24.2.45
Harris, S. N.	5.6.45	Holden, N. N.	21.3.45	Ings, J. T.	30.5.45
Harris, W. L.	26.2.45	Holland, H. W.	15.6.45	Ireland, G. A.	15.3.45
Harrison, W. R.	16.3.45	Holland, J.	2.5.45	Irving, R. F.	2.6.45
Harstorff, D. P.	5.6.45	Holland, L. U.	6.7.45	Irwin, L. R.	
Harvey, G. E. O.	8.3.45	Holier, H. F.	12.5.45	See entry for Erwin, L. R.	
Harvey, H. F.	11.5.43	Holme, C.	7.6.45	Isbel, C. E.	25.3.45
Harwood, F.	31.3.45	Holmes, R. F.	12.6.45	Izzard, C. H. M.	19.3.45
Hasluck, L. N.	6.4.44	Holst, E. J.	20.3.45	Jackaman, G. E.	2.6.45
Hasted, J. J.	29.1.45	Honor, B.	8.4.45	Jackes, W. K.	15.3.45
Hastie, L. J.	11.3.45	Hood, R. J.	5.12.44	Jacks, R. J.	11.4.45
Hawkins, C. A.	4.6.45	Hooper, W. R.	21.5.45	Jackson, F. P.	2.7.45
Hay, C. G.	18.2.45	Hopkins, A. G.	10.4.45	Jackson, J.	29.4.45
Haye, L. J.	8.2.45	Hopkins, W. R.	25.7.45	Jackson, Leonard W.	16.4.45
Hayes, J. W.	13.5.45	Horder, R. J.	9.7.45	Jackson, Leslie E.	8.7.45
Hayes, W. C.	12.5.45	Horne, G. D.	5.11.44	Jacobs, C. J.	22.6.45
Hazelgrove, M. B. F.	27.1.45	Horne, N.	1.4.45	Jacobs, G. W.	9.4.45
Headford, F. W.	10.4.45	Hotchin, D. P.	7.3.45	Jacobson, A.	24.12.44
Heaslop, J. E.	19.7.45	Hotston, L.	6.6.45	James, G. L.	12.2.45

James, J. R.	6.7.45	Kemp, H. A. J.	5.4.45	Learmonth, R. G.	6.3.45
James, R. W.	2.4.45	Kemp, M. W.	4.4.45	Lebeau, W. H.	24.1.45
Jantke, R. J.	21.3.45	Kent, E. J.	24.4.45	Ledwidge, F. B.	12.3.45
Jarrett, P.	20.4.45	Kerr, J. R.	15.2.45	Lee, D. H.	4.6.45
Jeavons, J. A.	14.7.45	Kerris, J. L.	26.6.45	Leedham, C. A.	18.2.45
Jeffrey, R. L.	6.5.45	Kilminster, E. G.	4.12.44	LeFevre, R.	6.5.45
Jeffrey, V. A.	13.2.45	Kilpatrick, C. H.	22.3.45	Leinster, V. P.	22.2.45
Jenyns, N. W.	12.6.45	Kilpatrick, J.	3.4.45	Leith, F. A.	22.5.45
Jesperson, T. F.	1.3.45	Kinder, J. W.	10.6.45	Lennon, V. J.	7.2.45
Jewiss, A. C.	13.7.45	King, C. H.	18.7.45	Lester, J.	30.3.45
Jillett, R. E.	5.6.45	King, E.	10.6.45	Lethbridge, T. C.	15.7.45
Johnson, C. G.	11.2.45	King, J. S.	13.6.45	Lever, A. L.	2.6.45
Johnson, H. L.	14.3.45	King, P. C.	17.6.45	Levey, R. E.	14.6.45
Johnson, H. V.	29.6.45	King, R. A.	12.5.45	Levis, H.	16.6.45
Johnson, S. H.	22.6.45	Kingsley, C. M.	2.6.45	Lewis, C. W. G.	17.1.45
Johnson, S. R.	28.2.45	Kinnon, V. R.	7.6.45	Lewis, F. A.	24.3.45
Johnson, A. E.	16.2.45	Kirby, E. A. N.	19.4.45	Lewis, J.	19.4.45
Johnston, A. B.	10.5.45	Kline, J.	16.2.45	Ley, P.	28.4.45
Johnston, C. A.	4.6.45	Knapp, W. G.	15.6.45	Light, J. W.	15.2.45
(served as Johnston, V.)		Knight, H. E.	1.5.45	Lillyman, J. A.	17.6.45
Johnston, C. S.	14.7.45	Knight, V.	16.2.45	Lindqvist, L. R.	29.5.45
Johnston, S. G.	21.4.45	Knight, H. R.	30.1.45	Lindsay, R. L.	18.6.45
Johnston, V.		Knowles, J.	20.2.45	Lister, A. W.	15.6.45
See entry for Johnston, C. A.		Knox, J. W.	22.3.45	Livet, V. L.	7.4.45
Jones, A. F.	2.6.45	Kohler, L. G.	27.3.45	Livingstone, H. H.	28.3.45
Jones, D. H.	13.7.45	Kopanica, J. F.	5.8.45	Lloyd, H. G.	5.6.45
Jones, F. J.	23.5.45	Krieger, L. C.	24.2.45	Loader, K. M.	13.5.45
Jones, H. B.	5.6.45	Kroschel, E. M.	18.1.45	Loan, J. B.	19.1.45
Jones, K.	17.5.45	Kyte, H. G.	18.6.45	Lobegeiger, J.	14.3.45
Jones, W. N.	26.2.45	Laidlaw, A. J.	10.4.45	(served as Randoll, J.)	
Jordan, W. A.	26.5.45	Lake, G.	8.4.45	Lock, B. C.	18.2.45
Joseland, K. A.	1.11.44	Lake, W. T.	25.5.45	Locke, J.	20.3.45
Joynes, C.	7.6.45	Lambert, G.	8.3.45	Logan, R. W. B.	26.3.45
Jubelski, C. W. M.	16.6.45	Lancaster, W. J.	7.6.45	Longbottom, H.	11.2.45
(served as Anderson,		Lane, D. R.	15.1.45	Longley, H.	5.7.45
C. W. M.)		Lane, T. H.	18.4.45	Louray, F. L.	3.6.45
Juchau, R. F.	23.7.45	Lang, J. A.	7.2.45	Love, W. H.	18.11.44
Jukes, C. G. H.	23.7.45	Langton, C. G.	25.5.45	Loveridge, A. A.	9.1.45
Jury, S. H. J.	15.3.45	Larcombe, C. T.	28.2.45	Lowe, A. J.	17.3.45
Justice, A. J.	21.3.45	Larner, V. G.	3.3.45	Lowe, J. T.	15.6.45
Kane, G. F.	12.1.45	Last, A. B.	10.7.45	Ludbey, R. B.	5.11.43
Kavanagh, L. M.	15.2.45	Launder, F. A.	24.5.45	Lumby, V. A.	4.3.45
Kealey, J. V.	30.7.45	Law, A. W.	21.3.45	Lupton, L.	8.4.45
Kearney, J.	24.5.45	Law, R. T.		Lupton, S. J.	5.6.45
Keating, E. J.	5.2.45	See entry for O'Hara, R. T.		Luton, H. W.	4.7.45
Keating, M.	5.2.45	Lawrence, A. S.	18.6.45	(served as McCormick, H.	
Keating, W. M.	3.2.45	Le Clercq, A. E.	4.3.45	W.)	
Keay, V. A.	10.5.45	Le Cussan, E. W.	8.3.45	Lynch, J. J.	20.6.45
Keays, D. C.	19.3.45	Lea, R.	22.3.45	Lyne, G.	4.6.45
Kelly, S. J.	7.6.45	Leadbeatter, W. C.	15.5.45	Lynton, R. L. M.	6.6.45
Kelly, F. W.	21.6.45	Lear, H. B.	17.3.45	Lysaght, H. W.	4.7.45
Kelly, B. H.	8.5.45	Lear, J.	17.6.45	Lytton, H.	15.5.45

Maben, R. R.	31.5.45	Matchett, H. D.	22.7.45	McIntosh, G. H.	11.2.45
Mabin, D. W.	14.2.45	Mathew, A. W.	2.6.45	(served as Hodges, G. until	
Macadam, S. J. A.	3.4.45	Matson, D.		11.10.42)	
Macaulay, W. A.	29.4.45	See entry for Stirling, D. H.		McIver, C. A.	19.8.44
MacDonald, L.	30.5.45	Matthews, L. C.	2.3.44	McIver, G. D.	26.2.45
MacDonald, R. H.	21.2.45	Maunsell, J. F.	19.3.45	McKean, I.	14.6.45
Mackay, F. J.	8.11.42	Maurice, C. M.		McKelvie, M.	24.4.45
Mackay, Theodore		See entry for Ghananburgh,		McKenna, C. R.	1.2.45
R. B.	11.5.43	C. M. M.		McKenzie, W. J.	7.4.45
(served as MacKenzie, D. S.)		Mawhinney, G. B.	20.1.45	McKerrow, E. A.	28.6.45
Mackay, Thomas	2.6.45	May, D. J.	3.8.45	McKinnon, V. H.	14.4.45
MacKenzie, C.	20.4.45	McAppion, H. E.	4.6.45	McLachlan, K. J.	20.6.45
MacKenzie, Douglas		McCall, K. B.	12.4.45	McLachlan, T. D.	31.5.45
H.	22.6.45	McCallum, H. D.	17.4.45	McLaughlin, B. L.	18.3.45
Mackenzie, Duncan	26.2.45	McCardle, P. E. J.	20.4.45	McLaughlin, R. G.	31.3.45
MacKenzie, D. S.		McCarthy, John F.	9.4.45	McLeenan, L. A.	22.5.45
See entry for Mackay,		McCarthy, Joseph F.	1.6.45	McLellan, A. P.	2.6.45
Theodore R. B.		McCarthy, L.	2.3.45	McLennan, L. H.	22.5.45
Mackie, A. G.	13.5.45	McClintock, W. A.	22.3.45	McLeod, C. J.	14.5.45
MacKinnon, D. C.	1.7.45	McClounan, R. L.	9.6.45	McLeod, J. R.	9.3.45
Macklin, K. G.	17.5.45	McConnell, A.	9.6.45	McLeod, W.	28.2.45
Macmeikan, D. J. G.	18.7.45	McConville, J. H.	16.4.45	McMahon, J.	10.7.45
Maconachie, R. D.	5.6.45	McCorley, K.	22.7.45	McManus, S. J. A.	27.3.45
MacPherson, S. D.	19.3.45	McCormack, R. A.	15.4.45	McMartin, J.	7.8.45
Madden, W.	13.7.45	McCormick, H. W.		McNab, R.	
Maddison, J. W.	7.3.45	See entry for Luton, H. W.		See entry for Stewart, B. P.	
Maddock, N. L.	24.7.45	McCracken, W. E.	4.8.45	McNaughton, D.	28.6.46
Maguire, J.	7.6.45	McCrum, A.	25.3.45	McSweeney, J. M.	29.12.44
Mahoney, J.	14.2.45	McCulloch, C. R.	1.3.45	Meagher, G. F.	29.5.45
Mahony, K. P.	24.1.45	McCullough, W.	20.4.45	Meek, E. L.	14.7.45
Main, C. D.	5.6.45	McDonald, A.	5.2.43	Meek, D. R.	18.3.45
Mainstone, C. D.	17.3.45	McDonald, C. H.	3.6.45	Menzies, H. W.	28.5.45
Maizey, C. W.	18.7.45	McDonald, F. R. A.	30.3.45	Mercer, R. L.	4.5.45
Makim, G. J.	17.6.45	McDonald, G. A.	26.12.44	Meredith, D. H.	15.4.45
Malin, W. M.	7.6.45	McDonald, W. B.	13.8.45	Merritt, R. L.	7.6.45
Manks, E. F.	1.6.45	McDonough, J. B.	15.3.45	Midgley, J. J.	16.3.45
Mann, C. N.	2.3.45	McEwan, R. I.	8.7.45	Midlane, D. L.	5.6.45
Mann, W. R.	6.7.45	McEwen, G. A.	1.6.45	Mildenhall, J. S.	9.6.45
Manton, L. C.	22.7.45	McFarlane, J.	20.6.45	Millar, S. B.	29.4.45
Marr, S.	28.3.45	McGeary, E. D.	21.6.45	Miller, A. M.	26.3.45
Marsh, C. K.	8.11.44	McGee, H. A.	25.2.45	Milliken, W. E.	12.2.45
Marsh, W. R.	16.3.45	McGee, W. A.	14.4.45	Mills, J. K.	18.5.45
Marsh, H. A.	8.6.45	McGill, L.	11.4.45	Milne, G. W. H.	14.2.45
Marshall, A.	7.6.45	McGlinn, A. J.	9.7.45	Milne, R. A.	13.4.45
Marshall, J. L.	2.6.45	McGowan, W. J.	3.4.45	Mitchell, A. L.	22.6.45
Marshall, L. F.	5.11.42	McGrath, P. J.	25.4.45	Mitchell, E. E. J.	28.3.45
Marshall, P. O.	3.4.45	McGregor, J. A.	3.5.45	Mitchell, J. W.	20.2.45
Martin, F. J.	4.12.44	McGregor, R.	2.4.45	Mitchell, R. J.	22.6.45
Martin, James T.	18.3.45	McGuire, A. D.	14.7.45	Mitchell, Walter	
Martin, John W.	13.2.45	McHenery, L. G.	7.5.45	Edward	10.5.45
Martin, M. F. J.	4.10.43	McIlhagga, W. J.	19.6.45	Mitchell, Walter	
Maskey, L. W.	9.8.45	McIlroy, K. A.	5.7.45	George	5.2.45

Molan, D. T.	20.5.45	Nagle, M. J.	15.6.45	O'Keefe, H. J.	25.7.45
Molde, K. C.	-.5.45	Nash, C. O.	23.3.45	Olive, E. R. J.	18.5.45
(served as Dawson, L. K.)		Nazzari, F.	24.4.45	Oliver, J.	16.3.45
Molloy, J.	3.5.45	Neal, C. S.	2.10.44	Ollis, J. N.	16.2.45
Molony, S. W.	13.1.45	Neal, F. W.	5.6.45	O'Loughlan, G. J.	4.6.45
Monaghan, H. J.	29.3.45	Neal, K. T.	14.4.45	Olver, K. F.	17.2.45
Mongan, D.	30.10.44	Neal, R.	25.5.45	O'Malley, G. F.	17.2.45
Monley, F. J.	22.2.45	Neale, D. M.	9.3.45	O'Meara, J. J.	9.6.45
Monro, W.	27.5.45	Neale, S. E.	28.2.45	O'Neale, J. T.	3.6.45
Moore, Alan W.	29.3.45	Neale, T. S.	14.9.42	O'Neil, L.	16.12.44
Moore, Albert C.	10.4.45	Neaves, G. M.	7.6.45	O'Neill, C. F.	19.3.45
Moore, C. G.	27.5.45	Negri, P. J.	21.1.45	O'Rourke, T. J.	31.5.45
Moore, Edward G.	4.6.45	Neilson, R. R.	18.11.44	Orr, J. S.	4.3.45
Moore, Edwin J.	1.7.45	Newhouse, F.	12.7.45	Orr, E. J. K.	20.3.45
Moore, J. E.	20.3.45	Newlands, T. S.	5.3.45	Ortloff, F. C.	18.2.45
Moore, L. C.	28.4.45	Newling, R. W.	13.6.45	Osborne, S. A.	21.6.45
Moore, M. F.	13.2.45	Newman, C. W.	11.3.45	Osgood, A.	7.3.45
Moore, R. J.		Newson, J. A.	6.6.45	Otter, L. T.	2.4.45
See entry for Temple, R. J.		Ney, W. C.	2.5.45	Ovens, H.	5.6.45
Moore, S. L.	3.1.45	Nicholls, S. T. A.	1.2.45	Ower, W. J.	18.7.45
Moore, T. A.	31.3.45	Nicholson, E. C.	11.6.45	Page, R. A.	17.2.45
Moran, J. P.	7.4.45	Nicholson, G.	26.1.45	Pallister, R.	5.1.45
Moran, R. K.	28.6.45	Nicholson, J. F. D.	15.2.45	Palmer, A.	11.6.45
Morgan, E.	22.3.45	Nink, L.	20.6.45	Palmer, D.	13.2.45
Morgan, H. C. B.	10.4.45	Nixon, J. H.	1.2.45	Palmer, H. W.	27.3.45
Morgan, L. C.	21.2.45	Noakes, A. H.	13.2.45	Palmer, N. W.	7.6.45
Morgan, L. G.	5.4.45	Noakes, A. W.	27.3.45	Palmer, S. J.	19.4.45
Morgan, N. L.	9.6.45	Noble, F. R.	26.5.45	Panton, O. W.	20.6.45
Morland, R. G.	20.3.45	Nolan, G.	18.6.45	Parfrey, T. H.	10.6.45
Morris, H.	17.1.45	Noon, J. T.	15.3.45	Parham, A. G.	29.6.45
Morris, R. W.	23.6.45	Noonan, E. G.	31.7.45	Parker, N. L.	19.3.45
Morriss, G. B.	9.5.45	Noonan, W. A.	23.7.45	Parkinson, D. S.	19.2.45
Mortimer, C. H.	23.5.45	Nunn, J. O.	9.2.45	Parnell, R. J.	29.5.45
Mortimer, H. W.	17.2.45	Oakeshott, J. B.	27.8.45	Parsons, J. W.	12.7.45
Morton, H. A.	31.3.45	Oakley, J. H.	23.5.45	Partridge, N. E.	4.7.45
Motley, L.	5.6.45	Obee, A. L.	23.4.45	Pascoe-Pearce, B.	15.8.45
Moule-Probert, J.	10.5.45	O'Brien, F.	23.5.45	Pashen, J. W.	3.2.45
Mulligan, R. P.	21.2.45	O'Brien, M. V.	22.6.45	Passmore, E. W.	13.2.45
Mulray, W. P.	6.4.45	O'Brien, W. M.	1.4.45	Paterson, S.	16.3.45
Mulvogue, R. H.	5.3.45	O'Connell, J.	14.1.45	Patten, C. E.	4.3.45
Mumme, L. W.	2.3.45	O'Connor, A. H.	26.2.45	Patterson, R. A.	29.5.45
Munford, F. A.	6.2.45	O'Connor, G.	7.3.45	Patterson, T. B.	18.6.45
Munro, E. L.	3.8.45	O'Connor, H. B.	27.7.45	Patterson, H. A.	21.6.45
Munro, J. F.	28.5.45	O'Connor, J. H.	11.4.45	Patteson, E.	22.2.45
Munro, L. A.	1.6.45	O'Connor, R. M.	15.6.45	Paulett, L.	29.7.45
Murnane, W. J.	26.1.43	O'Donnell, T. E.	28.5.45	Pawson, C.	19.4.45
Murray, D. A.	25.3.45	O'Donohue, E. J.	11.8.45	Paxman, C.	10.6.45
Murray, G. B.	21.4.45	Ogilvie, D. J.	30.6.45	Payne, H. J.	4.6.45
Murray, L. W.	18.10.42	O'Hara, R. T.	25.5.45	Peach, J. T.	16.7.45
Murray, Richard	20.5.45	(served as Law, R. T.)		Peacock, C. K.	15.3.45
Murray, Ronald J.	10.3.45	O'Hara, M. T.	29.5.45	Pearce, J. S.	7.6.45
Myers, C. D.	29.4.45	Ohlson, F. J.	2.2.45	Pearce, K. J.	8.6.45

Pearce, W. H.	1.4.45	Pryor, D. R.	16.4.45	Rickerby, K. W.	19.6.45
Peck, F.	16.3.45	Purcell, J. S.	17.6.45	Ridler, C. J. A.	5.3.45
Pederson, P. M.	21.1.45	Purdon, T.	18.3.45	Righetti, L. J.	17.2.45
Pegnall, C. W.	2.5.45	Pursell, A. L.	6.4.45	Ring, R.	29.6.45
Peoples, D. J.	9.2.45	Purtill, J. F.	20.4.45	Robbins, T. H.	4.6.45
Pepper, C. D.	30.5.45	Purvis, R. C.	4.6.45	Roberts, F.	23.6.45
Pepper, G. D.	10.3.45	Quailey, A. C.	16.2.45	Roberts, Hubert A.	5.3.45
Percival, E. J.	25.2.45	Quintal, E. A.	2.2.45	Roberts, Harold E.	26.3.45
Perrott, C. E.	15.2.45	Radcliffe, K. E.	28.9.44	Roberts, L. J.	13.2.45
Perry, J. C.	28.5.45	Radford, C.	26.2.45	Roberts, Stanley	19.6.45
Perry, K. G.	18.2.45	Radnedge, G.	20.6.45	Roberts, Sydney	21.5.45
Perry, W. G.	5.6.45	Rae, J.	13.7.45	Roberts, W. F.	30.3.45
Perry-Circuitt, E. F.	17.4.45	Raison, V. R.	2.6.45	Robertson, E. E.	23.5.45
Peters, C. J.	7.6.45	Raleigh, J.	23.7.45	Robertson, F. H.	11.7.45
Peters, K. A.	7.6.45	Ralph, B. D.	18.2.45	Robertson, G. C.	22.3.45
Peterson, J. W.	8.7.45	Ralph, W. D.	12.1.45	Robertson, R. J.	20.6.45
Phelan, M. J.	27.6.45	Ramsay, G. A.	21.7.45	Robins, C. W.	9.2.45
Phelps, R. L.	12.4.45	Randoll, J.		Robinson, B. A.	23.5.45
Phillips, B.	3.6.45	See entry for Lobegeiger, J.		Robinson, Frank	10.4.45
Phillips, E. J.	27.4.45	Rankin, C. F.	18.4.45	Robinson, Frank Gordon	
Phillips, R.	26.7.45	Rankin, C. W.	16.2.45	Blanchard	14.2.45
Phillips, W. A.	22.1.45	Rankin, G. H.	19.4.45	Robinson, G. B.	8.3.45
Picken, J.	3.4.43	Rankin, J. R.	15.3.45	Robinson, H.	4.6.45
Pickering, J. A.	27.3.45	Raphael, H. N.	2.6.45	Robinson, J. F.	29.6.45
Picone, D. G.	27.8.45	Ratcliff, R. B.	8.5.45	Rochford, F.	30.3.45
Pile, E. N.	13.6.45	Rawlings, B. A.	15.4.45	Rodgers, E. A.	7.6.45
Piper, R.	21.5.45	Raymond, K. M.	10.2.45	Rodriguez, J. F.	4.2.45
Platford, J.	23.5.45	Rea, E. H.	1.6.45	Roebuck, J. T.	16.5.45
Platt, S. H.	26.5.45	Read, W. G.	15.7.45	Rogers, J. S.	17.7.45
Player, G. C.	7.6.45	Reading, T. A.	11.8.45	Rolls, W. F.	9.4.45
Plewes, K. A.	15.3.45	Reardon, F. W.	9.6.45	Rooke, D. R.	6.4.45
Plunkett, G. W.	14.6.45	Reay, S. V. J.	8.2.45	Rooke, R. G.	19.6.45
Plunkett, J.	3.4.45	Redman, W. H.	12.8.42	Ross, D.	23.5.45
Pogson, C. R.	15.6.45	Reed, E. A.	19.9.43	Ross, J. H. N.	10.2.45
Pontin, R. W.	26.6.45	Reid, D. A.	29.6.45	Ross, W.	12.2.45
Pope, J. G.	2.3.45	Reid, F. C. D.	20.6.45	Rouse, J. F.	2.6.45
Porritt, N. A.	20.5.45	Reid, W.	27.12.44	Rouse, M. H.	17.3.45
Porteous, A. A.	3.11.44	Reid, R. D.	27.2.45	Rowan, H. J.	24.5.45
Potter, N.	25.3.45	Reilly, V. A.	2.6.45	Rowe, C. H.	5.6.45
Powell, C. A.	3.9.44	Reither, H.	8.8.45	Rowley, B.	16.3.45
Powell, L. V.	29.7.45	Reitze, H.	30.5.45	Ruane, R. M.	25.6.45
Powell, K. N.	17.6.45	Renaud, E. C.	14.3.45	Rudd, W. T.	13.7.45
Power, C. G. R.	20.7.45	Rendall, D.	9.6.45	Rummell, V. C.	18.3.45
Power, R. G.	8.5.45	Rennie, O. A.	7.6.45	Rundle, C. A.	5.7.45
Praetz, N. H.	7.6.45	Reynolds, C.	5.6.45	Ruscoe, G.	2.6.45
Prendergast, J. J.	18.6.45	Richards, Evan	7.6.45	Rush, M. J.	8.2.45
Pride, V. H.	27.5.45	Richards, Edward M.	18.3.45	Russell, A. W.	23.5.45
Priest, H. E.	6.4.45	Richards, R. M.	11.2.45	Ryan, James Gregory	18.4.45
Priester, F.	22.3.45	Richardson, Jack L.	4.6.45	Ryan, James Joseph	5.4.45
Pringle, F. W.	14.2.45	Richardson, John G.	23.5.45	Ryan, R. T.	7.6.45
Prior, L.	18.4.45	Richardson, L. W.	18.6.45	Ryan, W. A.	4.6.45
Prosser, W. R.	15.2.45	Richmiller, K. J.	30.4.45	Sadler, R. E. H.	1.6.45

Salter, P. J.	14.2.45	Sinnamon, F.	7.6.45	Sorby, W. T.	20.1.45
Sampson, H. R.	23.3.45	Skews, R. M.	7.6.45	Sotheron, B. E.	3.4.45
Sandercock, H. A.	3.4.45	Skinner, E. K.	16.6.45	Soutar, G. A. J.	2.6.45
Sankowsky, R. H.	15.2.45	Skinner, G. T.	17.1.45	Speake, C. R.	25.5.45
Savage, E.	10.6.45	Skinner, J. F.	15.8.45	Spears, N.	13.11.42
Savage, T.	30.1.45	Skinner, T. R.	17.4.45	Spence, R. H. C.	31.5.45
Sawford, B. G.	11.4.45	Slatter, A. J.	23.3.45	Spencer, H. F.	27.3.45
Scambrey, W. E.	20.3.45	Sleep, J.	6.7.45	Sproul, L. J.	3.5.45
Schibeci, D.	13.6.45	Sligar, G. W.	5.2.45	Spurling, T.	11.3.45
Schiphorst, A.	17.3.45	Sligo, N.	31.8.42	Spurway, R. S.	21.4.45
Schmutter, W. J.	18.7.45	Slip, E. C.	17.3.45	St Leon, G.	3.6.45
(served as Smoother, W. J.)		Small, Robert Darcy	23.6.45	Stace, R. A.	7.6.45
Scholefield, R. B.	18.7.45	Small, Robert Percy	8.4.45	Stacy, R. L.	25.7.45
Schutt, L. V.	2.4.45	Smalldon, H. J.	4.7.45	Staggs, F. L.	31.3.45
Scollen, T. P.	7.5.45	Smeeton, B. L. J.	15.2.45	Standring, H. C.	8.4.45
Scott, C.	14.4.45	Smith, Alan C.		Stanley, J. R.	25.5.45
Scott, James	19.1.45	See entry for Collins, A. C.		Stanley, R.	8.2.45
Scott, John M.	28.2.45	Smith, Albert A.	25.3.45	Stanton, A. J.	16.7.45
Scully, J. S.	20.3.45	Smith Alexander J.	14.4.45	Stanton, E.	18.3.45
Searle, L. E.	7.6.45	Smith, Andrew W. L.	29.1.45	Stanwell, O. M.	12.3.45
Seeley, J. W.	5.1.45	Smith, C. T.	24.3.45	Stapleton, T. N.	18.12.44
Sefton, B. L.	1.3.45	Smith, Edward Isaacs	15.3.45	Starkie, J. D. F.	10.5.45
Sefton, I. G.	4.4.45	Smith, Edward Walter	5.5.45	Starky, C. B.	17.1.45
Sevier, J.	7.6.45	(served as Andrews, S.		Steel, J. A.	25.6.45
Sewell, A. E.	5.3.45	until 11.5.42)		Steele, A. R.	10.5.45
Shackell, J. H.	14.4.45	Smith, Elwin S.	14.7.45	Steen, W. S.	15.7.45
Sharp, W.	1.4.45	Smith, Ernest	8.3.43	Steinbeck, W. J.	15.7.45
Shaw, A. D.	10.6.45	Smith, Francis Albert		Stevens, Charles	13.12.44
Shaw, R.	19.7.44	Oliver	7.6.45	Stevens, Clarence	
Shaw, G.	19.4.45	Smith, Francis Sidney	17.5.45	C. H.	18.4.45
Shaw, D. R.	17.3.45	Smith, George	7.6.45	Stevens, J. J.	19.4.45
Sheard, W. A.	15.5.45	Smith, George Jesse		Stevenson, T. S.	11.2.45
Shearman, S. G.	31.3.45	Howe	4.6.45	Stewart, A. B.	4.2.45
Sheedy, R. H.	27.3.45	Smith, Gordon A.	8.3.45	Stewart, B. P.	29.1.45
Shelvock, C. B.	17.4.45	Smith, H. V. G.	1.6.45	(served as McNab, R.)	
Shepherd, G. A.	2.8.45	Smith, Jack D.	16.3.45	Stewart, Herbert J.	25.5.45
Shepherd, W. P.	5.6.45	Smith, James S.	13.3.45	Stewart, Henry T. H.	21.6.45
Sherman, M. O.	16.3.45	Smith, John B. I.	13.2.45	Stewart, P.	8.7.45
Sherring, F.	12.2.45	Smith, M. H.	1.12.44	Stewart, S. K.	25.12.44
Sherwood, S.	22.4.45	Smith, O.	27.6.45	Stewart, W.	14.5.45
Shields, E. J.	7.6.45	Smith, Reginald E.	31.3.45	Stirling, C.	16.6.45
Shields, R.	21.11.44	Smith, Robert J. V.	10.11.42	Stirling, D. H.	15.7.45
Shipsides, R. A.	3.4.45	Smith, T. E.	18.12.44	(served as Matson, D.)	
Shirley, A. F.	10.5.45	Smith, William Henry	5.3.45	Stirling, G. M	23.5.45
Short, E. R.	26.4.45	Smith, William James	14.4.45	Stockley, R. R. W.	1.3.45
Short, M. N.	13.7.45	Smith, William Samuel		Stolarski, C. D.	24.3.45
Simpson, Henry J.	2.6.45	Charles	7.6.45	Stone, H. D.	12.5.45
Simpson, Herbert J.	10.2.45	Smoother, W. J.		Stone, R. D.	17.2.45
Simpson, L. P.	10.3.45	See entry for Schmutter, W. J.		Storey, G. J.	27.3.45
Simpson, S. A.	24.3.45	Smyth, C. G.	7.5.45	Strachan, G.	6.4.45
Sinclair, Ivan A. D.	5.8.45	Solomon, J. H.	11.2.45	Strang, P. M.	20.2.45
Sinclair, Ivor M.	9.3.45	Sommerville, A. C.	14.4.45	Strout, E. A.	28.3.45

Stuchbury, I.	17.11.44	Thoroughgood, H. J.	10.2.45	Walsh, F. V.	4.3.45
Sullivan, D.	18.1.45	Thorpe, H.	8.4.45	Walsh, L. J.	22.1.45
Sullivan, R. E.	31.3.45	Thurston, H. W.	11.3.45	Walter, R. W.	24.6.45
Sullivan, R. H.	17.6.45	Tickle, W.	24.2.45	Walters, A. F.	18.2.45
Sutton, J. E.	23.3.45	Tierney, J. E.	17.6.45	Walters, L. E.	4.3.45
Swan, C. W.	5.3.45	Tierney, M. J.	2.6.45	Walton, D. R.	7.6.45
Swan, W. A.	1.2.45	Tinning, R. J.	23.5.45	Wapling, J. H.	22.5.45
Swift, D. S.	30.6.45	Tipping, N. A.	4.7.45	Ward, M. A.	10.6.45
Sykes, R. W.	11.7.45	Tolliday, A. S.	18.2.45	Ward, R.	22.4.45
Syme, A. J.	4.6.45	Tomkyns, E. A.	25.6.45	Ward, S. W.	2.4.45
Symes, A. V. J.	11.4.45	Toms, H.	2.4.45	Wardale-Greenwood,	
Symons, G. H.	10.4.45	Toohey, C. J.		Rev. H.	12.7.45
Tait, R.	16.3.45	See entry for Hackland,		Wardman, J.	10.6.44
Tanko, V. K.	7.2.45	E. C. C.		Warner, B.	15.6.44
Tanner, V. G.	21.2.45	Toombs, R. E.	23.5.45	Warren, H. J.	22.3.45
Tanzer, H. J.	2.6.45	Travis, J. H.	2.6.45	Warren, J. M.	14.6.45
Tapper, S. G.	6.3.45	Treseder, H. A.	12.5.45	Warrington, C. W.	14.5.45
Taylor, A. A.	13.3.45	Trevillien, R. G.	25.1.45	Wastnidge, R.	13.2.45
Taylor, D.	1.4.45	Trigwell, A. G.	4.5.45	Waterhouse, A.	30.1.45
Taylor, George Lane	7.6.45	Trinder, L. G.	5.6.45	Waters, A. J. L.	9.6.45
Taylor, George William	2.3.45	Trodd, R. J.	22.10.44	Watson, Clarence	14.3.45
Taylor, Gordon		Tuckerman, J. H.	18.6.45	Watson, Charles Y.	6.3.45
Creswell	14.4.45	Tully, N. M.	1.7.45	Watson, F. W.	4.7.45
Taylor, Gordon James	12.4.45	Turner, A. J.	19.6.45	Watson, T. N.	15.12.44
Taylor, Horace B.	4.6.45	Turner, E. H.	18.6.45	Watson, W. J. H.	23.3.45
Taylor, Henry T.	5.6.45	Turner, K. M.	15.7.45	Watters, L. L.	22.12.44
Taylor, I.	3.5.45	Turner, N.	23.3.45	Watts, D. L.	20.7.45
Taylor, J. A.	5.2.45	Turner, Harold		Watts, E. R.	17.6.45
Taylor, N. H.	5.6.45	Raymond	8.5.45	Watts, T. J.	15.3.45
Taylor, T. C.	26.7.45	Turner, Harold		Weatherby, W. S.	15.7.45
Taylor, W. C.	8.5.45	Robert	18.2.45	Webber, S. A.	10.8.45
Telford, G. F.	12.12.44	Turner, R. E.	25.1.45	Webster, A. G.	2.6.45
Temple, R. J.	3.4.45	Twiss, R. T.	15.10.44	Weeks, F. N.	4.2.45
(served as Moore, R. J.)		Tyres, K. H.	5.2.45	Wehl, F. G.	2.8.45
Tennyson, B. G.	7.5.45	Tyrrell, A.	24.6.45	Weir, S. J.	15.7.45
Terrett, E.	7.8.45	Tyrrell, Reginald C.	23.7.45	Weissel, G.	23.5.45
Thistlethwaite, V.	15.7.45	Tyrell, Ronald C.	7.2.45	Welch, W. A.	9.6.45
Thomas, A. D.	10.8.44	Varrie, G. B.	7.6.45	Wellard, C. J.	8.6.45
Thomas, E.	21.3.45	Vaughan, W. J.	30.7.45	Wells, G. D. W.	5.7.45
Thomas, J. O.	15.5.45	Veal, R. J.	8.3.45	Wells, H. G.	4.3.45
Thomas, M. G.	26.5.45	Victorsen, L. M.	18.3.45	West, J. S.	20.2.45
Thompson, Rev. A. H.	19.6.45	Vogele, G. L.	14.2.45	Weston, W. E.	14.3.45
Thompson, F.	10.6.45	Vollheim, E. C. N.	12.2.45	Westwood, B.	1.7.45
Thompson, R. J. E.	30.3.45	Wachner, E. C.	24.3.45	Wheeler, J. E.	28.6.45
Thompson, V. R.	23.5.45	Waddington, G.	10.6.44	Whereat, M. C.	22.3.45
Thompson, W.	4.3.45	Walker, E. T.	9.6.45	White, A. M.	
Thomson, A.	13.1.45	Walker, J. S.	19.2.45	See entry for Adams, A. M.	
Thomson, E. F.	1.4.45	Walker, N. G.	11.2.45	White, B.	6.4.45
Thonder, W. C.	19.6.45	Walker, R. G.	2.7.45	White, C. H.	6.4.45
Thorley, I. E.	4.3.45	Wall, R. H.	1.3.45	White, J. A.	5.6.45
Thorneycroft, C. H.	30.10.44	Wallace, H. W.	19.1.45	White, L. A.	10.6.45
Thorns, A. S.	8.8.45	Waller, T.	5.6.45	White, S. H.	6.2.45

Whitehead, B. C.	13.7.45	William	9.2.45	Woodford, C. A.	30.5.45
Whitehead, W.	15.2.45	Wilson, George	20.1.45	Woodley, E. G.	5.8.45
Whitelaw, J. R.	26.7.45	Wilson, George		Woodley, F. E.	6.2.45
Whiting, W. G.	17.7.45	Edward	13.5.45	Woods, C. J.	8.2.45
Whybird, J. A.	14.7.45	Wilson, H.	16.3.45	Woods, F. H.	6.7.45
Whyman, H. A.	24.3.45	Wilson, L. A.	30.12.44	Woods, M. P.	10.3.45
Whyte, R. J. R.	5.6.45	Wilson Robert J.	24.7.45	Woolard, A. I.	6.3.45
Wilkes, H. R.	4.6.45	Wilson, Roderick S.	13.5.45	Woolnough, A. W. J.	15.2.45
Wilkie, J.	17.5.45	Wilson, Ronald M.	25.12.44	Worby, R. P.	19.6.45
Wilkins, G. H.	9.4.45	Wilson, S. C.	16.6.45	Worland, N. C.	15.2.45
Wilkins, K.	3.2.45	Winks, A. K.	7.7.45	Wraight, D. C. C.	11.2.45
Wilkinson, D. L.	8.8.45	Winning, H.	7.2.45	Wright, Cyril	8.6.45
Williams, A. T.	5.7.45	Winter, S. C.	2.3.45	Wright, Colin L.	13.6.45
Williams, G. E.	15.2.45	Winterbottom, A.	5.6.45	Wright, F. P.	12.6.45
Williams, H. P.	14.4.45	(served as Winters, T.)		Wright, T. J.	16.1.45
Williamson, L. R.	4.6.45	Winters, T.		Wrigley, Keith H.	25.7.45
Willmott, A. C.	29.6.45	See entry for		Wrigley, Kenneth G.	26.2.45
Wilmott, A. J.	10.1.45	Winterbottom, A.		Wye, F. R. C.	21.3.45
Willmott, K. W. A.	15.5.45	Wiseman, E. W.	10.6.45	Wynn, W. E.	21.3.45
Wilson, Albert	2.7.45	Wiseman, R. H.	30.7.45	Yates, G.	9.3.45
Wilson, Albert		Witt, K. C.	20.4.45	Young, A. D.	16.3.45
Edward	29.11.44	Wolfe, E. J.	2.7.45	Young, C. F.	27.7.45
Wilson, Charles W.	23.5.45	Wolfe, G.	7.6.45	Young, David	26.5.45
Wilson, Clarence B.	23.5.45	Wolter, G. J.	3.2.45	Young, Donald G. C.	21.6.45
Wilson, D. G.	21.3.45	Wood, R. B.	2.11.44	Young, J. S.	4.4.45
Wilson, Edward	27.3.45	Woodall, J.	7.6.45	Young, T. O.	10.6.45
Wilson, Edward		Woodcroft, K. R.	10.12.45	Zinn, A. C.	20.11.44

Source: Dr Richard Reid, *Sandakan 1942–1945*, Department of Veterans' Affairs, Canberra, 2008

BRITISH (658 MEN)

Name	Date of death				
Allen, J.	21.2.45	Barker, M. E.	27.1.45	Benn, E. T.	12.5.45
Allson, K. G.	12.7.45	Barlow, W. J.	25.1.45	Bennett, R. J.	15.12.44
Allsop, K. H.	14.3.45	Barnes, F. W.	15.6.45	Bentley,W. P.	21.3.45
Amoss, A. C.	4.2.45	Barnes, L. S.	22.4.45	Bessant, J. W.	1.5.45
Anderton, W. C.	2.3.45	Bartlett, A. E.	21.3.45	Bird, C. G.	12.8.45
Andrews, H.	27.3.45	Bassett, E.	6.3.45	Bird, F. L.	11.3.45
Aplin, C. E.	24.7.45	Bates, E. C. S.	27.5.45	Bird, M. C.	21.3.45
Archibald, T. M.	15.2.45	Batty, L. G.	21.4.45	Bishop, E. G.	1.2.45
Ashlin, B.	12.3.45	Baulcombe, H. J.	21.3.45	Black, L. W.	3.6.45
Ashmore, H.	10.3.45	Bayer, J. H.	2.8.45	Blazley, T. W.	1.7.44
Austin, T. H.	16.7.45	Beale, E. P.	4.4.45	Bluck, H. G.	22.5.45
Aynsley, F. A.	16.6.45	Beardshaw, H.	-.5.45	Blyth, J. W.	1.7.45
Baguley, L.	26.7.45	Beardsley, J.	17.6.45	Booth, F.	6.3.45
Bagwell, A. A. C.	7.6.45	Beck, J. T.	20.6.45	Bourne, R.	10.3.45
Baker, T. C.	21.3.45	Beever, E.	30.6.45	Boutcher, D. G.	14.4.45
Baker, W. G.	28.3.45	Bell, A.	9.6.45	Bowden, J. A.	16.7.45
Bareham, W. J.	1.3.45	Bellamy, H. W.	14.6.45	Boyd, J.	15.2.45

Brackenbury, K. S.	19.6.45	Collins, A. E.	28.2.45	Fairgray, N.	27.4.45
Brady, C.	17.3.45	Collins, D. G.	8.3.45	Faulks, C. H.	20.2.45
Bramley, C. A.	22.3.45	Coombs, J.	22.2.45	Feltham, M. R.	29.3.45
Bratt, F.	14.3.45	Coppin, E. J.	21.12.44	Fenn, N.	4.4.45
Brett, P. J.	30.3.45	Cosham, K. F.	9.1.45	Fenner, R. A.	20.2.45
Broadbent, F.	30.6.45	Cossens, R. E.	5.1.45	Fielding, T. O.	29.3.45
Brom, C. E.	29.1.45	Cossey, C. E.	10.3.45	Filbey, C. H.	10.2.45
Broom, C. L.	23.3.45	Costello, M. T.	6.1.45	Fillingham, W.	29.3.45
Brown, A. E.	2.3.45	Cox, A.	17.3.45	Finch, R. F.	20.4.45
Brown, L. D.	6.3.45	Cox, J. W.	19.2.45	Finnigan, W.	15.7.45
Brown, R. H.	27.1.45	Cressey, S. W.	28.4.45	Fisher, E.	17.2.45
Brown, W.	22.4.45	Crombie, R.	18.6.45	Fisher, T. W. S.	4.4.45
Buckingham, H. F.	22.7.45	Crone, J. K.	4.3.45	Fishwick, W.	26.12.44
Buckle, H.	6.3.45	Crook, A. L.	30.3.45	Fitzgerald, H. J.	12.6.45
Bull, W. G.	19.3.45	Crow, W. S.	27.6.45	Fletcher, J.	22.3.45
Bundock, G. E.	21.6.45	Cryer, E.	28.3.45	Fletcher, S. N.	14.5.45
Burdett, N.	23.7.45	Cunningham, E.	14.6.45	Flinn, M. M.	13.2.45
Burgess, H. G.	14.3.45	Curtis, R. S.	21.3.45	Foley, M.	4.6.45
Burgess, R.	7.6.45	Daniels, F. L. K.	27.8.45	Ford, E.A.	13.3.45
Burgess, R. R.	12.4.45	Darby, P. E.	22.6.45	Forster, J. J.	16.6.45
Burke, G.	29.3.45	Davey, W.	16.4.45	Foster, E.	4.3.45
Burroughs, J. G.	27.3.45	Davies, C. A. C.	28.4.45	Foster, L.	12.2.45
Butt, H. J.	29.9.43	Davies, J. I.	10.3.45	Frampton, E. J.	15.4.45
Camberg, D.	13.2.45	Davies, L.	18.6.45	Frater, A.	4.7.45
Campbell, T. M.	1.6.43	Davies, T. B.	28.2.45	Freeman, P. R. C.	4.5.45
Campling, F. S.	30.12.44	Davis, E.	13.3.45	Frost, D. A.	26.3.45
Cann, W. G.	24.2.45	Davison, G. M.	17.3.45	Frost, N.	21.1.45
Carson, C.	29.3.45	Deacon, W. J.	19.6.45	Gallagher, J.	24.3.45
Cartwright, E.	6.4.45	Dennison, A. C.	17.6.45	Gane, J.	8.7.45
Carver, P.	12.7.45	Doe, J. H.	7.1.45	Gardiner, A. L.	19.3.45
Castle, S. H. L.	30.6.45	Drew, J. S.	24.7.45	Gardner, H. D.	13.3.45
Challis, G.	3.4.45	Drew, R. E.	19.5.45	Garman, H.	16.2.45
Chapple, I.	21.4.45	Dunnett, J.	16.4.45	Garrad, E. F.	16.2.45
Charles, J.	8.2.45	Durham, J. A.	22.3.44	Gates, A. I.	16.3.45
Charlesworth, R. S.	24.2.45	Durrant, R. J.	29.3.45	Gavigan, E. P.	4.12.44
Cherry, F. A.	9.7.45	Dyer, W. V.	22.2.45	Geddes, W.	14.4.45
Chinchen, H. J.	5.5.45	Eaden, R. S.	4.2.45	Gibbs, C. F.	8.2.45
Chopping, G. N.	27.8.45	East, E. J.	29.5.45	Giffen, W.	5.6.45
Clark, A. C.	29.7.45	Edden, S. V.	17.2.45	Gilder, A. J.	29.4.45
Clark, H. E.	8.3.45	Edwards, J.	16.4.45	Glover, J. B.	26.9.44
Clark, R. W. J.	2.4.45	Edwards, S. E.	12.6.45	Godlonton, A. G.	21.4.45
Clarke, H. B.	13.2.45	Efford, P. H.	27.2.45	Gollop, W. D.	10.3.45
Clayton, J.	11.6.45	Elder, A. H.	21.3.45	Goodwin, F. R.	27.8.45
Cliff, R.	11.12.44	Elliott, D. V.	31.3.45	Gordon, H. C.	21.2.45
Cliff, S.	18.2.45	Endersby, R. W.	19.2.45	Gould, W. J.	7.1.45
Clouter, F. J.	19.2.45	Engstrom, R. C. B.	16.4.45	Graham, A.	19.3.45
Coffin, E.	29.5.45	Epstine, A.	7.6.45	Granger, H. P.	7.6.45
Coggon, H.	7.5.45	Evans, F. G.	22.5.45	Gray, J. D.	24.3.45
Coghlan, N.	23.6.43	Evans, J. W.	4.5.43	Green, H.	18.4.45
Cole, E. F.	8.12.44	Evans, T. F.	22.5.45	Green, H. W.	8.3.45
Cole, F. G. H.	14.2.45	Eyles, W. A. R.	23.3.45	Green, T. W.	22.3.45
Cole, P. W.	14.6.45	Failes, C. E.	7.6.45	Gregson, A.	28.3.45

Grewcock, L. H.	6.6.45	Hoof, A.	21.3.45	Lane, A.	23.2.45
Grice, R. W.	15.2.45	Hopkinson, H.	25.4.45	Lanham, H.	17.3.45
Griffiths, D. M.	6.3.45	Horrell, F.	21.3.45	Larter, G. R.	13.3.45
Griffiths, E. S.	25.2.45	Hudgell, H. E.	28.2.45	Latham, R.	2.4.45
Griffiths, I.	1.4.45	Hughes, A. J.	5.6.45	Law, D. R.	6.4.45
Groundon, F. G.	5.4.45	Hughes, B. F.	10.3.45	Lawrence, E. G.	30.6.45
Groves, F.	25.7.45	Hughes, D. J.	2.5.45	Lealand, J.	8.3.45
Guerin, D.	18.2.45	Humphreys, J. H.	19.3.45	Leclercq, R. R.	12.5.45
Guy, G.	2.4.45	Humphries, W. G.	24.3.45	Lee, R.	22.1.45
Hall, J. E. W.	14.4.45	Hutchinson, J.	8.2.45	LeFevre, R.	22.6.45
Hall, L.	22.2.45	Iles, R. J.	22.4.45	Leslie, G.	31.12.44
Hall, R.	23.4.45	Ingham, H.	17.3.45	Lester, C. F.	16.3.45
Hall, R. J.	21.12.44	Ireland, H. S.	16.1.45	Levins, P.	17.6.45
Hallsey, G. T.	28.2.45	Jacobi, H. C.	11.6.45	Lewis, V. A.	22.1.45
Hammond, B. I.	2.3.45	Jacobs, A.	27.2.45	Linge, A. J.	16.3.45
Hanley, J.	9.6.45	James, H. O.	16.6.45	Litten, A. J. E.	13.2.45
Hannant, N. J.	20.1.45	Jamieson, J.	14.7.45	Littlewood, E. L.	30.3.45
Hardacre, G.	22.10.44	Jardine, A.	12.3.45	Lockhart, J.	22.7.45
Hardman, J.	9.6.45	Jazewcis, W.	5.4.45	Lomas, G. T.	3.3.45
Harold, R. R.	24.6.45	Jefferies, J. P.	28.2.45	Long, G.	29.12.44
Harrington, D. F.	19.3.45	Jefferson, H. T. A.	16.2.45	Longhurst, L. E.	22.3.45
Harris, B.	19.1.44	Jewell, W. J.	2.7.45	Longworth, T.	7.3.45
Harris, C. W.	10.4.45	Johnson, E.	14.6.45	Lucas, C. R. G.	25.4.45
Harris, J.	9.6.45	Johnson, J. E.	17.2.45	Luscott, T.	27.2.45
Harrison, H.	26.3.45	Johnson, K. A.	20.6.45	Mace, A. F.	9.5.45
Harrold, J. G.	14.7.45	Jones, B. P.	14.2.45	Madeley, J. W.	1.3.45
Hart, M.	7.7.45	Jones, C.	12.6.45	Maguire, C.	20.6.45
Haslam, S. J.	13.6.45	Jones, E. B.	14.1.45	Maguire, J.	9.4.45
Hawkins, C.	8.3.45	Jones, J. H.	27.3.45	Mahon, E. O.	14.3.45
Hawkins, E. R.	5.7.45	Jones, M. P.	9.2.45	Maitland, T.	11.5.45
Hayward, S. A.	24.2.45	Jones, T.	23.3.45	Mannix, J.	31.3.45
Hazeltine, J.	12.6.45	Jones, T.	29.3.45	Marriott, P. C.	13.2.45
Hazzard, E. J.	1.4.45	Jones, T.	3.3.45	Marsden, J.	10.3.45
Henshall, N. H.	18.3.45	Jones, W. F.	4.10.44	Marsh, E. A.	11.12.44
Hester, W. V.	11.7.45	Jordan, F. J.	21.7.45	Martin, J. R.	31.3.45
Heywood, C. J.	15.2.45	Keable, L. A.	24.2.45	Mason, W.	22.3.45
Hickson, F.	5.4.45	Kearney, F. W.	8.7.45	Matthews, T.	30.4.45
Hill, J.	12.6.45	Keaveney, P. E.	7.6.45	Matthews, T. R.	15.6.45
Hill, W. R.	1.3.45	Keeble, N.	26.3.45	Maylam, H. E.	3.4.45
Hirstle, L.	16.1.45	Kelly, H. A.	15.2.45	McArthur, P.	16.4.45
Hitchens, R.	27.8.45	Kemp, H. A. J.	12.3.45	McCandless, J. R.	21.6.45
Hobbs, F. W.	26.11.44	Kennerley, K.	3.4.45	McComisky, H.	15.6.45
Hodges, T.	16.9.44	Kent, G. H.	5.3.45	McConnell, W. S.	31.3.45
Hodgkinson, D.	16.6.45	Kibble, E. T.	15.7.45	McCulloch, W. H.	7.7.45
Hodgkinson, F.	8.3.45	Kidby, H. G.	22.2.45	McDermott, T. H.	7.6.45
Hodgson, R.	30.4.45	Kitchingham, T.	2.12.44	McDonald, C. H.	22.2.45
Hodkinson, J. E.	19.5.45	Kleiser, E. L.	8.12.44	McDonald, J. A.	14.3.45
Hoggett, W. V.	25.7.45	Knapper, G. W.	27.4.45	McGough, M.	6.5.45
Holben, R. J.	9.2.45	Knowles, J. H.	8.4.45	McGregor, N. E.	1.12.44
Holder, C. J.	15.2.45	Knutton, H.	11.3.45	McKeon, L.	17.2.45
Holder, H. J.	6.3.45	Laing, R.	14.1.45	McLellan, R. C.	27.3.45
Holman, R. F.	27.3.45	Lambert, G.	2.4.45	McMeechan, C.	19.4.45

McMenemy, D.	23.5.45	Pask, J. K.	21.2.45	Rickard, T.	18.7.45
McNab, C. P.	5.2.45	Passey, F. M.	26.12.44	Robb, H. S.	30.3.45
McNee, S. R.	16.10.44	Patchesa, H. A.	7.6.45	Roberts, B.	-.3.45
Mears, R. M.	5.4.45	Paterson, L.	6.2.45	Roberts, O. G.	7.6.45
Mellor, E.	14.6.45	Paterson, R.	6.5.45	Roberts, R. J.	21.7.45
Mellor, S.	6.3.45	Patrick, F. W.	23.4.45	Roberts, W. L.	28.1.45
Merchant, A. H.	13.5.45	Payne, B.	30.3.45	Robinson, A. W.	7.6.45
Middleton, N.	8.1.45	Payne, W. E.	31.12.44	Robson, J. R.	18.2.45
Mileman, A. E.	11.3.45	Pearce, C.	4.4.45	Rocker, S. S.	3.7.45
Miles, G. A.	14.7.45	Pearson, C. B.	27.6.45	Rodden, M. J.	30.4.45
Millar, P. R.	28.3.45	Peat, J. H.	13.3.45	Rogers, E. R.	3.6.45
Millard, W. E.	9.7.45	Peel, J.	17.3.45	Rogers, J. W.	27.2.45
Miller, D. C.	24.5.45	Pelan, H. G.	4.5.45	Rolfe, I. D.	11.2.45
Miller, H. L.	4.2.45	Pennell, R. W.	21.2.45	Rooker, J. H.	9.8.45
Mills, J. F. D.	30.6.45	Penrose, S. H.	22.6.45	Rookwood, L. J.	31.3.45
Milton, H. E.	23.3.45	Perkins, J. W. F.	17.3.45	Ross, J. G.	29.3.45
Mitchell, A. W.	13.2.45	Perry, G. H.	31.3.45	Rouchy, J. F.	5.3.45
Moore, D.	26.3.45	Perry, H. S.	2.3.45	Rowarth, J. G.	9.5.45
Moore, F. W. A.	1.6.45	Petheram, K. D. G.	17.3.45	Rowland, J. D.	13.5.43
Moore, J. E.	25.1.45	Petherwick, N. G.	12.4.45	Russell, H. G.	1.5.45
Moore, T. A.	23.3.45	Phillips, D. G.	28.4.45	Russell, J.	14.2.45
Morris, L.	15.2.45	Phillips, J. W.	3.4.45	Sadler, F. E.	25.3.45
Morris, R. S.	23.2.45	Picot, E. J.	30.6.45	Said, A.	7.3.45
Morris, R.	21.2.45	Pimblett, E.	3.2.45	Salter, A. H.	21.3.45
Morrison, H. M. A.	5.4.45	Pittendreigh, W.	10.5.45	Sampson, F. S.	14.4.45
Morriss, G. B.	3.4.43	Platt, J. S.	18.2.45	Sanders, T. W.	14.4.45
Morton, F.	14.2.45	Plummmer, H. W.	7.6.45	Sands, A. M.	15.6.45
Myers, S.	30.3.45	Polden, L. W.	5.6.45	Sarginson, J. E.	11.4.45
Nathan, G. M.	15.4.45	Portsmouth, R. A.	14.2.45	Saunders, R. W.	13.3.45
Newall, J. E.	20.4.45	Potter, A. H.	5.3.45	Saville, W.	29.1.45
Newman, F. K.	8.3.45	Potter, A. A.	27.11.44	Scott, J. G.	16.4.45
Newman, F. R.	13.7.45	Potts, L. G.	14.7.45	Scott, R. C.	12.3.45
Newton, A. H.	7.2.45	Powell, J. F.	10.5.45	Scott, T.	4.9.44
Nicholas, J. L.	27.3.45	Pratt, J. C.	8.4.45	Seal, C. A.	9.1.45
Nickson, S. D.	20.7.45	Prentice, D. E.	11.8.45	Seckington, E.	7.3.45
Noble, J.	1.4.45	Presland, R. A.	20.12.44	Shackleton, N.	12.3.45
Northfield, A.	12.6.45	Price, D. J.	13.3.45	Sharp, H.	14.3.45
Norton, B.	21.2.45	Price, G. R.	16.2.43	Shatwell, C.	15.6.45
Oakham, G. J.	5.6.45	Priddle, G. F.	27.7.45	Shaw, A.W.	13.5.45
O'Connor, J. H.	20.1.45	Privett, D. E.	3.6.45	Shaw, G. P.	2.6.45
Olding, A. E.	5.4.45	Prouten, G.	3.7.45	Shaw, R.	14.6.45
Oldroyd, H. G.	25.4.45	Ramsay, H. J.	30.3.45	Shearsmith, D.	18.5.43
Oliver, H. S.	19.6.45	Ramsay, J. O.	25.11.44	Sherriff, F. C.	28.3.45
Ormond, W. J.	21.3.45	Ransome, H.	27.3.45	Shipley, G.	6.3.45
Orr, H.	28.3.45	Ratcliffe, W. W.	3.1.45	Shippen, J. W.	7.6.45
O'Shea, D. M. P.	28.3.45	Read, J.	18.5.45	Shrubshall, W. F.	5.3.45
Palmer, H. J.	15.6.45	Redman, C.	16.2.45	Shuffleton, J. A.	2.6.45
Parfitt, A. W. C.	21.4.43	Reeves, G. F.	15.3.45	Sime, J. R.	13.4.45
Parker, F. H.	20.3.45	Reid, K. W.	23.1.45	Simm, J.	9.5.45
Parker, L. N. J.	8.3.45	Rennie, G.	8.11.43	Simmonds, T. J. N.	25.2.45
Parker, R. Co.	14.2.45	Richard, T. H.	16.2.45	Simpson, B.	23.1.45
Parsons, F. J. H.	26.4.45	Richards, L. L.	15.6.45	Simpson, G. A.	21.4.45

Simpson, G. W.	7.4.45	Tester, E. J. R.	27.3.45	Webster, W.	5.6.45
Sims, E.	24.3.45	Thomas, B.	8.6.44	Webster, W. B.	16.7.45
Slade, A. E.	15.5.45	Thomas, H. J.	8.3.45	Weller, E. H.	9.3.43
Slater, J. E.	20.3.45	Thompson, E. H.	5.2.45	Wells, E. W.	14.4.45
Small, J. N.	14.4.45	Thompson, R.	27.12.44	Wells, F. G.	5.4.45
Smith, A. E. W.	13.3.45	Thompson, S. T.	3.8.45	Weston, S.	14.6.45
Smith, A. C.	4.10.44	Thornett, A. W. J.	9.2.45	White, C. E.	1.12.44
Smith, G.	30.7.45	Thoroughgood, C. R.	24.4.45	White, S. J.	30.7.45
Smith, G. B.	1.7.45	Thorpe, A. G.	1.3.45	Whitehead, R. M.	16.2.45
Smith, J. B. I.	12.3.45	Thurston, R. G.	3.1.45	Whiteside, R. M.	3.3.45
Smith, J. T.	12.3.45	Titley, J.	13.4.45	Whittle, T. C.	7.5.45
Smith, J. H.	15.7.44	Tomkinson, D.	1.9.44	Whittle, W.	13.3.45
Smith, S. J.	7.3.45	Tonkin, J.	2.3.45	Wilkie, J. M.	15.3.45
Smith, T. D.	9.7.45	Tonkinson, J. S.	18.4.45	Wilkinson, J.	11.2.45
Sneddon, T.	21.2.45	Tovey, G. H.	25.2.45	Wilkinson, W. A.	25.4.45
Sommerville, A. C.	26.5.43	Toye, J. W. A.	28.3.45	Williams, A. E.	15.2.45
Soorier, M. K.	19.5.45	Trickett, E. S.	30.11.44	Williams, C. R.	28.3.45
Southwell, J. R.	6.2.45	Tritton, V. J.	5.2.45	Williams, C. E.	28.2.45
Spencer, F. I.	6.2.45	Tugwell, W. P.	8.12.44	Williams, J. L.	20.3.45
Sperring, A. J.	6.5.45	Turland, P. C.	14.6.45	Williams, R. H.	16.2.45
Stammers, A. G.	12.6.43	Turnbull, E. D.	5.6.45	Williams, S.	21.7.45
Stapeley, O. W.	21.2.45	Tutty, J. G.	17.3.45	Williams, T. H.	4.6.45
Starmer, W. C.	8.4.45	Tyrrell, A.	15.3.45	Williamson, J.	2.4.45
Stephens, J. C.	12.6.45	Umpleby, E.	18.3.45	Willis, E. R.	23.4.45
Stephens, J.	14.6.45	Urry, F.	24.3.45	Willis, F. A. J.	15.6.45
Stephenson, A.	23.3.45	Varney, H. L.	28.5.45	Willmoth, A. W.	26.3.45
Stevenson, A. B.	2.7.45	Venton, C. L.	22.4.44	Wilson, C. J.	14.6.45
Sticklee, H. S.	4.1.45	Vickerman, H.	25.3.45	Wilson, G.	14.2.45
Stockwell, W. J.	26.1.45	Waidson, F.	27.3.45	Wilson, G. E.	28.3.45
Street, A.	15.7.45	Waite, S. A.	11.6.45	Wilson, J.	17.4.45
Summerfield, V.	21.3.45	Wakefield, A. L. B.	25.5.45	Wilson, L.	23.5.45
Sweeney, E.	30.3.45	Walker, J. S.	17.2.45	Winder, C. G.	27.2.45
Sweeney, M.	8.6.45	Walker, N. G.	2.6.45	Wiper, T.	1.6.45
Sweeting, A. J.	20.2.45	Wallace, R. A.	21.1.45	Wood, W. H.	28.6.45
Swindell, G.	18.2.45	Walmsley, M. W.	4.2.45	Woods, A. A.	21.3.45
Symonds, A. G.	12.12.44	Wanless, Rev. J. T.	15.3.45	Woods, E. A.	2.5.45
Tabberer, J. H.	18.7.45	Ware, J.	12.1.45	Woolbar, R. C.	3.4.45
Tampin, G. W.	11.3.45	Warner, S. L.	8.7.45	Woolf, W. H.	9.6.45
Tant, F. C.	13.7.45	Waterhouse, C.	9.3.45	Wragg, E.	24.6.45
Tasker, E. L.	14.3.45	Watkins, K. O.	1.8.45	Wright, A. E.	20.3.45
Taylor, A. L.	28.2.45	Watson, A. J.	30.4.43	Wright, K.	17.3.45
Taylor, C.	30.6.45	Watson, W. T. T.	11.6.45	Wright, S. W.	22.4.45
Taylor, E. W.	13.3.45	Watts, J. T.	14.4.45	York, R.	6.2.45
Taylor, J. C.	4.8.45	Watts, R.	3.4.45	York, R. W. J.	7.6.45
Taylor, W.	27.2.45	Waud, K. J.	3.5.45	Young, P. H.	26.7.45
Teasdale, W. J.	20.2.45	Webb, D. T.	14.2.45		
Tennent, B. G. R.	26.3.45	Webb, H. L.	18.3.45		

Source: Ron Taylor, historian and site manager, www.roll-of-honour.org.uk

APPENDIX 2

LIST OF SENTENCES IN THE TRIALS
OF THE SANDAKAN UNDERGROUND

DEATH

Abin, Sgt
Azcona, Felix
Funk, Alex
bin Gungau, Matusup
Lagan, Detective Ernesto
Matthews, Captain Lionel
Ming, Heng Joo
Singh, Jemadar Ujagar
Sing, Wong Mu

IMPRISONMENT

FIFTEEN YEARS
Damodaran
Mavor, Gerald
Taylor, Dr James
Yangsalang, Sgt Maj.
Yusop, Sgt

TWELVE YEARS
Dal Kiu Fook, Peter
Raymond
Salleh, Mohammed
Wells, Lt Rod

TEN YEARS
Apostol, Lamberto
Kong, Ng Ho
Weynton, Lt Gordon

EIGHT YEARS
Guriaman, Inspector Samuel
Seng, Amigaw

Seng, Soh Kem
Syn, Chin Piang (alias Chin
Chee Kong)

SEVEN YEARS
Leong, Peter
Majinal, Dick

SIX YEARS
Chang Ting Kiang, Henry
Funk, Paddy
Joo, Chan Tian
Kassiou
Richards, Cpl J.
Stevens, Sgt A.

FIVE YEARS
Chow, Foo Seng
Jakariah
Si Dik

FOUR YEARS
Funk, Johnny
Gorokon
Lumatep
Marshall, Spr Don
Ping, Chan
Tang, Felix

THREE YEARS
Aruliah, Samuel
Martin, Sig. Frank
Phillips, Mr
Tahir, Mohammed

TWO AND A HALF YEARS
Ching, Lau Bui
Kui, Ngui Ah

TWO YEARS
Davis, Pte S. G.
Jensen, Spr Carl
Kassim
Mills, Cpl Cyril
Min, Surat

ONE AND A HALF YEARS
Blain, Sgt A. M.
Davis, Spr R.
Graham, Cpl T. G.
Holly, Sgt R. B.
James, S/Sgt J. H.
Roffely, Cpl L. A. D.
Small, Cpl Arnold

ONE YEAR
Chai, Goh Teck
Dahlan
Kai
Laband, Dr J. F.
Rice-Oxley, Major
Seng, Goh Teck

SIX MONTHS
McDonough, Sgt W. J.
Rumble, Pte E. H.

Source: Don Wall, *Sandakan: The Last March*, Sydney, 2003

APPENDIX 3

LIST OF BORNEO NATIVES
WHO HELPED PRISONERS

NAME	DESCRIPTION
Orang Tuan Gundi	Headman of the village that harboured and fed L/Cpl Moxham, ltes Short, Botterill and Anderson (died of illness).
Barigah	Found the above-named escapees; aided in harbouring and feeding, also in handing them over to SRD party.
Sumping	Same as Barigah.
Ladooma	Same as Barigah.
Magador	Same as Barigah.
Kantong	Same as Barigah.
Ginssas bin Gangass	Found WO Sticpewich and Pte Reither and took them to Dihil, where they were harboured, fed and eventually taken to SRD.
Adihil bin Ambilid	Harboured and fed Sticpewich and Reither after their escape and helped Sticpewich to reach SRD.
Limbuang	Assisted in taking Sticpewich to SRD.
Galenty	Acted as spy for Sticpewich and contacted SRD with note from him.
Gopokau	Passed food to PW in Ranau area under the noses of the Jap guards.
Galunting	Helped to carry Sticpewich's belongings when he travelled to SRD r.v.
Ingurru	Passed food to PW in Ranau area on four occasions.
Balabiu	Nine-year-old girl who passed food on two occasions to PW on the 'death track'.
Darumsai	Aided Dihil in giving food to Sticpewich and Reither in the Ranau area after escape.
Peluia	Passed food to PW in Ranau market and in the area. Handed locket to me belonging to deceased PW.
Tima	Gave food to PW for period of two weeks.
Singki	Gave food to PW in Ranau area during air raids.

Ganung	Gave food to members of work parties at Ranau.
Janan	Gave food to PW during air raid, received articles from PW belonging to NX 52402 Pte W. G. Read and NX 68861 Dvr L. E. Hardy. Articles handed to 8 AAWGU by me for despatch 02E.
Hosina	Gave rice to PW between Ranau and Paginatan.
Rijan	Gave food to PW on working party, stated PW wore hat marked NX 6591 J. Pearson.
Amir	Gave food to vegetable party at Ranau.
Lasa	Gave food to PW on track between Ranau and Nelapak.
Hikandoa	Gave food to PW on track near Ranau.
Patuk	Gave food to PW on death track near Ranau.
Kg of Matang	Many villagers assisted PW with food, etc. in Ranau area. I made a payment to the village.
Balinti	Gave food to PW on firewood party at Ranau.
Galitang	Gave food to PW in Ranau area over period of a month on his way to school.
Burih	Gave food to starving PW when she was living in jungle close to track in the Paginatan area. Well known to the PW and addressed as 'Mumma' by them. Her husband died of malnutrition.
Hussin	Found two Australian and two British PW near Telupid. Australian PW were NX 78229 Pte Dawson L. K. and NX 34384 Gnr Fuller, E. J. The PW were taken to Kg Komansi, fed and harboured but all unfortunately died. Effects handed in prior to my visit.
Onsi and Village of Kemansi	Harboured and fed the four escapees enumerated above. Bodies recovered by 31 AAWGU.
Kaingal	Brought food to Short, Botterill and Moxham when they were being harboured in the Ranau area.
Guok	Same as Kaingal.
Kuntiwau	Gave food to Ginsas for Sticpewich and Reither.
Kalindai	Gave food to PW working in Ranau kedais.
Dun Kin	Gave PW food when they worked in Ranau kedais.
Gangau	Brought food to hiding place of Moxham, Short, Botterill and Anderson.
Ansangan	Same as Gangau.
Geronsi	Gave food to firewood party in Ranau area.
Ikul	Gave food to PW on rice-carrying party.
Saidin	Same as Ikul but on different rice party.
Jamin	Gave food to wood-gathering party near Ranau.
Surap	Took food to Sticpewich at his hiding place.

Aubin	Brought food to Sticpewich after his escape.
Limboo	Same as Aubin.
Sigindai	Gave food to PW in Ranau area.
Halima binte Binting	Widow of Matasup bin Gungau who helped Capt. Matthews, Dr J. P. Tayor and others in regard to the smuggling in of supplies to the Mile 8 camp and assisted in the radio and escape activities.
Halima binte Amat	Widow of the late Wong Mu Sing. This man was a spy for the Filipino guerrillas and assisted Capt. Matthews, Dr Taylor and helpers, particularly in regard to the escape of the eight Australian PW from Berhala Island in 1943.
Koram (NBAC) MBE	This NCO was stationed in the Sandakan area and played a big part in assisting Dr Taylor and Capt. Matthews and was one of the leading figures concerned in the escape of the Australian PW from Berhala Island in 1943.
Johnny Funk	Obtained radio parts for Capt. Matthews and assisted the late Heng Joo Ming, who harboured and fed NX 58809 Sjt W. Wallace when he escaped from Mile 8 camp. Also assisted in preparing maps of Sandakan for intelligence purposes. Was arrested and tortured by Japanese and sentenced at Kuching to four years' imprisonment.
Tau Bui Ching	Gave money and radio parts to Ernesto Lagan, who was one of Dr Taylor's chief assistants. Lagan was executed at Kuching by the Japanese. Tau Bui Ching was sentenced to two and a half years' imprisonment at Kuching.
Chan Tian Joo	Acted as treasurer for a fund being collected on behalf of escaped PW. Contributed money, food, cooking utensils and assisted in sending parcels into Mile 8 camp. He was also concerned in the passing of radio news. Was sentenced to six years' imprisonment at Kuching at mass trial.
Chin Piang Syn, also known as Chin Chee Kong	Assisted Dr Taylor, Heng Joo Ming and Capt. Matthews in many ways. Particularly in regard to the escape of Sgt Wallace and the other PW who escaped from Berhala Island in 1943. Had made preliminary arrangements to assist Sjt Blain and party to escape but was arrested before escape could be put into operation. Travelled to Sitangki (P. I.) with Wong Mu Sing before Berhala escapes took place in order to ensure that there was no trickery. Assisted in food smuggling, etc. and carried notes between camps. Was sentenced to eight years' imprisonment in Kuching in February 1944.

Siti Binte Jakariah	This woman was the de facto wife of the late Heng Joo Ming. Joo Ming was executed with Capt. Matthews at Kuching. He took a leading part in Dr Taylor's organisation, helped in obtaining radio parts, money, etc. and harboured Sjt Wallace after his escape. Gave considerable aid to Australian PW.
Magdalene Funk	Widow of the late Alex Funk, who was executed by the Japanese at Kuching along with Capt. L. C. Matthews. Alex Funk smuggled food, medicine, radio parts, etc. into the camp. He also obtained a revolver with nine rounds of ammunition, which he gave to Capt. Matthews. He assisted in giving food to a party of five Australian PW, who were eventually recaptured by the Japanese after escaping from the Mile 8 camp. Alex Funk was closely connected with Dr Taylor's organisation.
Taciana Teresa Bazan – formerly Mrs F. Azcona	This woman, now remarried, was formerly the widow of Felix Azcona, who was one of the eight men executed with Capt. Matthews. Felix Azcona assisted the Australian PW in many ways.
Chang Siew Ha	Widow of the late Soh Kim Seng, who died at Kuching while serving a sentence of imprisonment because of his aid to the Australian PW at the Mile 8 camp. He assisted Dr Taylor in many ways but in particular by preparing intelligence maps and passing food and medicine to the PW.
Katherine E. Lagan	Widow of the late Ernesto Lagan, who was executed at Kuching and was one of the leading figures in the assistance group. Ernesto Lagan was concerned in all aspects of the assistance group, mainly smuggling of food, medicines, radio parts and money. He collected considerable amounts of money for the PW and played a leading part in the escapes from Berhala, etc. He was closely associated with the Filipino spy Wong Mu Sing.
Ng Ho Kong	This man was concerned in sending radio parts, food and letters to the PW. He contacted Sjt Stevens at the power plant and was a contact for Chan Ping, who was in charge of the power plant. Ng Ho Kong was sentenced to ten years' imprisonment at Kuching because of the part he played in assisting the Australian PW.
Asadi bin Ajan	Gave food to the PW working parties in the Sandakan area. Was employed by NBT Co.
Nurse Phoebe Lai	Gave food and money to Australian PW when they were

	working at the NBT Co. sawmill. She also gave them food and medicines to take back to the Mile 8 camp.
Chan Ping	This man was in charge of the power plant at the Mile 8 camp. A party of Australian PW was allotted to him and lived with him. Chan Ping used to give food to the PW and also was a link for sending communications from the camp to Sandakan town. He brought parcels from Mr Mavor, containing radio parts, etc. into the camp. Ng Ho Kong was the middle link between Mavor and Chan Ping. The power plant was an important factor for the working of the camp secret radio receiving set. Chan Ping was sentenced to four years' imprisonment at Kuching.
Wong Yun Siew	This man obtained radio parts for the PW and also smuggled food and escape route plans to them. He was one of those included in the mass arrests. He was able to escape trial at Kuching by feigning insanity and was released from Sandakan jail after serving four months.
Goh Teck Seng	This man, together with his brother, Goh Teck Chai, and Foo Seng Chow, harboured and fed five members of 2/29BN, led by the late VX 48685 Cpl W. F. Fairey, for a period of seven months after their escape from the Mile 8 camp. This man was sentenced to one year's imprisonment at Kuching.
Goh Teck Chai	Same as for Goh Teck Seng.
Mohammed Salleh	This man was employed as a watchman at Berhala Island. When he went to Sandakan town, he used to bring parcels, etc. back to the PW on behalf of Dr Taylor's organisation. When the eight PW (Capt. Steele's party) were at liberty prior to their movement to the P.I., Salleh and others kept them alive by bringing food to them. He was sentenced to 12 years' imprisonment at Kuching.
Mansia	Gave food to the PW in the Ranau area on several occasions.
Henry Chang	
Ting Kiang	This man carried messages from Sandakan town to the PW camp. He was also concerned in the smuggling of food. When Sjt Wallace escaped, he carried messages from him to another PW in the Mile 8 camp. At the time of his arrest, he was making plans to assist another party of PW to escape. Was sentenced to six years' imprisonment at Kuching, by Japs.
Foo Seng Chow	Same as for Goh Teck Seng with the exception that Foo was sentenced to five years' jail.

Peter Raymond
Lai Kui Fook
    Was a contact between Dr Taylor and Capt. Matthews.
He carried many parcels of food, medicines and money to
the Mile 8 camp and gave Capt. Matthews a map of the
roads and installations. He received a sentence of 12 years'
imprisonment at Kuching.

Bernard Quadra
    A brother of Alberto Quadra, who took the Berhala Island
escapees to the Philippines in a small craft. Mr B. Quadra
gave information to me on behalf of his brother, who is
now at Siasa at the P.I.

Lamberto Apostol
    This man held the appointment of Superintendent at
the Govt Experimental Farm. He was concerned in the
smuggling of food, money and radio parts. He also helped
in passing the news sheets. He was sentenced to ten years'
imprisonment at Kuching.

Kwang Chu Ming
    This man, together with his brother, Kwang Ming Ming,
contributed money to a fund to aid the PW. They also
gave food to them. Kwan Ming Ming was absent in Hong
Kong at the time of my interrogation. The Kwang brothers
were not sentenced to imprisonment. Chu was fined
two thousand dollars and Ming was fined one thousand
dollars.

Peter Leong
    Assisted Ernesto Lagan, one of the principals of the
Dr Taylor organisation. He drew maps, etc. that were
eventually given to Capt. Matthews. He was sentenced to
seven years' imprisonment.

Samuel Aruliah
    Was concerned in the construction of the camp radios
and smuggled parts into the Mile 8 camp. He also took
part in the passing of communications between the Mile 8
camp and Berhala Island. He was sentenced to three years'
imprisonment by the Japs at Kuching.

Ngui Ah Kui
    Changed Australian currency into Jap dollars on behalf of
the Australian PW. Also gave a radio valve to Ng Ho Kong
for the PW's receiving set. He was sentenced to two and a
half years' imprisonment at Kuching.

Chow Yee Soo
    This woman is the widow of the late Lo Hoi Tshi. He
was arrested by the Japs mainly because of the monetary
aid that he gave to a fund being collected by Dr Taylor's
organisation on behalf of the PW. He was released
after paying a fine of two thousand dollars and died at
Sandakan in June 1945.

Chu Li Tsia
    Supplied food for a period of three days to a party of
six escaped Australian PW led by X15175 Cpl H. R.

	Trackson. He was arrested and beaten by the Japanese and released after paying a fine of fifty dollars.
Yau Siak Chau	Contributed money and food to aid the Berhala Island escapees. Was arrested by Japs and released after paying a fine of one thousand dollars.
Wong Wee Man	Contributed money to fund being raised to assist the Berhala Island escapees. Was fined two thousand dollars.
Mrs Mabel Liu	Contributed money to Dr Taylor's organisation. Was never arrested.
Cha Chin Nam	Gave food to PW working near Sandakan aerodrome.
Jakariah	Acted as boatman with Si Dick and transferred Sjt Wallace, an escaped Australian PW, from Sandakan to Berhala Island. Was sentenced to five years' imprisonment at Kuching by the Japanese court.
Simon Yong	Gave food and radio parts to the Australian PW in the Sandakan area.
Yusop	A Sjt in the North Borneo Armed Constabulary, organised the collection of money and foodstuffs for the PW at Mile 8 camp. Also acted as contact between the camp and Sandakan town. Was sentenced to 15 years' jail by the Japanese court at Kuching.
Guriaman	An inspector in the NEAC and one of Constabulary group that gave assistance. Was sentenced to eight years' jail.
Damodaran	This man is a clerk at Sandakan Civil Jail. He contributed sums of money and also gave food through the Constabulary members for the Mile 8 camp. He also sent writing paper to Capt. Matthews. He received a sentence of 15 years' imprisonment from the Jap court at Kuching.
Wong Hiong	Eyewitness to crucifixion of PW; also the execution of the last remaining PW at Mile 8 camp.
Ali Asa	Worked for Japs at Mile 8 camp up until the time when the last PW died.
Lap	Found Gnr Owen Campbell 2/10 Fd Regt in the Maunad area after Campbell had escaped from the Japanese while on the second Sandakan–Ranau Death March.
Ambiau	One of the natives responsible for the rescue of Gnr Campbell in the Maunad area.
Salium	As for Ambiau.
Amit	When Pte Braithwaite was rescued by Abing, Amit's father-in-law, he was taken to Amit's house. Amit assisted in his eventual return to Allied hands.
Orang Kulang	The main person responsible for the rescue of Gnr Campbell. He took him to the SRD party and was largely

	responsible for his movement out to sea to meet Allied aircraft.
Galunting	As for Lap.
Sagan	One of the natives responsible for the rescue of Pte Braithwaite in the Sapi area after his escape from the Japanese on the second Sandakan–Ranau Death March.
Omar	As for Sagan.
Sapan	As for Sagan.
Mangulong	As for Sagan.
Loreto Padua	As for Sagan.
Floro Mananay	Gave assistance to Cpl Fairey's party of escaped PW. He harboured them for ten days. Mr Mananay later died from illness and his widow is now in poor circumstances.
Paddy Funk	The younger of the three Funk brothers who gave considerable assistance to the PW at Mile 8 camp. Was endeavouring to aid a party of PW to escape at the time of his arrest by the Japanese. Was sentenced to six years' imprisonment at Kuching.
Jenny bin Sarudin	Gave food and medicine over a period of four months to the PW when they were working at the NBT Co. Sandakan.
Yang Salang	Formerly Sgt Major NBAC. This man was one of the members of the Constabulary organisation that gave varied assistance to the PW in the Sandakan area. Is at present serving a sentence of imprisonment following information from Dr J. P. Taylor that he divulged information while undergoing interrogation by the Japanese concerning the Dr Taylor–Capt. Matthews organisation.
Ismail bin Awang Raman; Kuting; Main; Mohamet Tassim; Omar; Deexee Richard; Dahtan	Employees of the NBT Co. who passed food to the PW when they went there on working parties.
Daiman bin Barang	An investigation was held surrounding the circumstances under which this police recruit was wounded while operating with the SRD unit in the Kudat area.
Lewah binte Mandadus	Widow of the late Kassiou, who died at Kuching while serving a sentence of imprisonment for aiding the Australian PW in the Sandakan area.
Bintang binte Udung	Widow of the late Cpl Abin NEAC, who was executed at Kuching with the late Capt. L. C. Matthews AIF. This was the NCO in charge of the Mile 8 police post who gave so

| | much valuable assistance to the Australian PW. |
| Wong Yui Yin | This woman is the widow of, and was the lawful wife of, the late Heng Joo Ming, who was executed at Kuching in 1944 with the late Capt. L. C. Matthews AIF and the other natives who paid for their assistance to the Australian PW with their lives. |

Source: Awards to Helpers, British North Borneo, Major Jackson's report, NAA MP742/1 328/1/32

ACKNOWLEDGEMENTS

Recalling the lives of young men who died on the Sandakan Death Marches was a sad and difficult experience for the families of victims. Yet many gave their time willingly, aware of the importance to posterity of the events that led to the untimely deaths of their husbands, brothers, sons and nephews. I thank them from my heart.

My particular thanks go to: Richard Braithwaite; Maureen Devereaux; Claudia Edwards; Christopher Elliott; Margaret Fisher; June Fowler-Smith; Tony Hall; Gwen Hammon; Heather Harrison-Lawrence; Antonia Hayes; Anthony Hazzard; Doreen Hurst; Brenda Kingen; David Matthews; Senator Anne McEwen; Steve Mockridge; Bill Molloy; Sue Moxham; Holly Norton; Bob and Cathie Oakeshott; Jeffrey Phillips; Diane Rowe; Betty and David Seccombe; Teresa Stephens; Ben Sticpewich; Derek Taylor; Peter Wilkins; Claire Woods; George Worrall; and Rod York.

I'm also deeply grateful to several servicemen who survived imprisonment in Kuching or Outram Road Gaol, or who otherwise participated in the Pacific War, and offered their memories and knowledge. These are: Ross McCowan; Russ Ewin; Leslie Bunn Glover; Warwick Johnstone; Tony White; and Bill Young.

The scale and scope of this project could not have been possible without the forensic research skills of Glenda Lynch in

Canberra, who was indispensable in assisting me go through thousands of documents. I also thank: Leticia Quintana, for her early work on the subject; Doreen Hurst (née Funk), for her thoughtfulness in putting me in touch with so many people in Borneo; and Brian Hales, a relative of a victim of the marches, who generously supplied his library. Mark Friezer, an old friend who accompanied my group on the journey across Borneo, took some beautiful portraits of native people, three of which appear in this book – and I thank him for his permission to use them. I also thank my niece Georgia Arnott, who spent days transcribing recordings of interviews – a long and arduous job.

I owe an equal debt of gratitude to the people in Borneo, many of whom helped me with my research in all sorts of ways. A great source of information was Tham Yau Kong and his trekking team, who guided my group along the approximate Death March route. On the way, several native people gave their time and knowledge, chiefly Domima binte Akui, Yumpil and Zudin. In Kota Kinabalu, too, Irene Benggon Charuruks, Jerry Ipang Ganggal, Bryan Lai and members of the Azcona and other families went out of their way to assist.

My sincere appreciation and thanks to everyone involved in this book at Random House, for their professionalism and excellence every step of the way; in particular to Kevin O'Brien, an editor of stoic brilliance, and Alison Urquhart, the publisher every writer longs for. And an open-ended thank you to my wonderful agent Jane Burridge, an expert in the Known Unknowns of the publishing business.

Several people were very helpful through their knowledge of, or access to information about, the Sandakan Death Marches and the prisoners' stories, or in other critical ways. These were:

Michele Cunningham; Christopher Dawson; Don Featherstone; Shirley Ham; Eric McDonald; John Miles; Stella Moo-Tan; Dr Narrelle Morris; Peter Rubinstein; Kevin Smith; Graham Swain AM; Barry Tinkler; Bruce Venables; and Gwenda Zappala.

I also acknowledge my debt to the pioneering research of authors of previous books on Sandakan, notably Kevin Smith, Lynette Silver and Don Wall.

The staff of the Australian War Memorial, the National Archives of Australia, the National Archives of Great Britain and the State Archives of Sabah were unfailingly cooperative. These reference libraries had a great deal more information than I had anticipated and were critical in piecing the story together.

Friends were wonderfully supportive, and I thank especially the members of our Sandakan trekking team: Drew Blomfield; Reg Carter; Mark Friezer; Robert Jarrett; Alex Kristenson; and Tony Rees (who was there in spirit).

Finally, once again, my love and thanks to my family – especially my wife, Marie, and son, Ollie, veterans of a few histories, who have always been with me in spirit.

REFERENCES

PART 1: BEFORE

Chapter 1: Singapore Lost

1. 8th Division war diary, AWM 52 1/5/17, www.awm.gov.au/collection/war_diaries/second_world_war/diary.asp?levelID=607.
2. Aldrich, p. 64.
3. Lieutenant Colonel Charles Anderson, Citation, Victoria Cross, *The London Gazette*, 13 February 1942: www.london-gazette.co.uk/issues/35456/supplements/749.
4. Major General Gordon Bennett's Report on Malayan Campaign, March 1942, NAA A5954 264/3.
5. Yamamoto, p. 13.
6. Tony White, interview, 2010.
7. 'Singapore Reflections': Captain Hartley James Walker's first-hand account of the events in the months leading up to the fall of Singapore in early 1942, monograph, AWM F940.5425 W179s.
8. Lodge, pp. 165–7.
9. Quoted in Smyth, p. 226.
10. Ibid., p. 228.
11. Quoted in Thompson, p. 9.
12. Ibid., p. 10.
13. 8th Division war diary, AWM 52 1/5/17, www.awm.gov.au/collection/war_diaries/second_world_war/diary.asp?levelID=607.
14. Japanese leaflet, dropped on Singapore, 10–11 February 1942, Ernest Hazzard's private papers.
15. 'Singapore Reflections': Captain Hartley James Walker's first-hand account of the events in the months leading up to the fall of Singapore in early 1942, monograph, AWM F940.5425 W179s.
16. Ibid.
17. Ibid.
18. Governor Thomas cable quoted on the COFEPOW website: www.cofepow.org.uk.
19. 'The Alexandra Hospital Massacre', WW2 People's War, BBC website: www.bbc.co.uk/ww2peopleswar/stories/60/a8515460.shtml.

20. Thompson, pp. 333–4.
21. Quoted in Smyth, p. 236.
22. Ibid.
23. Summary of Malayan Campaign by Lieutenant Colonel Kappe, Commanding 8th Division Signals, AWM 54 553/5/5.
24. See Bennett, *Why Singapore Fell.*
25. Percival, pp. 289, 292.
26. Ibid.
27. *Jatisari Journal*, Vol. 111, in Percival's private papers, quoted in Smyth, p. 241.
28. Percival's private papers, quoted in Smyth, p. 242.
29. 8th Division war diary, AWM 52 1/5/17, www.awm.gov.au/collection/war_diaries/second_world_war/diary.asp?levelID=607.
30. Thompson, pp. 348–9.
31. Quoted in ibid., p. 356.
32. Major General Gordon Bennett's Report on Malayan Campaign, March 1942, NAA A5954 264/3.
33. Yoji, p. 195.
34. Major General Gordon Bennett's Report on Malayan Campaign, March 1942, NAA A5954 264/3.
35. Yoji, p. 197.
36. Kappe Report, 'Remembering 1942: 15 February 1942, The Fall of Singapore', Australian War Memorial website: www.awm.gov.au/atwar/remembering1942/singapore/documents.asp.

Chapter 2: The Boat

1. Hastings, p. 53.
2. See Tanaka, *Hidden Horrors.*
3. Russ Ewin, interview, 2010.
4. Report of Captain R. E. Steele, Sergeant Walter Wallace and Sergeant R. J. Kennedy, prepared 16–23 March 1944, AWM 226 9, P1100876.
5. Preliminary interrogation of Owen Campbell, AWM 54 1010/1/2.
6. Blackburn. These excerpts from: www.theage.com.au/entertainment/books/the-whistle-blown-on-changi-20120204-1qyfl.html#ixzz1mCqzuNfs.
7. Shigenori Togo to Allied enquiries, 29 January 1942. See Clause 1098, International Military Tribunal for the Far East: www.ibiblio.org/hyperwar/PTO/IMTFE/IMTFE-8.html.
8. Quoted in Silver, *Sandakan*, pp. 33–4.
9. Quoted in Ewin, p. 70.
10. Connolly and Wilson, p. 165.
11. Tom Burns' diary, NAA B3856 144/14/140.

12. Smith, *Borneo*, p. 47.
13. Tom Burns' diary, NAA B3856 144/14/140.
14. Tony White, interview, 2010.
15. Ibid.; and Connolly and Wilson, p. 166.
16. Goodwin, p. 146.
17. Rod Wells' statement, AWM 54 1010/4/146.
18. Tom Burns' diary, NAA B3856 144/14/140.
19. Silver, *Sandakan*, p. 37.
20. Tony White, interview, 2010.
21. Richard Braithwaite, statement, AWM 54 1010/4/19.
22. Tom Burns' diary, NAA B3856 144/14/140.
23. *Prisoners of War*, Richard Braithwaite radio interview.
24. Tom Burns' diary, NAA B3856 144/14/140.

Chapter 3: British North Borneo

1. *The British North Borneo Herald*, 1 July 1941.
2. Ibid., 1 May 1941.
3. Ibid.
4. Ibid., 1 July 1941.
5. Furness, p. 1.
6. Ibid., p. 14.
7. Moffitt, p. 38.
8. Tanaka, pp. 12–13.
9. Quoted in Wong Tze Ken, p. 2.
10. Wong Tze Ken, pp. 6–7.
11. *The British North Borneo Herald*, 1 July 1941.
12. Quoted in Wong Tze Ken, p. 13.
13. Wong Tze Ken, p. 13.
14. *Official Gazette*, Legislative Council of British North Borneo, 1938 (undated).
15. Ibid.
16. Wong Tze Ken, p. 11.
17. Ibid., p. 35.
18. Borneo reports, cables to the secretary of state for the colonies, National Archives, Kew, United Kingdom, WO 208/1489.
19. Ibid.
20. Ibid.
21. Ibid.
22. Ibid.
23. Ibid.
24. Ibid.
25. Diary of George Woolley, quoted in Wong Tze Ken, p. 50.

Chapter 4: No. 1 Prisoner of War Camp
1. Matthews, p. 107.
2. *Prisoners of War*, Richard Braithwaite radio interview.
3. Jackson report, NAA MP742/1 328/1/32.
4. Richard Braithwaite, 'Shelter in Time of War', *Wartime* magazine, October 2010, No. 52.
5. Ibid.
6. Ibid.
7. Richard Braithwaite, statement, AWM 54 1010/4/19.
8. Tom Burns' diary, NAA B3856 144/14/140.
9. Quoted in Silver, *Sandakan*, p. 52.
10. Jackson report, NAA MP742/1 328/1/32.

Chapter 5: Officers and Men
1. Wong Tze Ken, p. 65.
2. Ibid., pp. 65-6.
3. Matthews, p. 2.
4. Ibid., p. 9.
5. Ibid., p. 38.
6. Quoted in ibid., p. 35.
7. Pamela Wells and Keith R. Colwill, *The Age*, Rod Wells obituary, 5 December 2003.
8. Ibid.
9. Pamela Wells' address to Sandakan Memorial Service in Bendigo, 2004, quoted in Matthews, p. 127.
10. Stan Woods' private papers.
11. Ibid.
12. Ibid.
13. Ibid.
14. Ibid.
15. Ibid.
16. Russ Ewin, interview, 2011.
17. *Prisoners of War*, Richard Braithwaite radio interview.
18. Justice Athol Moffitt address, transcript, 1987 National Conference of Veterans, Canberra.
19. Richard Braithwaite (son), interview, 2010.
20. Ibid.
21. Tom Burns' diary, NAA B3856 144/14/140.
22. Anthony Hill, Billy Young and the Dead End Kids, Sandakan POW Families Oration, 27 May 2011.
23. Ibid.
24. Michael Keating, service record, NAA B883 NX68380.
25. Bill Keating, service record, NAA B883 NX5829.

PART 2: THE CAMP

Chapter 6: First Escapes

1. Report of Captain R. E. Steele, Sergeant Walter Wallace and Sergeant R. J. Kennedy, prepared 16–23 March 1944, AWM 226 9, P1100876.
2. Ibid.
3. Smith, *Escapes and Incursions*, p. 20.
4. Ibid., p. 31.
5. Tom Burns' diary, NAA B3856 144/14/140.
6. Suga address to court, AWM 54 1010/6/59.

Chapter 7: The Commandant

1. Richard Braithwaite, statement, AWM 54 1010/4/19.
2. Quoted in Wall, *Kill the Prisoners*, p. 85.
3. Smith, *Borneo*, p. 87.
4. Stan Woods' private papers.
5. Smith, *Borneo*, p. 64.
6. Anthony Hill, Billy Young and the Dead End Kids, Sandakan POW Families Oration, 27 May 2011.
7. Ibid.
8. *Prisoners of War*, Richard Braithwaite radio interview.
9. According to Bunny Glover, dugongs were occasionally eaten; and Rod Wells told the War Crimes Tribunal that the prisoners purchased two or three yaks. Quoted in Matthews, p. 122.
10. Smith, *Borneo*, p. 71.
11. Tom Burns' diary, NAA B3856 144/14/140.
12. Quoted in Cunningham, p. 25.
13. *Prisoners of War*, Richard Braithwaite radio interview.
14. Ibid.
15. War Crimes Borneo trial transcripts for Hoshijima Susumi, NAA MP742/1 336/1/1180.
16. Tanaka, p. 22.
17. Ibid., p. 19.
18. Quoted in Cunningham, p. 26.
19. Cunningham, p. 25.
20. Affidavits by Japanese personnel in connection with charges arising from Sandakan–Ranau death march with comments by Bill Sticpewich, AWM 54 1010/4/174.
21. *Prisoners of War*, Richard Braithwaite radio interview.
22. Wall, *Sandakan*, p. 17.

23. Cunningham, p. 26.
24. Smith, *Borneo*, p. 67.
25. Tom Burns' diary, NAA B3856 144/14/140.
26. Quoted in Cunningham, p. 80.
27. Ibid.

Chapter 8: The Drome

1. Tanaka, p. 13.
2. Wall, *Sandakan*, p. 11.
3. Report of Captain R. E. Steele, Sergeant Walter Wallace and Sergeant R. J. Kennedy, prepared 16–23 March 1944, AWM 226 9, P1100876.
4. Tom Burns' diary, NAA B3856 144/14/140.
5. Report of Captain R. E. Steele, Sergeant Walter Wallace and Sergeant R. J. Kennedy, prepared 16–23 March 1944, AWM 226 9, P1100876.
6. As recorded in Silver, *Sandakan*, p. 66.
7. Smith, *Borneo*, pp. 80–1.
8. As recorded in Silver, *Sandakan*, pp. 66–7.
9. Affidavits by Japanese personnel in connection with charges arising from Sandakan–Ranau death march with comments by Bill Sticpewich, AWM 54 1010/4/174.
10. Richard Braithwaite, statement, AWM 54 1010/4/19.
11. Wall, *Sandakan*, p. 21.
12. Ewin, p. 75.
13. Quoted in Wall, *Sandakan*, pp. 21–2.

Chapter 9: Flesh and Bone

1. See Ham, *Kokoda*.
2. As observed by Chinese citizen Heng Joo Ming.
3. Keegan, p. 275.
4. Report of Captain R. E. Steele, Sergeant Walter Wallace and Sergeant R. J. Kennedy, prepared 16–23 March 1944, AWM 226 9, P1100876.
5. Ibid.
6. Richard Braithwaite, statement, AWM 54 1010/4/19.
7. Ibid.
8. Ibid.
9. Silver, *Sandakan*, p. 68.
10. Ibid., p. 69.
11. Smith, *Borneo*, p. 80.
12. Stan Woods' private papers.
13. Ibid.
14. Tom Burns' diary, NAA B3856 144/14/140.

15. Report of Captain R. E. Steele, Sergeant Walter Wallace and Sergeant R. J. Kennedy, prepared 16–23 March 1944, AWM 226 9, P1100876.
16. Bill Sticpewich's private papers; Affidavits by Japanese personnel in connection with charges arising from Sandakan–Ranau death march with comments by Bill Sticpewich, AWM 54 1010/4/174.

Chapter 10: The Cage

1. James Darlington, service record, NAA B883 NX40325.
2. Report of Captain R. E. Steele, Sergeant Walter Wallace and Sergeant R. J. Kennedy, prepared 16–23 March 1944, AWM 226 9, P1100876.
3. Richard Braithwaite, statement, AWM 54 1010/4/19.
4. Silver, *Sandakan*, p. 97.
5. Affidavits by Japanese personnel in connection with charges arising from Sandakan–Ranau death march with comments by Bill Sticpewich, AWM 54 1010/4/174.
6. Tanaka, p. 35.
7. Richard Braithwaite, statement, AWM 54 1010/4/19.
8. Quoted in Tanaka, p. 36.
9. Keith Botterill, statement, AWM 54 1010/4/17.
10. Affidavits by Japanese personnel in connection with charges arising from Sandakan–Ranau death march with comments by Bill Sticpewich, AWM 54 1010/4/174.
11. See reference in Tanaka, p. 37.
12. Anthony Hill, Billy Young and the Dead End Kids, Sandakan POW Families Oration, 27 May 2011.
13. Report of Captain R. E. Steele, Sergeant Walter Wallace and Sergeant R. J. Kennedy, prepared 16–23 March 1944, AWM 226 9, P1100876.

PART 3: RESISTANCE

Chapter 11: The Radio

1. Report by Wells on the activities of B Force for July 1942 to July 1943, NAA B3856 144/14/58.
2. Jackson report, NAA MP742/1 328/1/32.
3. Report by Wells on the activities of B Force for July 1942 to July 1943, NAA B3856 144/14/58.
4. Quoted in Silver, *Blood Brothers*, p. 117.
5. Report by Wells on the activities of B Force for July 1942 to July 1943, NAA B3856 144/14/58.

6. Silver, *Sandakan*, p. 90.
7. Quoted in Matthews, p. 130.
8. Ibid., p. 131.
9. Silver, *Sandakan*, p. 90.
10. Smith, *Borneo*, p. 89.
11. Lionel Matthews, Award of George Cross, VX24597, AWM 119 211.
12. Report by Wells on the activities of B Force for July 1942 to July 1943, NAA B3856 144/14/58.

Chapter 12: The Underground

1. Quoted in Hurst, p. 38.
2. Silver, *Blood Brothers*, p. 120.
3. Tony White, interview, 2010.
4. Correspondence between Jackson and Christopher Lagan concerning Ernesto Lagan, AWM Private Record PR86/144.
5. Jerry Ipang Ganggal, letter, 19 March 2011.
6. Report by Wells on the activities of B Force for July 1942 to July 1943, NAA B3856 144/14/58.
7. Jackson report, NAA MP742/1 328/1/32.
8. Ibid.
9. Ibid.
10. Ibid.

Chapter 13: The Berhala Eight

1. Laffin, p. 102.
2. Ibid.
3. Ibid.
4. Press release written by Lieutenant Pynt re. Major Blow and Captain McLaren, AWM 54 779/10/1.
5. Ibid.
6. Alan Powell, Australian Dictionary of Biography online: http://adb.anu.edu.au/biography/mclaren-robert-kerr-11001.
7. Quoted in Smith, *Escapes and Incursions*, p. 55.
8. See Tahir Matusin, *The Borneo Post*, 29 September 1998; this account quoted in Smith, *Escapes and Incursions*, p. 72.
9. Recounted in Smith, *Escapes and Incursions*, p. 73.
10. Ibid., p. 73.
11. Press release written by Lieutenant Pynt re. Major Blow and Captain McLaren, AWM 54 779/10/1.
12. Smith, *Escapes and Incursions*, p. 74.
13. Laffin, p. 102.

14. Quoted in Smith, *Escapes and Incursions*, p. 76.
15. Press release written by Lieutenant Pynt re. Major Blow and Captain McLaren, AWM 54 779/10/1.
16. Quoted in Smith, *Escapes and Incursions*, p. 78.
17. Press release written by Lieutenant Pynt re. Major Blow and Captain McLaren, AWM 54 779/10/1.

Chapter 14: Guerillas

1. Interview with Steele, quoted in Smith, *Escapes and Incursions*, p. 79.
2. Smith, *Escapes and Incursions*, p. 80.
3. Ibid., p. 81.
4. Report of Captain R. E. Steele, Sergeant Walter Wallace and Sergeant R. J. Kennedy, prepared 16–23 March 1944, AWM 226 9, P1100876.
5. *Daily Mirror*, 27 December 1973.
6. Ibid.
7. Report of Captain R. E. Steele, Sergeant Walter Wallace and Sergeant R. J. Kennedy, prepared 16–23 March 1944, AWM 226 9, P1100876.
8. Press release written by Lieutenant Pynt re. Major Blow and Captain McLaren, AWM 54 779/10/1.
9. Ibid.
10. *Daily Mirror*, 27 December 1973.
11. Laffin, p. 104.
12. Official History of the Operations and Administration of Special Operations – Australia, Vol. 1 – Organisation – copy no. 1, NAA A3269 O7/A.
13. Ibid.
14. Silver, *Sandakan*, p. 143.
15. Official History of the Operations and Administration of Special Operations – Australia, Vol. 1 – Organisation – copy no. 1, NAA A3269 O7/A.
16. Matthews, p. 139.
17. Paddy Funk, notes sent to David Matthews, quoted in Matthews, pp. 141–2.

Chapter 15: Arrivals

1. Silver, *Sandakan*, p. 125.
2. John Oakeshott's private papers.
3. Barton Wagner, letter to Mrs Enid Oakeshott, 5 January 1946, John Oakeshott's private papers.
4. Major John Fairley, letter to Mrs Enid Oakeshott, 22 July 1946, John Oakeshott's private papers.

5. General report on the activities of B Force in Borneo, July 1942 to July 1943, E Force escaper parties, AWM 54 554/3/1.
6. Major John Tulloch MBE, 'Sandakan to Ranau and the Death Marches', *Royal Artillery Gunner* magazine, Spring 2011.
7. Firkins, *From Hell to Eternity.*
8. Extract from Brigadier R. J. Lewendon, 'Gunners in Java', *The Gunner*, 1942.
9. Ernest Hazzard's private papers.
10. Steve Mockridge, letter to author, 2011.
11. Jeffrey Phillips' private papers.

Chapter 16: Betrayal

1. *Prisoners of War*, Richard Braithwaite radio interview.
2. Matthews, p. 142.
3. Correspondence between Jackson and Christopher Lagan concerning Ernesto Lagan, Private Record PR86/144; statement by Dr James Taylor, NAA.
4. Ibid.

Chapter 17: The Kempei-Tai

1. Affidavits by Japanese personnel in connection with charges arising from Sandakan–Ranau death march with comments by Bill Sticpewich, AWM 54 1010/4/174.
2. Silver, *Sandakan*, p. 132.
3. Melvyn Funk, address at Memorial Service, Burwood, Sydney, 1 August 2004.
4. Jackson report, NAA MP742/1 328/1/32.
5. Melvyn Funk, address at Memorial Service, Burwood, Sydney, 1 August 2004.
6. Tanaka, pp. 26–7.
7. Ibid., p. 27.
8. Quoted in Matthews, p. 154.
9. US Department of Agriculture, reporduced on the Livestrong website: www.livestrong.com.
10. Rod Wells, statement, AWM 54 1010/4/146.
11. Jackson report, NAA MP742/1 328/1/32.
12. Fred Simpson, Radio talk with Dr Taylor of Sandakan, NAA SP300/3 924.
13. Ibid.
14. Rod Wells, statement, AWM 54 1010/4/146.
15. Ibid.

16. Ibid.
17. Quoted in Matthews, p. 152.
18. Ibid.
19. Ibid.
20. Melvyn Funk, address at Memorial Service, Burwood, Sydney, 1 August 2004.
21. Jackson report, NAA MP742/1 328/1/32.
22. Ibid.
23. Ibid.
24. Ibid.
25. Ibid.
26. Silver, *Sandakan*, p. 137.

Chapter 18: Mountain Revolt
1. Hall, p. 7.
2. Quoted in ibid., p. 10.
3. Hall, pp. 21–2.
4. Ibid., p. 28.
5. Suarez's letter certifying Kwok, 11 May 1943, quoted in Hall, p. 33.
6. Ibid., p. 34.
7. Hall, p. 47.
8. Ibid., p. 60.

Chapter 19: Kuching
1. Quoted in Hall, p. 70.
2. Ibid., p. 69.
3. Hall, p. 76.
4. Python file, Borneo, copy I, NAA A3269 A7/A.
5. Ibid.
6. Hall, p. 82.
7. Steve Mockridge letter, quoted in Matthews, pp. 159–160.
8. Silver, *Sandakan*, p. 147.
9. Ooi, p. 317.
10. Ewin, p. 88.
11. Ibid., p. 90.
12. Ooi, p. 636.
13. Allan Walker.
14. Ooi, p. 389.
15. Ibid., p. 380.
16. Ibid., p. 309.
17. Ibid., pp. 412–13.

18. Ibid., pp. 373, 393.
19. Johnston et al., p. 16.
20. See Cunningham, p. 50.
21. Johnston et al., quoted in Cunningham, p. 57.
22. Johnston et al., p. 44.
23. Cunningham, pp. 61–2.
24. Ibid., p. 65.
25. Ibid., p. 78.
26. Melvyn Funk, address at Memorial Service, Burwood, Sydney, 1 August 2004.
27. Quoted in Matthews, p. 163.
28. Report by Wells on the activities of B Force for July 1942 to July 1943, NAA B3856 144/14/58.
29. Ibid.

Chapter 20: Execution

1. Matthews, p. 164.
2. Sumaga Yoshiro, statement on the execution of Captain L. C. Matthews, NAA MP742/1 336/1/1854.
3. Captain Watanabe Haruo, ibid.
4. Sumaga Yoshiro, ibid.
5. Tanaka, pp. 29–31.
6. Sumaga Yoshiro, statement on the execution of Captain L. C. Matthews, NAA MP742/1 336/1/1854.
7. Captain Watanabe Haruo, ibid.
8. Rod Wells, statement, AWM 54 1010/4/146.
9. Ibid.
10. Ibid.
11. Ibid.
12. Tanaka, p. 29.
13. Jackson report, NAA MP742/1 328/1/32.
14. Quoted in Matthews, p. 169.
15. Ibid., pp. 169–170.
16. Captain Watanabe Haruo, statement on the execution of Captain L. C. Matthews, NAA MP742/1 336/1/1854.
17. Sumaga Yoshiro and Captain Watanabe Haruo, ibid.
18. Matthews, p. 175.
19. Sumaga Yoshiro and Captain Watanabe Haruo, statement on the execution of Captain L. C. Matthews, NAA MP742/1 336/1/1854.
20. Matthews, p. 176; Silver, *Sandakan*, p. 175.
21. Ito Kasuo, statement on the execution of Captain L. C. Matthews, NAA MP742/1 336/1/1854.

22. Kurata Kizo, ibid.
23. Captain Watanabe Haruo, ibid.
24. Matthews, pp. 176–7.
25. Roy 'Slim' Kent, 'One Australian's Story', quoted in Matthews, pp. 176–7.
26. Ibid.
27. Quoted in Matthews, p. 178.

Chapter 21: Rescue?

1. Quoted in Cunningham, p. 96.
2. Ibid., p. 97.
3. Python file, Borneo, copy I, NAA A3269 A7/A.
4. Tanaka, pp. 32–3.
5. Smith, *Borneo*, pp. 326–7.
6. Ibid.
7. Python file, Borneo, copy I, NAA A3269 A7/A.
8. Ibid.
9. Ibid.
10. Sutherland, US Army chief of staff, to commander, Allied Landforces, 28 October 1943, NAA A1196 1/501/507.
11. Donald Wilson, brigadier general, chief of staff, to the chief of staff, RAAF Headquarters, Victoria Barracks, 14 January 1944, NAA A1196, 1/501/507.
12. Dunn, p. 187.
13. Ibid., p. 188.
14. Chief of the general staff, Victoria Barracks, to the chief of the air staff, 'Aircraft for Training – 1 Aust Parachute Bn', 1 November 1944, NAA A1196 1/501/507.
15. Cypher message from NE Area to the RAAF Headquarters, 25 November 1944, NAA A1196 1/501/507.
16. KINGFISHER file, copy I, Sandakan, Borneo, NAA A3269 A22/A.
17. Ibid.
18. Ibid.
19. Ibid.
20. Ibid.
21. Smith, *Borneo*, p. 328.

PART 4: THEY MARCH

Chapter 22: New Year 1945

1. Affidavits by Japanese personnel in connection with charges arising from Sandakan–Ranau death march with comments by Bill Sticpewich, AWM 54 1010/4/174.
2. Richard Braithwaite, statement, AWM 54 1010/4/19. Braithwaite estimated about 35 killed and wounded.
3. Affidavits by Japanese personnel in connection with charges arising from Sandakan–Ranau death march with comments by Bill Sticpewich, AWM 54 1010/4/174.
4. Ibid.
5. Quoted in Firkins, *From Hell to Eternity*, p. 93.
6. Ibid.
7. See ibid., pp. 99–100.
8. Keith Botterill, statement, AWM 54 1010/4/17.
9. Ibid.
10. Tony White, interview, 2010.
11. Quoted in Firkins, *From Hell to Eternity*, p. 99.
12. Affidavits by Japanese personnel in connection with charges arising from Sandakan–Ranau death march with comments by Bill Sticpewich, AWM 54 1010/4/174.
13. Ibid.
14. Smith, *Borneo*, p. 100.
15. Quoted in ibid., p. 100.

Chapter 23: The First March

1. Quoted in Firkins, *From Hell to Eternity*, p. 103.
2. Kiyoshi, p. 154.
3. From the journal of Taiwan POW Camp HQ in Taihoku, entry 1, August 1944: Extreme measures for POWs sent to the chief of staff of the 11th Unit (Formosa POW security No. 10), quoted in Daws, p. 325.
4. Daws, pp. 324–5.
5. Toru Fukubayashi, 'POW Camps in Japan Proper', POW Research Network Japan: www.powresearch.jp/en/archive/camplist/index.html.
6. Daws, p. 324.
7. Ibid.
8. Ibid., p. 325.
9. Ibid.

10. Ibid., p. 83.
11. War Crimes Borneo trial transcripts for General Baba Masao, NAA MP742/1 336/1/1180.
12. Ibid.
13. Jackson report, NAA MP742/1 328/1/32.
14. Ibid.
15. Ibid.
16. Ibid.
17. Ibid.
18. Ibid.
19. Tanaka, p. 48.
20. Silver, *Sandakan*, p. 212.
21. Affidavits by Japanese personnel in connection with charges arising from Sandakan–Ranau death march, AWM 54 1010/4/174.

Chapter 24: White Porters

1. Jackson report, NAA MP742/1 328/1/32.
2. Ibid.
3. Ibid.
4. Tham Yau Kong and his team, villages and tribal people encountered on the track, interviews, 2011.
5. Keith Botterill, statement, AWM 54 1010/4/17.
6. Ibid.
7. Silver, *Sandakan*, p. 213.
8. Keith Botterill, statement, AWM 54 1010/4/17.
9. Ibid.
10. Ibid.
11. Quoted in Smith, *Borneo*, p. 127.
12. Tanaka, p. 49.
13. Jackson report, NAA MP742/1 328/1/32.
14. Keith Botterill, statement, AWM 54 1010/4/17.
15. Verbal evidence of Bill Sticpewich, Keith Botterill and Bill Moxham, AWM 54 1010/3/98.
16. Ibid.
17. Quoted in Tanaka, p. 51.
18. Silver, *Sandakan*, p. 227.
19. Yumpil bin Yaron, interview, near Paginatan, 2011.
20. Ibid.
21. Ibid.
22. Local woman, interview, village near Ranau, 2011.
23. Zudin, interview, village near Paginatan, 2011.
24. Domima binte Akui, interview, Paginatan, 2011.

25. Smith, *Borneo*, p. 129.
26. Figures vary according to source; these are drawn from Smith, *Borneo*, pp. 127–8.

Chapter 25: The Guards

1. Jackson report, NAA MP742/1 328/1/32.
2. Quoted in Smith, *Borneo*, p. 156.
3. See, respectively, Smith, *Borneo*, pp. 127–9; Silver, *Sandakan*, p. 229; and Jackson report, NAA MP742/1 328/1/32.
4. Verbal evidence of Bill Sticpewich, Keith Botterill and Bill Moxham, AWM 54 1010/3/98.
5. Brinkman family's private papers, supplied by Shirley Mills, Brinkman's cousin, 23 January 2011.
6. Verbal evidence of Bill Sticpewich, Keith Botterill and Bill Moxham, AWM 54 1010/3/98.
7. Quoted in Firkins, *From Hell to Eternity*, p. 114; see also Keith Botterill, statement, AWM 54 1010/4/17.
8. Figures vary according to source; these are drawn from Silver, *Sandakan*, p. 229.
9. Quoted in Firkins, *From Hell to Eternity*, p. 115.
10. Quoted in Wall, *Sandakan*, p. 74.
11. War Crimes Borneo trial transcripts for Yamamoto Shoichi, NAA MP742/1 336/1/1180.
12. War Crimes Borneo trial transcripts for Takakuwa Takuo, ibid.

Chapter 26: An Example

1. Verbal evidence of Bill Sticpewich, Keith Botterill and Bill Moxham, AWM 54 1010/3/98.
2. Trial of Kitamura Kotaro, Kawakami Koyashi and Suzuki Saburo, statement by Keith Botterill, 1946, AWM 54 1010/6/30. This is Botterill's perjured statement, as it was Suzuki Taichi, not Suzuki Saburo, who tortured Cleary.
3. Ibid.
4. Ibid.
5. Jackson report, NAA MP742/1 328/1/32.
6. Trial of Kitamura Kotaro, Kawakami Koyashi and Suzuki Saburo, statement by Keith Botterill, 1946, AWM 54 1010/6/30.
7. Ibid.
8. Quoted in Silver, *Sandakan*, p. 224.
9. Trial of Kitamura Kotaro, Kawakami Koyashi and Suzuki Saburo, defending officer, address to the court, 1946, AWM 54 1010/6/30.

Chapter 27: Self-Sacrificed

1. Richard Murray, service record, NAA B883 NX33361.
2. Keith Botterill, service record, NAA B883 NX42191.
3. Silver, *Sandakan*, p. 230.
4. According to Silver, *Sandakan*, p. 231.
5. Trial of Kitamura Kotaro, Kawakami Koyashi and Suzuki Saburo, statement by Keith Botterill, 1946, AWM 54 1010/6/30.
6. Quoted in Silver, *Sandakan*, p. 234.
7. Verbal evidence of Bill Sticpewich, Keith Botterill and Bill Moxham, AWM 54 1010/3/98.
8. Silver, *Sandakan*, p. 235.
9. Trial of Kitamura Kotaro, Kawakami Koyashi and Suzuki Saburo, statement by Keith Botterill, 1946, AWM 54 1010/6/30.
10. Affidavits by Japanese personnel in connection with charges arising from Sandakan–Ranau death march with comments by Bill Sticpewich, AWM 54 1010/4/174.

Chapter 28: Rescue?

1. Quoted in Moffitt, p. 250.
2. AGAS I file, Borneo, copy I, February–September 1945, NAA A3269 A1/A.
3. Ibid.
4. Warwick Johnstone, interview, 2011.
5. Moffitt, p. 250.
6. Ibid.
7. AGAS I file, Borneo, copy I, February–September 1945, NAA A3269 A1/A.
8. Ibid.
9. Ibid.
10. Ibid.
11. Ibid.
12. Ibid.
13. Ibid.
14. Operations in Borneo: Report, National Archives, Kew, United Kingdom, DEFE 2/1171.
15. Ibid.
16. James, essay in Stockings.
17. Ibid.
18. Ibid.
19. Ibid.
20. Ibid.
21. Ibid.
22. Ibid.
23. Operations in Borneo: Report, National Archives, Kew, United Kingdom, DEFE 2/1171.

24. Ibid.
25. Ibid.
26. *Prisoners of War*, Richard Braithwaite radio interview.

Chapter 29: The Second March

1. Silver, *Sandakan*, p. 243.
2. Jackson report, NAA MP742/1 328/1/32.
3. Tanaka, pp. 53–4.
4. Jackson report, NAA MP742/1 328/1/32.
5. Quoted in Silver, *Sandakan*, pp. 242–3.
6. Jackson report, NAA MP742/1 328/1/32.
7. Smith, *Borneo*, p. 137.
8. Owen Campbell, statement, AWM 54 1010/4/27.
9. Quoted in Smith, *Borneo*, p. 137.
10. *Prisoners of War*, Richard Braithwaite radio interview.
11. Jackson report, NAA MP742/1 328/1/32.
12. Ibid.
13. Ibid.
14. Nelson Short, statement, AWM 54 1010/4/129.
15. Fukishima Masao, statement, AWM 54 1010/4/174.
16. Jackson report, NAA MP742/1 328/1/32.
17. Shoji Shinsuke, statement, AWM 54 1010/4/174.
18. Ibid.
19. Nagahiro Masao, statement, ibid.
20. Nakayama Tamao, statement, ibid.
21. Nelson Short, statement, AWM 54 1010/4/129.
22. Jackson report, NAA MP742/1 328/1/32.

Chapter 30: Two

1. Jackson report, NAA MP742/1 328/1/32.
2. AGAS [Projects] Intelligence Reports, Borneo, February–September 1945, NAA A3269 A5/A.
3. *The Sunday Mail*, 11 June 1989.
4. June Fowler-Smith, interview, 2012.
5. Wall, *Sandakan*, p. 93.
6. Emmett family's private papers.
7. Owen Campbell, statement, AWM 54 1010/4/27.
8. Ibid.
9. Copy by Australian War Correspondent (Fred Simpson) reporting from Sandakan, Labuan, Wewak and Tarakan Areas, 1944–45, AWM 54 773/4/11.

10. Owen Campbell, statement, AWM 54 1010/4/27.
11. Ibid.
12. Ibid.
13. Wall, *Sandakan*, p. 93.
14. Owen Campbell, statement, AWM 54 1010/4/27.
15. Ibid.
16. Orang Tuan Kulang's statement to Lieutenant Colonel Jackson, 11, 16 January 1947, AWM Private Record PR84/231.
17. Ibid.
18. Secret message dated 24 July 1945 regarding the interrogation of Campbell, AWM 54 1010/1/2.
19. Owen Campbell, statement, AWM 54 1010/4/27.
20. Ibid.
21. Ibid.
22. Silver, *Sandakan*, p. 254.
23. War Crimes and Trials – General, Estimates of Australian prisoners by areas, AWM 54 1010/1/2.
24. *Prisoners of War*, Richard Braithwaite radio interview.
25. Ibid.
26. War Crimes and Trials – General, Estimates of Australian prisoners by areas, AWM 54 1010/1/2.
27. *Prisoners of War*, Richard Braithwaite radio interview.
28. Ibid.
29. Ibid.
30. Quoted in *Weekend Australian*, 25–26 July 1992.
31. War Crimes and Trials – General, Estimates of Australian prisoners by areas, AWM 54 1010/1/2.
32. Ibid.
33. *Prisoners of War*, Richard Braithwaite radio interview.
34. Richard Braithwaite, interrogation report, NAA B3856 144/1/228.
35. *Prisoners of War*, Richard Braithwaite radio interview.

Chapter 31: The Chaplain

1. Harold Wardale-Greenwood, war-service dossier, NAA B883 VX38675.
2. Ibid.
3. Smith, *Borneo*, p. 165.
4. Silver, *Sandakan*, p. 100.
5. Quoted in Wall, *Sandakan*, p. 99.

Chapter 32: The Last Jungle Camp

1. Bill Sticpewich, statement titled 'Prelude to the Sandakan–Ranau march', AWM 54 1010/4/174.
2. Silver, *Sandakan*, p. 237.
3. Jackson report, NAA MP742/1 328/1/32.
4. Verbal evidence of Bill Sticpewich, Keith Botterill and Bill Moxham, AWM 54 1010/3/98.
5. Ibid.
6. Bill Sticpewich, statement beginning 'I was at Singapore', AWM 54 1010/4/174.
7. Ibid.; Jackson report, NAA MP742/1 328/1/32.
8. Wall, *Sandakan*, p. 100.
9. Smith, *Borneo*, p. 165.
10. Jackson report, NAA MP742/1 328/1/32.
11. Ibid.
12. Smith, *Borneo*, p. 165.

Chapter 33: Three

1. Silver, *Sandakan*, pp. 27–8.
2. Recounted in Silver, *Sandakan*, pp. 28–9.
3. Bill Moxham, statement, AWM 54 1010/4/107.
4. Ibid.
5. Quoted in Silver, *Sandakan*, p. 272.
6. Bill Sticpewich, statement beginning 'I was at Singapore', AWM 54 1010/4/174.
7. Keith Botterill, statement, AWM 54 1010/4/17.
8. Smith, *Borneo*, pp. 165–6.
9. Silver, *Sandakan*, p. 279.
10. Jackson report, NAA MP742/1 328/1/32.
11. Quoted in Silver, *Sandakan*, p. 273.
12. Jackson report, NAA MP742/1 328/1/32.
13. Ibid.
14. Bill Moxham, statement, AWM 54 1010/4/107.
15. Ibid.
16. Ibid.
17. Ibid.
18. Smith, *Borneo*, p. 264.
19. Jackson report, NAA MP742/1 328/1/32.
20. Silver, *Blood Brothers*, p. 256.
21. Quoted in Wall, *Sandakan*, p. 113; Silver, *Blood Brothers*, p. 258.
22. Jackson report, NAA MP742/1 328/1/32.
23. Ibid.

24.   Quoted in Smith, *Borneo*, p. 339.
25.   Bill Moxham, statement, AWM 54 1010/4/107.

Chapter 34: One
1.   Silver, *Sandakan*, p. 271.
2.   Verbal evidence of Bill Sticpewich, Keith Botterill and Bill Moxham, AWM 54 1010/3/98.
3.   Jackson report, NAA MP742/1 328/1/32.
4.   Smith, *Borneo*, p. 266.
5.   Quoted in ibid., p. 266.
6.   Affidavits by Japanese personnel in connection with charges arising from Sandakan–Ranau death march with comments by Bill Sticpewich, AWM 54 1010/4/174.
7.   Bill Sticpewich, statement beginning 'I was at Singapore', AWM 54 1010/4/174.
8.   Ibid.
9.   Ibid.
10.   Ibid.
11.   Affidavits by Japanese personnel in connection with charges arising from Sandakan–Ranau death march with comments by Bill Sticpewich, AWM 54 1010/4/174.
12.   Bill Sticpewich, statement beginning 'I was at Singapore', AWM 54 1010/4/174.
13.   As recounted in Silver, *Sandakan*, pp. 279–280.
14.   Jackson report, NAA MP742/1 328/1/32.
15.   Bill Sticpewich, statement beginning 'I was at Singapore', AWM 54 1010/4/174.
16.   Silver, *Sandakan*, p. 283.

Chapter 35: Mati Mati
1.   Quoted in Smith, *Borneo*, p. 167.
2.   Quoted in Silver, *Sandakan*, p. 280.
3.   Smith, *Borneo*, p. 168.
4.   Ibid.
5.   Silver, *Sandakan*, p. 8.
6.   Smith, *Borneo*, p. 170.
7.   Beppu Yoichi, statement, AWM 54 1010/4/174.
8.   Ibid.
9.   Matsuda Nobunaga, statement, ibid.
10.   Hirouchi, statement, ibid.
11.   Okada Toshiharu, statement, ibid.

12. Morioka Teikichi, statement, ibid.
13. Okada Toshiharu, statement, ibid.
14. Yasuyama Eikichi, statement, ibid.
15. Affidavits and Sworn Statements, ibid.
16. Toyoka Eijiro, statement, ibid.
17. Tomiyama, statement, ibid.
18. Fukishima Masao, statement, ibid.
19. Toyoka Eijiro, statement, ibid.
20. Matsuba Shokichi, statement, ibid.
21. Takeuchi Yoshimitsu, statement, ibid.
22. Oyama, statement, ibid.
23. Beppu Yoichi, statement, ibid.
24. Yamamoto Jiro, statement, ibid.
25. Nagahiro Masao, statement, ibid.
26. Hashimoto Masao, statement, ibid.
27. Nakayama Tamao, statement, ibid.
28. Beppu Yoichi, statement, ibid.

Chapter 36: The Last

1. Jackson report, NAA MP742/1 328/1/32.
2. Alleged crucifixion of British POW: evidence of Wong Hiong, National Archives, Kew, United Kingdom, WO 325/120.
3. Jackson report, NAA MP742/1 328/1/32.
4. Quoted in Wall, *Sandakan*, p. 118.
5. AGAS I file, Borneo, copy I, February–September 1945, NAA A3269 A1/A.
6. Silver, *Sandakan*, p. 260.
7. Jackson report, NAA MP742/1 328/1/32.

Chapter 37: Crucified

1. Alleged crucifixion of British POW: evidence of Wong Hiong, National Archives, Kew, United Kingdom, WO 325/120.
2. See the Find a Grave website: www.findagrave.com/cgi-bin/fg.cgi?page=gr&GRid=39866328.
3. War Crimes – Sandakan, Borneo – Crucifixion, NAA MP375/14 WC20.
4. Alleged crucifixion of British POW: evidence of Wong Hiong, National Archives, Kew, United Kingdom, WO 325/120.
5. Ham, *Kokoda*, pp. 344–8.
6. Interrogation report submitted by Captain Mort, obtained from the four Australian prisoners of war recovered from Ranau, AWM 54 779/3/82.

7.   Alleged crucifixion of British POW: evidence of Wong Hiong, National Archives, Kew, United Kingdom, WO 325/120.

8.   Tanaka, p. 64.

9.   War Crimes – Sandakan, Borneo – Crucifixion, NAA MP375/14 WC20.

10. War Crimes – Sandakan, Borneo – Crucifixion: Interrogation of Goto Yoshitaro, ibid.

11. War Crimes – Sandakan, Borneo – Crucifixion: Interrogation of Nishikawa Yoshinori, ibid.

12. Jackson report, NAA MP742/1 328/1/32.

13. Alleged crucifixion of British POW: evidence of Wong Hiong, National Archives, Kew, United Kingdom, WO 325/120.

14. Ibid.

15. Jackson report, NAA MP742/1 328/1/32.

16. Alleged crucifixion of British POW: evidence of Wong Hiong, National Archives, Kew, United Kingdom, WO 325/120.

PART 5: REVELATION

Chapter 38: Surrender

1.   Emperor Hirohito's speech of Surrender, quoted in Ham, *Hiroshima Nagasaki*, pp. 400–2.

2.   Quoted in Ham, *Hiroshima Nagasaki*, pp. 400–2.

3.   AGAS III file, Borneo, February–September 1945, NAA A3269 A3/A.

4.   AGAS report: evacuation of PWs in British North Borneo and list of enemy agents and collaborators, National Archives, Kew, United Kingdom, Y-HS 1/246.

5.   Ibid.

6.   AGAS III file, Borneo, February–September 1945, NAA A3269 A3/A.

7.   Ibid.

8.   Ibid.

9.   Ibid.

10. Ibid.

11. Battleship Missouri Memorial website: www.ussmissouri.com/page.aspx?pid=406.

12. Truman Papers, Historical File, 1924–1953, General, Harry S. Truman Library and Museum, Missouri, Box 188.

13. Ooi, p. 625.

14. Ibid., p. 636.

15. Keith, pp. 175–6.

16. Russ Ewin, interview, 2010.
17. Wall, *Sandakan*, p. 126.
18. Report on investigation into fate of allied POWs and internees in British Borneo, National Archives, Kew, United Kingdom, WO 325/52.
19. Tanaka, p. 68.
20. Ibid., p. 67.
21. Wall, *Sandakan*, p. 128.
22. Ibid.
23. AGAS III file, Borneo, February–September 1945, NAA A3269 A3/A.
24. Ibid.
25. Ibid.
26. Ross McCowan, letter to author, 24 January 2011.
27. Ibid.
28. Richard Braithwaite, interrogation report, NAA B3856 144/1/228.
29. Ibid.
30. *Prisoners of War*, Richard Braithwaite radio interview.

Chapter 39: Relics

1. Captain Leonard Darling, History of Allied PW in British Borneo, 16–20 November 1945, AWM 54 1010/9/111.
2. Bill Sticpewich, statement, AWM 54 1010/4/134.
3. Captain Leonard Darling, History of Allied PW in British Borneo, 16–20 November 1945, AWM 54 1010/9/111.
4. Ibid.
5. Ibid.
6. Ibid.
7. Ibid.
8. Ibid.
9. Silver, *Sandakan*, p. 294.
10. Captain Leonard Darling, History of Allied PW in British Borneo, 16–20 November 1945, AWM 54 1010/9/111.
11. Report re: search Ranau–Sandakan track, NAA MP742/1 132/1/529.
12. Captain Leonard Darling, History of Allied PW in British Borneo, 16–20 November 1945, AWM 54 1010/9/111.
13. Ibid.; see also Russell report, Services Reconnaissance Detachment – report on prisoners of war Borneo, NAA B3856 144/14/83.
14. Captain Leonard Darling, History of Allied PW in British Borneo, 16–20 November 1945, AWM 54 1010/9/111.
15. AGAS report: evacuation of PWs in British North Borneo and list of enemy agents and collaborators, National Archives, Kew, United Kingdom, Y-HS 1/246.

16. Captain Leonard Darling, History of Allied PW in British Borneo, 16–20 November 1945, AWM 54 1010/9/111; see also Russell report, Services Reconnaissance Detachment – report on prisoners of war Borneo, NAA B3856 144/14/83.

17. Report re: search Ranau–Sandakan track, NAA MP742/1 132/1/529.

18. Jackson report, NAA MP742/1 328/1/32.

19. Silver, *Sandakan*, p. 318.

20. *The Sydney Morning Herald, The Daily Telegraph*, 21 December 1946.

21. Tom Burns' diary, NAA B3856 144/14/140.

22. Report re: search Ranau–Sandakan track, recovery of 109 bodies, Sticpewich, statement, 31 Australian War Graves Unit, NAA MP742/1 132/1/529.

23. Ibid.

24. Ibid.

25. Ibid.

26. Report re: search Ranau–Sandakan track, recovery of 109 bodies, research of Sandakan–Ranau Rentis, Ranau Area and Paginatan by Warrant Officer Bill Sticpewich, NAA MP742/1 132/1/529.

27. Report re: search Ranau–Sandakan track, recovery of 109 bodies, Sticpewich, statement, 31 Australian War Graves Unit, ibid.

28. Ibid.

Chapter 40: The Trials

1. Affidavits by Japanese personnel in connection with charges arising from Sandakan–Ranau death march with comments by Bill Sticpewich, AWM 54 1010/4/174.

2. Statements by WO1 Sticpewich, NAA B3856 144/1/372 Part 3.

3. Affidavits by Japanese personnel in connection with charges arising from Sandakan–Ranau death march with comments by Bill Sticpewich, AWM 54 1010/4/174.

4. Ibid.

5. Ibid.

6. Ibid.

7. Ibid.

8. Ibid.

9. Ibid.

10. Ibid.

11. Ibid.

12. Ibid.

13. Captain Barr, Legal officer attached to 9 Australian Division, to DDLA HQ Morotai Force, January 1946, AWM 54 1010/4/174.

14. Ibid.

15.   Moffitt, p. 74.

16.   War Crimes Borneo trial transcripts for Takakuwa Takuo, NAA MP742/1 336/1/1180.

17.   Ibid.

18.   Ibid.

19.   Moffitt, p. 121.

20.   Ibid., p. 119.

21.   Captain Hoshijima Susumi, trial and execution, NAA MP742/1 336/1/707.

22.   Moffitt, p. 71.

23.   Ibid., p. 72.

24.   Ibid., p. 73.

25.   Ibid.

26.   Ibid., p. 79.

27.   War Crimes Borneo trial transcripts for Hoshijima Susumi, NAA MP742/1 336/1/1180.

28.   Quoted in 'The Sandakan Tragedy and War Trials', an address by Athol Moffitt, 1987 National Conference of the Veterans' Review Board.

29.   War Crimes Borneo trial transcripts for Hoshijima Susumi, NAA MP742/1 336/1/1180.

30.   Moffitt, p. 89.

31.   War Crimes Borneo trial transcripts for Hoshijima Susumi, NAA MP742/1 336/1/1180.

32.   Ibid.

33.   Ibid.

34.   Moffitt, p. 92.

35.   Ibid., p. 94.

36.   Ibid., p. 100.

37.   Quoted in ibid., p. 100.

38.   Ibid., p. 102.

39.   War Crimes Borneo trial transcripts for General Baba Masao, NAA MP742/1 336/1/1180.

40.   Ibid.

41.   Bill Sticpewich's private papers.

42.   War Crimes Borneo trial transcripts for General Baba Masao, NAA MP742/1 336/1/1180.

43.   Silver, *Sandakan*, p. 305.

44.   Ibid.

45.   Steve Meacham, *The Sydney Morning Herald*, 13 March 2012: www.smh.com.au/national/vc-award-would-be-based-on-lies-military-historian-warns-20120312-1uwh4.html#ixzz1ozhLUIPD.

46.   Silver, *Sandakan*, p. 349.

47.   War Crimes Borneo trial transcripts for Toyoda Kokishi, NAA MP742/1 336/1/1180.

48. Steve Meacham, *The Sydney Morning Herald*, 13 March 2012: www. smh.com.au/national/vc-award-would-be-based-on-lies-military-historian-warns-20120312–1uwh4.html#ixzz1ozhLUIPD.

49. Execution of Captain L. C. Matthews and ill-treatment of prisoners of war by Kempei Tai at Sandakan, NAA MP742/1, 336/1/1854.

50. Ill-treatment and torture of prisoners of war at Sandakan by Kempei Tai, NAA MP742/1 336/1/1943.

51. Execution of Captain L. C. Matthews and ill-treatment of prisoners of war by Kempei Tai at Sandakan, NAA MP742/1, 336/1/1854.

52. Ibid.

53. War Crimes Military Tribunal of Yamawaki Masataka and Watanabe Haruo, Manus, 30 October to 16 November 1950, NAA A471 81957.

54. Ibid.

55. Tanaka, pp. 70–1.

Chapter 41: The People

1. *People* magazine, 17 January 1951.

2. Jackson report, NAA MP742/1 328/1/32.

3. Quoted in Silver, *Sandakan*, pp. 331–2.

4. AGAS I file, Borneo, copy I, February–September 1945, NAA A3269 A1/A.

5. Ibid.

6. Ibid.

7. Ibid.

8. Silver, *Sandakan*, p. 330.

9. Awards to Helpers, British North Borneo, NAA MP742/1 66/1/578A.

10. *People* magazine, 27 August 1952.

11. Lieutenant Colonel Jackson, MBE, ED, 3 Pw Contact and Inquiry Unit, AWM Private Record PR84/231.

12. AGAS I file, Borneo, copy I, February–September 1945, NAA A3269 A1/A.

13. Awards to Helpers, British North Borneo, NAA MP742/1 66/1/578A.

14. Ibid.

15. Lieutenant Colonel Jackson, MBE, ED, 3 Pw Contact and Inquiry Unit, AWM Private Record PR84/231.

16. Ibid.

17. Awards to Helpers, British North Borneo, NAA MP742/1 66/1/578A.

18. Ibid.

19. Ibid.

20. Chifley to Blain, letter, 9 May 1947, in Jackson report, NAA MP742/1 328/1/32.

21. Correspondence between Jackson and Christopher Lagan concerning Ernesto Lagan, AWM Private Record PR86/144.

22. *People* magazine, 27 August 1952.
23. Malcolm MacDonald, speech, 17 September 1946, in Jackson report, NAA MP742/1 328/1/32.

Chapter 42: Home

1. Tony White's private papers.
2. Ibid.
3. Stan Woods' private papers.
4. Statements made by Bombardier Braithwaite and Gunner Campbell, NAA B3856, 144/1/246.
5. Royal condolence letter to families of POWs, National Archives, Kew, United Kingdom, Y-FCO 24/1181.
6. Frank Anderson service record, NAA B883 QX6866.
7. *Prisoners of War*, Richard Braithwaite radio interview.
8. Les Mockridge's private papers.
9. Jeffrey Phillips, interview, 2011.
10. Rose Barry, letter to author, 12 January 2011.
11. *The Age*, 15 August 2005.
12. Cases cited in Wall, *Sandakan*, p. 130.
13. John Oakeshott's private papers.
14. Ibid.
15. Ibid.
16. See 'The Dream Strike', *Daily Express*, Sabah, Sunday 23 August 2009.
17. Bob Oakeshott, interview, 2011.
18. Betty Seccombe, letter to author, 3 July 2011.
19. June Fowler-Smith, interview, 2012.
20. Barrie Whitehead's private papers, Lieutenant John Fuller, letter to Mrs Whitehead.
21. Ibid., unknown officer, letter to Mrs Whitehead.
22. Ibid., Ken Mosher, letter to Mrs Whitehead.
23. Ibid., Dick Braithwaite, letter to Mrs Whitehead.
24. Claire Woods, interview, 2011.
25. Stan Woods' private papers.
26. Blythe, p. 73.
27. Christopher Elliott's private papers, quoted in Elliott.
28. Ibid.
29. Ibid.
30. Blythe, p. 73.
31. Stephens family's private papers.
32. Ibid.
33. Ibid.
34. Ibid.
35. Phillips family's private papers.

36. Jeffrey Phillips, interview, 2011.
37. Ibid.
38. Ibid.
39. Ibid.
40. Rod York's private papers.
41. Ibid.
42. Ibid.
43. Dawson, *To Sandakan*, p. 107.
44. Stan Woods' private papers.
45. Ibid.
46. Ibid.
47. Steve Mockridge, interview, 2011.
48. Ibid.
49. Ibid.
50. Mockridge family's private papers, E. P. Beale, letter to Les Mockridge, 11 March 1946.
51. Steve Mockridge, interview, 2011.
52. Mockridge family's private papers.
53. *The Sydney Morning Herald*, 16 December 1996.
54. *The Age*, 5 December 2003.
55. Ibid.
56. Barry Tinkler, interview, 2011.
57. Bill Young, interview, 2011.
58. Compensation – Natives, North Borneo, NAA SP459/1 434/1/1727.
59. James Patrick Taylor file, NAA B510, 292.
60. Ibid.
61. Ibid.
62. Ibid.
63. Lionel Matthews, Award of George Cross, VX24597, AWM 119 211.
64. Ibid.
65. Ibid.
66. *The Argus* (Melbourne), 15 January 1948.
67. *The Bulletin*, 21 March 1956.
68. Laffin, pp. 102–3.
69. *The Sydney Morning Herald*, 26 January 2001.
70. Ibid. Blow is survived by his wife, Sonya, and their two children, Andrew and Nicole, and by a son of his first marriage, John. Blow's sister-in-law, Sheila Ross, wrote a book about him, *And Tomorrow Freedom* (Allen & Unwin, 1989).
71. Athol Moffitt's private papers, Blow, letter to Moffitt, 11 July 1987.
72. Ibid.
73. List of Awards for Services rendered whilst Prisoners of War, AWM 119 173 Part 1.
74. Statements by WO1 Sticpewich, NAA B3856 144/1/372 Part 3.

75.   *Prisoners of War*, Richard Braithwaite radio interview.
76.   Ibid.
77.   *The Chronicle*, 9 March 1999.
78.   *Prisoners of War*, Richard Braithwaite radio interview.
79.   Ibid.
80.   Ibid., Joyce Braithwaite radio interview.
81.   Ibid.
82.   Silver, *Sandakan*, p. 349.
83.   *The Sydney Morning Herald*, 13 March 2012. Botterill's lies about Cleary's death should disqualify the latter from consideration for the award of a posthumous Victoria Cross, according to Silver's case before Australia's Defence Honours and Awards Tribunal. In 2012, the Tribunal was investigating whether 13 cases deserved posthumous consideration for the award. Yet Botterill's perjury was surely irrelevant to the inquiry. While nobody doubts that Cleary died after horrific torture, his shocking ordeal does not meet the criteria for the award, which honours 'most conspicuous bravery, or some daring or pre-eminent act of valour or self-sacrifice . . . in the face of the enemy'. Cleary died not in the line of battle, or trying to escape, but powerless, helpless, flung about in the grip of his monstrous persecutors. The question of who murdered him is irrelevant to the question of whether or not Cleary is eligible for a posthumous Victoria Cross. He is not.
84.   Bill Keating, service record, NAA B883 NX5829.
85.   Quoted in *The Canberra Times*, 2 August 1993.
86.   Quoted in *The Australian*, 2 August 1993.
87.   General Sir Thomas Blamey, speech to Second Annual Conference of the Australian Armoured Corps, 19 November 1947, quoted in Forbes, p. 542.
88.   Operational plan for relief of Australian POW Borneo – 1945, NAA A5954 265/6.
89.   *The Sun-Herald*, 4 December 1947 and *The Herald* (Melbourne), 4 December 1947.
90.   Operational plan for relief of Australian prisoners of war in Borneo, 1945, draft reply to Parliamentary question by Mr Falkinder MP regarding General Blamey's public statement, NAA A663 O148/2/470.
91.   Operational plan for relief of Australian POW Borneo – 1945, NAA A5954 265/6.
92.   Quoted in 'The Sandakan Tragedy and War Trials', an address by Athol Moffitt, 1987 National Conference of the Veterans' Review Board.
93.   Quoted in Christopher Dawson, 'Why Our Prisoners of War in Borneo in World War II Could Not Be Rescued', *United Service*, Vol. 52, No. 9, 2000.

94.   Ibid.
95.   Ibid.
96.   Ibid.
97.   Ibid.
98.   *Prisoners of War*, Richard Braithwaite radio interview.
99.   Ueno, pp. 79–81.
100. Ibid., pp. 101–2.

BIBLIOGRAPHY

PRIMARY SOURCES

Documents

Australian War Memorial
AWM 52 1/5/17, Second World War Diaries of the 8th Australian Division, General Staff Branch

AWM 52 1/5/19, Second World War Diaries of the 8th Australian Division, No. 1 Prisoner of War Camp Changi

AWM 52 4/2/10, 2/10th Field Regiment, brief history

AWM 52 4/2/15, 2/15th Field Regiment, brief history

AWM 52 7/16/8, 8th Division Signals, war diary

AWM 52 10/32/25, 8th Division Amn Sub Park, war diary

AWM 52 11/12/18, 2/9th Australian Field Ambulance, war diary

AWM 52 11/12/19, 2/10th Australian Field Ambulance, war diary

AWM 54 424/4/7, Special reports and interrogations re. natives – Sandakan and Borneo, 1943–45

AWM 54 553/5/5, Campaign in Malaya and Singapore – Reports, Summary of Malayan Campaign by Lieutenant Colonel Kappe, Commanding 8th Division Signals

AWM 54 554/3/1, General report on the activities of B Force in Borneo, July 1942 to July 1943, E Force escaper parties

AWM 54 554/3/2, 8th Division in Captivity – B Force (Borneo): Information regarding Allied prisoners of war Sandakan, Jesselton and Ranau

AWM 54 554/6/1, Report on E Force AIF – POW, Malaya by Major J. G. Fairley, 1945

AWM 54 554/11/23, 8th Division in Captivity – Changi and Singapore Island: Report covering, as fully as possible, the history of the medical services, AIF Malaya after the capitulation of Singapore

AWM 54 773/4/11, Copy by Australian War Correspondent (Fred Simpson) reporting from Sandakan, Labuan, Wewak and Tarakan Areas, 1944–45

AWM 54 779/3/82, Prisoners of War and Internees – Examinations and Interrogations: Information – Allied Prisoners of War, Interrogation report submitted by Capt T. L. Mort, OC 3PW Contact and Inquiry teams, obtained from the four Australian recovered PWs ex Ranau

AWM 54 779/10/1, Prisoners of War and Internees – Escapes: Escaped Australian Prisoners of War, Copy of public relations story written by Major Blow and Captain McLaren

AWM 54 1010/1/2, War Crimes and Trials – General, Estimates of Australian prisoners by areas

AWM 54 1010/1/2, War Crimes and Trials – General, Preliminary interrogation of QX 14380 Owen Colin Campbell, 2/10th Field Regiment AIF, 28 July 1945, escaped from Sandakan Area, British North Borneo

AWM 54 1010/1/2, War Crimes and Trials – Secret message dated 24 July 1945 regarding the interrogation of Campbell

AWM 54 1010/3/98, War Crimes and Trials – Transcripts of Evidence: verbal evidence of W/O W. H. Sticpewich, Pte Keith Botterill, Cpl W. O. Moxham

AWM 54 1010/4/17, War Crimes and Trials – Affidavits and Sworn Statements, Report by Keith Botterill

AWM 54 1010/4/19, War Crimes and Trials – Affidavits and Sworn Statements, Report by James Richard Braithwaite

AWM 54 1010/4/27, War Crimes and Trials – Affidavits and Sworn Statements, Report by Owen Campbell

AWM 54 1010/4/107, War Crimes and Trials – Affidavits and Sworn Statements, Report by Bill Moxham

AWM 54 1010/4/129, War Crimes and Trials – Affidavits and Sworn Statements, Report by Nelson Short

AWM 54 1010/4/134, War Crimes and Trials – Affidavits and Sworn Statements, Report by Bill Sticpewich

AWM 54 1010/4/146, War Crimes and Trials – Affidavits and Sworn Statements, Report by Lieutenant Rod Wells

AWM 54 1010/4/174, War Crimes and Trials – Affidavits and Sworn Statements: Captain Barr, Legal officer attached to 9 Australian Division, to DDLA HQ Morotai Force, January 1946

AWM 54 1010/4/174, War Crimes and Trials – Affidavits and Sworn Statements: Affidavits by Japanese personnel in connection with charges arising from Sandakan–Ranau death march with comments by Warrant Officer W. H. Sticpewich covering prelude to march, War Crimes and events by Warrant Officer W. H. Sticpewich

AWM 54 1010/4/174, War Crimes and Trials – Affidavits and Sworn Statements: Affidavits by Japanese personnel in connection with charges arising from Sandakan–Ranau death march with comments by Warrant Officer W. H. Sticpewich: Beppu Yoichi statement

AWM 54 1010/4/174, War Crimes and Trials – Affidavits and Sworn Statements: Affidavits by Japanese personnel in connection with charges arising from Sandakan–Ranau death march with comments by Warrant Officer W. H. Sticpewich: Fukishima Masao statement

AWM 54 1010/4/174, War Crimes and Trials – Affidavits and Sworn Statements: Affidavits by Japanese personnel in connection with charges arising from Sandakan–Ranau death march with comments by Warrant Officer W. H. Sticpewich: Hashimoto Masao statement

AWM 54 1010/4/174, War Crimes and Trials – Affidavits and Sworn Statements: Affidavits by Japanese personnel in connection with charges arising from Sandakan–Ranau death march with comments by Warrant Officer W. H. Sticpewich: Hirouchi statement

AWM 54 1010/4/174, War Crimes and Trials – Affidavits and Sworn Statements: Affidavits by Japanese personnel in connection with charges arising from Sandakan–Ranau death march with comments by Warrant Officer W. H. Sticpewich: Matsuba Shokichi statement

AWM 54 1010/4/174, War Crimes and Trials – Affidavits and Sworn Statements: Affidavits by Japanese personnel in connection with charges arising from Sandakan–Ranau death march with comments by Warrant Officer W. H. Sticpewich: Matsuda Nobunaga statement

AWM 54 1010/4/174, War Crimes and Trials – Affidavits and Sworn Statements: Affidavits by Japanese personnel in connection with charges arising from Sandakan–Ranau death march with comments by Warrant Officer W. H. Sticpewich: Morioka Teikichi statement

AWM 54 1010/4/174, War Crimes and Trials – Affidavits and Sworn Statements: Affidavits by Japanese personnel in connection with charges arising from Sandakan–Ranau death march with comments by Warrant Officer W. H. Sticpewich: Nagahiro Masao statement

AWM 54 1010/4/174, War Crimes and Trials – Affidavits and Sworn Statements: Affidavits by Japanese personnel in connection with charges arising from Sandakan–Ranau death march with comments by Warrant Officer W. H. Sticpewich: Nakayama Tamao statement

AWM 54 1010/4/174, War Crimes and Trials – Affidavits and Sworn Statements: Affidavits by Japanese personnel in connection with charges arising from Sandakan–Ranau death march with comments by Warrant Officer W. H. Sticpewich: Okada Toshiharu statement

AWM 54 1010/4/174, War Crimes and Trials – Affidavits and Sworn Statements: Affidavits by Japanese personnel in connection with charges arising from Sandakan–Ranau death march with comments by Warrant Officer W. H. Sticpewich: Oyama statement

AWM 54 1010/4/174, War Crimes and Trials – Affidavits and Sworn Statements: Affidavits by Japanese personnel in connection with charges arising from Sandakan–Ranau death march with comments by Warrant Officer W. H. Sticpewich: Shoji Shinsuke statement

AWM 54 1010/4/174, War Crimes and Trials – Affidavits and Sworn

Statements: Affidavits by Japanese personnel in connection with charges arising from Sandakan–Ranau death march with comments by Warrant Officer W. H. Sticpewich: Takeuchi Yoshimitsu statement

AWM 54 1010/4/174, War Crimes and Trials – Affidavits and Sworn Statements: Affidavits by Japanese personnel in connection with charges arising from Sandakan–Ranau death march with comments by Warrant Officer W. H. Sticpewich: Tomiyama statement

AWM 54 1010/4/174, War Crimes and Trials – Affidavits and Sworn Statements: Affidavits by Japanese personnel in connection with charges arising from Sandakan–Ranau death march with comments by Warrant Officer W. H. Sticpewich: Toyoka Eijiro statement

AWM 54 1010/4/174, War Crimes and Trials – Affidavits and Sworn Statements: Affidavits by Japanese personnel in connection with charges arising from Sandakan–Ranau death march with comments by Warrant Officer W. H. Sticpewich: Yamamoto Jiro statement

AWM 54 1010/4/174, War Crimes and Trials – Affidavits and Sworn Statements: Affidavits by Japanese personnel in connection with charges arising from Sandakan–Ranau death march with comments by Warrant Officer W. H. Sticpewich: Yasuyama Eikichi statement

AWM 54 1010/6/30, War Crimes and Trials – Summary of Proceedings: Trial of Kitamura Kotaro, Kawakami Koyashi and Suzuki Saburo, statement by Keith Botterill, 1946

AWM 54 1010/6/59, War Crimes and Trials – Summary of Proceedings: Suga address to court

AWM 54 1010/9/111, History of Allied PW in British Borneo by Captain L. G. Darling, PWLO 9 Aust Div, dated 16–20 November 1945

AWM 57 3/36, Allied Geographical Section, South-West Pacific Area, Terrain Handbook 60, Sandakan

AWM 67 3/383, Official History, 1939–45 War, Records of Gavin Long: Sticpewich, W. H. WO1

AWM 93 50/2/23/483, War of 1939–45, Correspondence regarding a letter written by W/O H. Sticpewich

AWM 119 154, AIF – Malaya Operational Awards, WO1 Bill Sticpewich

AWM 119 173 Part 1, List of Awards for Services rendered whilst Prisoners of War

AWM 119 211, Award of George Cross, VX24597, Captain Lionel C. Matthews MC, 8th Australian Division

AWM 226 9, P1100876, Report of Captain R. E. Steele, Sergeant Walter Wallace and Sergeant R. J. Kennedy, prepared 16–23 March 1944

AWM F940.5425 W179s, monograph, 'Singapore Reflections': Captain Hartley James Walker's first-hand account of the events in the months leading up to the fall of Singapore in early 1942

Private Record PR00637, Private papers of Bill Sticpewich

Private Record PR01378, Private papers of Athol Moffitt

Private Record PR84/144, Private papers of Harry Jackson
Private Record PR84/231, Jackson, Harold W. S. (Lieutenant Colonel), MBE, ED, 3 Pw Contact and Inquiry Unit
Private Record PR84/231, Jackson, Harold W. S. (Lieutenant Colonel), Correspondence and statement – Orang Kulang, 11, 16 January 1947
Private Record PR86/144, Jackson, Harold W. S. (Lieutenant Colonel), Correspondence between Jackson and Christopher Lagan concerning Ernesto Lagan

Harry S. Truman Library and Museum, Missouri, United States
Truman Papers, Historical File, 1924–1953, Box 188 General

Imperial War Museum, Southwark, London, United Kingdom
EGL/1, Letter cards from Lawrence, sent from Sandakan camp, c.1945

National Archives of Australia
NAA 3DRL/7408, Funk's statement relating his capture, torture and interrogation by the Kempei-tai in 1943, the death of Captain Matthews, the Sandakan–Ranau death march and liberation, note on his death, 1981
NAA A446 1969/65043, Agnes Patricia Funk
NAA A463 1968/4056, Alec and Johnny Funk
NAA A471 22870, Bill Sticpewich, 8th Division Ammunition Column, date of court martial 13 March 1941
NAA A471 81957, War Crimes – Military Tribunal – Yamawaki Masataka (General): Watanabe Haruo (Captain): Unit – Borneo Defence Army: Place and date of Tribunal – Manus, 30 October to 16 November 1950
NAA A518 A320/3/1 Part 2, War damage compensation to natives – Policy
NAA A649 52/600/512, Compensation and reward for residents of British North Borneo who helped POWs
NAA A663 O148/2/470, Operational plan for relief of Australian prisoners of war in Borneo, 1945, draft reply to Parliamentary question by Mr Falkinder MP regarding General Blamey's public statement
NAA A705 55/1/912, Honours and awards, Leading Aircraftman Jack Wong Sue, Recommendation for DCM
NAA A1196 1/501/507, Paratroop Training Unit – Availability of aircraft: Sutherland, US Army chief of staff, to commander, Allied Landforces, dated 28 October 1943
NAA A1196 1/501/507, Paratroop Training Unit – Availability of aircraft: Donald Wilson, brigadier general, chief of staff, to the chief of staff, RAAF Headquarters, Victoria Barracks, dated 14 January 1944
NAA A1196 1/501/507, Paratroop Training Unit – Availability of aircraft: Memo from the chief of the general staff, Victoria Barracks, to the chief of the air staff titled 'Aircraft for Training – 1 Aust Parachute Bn', dated 1 November 1944

NAA A1196 1/501/507, Paratroop Training Unit – Availability of aircraft: Cypher message from NE Area to the RAAF Headquarters, dated 25 November 1944

NAA A1379 EPJ463, Dr James Patrick Taylor – British North Borneo

NAA A3269 A1/A, AGAS I file, copy I, British North Borneo, February–September 1945

NAA A3269 A1/B, AGAS I file, copy II, British North Borneo, February–September 1945

NAA A3269 A1–A9, AGAS I, II files, British North Borneo, February–September 1945

NAA A3269 A3/A, AGAS III file, British North Borneo, February–September 1945

NAA A3269 A5/A, AGAS [Projects] Intelligence Reports, British North Borneo, February–September 1945

NAA A3269 A7/A, PYTHON file, Borneo, copy I

NAA A3269 A7/B, PYTHON file, Borneo, copy II

NAA A3269 A22/A, A22B, KINGFISHER file, Sandakan, Borneo, 1944–45

NAA A3269 A31/B, Supplement to static report on British North Borneo Area, Geographical information

NAA A3269 O7/A, Q1–Q11, The Official History of the Operations and Administration of Special Operations – Australia (SOA), also known as the Inter-Allied Services Department (ISD) and Services Reconnaissance Department (SRD), Vols 1–5

NAA A5954 264/3, Major General Gordon Bennett's Report on Malayan Campaign, March 1942

NAA A5954 265/6 Operational plan for relief of Australian POW Borneo – 1945

NAA A5954 676/9, Borneo – Relief of Australian POW, 1945

NAA A9301 83783, Jack Wong Sue, service number 83783

NAA B503 N467, Keith Botterill NX42181 – POW Trust Fund application

NAA B503 N4635, Nelson Short NX58617 – POW Trust Fund application

NAA B503 Q285, Owen Campbell QX14380 – POW Trust Fund application

NAA B503 Q1728, Bill Sticpewich QX9538 – POW Trust Fund application

NAA B510 292, James Patrick Taylor file

NAA B883 NX5829, Bill Keating, service record

NAA B883 NX33361, Richard Murray, service record

NAA B883 NX40325, James Darlington, service record

NAA B883 NX42191, Keith Botterill, service record

NAA B883 NX45378, James Braithwaite, service record

NAA B883 NX58617, Nelson Short, service record

NAA B883 NX68380, Michael Keating, service record

NAA B883 NX19750, Bill Moxham, service record

NAA B883 NX72757, Tom Burns, service record

NAA B883 NX76184, George Cook, service record

NAA B833 NX76223, John Oakeshott, service record

NAA B883 QX4648, Rex Blow, service record

NAA B883 QX6380, Domenic Picone, service record

NAA B883 QX6866, Frank Anderson, service record

NAA B883 QX14380, Owen Campbell, service record

NAA B833 QX21058, Robert McLaren, service record

NAA B833 VX24597, Lionel Matthews, service record

NAA B883 VX38675, Harold Wardale-Greenwood, service record

NAA B2455, Harold Wardale-Greenwood file

NAA B3856 140/11/2073, Captain Lionel Matthews, VX24597

NAA B3856 144/1/228, Interrogation report, Bdr Braithwaite J. R., NX45378 – PoW recovered from Borneo

NAA B3856, 144/1/244, Gunner Owen Campbell and others – statements concerning prisoners of war known or believed to have died while in enemy custody including Sandakan

NAA B3856, 144/1/246, Statements made by Australian Prisoners of War recovered from Japanese hands in Borneo, Statements – NX45378 Bdr Braithwaite J. R. and QX14380 Gnr Campbell O. C. – Lists of Casualties/ Prisoners of War

NAA B3856 144/1/372 Part 3, Statements by WO1 Sticpewich

NAA B3856 144/14/14, Information extracted from interrogation reports regarding escaped POWs

NAA B3856 144/14/58, Report by recovered prisoner of war Lieutenant Wells R. G., Signals 8 Australian Division, on the activities of B Force for period July 1942 to July 1943

NAA B3856 144/14/83, Russell report, Services Reconnaissance Detachment – report on prisoners of war Borneo

NAA B3856 144/14/140, War Crimes – Sandakan – Borneo – Documents found in mass grave of 23 Australian prisoners of war, Personal diary thought to belong to Tom Burns, NX72757 2/20th Bn AIF

NAA J25 1972/20491, Paddy Henry Funk

NAA J1795 6/393, Domenic Picone, military officer's record of service

NAA MP375/14 WC20, War Crimes – Sandakan, Borneo – Crucifixion

NAA MP375/14 WC20, War Crimes – Sandakan, Borneo – Crucifixion: Interrogation of Goto Yoshitaro

NAA MP375/14 WC20, War Crimes – Sandakan, Borneo – Crucifixion: Interrogation of Nishikawa Yoshinori

NAA MP508/1 56/704/27, Department of Army: Applications for a commission in the Australian Army Chaplains Department, Harold Wardale-Greenwood

NAA MP729/8 44/431/101, Recovered Australian POW ex Borneo – information and reports

NAA MP742/1 66/1/513, Assistance by natives to Australian prisoners of war in Borneo

NAA MP742/1 66/1/572, Rewards for Helpers (Andu bin Patrick, et al.), British North Borneo

NAA MP742/1 66/1/578A, Awards to Helpers, British North Borneo

NAA MP742/1 81/1/801, Question of Financial Recompense and Honour to Hon. Dr J. P. Taylor

NAA MP742/1 132/1/465, Australian POWs shot and buried at Sandakan

NAA MP742/1 132/1/529, Report re: search Ranau–Sandakan track, recovery of 109 bodies, Sticpewich, statement, 31 Australian War Graves Unit

NAA MP742/1 132/1/529, Report re: search Ranau–Sandakan track, recovery of 109 bodies, research of Sandakan–Ranau Rentis, Ranau Area and Paginatan by Warrant Officer Bill Sticpewich

NAA MP742/1 328/1/32, Awards to Helpers, British North Borneo, Major Jackson's report

NAA MP742/1 336/1/707, War Crimes – Military Tribunal – Captain Hoshijima Susumi, trial and execution

NAA MP742/1 336/1/1180, War Crimes Borneo trial transcripts (statements, interrogation reports, evidence, etc.) for Baba Masao

NAA MP742/1 336/1/1180, War Crimes Borneo trial transcripts (statements, interrogation reports, evidence, etc.) for Hoshijima Susumi

NAA MP742/1 336/1/1180, War Crimes Borneo trial transcripts (statements, interrogation reports, evidence, etc.) for Takakuwa Takuo

NAA MP742/1 336/1/1180, War Crimes Borneo trial transcripts (statements, interrogation reports, evidence, etc.) for Yamamoto Shoichi

NAA MP742/1 336/1/1470, Report by Indonesian soldiers and QX9538, WO1 Bill Sticpewich

NAA MP742/1, 336/1/1854, War Crimes – Execution of Captain L. C. Matthews and ill-treatment of prisoners of war by Kempei Tai at Sandakan

NAA MP742/1 336/1/1854, War Crimes – Execution of Captain L. C. Matthews, Ito Kasuo statement

NAA MP742/1 336/1/1854, War Crimes – Execution of Captain L. C. Matthews, Kurata Kizo statement

NAA MP742/1 336/1/1854, War Crimes – Execution of Captain L. C. Matthews, Sumaga statement

NAA MP742/1 336/1/1854, War Crimes – Execution of Captain L. C. Matthews, Watanabe statement

NAA MP742/1 336/1/1943, War Crimes – Ill-treatment and torture of prisoners of war at Sandakan by Kempei Tai

NAA MP927/1 A274/1/1, Johnny Funk, medical history sheets

NAA MP927/1 A274/1/54, Sandakan Death March – Sergeant Jack Wong Sue

NAA MT885/1 S/8/2541, Bill Sticpewich, application for a commission
NAA MT929/2 V1957/60584, Lillian Funk, wife of Johnny
NAA SP300/3 924, Radio talk presented by ABC War Correspondent Fred
    Simpson with Dr Taylor of Sandakan
NAA SP459/1 434/1/1727, Compensation – Natives, North Borneo
NAA SP459/1 495/3/1850, Reimbursement – Loss of equipment and personal
    belongings, NX76223 Captain John Oakeshott

The National Archives, Kew, London, United Kingdom
CAB 84/70, Operations in Borneo, Note by Secretary, 1945
CAB 84/71, Operations in Borneo, Note by Secretary, 1945
X-HS 1, Papers on the establishment and operations of Special Operations
    Australia (SOA), known as the Services Reconnaissance Department
    (SRD), 1941–46
X-WO 357/5, Convicted Japanese war criminals held in prison in Borneo,
    Changi Gaol, Civil Prison (Hong Kong), Johore State Prison, Outram
    Road Gaol (Singapore), Padu, Penang, Rangoon Gaol, Sandakan, Stanley
    Gaol (Hong Kong) and Taiping Gaol, 1946–48
Y-CAB 106/124, Report on operations in Borneo, 1 May 1945–15 Aug 1945,
    by General Blamey, Commander Allied Land Forces, South West Pacific
    Area
Y-CAB 120/818, General MacArthur, 1943–45
Y-CAB 121/717, Operations in Borneo, 1945–46
Y-CAB 127/32, Telegrams between the Prime Minister, Mr Curtin
    (Prime Minister of Australia) and General MacArthur on command
    arrangements in the Pacific, 1944
Y-CO 531/31/10, Civil Affairs Policy in British Borneo: directive to General
    MacArthur, Allied C-in-C, S W Pacific, 1945
Y-CO 531/31/30, Conditions in Borneo: reports and correspondence from
    Brigadier C. F. MacAskie, Chief civil affairs officer, 1945–47
Y-CO 531/43/9, North Borneo War Victim's Fund: Establishment for the
    relief of Asiatics killed during the Japanese Occupation, 1947–48
Y-CO 825/43/13, Borneo military administration: directive for General
    MacArthur, 1944
Y-CO 825/48/9, Liberation of British Borneo: proposed message to be sent to
    people of Labuan from HM the King, 1945
Y-CO 852/665/3, Estimated needs for relief and rehabilitation of the Far East:
    Borneo, 1945
Y-CO 968/9/8, War intelligence telegrams: Malaya and North Borneo, 1943
Y-CO 980/129, Reports on Japanese internment camp at Berhala (Haraba)
    Island near Sandakan in British North Borneo, 1944
Y-CO 980/229, Lists of prisoners of war and civilian internees reported to be
    in Borneo, 1945
Y-DEFE 2/1171, Operations in Borneo: report, 1944

Y-FCO 24/1181, Memorial to prisoners of war of the Japanese who died on Sandakan/Ranau death march in 1944–45 in North Borneo, Malaysia, Royal condolence letter to families of POWs, 1971

Y-HS 1/244, Monthly situation report Sarawak and Borneo; SWPA monthly report; SRD operations quarterly; weekly sitreps and SRD operations; Melbourne sitreps; summary of operations, August 1944–May 1945

Y-HS 1/246, 'The Great Frustration', AGAS report: evacuation of PWs in British North Borneo and list of enemy agents and collaborators, 1942–45

Y-HS 1/251, SRD operations in Borneo in support of OBOE; ROBIN/ PLATYPUS and others, 1945

Y-HS 7/99, Evaluation report of Special Operations Australia by Lt. Col. A. Trappes-Lomax, 1946

Y-HS 8/951, Special Operations Australia (SOA) in Borneo and Sarawak, 1944–45

Y-WO 32/14547, Prisoners of War: General (Code 91 A): Reports on Prisoner of War Camps in Borneo, 1944–45

Y-WO 32/14553, Overseas: Borneo (Code 0/BC): Reports on Prisoner of War Camps in Borneo, 1945–46

Y-WO 106/3434, British Borneo: draft directive on civil affairs, 1943–45

Y-WO 106/3454, Operations in Borneo: information for Brigadier Haydon, 1945

Y-WO 203/2071, The relief of Australians in Borneo, 1945

Y-WO 203/2204, Borneo: report by Australian military forces on British Borneo Civil Affairs unit, 1945

Y-WO 203/6188, British military administration British Borneo: monthly reports, 1945–46

Y-WO 208/98, North Borneo: Terrain Study Volume 2, 1944

Y-WO 208/1489, Borneo, reports, mainly cables to the secretary of state for the colonies, 1941–45

Y-WO 220/118, Borneo C.A. Unit, 1944–45

Y-WO 252/514, Special report: Labuan, Sandakan and Tarakan areas of North Borneo, 1944

Y-WO 252/1242, Sandakan, North Borneo, 1945

Y-WO 325/39, Kuching Camp, Borneo: ill treatment of POWs and civilians, 1945–46

Y-WO 325/52, Report on investigation into fate of allied POWs and internees in British Borneo, 1945

Y-WO 325/120, Sandakan, Borneo: alleged crucifixion of British POW, 1947

Y-WO 325/148, Japanese atrocities in Borneo, 1945–46

Sabah State Archives, Kota Kinabalu, Sabah, Malaysia

An assortment of local newspapers and documents, including *The British North Borneo Herald* (1935–1941)

Interviews

Interviews/Conversations with Author (2010–12)

Agnes Agama – email
Domima binte Akui – on Death March route, Sabah
Ramlin Alim – Kota Kinabalu
Rose Barry – correspondence
Richard Braithwaite (son of Richard Braithwaite, survivor) – Sydney, Lismore
Irene Benggon Chururuks – email and Kota Kinabalu
Rebecca Coghlan – email
Michele Cunningham – email/telephone
Christopher Dawson – Sydney
Maureen Devereaux – Sydney
Dusun people – on Death March route, Sabah
Claudia Edwards – email
Christopher Elliott – London
Russ Ewin – Sydney
Margaret Fisher – telephone
Ron Ferguson – telephone
June Fowler-Smith – telephone
Brian Hales – Sydney
Tony Hall – email
Gwen Hammon – email
Heather Harrison-Lawrence – Reading, United Kingdom
Antonia Hayes – email
June Healy – Sydney
Anthony Hazzard – London
Doreen Hurst – email
Warwick Johnstone – Sydney
Brenda Kingen – email
Tham Yau Kong (and colleagues) – Sabah
Bryan Lai – Kota Kinabalu
Ross McCowan – correspondence/meeting
Eric McDonald – Canberra, email
Senator Anne McEwen – Adelaide
David Matthews – Adelaide
Steve Mockridge – London
Bill Molloy – telephone
Stella Moo-Tan – Kota Kinabalu
Dr Narrelle Morris – email
Sue Moxham – telephone
Holly Norton – email
Bob Oakeshott – Sydney

Jeffrey Phillips – London
Diane Rowe – Sydney
Ryan Rowland – email
Peter Rubinstein – Sydney
Betty Seccombe – correspondence
David Seccombe – London
Kevin Smith – Sydney
Teresa Stephens – Essex, United Kingdom
Ben Sticpewich – Sydney and Canberra
Graham Swain – email
Peter Tan – Kota Kinabalu
Derek Taylor – email
Barry Tinkler – telephone
Tony White – Lismore
Peter Wilkins – Sydney
Claire Woods – email and telephone
Robin Wookey – Sydney
George Worrall – London
Rod York – Brighton, United Kingdom
Bill Young – Sydney
Yumpil bin Yaron – on Death March route, Sabah
Gwenda Zappala – email
Zudin – on Death March route, Sabah

Newspapers and Magazines

The Advertiser (Adelaide)
The Age (Melbourne)
The Argus (Melbourne)
The Australian
The Borneo Bugle (Borneo Prisoner of War Relatives Group's newsletter)
The Borneo Post
The British North Borneo Herald
The Bulletin
The Canberra Times
The Chronicle
Daily Express (Sabah)
Daily Mirror
The Daily Telegraph
The Gunner
The Herald (Melbourne)
The London Gazette
Official Gazette (Legislative Council of British North Borneo)

People magazine
POW News
Royal Artillery Gunner magazine
The Sabah Society (newsletter)
Sandakan Families Newsletter (Australia)
Dr Kevin Smith Newsletter (Australia)
The Sunday Mail (Brisbane)
The Sun-Herald (Sydney)
The Sydney Morning Herald
United Service (Journal of the Royal United Service Institute)
Wartime magazine
Weekend Australian

Private Papers

Australia
Richard Braithwaite
Brinkman family
Emmett family
Les Hales and family
Athol Moffitt
John Oakeshott and family
Bill Sticpewich and family
Barrie Whitehead and family
Stan Woods and family
Keith Wookey

Sabah
Azcona family
Funk family
Jerry Ipang Ganggal
Peter and Bryan Lai

United Kingdom
Christopher Elliott and family
Heather Harrison-Lawrence and family
Ernest Hazzard and family
Les Mockridge and family
Arthur Percival
Jeffrey Phillips and family
Joe Stephens and family
Rod York and family

Speeches

Melvyn Funk, address at Memorial Service, Burwood, Sydney, 1 August 2004

Anthony Hill, Billy Young and the Dead End Kids, Sandakan POW Families Oration, 27 May 2011

Justice Moffitt address, 1987 Conference of Veterans

Rusty Priest, address at the Sandakan Memorial in Burwood Park, 6 August 2006

Tom Uren, address on Sandakan at Burwood Park, Sydney, 1 August 2004

SECONDARY SOURCES

Published Books

Adam-Smith, Patsy, *Prisoners of War: From Gallipoli to Korea*, Viking Penguin, Melbourne, 1992

Aldrich, Richard, *Intelligence and the War Against Japan: Britain, America and the Politics of Secret Service*, Cambridge University Press, Cambridge, 2000

Arvier, Robyn (ed.), *Don't Worry About Me: Wartime Letters of the 8th Division A.I.F.*, Robyn Arvier, Riverside, Tasmania, 2004

Barker, Theo, *Signals: A History of the Royal Australian Corps of Signals 1788–1947*, Royal Australian Corps of Signals Committee, 1987

Bennett, Gordon, *Why Singapore Fell*, Angus & Robertson, Sydney, 1944

Blackburn, Kevin, *The Sportsmen of Changi*, New South Books, Sydney 2012

Bleakley, Jack, *The Eavesdroppers: The Best Kept Secrets of World War 2*, Jack Bleakley, Melbourne, 1992

Blythe, R., *Private Words: Letters and Diaries from the Second World War*, Penguin Books, London, 1993

Champion, Rachel, *No Lost Battalion: An Oral History of the 2/29th Battalion AIF*, Slouch Hat Publications, Rosebud, Victoria, 2005

Christie, Robert W., *A History of the 2/29 Battalion, 8th Australian Division AIF*, 2/29 Battalion AIF Association, Malvern, Victoria, 1983

Connolly, Ray and Bob Wilson (eds), *Medical Soldiers: 2/10 Field Ambulance 8 Div., 1940–45*, 2/10 Australian Field Ambulance Association, Kingsgrove, New South Wales, 1985

Courtney, G. B. ('Gruff'), *Silent Feet: The History of 'Z' Special Operations 1942–1945*, R. J. & S. P. Austin, Melbourne, 1993

Cunningham, Michele, *Defying the Odds: Surviving Sandakan and Kuching*, Lothian Books, Melbourne, 2006

Daws, Gavan, *Prisoners of the Japanese: POWs of World War II in the Pacific*, Scribe Publications, Melbourne, 1994

Dawson, Christopher (ed.), *To Sandakan: The Diaries of Charlie Johnston,*

Prisoner of War 1942–45, Allen & Unwin, Sydney, 1995

Drea, Edward, *MacArthur's Ultra: Codebreaking and the War Against Japan, 1942–1945*, University Press of Kansas, Kansas City, 1993

Dunn, J. B. 'Lofty', *Eagles Alighting: A History of 1 Australian Parachute Battalion*, 1 Australian Parachute Battalion Association, Melbourne, 1999

Firkins, Peter, *Borneo Surgeon: A Reluctant Hero – The Life of Dr James Patrick Taylor*, Hesperian Press, Perth, Western Australia, 1995

From Hell to Eternity, Westward Ho Publishing Co., Perth, 1979

Forbes, Cameron, *Hellfire: The Story of Australia, Japan and the Prisoners of War*, Pan Macmillan Australia, Sydney, 2005

Furness, William, 'Folk-Lore in Borneo', Kessinger, Montana, 2010

Glover, Leslie Bunn, *The Boy from Bowen: Diary of a Sandakan POW*, Kristan Enterprises Pty Ltd, Robina, Queensland, 2011

Godfrey, Rupert, *The Years that the Locusts Have Eaten: War Diary and Sermons, 1941–45*, Heather Godfrey, Suffolk, United Kingdom, 2003

Goodwin, Robert, *Mates and Memories, Recollections of the 2/10 Field Regiment*, Boolarong Press with 2/10th Field Regiment Association, Brisbane, 1995

Hall, Maxwell, *Kinabalu Guerrillas: An Account of the Double 10th Uprising Against the Japanese Invaders in North Borneo*, Opus Publication, Kota Kinabalu, 2009

Ham, Paul, *Hiroshima Nagasaki*, HarperCollins, Sydney, 2011

Kokoda, HarperCollins, Sydney, 2003

Harrison, Tom, *World Within: A Borneo Story*, The Cresset Press, London, 1959

Hastings, Max, *Retribution: The Battle for Japan, 1944–45*, Alfred A. Knopf, New York, 2008

Hearder, Rosalind, *Keep the Men Alive: Australian POW Doctors in Japanese Captivity*, Allen & Unwin, Sydney, 2009

Holland, Frank, *El Tigre: Wartime Rescue Operations in New Britain; 'Z' Special Unit Operations in Portuguese Timor and Borneo*, Oceans Enterprises, Yarram, Victoria, 1999

Jacobs, James W. and Reginald James Bridgland (eds), *Through: The Story of Signals 8 Australian Division and Signals AIF Malaya*, 8 Division Signals Association, Sydney, 1949

James, Karl, 'The Unnecessary Waste: Australians in the Late Pacific Campaigns', essay in Craig Stockings (ed.), *Anzac's Dirty Dozen: 12 Myths of Australian Military History*, NewSouth Publishing, Sydney, 2012

Johnson, William Wallace, *Ripcord Australia*, ACPA, Eastwood, New South Wales, 1984

Johnston, Don, Jock Britz, George Forbes and H. S. Clayton, *Borneo Burlesque*, Department of Veterans' Affairs, Canberra, 2011

Keegan, John, *The Second World War*, Penguin, New York, 2005

Keith, Agnes Newton, *Beloved Exiles*, Little Brown & Co., Boston, 1972

Kiyosawa, Kiyoshi, *A Diary of Darkness: The Wartime Diary of Kiyosawa Kiyoshi*, Eugene Soviak and Kamiyama Tamie (trans.), Eugene Soviak (ed.), Princeton University Press, Princeton, 1999

Laffin, John, *Australians at War: Special and Secret*, Time Life/McKay, London, 1990

Lodge, A. B., 'Bennett, Henry Gordon (1887–1962)', *Australian Dictionary of Biography*, Vol. 13, Melbourne University Press, Melbourne, 1993

Magarry, William Ronald, *The Battalion Story: 2/26th Battalion, 8th Division, AIF*, W. R. Magarry, Jindalee, Queensland, 1994

Mant, Gilbert, *Grim Glory; With a Foreword by H. Gordon Bennett*, Currawong, Sydney, 1942

Massacre at Parit Sulong, Kangaroo Press, Kenthurst, New South Wales, 1995

Matthews, David, *The Duke: A Hero's Hero at Sandakan*, Seaview Press, West Lakes, South Australia, 2008

McKernan, Michael, *This War Never Ends: The Pain of Separation and Return*, University of Queensland Press, Brisbane, 2001

Moffitt, Athol, *Project Kingfisher*, Angus & Robertson, Sydney, 1989

Nelson, Hank, *Prisoners of War: Australians Under Nippon*, ABC, Sydney, 1985

Newman, Carolyn, *Legacies of our Fathers: World War II Prisoners of the Japanese – Their Sons and Daughters Tell Their Stories*, Thomas C. Lothian, Melbourne, 2005

Ooi, Keat Gin, *Japanese Empire in the Tropics: Selected Documents and Reports of the Japanese Period in Sarawak, Northwest Borneo, 1941–1945*, Ohio University Center for International Studies, Monographs in International Studies, SE Asia Series 101, Ohio, 1998

Penfold, A. W., Bayliss, W. C., Crispin, K. E., *Galleghan's Greyhounds: The Story of the 2/30th Australian Infantry Battalion, 22nd November, 1940–10th October, 1945*, 2/30th Battalion AIF Association, Halstead Press, Sydney, 1949

Percival, Arthur, *The War in Malaya*, Eyre & Spottiswoode, London, 1949

Reid, Richard, *Laden, Fevered, Starved – The POWs of Sandakan, North Borneo, 1945*, Commonwealth Department of Veterans' Affairs, Canberra, 1999

Sandakan 1942–1945, Commonwealth Department of Veterans' Affairs, Canberra, 2008

Richards, Charles Rowland Bromley 'Rowley' and Marcia McEwan, *The Survival Factor*, Kangaroo Press, Kenthurst, New South Wales, 1989

Ross, Sheila, *And Tomorrow Freedom*, Allen & Unwin, Sydney, 1989

Shim, P. S., *Inland People of Sabah: Before, During and After Nunuk Ragang*, Cultural Heritage of North Borneo, Kota Kinabalu, 2007

Silver, Lynette Ramsay, *Blood Brothers: Sabah and Australia 1942–45*, Opus
    Publications, Kota Kinabalu, 2010
    Sandakan: A Conspiracy of Silence, Opus Publications, Kota Kinabalu,
    2007
Smith, Kevin, *Borneo: Australia's Proud but Tragic Heritage*, K. R. & H.
    Smith, Armidale, New South Wales, 1999
    Escapes and Incursions, K. R. & H. Smith, Armidale, New South Wales,
    2006
    Stories from Sandakan: 2/18th Battalion, K. R. & H. Smith, Armidale,
    New South Wales, 2011
Smyth, Sir John, *Percival and the Tragedy of Singapore*, Macdonald & Co.,
    London, 1971
Sweeting, A. J., 'Camps in Borneo, Japan and Elsewhere', in Lionel Wigmore,
    The Japanese Thrust: Australia in the War of 1939–1945, Series One, Army,
    Vol IV, Canberra, 1957
Tanaka, Yuki, *Hidden Horrors: Japanese War Crimes in World War II*,
    HarperCollins Publishers, Boulder, Colorado, 1996
Thomason, William, *March to Ranau: Australian Servicemen at Sandakan,
    Borneo, 1943–1945*, Bendigo Militaria Museum, Bendigo, Victoria, 1989
Thompson, Peter, *The Battle for Singapore*, Piatkus Books, London, 2005
Ueno, Itsuyoshi, *An End to a War: A Japanese Soldier's Experience of the
    1945 Death Marches of North Borneo*, Mika Reilly (trans.), Richard W.
    Braithwaite (ed.), Opus Publications, Kota Kinabalu, 2012
Uhr, Janet Margaret, *Against the Sun: The AIF in Malaya, 1941–42*, Allen &
    Unwin, Sydney, 1998
Venables, Max, *From Wayville to Changi and Beyond*, M. Venables, Glenelg
    North, South Australia, 2002
Walker, Allan S., *Middle East and Far East: Australia in the War 1939–1945*,
    Series 5 (Medical), Vol. 2, Australian War Memorial, Canberra, 1953
Wall, Don, *Kill the Prisoners*, Sydney, 1997
    Sandakan: The Last March, Sydney, 2003
    Singapore and Beyond, 2/20 Battalion Association, Cowra, New South
    Wales, 1985
Whitelocke, Cliff and George O'Brien, *Gunners in the Jungle: A Story of the
    2/15 Field Regiment Royal Australian Artillery, 8 Division, Australian
    Imperial Force*, 2/15 Field Regiment Association, Eastwood, New South
    Wales, 1983
Wong Sue, Jack, *Blood on Borneo*, L. Smith (WA) Pty Ltd t/a Jack Sue WA
    Skindivers Publication, Bayswater, Western Australia, 2001
Wong Tze Ken, Danny, *Historical Sabah: The War*, Opus Publications, Kota
    Kinabalu, 2010
Yamamoto, Tsunemato, with Minoru Tanaka (co-auth.), Justin Stone
    (co-auth., ed.), *Bushido: The Way of the Samurai* (based on *The Hagakure*),

Square One Publishers, Garden City Park, New York, 2001
Yoji, Akashi, 'General Yamashita Tomoyuki: Commander of the 25th
Army' (essay) in B. Farrell and S. Hunter (eds), *Sixty Years On: The Fall of Singapore Revisited*, Times Media Private, Singapore, 2002

Radio Programs
Prisoners of War: Australians Under Nippon, Sandakan veterans interviewed by
Tim Bowden, ABC, Sydney, 1983

Unpublished Books
Azcona, Ricky, 'Story of the Azcona Family During the Second World War',
Bryan Lai (ed.), personal memoir
Braithwaite, Richard, with Harry Jackson, Keith Botterill, Bill Young
(co-auths), 'Long Ago in Borneo', personal memoir
Elliott, Christopher, 'In the Shadow of Kinabalu', privately published memoir
Ewin, Russ, 'Ballygawley to Belrose', personal memoir
Ganggal, Jimon bin, 'Recollection of Jimon of his Account during WW2',
personal memoir
Hurst, Doreen, 'Sandakan', family memoir
Lai, Bryan Paul, 'The Quiet Hero of Sandakan, North Borneo', memoir of
Peter Raymond Lai
Young, Bill, 'My War in Pictures, My Thoughts in Verse', Sydney, undated

Websites
Australian Dictionary of Biography: http://adb.anu.edu.au
Australian War Memorial: www.awm.gov.au
Australian War Memorial, war diaries of the 2/18th, 2/19th, 2/20th, 2/26th,
2/29th, 2/30th Australian Infantry Battalions and 8th Division: www.
awm.gov.au/collection/records/awm52
Battleship Missouri Memorial: www.ussmissouri.com
BBC, WW2 People's War: www.bbc.co.uk/history/ww2peopleswar
Borneo Exhibition Group: www.begwa.org
COFEPOW: www.cofepow.org.uk
Find a Grave: www.findagrave.com
The London Gazette: www.london-gazette.co.uk
POW Research Network Japan: www.powresearch.jp
Roll of Honour – Britain at War: www.roll-of-honour.org.uk
Veterans UK: www.veterans-uk.info/service_records/service_records.html

INDEX

3T

shouted "Sit down, Cross your legs", I didn't unde-
stand the last part but they anyway crossed
my legs. "Head down!" pushing my head
against the ~~b~~ rear end of another detainee.
like a chicken. A female voice was shouting
all the way to the Camp, "No Talking", and
a male voice, "Do not ~~talk~~", and an
Arabic translator ██████ [1,3]
[1,3] ██████, "Keep your head down",
I was completely annoyed by the American
way of talking, I hoped I had the option
not to listen 'to those guards, and stayed
that way ~~for~~ **GUANTÁNAMO** I got cured
by meeting **DIARY** erican people.
Although I u   giving orders
with two different way "DO NOT TAK" or
"No talking". It was interesting. Now, the
chains in my ankles cut the blood off to my
feet. My feet became numb. I heard only
moaning and crying of other detainees.
Beating was the order of the trip. I was
not spared, the guard kept hitting me
on my head, and ~~squeeze~~ squeeze my neck against
the rear end of the other detainee. But
I don't blame him as much as I do the
poor, and pain~~ful~~ detainee, who was crying, and
kept moving, and so ~~rose~~ raised my head.
Detainees told me ~~so~~ that we took a fairy
during the trip, but I didn't notice.

~~UNCLASSIFIED~~

ALSO BY LARRY SIEMS

*The Torture Report: What the Documents Say
about America's Post-9/11 Torture Program*

*Between the Lines: Letters between Undocumented Mexican
and Central American Immigrants and Their Families and
Friends*

GUANTÁNAMO DIARY

MOHAMEDOU OULD SLAHI

EDITED BY LARRY SIEMS

CANONGATE
Edinburgh · London

Published in Great Britain in 2015 by Canongate Books Ltd,
14 High Street, Edinburgh EH1 1TE

www.canongate.tv

1

First published in the United States by Little, Brown and Company, Hachette
Book Group, Inc, 1290 Avenue of the Americas, New York, NY 10104

British Library Cataloguing-in-Publication Data
A catalogue record for this book is available on
request from the British Library

ISBN 978 1 78211 284 6
Export ISBN 978 1 78211 606 6

Printed and bound in Great Britain by Clays Ltd, St Ives plc

MIX
Paper from
responsible sources
FSC
www.fsc.org   FSC® C018072

Mohamedou would like to dedicate his writing to the memory of his late mother, Maryem Mint El Wadia, and he would also like to express that if it weren't for Nancy Hollander and her colleagues Theresa Duncan and Linda Moreno, he couldn't be making that dedication.

you keep me in jail, so why should I cooperate? I said so not knowing that Americans use torture to facilitate interrogation. Of course, I was very tired from being taken to interrogation every day. My back was just conspiring against me. I sought Medical help, "You're not allowed to sit for so long time" said the ████ ████ physiotherapist, "Pls, tell my interrogators so by they make sit for long hours almost every day", "I will write a note but I can not sure whether it will have effect" she replied. Feb 03 ███ washed his hands off me, "I am going to leave but if you're ready to talk about ~~my~~ your telephone conversations request me. I'll come back" he said, "~~Be sure~~ I assure you that I am not going to talk ~~about~~ anything unless you answer my question - why I am here?", ███ asked me to dedicate an English copy of Koran to him, which I happily did and off he went. I never heard about ████████ after that, ███ and I to "not" working together but he was an over-baring person. I don't think in a negative way. ███ just had tons of reports with all Kind of evil theories. The ~~so~~ mis-mash of what-ifs was mainly fueled with prejudices, ~~and~~ hatered, and ignorance toward the Islamic Religion. "I am working on showing you

Contents

80

I hungrily started to read the letter but soon I got chocked. The letter was a cheap forgery, it was not from my family. It was the production of the Intel community. "Dear brothers what I received no letter, I am sorry!", "Bastards, they have done so with other detainees" said a detainee. But the forgery was so clumzy and unprofessional that no fool would fall for it. First, I have no brother of mine with that name, second, my name was misspelled, third my family doesn't live where the correspondent mention but close enough, forth I know not only the hand-writing of every single member of my family, I also know every phrases his ideas. The letter was kind of a sermon, "Be patient like your ancestors, and have faith that Allah is going to reward you". I was so mad at this attempt to fraud me, and play with my emotions. Next day, ▓ pulled me for interrogation. "How is your family doing?", "I hope they're doing well", "I've been working to get you the letter!", "Thank you very much, good effort, but if you guys want to forge a mail let me give some advices", "What are you talking about?", I smiled "if don't really know is okay, but it was cheap to forge a message and make me believe I have contact with my dear family!" I said handing him

A Timeline of Detention

January 2000	After spending twelve years studying, living, and working overseas, primarily in Germany and briefly in Canada, Mohamedou Ould Slahi decides to return to his home country of Mauritania. En route, he is detained twice at the behest of the United States—first by Senegalese police and then by Mauritanian authorities—and questioned by American FBI agents in connection with the so-called Millennium Plot to bomb LAX. Concluding that there is no basis to believe he was involved in the plot, authorities release him on February 19, 2000.
2000–fall 2001	Mohamedou lives with his family and works as an electrical engineer in Nouakchott, Mauritania.
September 29, 2001	Mohamedou is detained and held for two weeks by Mauritanian authorities and again questioned by FBI agents about the Millennium Plot. He is again released, with Mauritanian authorities publicly affirming his innocence.
November 20, 2001	Mauritanian police come to Mohamedou's home and ask him to accompany them for further questioning. He voluntarily complies, driving his own car to the police station.
November 28, 2001	A CIA rendition plane transports Mohamedou from Mauritania to a prison in Amman, Jordan, where he is interrogated for seven and a half months by Jordanian intelligence services.

July 19, 2002	Another CIA rendition plane retrieves Mohamedou from Amman; he is stripped, blindfolded, diapered, shackled, and flown to the U.S. military's Bagram Air Base in Afghanistan. The events recounted in *Guantánamo Diary* begin with this scene.
August 4, 2002	After two weeks of interrogation in Bagram, Mohamedou is bundled onto a military transport with thirty-four other prisoners and flown to Guantánamo. The group arrives and is processed into the facility on August 5, 2002.
2003–2004	U.S. military interrogators subject Mohamedou to a "special interrogation plan" that is personally approved by Defense Secretary Donald Rumsfeld. Mohamedou's torture includes months of extreme isolation; a litany of physical, psychological, and sexual humiliations; death threats; threats to his family; and a mock kidnapping and rendition.
March 3, 2005	Mohamedou handwrites his petition for a writ of habeas corpus.
Summer 2005	Mohamedou handwrites the 466 pages that would become this book in his segregation cell in Guantánamo.
June 12, 2008	The U.S. Supreme Court rules 5–4 in *Boumediene v. Bush* that Guantánamo detainees have a right to challenge their detention through habeas corpus.
August–December 2009	U.S. District Court Judge James Robertson hears Mohamedou's habeas corpus petition.
March 22, 2010	Judge Robertson grants Mohamedou's habeas corpus petition and orders his release.
March 26, 2010	The Obama administration files a notice of appeal.
November 5, 2010	The DC Circuit Court of Appeals sends Mohamedou's habeas corpus case back to U.S. district court for rehearing. That case is still pending.
Present	Mohamedou remains in Guantánamo, in the same cell where many of the events recounted in this book took place.

Notes on the Text, Redactions, and Annotations

This book is an edited version of the 466-page manuscript Mohamedou Ould Slahi wrote by hand in his Guantánamo prison cell in the summer and fall of 2005. It has been edited twice: first by the United States government, which added more than 2,500 black-bar redactions censoring Mohamedou's text, and then by me. Mohamedou was not able to participate in, or respond to, either one of these edits.

He has, however, always hoped that his manuscript would reach the reading public—it is addressed directly to us, and to American readers in particular—and he has explicitly authorized this publication in its edited form, with the understanding and expressed wish that the editorial process be carried out in a way that faithfully conveys the content and fulfills the promise of the original. He entrusted me to do this work, and that is what I have tried to do in preparing this manuscript for print.

Mohamedou Ould Slahi wrote his memoir in English, his fourth language and a language he acquired largely in U.S. custody, as he describes, often amusingly, throughout the book. This is both a significant act and a remarkable achievement in itself. It is also a choice that creates or contributes to some of the work's most important literary effects. By my count, he deploys a vocabulary of under seven thousand words—a lexicon about the size of the one that powers the Homeric epics. He does so in ways that sometimes echo those epics, as when he repeats formulaic phrases for recurrent phenomena and events. And he does so, like the creators of the epics, in ways that manage to deliver an enormous range of action and emotion. In the editing process, I have tried above all to preserve this feel and honor this accomplishment.

At the same time, the manuscript that Mohamedou managed to compose in his cell in 2005 is an incomplete and at times fragmentary draft. In some sections the prose feels more polished, and in some the handwriting looks smaller and more precise, both suggesting possible previous drafts; elsewhere the writing has more of a first-draft sprawl and urgency. There are significant variations in narrative approach, with less linear storytelling in the sections recounting the most recent events—as one would expect, given the intensity of the events and proximity of the characters he is describing. Even the overall shape of the work is unresolved, with a series of flashbacks to events that precede the central narrative appended at the end.

In approaching these challenges, like every editor seeking to satisfy every author's expectation that mistakes and distractions will be minimized and voice and vision sharpened, I have edited the manuscript on two levels. Line by line, this has mostly meant regularizing verb tenses, word order, and a few awkward locutions, and occasionally, for clarity's sake, consolidating or reordering text. I have also incorporated the appended flashbacks within the main narrative and streamlined the manuscript as a whole, a process that brought a work that was in the neighborhood of 122,000 words to just under 100,000 in this version. These editorial decisions were mine, and I can only hope they would meet with Mohamedou's approval.

Throughout this process, I was confronted with a set of challenges specifically connected with the manuscript's previous editing process: the government's redactions. These redactions are changes that have been imposed on the text by the same government that continues to control the author's fate and has used secrecy as an essential tool of that control for more than thirteen years. As such, the black bars on the page serve as vivid visual reminders of the author's ongoing situation. At the same time, deliberately or not, the redactions often serve to impede the sense of narrative, blur the contours of characters, and obscure the open, approachable tone of the author's voice.

Because it depends on close reading, any process of editing a censored text will involve some effort to see past the black bars and erasures. The annotations that appear at the bottom of the page throughout the text are a kind of record of that effort.

These notes represent speculations that arose in connection with the redactions, based on the context in which the redactions appear, information that appears elsewhere in the manuscript, and what is now a wealth of publicly available sources about Mohamedou Ould Slahi's ordeal and about the incidents and events he chronicles here. Those sources include declassified government documents obtained through Freedom of Information Act requests and litigation, news reports and the published work of a number of writers and investigative journalists, and extensive Justice Department and U.S. Senate investigations.

I have not attempted in these annotations to reconstruct the original redacted text or to uncover classified material. Rather, I have tried my best to present information that most plausibly corresponds to the redactions when that information is a matter of public record or evident from a careful reading of the manuscript, and when I believe it is important for the overall readability and impact of the text. If there are any errors in these speculations, the fault is entirely mine. None of Mohamedou Ould Slahi's attorneys holding security clearances has reviewed these introductory materials or the footnotes, contributed to them in any way, or confirmed or denied my speculations contained in them. Nor has anyone else with access to the unredacted manuscript reviewed these introductory materials or the footnotes, contributed to them in any way, or confirmed or denied my speculations contained in them.

So many of the editing challenges associated with bringing this remarkable work to print result directly from the fact that the U.S. government continues to hold the work's author, with no satisfactory explanation to date, under a censorship regime that prevents him from participating in the editorial process. I look forward to the day when Mohamedou Ould Slahi is free and we can read this work in its entirety, as he would have it published. Meanwhile I hope this version has managed to capture the accomplishment of the original, even as it reminds us, on almost every page, of how much we have yet to see.

Introduction

by Larry Siems

In the summer and early fall of 2005, Mohamedou Ould Slahi handwrote a 466-page, 122,000-word draft of this book in his single-cell segregation hut in Camp Echo, Guantánamo.

He wrote it in installments, starting not long after he was finally allowed to meet with Nancy Hollander and Sylvia Royce, two attorneys from his pro bono legal team. Under the strict protocols of Guantánamo's sweeping censorship regime, every page he wrote was considered classified from the moment of its creation, and each new section was surrendered to the United States government for review.

On December 15, 2005, three months after he signed and dated the manuscript's last page, Mohamedou interrupted his testimony during an Administrative Review Board hearing in Guantánamo to tell the presiding officers:

> *I just want to mention here that I wrote a book recently while in jail here recently about my whole story, okay? I sent it for release to the District [of] Columbia, and when it is released I advise you guys to read it. A little advertisement. It is a very interesting book, I think.*[1]

But Mohamedou's manuscript was not released. It was stamped "SECRET," a classification level for information that could cause serious damage to national security if it becomes public, and "NOFORN," meaning it can't be shared with any foreign nationals or intelligence services. It was deposited in a secure facility near Washington, DC, accessible only to those with a full security clearance and an official "need to know." For more than six years, Mohamedou's attorneys carried out litigation and negotiations to have the manuscript cleared for public release.

During those years, compelled largely by Freedom of Information Act litigation spearheaded by the American Civil Liberties Union, the U.S. government released thousands of secret documents that described the treatment of prisoners in U.S. custody since the September 11, 2001, terrorist attacks. Many of those documents hinted at Mohamedou's ordeal, first in the hands of the CIA, and then in the hands of the U.S. military in Guantánamo, where a "Special Projects Team" subjected him to one of the most stubborn, deliberate, and cruel interrogations in the record. A few of those documents contained something else as well: tantalizing samples of Mohamedou's voice.

One of these was in his own handwriting, in English. In a short note dated March 3, 2005, he wrote, "Hello. I, Mohamedou Ould Slahi, detained in GTMO under ISN #760, herewith apply for a writ of habeas corpus." The note concluded simply, "I have done no crimes against the U.S., nor did the U.S. charge me with crimes, thus I am filing for my immediate release. For further details about my case, I'll be happy for any future hearings."

Another handwritten document, also in English, was a letter to his attorney Sylvia Royce dated November 9, 2006, in which he joked, "You asked me to write you everything I told my interrogators. Are you out of your mind? How can I render uninterrupted interrogation that has been lasting the last 7 years? That's like asking Charlie Sheen how many women he dated." He went on:

Yet I provided you everything (almost) in my book, which the government denies you the access to. I was going to go deeper in details, but I figured it was futile.

To make a long story short, you may divide my time in two big steps.

(1) Pre-torture (I mean that I couldn't resist): I told them the truth about me having done nothing against your country. It lasted until May 22, 2003.

(2) Post-torture era: where my brake broke loose. I yessed every accusation my interrogators made. I even wrote the infamous confession about me planning to hit the CN Tower in Toronto, based on SSG ▉▉▉▉▉▉▉ advice. I just wanted to get the monkeys off my back. I don't care how long I stay in jail. My belief comforts me.[2]

The documents also included a pair of transcripts of Mohamedou's sworn testimony before detainee review boards in Guantánamo. The first—and the first sample of his voice anywhere in the documents—is from his Combatant Status Review Tribunal (CSRT) hearing; the date is December 8, 2004, just months after his so-called "special interrogation" ended. It includes this exchange:

Q: Can I get your response to the very first allegation that you are a member of the Taliban or al Qaida?

A: The Taliban, I have nothing to do with them whatsoever. Al Qaida, I was a member in Afghanistan in 91 and 92. After I left Afghanistan, I broke all my relations with al Qaida.

Q: And you've never provided them money, or any type of support since then?

A: Nothing whatsoever.

Q: Ever recruited for them?

A: No, not at all; no trying to recruit for them.

Q: You said that you were pressured to admit you were involved in the Millennium plot, right?

A: Yes.

Q: To whom did you make that confession?

A: To the Americans.

Q: And what do you mean by pressure?

A: Your honor, I don't wish to talk about this nature of the pressure if I don't have to.

Q: Tribunal President: You don't have to; we just want to make sure that you were not tortured or coerced into saying something that wasn't true. That is the reason he is asking the question.

A: You just take from me I am not involved in such a horrible attack; yes I admit to being a member of al Qaida, but I am not willing to talk about this. The smart people came to me and analyzed this, and got the truth. It's good for me to tell the truth, and the information was verified. I said I didn't have anything to do with this. I took and passed the polygraph, and they said I didn't have to speak of this anymore. They said please don't speak of this topic anymore, and they haven't opened it up to this topic for a year now.

Q: So no U.S. authorities abused you in any way?

A: I'm not willing to answer this question; I don't have to, if you don't force me to.[3]

The other transcript comes from the 2005 Administrative Review Board hearing where he announced he had written this book. A year had passed since the CSRT hearing, a year when he was finally allowed to meet with attorneys, and when he somehow found the distance and the stamina to write down his experience. This time he speaks freely of his odyssey, not in fear or in anger, but in a voice inflected with irony and wit. "He was very silly," Mohamedou says of one of his interrogator's threats, "because he said he was going to bring in black people. I don't have any problem with black people, half of my country is black people!" Another interrogator in Guantánamo known as Mr. X was covered head to toe "like in Saudi Arabia, how the women are covered," and wearing "gloves, O.J. Simpson gloves on his hands." Mohamedou's answers are richly detailed, for deliberate effect and for an earnest purpose. "Please," he tells the board, "I want you guys to understand my story okay, because it really doesn't matter if they release me or not, I just want my story understood."[4]

We do not have a complete record of Mohamedou's effort to tell his story to the review board at that hearing. Just as he begins to describe what he experienced in Guantánamo during the summer of 2003, "the recording equipment began to malfunction," notes a boldface interruption in the transcript. For the lost section, in which "the detainee discussed how he was tortured while here at GTMO by several individuals," the document offers instead "the board's recollection of that 1000 click malfunction":

> *The Detainee began by discussing the alleged abuse he received from a female interrogator known to him as* ▆▆▆▆▆▆▆▆. *The Detainee attempted to explain to the Board* ▆▆▆▆▆▆▆▆ *actions but he became distraught and visibly upset. He explained that he was sexually harassed and although he does like women he did not like what* ▆▆▆▆▆▆▆▆ *had done to him. The Presiding Officer noticed the Detainee was upset and told him he was not required to tell the story. The Detainee was very appreciative and elected not to elaborate on the alleged abuse from* ▆▆▆▆▆▆▆▆.
>
> *The Detainee gave detailed information regarding the alleged abuse from* ▆▆▆▆▆▆▆▆ *and* ▆▆▆▆▆▆▆▆. *The Detainee*

stated that ▮▮▮▮▮▮▮▮ *and* ▮▮▮▮▮▮▮▮ *entered a room with
their faces covered and began beating him. They beat him so badly
that* ▮▮▮▮▮▮▮▮ *became upset.* ▮▮▮▮▮▮▮▮ *did not like
the treatment the Detainee was receiving and started to sympathize
with him. According to the Detainee,* ▮▮▮▮▮▮▮▮ *was crying and
telling* ▮▮▮▮▮▮▮▮ *and* ▮▮▮▮▮▮▮▮ *to stop beating him.
The Detainee wanted to show the Board his scars and location of
injuries, but the board declined the viewing. The Board agrees that
this is a fair recap of the distorted portion of the tape.[5]*

We only have these transcripts because in the spring of 2006, a
federal judge presiding over a FOIA lawsuit filed by the Associated
Press ordered them released. That lawsuit also finally compelled
the Pentagon, four years after Guantánamo opened, to publish an
official list of the men it was holding in the facility. For the first
time, the prisoners had names, and the names had voices. In the
transcripts of their secret hearings, many of the prisoners told stories that undercut claims that the Cuban detention camp housed
"the worst of the worst," men so dangerous, as the military's presiding general famously declared as the first prisoners were landing
at the camp in 2002, they would "gnaw hydraulic lines in the back
of a C-17 to bring it down."[6] Several, like Mohamedou, broached
the subject of their treatment in U.S. custody.

The Pentagon doubled down. "Detainees held at Guantánamo
are terrorist trainers, bomb-makers, would-be suicide bombers,
and other dangerous people," a military spokesman again asserted
when the transcripts became public. "And we know that they're
trained to lie to try to gain sympathy for their condition and to
bring pressure against the U.S. government."[7] A year later, when
the military released the records of Guantánamo's 2006 Administrative Review Board hearings, Mohamedou's transcript was
missing completely. That transcript is still classified.

Mohamedou's manuscript was finally cleared for public release, and a member of his legal team was able to hand it to me on a disk labeled "Slahi Manuscript—Unclassified Version," in the summer of 2012. By then, Mohamedou had been in Guantánamo for a decade. A federal judge had granted his habeas corpus petition two years before and ordered him released, but the U.S government had appealed, and the appeals court sent his petition back down to the federal district court for rehearing. That case is still pending.

Mohamedou remains to this day in the same segregation cell where he wrote his Guantánamo diary. I have, I believe, read everything that has been made public about his case, and I do not understand why he was ever in Guantánamo in the first place.

Mohamedou Ould Slahi was born on December 31, 1970, in Rosso, then a small town, now a small city, on the Senegal River on Mauritania's southern border. He had eight older siblings; three more would follow. The family moved to the capital, Nouakchott, as Mohamedou was finishing primary school, and his father, a nomadic camel trader, died not long after. The timing, and Mohamedou's obvious talents, must have shaped his sense of his role in the family. His father had taught him to read the Koran, which he had memorized by the time he was a teenager, and he did well in high school, with a particular aptitude for math. A 2008 feature in *Der Spiegel* describes a popular kid with a passion for soccer, and especially for the German national team—a passion that led him to apply for, and win, a scholarship from the Carl Duisberg Society to study in Germany. It was an enormous leap for the entire family, as the magazine reported:

Slahi boarded a plane for Germany on a Friday in the late summer of 1988. He was the first family member to attend a university—abroad, no less—and the first to travel on an airplane. Distraught by the departure of her favorite son, his mother's goodbye was so tearful that Mohamedou briefly hesitated before getting on his flight. In the end, the others convinced him to go. "He was supposed to save us financially," his brother [Y]ahdih says today.[8]

In Germany, Mohamedou pursued a degree in electrical engineering, with an eye toward a career in telecom and computers, but he interrupted his studies to participate in a cause that was drawing young men from around the world: the insurgency against the communist-led government in Afghanistan. There were no restrictions or prohibitions on such activities in those days, and young men like Mohamedou made the trip openly; it was a cause that the West, and the United States in particular, actively supported. To join the fight required training, so in early 1991 Mohamedou attended the al-Farouq training camp near Khost for seven weeks and swore a loyalty oath to al-Qaeda, the camp's operators. He received light arms and mortar training, the guns mostly Soviet made, the mortar shells, he recalled in his 2004 Combatant Status Review hearing, made in the U.S.A.

Mohamedou returned to his studies after the training, but in early 1992, with the communist government on the verge of collapsing, he went back to Afghanistan. He joined a unit commanded by Jalaluddin Haqqani that was laying siege to the city of Gardez, which fell with little resistance three weeks after Mohamedou arrived. Kabul fell soon thereafter, and as Mohamedou explained at the CSRT hearing, the cause quickly turned murky:

Right after the break down of [the] Communists, the Mujahiden themselves started to wage Jihad against themselves, to see who would be in power; the different factions began to fight against each other. I decided to go back because I didn't want to fight against other Muslims, and found no reason why; nor today did I see a reason to fight to see who could be president or vice-president. My goal was solely to fight against the aggressors, mainly the Communists, who forbid my brethren to practice their religion.

That, Mohamedou has always insisted, marked the end of his commitment to al-Qaeda. As he told the presiding officer at his CSRT:

Ma'am, I was knowledgeable I was fighting with al Qaida, but then al Qaida didn't wage Jihad against America. They told us to fight with our brothers against the Communists. In the mid-90's they wanted to wage Jihad against America, but I personally had nothing to do with that. I didn't join them in this idea; that's their problem. I am completely out of the line between al Qaida and the U.S. They have to solve this problem themselves; I am completely independent of this problem.[9]

Back in Germany, Mohamedou settled into the life he and his family in Nouakchott had planned. He completed his degree in electrical engineering at the University of Duisburg, his young Mauritanian wife joined him, and the couple lived and worked in Duisburg for most of the 1990s. During that time, though, he remained friends or kept in touch with companions from the Afghanistan adventure, some of whom maintained al-Qaeda ties. He also had his own direct association with a prominent al-Qaeda member, Mahfouz Ould al-Walid, also known as Abu Hafs al-Mauritani, who was a member of al-Qaeda's Shura Council and one of Osama bin Laden's senior theological advisers. Abu Hafs is a distant cousin of Mohamedou, and also a brother-in-law through his marriage to Mohamedou's wife's sister. The two were in occasional phone contact while Mohamedou was in Germany—a call from Abu Hafs, using bin Laden's satellite phone, caught the ears of German intelligence in 1999—and twice Mohamedou helped Abu Hafs transfer $4,000 to his family in Mauritania around the Ramadan holidays.

In 1998, Mohamedou and his wife traveled to Saudi Arabia to perform the hajj. That same year, unable to secure permanent residency in Germany, Mohamedou followed a college friend's recommendation and applied for landed immigrant status in Canada, and in November 1999 he moved to Montreal. He lived for a time with his former classmate and then at Montreal's large al Sunnah mosque, where, as a *hafiz*, or someone who has memorized the Koran, he was invited to lead Ramadan prayers when the imam was traveling. Less than a month after he arrived in Montreal, an Algerian immigrant and al-Qaeda member named Ahmed Ressam was arrested entering the United States with a car laden with explosives and a plan to bomb Los Angeles International Airport on New Year's Day, as part of what became known as the Millennium Plot. Ressam had been based in Montreal. He left the city before Mohamedou arrived, but he had attended the al Sunnah mosque and had connections with several of what Mohamedou, at his CSRT hearing, called his classmate's "bad friends."

Ressam's arrest sparked a major investigation of the Muslim immigrant community in Montreal, and the al Sunnah mosque community in particular, and for the first time in his life, Mohamedou was questioned about possible terrorist connections. The

Royal Canadian Mounted Police "came and interrogated me," he testified at his 2005 Administrative Review Board hearing.

> *I was scared to hell. They asked me do I know Ahmed Ressam, I said, "No," and then they asked do you know this guy and I said, "No, No." I was so scared I was shaking. . . . I was not used to this, it was the first time I had been interrogated and I just wanted to stay out of trouble and make sure I told the truth. But they were watching me in a very ugly way. It is okay to be watched, but it is not okay to see the people who are watching you. It was very clumsy, but they wanted to give the message that we are watching you.*

Back in Mauritania, Mohamedou's family was alarmed. " 'What are you doing in Canada?' " he recalled them asking. "I said nothing but look[ing] for a job. And my family decided I needed to get back to Mauritania because this guy must be in a very bad environment and we want to save him." His now ex-wife telephoned on behalf of the family to report that his mother was sick. As he described to the Review Board:

> *[She] called me and she was crying and she said, "Either you get me to Canada or you come to Mauritania." I said, "Hey, take it easy." I didn't like this life in Canada, I couldn't enjoy my free-dom and being watched is not very good. I hated Canada and I said the work is very hard here. I took off on Friday, 21 January 2000; I took a flight from Montreal to Brussels, then to Dakar.[10]*

With that flight, the odyssey that will become Mohamedou's *Guantánamo Diary* begins.

It begins here because from this moment forward, a single

force determines Mohamedou's fate: the United States. Geographically, what he calls his "endless world tour" of detention and interrogation will cover twenty thousand miles over the next eighteen months, starting with what is supposed to be a homecoming and ending with him marooned four thousand miles from home on a Caribbean island. He will be held and interrogated in four countries along the way, often with the participation of Americans, and always at the behest of the United States.

Here is how the first of these detentions is described in a timeline that U.S. District Judge James Robertson included in his declassified 2010 order granting Mohamedou's habeas corpus petition:

Jan 2000   *Flew from Canada to Senegal, where brothers met him to take him to Mauritania; he and brothers were seized by* ███████████ *authorities, and were questioned about the Millennium plot. An American came and took pictures; then, someone he presumed was American flew him to Mauritania, where he was questioned further by Mauritanian authorities about the Millennium plot.*

Feb 2000   *Interrogated by* ███ *re Millennium plot*

2/14/2000   ████████████ *released him, concluding there was no basis to believe he was involved in the Millennium plot.*

"The Mauritanians said, 'We don't need you, go away. We have no interest in you,'" Mohamedou recalled, describing that release at his ARB hearing. "I asked them what about the Americans? They said, 'The Americans keep saying you are a link but they don't give us any proof so what should we do?'"

But as Judge Robertson chronicled in his timeline, the Mauritanian government summoned Mohamedou again at the United States' request shortly after the 9/11 terrorist attacks:

9/29/2001	*Arrested in Mauritania; authorities told him* ▮▮▮▮▮ ▮▮▮▮▮ *arrest because Salahi was allegedly involved in Millennium plot.*
10/12/2001	*While he was detained, agents performed a search at his house, seizing tapes and documents.*
10/15/2001	*Released by* ▮▮▮▮▮▮ *authorities.*[11]

Between those two Mauritanian arrests, both of which included interrogations by FBI agents, Mohamedou was living a remarkably ordinary and, by his country's standards, successful life, doing computer and electronics work, first for a medical supply company that also provided Internet services, and then for a similarly diversified family-owned import business. But now he was nervous. Although he was free and "went back to his life," as he explained to the ARB:

> *I thought now I will have a problem with my employer because my employer would not take me back because I am suspected of terrorism, and they said they would take care of this. In front of me while I was sitting [there] the highest intelligence guy in Mauritania called my employer and said that I was a good person, we have no problem with [him] and we arrested him for a reason. We had to question him and we have questioned him and he is good to go, so you can take him back.*[12]

His boss did take him back, and just over a month later, Mohamedou's work would take him to the Mauritanian Presidential Palace, where he spent a day preparing a bid to upgrade President Maaouya Ould Sid'Ahmed Taya's telephone and computer systems. When he got home, the national police appeared again, telling him he was needed once more for questioning. He asked them to wait while he showered. He dressed, grabbed his keys—he went voluntarily, driving his own car to police headquarters—and told his mother not to worry, he would be home soon. This time, though, he disappeared.

For almost a year, his family was led to believe he was in Mauritanian custody. His oldest brother, Hamoud, regularly visited the security prison to deliver clean clothes and money for Mohamedou's meals. A week after Mohamedou turned himself in, however, a CIA rendition flight had spirited him to Jordan; months later, the United States had retrieved him from Amman and delivered him to Bagram Air Base in Afghanistan and, a few weeks after that, to Guantánamo. All this time, his family was paying for his upkeep in the Nouakchott prison; all this time, the prison officials pocketed the money, saying nothing. Finally, on October 28, 2002, Mohamedou's youngest brother, Yahdih, who had assumed Mohamedou's position as the family's European breadwinner, picked up that week's edition of *Der Spiegel* and read that his brother had by then "been sitting for months in a wire cage in the U.S. prison camp in Guantánamo."

Yahdih was furious—not, he remembers, at the United States but at the local authorities who had been assuring the family they had Mohamedou and he was safe. "Those police are bad people, they're thieves!" he kept yelling when he called his family with the news. "Don't say that!" they panicked, hanging up. He called them back and started in again. They hung up again.

Yahdih still lives in Düsseldorf. He and I met last year over a series of meals in a Moroccan restaurant on Ellerstraße, a center for the city's North African community. Yahdih introduced me to several of his friends, mainly young Moroccans, many of them, like Yahdih, now German citizens. Among themselves they spoke Arabic, French, and German; with me, like Yahdih, they gamely tried English, laughing at one another's mistakes. Yahdih told a classic immigrant's joke, in Arabic for his friends and then translating for me, about an aspiring hotel worker's English test. "What do you say if you want to call someone over to you?" the applicant is quizzed. "Please come here," he answers. "What if you want him to leave?" The applicant pauses, then brightens. "I go outside and tell him, 'Please come here!'"

In Düsseldorf, Yahdih and I spent an entire meal sorting and labeling photographs of siblings, sisters- and brothers-in-law, nieces and nephews, many living in the family's multigenerational household in Nouakchott. During his 2004 CSRT hearing, Mohamedou explained his disinterest in al-Qaeda after he returned to Germany by saying, "I had a big family to feed, I had 100 mouths to feed." It was an exaggeration, but only by half, maybe. Now Yahdih bears a large share of that responsibility. Because activism can be a risky business in Mauritania, he has also assumed the family lead in advocating for Mohamedou's release. During our last meal together, we watched YouTube videos of a demonstration he helped organize in Nouakchott last year outside the Presidential Palace. The featured speaker, he pointed out, was a parliament minister.

A few days before I visited Yahdih, Mohamedou had been allowed one of his twice-yearly calls with his family. The calls are arranged under the auspices of the International Committee of the Red Cross and connect Mohamedou with the family household in Nouakchott and with Yahdih in Germany. Yahdih told me he had recently written to the Red Cross to ask if the number of calls could be increased to three a year.

The first of these calls took place in 2008, six and a half years after Mohamedou disappeared. A reporter for *Der Spiegel* witnessed the scene:

At noon on a Friday in June 2008, the Slahi family convenes at the offices of the International Red Cross (IRC) in the Mauritanian capital Nouakchott. His mother, brothers, sisters, nephews, nieces and aunts are all dressed in the flowing robes they would normally wear to a family party. They have come here to talk to Mohamedou, their lost son, by telephone. The Joint Task Force in Guantanamo has granted its approval, with the IRC acting as go-between. Thick carpets cover the stone floor and light-colored curtains billow at the windows of the IRC office.

"My son, my son, how are you feeling?" his mother asks. "I am so happy to hear you." She breaks into tears, as she hears his voice for the first time in more than six years. Mohamedou's older brother speaks with him for 40 minutes. Slahi tells his brother that he is doing well. He wants to know who has married whom, how his siblings are doing and who has had children. "That was my brother, the brother I know. He has not changed," Hamoud Ould Slahi says after the conversation.[13]

From what Yahdih tells me, the conversations remain more or less the same five years later, though two things have changed. The calls are now Skype calls, so they can see one another. And they are now missing Mohamedou's and Yahdih's mother. She died on March 27, 2013.

The lead editorial in the *New York Daily News* on March 23, 2010, was titled "Keep the Cell Door Shut: Appeal a Judge's Outrageous Ruling to Free 9/11 Thug." The editorial began:

It is shocking and true: a federal judge has ordered the release of Mohamedou Ould Slahi, one of the top recruiters for the 9/11 attacks — a man once deemed the highest-value detainee in Guantanamo.

That ruling was Judge James Robertson's then still-classified memorandum order granting Mohamedou's habeas corpus petition—the petition Mohamedou handwrote in his Camp Echo cell five years before. Without access to that order or to the legal filings or court hearing that resulted in the order, the newspaper's editorial board nevertheless conjectured that a judge was letting "a terrorist with the blood of 3,000 on his hands" go free, adding contortedly, "he possibly being a man whose guilt was certain but unprovable beyond a reasonable doubt thanks to squeamishness over evidence acquired under rough treatment." Expressing confidence that Mohamedou was "squeezed appropriately hard after 9/11" and that his treatment made the country safer, the editors urged the Obama administration to appeal the order, adding, "What was the rush to release? The judge could have waited, should have waited, for the country to understand why this had to happen before exercising his legal authority."[14]

Two weeks later, the court released a declassified, redacted version of Judge Robertson's order. A section of the opinion summarizing the government's arguments for why Mohamedou must remain in Guantánamo included a footnote that might have surprised the newspaper's readers:

> *The government also argued at first that Salahi was also detainable under the "aided in 9/11" prong of the AUMF, but it has now abandoned that theory, acknowledging that Salahi probably did not even know about the 9/11 attacks.*[*15]

That certainly would make it a stretch to call Mohamedou a "9/11 thug." It is also a stretch, by any measure, to call a

---

* The AUMF, or Authorization for Use of Military Force, is the September 14, 2001, law under which Guantánamo operates. It authorizes the judgment ordering a man freed nine years after he was taken into custody a "rush to release." But there is a truth at the heart of that *Daily News* editorial—and much of the press coverage about Mohamedou's case—and that truth is confusion. Nine years is now thirteen, and the country seems to be no closer to understanding the U.S. government's case for holding Mohamedou than when Judge Robertson, the one judge who has thoroughly reviewed his case, ordered him released.

This much seems clear from the available record: Mohamedou's time in U.S. custody did not begin with allegations that he was a top 9/11 recruiter. When he was questioned by FBI agents on his return to Mauritania in February 2000, and again a few weeks after the 9/11 attacks, the focus was on the Millennium Plot. This appears to have been the case for his rendition to Jordan as well: "The Jordanians were investigating my part in the Millennium plot," Mohamedou told the Administrative Review Board in 2005. "They told me they are especially concerned about the Millennium plot."

By the time the CIA delivered Mohamedou to Jordan, though, Ahmed Ressam had been cooperating for months with the Justice Department in the United States, and by the time the CIA retrieved Mohamedou eight months later, Ressam had testified in two terrorism trials and provided the names of more than 150 people involved in terrorism to the U.S. government and the governments of six other countries. Some of those people were Guantánamo detainees, and the U.S. government has used Ressam's statements as evidence against them in their habeas cases.

---

president "to use all necessary and appropriate force against those nations, organizations, or persons he determines planned, authorized, committed, or aided the terrorist attacks that occurred on September 11, 2001, or harbored such organizations or persons, in order to prevent any future acts of international terrorism against the United States by such nations, organizations or persons."

Not so with Mohamedou. Ressam "conspicuously fails to implicate Salahi," Robertson noted in his habeas opinion.

The CIA would have known this. The agency would also have known if the Jordanians had uncovered anything linking Mohamedou to the Millennium Plot, the September 11 attacks, or any other terrorist plots. But the CIA apparently never provided any information from his interrogation in Amman to Guantánamo prosecutors. In a 2012 interview with the Rule of Law Oral History Project at Columbia University, Lt. Col. Stuart Couch, the Marine prosecutor assigned to build a case against Mohamedou in Guantánamo, said that the CIA showed him no intelligence reports of its own, and most of the reports the agency did share with him came from Mohamedou's Guantánamo interrogation. "He had been in their custody for six months. They knew I was the lead prosecutor. They knew we were contemplating a capital case. If we could have found his connection to 9/11, we were going to go for the death penalty."

"So something must have gone on," Stuart Couch surmised in that interview. "Slahi was in the custody of the CIA, and they must have felt like they got as much information out of him as they could, or the information they had didn't pan out to his significance, and they just kind of threw him over to U.S. military control at Bagram, Afghanistan."[16]

There is a chilling passage in the 2004 CIA inspector general's investigation report *Counterterrorism and Detention Interrogation Activities, September 2001–October 2003*, one of only two unredacted passages in a four-page blacked-out section of the report headed "Endgame." It says:

> *The number of detainees in CIA custody is relatively small by comparison with those in military custody. Nevertheless, the Agency, like the military, has an interest in the disposition of*

detainees and a particular interest in those who, if not kept in isolation, would likely have divulged information about the circumstances of their detention.[17]

In early 2002, not even Mohamedou's family knew he was in Jordan. Few people anywhere knew that the United States was operating a rendition, detention, and interrogation program, and that it was doing so not just with the assistance of long-standing allies like the Jordanian intelligence service but also with the cooperation of other, shakier friends. Mauritania was such a friend. In 2002, Mauritania's president and multi-decade ruler Ould Taya was under fire internationally for his country's human rights record, and at home for his close cooperation with the United States' antiterrorism policies. That Mohamedou had been questioned by FBI agents in his own country in 2000 had been controversial enough to attract the press. What if he had returned to the country in mid-2002 with stories that he had been turned over to the Americans without extradition proceedings, in violation of an explicit Mauritanian constitutional protection; that the CIA had delivered him in secret to Jordan; and that he had been interrogated for months in a Jordanian prison?

In any case, there is no indication that when a U.S. military C-17 carrying Mohamedou and thirty-four other prisoners landed in Guantánamo on August 5, 2002, the thirty-one-year-old Mauritanian was an especially high-value detainee. He would have stood out if so: an article published two weeks later in the *Los Angeles Times* titled "No Leaders of al Qaeda Found at Guantánamo Bay, Cuba" quoted government sources who said that there were "no big fish" in custody there, and the island's nearly six hundred detainees were not "high enough in the command and control structure to help counter-terrorism experts unravel al Qaeda's tightknit cell and security system."[18] A top secret CIA audit of the facility around the same time reportedly echoed those conclusions. When journalists visited the camp that August, the commander of Guantánamo's detention operations told them his own uniformed officers were questioning the continuing designation of detainees as "enemy combatants" as opposed to prisoners of war entitled to Geneva convention protections. The Pentagon's solution was to replace that commander and ratchet up the camp's intelligence operations.

Almost immediately a schism opened between military interrogators and the FBI and Criminal Investigation Task Force agents who had generally been leading prisoner interviews in Guantánamo. In September and October, over the fierce objections of the FBI and CITF agents, the military set up its first "Special Projects Team" and developed a written plan for the interrogation of the Saudi prisoner Mohammed al-Qahtani. That plan incorporated some of the "enhanced interrogation techniques" the CIA had been employing for several months in its own secret prison. Under the plan, which was implemented in fits and starts through the fall and finally, with the signed authorization of Defense Secretary Rumsfeld, in a harrowing fifty-day barrage starting in November, military interrogators subjected Qahtani to a round-the-clock regime of extreme sleep deprivation, loud music and white noise, frigid temperatures, stress positions, threats, and a variety of physical and sexual humiliations.

It was during this time, as the struggle over interrogation methods was playing out in the camp, that a link surfaced between Mohamedou Ould Slahi and the 9/11 hijackers. "September 11, 2002, America arrested a man by the name of Ramzi bin al-Shibh, who is said to be the key guy in the September 11th attacks," Mohamedou recounted at his 2005 ARB hearing.

It is exactly one year after September 11, and since his capture my life has changed drastically. The guy identified me as the guy that he saw in October 1999, which is correct, he was in my house. He said that I advised him to go to Afghanistan to train. Okay, then his interrogator ████████████ *from the FBI asked him to speculate who I was as a person. He said I think he is an operative of Usama Bin Laden and without him I would never have been involved in September 11th.*[19]

Bin al-Shibh had been the target of an international manhunt since 9/11 for his alleged role in coordinating the "Hamburg cell" of hijackers. He was transferred to CIA custody immediately after his capture in a shoot-out in a suburb of Karachi and was held first in the CIA's "Dark Prison" in Afghanistan and then, through the fall, in a prison near Rabat, Morocco. During interrogations in one of those facilities, bin al-Shibh told of a chance meeting with a stranger on a train in Germany, where he and two friends talked of jihad and their desire to travel to Chechnya to join the fight against the Russians. The stranger suggested they contact Mohamedou in Duisburg, and when they did, Mohamedou put them up for a night. "When they arrived," the 9/11 Commission recorded in a description drawn from intelligence reports from those interrogations, "Slahi explained that it was difficult to get to Chechnya at the time because many travelers were being detained in Georgia. He recommended they go through Afghanistan instead, where they could train for jihad before traveling to Chechnya."[20]

Bin al-Shibh did not assert that Mohamedou sent him to Afghanistan to join a plot against the United States. Lt. Col. Couch, who saw the bin al-Shibh intelligence report, recalled in the 2012 interview, "I never saw any mention that it was to attack America. I never saw the fact that Ramzi Bin al-Shibh had said, 'We told him what we wanted to do, and he said, "This is where you need to go train."' It was sort of, 'This is where you can get training.'"[21] During Mohamedou's habeas proceedings, the U.S. government did not argue that he had persuaded the men to join bin Laden's plot; rather, the government alleged that in suggesting that the men seek training in Afghanistan—something Mohamedou had learned was necessary to join an earlier fight involving Russians—he was serving in general as an al-Qaeda recruiter. Judge Robertson disagreed, finding that the record showed only that "Salahi provided lodging for three men for one night in Germany, that one of these was Ramzi bin al-Shibh, and that there was discussion of jihad and Afghanistan."[22]

Stuart Couch received bin al-Shibh's intelligence reports when he was assigned Mohamedou's case in the fall of 2003. The reports, and the assignment itself, had particular significance for the former Marine pilot: his close friend Michael Horrocks, a fellow refueling tanker pilot in the Marines, was the copilot on the United Airlines flight that the 9/11 hijackers used to bring down the World Trade Center's South Tower. That event had drawn Stuart Couch back to active service. He joined the Guantánamo military commission's team of prosecutors with a purpose, hoping, as he explained in a 2007 *Wall Street Journal* profile, "to get a crack at the guys who attacked the United States."[23]

Soon he was looking at batches of intelligence reports from another source, Mohamedou himself, the fruit of what military interrogators were already touting as their most successful Guantánamo interrogation. Those reports contained no information about the circumstances of that interrogation, but Lt. Col. Couch had his suspicions. He had been told that Mohamedou was on "Special Projects." He had caught a glimpse, on his first visit to the base, of another prisoner shackled to the floor in an empty interrogation booth, rocking back and forth as a strobe light flashed and heavy metal blared. He had seen this kind of thing before: as a Marine pilot, he had endured a week of such techniques in a program that prepares U.S. airmen for the experience of capture and torture.

Those suspicions were confirmed when the lieutenant colonel's investigator, a Naval Criminal Investigative Service (NCIS) agent, gained access to military interrogators' files. Those files included the Special Projects Team's daily memoranda for the record, the interrogators' detailed accounts not only of what was said in each session but also of how the information was extracted.

Those records remain classified, but they are summarized in the U.S. Senate Armed Services Committee's 2008 *Inquiry into the Treatment of Detainees in U.S. Custody* and the Justice Department's own 2008 review of interrogations in Guantánamo, Afghanistan, and Iraq. Those reports document a "special interrogation" that followed a second painstaking, Rumsfeld-approved plan and unfolded almost exactly as Mohamedou describes it in his *Guantánamo Diary*. Among the specific documents described in those reports are two that, when Stuart Couch uncovered them in early 2004, convinced him that Mohamedou had been tortured.

The first was a fake State Department letter Mohamedou had been presented in August 2003, which was clearly meant to exploit his close relationship with his mother. In its report, the Senate Armed Services Committee describes "a fictitious letter that had been drafted by the Interrogation Team Chief stating that his mother had been detained, would be interrogated, and if she were uncooperative she might be transferred to GTMO. The letter pointed out that she would be the only female detained at 'this previously all-male prison environment.'"

The second was an October 17, 2003, e-mail exchange between

one of Mohamedou's interrogators and a U.S. military psychiatrist. In it, the committee found, the interrogator "stated that 'Slahi told me he is "hearing voices" now.... He is worried as he knows this is not normal.... By the way... is this something that happens to people who have little external stimulus such as daylight, human interaction etc???? Seems a little creepy.'" The psychologist responded, "Sensory deprivation can cause hallucinations, usually visual rather than auditory, but you never know.... In the dark you create things out of what little you have."[24]

In a 2009 interview, Lt. Col. Couch described the impact of these discoveries:

> *Right in the middle of this time, when I had received this information from the NCIS agent — the documents, the State Department letterhead — and it was at the end of this, hearing all of this information, reading all this information, months and months and months of wrangling with the issue, that I was in church this Sunday, and we had a baptism. We got to the part of the liturgy where the congregation repeats — I'm paraphrasing here, but the essence is that we respect the dignity of every human being and seek peace and justice on earth. And when we spoke those words that morning, there were a lot of people in that church, but I could have been the only one there. I just felt this incredible, alright, there it is. You can't come in here on Sunday, and as a Christian, subscribe to this belief of dignity of every human being and say I will seek justice and peace on the earth, and continue to go with the prosecution using that kind of evidence. And at that point I knew what I had to do. I had to get off the fence.[25]*

Stuart Couch withdrew from Mohamedou's case, refusing to proceed with any effort to try him before a military commission.

No charge sheet has ever been drawn up against Mohamedou

Ould Slahi in Guantánamo, no military commission defense attorney was ever appointed to his case, and it appears there have been no further attempts to prepare a case for prosecution. The *Daily News* editorial decrying Judge Robertson's habeas decision attributes this to "squeamishness" over using "evidence acquired under rough treatment," but it is not at all clear that Mohamedou's brutal Guantánamo interrogation yielded any evidence that he had a hand in any criminal or terrorist activities. At his 2005 ARB hearing, he told of manufacturing confessions under torture, but the interrogators themselves must have discounted what they knew to be induced confessions; what they passed along in their scrubbed intelligence reports consisted instead, Stuart Couch has said, of a kind of "Who's Who of al Qaeda in Germany and all of Europe."[26]

Just as his extreme treatment is often cited as an indicator of his guilt, so those intelligence reports have come to serve as a kind of after-the-fact proof that Mohamedou himself must be among the Who's Who. And yet, Stuart Couch has suggested, Mohamedou's knowledge seems to have been little better than his interrogators'. "I think, if my recollection is right, that most of them had already been known to the intelligence services when he was being questioned," Couch noted in the 2012 interview, adding:

> *I've got to be clear on something. When you read the intelligence reports given up by Slahi, he doesn't implicate himself in anything. The only way he implicates himself is by his knowledge of these people. He never implicates himself in any of what I would consider to be an overt act that was part of the al-Qaeda conspiracy to attack the United States on 9/11.*[27]

Nor, it seems, have U.S. intelligence services unearthed anything else implicating Mohamedou in other terrorist plots or attacks. In a 2013 interview, Colonel Morris Davis, who became chief prosecutor for the Guantánamo military commissions in 2005, described a last-ditch effort, almost two years after Stuart Couch withdrew from Mohamedou's case, to develop some kind of charge against Mohamedou. Colonel Davis's real target at the time was not Mohamedou, who by then hardly even registered on the prosecutorial radar, but rather the prisoner the military had moved into the hut next door to Mohamedou's to mitigate the effects of his torture and almost two years of solitary confinement. That prisoner would not accept a plea bargain, however, unless Mohamedou received a similar offer. "We had to figure some kind of similar deal for Slahi," Colonel Davis said in that interview, "which meant we had to find *something* we could charge him with, and that was where we were having real trouble."

When Slahi came in, I think the suspicion was that they'd caught a big fish. He reminded me of Forrest Gump, in the sense that there were a lot of noteworthy events in the history of al-Qaida and terrorism, and there was Slahi, lurking somewhere in the background. He was in Germany, Canada, different places that look suspicious, and that caused them to believe that he was a big fish, but then when they really invested the effort to look into it, that's not where they came out. I remember a while after I got there, in early 2007, we had a big meeting with the CIA, the FBI, the Department of Defense, and the Department of Justice, and we got a briefing from the investigators who worked on the Slahi case, and their conclusion was there's a lot of smoke and no fire.[28]

When Mohamedou's habeas corpus petition finally came before the federal court in 2009, the U.S. government did not try to argue that he was a major al-Qaeda figure or that he had a hand in any al-Qaeda plans or attacks. As the DC Circuit Court of Appeals wrote in its subsequent review of the case:

> *The United States seeks to detain Mohammedou Ould Salahi on the grounds that he was "part of" al-Qaida not because he fought with al-Qaida or its allies against the United States, but rather because he swore an oath of allegiance to the organization, associated with its members, and helped it in various ways, including hosting its leaders and referring aspiring jihadists to a known al-Qaida operative.*[29]

When Judge Robertson heard Mohamedou's petition in 2009, the DC district courts presiding over Guantánamo habeas cases were judging the question of whether a petitioner was part of al-Qaeda based on whether the government could show that the petitioner was an active member of the organization at the time he was detained. Mohamedou had joined al-Qaeda in 1991 and sworn a loyalty oath to the organization at that time, but that was a very different al-Qaeda, practically an ally of the United States; Mohamedou has always maintained that the fall of the communist government in Afghanistan marked the end of his participation in the organization. In his habeas proceedings, the government insisted that his occasional contacts and interactions with his brother-in-law and cousin Abu Hafs and a handful of other friends and acquaintances who had remained active in al-Qaeda proved that Mohamedou was still a part of the organization. While a few of those interactions involved possible gestures of support, none, Robertson suggested, rose to the level of criminal material support for terrorism, and overall, Mohamedou's contacts with these people were so sporadic that "they tend to support Salahi's submission that he was attempting to find the appropriate balance—avoiding close relationships with al Qaida members, but also trying to avoid making himself an enemy."

Judge Robertson's decision granting Mohamedou's habeas corpus petition and ordering his release came at a critical moment: as of April 1, 2010, the U.S. government had lost thirty-four out of forty-six habeas cases. In appeals of several of those cases, the government persuaded the DC Circuit Court of Appeals to accept a looser standard for judging whether a petitioner was "part of" al-Qaeda; now, as the appellate court explained in reversing Judge Robertson's order and remanding the case to district court for rehearing, the government no longer needed to show that a Guantánamo prisoner was carrying out al-Qaeda orders or directions at the time he was taken into custody.

In its opinion, the appeals court was careful to delineate "the precise nature of the government's case against Salahi." "The government has not criminally indicted Salahi for providing material support to terrorists or the 'foreign terrorist organization' al-Qaida," the court emphasized. "Nor," it added, "does the government seek to detain Salahi under the AUMF on the grounds that he aided the September 11 attacks or 'purposefully and materially support[ed]' forces associated with al-Qaeda 'in hostilities against U.S. Coalition partners.'" Rather, when Mohamedou's habeas corpus case is reheard in federal court, the government will likely again be arguing that his sporadic interactions with active al-Qaeda members in the 1990s mean that he too remained a member. Under the new standard, the court wrote, "Even if Salahi's connections to these individuals fail independently to prove that he was 'part of' al-Qaida, those connections make it more likely that Salahi was a member of the organization when captured and thus remain relevant to the question of whether he is detainable."[30]

Ironically, when a district court rehears the case, the government will likely face questions about what it has always contended is the most damaging of those connections, Mohamedou's relationship with his cousin and brother-in-law Abu Hafs. As a member of bin Laden's Shura Council, Abu Hafs had a $5 million bounty on his head from the United States in the late 1990s, a figure that increased to $25 million after the September 11, 2001, terrorist attacks. For years, though, the United States has known that Abu Hafs opposed those attacks; the 9/11 Commission reported that he "even wrote Bin Laden a message basing opposition to those attacks on the Qur'an." After the attacks, Abu Hafs left Afghanistan for Iran, where Iranian authorities placed him under a soft form of house arrest for more than a decade. In April 2012, Iran repatriated Abu Hafs to Mauritania. He was held for two months in a Mauritanian prison, during which he reportedly met with an international delegation that included Americans, condemned the 9/11 attacks, and renounced his ties to al-Qaeda. He was released in July 2012 and has been living since then as a free man.

I have not met Mohamedou Ould Slahi. Other than sending him a letter introducing myself when I was asked if I would help to bring his manuscript to print—a letter I do not know if he received—I have not communicated with him in any way.

I did request to meet with him at least once before submitting the completed work to make sure my edits met with his approval. The answer from the Pentagon was brief and absolute. "Visiting or otherwise communicating with any detainee in the detention facility in Guantanamo, unless you are legal counsel representing the detainee, is not possible," a public affairs officer wrote.

"As you are aware, the detainees are held under the Law of War. Additionally, we do not subject detainees to public curiosity."

The phrase "public curiosity" comes from one of the pillars of the Law of War, the 1949 Geneva Convention Relative to the Treatment of Prisoners of War. Article 13 of the convention, "Humane Treatment of Prisoners," says:

> *Prisoners must at all times be humanely treated. Any unlawful act or omission by the Detaining Power causing death or seriously endangering the health of a prisoner of war in its custody will be prohibited, and will be regarded as a serious breach of the present Convention. . . .*
>
> *Prisoners must at all times be protected, particularly from acts of violence or intimidation and against insults and public curiosity.*
>
> *Measures of reprisal against prisoners of war are prohibited.*

I had proposed a confidential meeting, under strict security protocols, to make sure the edited version of Mohamedou's work—a work he specifically wrote for a public readership— accurately represents the original content and intent. For years that work itself was withheld, under a censorship regime that has not always served Geneva's purposes.

Censorship has been integral to the United States' post-9/11 detention operations from the start. It has been purposeful, not once but twice: first, to open a space for the abuse of prisoners, and then to conceal that those abuses happened. In Mohamedou's case, those abuses include enforced disappearance; arbitrary and incommunicado detention; cruel, inhuman, and degrading treatment; and torture. We know this thanks to a documentary record that was also, for years, rigorously suppressed.

I do not know to what extent personal and institutional

interests in covering up those abuses have contributed to Mohamedou's continuing imprisonment. I do know that in the five years I have spent reading the record about his case, I have not been persuaded by my government's vague and shifting explanations for why he is in Guantánamo, or by the assertions of those who defend his now-thirteen-year detention by saying he is almost certainly, or possibly, a this or a that. My own sense of fairness tells me the question of what this or that may be, and of why he must remain in U.S. custody, should long ago have been answered. It would have been, I believe, if his *Guantánamo Diary* had not been kept secret for so long.

When Mohamedou wrote the manuscript for this book nine years ago, in the same isolated hut where some of the book's most nightmarish scenes had very recently happened, he set himself a task. "I have only written what I experienced, what I saw, and what I learned first-hand," he explains near the end. "I have tried not to exaggerate, nor to understate. I have tried to be as fair as possible, to the U.S. government, to my brothers, and to myself."

He has, from everything I have seen, done just that. The story he tells is well corroborated by the declassified record; he proves again and again to be a reliable narrator. He certainly does not exaggerate: the record contains torments and humiliations not included in the book, and he renders several of those he does include with considerable discretion. Even when the events he recounts are at their most extreme, his narration is tempered and direct. The horrors of those events speak for themselves.

That is because his real interest is always in the human dramas of these scenes. "The law of war is harsh," Mohamedou writes early on.

If there's anything good at all in a war, it's that it brings the best and the worst out of people: some people try to use the lawlessness to hurt others, and some try to reduce the suffering to the minimum.

In chronicling his journey through the darkest regions of the United States' post-9/11 detention and interrogation program, his attention remains on his interrogators and guards, on his fellow detainees, and on himself. In his desire "to be fair," as he puts it, he recognizes the larger context of fear and confusion in which all these characters interact, and the much more local institutional and social forces that shape those interactions. But he also sees the capacity of every character to shape or mitigate the action, and he tries to understand people, regardless of stations or uniforms or conditions, as protagonists in their own right. In doing so, he transforms even the most dehumanizing situations into a series of individual, and at times harrowingly intimate, human exchanges.

This is the secret world of Guantánamo — a world of startlingly premeditated brutalities and of incidental degradations, but also a world of ameliorating gestures and kindnesses, of acknowledgments and recognitions, of mutual curiosities and risky forays across deep divides. That Mohamedou managed to experience all of this despite four years of the most arbitrary treatment imaginable and in the midst of one of Guantánamo's most horrendous interrogations says a great deal about his own character and his humanity. It says even more about his skills as a writer that he was able, so soon after the most traumatic of those experiences, to create from them a narrative that manages to be both damning and redeeming.

And yet this is not what impressed me most, as a reader and as a writer, when I first opened the file with Mohamedou's handwritten manuscript of *Guantánamo Diary*. What arrested me were characters and scenes far removed from Guantánamo: The hard-luck stowaway in a Senegalese prison. A sunset in Nouakchott after a Saharan dust storm. A heartbreaking moment of homesickness during a Ramadan call to prayer. The airport approach over Nouakchott's shantytowns. A rain-glazed runway in Cyprus. A drowsy predawn lull on a CIA rendition flight. Here is where I first recognized Mohamedou the writer, his sharp eye for character, his remarkable ear for voices, the way his recollections are infused with information recorded by all five senses, the way he accesses the full emotional register, in himself and others. He has the qualities I value most in a writer: a moving sense of beauty and a sharp sense of irony. He has a fantastic sense of humor.

He manages all of this in English, his fourth language, a language he was in the process of mastering even as he wrote the manuscript. This accomplishment testifies to a lifelong facility and fascination with words. But it also stems, it is clear, from a determination to engage, and to meet his environment on its own terms. On one level, mastering English in Guantánamo meant moving beyond translation and interpretation, beyond the necessity of a third person in the room, and opening the possibility that every contact with every one of his captors could be a personal exchange. On another, it meant decoding and understanding the language of the power that controls his fate—a power, as his twenty-thousand-mile odyssey of detention and interrogation vividly illustrates, of staggering influence and reach. Out of this engagement comes a truly remarkable work. On the one hand, it is a mirror in which, for the first time in anything I have read from Guantánamo, I have recognized aspects of myself, in both the characters of my compatriots and of those my country is holding captive. On another, it is a lens on an empire with a scope and impact few of us who live inside it fully understand.

For now, that power still controls Mohamedou's story. It is present in these pages in the form of more than 2,600 black-box redactions. These redactions do not just hide important elements of the action. They also blur Mohamedou's guiding principles and his basic purpose, undercutting the candor with which he addresses his own case, and obscuring his efforts to distinguish his characters as individuals, some culpable, some admirable, most a complex and shifting combination of both.

And it is present above all in his continuing, poorly explained imprisonment. Thirteen years ago, Mohamedou left his home in Nouakchott, Mauritania, and drove to the headquarters of his national police for questioning. He has not returned. For our collective sense of story and of justice, we must have a clearer understanding of why this has not happened yet, and what will happen next.

Guantánamo lives on unanswered questions. But now that we have *Guantánamo Diary*, how can we not at least resolve the questions in Mohamedou's case?

When we do, I believe there will be a homecoming. When that happens, the redactions will be filled in, the text will be reedited and amended and updated as Mohamedou himself would have it, and we will all be free to see *Guantánamo Diary* for what it ultimately is: an account of one man's odyssey through an increasingly borderless and anxious world, a world where the forces shaping lives are ever more distant and clandestine, where destinies are determined by powers with seemingly infinite reach, a world that threatens to dehumanize but fails to dehumanize — in short, an epic for our times.

103

comfort items, except for a thin iso-mat and a very thin, small, and worn-out blanket. I was deprived from my books, which I owned. I was deprived from my Koran. I was deprived from my soap. I was deprived from my toothpaste - maybe -, I was deprived from the roll of toilet paper I had. The cell - better the box - was cooled down that I was shaking most of the time. I was forbidden from seeing the light of the day. Every once in a while they gave me a rec-time in the night to keep me from seeing or interacting with any detainees. I was living litterally in tenor, I don't remember having slept one night quietly, and that if they gave me a break, which was rarely. For the next seventy days to come I hadn't known the sweetness of sleeping. Interogation for 24-hours, three, and some times, four shifts a day. I rarely got a day-off, "If you start to coop-erate you'll have some sleep, and hot meals" █████ used to tell me repeatedly. The Last visit of ICRC: After a couple days of my tranfer █████ from ICRC showed up at my cell and asked me whether I wanted to write a teller, "yes!" I said, █████ handed a paper and I wrote, "Mama I Love you, I just wanted to tell you that I love you! "

After that visits I never saw the ICRC for more than a year. They tried to see me but in vain. "You started to torture me, but you don't know how much I can take. You might end up killing me," I said when ▮▮ and ▮▮ pulled me for interrogation, "We do recommand things, but we don't have 'the final decision'" ▮▮ said, "I just want to warn you, I am suffering b/ of the harsh conditions you expose me to, I already have sciatic nerve ~~crisis~~ attack. And torture will not make me more cooperative"; "According to my experience you will cooperate. We are stronger than you, a ...ces" ▮▮ said. ▮▮ never w ...name, but he got busted, when mistakenly one of um colleague called him with his name. He doesn't know that I know his name, but well I do. ▮▮ grew worse with every day passing by. He started to lay me out my case — He started with the story of ▮▮, and me having recruit him for sep11 attack. "Why should he lie to us" ▮▮ said, "I don't know". "All you have to say is, I don't remember, I don't know, I have done nothing. You think you are going to impress an American jury with these word. In the eyes of Americans you are doomed. Just looking at you in orange suits, chains, being muslim, and Arabic is enough to convict you" ▮▮ said "That is injust", "We know that you are criminal"

|11

██████████████████████████████████████

██████ . I have a great body." Every once in a while ████ offered me to other side of the coin," If you start to cooperate, I am gonna stop harassing you? otherwise I will be doing the same with you and worse every day. I am ████████ and that why my gov't designated me to this job. I've been always successful. Having sex with somebody is not considered as torture" ███ was leading the monolog ████████. Every now and then the ████████ entered the room, and try to make me speak," you cannot defeat us, we have so many people, and we keep humilate you with America ██████", "I have a ████████ friend, I'm gonna bring tomorrow to help me" ████ said, "At least, cooperate" said ████ wryly. ████ didn't undress me but ████ was touching my private parts with ███ body. In the late afternoon, an other torture squad started with other poor detainee. I could hear loud music playing. "Do you want me to send you to that team or are you gonna cooperate" said ████, but I didn't answer. The guards wryly used to call █████████████████ ████████████████ b/c the most of the torture took place in those buildings, and in the nights. When the darkness started to cover the sorry camp, ███ ████████ sent me back to my cell. "Today is just the begin, what's coming is worse and that is every day" ████████ Doctor Routine check: In order ████ to see how much ^torture a detainee

ONE

Jordan-Afghanistan-GTMO

July 2002-February 2003

The American Team Takes Over...Arrival at Bagram...
Bagram to GTMO...GTMO, the New Home...One
Day in Paradise, the Next in Hell

██████████████, July ██, 2002, 10 p.m.*

The music was off. The conversations of the guards faded
away. The truck emptied.

I felt alone in the hearse truck.

The waiting didn't last: I felt the presence of new people, a
silent team. I don't remember a single word during the whole
rendition to follow.

---

* It becomes clear, from an unredacted date a few pages into the manuscript, that the action begins late in the evening on July 19, 2002. MOS
manuscript, 10. A Council of Europe investigation has confirmed that a
CIA-leased Gulfstream jet with the tail number N379P departed Amman,
Jordan, at 11:15 p.m. that night for Kabul, Afghanistan. An addendum to
that 2006 report listing the flight records is available at http://assembly.coe.
int/CommitteeDocs/2006/20060614_Ejdoc162006PartII-Appendix.pdf.

EDITOR'S NOTE ON THE FOOTNOTES: None of Mohamedou
Ould Slahi's attorneys holding security clearances has reviewed the
footnotes in this book, contributed to them in any way, or confirmed or
denied my speculations contained in them. Nor has anyone else with access

A person was undoing the chains on my wrists. He undid the first hand, and another guy grabbed that hand and bent it while a third person was putting on the new, firmer and heavier shackles. Now my hands were shackled in front of me.

Somebody started to rip my clothes with something like a scissors. I was like, What the heck is going on? I started to worry about the trip I neither wanted nor initiated. Somebody else was deciding everything for me; I had all the worries in the world but making a decision. Many thoughts went quickly through my head. The optimistic thoughts suggested, Maybe you're in the hands of Americans, but don't worry, they just want to take you home, and to make sure that everything goes in secrecy. The pessimistic ones went, You screwed up! The Americans managed to pin some shit on you, and they're taking you to U.S. prisons for the rest of your life.

I was stripped naked. It was humiliating, but the blindfold helped me miss the nasty look of my naked body. During the whole procedure, the only prayer I could remember was the crisis prayer, *Ya hayyu! Ya kayyum!* and I was mumbling it all the time. Whenever I came to be in a similar situation, I would forget all my prayers except the crisis prayer, which I learned from life of our Prophet, Peace be upon him.

One of the team wrapped a diaper around my private parts. Only then was I dead sure that the plane was heading to the U.S. Now I started to convince myself that "every thing's gonna be alright." My only worry was about my family seeing me on TV in such a degrading situation. I was so skinny. I've been always, but never *that* skinny: my street clothes had become so loose that I looked like a small cat in a big bag.

---

to the unredacted manuscript reviewed the footnotes, contributed to them in any way, or confirmed or denied my speculations contained in them.

When the U.S. team finished putting me in the clothes they tailored for me, a guy removed my blindfold for a moment. I couldn't see much because he directed the flashlight into my eyes. He was wrapped from hair to toe in a black uniform. He opened his mouth and stuck his tongue out, gesturing for me to do the same, a kind of AHH test which I took without resistance. I saw part of his very pale, blond-haired arm, which cemented my theory of being in Uncle Sam's hands.

The blindfold was pushed down. The whole time I was listening to loud plane engines; I very much believe that some planes were landing and others taking off. I felt my "special" plane approaching, or the truck approaching the plane, I don't recall anymore. But I do recall that when the escort grabbed me from the truck, there was no space between the truck and the airplane stairs. I was so exhausted, sick, and tired that I couldn't walk, which compelled the escort to pull me up the steps like a dead body.

Inside the plane it was very cold. I was laid on a sofa and the guards shackled me, mostly likely to the floor. I felt a blanket put over me; though very thin, it comforted me.

I relaxed and gave myself to my dreams. I was thinking about different members of my family I would never see again. How sad would they be! I was crying silently and without tears; for some reason, I gave all my tears at the beginning of the expedition, which was like the boundary between death and life. I wished I were better to people. I wished I were better to my family. I regretted every mistake I made in my life, toward God, toward my family, toward anybody!

I was thinking about life in an American prison. I was thinking about documentaries I had seen about their prisons, and the harshness with which they treat their prisoners. I wished I were blind or had some kind of handicap, so they would put me in isolation and give me some kind of humane treatment and protection. I was thinking, What will the first hearing with the judge be like? Do I have a chance to get due process in a country so full of hatred against Muslims? Am I really already convicted, even before I get the chance to defend myself?

I drowned in these painful dreams in the warmth of the blanket. Every once in a while the pain of the urine urge pinched me. The diaper didn't work with me: I could not convince my brain to give the signal to my bladder. The harder I tried, the firmer my brain became. The guard beside me kept pouring water bottle caps in my mouth, which worsened my situation. There was no refusing it, either you swallow or you choke. Lying on one side was killing me beyond belief, but every attempt to change my position ended in failure, for a strong hand pushed me back to the same position.

I could tell that the plane was a big jet, which led me to believe that flight was direct to the U.S. But after about five hours, the plane started to lose altitude and smoothly hit the runway. I realized the U.S. is a little bit farther than that. Where are we? In Ramstein, Germany? Yes! Ramstein it is: in Ramstein there's a U.S. military airport for transiting planes from the middle east; we're going to stop here for fuel. But as soon as the plane landed, the guards started to change my metal chains for plastic ones that cut my ankles painfully on the short walk to a helicopter. One of the guards, while pulling me out of the plane, tapped me on the shoulder as if to say, "you're gonna be alright." As in agony as I was, that gesture gave me hope that there were still some human beings among the people who were dealing with me.

When the sun hit me, the question popped up again: Where am I? Yes, Germany it is: it was July and the sun rises early. But why Germany? I had done no crimes in Germany! What shit did they pull on me? And yet the German legal system was by far a better choice for me; I know the procedures and speak the language. Moreover, the German system is somewhat transparent, and there are no two and three hundred years sentences. I had little to worry about: a German judge will face me and show me whatever the government has brought against me, and then I'm going to be sent to a temporary jail until my case is decided. I won't be subject to torture, and I won't have to see the evil faces of interrogators.

After about ten minutes the helicopter landed and I was taken into a truck, with a guard on either side. The chauffeur and his neighbor were talking in a language I had never heard before. I thought, What the heck are they speaking, maybe Filipino? I thought of the Philippines because I'm aware of the huge U.S. Military presence there. Oh, yes, Philippines it is: *they* conspired with the U.S. and pulled some shit on me. What would the questions of *their* judge be? By now, though, I just wanted to arrive and take a pee, and after that they can do whatever they please. Please let me arrive! I thought; After that you may kill me!

The guards pulled me out of the truck after a five-minute drive, and it felt as if they put me in a hall. They forced me to kneel and bend my head down: I should remain in that position until they grabbed me. They yelled, "Do not move." Before worrying about anything else, I took my most remarkable urine since I was born. It was such a relief; I felt I was released and sent back home. All of a sudden my worries faded away, and I smiled inside. Nobody noticed what I did.

About a quarter of an hour later, some guards pulled me and towed me to a room where they obviously had "processed" many detainees. Once I entered the room, the guards took the gear off my head. Oh, my ears ached so badly, and so did my head; actually my whole body was conspiring against me. I could barely stand. The guards started to deprive me of my clothes, and soon I stood there as naked as my mother bore me. I stood there for the first time in front of U.S. soldiers, not on TV, this was for real. I had the most common reaction, covering my private parts with my hands. I also quietly started to recite the crisis prayer, *Ya hayyu! Ya kayyum!* Nobody stopped me from praying; however, one of the MPs was staring at me with his eyes full of hatred. Later on he would order me to stop looking around in the room.

A ███████████████████████████ medic gave me a quick medical check, after which I was wrapped in Afghani cloths. Yes, Afghani clothes in the Philippines! Of course I was chained, hands and feet tied to my waist. My hands, moreover, were put in mittens. Now I'm ready for action! What action? No clue!

The escort team pulled me blindfolded to a neighboring interrogation room. As soon as I entered the room, several people started to shout and throw heavy things against the wall. In the melee, I could distinguish the following questions:

"Where is Mullah Omar?"

"Where is Usama Bin Laden?"

"Where is Jalaluddin Haqqani?"

A very quick analysis went through my brain: the individuals in those questions were leading a country, and now they're a bunch of fugitives! The interrogators missed a couple of things. First, they had just briefed me about the latest news: Afghanistan is taken over, but the high level people have not been captured. Second, I turned myself in about the time when the war against terrorism started, and since then I have been in a Jordanian prison, literally cut off from the rest of the world. So

how am I supposed to know about the U.S. taking over Afghanistan, let alone about its leaders having fled? Not to mention
where they are now.

I humbly replied, "I don't know!"

"You're a liar!" shouted one of them in broken Arabic.

"No, I'm not lying, I was captured so and so, and I only know
Abu Hafs..." I said, in a quick summary of my whole story.*

"We should interrogate these motherfuckers like the Israelis do."

"What do they do?" asked another.

"They strip them naked and interrogate them!"

"Maybe we should!" suggested another. Chairs were still
flying around and hitting the walls and the floor. I knew it was
only a show of force, and the establishment of fear and anxiety.
I went with the flow and even shook myself more than necessary. I didn't believe that Americans torture, even though I had
always considered it a remote possibility.

"I am gonna interrogate you later on," said one, and the U.S.
interpreter repeated the same in Arabic.

"Take him to the Hotel," suggested the interrogator. This
time the interpreter didn't translate.

---

* Abu Hafs, whose name appears here and elsewhere in the manuscript
unredacted, is MOS's cousin and former brother-in-law. His full name is
Mahfouz Ould al-Walid, and he is also known as Abu Hafs al-Mauritani.
Abu Hafs married the sister of MOS's former wife. He was a prominent
member of al-Qaeda's Shura Council, the group's main advisory body, in
the 1990s and up until the September 11, 2001, terrorist attacks in the
United States. It has been widely reported that Abu Hafs opposed those
attacks; the 9/11 Commission recorded that "Abu Hafs the Mauritanian
reportedly even wrote Bin Ladin a message basing opposition to the attacks
on the Qur'an." Abu Hafs left Afghanistan after the 9/11 attacks and spent
the next decade under house arrest in Iran. In April 2012 he was extradited
to Mauritania, where he was held briefly and then released. He is now a
free man. The relevant section of the 9/11 Commission report is available
at http://govinfo.library.unt.edu/911/report/911Report_Ch7.pdf.

And so was the first interrogation done. Before the escort grabbed me, in my terrorizing fear, I tried to connect with the interpreter.

"Where did you learn such good Arabic?" I asked.

"In the U.S.!" he replied, sounding flattered. In fact, he didn't speak good Arabic; I just was trying to make some friends.

The escort team led me away. "You speak English," one of them said in a thick Asian accent.

"A little bit," I replied. He laughed, and so did his colleague. I felt like a human being leading a casual conversation. I said to myself, Look how friendly the Americans are: they're gonna put you in a Hotel, interrogate you for a couple of days, and then fly you home safely. There's no place for worry. The U.S. just wants to check everything, and since you're innocent, they're gonna find that out. For Pete's sake, you're on a base in Philippines; even though it's a place at the edge of legality, it's just temporary. The fact that one of the guards sounded Asian strengthened my wrong theory of being in the Philippines.

I soon arrived, not at a Hotel but at a wooden cell with neither a bathroom nor a sink. From the modest furniture—a weathered, thin mattress and an old blanket—you could tell there had been somebody here. I was kind of happy for having left Jordan, the place of randomness, but I was worried about the prayers I could not perform, and I wanted to know how many prayers I missed on the trip. The guard of the cell was a small, skinny white ▇▇▇▇, a fact which gave me more comfort: for the last eight months I had been dealt with solely by big, muscular males.*

---

* Context suggests the guard may be female. Throughout the manuscript, it appears that the pronouns *she* and *her* are consistently redacted, and *he* and *his* appear unredacted.

I asked ▇▇▇ about the time, and ▇▇▇ told me it was about eleven, if I remember correctly. I had one more question.

"What day is it?"

"I don't know, every day here is the same," ▇▇▇ replied. I realized I had asked too much; ▇▇▇ wasn't even supposed to tell me the time, as I would learn later.

I found a Koran gently placed on some water bottles. I realized I was not alone in the jail, which was surely not a Hotel.

As it turned out, I was delivered to the wrong cell. Suddenly, I saw the weathered feet of a detainee whose face I couldn't see because it was covered with a black bag. Black bags, I soon would learn, were put on everybody's heads to blindfold them and make them unrecognizable, including the writer. Honestly, I didn't want to see the face of the detainee, just in case he was in pain or suffering, because I hate to see people suffering; it drives me crazy. I'll never forget the moans and cries of the poor detainees in Jordan when they were suffering torture. I remember putting my hands over my ears to stop myself from hearing the cries, but no matter how hard I tried, I was still able to hear the suffering. It was awful, even worse than torture.

The ▇▇▇▇ guard at my door stopped the escort team and organized my transfer to another cell. It was the same as the one I was just in, but in the facing wall. In the room there was a half-full water bottle, the label of which was written in Russian; I wished I had learned Russian. I said to myself, a U.S. base in the Philippines, with water bottles from Russia? The U.S. doesn't need supplies from Russia, and besides, geographically it makes no sense. Where *am* I? Maybe in a former Russian Republic, like Tajikstan? All I know is that I don't know!

The cell had no facility to take care of the natural business. Washing for prayer was impossible and forbidden. There was no clue as to the *Kibla*, the direction of Mecca. I did what I

could. My next door neighbor was mentally sick; he was shouting in a language with which I was not familiar. I later learned
that he was a Taliban leader.

Later on that day, July 20, 2002, the guards pulled me for
routine police work, fingerprints, height, weight, etcetera. I was
offered ▮▮▮▮▮▮▮▮ as interpreter. It was obvious that Arabic
was not ▮▮▮ first language. ▮▮▮ taught me the rules: no
speaking, no praying loudly, no washing for prayer, and a bunch
of other nos in that direction.* The guard asked me whether I
wanted to use the bathroom. I thought he meant a place where
you can shower; "Yes," I said. The bathroom was a barrel filled
with human waste. It was the most disgusting bathroom I ever
saw. The guards had to watch you while you were taking care of
business. I couldn't eat the food—the food in Jordan was, by far,
better than the cold MREs I got in Bagram—so I didn't really
have to use the bathroom. To pee, I would use the empty water
bottles I had in my room. The hygienic situation was not exactly
perfect; sometimes when the bottle got filled, I continued on the
floor, making sure that it didn't go all the way to the door.

For the next several nights in isolation, I got a funny guard
who was trying to convert me to Christianity. I enjoyed the
conversations, though my English was very basic. My dialogue
partner was young, religious, and energetic. He liked Bush ("the
true religious leader," according to him); he hated Bill Clinton
("the Infidel"). He loved the dollar and hated the Euro. He had
his copy of the bible on him all the time, and whenever the
opportunity arose he read me stories, most of which were from
the Old Testament. I wouldn't have been able to understand
them if I hadn't read the bible in Arabic several times—not to
mention that the versions of the stories are not that far from the

---

* Again, redacted pronouns suggest the interpreter is female.

ones in the Koran. I had studied the Bible in the Jordanian prison; I asked for a copy, and they offered me one. It was very helpful in understanding Western societies, even though many of them deny being influenced by religious scriptures.

I didn't try to argue with him: I was happy to have somebody to talk to. He and I were unanimous that the religious scriptures, including the Koran, must have come from the same source. As it turned out, the hot-tempered soldier's knowledge about his religion was very shallow. Nonetheless I enjoyed him being my guard. He gave me more time on the bathroom, and he even looked away when I used the barrel.

I asked him about my situation. "You're not a criminal, because they put the criminals in the other side," he told me, gesturing with his hand. I thought about those "criminals" and pictured a bunch of young Muslims, and how hard their situation could be. I felt bad. As it turned out, later on I was transferred to these "criminals," and became a "high priority criminal." I was kind of ashamed when the same guard saw me later with the "criminals," after he had told me that I was going to be released at most after three days. He acted normally, but he didn't have that much freedom to talk to me about religion there because of his numerous colleagues. Other detainees told me that he was not bad toward them, either.

The second or the third night ▌▌▌▌▌▌▌▌ pulled me out of my cell himself and led me to an interrogation, where the same ▌▌▌▌▌▌▌▌▌▌▌▌ Arabic already had taken a seat. ▌▌▌▌▌▌ ▌▌▌▌▌▌▌▌▌▌▌▌▌▌▌▌▌▌▌▌▌▌▌▌▌▌▌▌▌ ▌▌▌▌▌▌▌▌▌▌▌▌▌▌▌▌▌▌▌▌▌▌▌▌▌▌. You could tell he was the right man for the job: he was the kind of man who wouldn't mind doing the dirty work. The detainees back in Bagram used to call him ████████████████; he reportedly was responsible for torturing even innocent individuals the government released.*

████████████ didn't need to shackle me because I was in shackles 24 hours a day. I slept, ate, used the bathroom while completely shackled, hand to feet. ████████████ opened a file in his hand ████████████████████████████████████ and started by means of the interpreter. ████████████ was asking me general questions about my life and my background. When he asked me, "What languages do you speak?" he didn't believe me; he laughed along with the interpreter, saying, "Haha, you speak German? Wait, we're gonna check."

Suddenly ████████████████████████████████ ████████████ the room ████████████████████ ██ ████████████. There was no mistaking it, he was ████████████ ██ ██ ████████████†

"Ja Wohl," I replied. ████████████████ was not ████████████ but his German was fairly acceptable, given that he spent ████ ██ ██. He confirmed to his colleague that my German was "████████████.

---

* At his December 15, 2005, Administrative Review Board (ARB) hearing, MOS described a U.S. interrogator in Bagram who was Japanese American and whom Bagram prisoners referred to as "William the Torturer." ARB transcript, 23. The lead interrogator here could be that interrogator. MOS's 2005 ARB hearing transcript is available at http://www.dod.mil/pubs/foi/operation_and_plans/Detainee/csrt_arb/ARB_Transcript_Set_8_20751-21016.pdf, p. 23 transcript, p. 206 in link.

† Context suggests the second interrogator addressed MOS in German.

Both looked at me with some respect after that, though the respect was not enough to save me from ▮▮▮▮▮▮▮▮ wrath.

▮▮▮▮▮▮▮▮ asked me where I learned to speak German, and said that he was going to interrogate me again later.

▮▮▮▮▮▮▮▮▮▮▮▮▮▮▮▮▮▮▮▮▮▮▮, "Wahrheit macht frei, the truth sets you free."

When I heard him say that, I knew the truth wouldn't set me free, because "Arbeit" didn't set the Jews free. Hitler's propaganda machinery used to lure Jewish detainees with the slogan, "Arbeit macht frei," Work sets you free. But work set nobody free.

▮▮▮▮▮▮▮▮ took a note in his small notebook and left the room. ▮▮▮▮▮▮▮ sent me back to my room and apologized ▮▮▮▮▮▮▮▮▮▮▮▮▮▮.*

"I am sorry for keeping you awake for so long,"

"No problem!" ▮▮▮ replied.

After several days in isolation I was transferred to the general population, but I could only look at them because I was put in the narrow barbed-wire corridor between the cells. I felt like I was out of jail, though, and I cried and thanked God. After eight months of total isolation, I saw fellow detainees more or less in my situation. "Bad" detainees like me were shackled 24 hours a day and put in the corridor, where every passing guard or detainee stepped on them. The place was so narrow that the barbed wire kept pinching me for the next ten days. I saw ▮▮▮▮▮▮▮▮▮▮▮▮▮▮▮▮ being force-fed; he was on a forty-five day hunger strike. The guards were yelling at him, and he was bouncing a dry piece of bread between his hands. All the detainees looked so worn out, as if they had been buried and after several days resurrected, but ▮▮▮▮▮▮▮▮▮▮▮▮ was a completely different story: he was bones without meat. It

---

* Context suggests the apology is directed to the interpreter.

reminded me of the pictures you see in documentaries about WWII prisoners.

Detainees were not allowed to talk to each other, but we enjoyed looking at each other. The punishment for talking was hanging the detainee by the hands with his feet barely touching the ground. I saw an Afghani detainee who passed out a couple of times while hanging from his hands. The medics "fixed" him and hung him back up. Other detainees were luckier: they were hung for a certain time and then released. Most of the detainees tried to talk while they were hanging, which made the guards double their punishment. There was a very old Afghani fellow who reportedly was arrested to turn over his son. The guy was mentally sick; he couldn't stop talking because he didn't know where he was, nor why. I don't think he understood his environment, but the guards kept dutifully hanging him. It was so pitiful. One day one of the guards threw him on his face, and he was crying like a baby.

We were put in about six or seven big barbed-wire cells named after operations performed against the U.S: Nairobi, U.S.S. Cole, Dar-Es-Salaam, and so on. In each cell there was a detainee called English, who benevolently served as an interpreter to translate the orders to his co-detainees. Our English was a gentleman from Sudan named ███████████████████. His English was very basic, and so he asked me secretly whether I spoke English. "No," I replied—but as it turned out I was a Shakespeare compared to him. My brethren thought that I was denying them my services, but I just didn't know how bad the situation was.

Now I was sitting in front of bunch of dead regular U.S. citizens. My first impression, when I saw them chewing without a break, was, What's wrong with these guys, do they have to eat so much? Most of the guards were tall, and overweight. Some of them were friendly and some very hostile. Whenever I realized that a guard was mean I pretended that I understood no English. I remember one cowboy coming to me with an ugly frown on his face:

"You speak English?" he asked.

"No English," I replied.

"We don't like you to speak English. We want you to die slowly," he said.

"No English," I kept replying. I didn't want to give him the satisfaction that his message arrived. People with hatred always have something to get off their chests, but I wasn't ready to be that drain.

Prayer in groups wasn't allowed. Everybody prayed on his own, and so did I. Detainees had no clues about prayer time. We would just imitate: when a detainee started to pray, we assumed it was time and followed. The Koran was available to detainees who asked for one. I don't remember asking myself, because the handling by the guards was just disrespectful; they threw it to each other like a water bottle when they passed the holy book through. I didn't want to be a reason for humiliating God's word. Moreover, thank God, I know the Koran by heart. As far as I recall, one of the detainees secretly passed me a copy that nobody was using in the cell.

After a couple of days, ███████████████████████ pulled me to interrogate me. ███████████████ acted as an interpreter.

"Tell me your story," ████████████ asked.

"My name is, I graduated in 1988, I got a scholarship to Germany...." I replied in very boring detail, none of which seemed to interest or impress ████████████. He grew tired and started to yawn. I knew exactly what he wanted to hear, but I couldn't help him.

He interrupted me. "My country highly values the truth.

Now I'm gonna ask you some questions, and if you answer truthfully, you're gonna be released and sent safely to your family. But if you fail, you're gonna be imprisoned indefinitely. A small note in my agenda book is enough to destroy your life. What terrorist organizations are you part of?"

"None," I replied.

"You're not a man, and you don't deserve respect. Kneel, cross your hands, and put them behind your neck."

I obeyed the rules and he put a bag over my head. My back was hurting bad lately and that position was so painful; ████████████ was working on my sciatic problem.* ████████████ brought two projectors and adjusted them on my face. I couldn't see, but the heat overwhelmed me and I started to sweat.

"You're gonna be sent to a U.S. facility, where you'll spend the rest of your life," he threatened. "You'll never see your family again. Your family will be f**cked by another man. In American jails, terrorists like you get raped by multiple men at the same time. The guards in my country do their job very well, but being raped is inevitable. But if you tell me the truth, you're gonna be released immediately."

I was old enough to know that he was a rotten liar and a man with no honor, but he was in charge, so I had to listen to his bullshit again and again. I just wished that the agencies would start to hire smart people. Did he really think that anybody would believe his nonsense? Somebody would have to be stupid: was he stupid, or did he think I was stupid? I would have respected him more had he told me, "Look, if you don't tell me what I want to hear, I'm gonna torture you."

---

* At his 2005 ARB hearing, MOS indicated that an interrogator nicknamed "William the Torturer" made him kneel for "very long hours" to aggravate his sciatic nerve pain and later threatened him. ARB transcript, 23.

Anyway, I said, "Of course I will be truthful!"

"What terrorist organizations are you part of?"

"None!" I replied. He put back the bag on my head and started a long discourse of humiliation, cursing, lies, and threats. I don't really remember it all, nor am I ready to sift in my memory for such bullshit. I was so tired and hurt, and tried to sit but he forced me back. I cried from the pain. Yes, a man my age cried silently. I just couldn't bear the agony.

███████████ after a couple of hours sent me back to my cell, promising me more torture. "This was only the start," as he put it. I was returned to my cell, terrorized and worn out. I prayed to Allah to save me from him. I lived the days to follow in horror: whenever ███████████ went past our cell I looked away, avoiding seeing him so he wouldn't "see" me, exactly like an ostrich. ███████████ was checking on everybody, day and night, and giving the guards the recipe for every detainee. I saw him torturing this other detainee. I don't want to recount what I heard about him; I just want to tell what I saw with my eyes. It was an Afghani teenager, I would say 16 or 17. ███████████ made him stand for about three days, sleepless. I felt so bad for him. Whenever he fell down the guards came to him, shouting "no sleep for terrorists," and made him stand again. I remember sleeping and waking up, and he stood there like a tree.

Whenever I saw ███████████ around, my heart started to pound, and he was often around. One day he sent a ███████████████████ interpreter to me to pass me a message.

"███████████ is gonna kick your ass."

I didn't respond, but inside me I said, May Allah stop you! But in fact ███████████ didn't kick my rear end; instead ███████████████ pulled me for interrogation.* He was a nice

---

* This appears to be the German-speaking interrogator who assisted in the earlier interrogation.

guy; maybe he felt he could relate to me because of the language. And why not? Even some of the guards used to come to me and practice their German when they learned that I spoke it.

Anyway, he recounted a long story to me. "I'm not like ███████████. He's young and hot-tempered. I don't use inhumane methods; I have my own methods. I want to tell something about American history, and the whole war against terrorism."

███████████ was straightforward and enlightening. He started with American history and the Puritans, who punished even the innocents by drowning them, and ended with the war against terrorism. "There is no innocent detainee in this campaign: either you cooperate with us and I am going to get you the best deal, or we are going to send you to Cuba."

"What? *Cuba?*" I exclaimed. "I don't even speak Spanish, and you guys *hate* Cuba."

"Yes, but we have an American territory in Guantánamo," he said, and told me about Teddy Roosevelt and things like that. I knew that I was going to be sent further from home, which I hated.

"Why would you send me to Cuba?"

"We have other options, like Egypt and Algeria, but we only send them the very bad people. I hate sending people over there, because they'll experience painful torture."

"Just send me to Egypt."

"You sure do not want that. In Cuba they treat detainees humanely, and they have two Imams. The camp is run by the DOJ, not the military."*

---

* Department of Justice. This is not true, of course. The Guantánamo Bay detention camp is located on the Guantánamo Bay Naval Base and is run by a U.S. military joint task force under the command of the U.S. Southern Command.

"But I've done no crimes against your country."

"I'm sorry if you haven't. Just think of it as if you had cancer!"

"Am I going to be sent to court?"

"Not in the near future. Maybe in three years or so, when my people forget about September 11." ▇▇▇▇▇▇▇ went on to tell me about his private life, but I don't want to put it down here.

I had a couple more sessions with ▇▇▇▇▇▇▇ after that. He asked me some questions and tried to trick me, saying things like, "He said he knows you!" for people I had never heard of. He took my email addresses and passwords. He also asked the ▇▇▇▇▇▇▇▇▇▇▇▇▇▇▇ who were present in Bagram to interrogate me, but they refused, saying the ▇▇▇▇▇▇ law forbids them from interrogating aliens outside the country.* He was trying the whole time to convince me to cooperate so he could save me from the trip to Cuba. To be honest, I preferred to go to Cuba than to stay in Bagram.

"Let it be," I told him. "I don't think I can change anything."

Somehow I liked ▇▇▇▇▇▇▇. Don't get me wrong, he was a sneaky interrogator, but at least he spoke to me according to the level of my intellect. I asked ▇▇▇▇▇▇▇ to put me inside the cell with the rest of the population, and showed him the injuries I had suffered from the barbed wire. ▇▇▇▇▇▇▇

---

* This could refer to agents of the German foreign intelligence service, the Bundesnachrichtendienst (BND). Press accounts indicate that MOS was interrogated by both German and Canadian intelligence agents in Guantánamo; later in the manuscript, in the scene where he meets with what appear to be BND interrogators in GTMO, MOS specifically references such a prohibition on external interrogations. See footnote on page 51; see also http://www.spiegel.de/international/world/from-germany-to -guantanamo-the-career-of-prisoner-no-760-a-583193-3.html; and http:// www.thestar.com/news/canada/2008/07/27/csis_grilled_trio_in_cuba.html.

approved: in Bagram, interrogators could do anything with you; they had overall control, and the MPs were at their service. Sometimes ▇▇▇▇▇▇▇ gave me a drink, which I appreciated, especially with the kind of diet I received, cold MREs and dry bread in every meal. I secretly passed my meals to other detainees.

One night ▇▇▇▇▇▇▇ introduced two military interrogators who asked me about the Millennium plot. They spoke broken Arabic and were very hostile to me; they didn't allow me to sit and threatened me with all kind of things. But ▇▇▇▇▇▇▇ hated them, and told me in ▇▇▇▇▇▇▇, "If you want to cooperate, do so with me. These MI guys are nothing." I felt myself under auction to whichever agency bids more!*

In the population we always broke the rules and spoke to our neighbors. I had three direct neighbors. One was an Afghani teenager who was kidnapped on his way to Emirates; he used to work there, which was why he spoke Arabic with a Gulf accent. He was very funny, and he made me laugh; over the past nine months I had almost forgotten how. He was spending holidays with his family in Afghanistan and went to Iran; from there he headed to the Emirates in a boat, but the boat was hijacked by the U.S. and the passengers were arrested.

---

* The interrogator's remark about military interrogators and MOS's reference to an interagency competition for control of his interrogation suggest that the interrogator may be from one of the civilian agencies, likely the FBI. The protracted interagency conflict between the FBI and the Pentagon's Defense Intelligence Agency over the military's interrogation methods has been widely documented and reported, most notably in a May 2008 report by the U.S. Department of Justice's Inspector General titled *A Review of the FBI's Involvement in and Observations of Detainee Interrogations in Guantanamo Bay, Afghanistan, and Iraq* (hereafter cited as DOJ IG). The report, which is available at http://www.justice.gov/oig/special/s0805/final.pdf, includes substantial sections devoted specifically to MOS's interrogation.

My second neighbor was twenty-year-old Mauritanian guy who was born in Nigeria and moved to Saudi Arabia. He'd never been in Mauritania, nor did he speak the Mauritanian dialect; if he didn't introduce himself, you would say he was a Saudi.

My third neighbor was a Palestinian from Jordan named ██████████. He was captured and tortured by an Afghani tribal leader for about seven months. His kidnapper wanted money from ██████████ family or else he would turn him over to the Americans, though the latter option was the least promising because the U.S. was only paying $5,000 per head, unless it was a big head. The bandit arranged everything with ██████████ family regarding the ransom, but ██████████ managed to flee from captivity in Kabul. He made it to Jalalabad, where he easily stuck out as an Arab mujahid and was captured and sold to the Americans. I told ██████████ that I'd been in Jordan, and he seemed to be knowledgeable about their intelligence services. He knew all the interrogators who dealt with me, as ██████████ himself spent 50 days in the same prison where I had been.

When we spoke, we covered our heads so guards thought we were asleep, and talked until we got tired. My neighbors told me that we were in Bagram, in Afghanistan, and I informed them that we were going to be transferred to Cuba. But they didn't believe me.

Around 10 a.m. on August ██, 2002 a Military unit, some armed with guns, appeared from nowhere.* The armed MPs

---

* It is clear from an unredacted date later in this chapter, as well as from official in-processing records, that MOS arrived in Guantánamo on August 5, 2002, which would make this scene the morning of August 4, 2002.

were pointing their guns at us from upstairs, and the others were shouting at the same time, "Stan' up, Stan' up..." I was so scared. Even though I expected to be transferred to Cuba some time that day, I had never seen this kind of show.

We stood up. The guards kept giving other orders. "No talking...Do not move...Ima fucking kill yo'...I'm serious!" I hated it when ▆▆▆▆▆▆▆ from Palestine asked to use the bathroom and the guards refused. "Don't move." I was like, Can't you just keep it till the situation is over? But the problem with ▆▆▆▆▆▆▆ was that he had dysentery, and he couldn't hold it; ▆▆▆▆▆▆▆ had been subjected to torture and malnutrition in Kabul during his detention by the Northern Alliance tribal leader. ▆▆▆▆▆▆▆ told me that he was going to use the bathroom anyway, which he did, ignoring the shouting guards. I expected every second a bullet to be released toward him, but that didn't happen. The bathroom inside our shared cells was also an open barrel, which detainees in punishment cleaned every day for every cell. It was very disgusting and smelled so bad. Being from a third world country, I have seen many unclean bathrooms, but none of them could hold a candle to Bagram's.

I started to shake from fear. One MP approached the gate of our cell and started to call the names, or rather the numbers, of those who were going to be transferred. All the numbers called in my cell were Arabs, which was a bad sign. The brothers didn't believe me when I told them we were going to be transferred to Cuba. But now I felt myself confirmed, and we looked at each other and smiled. Several guards came to the gate with a bunch of chains, bags, and other materials. They started to call us one by one, asking each detainee to approach the gate, where he got chained.

"███████████," one of the guards shouted. I proceeded to the gate like a sheep being led to her butcher. At the gate, a guard yelled, "Turn around!" which I did, and "Both hands behind!"

When I slid my hands through the bin hole behind my back, one of the guards grabbed my thumb and bent my wrist. "When you fuckin' move, I'm gonna break your hand." Another guard chained my hands and my feet with two separate chains. Then a bag was put over my head to blindfold me. The gate was opened, and I was roughly pushed and thrown over the back of another detainee in a row. Although I was physically hurt, I was solaced when I felt the warmth of another human being in front of me suffering the same. The solace increased when ████████████ was thrown over my back. Many detainees didn't exactly understand what the guards wanted from them, and so got hurt worse. I felt lucky to have been blindfolded, for one, because I missed a lot bad things that were happening around me, and for two, because the blindfold helped me in my day-dreaming about better circumstances. Thank ALLAH, I have the ability to ignore my surroundings and daydream about anything I want.

We were supposed to be very close to each other. Breathing was very hard. We were 34 detainees, all of whom were Arab except for one Afghani and one from the Maldives.* When we were put in a row, we were tied together with a rope around our upper arms. The rope was so tight that the circulation stopped, numbing my whole arm.

---

* In-processing height and weight records indicate that thirty-five detainees arrived in Guantánamo on August 5, 2002. The records of that group are available at http://www.dod.mil/pubs/foi/operation_and_plans /Detainee/measurements/ISN_680–ISN_838.pdf. An official list of all Guantánamo detainees is available at http://www.defense.gov/news /may2006/d20060515%20list.pdf.

We were ordered to stand up, and were pulled to a place where the "processing" continued. I hated it because ████ ████████ kept stepping on my chain, which hurt badly. I tried my best not to step on the chain of the man in front of me. Thank God the trip was short: somewhere in the same building we were set down next to each other on long benches. I had the feeling that the benches made a circle.

The party started with dressing the passengers. I got a headset that prevented me from hearing. It gave me such a painful headache; the set was so tight that I had the top of my ears bleeding for a couple of days. My hands were now tied to my waist in the front, and connected with a chain all the way to my feet. They connected my wrists with a six-inch hard plastic piece, and made me wear thick mittens. It was funny, I tried to find a way to free my fingers, but the guards hit my hands to stop moving them. We grew tired; people started to moan. Every once in a while one of the guards took off one of my ear plugs and whispered a discouraging phrase:

"You know, you didn't make any mistake: your mom and dad made the mistake when they produced you."

"You gonna enjoy the ride to the Caribbean paradise...." I didn't answer any provocation, pretending not to understand what he said. Other detainees told me about having been subject to such humiliation, too, but they were luckier; they understood no English.

My flipflops were taken away, and I got some made-in-China tennis shoes. Over my eyes they put really ugly, thick, blind-folding glasses, which were tied around my head and over my ears. They were similar to swimming goggles. To get an idea about the pain, put some old goggles around your hand and tie them tight, and stay that way for a couple of hours; I am sure you will remove them. Now imagine that you have those same goggles tied around your head for more than forty hours. To seal the dressing, a sticky pad was placed behind my ear.

Sometime during the processing we got a cavity search, to the laughter and comments of the guards. I hated that day when I started to learn my miserable English vocabulary. In such situations you're just better off if you don't understand English. The majority of the detainees wouldn't speak about the cavity searches we were subject to, and they would get angry when you started to talk about them. I personally wasn't ashamed; I think the people who did these searches without good reason should be ashamed of themselves.

I grew sick, tired, frustrated, hungry, nauseous, and all the other bad adjectives in the dictionary. I am sure I wasn't the only one. We got new plastic bracelets carrying a number. My number turned out to be 760, and my next ████████████████████. You could say my group was the 700 series.

████████████ used the bathroom a couple of times, but I tried not to use it. I finally went in the afternoon, maybe around 2 p.m.

"Do you like music?" the guard who was escorting me there asked when we were alone.

"Yes, I do!"

"What kind?"

"Good music!"

"Rock and Roll? Country?" I wasn't really familiar with these types he mentioned. Every once in a while I used to listen to German radio with different kinds of Western music, but I couldn't tell which one was which.

"Any good music," I replied. The good conversation paid off in the form that he took my blindfold off so that I could take care of my business. It was very tricky, since I had chains all around my body. The guard placed me gently back on the bench, and for the next couple of hours waiting was the order. We were deprived from the right of performing our daily prayers for the next forty-eight hours.

Around four p.m., the transport to the airport started. By then, I was a "living dead." My legs weren't able to carry me anymore; for the time to come, the guards had to drag me all the way from Bagram to GTMO.

We were loaded in a truck that brought us to the airport. It took five to ten minutes to get there. I was happy for every move, just to have the opportunity to alter my body, for my back was killing me. We were crowded in the truck shoulder-to-shoulder and thigh-to-thigh. Unluckily I was placed facing the back of the vehicle, which I really hate because it gives me nausea. The vehicle was equipped with hard benches so that the detainees sat back to back and the guards sat at the very end shouting, "No talking!" I have no idea how many people were in the truck; all I know is that one detainee sat on my right, and one on my left, and another against my back. It is always good to feel the warmth of your co-detainees, somehow it's solacing.

The arrival at the airport was obvious because of the whining of the engines, which easily went through the earplugs. The truck backed up until it touched the plane. The guards started to shout loudly in a language I could not differentiate. I started to hear human bodies hitting the floor. Two guards grabbed a detainee and threw him toward two other guards on the plane, shouting "Code"; the receiving guards shouted back confirming receipt of the package. When my turn came, two guards grabbed me by the hands and feet and threw me toward the reception team. I don't remember whether I hit the floor or was caught by the other guards. I had started to lose feeling and it would have made no difference anyway.

Another team inside the plane dragged me and fastened me on a small and straight seat. The belt was so tight I could not breathe. The air conditioning hit me, and one of the MPs was shouting, "Do not move, Do not talk," while locking my feet to the floor. I didn't know how to say "tight" in English. I was calling, "MP, MP, belt..." Nobody came to help me. I almost got smothered. I had a mask over my mouth and my nose, plus the bag covering my head and my face, not to mention the tight belt around my stomach: breathing was impossible. I kept saying, "MP, Sir, I cannot breathe!...MP, SIR, please." But it seemed like my pleas for help got lost in a vast desert.

After a couple minutes, ████████████ was dropped beside me on my right. I wasn't sure it was him, but he told me later he felt my presence beside him. Every once in a while, if one of the guards adjusted my goggles, I saw a little. I saw the cockpit, which was in front of me. I saw the green camo-uniforms of the escorting guards. I saw the ghosts of my fellow detainees on my left and my right. "Mister, please, my belt...hurt...," I called. When the shoutings of the guards faded away, I knew that the detainees were all on board. "Mister, please...belt...." A guard responded, but he not only didn't help me, he tightened the belt even more around my abdomen.

Now I couldn't endure the pain; I felt I was going to die. I couldn't help asking for help louder. "Mister, I cannot breathe..." One of the soldiers came and untightened the belt, not very comfortably but better than nothing.

"It's still tight..." I had learned the word when he asked me, "Is it tight?"

"That's all you get." I gave up asking for relief from the belt.

"I cannot breathe!" I said, gesturing to my nose. A guard appeared and took the mask off my nose. I took a deep breath and felt really relieved. But to my dismay, the guard put the

mask back on my nose and my mouth. "Sir, I cannot breathe...
MP...MP." The same guy showed up once more, but instead
of taking the mask off my nose, he took the plug out of my ear
and said, "Forget about it!" and immediately put the ear plug
back. It was harsh, but it was the only way not to smother. I
was panicking, I had just enough air, but the only way to survive was to convince the brain to be satisfied with the tiny bit
of air it got.

The plane was in the air. A guard shouted in my ear, "Ima
gonna give you some medication, you get sick." He made me
take a bunch of tablets and gave me an apple and a peanut butter
sandwich, our only meal since the transfer procedure began.
I've hated peanut butter since then. I had no appetite for anything, but I pretended I was eating the sandwich so the guards
don't hurt me. I always tried to avoid contact with those violent
guards unless it was extremely necessary. I took a bite off the
sandwich and kept the rest in my hand till the guards collected
the trash. As to the apple, the eating was tricky, since my hands
were tied to my waist and I wore mittens. I squeezed the apple
between my hands and bent my head to my waist like an acrobat
to bite at it. One slip and the apple is gone. I tried to sleep, but
as tired as I was, every attempt to take a nap ended in failure.
The seat was as straight as an arrow, and as hard as a stone.

After about five hours, the plane landed and our ghosts were
transferred to another, maybe bigger plane. It was stable in
the air. I was happy with every change, any change, hoping for
the betterment of my situation. But I was wrong, the new plane
wasn't better. I knew that Cuba was quite far, but I never
thought it to be that far, given the U.S.'s high speed airplanes.
At some point, I thought that the government wanted to blow
up the plane over the Atlantic and declare it an accident, since
all the detainees had been interrogated over and over and over.

But this crazy plan was the least of my worries; was I really worried about a little death pain, after which I would hopefully enter paradise with God's mercy? Living under God's mercy would be better than living under the U.S.'s mercy.

The plane seemed to be heading to the kingdom of far, far away. Feeling lessened with every minute going by; my body numbed. I remember asking for the bathroom once. The guards dragged me to the place, pushed inside a small room, and pulled down my pants. I couldn't take care of my business because of the presence of others. But I think I managed with a lot of effort to squeeze some water. I just wanted to arrive, no matter where! Any place would be better than this plane.

After I don't know how many hours, the plane landed in Cuba. The guards started to pull us out of the plane. "Walk!... Stop!" I couldn't walk, for my feet were unable to carry me. And now I noticed that at some point I had lost one of my shoes. After a thorough search outside the plane, the guards shouted, "Walk! Do not talk! Head down! Step!" I only understood "Do not talk," but the guards were dragging me anyway. Inside the truck, the guards shouted "Sit down! Cross your legs!" I didn't understand the last part but they crossed my legs anyway. "Head down!" one shouted, pushing my head against the rear end of another detainee like a chicken. A female voice was shouting all the way to the camp, "No Talking," and a male voice, "Do Not Talk," and an Arabic translator, ███████████ ████████████████████████████████████, "Keep your head down." I was completely annoyed by the American way of talking; I stayed that way for a long time, until I got cured by meeting other good Americans. At the same time, I was thinking about how they gave the same order two different ways: "Do not talk" and "No talking." That was interesting.

By now the chains on my ankles were cutting off the blood

to my feet. My feet became numb. I heard only the moaning and crying of other detainees. Beating was the order of the trip. I was not spared: the guard kept hitting me on my head and squeezing my neck against the rear end of the other detainee. But I don't blame him as much as I do that poor and painful detainee, who was crying and kept moving, and so kept raising my head. Other detainees told me that we took a ferry ride during the trip, but I didn't notice.

After about an hour we were finally at the promised land. As much pain as I suffered, I was very happy to have the trip behind me. A Prophet's saying states, "Travel is a piece of torture." This trip was certainly a piece of torture. Now I was only worried about how I was going to stand up if they asked me to. I was just paralyzed. Two guards grabbed me and shouted "Stan' up." I tried to jump but nothing happened; instead they dragged me and threw me outside the truck.

The warm Cuban sun hit me gracefully. It was such a good feeling. The trip started ▓▓▓▓▓▓▓▓▓▓▓▓▓▓▓▓▓▓▓ 10 a.m., and we arrived in Cuba around 12:00 or 1:00 a.m. ▓▓▓▓▓▓▓▓▓▓▓▓▓▓▓▓▓, which meant we spent more than thirty hours in an ice-cold airplane.* I was luckier than a ▓▓▓▓▓▓▓▓▓ brother who froze totally. He happened to ask the guard to turn down the A/C on the plane. The guard not

---

* In this passage, MOS describes a five-hour flight, a change of airplanes, and then a much longer flight. A 2008 investigation by the British human rights organization Reprieve found that transfers of prisoners from Bagram to Guantánamo typically involved a stop at the U.S. air base in Incirlik, Turkey, and the Rendition Project has found that a C-17 military transport plane, flight number RCH233Y, flew from Incirlik to Guantánamo on August 5, 2002, carrying thirty-five prisoners. See http://www.libertyse curity.org/IMG/pdf_08.01.28FINALPrisonersIllegallyRenderedtoGuanta namoBay.pdf; and http://www.therenditionproject.org.uk/pdf/PDF%20 154%20[Flight%20data.%20Portuguese%20flight%20logs%20to%20 GTMO,%20collected%20by%20Ana%20Gomes].pdf.

only refused to meet his wish, but he kept soaking him with water drops all the way to Cuba. The medics had to put him in a room and treat him with a blazing fire.

"When they started the fire, I said to myself, here you go, now they start the torture!" he told us. I laughed when he recounted his story in the ███████████████ the next morning.

I could tell they had changed the guard team for a better one. The old team used to say "Wader"; the new team says "Water." The old team used to say, "Stan' up," the new team, "Stand up." The old team was simply too loud.

I could also tell the detainees had reached their pain limit. All I heard was moaning. Next to me was an Afghani who was crying very loudly and pleading for help ██████████████ ████████████████████████████. He was speaking in Arabic, "Sir, how could you do this to me? Please, relieve my pain, Gentlemen!" But nobody even bothered to check on him. The fellow was sick back in Bagram. I saw him in the cell next to ours; he was vomiting all the time. I felt so bad for him. At the same time, I laughed. Can you believe it, I stupidly laughed! Not at him; I laughed at the situation. First, he addressed them in Arabic, which no guards understood. Second, he called them Gentlemen, which they were most certainly not.

In the beginning I enjoyed the sunbath, but the sun grew hotter with every minute that went by. I started to sweat, and grew very tired of the kneeling position I had to remain in for about six hours. Every once in a while a guard shouted, "Need water!" I don't remember asking for water, but it's likely that I did. I was still stuck with the blindfold, but my excitement about being in a new correctional facility with other human beings I could socialize with, in a place where there would be no torture or even interrogation, overwhelmed my pain; that and the fact that I didn't know how long the detention was going to last. And so I didn't open my mouth with any complaints or moans, while many brothers around me where moaning and even crying. I think that my pain limit had been reached a long time before.

I was dead last to be "processed"; people who got hurt on the plane probably had priority, such as ████████████████ ██████████. Finally two escorting guards dragged me into the clinic. They stripped me naked and pushed me into an open shower. I took a shower in my chains under the eyes of everybody, my brethren, the medics, and the Army. The other brothers who proceeded me were still stark naked. It was ugly, and although the shower was soothing, I couldn't enjoy it. I was ashamed and I did the old ostrich trick: I looked down to my feet. The guards dried me and took me to the next step. Basically the detainees went through a medical check, where they took note of everybody's biological description, height, weight, scars, and experienced the first interrogation inside the clinic. It was like a car production line. I followed the steps of the detainee who preceded me, and he followed somebody else's steps, and so on and so forth.

"Do you have any known diseases?" asked the young nurse.

"Yes, sciatic nerve and hypotension."

"Anything else?"

"No."

"Where did they capture you?"

"I don't understand," I replied. The doctor repeated the

nurse's question, but I still didn't understand. He spoke too quickly.

"Never mind!" the doctor said. One of my guards gestured to me, putting one of his hands over the other. Only then did I understand the doctor's question.

"In my country!"

"Where are you from?"

"Mauritania," I replied as the guards were dragging me to the next step. Medics are not supposed to interrogate detainees, but they do anyway. Personally I enjoy conversations with everybody and I couldn't care less about them breaking the rules.

It was cool and crowded inside the hospital. I was solaced by the fact that I saw detainees who were in the same situation as me, especially after they wrapped us in the orange uniform. Interrogators were disguised among the Medics to gather information.

"Do you speak Russian?" an old civilian, an Intel wreck of the cold war, asked me. He interrogated me a couple of times later on, and told me that he once worked with ████████████████, a Mujahideen leader in Afghanistan during the war with the Soviets who supposedly used to turn over Russian detainees to the U.S. "I interrogated them. They're now U.S. citizens, and among my best friends," he told me. He claimed to be responsible for a section of the GTMO Task Force. Interrogators like him were sneaking around, trying to converse "innocently" with the detainees. However, interrogators have a hard time mixing in with other people. They're simply very clumsy.

The escort led me to a room with many detainees and interrogators at work. "What's your name? Where are you from? Are you married?"

"Yes!"

"What's the name of your wife?" I forgot the name of my wife and several members of my family as well because of the persistent state of depression I had been in now for the last nine months. Since I knew that nobody was going to buy such a thing, I went, "Zeinebou," just a name that came to my mind.

"What languages do you speak?"

"Arabic, French, German."

"Sprechen Sie Deutsch?" asked the male interrogator in uniform who was helping ████████████████████████ typing in laptop.

"Bist du ████████████?" I asked him. ████████████ was shocked when I mentioned his name.

"Who told you about me?"

"████████████, from Bagram!" I said, explaining that in Bagram ████████████ told me about ████████████ in case I needed a German translator in GTMO.*

"We'll keep the conversation in English, but very simple," he said. ████████████ avoided me for the rest of his time in GTMO.

I was listening to the interrogation of a Tunisian fellow detainee.

"Did you train in Afghanistan?"

"No."

"You know if you lie, we're gonna get the information from Tunisia!"

"I am not lying!"

The medical check resumed. A ████████████████████ corpsman took a thousand and one tubes of blood off me. I thought I was going to pass out or even die. A blood pressure check showed 110 over 50, which is very low. The doctor

---

* MOS may be referring here to his German-speaking interrogator in Afghanistan.

immediately put me on small red tablets to increase my blood pressure. Pictures were taken. I hated the fact that my privacy was being disrespected in every way. I was totally under the mercy of somebody I didn't trust and who might be ruthless. Many detainees would smile for the camera. I personally never smiled, and I don't think that on that day, August 5th, 2002, any detainee did.

After the endless processing, the escort team took me out of the clinic. "Keep your head down!" It was already dark outside but I couldn't tell what time it was. The weather was nice. "Sit down." I sat outside for about thirty minutes before the escort team picked me up and put me in a room and locked me to the floor. I didn't notice the lock, nor had I ever been subject to it before. I thought the room was to be my future home.

The room was bare but for a couple of chairs and a desk. There was no sign of life. "Where are the other detainees?" I said to myself. I grew impatient and decided to go outside the room and try to find other fellow detainees, but as soon as I tried to stand up the chains pulled me down hard. Only then did I know that something was wrong with my assumptions. As it turned out, I was in the interrogation booth in ██████████ ██████████, a building with history.

All of a sudden three men entered the room: the older guy who spoke to me earlier in the clinic, an ██████████████ ████████████████████████████, and a ████████████████████ ██████████ who served as an interpreter.*

---

* The FBI led MOS's interrogations for his first several months in Guantánamo, waging a well-documented struggle to keep him out of the hands of military interrogators. "The FBI sought to interview Slahi immediately after he arrived at GTMO," the DOJ Inspector General reported. "FBI and task force agents interviewed Slahi over the next few months, utilizing rapport building techniques." At his 2005 ARB hearing, MOS described an "FBI guy" who interrogated him shortly after his arrival and told him,

"Comment vous vous appelez?" asked ▮▮▮▮▮▮▮▮ in a thick accent.

"Je m'appelle......" I answered, and that was the end of ▮▮▮▮▮▮▮▮▮▮▮▮▮▮▮▮▮▮▮. Interrogators always tend to bring the factor of surprise as a technique.

I glimpsed one of the guy's watches. It was nearly 1 a.m. I was in a state where my system had gotten messed up; I was wide awake in spite of more than forty-eight hours of sleeplessness. The interrogators wanted to use that weakness to facilitate the interrogation. I was offered nothing such as water or food.

▮▮▮▮▮▮▮▮ led the interrogation, and ▮▮▮▮▮▮▮▮▮▮▮ was a good translator. The other guy didn't get the chance to ask questions, he just took notes. ▮▮▮▮▮▮▮▮ didn't really come up with a miracle: all he did was ask me some questions I had been asked uninterruptedly for the past three years. ▮▮▮▮▮▮▮ spoke a very clear English, and I almost didn't need the translator. He seemed to be smart and experienced. When the night grew late, ▮▮▮▮▮▮▮▮ thanked me for my cooperation.

"I believe that you are very open," he said. "The next time we'll untie your hands and bring you something to eat. We will not torture you, nor will we extradite you to another country." I was happy with ▮▮▮▮▮▮▮ assurances, and encouraged in my cooperation. As it turned out, ▮▮▮▮▮▮▮ was either misleading me or he was unknowledgeable about the plans of his government.

The three men left the room and sent the escort team to me,

"We don't beat people, we don't torture, it's not allowed." That would appear to be the lead interrogator in this scene — and perhaps also the "older gentleman" who appears in a subsequent session. DOJ IG, 122; ARB transcript, 23.

which led me to my cell. It was in ██████████ Block, a block designed for isolation.* I was the only detainee who had been picked for interrogation from our entire group of thirty-four detainees. There was no sign of life inside the block, which made me think that I was the only one around. When the guard dropped me in the frozen-cold box I almost panicked behind the heavy metal door. I tried to convince myself, It's only a temporary place, in the morning they're going to transfer me to the community. This place cannot be for more than the rest of the night! In fact, I spent one whole month in ████████ ██████████.

It was around 2 a.m. when the guard handed me an MRE. I tried to eat what I could, but I had no appetite. When I checked my stuff I saw a brand new Koran, which made me happy. I kissed the Koran and soon fell asleep. I slept deeper than I ever had.

The shoutings of my fellow detainees woke me up in the early morning. Life was suddenly blown into ████████████████████ ██████████████████. When I arrived earlier that morning, I never thought that human beings could be possibly stored in a bunch of cold boxes; I thought I was the only one, but I was wrong, my fellow detainees were only knocked out due to the harsh punishment trip they had behind them. While the guards were

---

* The March 3, 2003, Camp Delta Standard Operating Procedures instructed that arriving prisoners be processed and held for four weeks in a maximum security isolation block "to enhance and exploit the disorientation and disorganization felt by a newly arrived detainee in the interrogation process" and "to [foster] dependence of the detainee on his interrogator." The document is available at http://www.comw.org/warreport/fulltext/gitmo-sop.pdf (hereafter cited as SOP).

serving the food, we were introducing us to ourselves. We couldn't see each other due to the design of the block but we could hear each other.

"Salam Alaikum!"

"Waalaikum Salam."

"Who are you?

"I am from Mauritania...Palestine...Syria...Saudi Arabia...!"

"How was the trip?"

"I almost froze to death," shouted one guy.

"I slept the whole trip," replied ███████████████████.

"Why did they put the patch beneath my ear?" said a third.

"Who was in front of me in the truck?" I asked. "He kept moving, which made the guards beat me all the way from the airport to the camp."

"Me, too," another detainee answered.

We called each other with the ISN numbers we were assigned in Bagram. My number was ████.* In the cell on my left was ███████████ from ███████████. He is about ██████ ██████████████████████████████████. Though Mauritanian, he had never really been in the country; I could tell because of his ██████ accent. On my right was the guy from the █████████. He spoke poor Arabic, and claimed to have been captured in Karachi, where he attends the University. In front of my cell they put the Sudanese, next to each other.†

---

* The number has already appeared unredacted, and the Department of Defense has officially acknowledged that MOS's ISN is 760. See, e.g., the publicly released DOD detainees list available at http://www.defense.gov/news/may2006/d20060515%20list.pdf.

† MOS may be referring here to Mohammed al-Amin (ISN 706), who was born in Mauritania but moved to Saudi Arabia for religious studies, and Ibrahim Fauzee (ISN 730), who is from the Maldives. Both arrived in

Breakfast was modest: one boiled egg, a hard piece of bread, and something else I don't know the name of. It was my first hot meal since I left Jordan. Oh, the tea was soothing! I like tea better than any food, and for as long as I can remember I've been drinking it. Tea is a crucial part of the diet of people from warmer regions; it sounds contradictory but it is true.

People were shouting all over the place in indistinct conversations. It was just a good feeling when everybody started to recount his story. Many detainees suffered, some more and some less. I didn't consider myself the worst, nor the luckiest. Some people were captured with their friends and their friends disappeared from the face of the earth; they most likely were sent to other allied countries to facilitate their interrogation by torture, such as the ███████████████████████████ ██████. I considered the arrival to Cuba a blessing, and so I told the brothers, "Since you guys are not involved in crimes, you need to fear nothing. I personally am going to cooperate, since nobody is going to torture me. I don't want any of you to suffer what I suffered in Jordan. In Jordan, they hardly appreciate your cooperation."

I wrongly believed that the worst was over, and so I cared less about the time it would take the Americans to figure out that I was not the guy they are looking for. I trusted the American justice system too much, and shared that trust with the detainees from European countries. We all had an idea about how the democratic system works. Other detainees, for instance those from the Middle East, didn't believe it for a second and trust the American system. Their argument lay on the growing

---

GTMO with MOS on August 5, 2002; both have since been released. See http://projects.nytimes.com/guantanamo/detainees/706-mohammad -lameen-sidi-mohammad; and http://projects.nytimes.com/guantanamo /detainees/730-ibrahim-fauzee.

hostility of extremist Americans against Muslims and the Arabs. With every day going by, the optimists lost ground. The interrogation methods worsened considerably as time went by, and as you shall see, those responsible for GTMO broke all the principles upon which the U.S. was built and compromised every great principle such as Ben Franklin's "They that give up essential liberty to obtain a little temporary safety deserve neither liberty nor safety."

All of us wanted to make up for months of forced silence, we wanted to get every anger and agony off our chests, and we listened to each other's amazing stories for the next thirty days to come, which was our time in ███████ Block. When we later got transferred to a different block, many fellow detainees cried for being separated from their new friends. I cried, too.

███████████████ escort team showed up at my cell.

"██████████!" said one of the MPs, holding the long chains in his hands. ███████████ is the code word for being taken to interrogation.* Although I didn't understand where I was going, I prudently followed their orders until they delivered me to the interrogator. His name was ████████████ ████████████████████████████ wearing a U.S. Army uniform. He is an ████████████████████████ ████████████████, a man with all the paradoxes you may imagine. He spoke Arabic decently, with a ██████████ accent; you could tell he grew up among ██████████ friends.†

---

* The word is likely "Reservation." It appears unredacted elsewhere throughout the manuscript. See, e.g., MOS manuscript, 69, 112, 122.

† Around this time, FBI-led interrogation teams often included members of the military's Criminal Investigation Task Force (CITF) and military

I was terrified when I stepped into the room in ██████████ building because of the CamelBak on ████████████ back, from which he was sipping. I never saw a thing like that before. I thought it was a kind of tool to hook on me as a part of my interrogation. I really don't know why I was scared, but the fact that I never saw ████████████ nor his CamelBak, nor did I expect an Army guy, all these factors contributed to my fear.

The older gentleman who interrogated me the night before entered the room with some candies and introduced ████████ ████████ to me, "I chose ████████████ because he speaks your language. We're going to ask you detailed questions about you ████████████████████. As to me, I am going to leave soon, but my replacement will take care of you. See you later." He stepped out of the room leaving me and ████████████ to work.

████████████ was a friendly guy. He was ████████████ in the U.S. Army who believed himself to be lucky in life. ████████████ wanted me to repeat to him my whole story, which I've been repeating for the last three years over and over. I got used to interrogators asking me the same things. Before the interrogator even moved his lips I knew his questions, and as soon as he or she started to talk, I turned my "tape" on. But

intelligence agents. The DOJ Inspector General's report records that "in May 2002, the military and the FBI adopted the 'Tiger Team' concept for interrogating detainees. According to the first GTMO case agent, these teams consisted of an FBI agent, an analyst, a contract linguist, two CITF investigators, and a military intelligence interrogator." The IG found that "the FBI withdrew from participation in the Tiger Teams in the fall of 2002 after disagreements arose between the FBI and military intelligence over interrogation tactics. Several FBI agents told the OIG that while they continued to have a good relationship with CITF, their relationship with the military intelligence entities greatly deteriorated over the course of time, primarily due to the FBI's opposition to the military intelligence approach to interrogating detainees." DOJ IG, 34.

when I came to the part about Jordan, ████████████ felt very sorry!

"Those countries don't respect human rights. They even torture people," he said. I was comforted: if ████████████ criticized cruel interrogation methods, it meant that the Americans wouldn't do something like that. Yes, they were not exactly following the law in Bagram, but that was in Afghanistan, and now we are in a U.S. controlled territory.

After ████████████ finished his interrogation, he sent me back and promised to come back should new questions arise. During the session with ████████████, I asked him to use the bathroom. "No. 1 or No. 2?" he asked. It was the first time I heard the human private business coded in numbers. In the countries I've been in, it isn't customary to ask people about their intention in the bathroom, nor do they have a code.

I never saw ████████████ in an interrogation again. The ████████████████ resumed his work a couple of days later, only the ████████████████ was now reinforced with ████████, ████████████████████ ████████. ████████████ was another friendly guy. He and ████████████ worked very well together. For some reason, ████████████ was interested in taking my case in hand. Although a military interrogator came with the team a couple of times and asked some questions, you could tell that ████████████ had the upper hand.*

The team worked on my case for over a month, on almost a daily basis. They asked me all kind of questions, and we spoke about other political topics beside the interrogation. Nobody ever threatened me or tried to torture me, and from my side I

---

* As the DOJ IG report makes clear, the FBI maintained overall control of the interrogation of MOS throughout 2002 and early 2003. DOJ IG, 122.

was cooperating with the team very well. "Our job is to take your statements and send them to the analysts in D.C. Even if you lie to us, we can't really tell right away until more information comes in," said ██████████.

The team could see very clearly how sick I was; the prints of Jordan and Bagram were more than obvious. I looked like a ghost.

"You're getting better," said the Army guy when he saw me three weeks after my arrival in GTMO. On my second or third day in GTMO I had collapsed in my cell. I was just driven to my extremes; the MREs didn't appeal to me. The Medics took me out of my cell and I tried to walk the way to the hospital, but as soon as I left ██████████████ I collapsed once more, which made the Medics carry me to the clinic. I threw up so much that I was completely dehydrated. I received first aid and got an IV. The IV was terrible; they must have put some medication in it that I have an allergy to. My mouth dried up completely and my tongue became so heavy that I couldn't ask for help. I gestured with my hands to the corpsmen to stop dripping the fluid into my body, which they did.

Later that night the guards brought me back to my cell. I was so sick I couldn't climb on my bed; I slept on the floor for the rest of the month. The doctor prescribed Ensure and some hypertension medicine, and every time I got my sciatic nerve crisis the corpsmen gave me Motrin.

Although I was physically very weak, the interrogation didn't stop. But I was nonetheless in good spirits. In the Block we were singing, joking, and recounting stories to each other. I also got the opportunity to learn about the star detainees, such as his excellence ████████████████████████████████████ ██████████████████████████████████████ fed us with the latest news and rumors from camp. ████████████

███████████████ had been transferred to our Block due to his "behavior."*

███████████████ told us how he was tortured in Kandahar with other detainees. "They put us under the sun for a long time, we got beaten, but brothers don't worry, here in Cuba there is no torture. The rooms are air-conditioned, and some brothers even refuse to talk unless offered food," he said. "I cried when I saw detainees blindfolded and taken to Cuba on TV. The American Defense Secretary spoke on TV and claimed these detainees are the most evil people on the face of the earth. I never thought that I would be one of these 'evil people,'" said

███████████████████████████████████████

████████████████ had been working as an ███████████

███████████████████████████████████████.

He was captured with four other colleagues of his in his domicile in ████████████████ after midnight under the cries of his children; he was pried off his kids and his wife. The same thing exactly happened to his friends, who confirmed his story. I heard tons of such stories and every story made me forget the last one. I couldn't tell whose story was more saddening. It even started to undermine my story, but the detainees were unanimous that my story was the saddest. I personally don't know. The German proverb says: "Wenn das Militar sich bewegt, bleibt die Wahrheit auf der Strecke." When the Military sets itself in motion, the truth is too slow to keep up, so it stays behind.

The law of war is harsh. If there's anything good at all in a war, it's that it brings the best and the worst out of people: some

---

* Context here suggests that the same Camp Delta block where arriving detainees were held for the first month also served as a punishment block for detainees from the general population.

people try to use the lawlessness to hurt others, and some try
to reduce the suffering to the minimum.

On September 4, 2002, I was transferred to ██████████████,
and so the interrogators ended the isolation and put me in with
general population. On the one hand, it was hard for me to
leave the friends I'd just made, and on the other hand I was
excited about going to a dead normal Block, and being a dead
average detainee. I was tired of being a "special" detainee, riding all over the world against my will.

I arrived in ██████████████ before sunset. For the first time
in more than nine months, I was put in a cell where I could see
the plain.* And for the first time I was able to talk to my fellow
detainees while seeing them. I was put in ██████████████
between two Saudis from the South. Both were very friendly
and entertaining. They had both been captured ██████████████
██████████████████████████. When the prisoners tried
to free themselves from the Pakistani Army, which was working on behalf of the U.S., one of them, an Algerian, grabbed
the AK47 of a ██████████████ guard and shot him. In the melee,
the ██████████████ detainees asserted control ██████████
██████████████████; the guards fled, and the detainees fled
too—just as far as where another ██████████████ U.S. division
was awaiting them, and they were captured again. The

---

* By "plain," I think MOS may mean the Cuban landscape surrounding
the camp. It appears from the manuscript that MOS was held in two or
three different blocks in Camp Delta over the next several months, including one block that housed detainees from European and North African
countries. MOS manuscript, 62. MOS indicated at his ARB hearing that
he was being held in Camp Two's Mike Block as of June 2003. ARB transcript, 26.

████████████████ event caused many casualties and injuries. I saw an Algerian detainee who was completely disabled due to the amount of bullets he had taken.

I had a good time in ██████████████████ at the beginning, but things started to get ugly when some interrogators started to practice torture methods on some detainees, though shyly. As far as I heard and saw, the only method practiced at first was the cold room, all night. I know a young Saudi man who was taken to interrogation every night and put back in his cell in the morning. I don't know the details of what exactly happened to him because he was very quiet, but my neighbors told me that he refused to talk to his interrogators ██████████ ██ also told me that he was also put in the cold room two nights in a row because he refused to cooperate.

Most of the detainees by then were refusing to cooperate after they felt they had provided everything relevant to their cases. People were desperate and growing tired of being interrogated all the time, without hope of an end. I personally was relatively new and wanted to take my chances: maybe my fellow detainees were wrong! But I ended up bumping into the same brick wall as anybody else. Detainees grew worried about their situation and the absence of a due process of law, and things started to get worse with the use of painful methods to extract information from detainees.

Around mid-September, 2002, an ██████████████████ ████████████████████████████████ pulled me to interrogation and introduced themselves as the team that was going to assess me for the next two months.*

---

* Because this occurred within the period during which the FBI had overall control of MOS's interrogation, this would likely be another FBI-led interrogation team; see footnote on p. 44.

"How long am I going to be interrogated?"

"As long as the government has questions for you!"

"How long is that?"

"I can only tell you that you will not spend more than five years here," said ████████████. The team was communicating with me through an Arabic interpreter who looked ████████ ████████████.

"I'm not ready to be asked the same questions again and again!"

"No, we have some new questions." But as it turned out they were asking me the very same questions I had been asked for the last three years. Even so, I was reluctantly cooperating. I honestly didn't see any advantages in cooperating, I just wanted to see how far things were going to go.

Around the same time another interrogator ████████████ ████████████ pulled me to interrogation. He was ████████████ ████████████████████████████████, an organized goatee, and spoke ████████████████████████████████ accent. ████████ ██ He was straightforward with me, and even shared with me what ██ about me. ████████████████████ was talking, and talking, and talking some more: he was interested in getting me to work for him, as he had tried with other North African Arabs.*

---

* This interrogator might be from the CIA. In 2013, the Associated Press reported that between 2002 and 2005, CIA agents in GTMO sought to recruit detainees to serve as informants and double agents for the United States. The CIA also helped facilitate interrogations by foreign intelligence agents in Guantánamo. Adam Goldman and Matt Apuzzo, "Penny Lane, GITMO's Other Secret CIA Facility," Associated Press, November 26, 2013, http://bigstory.ap.org/article/penny-lane-gitmos-other-secret-cia -facility.

"Next Thursday, I've arranged a meeting with the ▮▮▮▮ ▮▮▮▮▮▮▮▮▮▮▮. Are you going to talk to them?"

"Yes, I am." That was the first lie I detected, because ▮▮▮▮ ▮▮▮▮▮▮▮▮▮▮▮▮▮▮▮ had told me, "No foreign government is going to talk to you here, only us Americans!"* In fact, I heard about many detainees meeting with non-American interrogators, such as ▮▮▮▮▮▮▮▮▮▮▮▮▮▮▮▮▮▮▮▮▮▮▮▮▮▮▮ ▮▮▮▮▮▮▮▮▮▮▮▮▮▮▮▮▮▮▮▮▮▮▮▮▮▮▮▮▮▮▮▮▮▮▮ ▮▮▮▮▮▮▮▮▮▮▮▮▮▮▮▮▮▮▮▮▮▮ were helping the U.S. to extract information from the ▮▮▮▮▮▮▮ detainees. The ▮▮▮▮▮▮▮▮▮▮▮▮▮ interrogators and the ▮▮▮▮▮▮▮▮▮▮▮ ▮▮▮▮▮▮ threatened some of their interviewees with torture when they got back home.

"I hope I see you in another place," said the ▮▮▮▮▮▮▮▮ interrogator to ▮▮▮▮▮▮▮▮▮▮▮▮▮.

"If we see each other in Turkistan, you're gonna talk a lot!" the ▮▮▮▮▮▮▮ interrogator told ▮▮▮▮▮▮▮▮▮ ▮▮▮.†

But I was not afraid of talking to anyone. I had done no crimes against anybody. I even wanted to talk to prove my innocence, since the American motto was "GTMO detainees are guilty until proven innocent." I knew what was awaiting

---

* Likely the "older gentleman" or one of his other FBI interrogators.

† The quotations appear to be directed to two different detainees. The unredacted "Turkistan" in this passage suggests that MOS may be referring to the interrogations of ethnic Uighur detainees by Chinese intelligence agents in GTMO. These interrogations, which were reportedly preceded by periods of sleep deprivation and temperature manipulation, were first revealed in the May 2008 DOJ Inspector General's report, *A Review of the FBI's Involvement in and Observations of Detainee Interrogations in Guantanamo Bay, Afghanistan, and Iraq*. McClatchy Newspapers reported that the interrogations took place over a day and a half in September 2002. See http://www .mcclatchydc.com/2009/07/16/72000/uighur-detainees-us-helped -chinese.html.

me when it came to ███████████ interrogators, and I wanted to get things out off my chest.

The day came and the guards pulled me and took me ████████████████████████████, where detainees usually met ███ ██████████████████████████████████████. Two ████████ ██ gentlemen were sitting on the other side of the table, and I was looking at them, locked on the floor. ████████████████ ██ ████████, who played the bad guy role during the interrogation. Neither introduced himself, which was completely against the ████████████████████████; they just stood in front of me like ghosts, the same as the rest of the secret interrogators.*

"Do you speak German, or do we need an interpreter?" asked the ████████████████.

"I am afraid we don't," I replied.

"Well, you understand the seriousness of the matter. We've come from ████████████ to talk to you.

"People have been killed," continued the older man.

I smiled. "Since when are you allowed to interrogate people outside ████████████?"

"We are not here to discuss the judicial grounds of our questioning!"

"I might, sometime in the future, be able to talk to the press

---

* The visitors are likely German. In 2008, *Der Spiegel* reported that in September 2002, two members of the Bundesnachrichtendienst (BND) and one member of the Office for the Protection of the Constitution, Germany's foreign and domestic intelligence agencies, interviewed MOS for ninety minutes in Guantánamo. MOS appears to refer to two of those visitors, one older and one younger. John Goetz, Marcel Rosenbach, Britta Sandberg, and Holger Stark, "From Germany to Guantanamo: The Career of Prisoner No. 760," *Der Spiegel,* October 9, 2008, http://www.spiegel.de /international/world/from-germany-to-guantanamo-the-career-of -prisoner-no-760-a-583193.html.

and give you away," I said. "Though I don't know your names, I'll recognize your pictures, no matter how long it takes!"

"You can say whatever you want, you're not gonna hurt us! We know what we're doing," he said.

"So clearly you guys are using the lawlessness of this place to extract information out of me?"

███████ Salahi, if we wanted to, we could ask the guards to hang you on the wall and kick your ass!"* When he mentioned the crooked way he was thinking, my heart started to pound, because I was trying to express myself carefully and at the same avoid torture.

"You can't scare me, you're not talking to a child. If you continue speaking to me with this tone, you can pack your luggage and go back to ███████."

"We are not here to prosecute you or scare you, we would just be grateful if you would answer a couple of questions we have," said ███████.

"Look, I've been in your country, and you know that I was never involved in any kind of crimes. Plus, what are you worried about? Your country isn't even threatened. I've been living peacefully in your country and never abused your hospitality. I am very grateful for all that your country helped me with; I don't stab in the back. So what theater are you trying to play on me?"

███████ Salahi, we know that you are innocent, but we did not capture you, the Americans did. We are not here on behalf of the U.S. We work for ███████, and lately we stopped some bad plots. We know you cannot possibly know about these things. However, we only want to ask you about two individuals, ███████

---

* Probably "Herr Salahi." "Salahi" is a variant spelling of MOS's last name that is generally used in court documents in the United States.

██████, and we would be grateful if you would answer our questions about them."

"It's just funny that you've come all the way from ████████████ to ask about your own people! Those two individuals are good friends of mine. We attended the same mosques, but I don't know them to be involved in any terrorist operations."

The session didn't last much longer than that. They asked me how I was doing and about the life in the camp and bid me farewell. I never saw the ████████████ after that.

Meanwhile, the ██████████████████████████████ kept questioning me.

"Do you know this guy, ████████████████████████?" asked ████████████.

"No, I don't," I honestly answered.

"But he knows you!"

"I am afraid you have another file than mine!"

"No, I read your file very thoroughly."

"Can you show me his picture?"

"Yes. I'm going to show it to you tomorrow."

"Good. I might know him by another name!"

"Do you know about the American bases in Germany?"

"Why do you ask me about that? I didn't go to Germany to study the American bases, nor am I interested in them in any way!" I angrily replied.

"My people respect detainees who tell the truth!" ████████████ said, while ██████████████ took notes. I took the hint that he was calling me a liar in a stupid way. The session was terminated.

The next day ██████████████ reserved me in the ████████ ████████████████ and showed me two pictures. The first one turned out to be that of ████████████████████████████, who was suspected of having participated in the September 11 attack and who was captured ██████████████████████████████████.

The second picture was of ████████████████████ one of the September 11 hijackers. As to ███████████████, I had never heard of him or saw him, and as to ████████ ███████████████, I figured I've seen the guy, but where and when? I had no clue! But I also figured that the guy must be very important because █████████████ were running fast together to find my link with him.* Under the circumstances, I denied having seen the guy. Look at it, how would it have looked had I said I'd seen this guy, but I don't know when and where? What interrogator would buy something like that? Not one! And to be honest with you, I was as scared as hell.

The ████████ team reserved me again the next day and showed me the picture of ████████████, and I denied that I knew him, the same way I had the day before. My denial that I knew a man that I don't really know, I just saw him for a very short time once or twice and had no association whatsoever with him, gave fuel to all kind of wild theories linking me to the September 11 attack. The investigators were just drowning and were looking for any straw to grab, and I personally didn't exactly want to be that straw.

████████████████████████████████ said ████████. "████████████████████████████
████████████████████████████████
████████████████████████████████

---

* The first picture is likely of Ramzi bin al-Shibh, who was captured in a shoot-out in a suburb of Karachi, Pakistan, right around this time, on September 11, 2002. At his 2005 ARB hearing, MŌS told the panel, "September 11th, 2002, America arrested a man by the name of Ramzi Bin al Shibh, who is said to be the key guy in the September 11th attacks. It was exactly one year after 9/11, and since his capture my life has changed drastically." ARB transcript, 23.

[REDACTED]

[REDACTED]

[REDACTED]

"In the next few days!"

In the meantime I was transferred to [REDACTED] where I met the [REDACTED] for the first time. He was another one of the star detainees. [REDACTED] heard about my story, and like any [REDACTED], he wanted to have more information. On my side, I also wanted to converse with cultured people. As far as I could tell, [REDACTED] was a decent guy; I have a hard time picturing him as a criminal.

I stayed in [REDACTED] less than two weeks before I was transferred to [REDACTED] was filled with European and North African detainees. For the first time I got to know the [REDACTED] and the [REDACTED]

[REDACTED]

[REDACTED]

[REDACTED]

[REDACTED]

[REDACTED]

[REDACTED]

[REDACTED]

[REDACTED] in [REDACTED]

[REDACTED] before. I always wanted to know where I was going and why. I remember one time when the escorting team refused to tell me where I was going: I thought they were taking me to my execution.* When I entered [REDACTED]

---

* The extended redaction that follows is one of two multipage redactions in the manuscript. The second one, which occurs at the end of chapter 6,

seems to correspond to a polygraph examination that MOS took in the late
fall of 2003 (see footnotes on pp. 297 and 299). It is possible that this first
extended redaction concerns a polygraph examination as well. At his 2005
ARB hearing, as he is describing his FBI interrogations through the winter
of 2002, MOS said, "Then I took a polygraph and [Ramzi bin al-Shibh]
refused to take a polygraph for many reasons. It turns out he is very contradictory and he lies. They said that to me themselves. They said my credibility is high because I took the polygraph." After his capture on September
11, 2002, Ramzi bin al-Shibh was held and interrogated at several CIA
black sites. News reports suggest that bin al-Shibh was interrogated in a
CIA-run facility near Rabat, Morocco, in late September and through the
fall of 2002, and in 2010 the U.S. government acknowledged it possessed
videotapes of bin al-Shibh's 2002 interrogation in Morocco. See, e.g.,
http://www.nytimes.com/2010/08/18/world/18tapes.html; and http://
hosted.ap.org/specials/interactives/wdc/binalshibh/content.swf.

was accompanied by an
Arabic Interpreter ███████████████████████. He
was very weak in the language. ████████████████

███████████████████████████████████
███████████████████████████████████
███████████████████████████████████
███████████████████████████████████
███████████████████████████████████
███████████████████████████████████

After a couple of days, I was taken to interrogation.

"How are you?" said ████████████. It had been a long time since I'd seen him.

"Good!"

████████████████ were in ████████████████, when you agreed ████████████████████████████

███████████████████████████████████
███████████████████████████████████
███████████████████████████████████
███████████████████████████████████
███████████████████████████████████
███████████████████████████████████
███████████████████████████████████
███████████████████████████████████
███████████████████████████████████
███████████████████████████████████
███████████████████████████████████
███████████████████████████████████
███████████████████████████████████
███████████████████████████████████
███████████████████████████████████
███████████████████████████████████
███████████████████████████████████
███████████████████████████████████
███████████████████████████████████
███████████████████████████████████

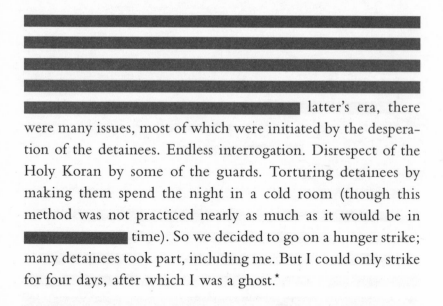

latter's era, there were many issues, most of which were initiated by the desperation of the detainees. Endless interrogation. Disrespect of the Holy Koran by some of the guards. Torturing detainees by making them spend the night in a cold room (though this method was not practiced nearly as much as it would be in ▮▮▮▮▮▮▮▮ time). So we decided to go on a hunger strike; many detainees took part, including me. But I could only strike for four days, after which I was a ghost.*

---

* Later in the manuscript, MOS writes that he participated in a hunger strike in September 2002, and news reports document a hunger strike in late September and October of that year (see, e.g., http://america.aljazeera. com/articles/multimedia/guantanamo-hungerstriketimeline.html, quoting an FBI document attributing that protest to anger over treatment by guards and the ongoing detention without trial or legal process). That hunger strike occurred toward the end of the tenure of Major General Michael E. Dunlavey, who was the commander of JTF-170, the intelligence operations in Guantánamo, from February through October 2002. He was succeeded by Major General Geoffrey D. Miller, who became commander of JTF-GTMO, which encompassed all Guantánamo operations, in November 2002. The Senate Armed Services Committee has documented at length the trend toward more abusive interrogations in October and November 2002, which included the development of the military's first "Special Interrogation Plan" for Mohammed al-Qahtani. On December 2, 2002, Secretary of Defense Donald Rumsfeld signed a memo authorizing interrogation methods including nudity, forced standing and stress positions, and twenty-hour interrogations. U.S. Senate Armed Services Committee, "Inquiry in the Treatment of Detainees in U.S. Custody," November 20, 2008, http://www.armed-services.senate.gov/imo/media/doc/Detainee-Report-Final_April-22-2009.pdf (hereafter cited as SASC).

"Don't break, you're gonna weaken the group," said my Saudi neighbor.

"I told you guys I'm gonna hunger strike, not that I'm gonna commit suicide. I'm gonna break," I replied.

██. He was the kind of man to be picked for the dirtiest job, when many others had failed. ███████████ was a very radical hater. He completely changed the detention policies in GTMO in all aspects.

██
██
██
██
██
██
██
██
██

██████████████████████████████████ One day in paradise, and the next in hell. Detainees of this level are completely under the mercy of their interrogators, which was very convenient for the interrogators. █████████████████████

██
██
██
██
██
██

████████████████████████████████

I was like, what the heck is going on, I've never been in trouble with the guards, and I am answering my interrogators and cooperating with them. But I missed that cooperation meant telling your interrogators whatever they want to hear.

*   *   *

I was put once more in ███████████████ end ███████████.*

An escort team appeared in ███████████████ in front of my cell.

"760 reservation!" they said.

"OK, just give me a second!" I put my clothes on and washed my face. My heart started to pound. I hated interrogation; I had gotten tired of being terrified all the time, living in constant fear day-in and day-out for the last thirteen months.

"Allah be with you! Keep your head on! They work for Satan!" yelled my fellow detainees to keep me together, as we always did when somebody got pulled for interrogation. I hated the sounds of the heavy metal chains; I can hardly carry them when they're given to me. People were always getting taken from the block, and every time I heard the chains I thought it would be me. You never know what's going to happen in the interrogation; people sometimes never came back to the block, they just disappeared. It happened to a Moroccan fellow detainee, and it would happen to me, as you're going to learn, God willing.

When I entered the room in ████████████████████, it was crowded with ███████████████████████
██
██.†

"Hi!"

---

* It is now around the end of 2002.

† The 2008 DOJ Inspector General's report identifies the two FBI agents who interview MOS from this point until he is turned over to the JTF-GTMO task force in May 2003 by the pseudonyms "Poulson" and "Santiago." Context suggests that the group in the room also includes a military interrogator and a French-speaking translator. According to the DOJ IG report, the team at this time also included a detective from the New York

"Hi!"

"I've chosen ███████████████ based on their experience and maturity. They'll be assessing your case from now on. There are a couple of things that need to be completed in your case. For instance, you didn't tell us everything about ████████████████████████. He's a very important guy ██████████████████."

"First, I told you what I know about ███████████████, even though I don't need to be providing you information about anybody. We're talking here about me. Second, in order to continue my cooperation with you, I need you to answer me one question: WHY AM I HERE? If you don't give me the answer, you can consider me a non-existent detainee." Later on I learned from my great lawyers ████████████████████ ████████████████ that the magic formulation of my request is a Petition for a Writ of Habeas Corpus. Obviously that phrase makes no sense to the average, mortal man like me. The average person would just say, "Why the hell are you locking me up?" I'm not a lawyer, but common sense dictates that after three years of interrogating me and depriving me of my liberty, the government at least owes me an explanation why it's doing so. What exactly is my crime?

"It makes no sense: It's like somebody who quits a 10-mile trip after traveling nine miles," said █████████████. It would have been more accurate had he said "a million mile trip after traveling one mile."

"Look, it's as simple as ABC: answer me the question and I'll cooperate with you fully!"

"I have no answer!" █████████ said.

"Neither do I!" I replied.

Police Department's Joint Terrorism Task Force, who interrogated Slahi with "Poulson" in January 2003. DOJ IG, 295–99.

"It says in the Koran somebody who kills one soul is considered to have killed all of humanity," said the French translator, trying to reach a breakthrough. I looked at him disrespectfully with the side of my face.

"I am not the guy you're looking for!" I said in French, and I repeated it in plain English.

███████████ started. "I am sure you're against killing people. We're not looking for you. We're looking for those guys who are out there trying to hurt innocents." He said this while showing me a bunch of ghostly pictures. I refused to look at them, and whenever he tried to put them under my sight I looked somewhere else. I didn't even want to give him the satisfaction of having taken a look at them. "Look, ███████ ███████████████ is cooperating, and he has a good chance of getting his sentence reduced to twenty-seven years—and ████████████████ is really a bad person. Somebody like you needs only to talk for five minutes, and you're a free man," said ███████████. He was everything but reasonable. When I contemplated his statement, I was like, God, a guy who is cooperating is gonna be locked up for 27 more years, after which he won't be able to enjoy any kind of life. What kind of harsh country is that? I am sorry to say that ████████ statement wasn't worth an answer. He and ██████████ tried to reason with the help of the MI guy, but there was no convincing me to talk.

You could tell that the interrogators were getting used to detainees who refused to cooperate after having cooperated for a while. Just as I was learning from other detainees how not to cooperate, the interrogators were learning from each other how to deal with non-cooperating detainees. The session was closed and I was sent back to my cell. I was satisfied with myself, since I now officially belonged to the majority, the non-cooperating detainees. I minded less being locked up unjustly for the rest of my life; what drove me crazy was to be expected to cooperate, too. You lock me up, I give you no information. And we both are cool.

▬▬▬▬▬▬▬▬▬ the sessions continued with the new team. ▬▬▬▬▬▬▬▬ rarely attended the sessions; "I won't come as long as you don't give us every piece of information you have," he once said. "Still, because we're Americans we treat you guys according to our high standards. Look at ▬▬▬▬▬▬▬▬▬, we're offering him the latest medical technology."

"You want just to keep him alive because he might have some Intels, and if he dies, they're gonna die with him!" I responded. U.S. interrogators always tended to mention free food and free medical treatment for detainees. I don't really understand what other alternatives they have! I personally have been detained in non-Democratic countries, and the medical treatment was the highest priority. Common sense dictates that if a detainee goes badly ill there will be no Intels, and he'll probably die.

We spent almost two months of argumentation. "Bring me to the court, and I'll answer all your questions," I would tell the team.

"There will be no court!" they would answer.

"Are you a Mafia? You kidnap people, lock them up, and blackmail them," I said.

"You guys are a law enforcement problem," said ▬▬▬▬▬▬. "We cannot apply the conventional law to you. We need only circumstantial evidence to fry you."

"I've done nothing against your country, have I?"

"You're a part of the big conspiracy against the U.S.!" said ▬▬▬▬▬▬▬.

"You can pull this charge on anybody! What have I done?"

"I don't know, you tell me!"

"Look, you kidnap me from my home in Mauritania, not from a battlefield in Afghanistan, because you suspected me of having been part of the Millennium Plot—which I am not, as you know by now. So what's the next charge? It looks to me as if you want to pull any shit on me."

"I don't want to pull any shit on you. I just wish you had access to the same reports as I do!" said ▮▮▮▮▮▮▮▮▮.

"I don't care what the reports say. I'd just like you to take a look at the reports from January 2000 linking me to the Millennium Plot. And you now know that I'm not a part of it, after the cooperation of ▮▮▮▮▮▮▮▮▮▮▮▮*

"I don't think that you are a part of it, nor do I believe that

---

* In this and the next paragraph, the subject could be Ahmed Ressam. Ressam was arrested as he tried to enter the United States from Canada in a car laden with explosives on December 14, 2000; he was convicted the following year of planning to bomb Los Angeles International Airport on New Year's Day 2001 as part of what became known as the Millennium Plot. In May 2001, after entering a guilty plea and before sentencing, Ressam began cooperating with U.S. authorities in exchange for assurances of a reduced sentence. A U.S. Court of Appeals later wrote that "Ressam continued cooperating until early 2003. Over the course of his two-year cooperation, he provided 65 hours of trial and deposition testimony, and 205 hours of proffers and debriefings. Ressam provided information to the governments of seven different countries and testified in two trials, both of which ended in convictions of the defendants. He provided names of at least 150 people involved in terrorism and described many others. He also provided information about explosives that potentially saved the lives of law enforcement agents, and extensive information about the mechanics of global terrorism operations." As MOS indicates here, Ressam never named or implicated him in any way in all those sessions. Ressam later recanted some of his testimony implicating others in the Millennium Plot. He originally received a twenty-two-year sentence with five years' supervision after his release. In 2010 the Ninth Circuit Court of Appeals ruled that sentence was too lenient and violated mandatory sentencing guidelines, and remanded the case to a federal judge for resentencing. The court's opinion is available at http://cdn.ca9.uscourts.gov/datastore/opinions/2010/02/02/09-30000.pdf.

you know ███████████████" But I do know that you know people who know ████████████" said ██████████.

"I don't know, but I don't see the problem if it is the case," I replied, "Knowing somebody is not a crime, no matter who he is."

A young Egyptian who was serving as interpreter that day tried to convince me to cooperate. "Look, I have come here sacrificing my time to help you guys, and the only way to help yourself is to talk," he said.

"Aren't you ashamed to work for these evil people, who arrest your brothers in faith for no reason than being Muslim?" I asked him. "████████, I am older than you are, speak more languages, I have a higher college grade, and I've been in many more countries than you have. I understand you're here to help yourself and make money. If you're trying to fool anybody, it's only yourself!" I was just so mad because he talked to me as if I were a child. ██████████████████████ were just staring.

These conversation took place again and again in different sessions. I kept saying, "You tell why I am here, I'll cooperate; you don't tell me, I'm not gonna cooperate. But we can talk about anything else beside interrogation."

████████████ welcomed that idea. He assured me that he was going to ask his boss to provide him the cause of my arrest, because he didn't know it himself. In the meantime he taught me a lot about American culture and history, the U.S. and Islam, and the U.S. and the Arab world. The team started to bring movies in; I saw *The Civil War*, Muslims in the U.S., and several other *Frontline* broadcasts regarding terrorism. "All of this shit happens because of hatred," he would say. "Hatred is the reason for all disasters."

██████████████, he was interested in getting information

as quickly as possible using classic police methods. He offered me McDonald's one day, but I refused because I didn't want to owe him anything. "The Army are fighting to take you to a very bad place, and we don't want that to happen!" he warned me.

"Just let them take me there; I'll get used to it. You keep me in jail whether or not I cooperate, so why should I cooperate?" I said this still not knowing that Americans use torture to facilitate interrogations. I was very tired from being taken to interrogation every day. My back was just conspiring against me. I even sought Medical help.

"You're not allowed to sit for such a long time," said the ▆▆▆▆▆▆▆▆▆▆▆ physiotherapist.

"Please tell my interrogators that, because they make me sit for long hours almost every day."

"I'll write a note, but I'm not sure whether it will have an effect," she replied.

It didn't. Instead, in February 2003, ▆▆▆▆▆▆▆ washed his hands of me.*

"I am going to leave, but if you're ready to talk about your telephone conversations, request me, I'll come back," he said.

"I assure you, I am not going to talk about anything unless you answer my question: Why am I here?"

---

* This may be the NYPD interrogator who the DOJ IG report indicates was part of the interrogation team in January 2003. The report describes an NYPD detective MOS identified as "Tom," who "told Slahi that if he did not explain certain phone calls he would be sent to a 'very bad place.'" DOJ IG, 299.

BEFORE

285

or crying. ~~HHt~~ Ultimately I ended up doing both. I kept reading the short message over and over. I knew it was for real ~~from~~ my mom not like the fake one I got one year ago. The only problem I couldn't respond the letter b/c I was still then not allowed to see the ICRC.

was the one who handed me that historical piece of paper.

The ~~First~~ Unofficial Laughter in the ocean of Tears:

▮ kept getting me English litterature ~~books~~ I enjoyed reading, most of them were Western. But I ~~remember~~ still remember one book called The Catcher in The Rye that made me laugh until my stomach hurt. I was a funny book. I ~~keep~~ tried to keep my laughter as low as possible and pushing it down, but the guards felt something _ "Are you crying?" asked me one of them _ "No, I am alright!" I responded. And since interrogators are not professional ~~come chairs~~, most of the humour they, some tie, came up with ~~with~~ a bunch of lame jokes that really didn't make me laugh, but I ~~forced~~ myself to always to an official smile.

▮ came on Sunday morning and waited outside the building. ▮ appeared before my cell ▮. I didn't recognize him. I thought he was a new interrogator. But he spoke I knew it was him. "Are ▮" _ "Don't worry. Your interrogator is waiting outside on you". _ I was overwhelmed and terrified at the same time. It was too much for me. ~~Look~~ ▮ led me outside the building where ▮

TWO

Senegal-Mauritania

January 21, 2000–February 19, 2000

The First Arrest in Senegal... An Escorted Homecoming... The First Interrogation in Mauritania... Getting Stuck in a Cul-de-Sac... The U.S. Dramatizes the Matter

A Mauritanian folktale tells us about a rooster-phobe who would almost lose his mind whenever he encountered a rooster.

"Why are you so afraid of the rooster?" the psychiatrist asks him.

"The rooster thinks I'm corn."

"You're not corn. You are a very big man. Nobody can mistake you for a tiny ear of corn," the psychiatrist said.

"I know that, Doctor. But the rooster doesn't. Your job is to go to him and convince him that I am not corn."

The man was never healed, since talking with a rooster is impossible. End of story.

For years I've been trying to convince the U.S. government that I am not corn.

It started in January 2000, when I was returning to Mauritania after living twelve years overseas. At 8 p.m. on ███████ ██████, my friends ████████████████████████████

dropped me off at Dorval Airport in Montreal. I took the night Sabena flight to Brussels and was continuing to Dakar the next afternoon.* I arrived in Brussels in the morning, sleepy and worn out. After collecting my luggage, I collapsed on one of the benches in the International area, using my bag as a pillow. One thing was sure: anybody could have stolen my bag, I was so tired. I slept for one or two hours, and when I woke up, I looked for a toilet where I could wash and a place to pray.

The airport was small, neat, and clean, with restaurants, duty-free shops, phone booths, Internet PCs, a mosque, a church, a synagogue, and a psych consulting bureau for atheists. I checked out all the God's houses, and was impressed. I thought, This country could be a place I'd want to live. Why don't I just go and ask for asylum? I'd have no problem; I speak the language and have adequate qualifications to get a job in the heart of Europe. I had actually been in Brussels, and I liked the multicultural life and the multiple faces of the city.

I left Canada mainly because the U.S. had pitted their security services on me, but they didn't arrest me, they just started to watch me. Being watched is better than being put in jail, I realize now; ultimately, they would have figured out that I am not a criminal. "I never learn," as my mom always put it. I never believed that the U.S. was evilly trying to get me in a place where the law has nothing to say.

The border was inches away. Had I crossed that border, I would never have written this book.

Instead, in the small mosque, I performed the ritual wash and

---

* MOS's 2004 Combatant Status Review Tribunal (CSRT) and 2005 Administrative Review Board hearing transcripts make clear the date is January 21, 2000. The CSRT transcript is available at http://online.wsj .com/public/resources/documents/couch-slahihearing-03312007.pdf. CSRT transcript, 6; ARB transcript, 16.

prayed. It was very quiet; the peacefulness was dominating. I felt so tired that I lay down in the mosque and read the Koran for some time and fell asleep.

I woke up to the movements of another guy who came to pray. He seemed to know the place and to have transited through this airport many times. ███████████████████████████ ████████████████. We greeted each other after he finished his prayer.

"What are you doing here?" he asked me.

"I'm transiting. I came from Canada, and am heading for Dakar."

"Where are you from?"

"Mauritania. What about you?'

"I'm from Senegal. I'm a merchant between my country and the Emirates. I'm waiting on the same flight as you."

"Good!" I said.

"Let's go rest. I'm a member of Club Such-and-Such," he suggested, I don't recall the name. We went to the club, and it was just amazing: TV, coffee, tea, cookies, a comfortable couch, newspapers. I was overwhelmed, and I spent most of the time sleeping on a couch. At some point, my new ████████████ friend wanted to have lunch, and woke me up to do the same. I was concerned I wouldn't be able to come back because I had no club card and they had just let me in because my ████████████ ████ friend flashed his membership card. However, my stomach's call was louder, and I decided to go outside and have some food. I went to the Sabena Airlines counter and asked for a free meal card, and found a restaurant. Most of the food was mixed with pork, so I decided on a vegetarian meal.

I went back to the club and waited until my friend and I were called to our flight, Sabena #502 to Dakar. I had chosen Dakar because it was by far cheaper than flying directly to

Nouakchott, Mauritania. Dakar is only about 300 miles from Nouakchott, and I arranged with my family to pick me up there. So far so good; people do it all the time.

During the flight, I was full of energy because I had had some quality sleep in Brussels airport. Next to me was a young French girl who lived in Dakar but was studying medicine in Brussels. I was thinking that my brothers might not make it to the airport on time, so I would have to spend some time in a hotel. The French girl benevolently enlightened me about the prices in Dakar, and how the Senegalese people try to overcharge strangers, especially the taxi drivers.

The flight took about five hours. We arrived around 11 p.m., and the whole formalities thing took about thirty minutes. When I took my bag from the baggage claim, I bumped into my ▮▮▮▮▮▮▮▮ friend, and we bid each other farewell.* As soon as I turned away carrying my bag, I saw my brother ▮▮▮▮▮▮▮▮ smiling; he obviously had seen me before I saw him. ▮▮▮▮▮▮▮▮ was accompanied by my other brother ▮▮▮▮▮▮▮▮ and two friends of theirs I didn't know. ▮▮▮▮▮▮▮▮ grabbed my bag and we headed toward the parking lot. I liked the warm night weather that embraced me as soon as I left the gate. We were talking, asking each other excitedly how things were going. As we crossed the road, I honestly cannot describe what happened to me. All I know is that in less than a second my hands were shackled behind my back and I was encircled by a bunch of ghosts who cut me off from the rest of my company. At first I thought it was an armed robbery, but as it turned out it was a robbery of another kind.

---

* Context and the events that follow make clear that this is the Senegalese businessman he spent time with in the Brussels airport.

"We arrest you in the Name of the Law," said the special agent while locking the chains around my hands.

"I'm arrested!" I called to the brothers I couldn't see anymore. I figured if they missed me all of a sudden it would be painful for them. I didn't know whether they heard me or not, but as it turned out, they had heard me indeed because my brother ████████████████ kept mocking me later and claiming that I am not courageous since I called for help. Maybe I'm not, but that's what happened. What I didn't know was that my two brothers and their two friends were arrested at the same time. Yes, their two friends, one who came with my brothers all the way from Nouakchott, and the other, his brother who lives in Dakar and just happened to ride with them to the airport, just in time to be arrested as a part of a "gang": What luck!

I honestly was not prepared for this injustice. Had I known the U.S. investigators were really so full of it, I wouldn't have left Canada, or even Belgium when I was transiting through. Why didn't the U.S. have me arrested in Germany? Germany is one of the closest allies of the U.S. Why didn't the U.S. have me arrested in Canada? Canada and the U.S. are almost the same country. The U.S. interrogators and investigators claimed that I fled Canada out of fear that I was going to be arrested, but that doesn't really make any sense. First of all, I left using my passport with my real name, after going through all formalities including all kinds of registrations. Secondly, is it better to be arrested in Canada or Mauritania? Of course in Canada! Or why didn't the U.S. have me arrested in Belgium, where I spent almost twelve hours?

I understand the anger and frustration of the U.S. about terrorist attacks. But jumping on innocent individuals and making them suffer, looking for fake confessions, doesn't help anybody. It rather complicates the problem. I would always tell the U.S.

agents, "Guys! Cool down! Think before you act! Just put a small percentage on the possibility that you might be wrong before you irreparably injure somebody!" But when something bad happens, people start to freak out and lose their composure. I've been interrogated throughout the last six years by over a hundred interrogators from different countries, and they have one thing in common: confusion. Maybe the government wants them to be that way, who knows?

Anyhow, the local police at the airport intervened when they saw the mêlée—the Special Forces were dressed in civilian suits, so there really was no differentiating them from a bunch of bandits trying to rob somebody—but the guy behind me flashed a magic badge, which immediately made the policemen retreat. All five of us were thrown in a cattle truck, and soon we got another friend, the guy I had met in Brussels, just because we bid each other farewell at the luggage carousel.

The guards got in with us. The leader of the group sat up front in the passenger seat, but he could see and hear us because the glass that usually separates the driver from the cattle wasn't there anymore. The truck took off like in a Hollywood chase scene. "You're killing us," one of the guards must have said, because the driver slowed down a little bit. The local guy who came to the airport with my brothers was losing his mind; every once in a while he spat some indistinct words conveying his worries and unhappiness. As it turned out the guy thought that I was a drug dealer and he was relieved when the suspicion turned out to be terrorism! Since I was the starring actor, I felt bad for causing so much trouble for so many people. My only solace was that I didn't mean to—and also, at that moment, the fear in my heart overwhelmed the rest of my emotions.

When I sat down on the rough floor, I felt better surrounded by the warmth of the company, including the Special Forces agents. I started to recite the Koran.

"Shut up!" said the boss in the front. I didn't shut up; I lowered my voice, but not enough for the boss. "Shut up!" he said, this time raising his baton to hit me. "You're trying to bewitch us out!" I knew he was serious, and so I prayed in my heart. I hadn't tried to bewitch anybody out, nor do I know how to do it, but Africans are some of the most gullible folks I ever knew.

The trip took between fifteen and twenty minutes, so it was shortly after midnight when we arrived at the Commissariat de Police. The masterminds of the operation stood behind the truck and got involved in a discussion with my Brussels friend. I didn't understand anything; they were speaking in the local language ██████.* After a short discussion, the guy took his heavy bags, and off he went. When I later asked my brothers what he told the police, they told me that he said he had seen me in Brussels and never before, and that he didn't know that I was a terrorist.

Now we were five persons jailed in the truck. It was very dark outside, but I could tell that people were coming and going. We waited between forty minutes and an hour in the truck. I grew more nervous and afraid, especially when the guy in the passenger seat said, "I hate working with the Whites," or rather he used the word 'Moors,' which made me believe that they were waiting on a Mauritanian team. I started to have nausea, my heart was a feather, and I shrank so small to hold myself together. I thought about all the kinds of torture I had heard of, and how much I could take tonight. I grew blind, a thick cloud built in front of my eyes, I couldn't see anything. I

---

* The language is likely Wolof; it is named again without redaction a few pages later. MOS manuscript, 436.

grew deaf; after that statement all I could hear was indistinct whispers. I lost the feeling of my brothers being with me in the same truck. I figured only God can help my situation. God never fails.

"Get out," shouted the guy impatiently. I fought my way through and one of the guards helped me jump down the step. We were led into a small room that was already occupied by mosquitoes, just in time for them to start their feast. They didn't even wait until we slept; they went right away about their business, tearing us apart. The funny thing about mosquitoes is that they're shy in small groups and rude in big ones. In small groups, they wait until you fall asleep, unlike in big groups, where they start to tease you right away, as if to say: "What can you do about it?" And in fact, nothing. The toilet was filthy as it could be, which made it an ideal environment for breeding mosquitoes.

I was the only chained person. "Did I beat you?" asked the guy while taking off the handcuffs.

"No, you didn't." When I looked I noticed I already had scars around my wrists. The interrogators started to pull us one by one for interrogation, starting with the strangers. It was a very long, scary, dark and bleak night.

My turn came shortly before the first daylight.

In the interrogation room there were two men ████████████

██

███████████████, a male interrogator and his recorder.* The ██████████ Police Chief was in charge of the police station, but

---

* The cast seems to consist of two men and two women: the Senegalese interrogator and his recorder, both male; and the Senegalese police chief and an American, who the redacted pronouns suggest are both female.

████ was not part of the interrogation; ████ looked so tired that ████ fell asleep several times out of boredom. The American ██████ was taking notes, and sometimes ████ passed notes to the interrogator. The interrogator was a quiet, skinny, smart, rather religious and deep thinking ████████.

"We have very heavy allegations against you," he said, pulling a thick stack of papers out of a bright yellow envelope. Before he had them halfway out, you could tell he had been reading the stuff many times. And I already knew what he was talking about, because the Canadians had already interviewed me.

"I have done nothing. The U.S. wants to dirty Islam by pinning such horrible things on Muslims."

"Do you know ██████████████████?"*

"No, I don't. I even think his whole story was a fake, to unlock the terrorism budget and hurt the Muslims." I was really honest about what I said. Back then I didn't know a whole lot of things that I do now. I believed excessively in Conspiracy Theories—though maybe not as much as the U.S. government does.

The interrogator also asked me about a bunch of other people, most of whom I didn't know. The people I did know were not involved in any crimes whatsoever, as far as I knew. Lastly, the Senegalese asked me about my position toward the U.S., and why I had transited through his country. I really didn't understand why my position toward the U.S. government should matter to anybody. I am not a U.S. citizen, nor did I ever apply to enter the U.S., nor am I working with the U.N. Besides, I could always lie. Or let's say I love the U.S., or I hate it, it doesn't really matter as long as I haven't done any crimes

---

* The question, given the pre-9/11 date of this interview and the reference to the Canadians, might refer to Ahmed Ressam. See footnote on p. 66.

against the U.S. I explained all this to the Senegalese interrogator with a clarity that left no doubt at all about my circumstances.

"You seem very tired! I suggest you go and have some sleep. I know it's hard," he said. Of course I was dead tired, and hungry and thirsty. The guards led me back to the small room where my brothers and the other two guys were lying on the floor, fighting against the most efficient Senegalese Air Force Mosquitoes ███████. I was no luckier than the rest. Did we sleep? Not really.

The interrogator and his assistant showed up early in the morning. They released the two guys, and took me and my brothers to the headquarters of the Ministère de L'Intérieur. The interrogator, who turned out to be a very high-level person in the Senegalese government, took me to his office and made a call to the Minister of Internal Affairs.

"The guy in front of me is not the head of a terrorist organization," he said. I couldn't hear what the minister said. "When it comes to me, I have no interest in keeping this guy in jail— nor do I have a reason," the interrogator continued. The telephone call was short and straightforward. In the meantime, my brothers made themselves comfortable, bought some stuff, and started to make tea. Tea is the only thing that keeps the Mauritanian person alive, with God's help. It had been a long time since any of us had eaten or drunk anything, but the first thing that came to mind was tea.

I was happy because the one-ton stack of paper the U.S. government had provided the Senegalese about me didn't seem to impress them; it didn't take my interrogator a whole lot of time to understand the situation. My two brothers started a conversation with him in Wolof. I asked my brothers what the conversation was about, and they said that the Senegalese government was not interested in holding me, but the U.S. was the one that was going to call the shots. Nobody was happy with that, because we had an idea of what the U.S. call would be like.

"We're waiting on some people from the U.S. embassy to show up," said the interrogator. Around eleven o'clock a black American ████████ showed up.* ████ took pictures, finger-prints, and the report the recorder had typed earlier that morn-ing. My brothers felt more comfortable around the black ████████ than the white ████████ from last night. People feel comfortable with the looks they are used to, and since about 50 percent of Mauritanians are black, my brothers could relate to them more. But that was a very naïve approach: in either case, black or white, ████████ would just be a messenger.

After finishing ████ work, ████████ made a couple of calls, pulled the interrogator aside and spoke to him briefly, and then ████ was gone. The inspector informed us that my brothers were free to go and that I was going to be held in contempt for some time.

"Do you think we can wait on him until he gets released?" my brother asked.

"I would suggest you guys go home. If he gets released, he will find his way." My brothers left and I felt abandoned and lonely, though I believe my brothers did the right thing.

For the next couple of days, the Senegalese kept interrogating me about the same things; the U.S. investigators sent them the questions. That was all. The Senegalese didn't hurt me in any way, nor did they threaten me. Since the food in jail was horrible, my brothers arranged with a family they knew in Dakar to bring me one meal a day, which they consistently did.

---

* Redacted pronouns suggest this, too, may be a woman.

My concern, as I say, was and still is to convince the U.S. government that I am not a corn. My only fellow detainee in the Senegalese jail had a different concern: to smuggle himself to Europe or America. We definitely had different Juliets. The young man from Ivory Coast was determined to leave Africa.

"I don't like Africa," he told me. "Many friends of mine have died. Everybody is very poor. I want to go to Europe or America. I tried twice. The first time I managed to sneak into Brazil when I outsmarted the port officials, but one African guy betrayed us to the Brazilian authorities, who put us in jail until they deported us back to Africa. Brazil is a very beautiful country, with very beautiful women," he added.

"How can you say so? You were in jail the whole time!" I interrupted him.

"Yes, but every once in a while the guards escorted us to look around, then took us back to jail," he smiled.

"You know, brother, the second time I almost made it to Ireland," he went on. "But the ruthless ███████████ kept me in the ship and made customs take me."

Sounds Columbus-y, I thought. "How did you get on board in the first place?" I wondered.

"It's very easy, brother. I bribed some of the workers at the port. Those people smuggled me onto a ship heading to Europe or America. It didn't really matter. I hid in the containers section for about a week until my provisions were gone. At that point, I came up and mingled with the crew. At first, they got very mad. The Captain of the ship headed to Ireland was so mad that he wanted to drown me."

"What an animal!" I interrupted, but my friend kept going.

"But after some time the crew accepted me, gave me food, and made me work."

"How did they catch you this time?"

"My smugglers betrayed me. They said the ship was heading nonstop to Europe. But we made a stop in Dakar and customs took me off of the ship, and here I am!"

"What's your next plan?"

"I'm gonna work, save some money, and try again." My fellow detainee was determined to leave Africa at any cost. Moreover, he was confident that one day he was going to put his feet in the promised land.

"Man, what you see on TV is not how real life looks like in Europe," I said.

"No!" he answered. "My friends have been successfully smuggled into Europe, and they have good lives. Good looking women and a lot of money. Africa is bad."

"You might as easily end up in jail in Europe."

"I don't care. Jail in Europe is good. Africa is bad."

I figured the guy was completely blinded by the rich world that deliberately shows us poor Africans a "paradise" we cannot enter, though he had a point. In Mauritania, the majority of the young people want to emigrate to Europe or the U.S. If the politics in African countries don't change radically for the better, we are going to experience a catastrophe that will affect the whole world.

His cell was catastrophic. Mine was a little better. I had a very thin worn-out mattress, but he had nothing but a piece of carton he slept on. I used to give him my food because when I get anxious I can't eat. Besides, I got good food from outside, and he got the bad food of the jail. The guards let us be together during the day and locked him up nights. My cell was always open. The day before I was extradited to Mauritania, the ambassador of Ivory Coast came to confirm the identity of my fellow detainee. Of course he had no papers whatsoever.

*   *   *

"We are releasing you!" the recorder who had been interrogating me for the last several days said happily.

"Thank you!" I interrupted him, looking in the direction of Mecca, and prostrating myself to thank God for being free.

"However, we have to turn you over to your country."

"No, I know the way, I'll do it on my own," I said innocently, thinking I didn't really want to go back to Mauritania, but maybe to Canada or somewhere else. My heart had been teased enough.

"I am sorry, we have to turn you over ourselves!" My whole happiness turned into agony, fear, nervousness, helplessness, confusion and other things I cannot describe. "Gather your stuff!" the guy said. "We're leaving."

I started to gather my few belongings, heartbroken. The inspector grabbed my bigger bag and I carried my small briefcase. During my arrest, the Americans had copied every single piece of paper I had and sent it all to Washington for analysis.

It was around 5 p.m. when we left the gate of the Commissariat de Police. Out front stood a Mitsubishi SUV. The inspector put my bags in the trunk, and we got into the back seat. On my left sat a guard I had never seen before, older and big boned. He was quiet and rather laid back; he looked straight ahead most of the time, only rarely scanning me quickly with the side of his eye. I hated it when guards would keep staring at me as if they had never seen a mammal before. On my right was the inspector who had been the recorder. In the passenger's seat sat the lead interrogator. The driver was a ████████████████████████████████ ██.*

---

* This character is described in the subsequent paragraphs, without redactions, as "the white driver," "the white guy," and "the American man."

From his tan you could tell he had spent some time in a warm place, but not in Senegal because the interrogator kept guiding him to the airport. Or maybe he was looking for best way, I couldn't tell. He spoke French with a heavy accent, though he was stingy in his conversation; he limited himself exactly within the necessary. He never looked at or addressed me. The other two interrogators tried to talk to me, but I didn't answer, I kept reading my Koran silently. Out of respect, the Senegalese didn't confiscate my Koran, unlike the Mauritanians, Jordanians, and Americans.

It took about 25 minutes to the airport. The traffic was quiet around and inside the terminal. The white driver quickly found a parking place. We got out of the truck, the guards carrying my luggage, and we all passed through the diplomatic way to the waiting room. It was the first time that I shortcut the civilian formalities while leaving one country to another. It was a treat, but I didn't enjoy it. Everybody seemed to be prepared in the airport. In front of the group the interrogator and the white guy kept flashing their magic badges, taking everybody with them. You could clearly tell that the country had no sovereignty: this was still colonization in its ugliest face. In the so-called free world, the politicians preach things such as sponsoring democracy, freedom, peace, and human rights: What hypocrisy! Still, many people believe this propaganda garbage.

The waiting room was empty. Everybody took a seat, and one of the Senegalese took my passport and went back and stamped it. I thought I was going to take the regular Air Afrique flight that was scheduled to Nouakchott that afternoon. But it didn't take very long to realize I had my own plane to myself. As soon as the guy returned with my stamped passport, all five of us stepped toward the runway, where a very small white

plane was already running its engines. The American man gestured for us to stay behind and he had a quick talk with the
pilot. Maybe the interrogator was with him, too, I can't remember. I was too scared to memorize everything.

Soon enough we were told to get in. The plane was as small
as it could be. We were four, and barely managed to squeeze
ourselves inside the butterfly with heads down and backs bent.
The pilot had the most comfortable place. She was a French
lady, you could tell from her accent. She was very talkative, and
rather on the older side, skinny and blond. She didn't talk to
me, but she exchanged some words with the inspector during
the trip. As it turned out, I later learned she told her friends in
Nouakchott about the secret package she delivered from Dakar.
The bigger guard and I squeezed ourselves, knees-on-faces, in
the back seat, facing the inspector, who had a little better seat
in front of us. The plane was obviously overloaded.

The Interrogator and the American man waited until they
made sure that the plane took off. I wasn't paying attention to
the conversations between the pilot and the inspector, but I
heard her at one point telling him that the trip was only 300
miles, and would take between 45 minutes and an hour, depending on the wind direction. That sounded so medieval. The
inspector tried to talk to me, but there was nothing to talk
about; to me everything was already said and done. I figured
he had nothing to say to help me, so why should I talk to him?

I hate traveling in small planes because they're shaky and I
always think the wind is going to blow the plane away. But this
time was different, I was not afraid. In fact I wanted the plane
to crash, and only me to survive. I would know my way: it was
my country, I was born here, and anybody would give me food
and shelter. I was drowned in my dreams, but the plane didn't

crash; instead it was getting closer and closer to its destination. The wind was in its favor. I was thinking about all my innocent brothers who were and still are being rendered to strange places and countries, and I felt solaced and not alone anymore. I felt the spirits of unjustly mistreated people with me. I had heard so many stories about brothers being passed back and forth like a soccer ball just because they have been once in Afghanistan, or Bosnia, or Chechnya. That's screwed up! Thousands of miles away, I felt the warm breath of these other unjustly treated individuals comforting me. I stuck all the time to my Koran, ignoring my environment.

My company seemed to have a good time checking the weather and enjoying the beach we had been flying along the whole time. I don't think that the plane had any type of navigation technologies because the pilot kept a ridiculously low altitude and oriented us with the beach. Through the window I started to see the sand-covered small villages around Nouakchott, as bleak as their prospects. There definitely had been a sandstorm earlier that day; People were just gradually daring to go outside. The suburbs of Nouakchott appeared more miserable than ever, crowded, poor, dirty, and free of any of life's crucial infrastructures. It was the Kebba ghetto I knew, only worse. The plane flew so low I could tell who was who among the people who were moving, seemingly disoriented, everywhere.

It had been long time since I had seen my country last—since August 1993, in fact. I was coming back, but this time as a terrorism suspect who was going to be hidden in some secret hole. I wanted to cry out loud to my people, "Here I am! I am not a criminal! I'm innocent! I am just the guy you knew, I'm no different!" But my voice was oppressed, just like in a nightmare.

I couldn't really recognize anything, the city plan had changed so radically.

I finally realized the plane was not going to crash, and I was not going to have the chance to talk to my people. It's amazing how hard it can be for someone to accept his miserable situation. The key to surviving any given situation is to realize that you are in it. Whether I wanted it or not, I was going to be delivered to the very people I didn't want to see.

"Can you do me a favor?" I asked the Inspector.

"Sure!"

"I'd like you to inform my family that I'm in the country."

"OK. Do you have the phone number?"

"Yes, I do." The inspector, against my expectation, indeed called my family and told them about my reality. Moreover, the Senegalese made an official press declaration stating that they turned me over to my country. Both the Mauritanians and Americans were pissed off about that.

"What did you tell the Inspector?" the Mauritanian DSE, the Directeur de la Sûrete de l'État, asked me later.[*]

"Nothing."

"You're lying. You told him to call your family." It didn't really take David Copperfield to figure out that the telephone call was intercepted.

The handover was quick. We landed near the back door of the airport, where two men were waiting, the Mauritanian Inspector and another freakin' big black guy, most likely brought to take care of business—just in case!

"Where is the Airport Police Chief?" the Inspector wondered, looking at his black colleague. I knew the Airport Police

---

[*] The Directeur de la Sûrete de l'État, which MOS abbreviates as DSE throughout the manuscript, is the director of the Mauritanian intelligence service.

Chief: he had once been in Germany, and I gave him shelter and helped him buy a Mercedes-Benz. I hoped he would show up, so he could see me and put in a good word for me. But he never showed. Nor would he have put in a good word for me: Mauritanian Intelligence is by far the highest law enforcement authority. But I felt like I was drowning, and I would have grabbed any straw I encountered.

"You will be escorted to the hotel to spend the rest of the night," said the Inspector to his guests.

"How are you?" he said ungenuinely, looking at me.

"I'm fine."

"Is that all he has?" he asked.

"Yes that's it." I was watching all my belongings on earth being passed around as if I'd already died.

"Let's go!" the inspector said to me. The black guy, who never took his eyes off me, carried the luggage and pushed me before him toward a dirty small room at the secret gate of the airport. In the room, the black dude unfolded his dirty black 100 year-old turban.

"Mask your face thoroughly with this turban," said the Inspector. Typically Mauritanian: the Bedouin spirit still dominates. The inspector should have foreseen that he would need a Turban to wrap my head, but in Mauritania organization is almost non-existent; everything is left to whim and chance. It was tricky, but I hadn't forgotten yet how to fold a turban around my head. It is something people from the desert must learn. The turban smelled of piled-up sweat. It was just disgusting to have it around your mouth and nose. But I obediently complied with the orders and held my breath.

"Don't look around," the inspector said when the three of us stepped out of the room toward the parked Secret Police car, a ▬▬▬▬▬▬▬. I sat in the passenger's seat, the inspector drove, and the black guy sat in the back seat, without saying a word. It was about sunset, but you couldn't tell exactly because the cloud of sand was covering the horizon. The streets were empty. I illegally looked around whenever the chance arose, but I could hardly recognize anything.

The trip was short, about ten minutes to the Security Police building. We stepped out of the car and entered the building, where another guard was waiting on us, ██████████████. The environment was an ideal place for mosquitoes, human beings are the strangers in that place: filthy toilet, dirty floor and walls, holes connecting all the rooms, ants, spiders, flies.

"Search him thoroughly," the inspector told ████████.

"Give me everything you have," ███████ respectfully asked me, wanting to avoid searching me. I gave ███████ everything I had except for my pocket Koran. The inspector must have realized I would have one, for ███████ came back and said, "Do you have a Koran?"

"Yes, I do."

"Give it to me! I told you to give me everything." By now the guard was growing afraid of being sent back again, so he searched me gently, but he didn't find anything but my pocket Koran. I was so sad, tired, and terrorized that I couldn't sit up straight. Instead I put my jacket on my face and fell on the inch-thick, worn-out 100-year-old mattress, the only object that existed in that room. I wanted to sleep, lose my mind, and not wake up until every bad thing was over. How much pain can I take? I asked myself. Can my family intervene and save me? Do they use electricity? I had read stories about people who were tortured to death. How could they bear it? I'd read about Muslim heroes who faced the death penalty, head up. How did they do it? I didn't know. All I knew was that I felt so small before all the big names I knew, and that I was scared to death.

Although the mosquitoes were tearing me apart, I fell asleep. Every once in a while I woke up and asked myself, Why don't they interrogate me right now, and do with me whatever they want, and everything will be over? I hate waiting on torture; an Arabic proverb says, "Waiting on torture is worse than torture." I can only confirm this proverb. I managed to perform my prayers, how I don't know.

Sometime around midnight I woke up to people moving around, opening and closing doors in an extraordinary manner. When the guard opened the door to my room, I glimpsed the face of a Mauritanian friend who happened to be with me a long time ago when I visited Afghanistan in 1992 during the struggle against communism. He looked sad and weathered, and must have gone through painful torture, I thought. I almost lost my mind, knowing for sure I was going to suffer at least as much as he had, given his close relationship with the Mauritanian president and the power of his family—qualities I don't have. I thought, The guy surely must have spoken about me, and that is the reason why they brought him here.

"Get up!" said the guards. "Put on your turban." I put on the dirty turban, gathered my last strength, and followed the guards to the interrogation room like a sheep being driven to its last destination, the slaughterhouse.

When I was driven past the guy I had seen earlier, I realized he was just a screwed-up guard who failed to keep his uniform the way it should be. He was sleepy and drowsy: they must have called him in the midst of his sleep, and he hadn't yet washed his face. It was not the friend I thought it was; anxiety, terror, and fear were dominating my mind. Lord have mercy! I was somewhat relieved. Did I commit a crime? No. Did my friend commit a crime? No. Did we conspire to committing a crime? No. The only thing we had done together was make a trip to Afghanistan in February 1992 to help the people fighting against communism. And as far as I was concerned that was not a crime, at least in Mauritania.

So why was I so scared? Because crime is something relative; it's something the government defines and re-defines whenever it pleases. The majority of people don't know, really, where the line is that separates breaking the law from not breaking it. If you get arrested, the situation worsens, because most people trust the government to have a good reason for the arrest. On top of that, if I personally had to suffer, I didn't want anybody to suffer with me. I thought they arrested my friend in connection with the Millennium Plot, if only because he had been in Afghanistan once.

I entered the interrogation room, which was the office of the DSE. The room was large and well-furnished: leather couch, two love-seats, coffee table, closet, one big desk, one leather chair, a couple of other chairs for unimportant guests, and, as always, the picture of the president conveying the weakness of the law and the strength of the government. I wished they had turned me over to the U.S.: at least there are things I could refer to there, such as the law. Of course, in the U.S. the government and politics are gaining more and more ground lately at the cost of the law. The government is very smart; it evokes terror in the hearts of people to convince them to give up their freedom and privacy. Still, it might take some time until the U.S. government overthrows the law completely, like in the third world and the communist regimes. But really that is none of my concern, and thank God my government doesn't possess the technology to track Bedouins in the vast desert.

There were three guys in the interrogation room: the DSE, his assistant, and his recorder. The DSE asked them to bring my stuff in. They thoroughly searched everything I had; no stone remained unturned. They didn't speak to me, they only spoke with each other, mostly in whispers, just to annoy the hell out of me. At the end of the search, they sorted out my papers and put aside the ones they thought interesting. Later on, they asked me about every single word in those papers.

"I am going to interrogate you. I just want to tell you as a forewarning that you better tell me the whole truth," the DSE said firmly, making a big effort to take a break from smoking his pipe, which he never took off his lips.

"I sure will," I answered.

"Take him back," the DSE dryly ordered the guards.

"Listen, I want you to tell me about your whole life, and how you joined the Islamic movement," said the DSE when the guards dragged my skeleton away from the mosquitoes and back into the interrogation room.

If you get arrested for the first time, chances are that you're not going to be forthcoming, and that's OK; even though you know you haven't done any crimes, it seems sensible. You're very confused, and you'd like to make yourself appear as innocent as possible. You assume you are arrested more or less on a reasonable suspicion, and you don't want to cement that suspicion. Moreover, questioning involves a lot of stuff nobody wants to talk about, like your friends and your private life. Especially when the suspicions are about things like terrorism, the government is very rude. In the interrogation you always avoid talking about your friends and your private, intimate life. And finally, you are so frustrated because of your arrest, and you really don't owe your interrogators anything. On the contrary, they owe you to show you the true cause of your detention, and it should be entirely up to you to comment then or to leave them be. If this cause is enough to hold you, you can seek professional representation; if not, well you shouldn't be arrested in the first place. That's how the civilized world works, and everything else is dictatorship. Dictatorship is governed by chaos.

To be honest with you, I acted like any average person: I tried to make myself look as innocent as a baby. I tried to protect the identities of every single person I knew, unless he or she was too well-known to the Police. The interrogations continued in this manner, but when they opened the Canadian file, things soured decidedly.

The U.S. government saw in my arrest and my rendition to Mauritania a once-in-a-blue-moon opportunity to unveil the plan of Ahmed Ressam, who back then was refusing to cooperate with the U.S. authorities. Furthermore, the U.S. wanted to learn in detail about my friends in both Canada and Germany, and even outside those countries. After all my cousin and brother ████████████████ was already wanted with a reward of U.S. $5,000,000.* The U.S. also wanted to learn more about the whole Jihadi issue in Afghanistan, Bosnia, and Chechnya.

---

* Ressam appears here unredacted. The wanted man, it is clear from context here and unredacted references elsewhere in the manuscript, is MOS's cousin and former brother-in-law Abu Hafs. Abu Hafs was wanted in connection with al-Qaeda attacks in the 1990s, with a $5 million reward under the FBI's Rewards for Justice Program. The reward for senior al-Qaeda figures increased to $25 million after the September 11, 2001, terrorist attacks. See, e.g., U.S. State Department, "Patterns of Global Terrorism," appendix D, May 21, 2002, http://www.state.gov/documents /organization/20121.pdf.

Expertise for free. For the aforementioned, and for other reasons I don't know, the U.S. drove my case as far as it could be driven. They labeled me "Mastermind of the Millennium Plot." They asked all countries to provide any tiny bit of information they possessed about me, especially Canada and Germany. And since I am already a "bad" guy, force must be applied to roast me.

To the dismay of the U.S. government, things were not really as they seemed, nor did the government achieve what it wanted. No matter how smart somebody plans, God's plan always works. I felt like 2Pac's "Me Against the World." And here's why.

All the Canadians could come up with was, "We have seen him with x and y, and they're bad people." "We've seen him in this and that mosque." "We have intercepted his telephone conversations, but there's nothing really!" The Americans asked the Canadians to provide them the transcripts of my conversations, but after they edited them. Of course it doesn't make sense to selectively take different passages from a whole conversation and try to make sense of them. I think the Canadians should have done one of two things: either refused to provide the Americans any private conversation that took place in their country, or provided them the whole conversation in its original form, not even translated.

Instead, out of the words the Canadians chose to share with their U.S. colleagues, U.S. interrogators magically stuck with two words for more than four years: Tea and Sugar.

"What do you mean by tea and sugar?"

"I mean tea and sugar." I cannot tell you how many times the U.S. asked me, and made other people ask me, this question. Another Mauritanian folktale recounts about a man who was born blind and who had one chance to get a glimpse of the world. All he saw was a rat. After that, whenever anybody tried to explain anything to the guy, he always asked, "Compare it with the rat: Is it bigger? smaller?"

Canadian intelligence wished I were a criminal, so they could make up for their failure when ▮▮▮▮▮▮▮▮▮▮ slipped from their country to the U.S. carrying explosives.* The U.S. blamed Canada for being a preparation ground for terrorist attacks against the U.S., and that's why Canadians Intel freaked out. They really completely lost their composure, trying everything to calm the rage of their big brother, the U.S. They began watching the people they believed to be bad, including me. I remember after ▮▮▮▮▮▮▮▮▮ plot, the Canadians tried to implant two cameras, one in my room, one in my roommate's. I used to be a very heavy sleeper. I heard voices but I couldn't tell what it was—or let's say I was too lazy to wake up and check on them. My roommate ▮▮▮▮▮▮▮▮▮ was different; he woke up and followed the noise. He laid low and watched until the tiny hole was through. The guy in the other room blew through the hole, and when he checked with his eye, he made eye contact with ▮▮▮▮▮▮▮.

▮▮▮▮▮▮▮▮▮ woke me up and told me the story.

"▮▮▮▮▮▮▮, I heard the same voices in my room." I said to him. "Let's check!" Our short investigation was successful: we found a tiny twin hole in my room.

"What should we do?" ▮▮▮▮▮▮▮ asked.

"We call the police," I said.

"Well, call them!" ▮▮▮▮▮▮▮ said. I purposely didn't use our telephone; instead, I went out and used a public phone, dialing 911. Two cops showed up, and I explained to them that our neighbor, without our consent, drilled two holes in our

---

* Again, the reference appears to be to Ahmed Ressam.

house, and we wanted him to be held for his illegal action toward us. Basically, we asked for a fair relief.

"Put some caulk inside the holes and the problem is solved," said one of the cops.

"Really? I didn't know that. Are you a carpenter?" I said. "Look! I didn't call you to give me advice on how to fix my house. There's an obvious crime behind this, trespassing and violation of our privacy. If you don't take care of us, we'll take care of ourselves. And by the way: I need you guys' business cards," I said. Each one silently produced a business card with the other cop's name and contact on the back of it. Obviously, those cops were following some idiot directions in order to deceive us, but for the Canadian Intel it was too late. For days to come we were just sitting and making fun of the plan.

The irony was that I lived in Germany for twelve years and they never provided any incriminating information about me, which was accurate. I stayed less than two months in Canada, and yet the Americans claimed that the Canadians provided tons of information about me. The Canadians don't even know me! But since all Intel work is based on what ifs, Mauritania and the U.S. started to interpret the information as they pleased, in order to confirm the theory that I was the mastermind of the Millennium Plot.

The interrogation didn't seem to develop in my favor. I kept repeating my Afghanistan Jihad story of 1991 and early 1992, which didn't seem to impress the Mauritanian interrogator. Mauritania doesn't give a damn about a trip to Afghanistan; they understand it very well. If you try to make trouble inside the country, however, you're going to be arrested, regardless of whether or not you've been in Afghanistan. On the other hand, to the American government a bare visit to Afghanistan, Bosnia, or Chechnya is worth watching you for the rest of your life and trying to lock you up. All the Arabic countries have the same approach as Mauritania, except the communist ones. I even think the communist Arab countries are at least fairer than the U.S. government in this regard, because they forbid their citizens to go to Jihad in the first place. Meanwhile, the U.S. government prosecutes people based on an unwritten law.

My Mauritanian interrogator was interested in my activities in Canada, which are non-existent in the criminal sense, but nobody was willing to believe me. All my answers to the question, "Have you done this or that while in Canada?" were, "No, No, No, No." And there we got completely stuck. I think I looked guilty because I didn't tell my whole story about Afghanistan, and I figured I had to fill that gap in order to make my case stronger. The interrogator had brought film equipment with him that day. As soon as I saw it, I started to shake: I knew that I would be made to confess and that they were going to broadcast me on the National TV, just like in October 1994, when the Mauritanian government arrested Islamists, made them confess, and broadcast their confessions.* I was so scared

---

* Throughout the manuscript, MOS refers several times to the political climate and events in Mauritania—in particular, to the close cooperation of President Maaouya Ould Sid'Ahmed Taya with the United States in the so-called War on Terror. Ould Taya came to power in a military coup in 1984 and became president in 1992. During his long tenure as head of state, Ould Taya carried out several waves of arrests of political opponents and Islamists like the one described here, in which more than ninety people, including a former government minister and ten religious leaders, were arrested and then amnestied after publicly confessing to membership in illegal organizations. A crackdown on Islamists in the army and education system led to a failed coup attempt in 2003, and Ould Taya was ultimately deposed in a successful coup in 2005. By that time, in part because of his support for U.S. antiterrorism polices, which included allowing the rendition of MOS, and his aggressive campaign against Islamists in Mauritania, Ould Taya had lost much of his public support. See http://www.nytimes .com/2005/08/08/international/africa/08mauritania.html?fta=y&_r=0; http://www.csmonitor.com/2005/0809/p07s02-woaf.html; and http://

my feet couldn't carry my body. You could tell there was a lot of pressure on my government.

"I've been very patient with you, boy," the interrogator said. "You got to admit, or I am going to pass you the special team." I knew he meant the torture team. "Reports keep coming every day from everywhere," he said. In the days before this talk I couldn't sleep. Doors kept getting opened and closed. Every move around me hit my heart so bad. My room was next to the archive, and through a small hole I could see some of the files and their labels; I started to hallucinate and read papers about me that didn't exist. I couldn't take anything anymore. And torture? No way.

"Look, Director! I have not been completely truthful with you, and I would like to share my whole story." I told him. "However, I don't want you to share the Afghanistan story with the U.S. government, because they don't understand this whole Jihad recipe, and I am not willing to put gas on the fire."

"Of course I won't," the DSE said. Interrogators are used to lying to people; the interrogator's whole job is about lying, outsmarting, and deception. "I can even send my recorder and my assistant away, if you'd like," he continued.

"No, I don't mind them around." The DSE called his driver and sent him to buy some food. He brought chicken salad, which I liked. It was my first meal since I left Senegal; it was now February 12, 2000.

"Is that all you're gonna eat?" wondered the DSE.

"Yes, I'm full."

"You don't really eat."

"That's the way I am." I started to recount my whole Jihad story in the most boring detail. "And as to Canada or an attack against the U.S., I have nothing to do with it," I finished. In the

www.ft.com/cms/s/0/23ab7cfc-0e0f-11da-aa67-00000e2511c8.html #axzz2vwtOwdNb.

days that followed I got, by far, better treatment and better food, and all the questions he asked me and all my answers were consistent in themselves and with the information he already knew from other sources. When the DSE knew that I was telling him the truth, he quit believing the U.S. reports to be the Gospel truth, and very much put them aside, if not in the garbage.

████████████████████████████ showed up to interrogate me. There were three of them, ██████████████████████████ ████████████████████████████. Evidently the Mauritanian authorities had shared all of my interviews with ████ ████████████, so that ████████ and the Mauritanians were at the same level of information.*

When the team arrived they were hosted at ████████████ ████████████████████████ gave me a forewarning the day they came to interrogate me.†

---

* Judging from MOS's 2005 ARB testimony, the date is around February 15, 2000, and these interrogators are likely Americans. MOS told the Administrative Review Board panel in 2005 that an American team consisting of two FBI agents and a third man from the Justice Department interrogated him over a two-day period near the end of his detention in Mauritania. His detention for questioning at the behest of the United States was widely reported in the local and international press; in a BBC report, Mauritanian officials confirmed that he was questioned by the FBI. ARB transcript, 17; http://news.google.com/newspapers?nid=1876&dat=20000 129&id=gzofAAAAIBAJ&sjid=5s8EAAAAIBAJ&pg=6848,4968256; http://news.bbc.co.uk/2/hi/africa/649672.stm.

† This might be the Presidential Palace. Elsewhere in the manuscript, MOS's American interrogators tout the United States' close relations with then-president Maaouya Ould Sid'Ahmed Taya, implying that they were hosted by the president and stayed at the Presidential Palace when they were carrying out investigations in the country. MOS manuscript, 130.

"Mohamedou, we have nothing on you. When it comes to us, you are a free man," he told me. "However, those people want to interrogate you. I'd like you to be strong, and to be honest with them."

"How can you allow foreigners to interrogate me?"

"It's not my decision, but it's just a formality," he said. I was very afraid, because I had never met American interrogators, though I anticipated that they would not use torture to coerce information. But the whole environmental setup made me very skeptical toward the honesty and humanity of the U.S. interrogators. It was kind of like, "We ain't gonna beat you ourselves, but you know where you are!" So I knew ▬▬▬▬▬ wanted to interrogate me under the pressure and threat of a non-democratic country.

The atmosphere was prepared. I was told what to wear and what to say. I never had the chance to take a shower or to wash my clothes, so I wore my some of my dirty clothes. I must have smelled terribly. I was so skinny from my confinement that my clothes didn't fit; I looked like a teenager in baggy pants. But as much as I was pissed, I tried to look as comfortable, friendly, and normal as I could.

▬▬▬▬▬▬▬▬▬▬▬▬▬▬▬▬ arrived around 8 p.m., and the interrogation room was cleaned for them. I entered the room smiling. After diplomatic greetings and introductions I sat down on a hard chair, trying to discover my new world.

The ▬▬▬▬▬▬▬▬ started to talk. "We have come from the States to ask you some questions. You have the right to remain calm. You may also answer some questions and leave others. Were we in the U.S., we would have provided you with a lawyer free of charge."

I almost interrupted his nonsense and said, 'Cut the crap, and ask me the questions!' I was like, 'What a civilized world!' In the room, there were only the ▆▆▆ interrogators with an Arabic interpreter. The Mauritanian interrogators stepped outside.

"Oh, thank you very much. I don't need any lawyer," I said.

"However, we would like you to answer our questions."

"Of course I will," I said. They started to ask me about my trip to Afghanistan during the war against communism, showed me a bunch of pictures, asked me questions about Canada, and hardly any questions about Germany. As to the pictures and Canada, I was completely truthful, but I deliberately withheld some parts of my two Afghanistan trips in January 1991 and February 1992. You know why? Because it is none of the U.S government's business what I had done to help my Afghani brothers against the communists. For Pete's sake, the U.S. was supposedly on our side! When that war was done I resumed my regular life; I hadn't broken any Mauritanian or German laws. I legally went to Afghanistan and came back. As for the U.S., I am not a U.S. citizen, nor have I been in the U.S. — so what law have I possibly broken? I understand that if I enter the U.S. and they arrest me for a reasonable suspicion, then I completely have to explain to them my position. And Canada? Well, they made a big deal out of me being in Canada, because some Arab guy had tried to attack them from Canada. I explained with definite evidence that I was not a part of it. Now F*ck off and leave me alone.

The ▆▆▆ interrogators told me that I wasn't truthful.

"No, I was," I lied. The good thing was that I didn't give a damn about what they thought. ▆▆▆▆▆▆ kept writing my answers and looking at me at the same time. I wondered, how could he do both? But later I learned that ▆▆▆ interrogators study your body language while you're speaking, which is nothing but bullshit.* There are many factors involved in an interrogation, and they differ from one culture to another. Since ▆▆▆▆▆▆▆▆▆▆▆▆ knows my entire case now, I suggest that ▆▆▆▆▆▆▆▆▆ should go back and check where he marked me as lying, just to check his competence. The U.S. interrogators also went outside their assignment and did what any interrogator would have done: they fished, asking me about Sudan, Nairobi, and Dar Es Salaam. How am I supposed to know about those countries, unless I have multiple doppelgängers?

▆▆▆▆▆▆▆▆▆▆▆▆▆▆ offered to have me work with them. I think the offer was futile unless they were dead sure that I was a criminal. I'm not a cop, but I understand how criminals can repent—but I personally had done nothing to repent for. The next day, about the same time, ▆▆▆▆▆▆▆▆▆▆▆▆ showed up once more, trying to get at least the same amount of information I had shared with the Mauritanians, but there was no persuading me. After all the Mauritanian authorities duly shared everything with them. The ▆▆▆▆▆▆▆▆▆▆▆ didn't push me in any uncivilized way; they acted rather friendly. The chief of the team said, "We're done. We're going back home," exactly like Umm 'Amr and her donkey.† ▆▆▆▆▆▆▆▆▆

---

* Because MOS's ARB testimony suggests this interrogation was led by the FBI, he may be referring here to the FBI in general and to one agent in particular. ARB transcript, 17. The FBI does list body language among possible deception clues in material posted on its website, and former FBI agents have written and spoken publicly on the subject. See, e.g., http://www.fbi.gov/stats-services/publications/law-enforcement-bulletin/june_2011/school_violence; and http://cjonline.com/news/local/2010-11-26/no_lie_ex_fbi_agent_spots_fibbers.

† The reference is to a pre-Islamic proverb about a cursed woman who is expelled from her tribe; the sense is of an unwanted person who goes away and is not seen again.

██████████ left Nouakchott, and I was released ██████████
██████.*

"Those guys have no evidence whatsoever," the DSE said sadly. He felt completely misused. The Mauritanians didn't want me delivered to them in the first place, because it was a no-win situation: if they found me guilty and they delivered me to the U.S., they were going to feel the wrath of the public; if not, they would feel the wrath of the U.S. government. In either case, the President was going to lose his office.

So in the end, something like this must of happened under the table:

"We found nothing on him, and you guys didn't provide us any evidence," the Senegalese must have said. "Under these circumstances, we can't hold him. But if you want him, take him."

"No, we can't take him, because we've got to get evidence on him first," answered the U.S. government.

"Well, we don't want to have anything to do with him," said the Senegalese.

"Turn him over the Mauritanians," the U.S. government suggested.

"No, we don't want him, just take him!" cried the Mauritanian government.

"You got to," said the U.S. government, giving the Mauritanians no choice. But the Mauritanian government always prefers keeping peace between the people and the government. They don't want any trouble.

"You are free to go," said the DSE.

"Should I give him everything?"

"Yes, everything," the DSE answered. He even asked me to

---

* The *New York Times* reported that MOS was released from Mauritanian custody on February 19, 2000. http://www.nytimes.com/2000/02/21 /world/terrorist-suspect-is-released-by-mauritania.html.

double-check on my belongings, but I was so excited I didn't check on anything. I felt as if the ghoul of fear had flown from my chest.

"Thank you very much," I said. The DSE ordered his assistant and recorder to drive me home. It was about 2 p.m. when we took off toward my home.

"You'd better not talk with journalists," said the inspector.

"No, I won't." And indeed, I never disclosed the scandal of foreign interrogators violating the sovereignty of my country to journalists. I felt so bad about lying to them.

"Come on, we have seen the ███████████████████ ████████████* God, those journalists are wizards.

"Maybe they were listening to my interrogation," I said unconvincingly.

I tried to recognize the way to my home, but believe me, I didn't recognize anything until the police car parked in front of our house and dropped me there. It had been almost seven years since I saw my family last.† Everything had changed. Children had become men and women, young people had become older. My strong mom had become weak. Nonetheless everybody was happy. My sister ████████████ and my former wife had hardly slept nights, praying to God to relieve my pains and sufferings. May God reward everybody who stood on my side.

Everybody was around, my aunt, the in-laws, friends. My family kept generously feeding the visitors, some of whom came just to congratulate me, some to interview me, some just to get

---

* MOS appears to be quoting a conversation with a particular journalist after his release.

† MOS left Mauritania in 1988 to study in Germany. He testified at his 2004 CSRT hearing that he visited his family in Mauritania for two or three weeks in 1993. CSRT transcript, 5.

to know the man who had made news for the last month. After the first few days, my family and I were making plans for my future. To make a long story short, my family wanted me to stay in the country, if only to see me every day and enjoy my company. I said to myself, Screw it, went out, found a job, and was enjoying looking into the pretty face of my mom every morning. But no joy is forever.

THREE

Mauritania

September 29, 2001–November 28, 2001

A Wedding and a Party...I Turn Myself In...Release
from Custody...The Camel Rests in Two Steps...The
Secret Police Show Up at My House... "Independence
Day"...A Flight to Jordan

It was a very busy day:* for one, I was involved in organizing the wedding of my lovely niece ██████████████,
and for two, I was invited to attend a big dinner organized
by a very important man in my tribe named ████████
██████████████. This man had unluckily been involved in a
terrible car accident, and had recently come back after spending some time in the U.S. for medical treatment. ████████
██████████████ enjoys a high respect among the people
from the South, and the dinner was to aid what we call The
Cadres of Trarza.†

In the morning I asked my boss to give me some money to

---

* The date, according to MOS's 2005 ARB testimony, is Saturday,
September 29, 2001. ARB transcript, 18.

† Trarza is the region of southern Mauritania that extends from the
Senegalese border north to the capital. It was also the name of a precolonial
emirate in the same region. The Cadres of Trarza appears to be a community organization.

help my sister with the wedding.* In Mauritania we have the bad habit of organizing everything on the whim, a heritage of rural life that all Mauritanians still deal with today. My job was to help transport the invited guests to the site where the wedding was taking place.

Weddings in the Islamic, Arabic World are not only different from one country to another, but within the same country there are all kinds of different customs. My niece's wedding followed the customs that are practiced by average prestigious families in southern Mauritania.

Most of the work is usually done by the guy. He investigates the would-be wife's background by unleashing the female relatives he trusts the most. The report of this "committee" will produce an assessment of the technical data of the girl, her attitude, her intellect, and the like; sometimes this investigation step can be skipped when the girl already has a good reputation.

The next step is dating, though that is different than the American model. The interested guy dates his would-be wife in her family's house, usually in the presence of other family

---

* MOS testified at his 2004 CSRT and 2005 ARB hearings that when he returned to Mauritania in 2000 he worked as an electronics and computer specialist, first for a medical equipment supply company and then, starting in July 2001, for a company named Aman Pêche in Nouakchott. "This is a French word for fish," he explained at his CSRT hearing. "This company was a company of people from my tribe, and they gave me more money to join them. They wanted to develop the business and to use me; I was just setting up at my office, because they didn't know what to do with me at first. They had many electronic devices they wanted me to take care of. I had just set up my office and installed the AC, and September 11th happened. Then America went crazy looking for leads; and I was the cousin of the right hand of Osama bin Laden, and oh, get him." CSRT transcript, 8; ARB transcript, 18.

members. The goal of these dates is for both to get to know each other. The dating can take between a couple of months and a couple of years, depending on the man and the girl. Some girls don't want to start a family before graduating from school, and some do — or let's say family pressure and the man compel her to start the family right away. On the other hand, most guys aren't ready for marriage; they just want to "reserve" the girl and go about their business until they are financially ready. The groom is usually older than the bride, sometimes even much older, but in a few cases the bride happens to be older, and sometimes much older. Mauritanians are relatively tolerant when it comes to age differences.

Before the guy officially asks for the hand of the girl, he secretly sends a good friend to the girl to ask her whether she might consider him. When that is established, the decisive step comes next: the guy asks the girl's mom whether she would accept him as the husband of her daughter. Guys only ask for the hand of a girl if they know they will more than likely be accepted, so sometimes the guy sends a trusted third person in order to avoid the embarrassment of being turned down. Only the mother of the girl can decide; most fathers have little say.

This step, though not official, is binding for both. Everybody now knows that ▆▆▆▆▆ is engaged to ▆▆▆▆▆▆▆. Premarital sex is not tolerated in Mauritania, and not only for religious reasons: many guys mistrust any girl who accepts having sex with them. They assume, If she accepts having sex with me, she would accept another man, and another man, in an endless sexual adventure. Although the Islamic religion treats males and females the same way in this regard, the society tends to accept premarital sex from men much more than women. You can compare it with cheating in the U.S.: the society tolerates it more if a man cheats than if a women does. I never met an American man who would forgive cheating, but I did meet many American women who would.

There is no party or engagement ring, but the fiancé is now entitled to give his wife-to-be presents. Before the engagement, a lady would not accept presents from a stranger.

The last step is the actual wedding, the date of which is set by agreement of both; each party can take as much as time as he or she needs, as long as it is reasonable. The man is expected to produce a dowry as a necessary formality, but it is not appropriate for the girl's family to ask for any sum; the whole thing must be left to the man and his financial possibilities. So dowries vary from a very modest to a relatively sinfully high amount. Once the man produces whatever his possibilities and judgment allow, many families will only take a small, symbolic amount and send the rest to the man's family, at least half of the dowry.

The wedding party traditionally takes place in the girl's family house, but lately some people have found a lucrative business in professionally organizing weddings in club-like houses. The Party begins with the *Akd*, the marriage agreement, which can be performed by any Imam or respected Sheikh. Mauritanians don't believe in governmental formalities, and so hardly anybody declares his marriage at a government institution unless it is for financial advantages, which rarely exist.

The wedding party equally drains both the groom's and bride's family. Traditionally, Mauritanians would party for seven full days, but the punishments of modern life cut those seven days back to one single night. Only the friends of the groom from his generation are allowed to attend the wedding, unlike women, who can be all different ages. At the party women don't mingle directly with men, though they can be in the same hall; each sex respects the spot of the other. However,

all the attendants talk to each other and enjoy the same entertainment that takes place in the middle of the hall, such as
sketches, music, and poetry. When I was a child, women and
men used to pass coded messages back and forth targeting a
particular individual who certainly understood the message; the
messages usually unfolded a funny situation that could happen
to anybody and that is somewhat embarrassing. The person's
friends would laugh at him or her, and he or she would have to
fight back targeting the anonymous person who sent the message. People don't do this teasing entertainment anymore.

During the wedding food and drinks are generously served.
The party traditionally closes with what they call the *Taweez-
Pillage*, which doesn't have anything with the literal meaning of
the words. It just describes the plot by the women to kidnap
the bride, and the brothers' efforts to prevent the act. The bride's
female friends are allowed to conspire and kidnap the bride and
hide her; it is the job of the groom and his friends to prevent
this event, and should the men fail in preventing the abduction,
it is their duty to find the bride and deliver her to her husband.
The bride must cooperate with her female friends, and she usually does, otherwise she'll be branded with all kinds of bad
adjectives. It sometimes takes many days for the males to find
the bride.

When the man succeeds in getting the bride the party is over,
and the bride is given to the groom. Both get escorted by their
closest friends in a long rally leading to the house of the new
family, while the rest of the attendants retreat to their own
homes.

The wedding of my beloved niece ███████████ would
have gone more or less like this. I wasn't supposed to attend the
party because I was way older than the groom, and in any case
I didn't have time. I had another interesting party waiting on

me. When I finished delivering the guests I checked with my mom on the situation. Everything seemed to be alright; my services no longer were required as far as I could see. The atmosphere of wedding was clearly going to take over.

When I got to the party, which was in the beautiful villa of ███████████████ in Tevrlegh Zeina, the warmth of companionship hit me gracefully. I didn't know the majority of the guests, but I spotted my beloved ████████████████████ ████████████████ drowned in the middle of the crowd. I right away fought through the crowd and sat beside ████████████.

He was happy to see me, and introduced me to the most remarkable guest. We retreated to the margin of the party with a few of his friends, and ██████████████████ introduced me to a friend of his, a young ████████████. The ████████████ asked ████████████████ and me whether he could defend ████████████████, who now was wanted by the U.S. authorities with a $25,000,000 reward.*

"What are you going to do for him? Reduce his sentence from 500 to 400 years?" I asked wryly. People in the other parts of the free world like Europe have problems understanding the draconian punishments in the U.S. Mauritania is not a country of law, so we don't have a problem understanding whatever the government does; even so, the Mauritanian legal code, when it is followed, is much more humane than the American. Why sentence somebody to 300 years when he is not going to live that long?

We were just talking like that, and enjoying the food that was generously served, when my cell phone rang. I pulled it out

---

* The conversation appears to center on Abu Hafs, who in the wake of the 9/11 attacks was now the subject of a $25 million bounty (see footnote on p. 94).

of my pocket and stepped aside. The display read the phone number of the DSE, the Directeur de la Sûrete de l'État.

"Hi," I answered.

"Mohamedou, where are you?" he said.

"Don't worry! Where are you?"

"I'm outside of my front door! I'd like to see you."

"Fine. Just hold on, I'm on my way!" I said. I took ████ ███████████████████████ aside.

"Look, ███████████████ called me, and I'm going to see him."

"As soon as he releases you, give me a buzz."

"Alright," I said.

The DSE was waiting in front of his house, but he was not alone: his assistant stood beside him, which was not a good sign.

"Salam Alaikum," I said, stepping outside my car.

"Waalaikum Assalam. You're gonna ride with me, and somebody else is going to drive your car."

"Fine." The Inspector and I rode with the DSE and headed toward the secret, well-known jail.

"Look, those people told us to arrest you."

"Why?"

"I don't know, but I hope you'll be free soon. This whole 9/11 attack thing is screwing up everybody." I didn't say a thing. I just let him and his assistant make small talk, to which I paid no attention. The DSE had already called and interrogated me twice in the two and a half weeks since the 9/11 attack, but obviously the American government was not satisfied with a yard; they wanted a mile at first, and then the whole Autobahn, as it turned out in the end.

They put me in the same room I had been in one and half years ago. The Inspector went out to brief the guards, which gave me the opportunity to give a quick call to ████████ ████████████████.

"I'm arrested," I whispered, and hung up without even waiting on his answer. Then I erased my whole phone book. Not that I had any hot numbers—all I had were some numbers of business partners in Mauritania and Germany—but I didn't want the U.S. government harassing those peaceful people just because I had their numbers in my phone. The funniest record I deleted read "PC Laden," which means computer store; the word for "store" in German just happens to be "Laden." I knew no matter how hard I would have tried to explain that, the U.S. interrogators would not have believed me. For Pete's sake, they always tried to pin things on me that I had nothing to do with!

"Give me your cell phone," the Inspector said when he returned. Among the belongings the Americans took back home with them later was that old, funny looking cell phone, but there were no numbers to check. As to my arrest, it was sort of like political drug-dealing: the FBI asked the U.S. President to intervene and have me arrested; in turn George W. Bush asked the vanishing Mauritanian President for a favor; on receiving the U.S. president's request, his Mauritanian colleague moved his police forces to arrest me.

"I really have no questions for you, because I know your case," the DSE said. Both the DSE and his assistant left, leaving me with the guards and oodles of mosquitoes.

After several days in the prison, the DSE came to my cell.

"Look! Those people want to know about ███████████ ███████████, and they said you were a part of the Millennium Plot."

"Well, ███████████████████████ are my friends in Germany, and as to the Millennium Plot, I had nothing to do with it."

"I'll give you a pen and paper, and you write whatever you know."

*　　*　　*

After two weeks of incarceration in the Mauritanian prison, two white U.S. interrogators ▇▇▇▇▇▇▇▇▇▇▇▇▇▇▇▇▇▇▇▇ ▇▇▇▇▇▇▇▇ came to the jail late one afternoon to interrogate me.*

Before ▇▇▇▇▇▇▇▇▇▇▇▇▇▇▇▇▇▇▇▇▇▇▇▇▇▇▇ met me, they asked the police to storm my house and office and confiscate anything that could give leads to my "criminal" activities. A special security team took me home, searched my house, and seized everything they thought might be relevant for the Americans. When the team arrived my wife was asleep, and they scared the hell out of her: she had never seen police searching somebody's house. Neither had I, for that matter, but I had no problem with the search except that it bothered my family. My neighbors didn't care much, first because they know me, and second because they know that the Mauritanian police are unjust. In a separate operation, another team searched the company where I worked. As it turned out, the Americans were not interested in any of the garbage except my work computer and the cellphone.

When I entered the interrogation room, the two Americans were sitting on the leather sofa, looking extremely angry. They must have been FBI, because the stuff they confiscated ended up on FBI's hands back in the States.

"Hi," I said, reaching out my hand. But both my hand and my "Hi" remained hanging in the air. ▇▇▇▇▇▇▇ seemed to be the leader. He pushed an old metal chair toward me.

"Do you see the picture on the wall?" ▇▇▇▇▇▇▇ said, pointing

---

* In his 2005 ARB testimony, MOS dates this interrogation as October 13, 2001, and speculates that these two interrogators are FBI, though "they are American, they may be anything." Accompanying the lead interrogator is an interrogator who "spoke German adequately but not very good," and "with a bad accent," who interprets during the interview. ARB transcript, 18.

at the President's picture, with ███████████ translating into German.

"Yes," I answered.

"Your president promised our president that you are going to cooperate with us," ████████ said. I thought, How cheap! I personally don't give a damn about either president; to me both are unjust and evil.

"Oh, yes! I surely will," I said, reaching for a drink on a table filled with all kinds of drinks and sweets. ████████ jerked the drink out of my hand.

"We are not here for a party," he said. "Look, I am here to find the truth about you. I'm not here to detain you."

"OK! You ask and I'll answer."

In the midst of this discourse, the tea guy surged into the room, trying to accommodate his angry guests. "Fuck off!" said ████████. ████████████████ very disrespectful toward poor people, an idiot, and a racist who had one of the lowest self-esteems in the world. For my part, I ignored all the curses he addressed me with and just stayed cool, though very thirsty, because the session lasted the whole night.

"Before 9/11 you called your younger brother in Germany and told him, 'Concentrate on your school.' What did you mean with this code?"

"I didn't use any code. I always advise my brother to concentrate on his school."

"Why did you call a satellite company in the U.S.?"

"Because we have our Internet connection from the U.S., and I needed support."

"Why did you call this hotel in Germany?"

"My boss asked me to make a reservation for one of his cousins."

"How many computers do you have?"

"Only my work computer."

"You're lying! You have a laptop."

"That's my ex-wife's."

"Where is your ex-wife living?"

"The DSE knows."

"OK, let's check this lie out." ▇▇▇▇ disappeared for several minutes, asking the DSE to search my ex-wife's house and seize the laptop.

"What if you're lying?"

"I am not."

"But what if?"

"I'm not."

Of course he threatened me with all kinds of painful torture should it turn out I was lying. "You know we have some black motherfuckers who have no mercy on terrorists like you," he said, and as he proceeded, racial references kept flying out of his mouth. "I myself hate the Jews..."—I didn't comment—"...But you guys come and hit our building with planes," he continued.

"That's between you and the people who did it. You must resolve your problem with them; I have nothing to do with it."

Every once in a while ▇▇▇▇ received a call, obviously from a lady. During that time the other German-speaking idiot came up with the most stupid questions.

"Check this out. This is a German newspaper writing about you guys," he said. I scanned a newspaper article about the extremist presence in Germany.

"Well, ▇▇▇▇▇▇ that's none of my problem. As you can see, I'm in Mauritania."

"Where is ███████████? Where is Noumane?" ████████ asked angrily.*

"I am not in Afghanistan, I'm in Mauritania—in prison. How can I possible know their whereabouts?"

"You're hiding him," he said. I was going to say, "Check up my sleeves," but I realized my situation didn't allow it.

"███████████████████████ said that he knew you!"

"I don't know ██████████████████████. There is nothing to change about that fact." In the meantime, the DSE and his assistant came back with my ex-wife's laptop. They weren't allowed into the interrogation room; they knocked at the door and ████████████ stepped outside. I looked with the side of my eyes and recognized the laptop bag. I was happy that they found the "big secret."

████████ returned. "What if I told you that they didn't find the laptop," he said, trying to be smarter than he is.

"All I can tell you is that I have no laptop," I said, letting him believe that I hadn't seen the case. He didn't ask anymore about the laptop after that. They mirrored all the hard disks and took them home, just to waste four years popping their eyes out of their heads looking for non-existent treasure. Tough luck!

"We have invaded Afghanistan and are killing everybody. Do you think that's OK?" ████████ asked.

"You know best what you're doing," I said.

---

* The "Noumane" in the interrogator's question may refer to Noumane Ould Ahmed Ould Boullahy, whose name appears in a footnote to Judge James Robertson's opinion granting MOS's habeas corpus petition. The footnote reads, "The government asserts that Salahi swore the oath to Osama bin Laden, and did so at the same time as Noumane Ould Ahmed Ould Boullahy, who went on to become one of bin Laden's bodyguards. There is no evidence that Salahi maintained, or that he ever had, any relationship with Boullahy." The opinion is available at https://www.aclu.org/files/assets/2010-4-9-Slahi-Order.pdf.

"Do you know Houari?"*

"No!"

"The Canadians said that they saw him with you. Either I am lying to you or they lied to me—or you're lying."

"I don't know him, but in the mosque, and in the café beneath it, I was always around many people I don't know."

"Why do you think we picked you up out of more than two million Mauritanians?"

"I don't know why. All I know is I haven't done anything against you."

"Write your name in Arabic." I wrote my name. For some reason, he kept taking pictures during the session. He really confused the hell out of me.

"Why did you call the UAE?"

"I didn't."

"So you think I am lying to you?"

"No, but I don't remember calling the UAE." As it turned out he did lie, but maybe unintentionally. I didn't call the UAE, but I did receive a call from a female friend of mine, ███████ ████████████, who tried desperately to bring me and my ex-wife back together. I couldn't remember this during the session, I was so nervous. But when I was released, my family helped me remember, so I went to the police on my own and explained the call to them, and another call my ███████ ████████████████████████ made to France to contact his medicine supplier in Paris. In real life, if I give my phone to somebody I trust, I don't ask him about the details of his call. But if you get arrested, you have to lay out your whole life, and something like "I don't remember" doesn't work.

During the session, ██████████████ called my family and me

---

* This name is written "Houari" in the manuscript. The interrogator may be referring to convicted Millennium Plot co-conspirator Mokhtar Hauoari.

all kind of names, and forbade me to drink from the goods that my people paid for—it was, after all, our taxes that made the U.S. guests comfortable. At the end of the session, when I was about to dehydrate, ███████████ hit me in the face with 1.5-liter water bottle and left the room. I didn't even feel the pain from a blow that almost broke my nose because of the relief of ███████████████████ leaving. ████████████ ████████████ didn't write anything, which struck me as strange because interrogators always want to write, but I believe that they recorded the session. ██████████ tried his best to repeat the curses that █████████ was generously producing. I think that █████████ was worthless to Mr. ███████; he just brought him along as a translator.

The Americans left ████████████, and the next day, the Mauritanian government released me without any charges. Furthermore, the DSE went to the Media Center and informed them that I was innocent and acquitted of every charge. The DSE's boss, the Directeur Général de la Sûreté Nationale,* offered me a loan in case I had any problems getting back to my job, and at the same time, the DSE called the President and Director General of my company and assured him that I am innocent and must resume my work.†

"We never doubted him for a second. He is welcome any time," my former boss answered. Still, the government was ordered by the U.S. to keep me under house arrest with no reason besides injustice and the misuse of power. I wasn't wor-

---

* Directeur Général de la Direction Générale de la Sûreté Nationale is abbreviated here and a few pages later in the manuscript as DG and spelled out in a footnote the second time. The Sûreté Nationale is the Mauritanian national police force; its director general is the country's top law enforcement official.

† In the manuscript, this is abbreviated PDG, short for the French title *président-directeur général*, the equivalent of president and CEO.

ried about getting a job after jail because I knew that Mauritanians were growing tired of Americans jumping on innocent people all around the world and trying to incriminate them. In fact, I got more job opportunities than I ever had in my life. My only worry was for my sister ███████████, who was suffering from depression and anxiety. My family of course was very happy to have me back, and so were my friends and relatives who kept coming to greet me and wish me good luck.

But the camel, as they say, rests in two steps.

Legend has it that an urban dweller rode a camel with a Bedouin. The Bedouin sat in front of the hump, and the urban dweller behind it so he could steady himself by grabbing the Bedouin. When they arrived home, the camel bent his front legs to come to rest, and the Bedouin, caught off guard, lost his equilibrium and fell to the ground. The urban dweller couldn't help laughing at the Bedouin.

The Bedouin looked at his friend and said, "Too soon to be happy: the camel rests in two steps." And indeed, as soon as the camel bent his rear legs to come to his final rest, the urban dweller fell on his face.

As far as I can remember, I never fell off a camel; however, as soon as I resumed my life, the U.S. government started conspiring with the Mauritanian government to kidnap me.

It was around 4 p.m. when I got back from work about a month later. It had been a long day, hot, and humid: one of those days. The Islamic calendar read Ramadan 4th, and so far everybody in the family was fasting except for the kids.*

---

* Ramadan 4th was Tuesday, November 20, in 2001.

It had been a remarkable workday. My company sent me to assess a relatively big project for our small company: we had been asked to give an estimate to network the Presidential Palace for both computers and telephones. I had made an appointment with the project coordinator for early that morning, and waiting outside his office was the order of the first half of the day. There are two things all government officials have in common: they don't respect appointments, and they never start work on time.

During Ramadan, most people party nights and sleep days. I hadn't partied last night, but I had stayed up late for another reason: namely I had a little familial fight with my beloved wife. I hate fights, and so I was depressed and couldn't sleep the whole night. As drowsy and sleepy I was, I still managed to be on the site of my rendezvous, though not punctually, with time enough to beat the coordinator by hours. His office was closed, and there was no free chair in the corridor, and so I had to put up with squatting on the floor with my back to the wall. I fell asleep many times.

Around noon ▉▉▉▉▉▉▉▉▉▉▉▉▉ showed up and took me to the Presidential Palace. I thought there would be a lot of formalities, especially for a "terrorist suspect" such as myself, but nothing like that happened. You had to give your name the day before, and when I showed the guards my ID they verified the visitors' list, where my name appeared with the appropriate clearance. I was shocked. But after all, only the Americans suspect me of terrorism, no other country. The irony is that I have never been in the States, and all the other countries I have been in kept saying, "The guy is alright."

As soon as I entered the sanctuary of the palace, I felt as if I were in another country. There was a garden inside with all kinds of flowers. Water fountains created a light drizzle. The weather was just cool and fine.

We went right to business. I went through many rooms on different floors and took some measurements, but we were stopped and advised to leave the actual palace because there was an official visit. We could stay inside the compound, and so I used that time and went to the palace's central telephone exchange to check on the infrastructure. The ███████████ ████████████████████████ and as friendly as most people from Atar. He was more of a security choice; the president trusts his own people most, which makes perfect sense. I felt depressed because the whole project needed much more work than what it said in the papers, and I needed help, professional help. I didn't want to mess around with the Presidential Palace. I would rather retreat completely than start selling them made-in-Timbuktu hi-tech equipment.

The ████████████████████ showed us the things we needed to see and disappeared to his guests. It was late, and the project coordinator asked for another appointment to finish the measurement work and the assessment of the needed infrastructure. ███████████████████ and I left with the intention of coming back tomorrow and finishing the work. By the time we left the gate, I was already tired, and like, Get me the hell outta here. I made a call to my boss and briefed him, and I even went to the office after that and told my colleagues what happened.

On the way home, ████████████████████████████ called me to make sure that I would be at dinner in his house. ██████ ██████████ is a ████████████████████████████ ██ ██████████. Besides, ████████████████ is an old friend of the family; I knew him and played cards with him when I was a child. Today ████████████████ was organizing a big dinner for his friends, including my brother, who was on vacation with us from Germany, and me. Right when ████████████ called, my car had a breakdown. I hated it when my As-Old-As-My-Grandpa car did that.

"Do you need me to come to you?" ██████████████ asked.

"No, I can see a garage not far from me. I'm sure they'll help me."

"Don't forget our Dinner Party, and remind ███████ ████████████!" he said.

A mechanic from the garage found that the benzene pipe to the carburetor was broken, and fixed it. In Mauritania people fix everything; in Germany, people replace everything. The mechanic wanted me to pay him more than I thought he ought to be paid, and so I did the thing I hate the most, negotiation, and paid him the amount we agreed on. One thing I like about Germany is that you don't need to negotiate; everything is labeled with a price. You could be mute and nonetheless be treated justly. The thing about negotiation is that most of the time somebody is going to be disadvantaged. Personally, I just want a fair price for both parties that makes each party happy.

When I arrived at my mom's home around 4 p.m., only my ████████████████ and my sister ██████████████ were there, and both were asleep.* My mom had gone outside to gather her scattered sheep; it was feeding time. I went inside the house and put on my bathrobe. On my way to the shower, my mom and two secret police guys surged almost simultaneously into the house.

"Salahi, the Director General wants to see you!"

"Why?"

---

* It becomes clear in a few paragraphs that the first family member mentioned here is an aunt.

"We don't know," said one of the guys.

"OK. I'm going to take a shower and change my clothes."

"OK!" said the guy, stepping out. "We're gonna wait on you outside." The secret police respected me highly since I turned myself in a couple of weeks ago; they knew I am not a person who flees. I had basically been under house arrest since 2000 but I could have fled the country anytime; I didn't, and didn't have any reason to. I took my shower and changed. In the meantime my aunt woke up because of the noise. My sister didn't wake up, as far as I remember, and that was good, because I was only worried about her and the extreme depression she had been suffering.

"I think the police called you because you bought a new TV, and they don't want you to watch TV. Don't you think?" said my mom innocently.

I smiled and said, "I don't think so, but everything is going to be alright." My mom was referring to the new satellite antenna I installed the night before to have better TV reception. The irony is that the ▆▆▆▆▆▆▆▆▆▆▆▆▆▆▆▆▆▆ was the one who helped me install the antenna.* When I was in prison the month before, he had asked me to find a job for him because the police paid him miserably. I promised him I would, and in the meantime, I wanted to offer him an opportunity to do some work for me, so I called him to help fix my antenna, and paid him adequately. That was the only way for a man like him to survive. I helped him get some work, and we were sipping tea and joking in my house.

"I didn't bring you to my house to arrest me," I said jokingly.

---

* That is, it appears that one of the officers who has been dispatched to bring MOS in for questioning was in MOS's home to help him install the satellite antenna the previous evening.

"I hope you will never be arrested," ███████████████████
said.

My mom's house is next to my brother's, with a short wall that separates them. I could simply have jumped to my brother's house, and escaped through his door that opens to a completely other street, and guess what? There would be no finding me, not only because so many people would shelter me, but also because the police agents would not have been interested in finding me. I even believe that the government would have been much happier saying to the U.S., "He fled, we couldn't find him."

You should know, Dear Reader, that a country turning over its own citizens is not an easy deal. The President wished he hadn't had to turn me over. I wonder why? After all it cost him his office afterward. I understand that if the U.S. captures me in Afghanistan and takes me to GTMO for whatever reason, my government cannot be blamed because I chose to go to Afghanistan. But kidnapping me from my house in my country and giving me to the U.S., breaking the constitution of Mauritania and the customary International Laws and treaties, that is not OK. Mauritania should have asked the U.S. to provide evidence that incriminates me, which they couldn't, because they had none. But even if the U.S. did so, Mauritania should try me according to the criminal code in Mauritania, exactly as Germany does with its citizens who are suspected of being involved in 9/11. On the other hand, if the U.S. says "We have no evidence," then the Mauritanian response should be something like, "Fu*k you!" But no, things don't work this way. Don't get me wrong, though: I don't blame the U.S. as much as I do my own government.

The secret police agents obviously wanted me to flee, especially ████████████████. But I wanted to keep it real—not to mention that the government itself assured my family that I had done nothing, and so my family always wanted me to go to the police whenever they asked to see me. The funny thing about "Secret Police" in Arab countries is that they are more known to the commoners than the regular police forces. I think the authorities in Arabic countries should think about a new nomenclature, something like "The Most Obvious Police."

There were four of them when I stepped outside the door with my mom and my aunt. My mom kept her composure, and started to pray using her fingers. As to my aunt, that was her first time seeing somebody taken by the police, and so she got crippled and couldn't say a word. She started to sweat heavily and mumbled some prayers. Both kept their eyes staring at me. It is the taste of helplessness, when you see your beloved fading away like a dream and you cannot help him. And same for me: I would watch both my mom and my aunt praying in my rearview mirror until we took the first turn and I saw my beloved ones disappear.

"Take your car, we hope you can come back home today," one of the guys had instructed me. "The DG might just ask you some questions." ▬▬▬▬▬▬▬▬ occupied my passenger seat, as sad as he could be.

"Salahi, I wish I were not part of this shit," he said. I didn't respond. I kept following the police car that was heading toward the secret, well-known jail. I had been incarcerated a couple times in the same illegal prison, and knowing it didn't make me like it. I hated the compound, I hated the dark, dirty room, I hated the filthy bathroom, and I hated everything about it, especially the constant state of terror and fear.

"Earlier today the Inspector was looking for you. You know the DSE is on a trip in Spain. The Inspector asked us who has your phone number. But I didn't say anything, even though I have it," ██████████████, trying to make himself feel better. The only other guy who had my phone number was the DSE, and obviously he didn't give it to anybody.

So here we are, at the gate of the resented prison. The ████████████ was in his office, looking at me with his dishonest smile, which he quickly changed into a frown.*

"We didn't have your phone number. The director is on a trip. He's coming in three days, and meanwhile we are going to hold you in contempt."

"Why? I'm really growing tired of being arrested for no reason. What do you want from me now? You've just released me," I said, frustrated and angry, especially since the guy who knows my case was not in the country.

"Why are you so scared? I never knew you like that," the ████████████ said.

"Look, you arrested me after 9/11, and the U.S. interrogators came here and interrogated me. After that you, when you realized that I'm innocent, you released me. I sort of understand the mass arrest after 9/11, but this arrest right now is not OK."

"Everything is gonna be alright. Give me your cell phone," the Inspector lied, smiling his usual forced smile. ████████████ had about as much clue as I did about the goal of my arrest because the government wouldn't have shared anything with him. I don't think that the Mauritanian government had reached a resolution on my case; the main guy ████████████ ████████████ was on a trip, and without him a decision could hardly be made. What the ████████████ and I both knew back then was that the U.S. asked Mauritania's then-president

---

* This person could be the "Inspector" referred to several times elsewhere in this scene.

to hold me; the Mauritanian president asked his Directeur Général de la Sûreté Nationale — who is now the president — to arrest me; and he in his turn ordered his people, led by the Inspector, to hold me in contempt.*

However, I think that the U.S. wasn't making a secret of its wish, namely to have me in Jordan, and so at the point of my arrest ████████████████████ two people knew the plan: the Mauritanian president and his DG. But since the U.S. was asking so much from its ally, the Mauritanian government needed some time to digest and confer. Turning me over to Jordan involved some serious things. The Mauritanian constitution would have to be broken. The Mauritanian President was hanging onto his office by a spider's thread, and any trouble would shake him heavily. The U.S. hadn't asked the Mauritanians to turn me over to them, which would make more sense; no, they wanted me in Jordan, and that was a big disrespect to the sovereignty of Mauritania. The Mauritanian government had been asking for evidence, any evidence, and the U.S. has failed to provide anything, and so arresting me in itself was burdensome for the government, let alone sending me to Jordan. The Mauritanian government sought incriminating evidences from the countries I had been in, Germany and Canada, and both countries provided only good conduct reports. For these and other reasons, the Mauritanian President needed his trusted guy, the DSE, before he took such a dangerous step.

I handed my cell phone to the Inspector, and he ordered the

---

* Mauritania's Directeur Général de la Sûreté Nationale in 2001 was Ely Ould Mohamed Vall. Vall, who served as director of the national police under President Maaouya Sid'Ahmed Ould Taya, seized power himself in a bloodless coup when Ould Taya was out of the country on August 3, 2005.

guards to take care of me and left. So I had to party with the guards instead of ▇▇▇▇▇▇▇▇▇▇ and the rest of my cousins.

In Mauritania, the guards of secret detainees are part of the Secret Police, and as much as they might sympathize with you, they would do anything they were ordered to, even if it involved taking your life. Such people are resented in the society because they are the arms of the dictatorship; without them the dictator is crippled. They must not be trusted. And yet I didn't feel any hatred toward them, just bad for them; they had the right to be as miserable as the majority of Mauritanians. Most of them knew me from previous arrests.

"I divorced my wife!" a young guard told me.

"Why, man? You have a daughter."

"I know but I don't have enough money to rent a place for my wife and me, and my wife got fed up with living in my mom's house. They just couldn't get along."

"But divorce? Come on!"

"What would you have done in my shoes?" I couldn't find any answer, because the simple Math was against me. They guy's salary was about 40 or 50 dollars a month, and in order to have a somewhat decent life he needed at least $1,000. All my guards had something in common: they all lived way below the poverty line, and without a supplementary job none of them could make it to the end of the month. In Mauritania, the gap between leading officers and enlisted agents is just too big.

"We have seen many people who have been here and ended up occupying very high level jobs in the government. We're sure you will, too," they always teased me. I'm sure they aspired to better jobs in the government, but I personally don't believe in working with a government that's not righteous; to me, the need for the miserable wages is not an excuse for the mischief they were doing under the color and authority of an unjust regime. In my eyes, they were as guilty as anybody else, no matter what excuses they may come up with.

Nonetheless, the Mauritanian guards, without exception, all expressed their solidarity with me and wished they didn't have to be the ones who had to do the job. They showed me all kinds of sympathy and respect, and they always tried to calm me down because I was worried about being turned over to the States and sent to a Military Tribunal. By then, the U.S. President was barking about putting terrorist suspects before military tribunals, and all kinds of other threats. I knew I would have no chance to be tried justly in a foreign military tribunal. We ate, prayed, and socialized together. We shared everything, food, tea, and we had a radio receiver to hear the news. We all slept in a big room with no furniture and an oodle of mosquitoes. Since it was Ramadan, we ate nights and stayed awake for the most part, and slept during the day. They were obviously directed to treat me that way; the ▄▄▄▄▄▄▄▄▄ sometimes joined us to check on things.

As scheduled, the DSE came back from his trip. "Hi," he greeted me.

"Hi."

"How are you doing?"

"Fine! Why are you arresting me?"

"Be patient! It's not a fire!" he said. Why did he speak about fire? I wondered. He didn't look happy at all, and I knew it wasn't me who was causing his unhappiness. I was completely depressed and terrorized, and so I fell sick. I lost my appetite and couldn't eat anything, and my blood pressure dropped gravely. The DSE called a doctor to check on me.

"You cannot fast. You have to eat," he said, prescribing some medicine. Since I couldn't stand up I had to urinate in a water bottle, and as to anything else, I didn't need to because I hadn't eaten anything. I really got very sick, and the Mauritanian government was completely worried that the Merchandise was going to vanish before the U.S. client took it. Sometimes I tried to sit up in order to eat a little bit, but as soon as I sat straight, I started to get dizzy and fell down. All that time I drank and ate what I could while lying on a thin mattress.

I spent seven days in Mauritanian custody. I didn't get any visits from my family; as I later learned, my family was not allowed to see me, and they were denied the knowledge of my whereabouts. On the eighth day, November 28, 2001, I was informed that I was going to be shipped to Jordan.

November 28th is Mauritanian Independence Day; it marks the event when the Islamic Republic of Mauritania supposedly received its independence from the French colonists in 1960. The irony is that on this very same day in 2001, the independent and sovereign Republic of Mauritania turned over one of its own citizens on a premise. To its everlasting shame, the Mauritanian government not only broke the constitution, which forbids the extradition of Mauritanian criminals to other countries, but also extradited an innocent citizen and exposed him to the random American Justice.

The night before the multilateral deal was closed between Mauritania, the U.S., and Jordan, the prison guards allowed me to watch the parade that was coming from downtown toward the Presidential Palace, the bands escorted by schoolboys carrying lighted candles. The sight awoke childhood memories of when I took part in the same parade myself, as a schoolboy, nineteen years before. Back then I looked with innocence at the event that marked the birth of the nation I happened to be part of; I didn't know that a country is not considered sovereign if it cannot handle its issues on its own.

*   *   *

The Secret Service is the most important government corps in the third world, and in some countries in the so-called free world as well, and so the DSE was invited to the ceremonial colors at the Presidential Palace in the morning. It was between 10 and 11 o'clock when he finally came in, accompanied by his assistant and his recorder. He invited me to his office, where he usually interrogates people. I was surprised to see him at all because it was a holiday. Although I was sick, my blood pressure rose so much from the unexpected visit that I was able to stand and go with them to the interrogation room. But as soon as I entered the office I collapsed on the big leather black sofa. It was obvious that my hyperactivity was fake.

The DSE sent all the guards home, and so I was left with him, his recorder, and his assistant. The guards gestured to me happily as they left the building, as if to say, "Congratulations!" They and I both thought that I was going to be released, though I was skeptical: I didn't like all the movements and telephone conversations that were going on around me.

The DSE sent his assistant away, and he came back with a couple of cheap things, clothes and a bag. Meanwhile the Recorder collapsed asleep in front of the door. The DSE pulled me into a room with nobody but us.

"We're going to send you to Jordan," he announced.

"Jordan! What are you talking about?"

"Their King was subject to a failed assassination attempt."

"So what? I have nothing to do with Jordan; my problem is with Americans. If you want to send me to any country, send me to the U.S."

"No, they want you to be sent to Jordan. They say you are the accomplice of ███████████████████████, though I know you have nothing to do with ████████████ or with September 11."

"So why don't you protect me from this injustice as a Mauritanian citizen?" I asked.

"America is a country that is based on and living with injustice," was his answer.

"OK, I would like to see the President!" I said.

"No, you can't. Everything is already irreversibly decided."

"Well, I want to say good-bye to my mom," I said.

"You can't. This operation is secret."

"For how long?"

"Two days, or maximum three. And if you choose, you don't need to talk to them," he added. "I really have no problem with that." I knew that he was speaking out of his rear end, because I was destined to Jordan for a reason.

"Can you assure me of when I'll be coming back?"

"I'll try. But I hope this trip to Jordan will add another positive testimony in your favor. The Senegalese, the Canadians, the Germans, and I myself believe that you're innocent. I don't know how many witnesses the Americans need to acquit you."

The DSE took me back to his office and tried several times to call his boss, the DG. When he finally reached him, the DG could not give a precise date for my return but assured him that it would be a couple of days. I don't know for sure, but I believe that the Americans outsmarted everybody. They just asked to get me to Jordan, and then there would be another negotiation.

"I don't know exactly," the DSE told me honestly when he got off the phone. "But look: today is Wednesday. Two days for interrogation, and one day for the trip. So you will be back here Saturday or Sunday."

He opened the bag that his assistant brought and asked me to try on the new cheap clothes. I put on the complete suit: a t-shirt, a pair of pants, jacket and plastic shoes. What a sight! Nothing fit; I looked like a skeleton dressed in a new suit. But who cared? At least I didn't.

Between the time when I got the decision and the time the U.S. turned me over to the Jordanian Special Forces, I was treated like a UPS package. I cannot describe my feelings: anger, fear, powerlessness, humiliation, injustice, betrayal.... I had never really contemplated escaping from jail, although I had been jailed unjustly four times already. But today I was thinking about it because I never, even in my dreams, considered I would be sent to a third country that is known throughout the world as a torture-practicing regime. But that was my only bullet, and if I used it and missed I would look very bad in the eyes of my government. Not that that mattered; they obviously would still comply with the U.S. even if I was an angel in their eyes. After all, I had turned myself in.

I looked around for ways to escape. Let's say I managed to get out of the building: I would need a taxicab as soon as I reached the main road. But I had no money on me to pay a cab, and I couldn't take one to a place where somebody knew me because those are the first places they're going to look. When I checked the doors, there was only one door that I would not have any reason to approach, so I asked to use the bathroom. In the bathroom I trimmed my beard and meditated about the other door. It was glass, so I could break it, but I knew the plan of the building; that door would lead to an armed guard who might shoot me dead right away. And even if I managed to sneak past the guard, I had to go around the Ministry for Internal Affairs that neighbors the main street, where there are always guards watching people coming and going. It would be impossible to go through the gate. Maybe, just maybe there's a possibility of jumping the wall, but was I strong enough to do that? No, I wasn't. But I was ready to pull all my strength together and make the impossible possible.

All these plans and thoughts were going through my head when I was using the bathroom. I looked at the roof, but there was no way to escape there; the roof was concrete. I finished cleaning and shaving and left. Outside of the bathroom there was a hall without roof; I thought I could maybe climb the wall and leave the compound by going from one roof to another. But there were two constraints: one, the wall was about 20 feet tall and there was nothing to grab onto in order to climb; and two, the whole compound could be encircled in a matter of minutes by the police, so that no matter where I landed I would be secure in police hands. I realized escape would remain an unrealized dream for somebody who suddenly found all doors before him closed except the door to heaven.

The DSE kept making calls to the incoming flight that carried the special mission team. "They should be here in about three hours. They're in Cyprus now!" he said. Normally he was not supposed to tell me where the plane was, or who was on the plane, or where I was going to be taken; the Americans wanted to maintain the terrorizing factors as harshly as possible. I should know nothing about what was happening to me. Being taken to an airport blindfolded, put in a plane, and taken to country that is an eleven hour flight away together make enough horrible factors that only people with nerves of steel would survive. But the DSE didn't care about telling me everything he knew. Not because he was worried about me, but because he knew for a fact that agreeing to such a horrible operation was at the same time agreeing to give up power. The turmoil against the Mauritanian President was already there, but the DSE knew this would certainly break the camel's back. I knew the same, and so I kept praying, "Oh, Lord please don't let people spill blood in my name!"

The DSE learned from the tower that the plane was expected around 7:00 or 7:30 p.m. The Recorder had been sleeping the whole time, so the DSE sent him home. It was around 6:00 p.m. when the DSE, his assistant, and I took off in the Director's luxurious Mercedes. He called the airport watch one more time to make the necessary arrangements to smuggle me securely without anybody noticing. I hoped his plan would fail and somebody would rat the government out.

The DSE headed in the opposite direction of the airport: he wanted to waste time and arrive at the airport about the same time as the Jordanian delegation. I was hoping that their plane would crash. Even though I knew it was replaceable, I wanted the plan to be postponed, like if you got news of your death and you wanted to postpone it. The DSE stopped at a grocery store and went in to buy some snacks for us to break the fast; sunset was going to catch us at the airport about the time of the unwelcome arrival. In front of the store stood a white U.N. truck. The driver had entered the store and left the engine running. I thought, with some luck I could possibly hijack it, and with some more luck I could get away, because the Benz would have little chance against the stronger body of the Toyota 4-wheel drive truck.

But I saw some drawbacks that discouraged me from the attempt. The hijacking would involve innocent parties: in the cab sat the family of the truck driver, and I was not ready to hurt innocent people. A hijacking would also involve neutralizing the Benz, which could cost the lives of two police officers. Although I wouldn't feel guilty about them getting themselves killed while trying to unjustly and illegally arrest me, I didn't want to kill anybody. And was I really physically able to execute the operation? I wasn't sure. Thinking of the operation was sort of daydreaming to distract myself from the horrible unknown that was awaiting me.

I should mention that in Mauritania the police don't have the Americans' extremely paranoid and vigilant technique of blind-folding, ear-muffing, and shackling people from head to toe; in that regard Mauritanians are very laid back. As a matter of fact, I don't think anybody is as vigilant as the Americans. I was even walking free when we arrived at the Airport, and I could have easily have run away and reached the public terminal before anybody could catch me. I could at least have forcibly passed the message to the public, and hence to my family, that I was kidnapped. But I didn't do it, and I have no explanation for why not. Maybe, had I known what I know today, I would have attempted anything that would have defeated the injustice. I would not even have turned myself in to begin with.

After the grocery stop, we took off straight to the airport. There was hardly any traffic due to the holiday; people had retreated peacefully, as usual on this day, to their homes. It had been eight days since I last saw the outside world. It looked bleak: there must have been a dust storm during the day that was just starting to give way in favor of the ocean breeze. It was a situation I had seen a thousand and one times, and I still liked it. It's like whenever the dust storm kills the city, the ocean breeze comes at the end of the day and blows the life back into it, and slowly but surely people start to come out.

The twilight was as amazing and beautiful as it had always been. I pictured my family already having prepared the Iftar fast-breaking food, my mom mumbling her prayers while duly working the modest delicacies, everybody looking for the sun to take its last steps and hide beneath the horizon. As soon as the Muezzin declares, "God is Great" everyone would hungrily grab something to drink. My brothers prefer a quick smoke and a cup of tea before anything; my sisters would drink first. None of my sisters smoke, smoking for a lady in my culture is not appropriate. The only absent person is me, but everybody's heart is with me, everybody's prayers are for me. My family thought it would be only a matter of several days before the government released me; after all, the Mauritanian authorities told my family that I have done nothing, they were just waiting until the Americans would see the truth and let me be. How wrong was my family! How wrong was I to put my faith in a bunch of criminals and put my fate in their country! I didn't seem to have learned anything. But regret didn't seem to help either: the ship had sailed.

The Mercedes was heading soundlessly to the airport, and I was drowned in my daydreams. At the secret gate, the Airport police chief was waiting on us as planned. I hated that dark gate! How many innocent souls have been led through that secret gate? I had been through it once, when the U.S. government brought me from Dakar and delivered me to my government twenty months earlier. Arriving at the gate put an end to my dreams about a savior or a miraculous sort of a superman who would stop the car, neutralize the police officers, and carry me home on his wings so I could catch my Iftar in the warmth of my mom's hut. There was no stopping God's plan, and I was complying and subduing completely to his will.

The Airport Police Chief looked rather like a camel herder. He was wearing a worn-out Boubou, the national dress, and an unbuttoned T-shirt.

"I told you I didn't want anybody to be around," said the DSE.

"Everything's alright," the chief said reluctantly. He was lazy, careless, naïve, and too traditional. I don't even think he had a clue about what was going on. He seemed to be a religious, traditional guy, but religion didn't seem to have any influence of his life, considering the wrong conspiracy he was carrying out with the government.

The Muezzin started to sing the amazing Azan declaring the end of the day, and hence the fast. "ALLAH is Great, Allah is great." "I testify there is no God but God," once, twice, and then twice, "I testify Mohamed is the messenger of God." "Come to pray, Come to pray, Come to flourish, Come to flourish," and then, twice, "God is Great" and "There is no God but God." What an amazing message! But guess what, dear Muezzin, I cannot comply with your call, nor can I break my fast. I wondered, Does this Muezzin know what injustice is taking place in this country?

There was no clean place around. All the miserable budget the government had approved for the restoration of the airport had literally been devoured by the agents the government put its trust in. Without saying anything, I went to the least dirty spot and started to perform my prayer. The DSE, his assistant, and the chief joined in. After I was done praying, the DSE offered me water and some sweet buns to break my fast; at that same moment the small business jet hit the runway. I had no appetite anyway, but the arriving plane sealed any need to eat. I knew I was not going to survive without eating, though, so I reached for the water and drank a little bit. I took a piece of the sweet bread and forced it inside my mouth, but the piece apparently landed in a cul-de-sac; my throat conspired against me and closed. I was losing my mind from terror, though I tried to act normally and regain my composure. I was shaking, and kept mumbling my prayers.

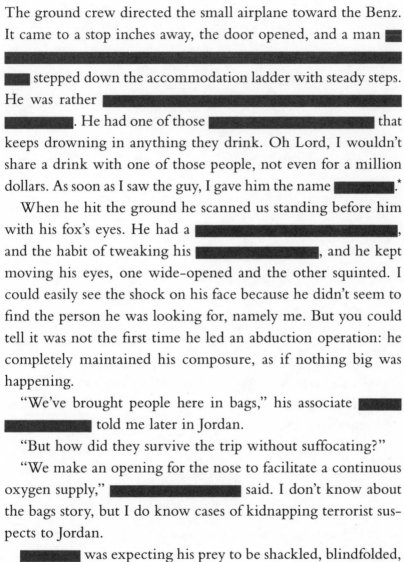

*   *   *

The ground crew directed the small airplane toward the Benz.
It came to a stop inches away, the door opened, and a man ▮
▮▮▮▮▮▮▮▮▮▮▮▮▮▮▮▮▮▮▮▮▮▮▮▮▮▮▮▮▮▮▮▮▮▮▮▮▮▮
▮▮▮ stepped down the accommodation ladder with steady steps.
He was rather ▮▮▮▮▮▮▮▮▮▮▮▮▮▮▮▮▮▮▮▮▮▮▮▮▮▮▮
▮▮▮▮▮▮▮▮. He had one of those ▮▮▮▮▮▮▮▮▮▮▮▮▮▮▮ that
keeps drowning in anything they drink. Oh Lord, I wouldn't
share a drink with one of those people, not even for a million
dollars. As soon as I saw the guy, I gave him the name ▮▮▮▮▮▮.*

When he hit the ground he scanned us standing before him
with his fox's eyes. He had a ▮▮▮▮▮▮▮▮▮▮▮▮▮▮▮▮▮▮▮▮,
and the habit of tweaking his ▮▮▮▮▮▮▮▮▮▮▮▮, and he kept
moving his eyes, one wide-opened and the other squinted. I
could easily see the shock on his face because he didn't seem to
find the person he was looking for, namely me. But you could
tell it was not the first time he led an abduction operation: he
completely maintained his composure, as if nothing big was
happening.

"We've brought people here in bags," his associate ▮▮▮▮▮
▮▮▮▮▮▮▮▮▮▮ told me later in Jordan.

"But how did they survive the trip without suffocating?"

"We make an opening for the nose to facilitate a continuous
oxygen supply," ▮▮▮▮▮▮▮▮▮▮▮▮▮▮▮ said. I don't know about
the bags story, but I do know cases of kidnapping terrorist suspects to Jordan.

▮▮▮▮▮▮▮▮ was expecting his prey to be shackled, blindfolded,

---

* MOS's nickname for the leader of the Jordanian rendition team, who
greets him here, seems to be "Satan," which appears unredacted twice later
in the scene. Context suggests the thing "that keeps drowning" might be
a mustache.

earmuffed. But me, standing before him in civilian clothes with eyes wide open like any human being, that struck him. No, that is not the way a terrorist looks—especially a high-level terrorist who was supposedly the brain behind the Millennium plot.

"Hi," he said; he obviously wasn't used to the beautiful Muslim greeting, "Peace be with you!" He quickly exchanged words with the DSE, though they didn't understand each other very well. The DSE wasn't used to the Jordanian dialect, nor was the Jordanian guest used to the Mauritanian way of speaking. I had an advantage over both of them: there is hardly any Arabic dialect I don't understand because I used to have many friends from different cultural backgrounds.

"He said he needs fuel," I explained to the DSE. I was eager to let my predator know *I am, I am.* I took my bag and showed my readiness to board, and that's when ████████ realized that I was the meager "terrorist" he was sent to pick up.

The DSE handed him my passport and a thin folder. At the top of the accommodation ladder there were two young men dressed in Ninja-like black suits who turned out to be the guards who were going to watch me during the longest eleven-hour trip of my life. I quickly spoke to the DSE in a manner I knew the ██████████ wouldn't understand.

"Tell him not to torture me."

"This is a good guy; I would like you to treat him appropriately!" the DSE said vaguely.

"We're going to take good care of him," answered the ████████ in an ambiguous statement.

The DSE gave me some food to eat during the flight. "No need, we have enough food with us," the ████████ said. I was happy, because I liked the Middle Eastern cuisine.

I took the seat that was reserved for me, and the leader of the operation ordered a thorough search while the plane was rolling on the runway. All they found was my pocket Koran, which they gave back to me. I was blindfolded and earmuffed, but the blindfold was taken away to allow me to eat when the plane reached its regular altitude. As much as I knew about the basics of telecommunication tools, I was terrorized when they put on the earphone-like earmuffs: I thought it was a new U.S. method to suck intels out of your brain and send them directly to a main computer which analyzes the information. I wasn't worried about what they would suck out of my brain, but I was worried about the pain I may suffer due to electrical shocks. It was silly, but if you get scared you are not you anymore. You very much become a child again.

The plane was very small, and very noisy. It could only fly for three to three-and-a-half hours, and then it had to take fuel. "They are in Cyprus," the DSE told me several hours before their arrival in Nouakchott; I figured the return would be by the same route, because such crimes have to be perfectly coordinated with the conspiring parties.

██████████ offered me a meal. It looked good, but my throat was stiff and I felt like I was trying to swallow rough stones. "Is that all?" ████████ wondered.

"I am alright, ████████," I said. ████████ literally means somebody who has performed the pilgrimage to Mecca, but in the Middle East you respectfully refer to anybody you don't know as ████████.* In Jordan they call every detainee ████████ in order to keep the names secret.

"Eat, eat, enjoy your food!" ████████ said, trying to give me some comfort to eat and stay alive.

"Thanks, ████████, I've eaten enough."

---

* It appears from the context that MOS is referring to the honorific "Hajji."

"Are you sure?"

"Yes, ▮▮▮▮▮▮," I replied. ▮▮▮▮▮▮▮ looked at me, forcing the most dishonest, sardonic smile I ever saw, exactly like he did when he stepped down out of the plane back in Nouakchott airport.

The guards collected the garbage and placed the tray table in the upright position. I had two of them watching me, one right behind my neck, and the second sitting next to me. The guy behind me was staring at me the whole time; I doubt he ever blinked his eyes. He must have been through some rough training.

"In my training, I almost lost my composure," one young recruit later told me in the Jordanian prison. "During the training, we took a terrorist and slew him in front of all the students. Some couldn't take it and burst out crying," he continued.

"Where did you guys train?" I asked him.

"An Arabic country, I cannot tell you which one." I felt nauseous, but tried my best to act in front of the guy as if everything were normal and he were a hero. "They want us to have no mercy with terrorists. I can kill a terrorist who is running away without wasting more than one bullet," he demonstratively claimed.

"Oh, that's great! But how do you know he is a terrorist? He might be innocent," I gauged.

"I don't care: if my boss said he is a terrorist, he is. I am not allowed to follow my personal judgment. My job is to execute." I felt so bad for my people and the level of cruelty and gruesomeness they have fallen into. Now I was standing for real before somebody who is trained to kill blindly whomever he is ordered to. I knew he wasn't lying, because I met a former Algerian soldier once who was seeking asylum in Germany, and he told me how gruesomely they dealt with the Islamists, too.

"During an ambush, we captured a sixteen-year-old teen-ager, and on the way to the jail our boss stopped, took him off the truck, and shot him dead. He didn't want him in jail, he wanted revenge," he told me.

I wondered why there was so much vigilance, given that I was shackled and there were two guards, two interrogators, and two pilots. Satan asked the guard who was sitting beside me to empty his seat, and ▓▓▓▓▓▓▓ sat beside me and started to inter-rogate me.*

"What's your name?"

"Mohamedou Ould Salahi."

"What's your nickname?"

"Abu Musab."

"What other nicknames do you have?"

"None!"

"Are you sure?"

"Yes, ▓▓▓▓▓!" I wasn't used to an interrogator from the Sham region, and I had never heard that accent in such a scary way. I find the Sham accent one of the sweetest in the Arabic language, but ▓▓▓▓▓▓▓ accent was not sweet. He was just evil: the way he moved, spoke, looked, ate, everything. During our short conversation we were almost shouting, but we could hardly hear one another because of the extremely loud whining of the engines. I hate small planes. I always feel as if I'm on the wing of a demon when I travel in them.

"We should stop the interrogation and resume it later on," he said. Thank you, old engines! I just wanted him out of my face. I knew there was no way around him, but just for the time being.

▓▓▓▓▓▓▓▓▓▓▓ around midnight GMT we landed in

---

* "Satan" appears here unredacted in the manuscript.

Cyprus. Was it a commercial airport or the military airport? I don't know. But Cyprus is one of the Mediterranean paradises on Earth.

The interrogators and the two pilots put their jackets on and left the plane, most likely for a break. It looked like it had been raining; the ground looked wet, and a light drizzle was caressing the ground. Every once in a while I stole a quick glimpse through the small, blurry window. The breeze outside gave away the presence of a cold winter on the island. I felt some noises that shook the small plane; it must have been the fuel cistern moving. I drowned in my daydreams.

I was thinking, Now the local police will suspect the plane, and hopefully search it. I am lucky because I'm breaking the law by transiting through a country without a transit visa, and I'll be arrested and put in jail. In the prison, I'll apply for asylum and stay in this paradise. The Jordanians can't say anything because they are guilty of trying to smuggle me. The longer the plane waits, the better my chances are to be arrested.

How wrong I was! How comforting a daydream can be! It was my only solace to help me ignore and forget the evilness that surrounded me. The plane indeed waited long enough, about an hour, but there was no searching the plane. I was non-existent in the passengers' list that the Jordanians gave to the local authorities. I even thought I saw police in thick black uniforms coming near the plane, but I was not to be spotted because I was sandwiched between two seats and had to keep my head down, so I looked like a small bag. I might be wrong though, and just saw them because I wanted the police to come and arrest me.

██████, his associate, and the two pilots came back and we took off. The pilots switched places. I saw the fat pilot sitting in front of ███████; he was almost as broad as he was tall. ████████ started a conversation with him. Although I couldn't hear the talk, I assumed it to be a friendly discussion between two mature men, which was good. ████████ grew tired like everybody else, except for the young guard who kept his never-blinking eyes pointed on me. Every once in a while he made a comment like, "Keep your head down!" and "Look down," but I kept forgetting the rules. I had the feeling that this would be my last flight, because I was certain I wouldn't make it through the torture. I thought about every member of my family, even my far nephews and nieces and my in-laws. How short is this life! In a blink of an eye, everything is gone.

I kept reading my Koran in the dim light. My heart was pounding as if it wanted to jump out of my mouth. I barely understood anything of what I was reading; I read at least 200 or 300 pages unconsciously. I was prepared to die, but I never imagined it would be this way. Lord have mercy on me! I think hardly anybody will meet death the way he or she imagined. We human beings take everything into consideration except for death; hardly anybody has death on his calendar. Did God really predestinate for me to die in Jordan at the hands of some of the most evil people in the world? But I didn't really mind being killed by bad people; before God they will have no case, I was thinking.

████████████████████ around 4 a.m. GMT. A fake peace dominated the trip between Cyprus and my unknown present destination. The bandits seemed to be exhausted from the previous day trip from Amman to Nouakchott, and that was a blessing for me. The plane started to lose altitude again, and finally landed in a place I didn't know. I think it was an Arabic country somewhere in the Middle East, because I think I spotted signs in Arabic through the small windows when I stole a quick glimpse off my guarding demon. It was still nighttime, and the weather seemed to be clear and dry; I didn't see any signs of winter.*

This time I did not hope for the police to search the airplane, because Arabic countries are always conspiring with each other against their own citizens. What treason! Nonetheless, any leak of information wouldn't hurt. But I didn't give that day-dream a second thought. We didn't stay long, though we went through the same procedure, ████████ and his two pilots going for a short break, and the same noises of taking on fuel that I heard in Cyprus. The plane took off to its final destination, Amman, Jordan. I don't think that we made any more stops, though I kept passing out and coming to until we arrived in Jordan.

Over ninety percent of Jordanians are Muslim. For them, as for all Muslims from the Middle East, fasting during Ramadan is the most important religious service. People who don't fast are resented in the society, and so many people fast due to social pressure even though they don't believe in religion. In Mauri-tania, people are much more relaxed about fasting, and less relaxed about prayer.

"Take your breakfast," said the guard. I think I had fallen asleep for a moment.

"No, thanks."

"It's your last chance to eat before the fast begins."

"No, I'm OK."

"Are you sure?"

"Yes, ████." They started to eat their breakfast, chewing like cows; I could even hear them through my earmuffs. I kept

---

* MOS indicated that the flight left Amman on the evening of Novem-ber 28, so it would now be early in the morning of November 29, 2001.

stealing glimpses toward the small windows until I saw the first daylight prying the darkness open.

"██████, I'd like to perform my prayer," I said to the guard. The guard had a little conversation with ██████████, who ordered him to take off one of my earmuffs.

"There is no opportunity to pray here. When we arrive, you and I are going to pray together," said ██████████. I was sort of comforted, because if he prays that was a sign that he was a believer, and so he wouldn't possibly hurt his "brother" in belief. And yet he didn't seem to have knowledge about his religion. Prayer must be performed on time in the best manner you can, at least in your heart. You cannot postpone it except for the reasons explained in the Islamic scriptures. In any case, the promised prayer with Satan never took place.*

---

* Again, "Satan" appears here in the manuscript unredacted.

FOUR

Jordan

November 29, 2001–July 19, 2002

The Hospitality of My Arab Brothers...Cat and Mouse: ICRC vs. Jordanian Intel...The Good News: I Supposedly Attempted to Kill the Mauritanian President... Bodybuilding Center: What I Know Kills Me...Unjust Justice

███████████████████████, around 7:00 a.m. local time.*

The small plane clumsily started to fight its way through the cloudy and cold sky of Amman. We finally hit the ground and came to a standstill. Everybody was eager to get the hell out of the plane, including me.

"Stand up," said one the guards, taking off the metal handcuffs that had already built a ring around my wrists. I was relieved, and sat silently talking to myself. "Look, they're friendly. They just wanted to make sure that you didn't do anything stupid in the plane; now that we arrived, there is no need for cuffs or earmuffs." How wrong I was! They just took the handcuffs off in order to handcuff me again behind my back and put on bigger earmuffs and a bag over my head, covering my neck. My

---

* It is still the morning of November 29, 2001 (see footnote on p. 148).

heart started to pound heavily, which raised my blood pressure and helped me to stand steadier on my feet. I started to mumble my prayers. This was the first time that I got treated this way. My pants started to slip down my legs because I was so skinny and had been virtually without food for at least a week.

Two new, energetic guards dragged me out of the plane. I twisted my feet when I reached the ladder; I couldn't see anything, nor did the stupid guards tell me anything. I fell face down, but the guards caught me before I hit the ladder.

"Watch out!" said ███████████████████, my future interrogator, to the guards. I memorized his voice, and when he later started to interrogate me, I recognized it from that day. I now knew that I had to step down the ladder until my feet hit the ground, and an ice-cold winter breeze hit my whole body. My clothes were not designed for this weather. I was wearing the worthless, made-in-a-cheap-country clothes I got from the Mauritanian authorities.

One of the guards silently helped my feet get into the truck that was parked inches away from the last step of the ladder. The guards squeezed me between them in the back seat, and off took the truck. I felt comforted; it was warm inside the truck, and the motor was quiet. The chauffeur mistakenly turned the radio on. The female DJ voice struck me with her Sham accent and her sleepy voice. The city was awakening from a long, cold night, slowly but surely. The driver kept accelerating and hitting the brakes suddenly. What a bad driver! They must have hired him just because he was stupid. I was moving back and forth like a car crash dummy.

I heard a lot of horns. It was the peak time for people who were going to work. I pictured myself at this very same time back home, getting ready for work, enjoying the new day, the morning ocean breeze through my open window, dropping my nephews off at their respective schools. Whenever you think life is going in your favor, it betrays you.

After about 40 or 45 minutes of painful driving, we took a turn, entered a gate, and stopped. The guards dragged me out of the truck. The cold breeze shook my whole body, though only for a very short time before we entered the building and I was left near a heater. I knew how the heater looked even with my eyes closed; I just sensed it was like the ones I had in Germany. Later on, I learned from the guards that the prison facility was built by a Swedish company.

"Do not move," said one of the guards before they both emptied out of the place. I stood still, though my feet could hardly carry me and my back hurt so bad. I was left there for about 15 or 20 minutes before ▓▓▓▓▓▓▓▓▓▓▓▓▓▓▓▓ grabbed me by the back of my collar, almost choking me to death. ▓▓▓▓▓▓▓▓▓▓▓▓▓▓ pushed me roughly up the stairs. I must have been on the ground floor, and he pushed me to the first.

Legend has it that Arabs are among the most hospitable folks on the face of the earth; both friends and enemies are unanimous about that. But what I would be experiencing here was another kind of hospitality. ▓▓▓▓▓▓▓▓▓▓▓▓▓▓▓ pushed me inside a relatively small room with a desk, a couple of chairs, and another guy sitting behind the desk and facing me. I baptized ▓▓▓▓▓▓▓▓▓▓▓ as soon as I saw him. He was a ▓▓▓ ▓▓▓▓▓▓▓▓▓▓▓▓▓▓▓▓▓▓▓▓▓▓▓▓▓▓▓▓▓▓▓▓▓. Like the rest of the guards, he was dressed in ▓▓▓▓▓▓▓▓▓▓▓ ▓▓▓▓▓▓▓▓ had a high-and-tight haircut.* You could see that he had been doing this work for some time: there were no

---

* At his 2005 ARB hearing, MOS indicated that throughout his time in the Jordanian prison, everyone on the prison staff wore military uniforms. ARB transcript, 22.

signs of humanity in his face. He hated himself more than anybody could hate him.

The first thing I saw were two pictures on the wall, the present King Abdullah and his extinguished father Hussein. Such pictures are the proof of dictatorship in the uncivilized world. In Germany I never saw anybody hang the picture of the president; the only time I saw his picture was when I was watching news, or driving around during elections, when they hang a bunch of candidates' pictures. Maybe I'm wrong, but I mistrust anybody who hangs the picture of his president, or any president who wins any elections with more than 80%. It's just ridiculous. On the other wall I read the time on a big hanging clock. It was around 7:30 a.m.

"Take your clothes off!" said ████████████████████████. I complied with his order except for my underwear. I was not going to take them off without a fight, no matter how weak it would be. But ██████████████████████ just handed me a clean, light blue uniform. Jordanians are materially much more advanced and organized than Mauritanians; everything in the prison was modest, but clean and neat. It was the first time I put on a prison uniform in my life. In Mauritania there is no specific uniform, not because Mauritania is a democratic country, but maybe because the authorities are too lazy and corrupt. A uniform is a sign of backwards and communist countries. The only so-called "democratic" country that has this technique of wrapping up detainees in uniforms is the U.S.; the Jordanians have adopted a 100% American system in organizing their prisons.

The young guy behind the table was rather fat. He was acting as a clerk, but he was a horrible one.

"What's your name? What's your address in Amman?"

"I am not from Amman."

"Where the hell are you from?"

"I am from Mauritania," I answered.

"No, I mean where do you live here in Jordan?"

"Nowhere!"

"Did they capture you while transiting through the airport?"

"No, Hajji took me from my country to question me for two days and bring me back."* I wanted to make it sound as harmless as possible. Besides, that's what I was told, even though I had the feeling now that I was being lied to and betrayed.

"How do you spell your name?" I spelled out my complete name, but the guy didn't seem to have gone to primary school. He wrote as if with Chinese chopsticks. He kept filling out one form after another and throwing the old ones in the garbage can.

"What have you done?"

"I've done nothing!"

Both burst out in laughter. "Oh, very convenient! You have done nothing but you are here!" I thought, What crime should I say in order to satisfy them?

I presented myself as a person who came all the way from Mauritania to provide intels about my friends. "█████████ told me he needed my help," I said. But then I thought, What a silly answer. If I were going to provide information freely, I could do so in Mauritania. The guards didn't believe me anyway; what criminal benevolently admits to his crime? I felt humiliated because my story sounded weird and untruthful.

In the bureaucratic chaos, the prison's commanding officer took the process in hand. He took my wallet and copied my personal data from my ID. He was a serious looking officer in his late thirties, light blond, Caucasian looking, with a dry face. It was obvious he was married to the cause. During my sojourn in the Dar Al Tawqif wa Tahqiq House† for Arrest and

---

* "Hajji" appears here unredacted.

† The Arabic phrase itself appears to be a transliteration of the phrase "house of arrest and detention." In its 2008 report "Double Jeopardy: CIA

Interrogation, I kept seeing him working day and night and sleeping in the prison. Most of the guards do. They work ███

███ rarely left the facility. I would catch him sneakily trying to look through the bin hole without me noticing him.* ████████████████████████ was an ████████ in what they call the al Jaish Al Arabi, the Arab Legion. I was thinking, What a masquerade! If this is the protector of us Arabs, we screwed up! As an Arabic saying has it, "Her protector is her assailant."

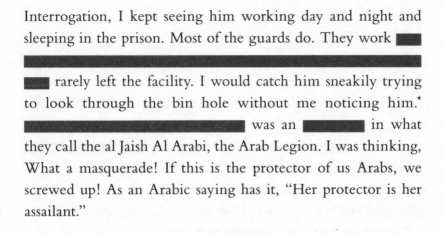

Renditions to Jordan," Human Rights Watch recorded that "from 2001 until at least 2004, Jordan's General Intelligence Department (GID) served as a proxy jailer for the U.S. Central Intelligence Agency (CIA), holding prisoners that the CIA apparently wanted kept out of circulation, and later handing some of them back to the CIA." Human Rights Watch reported that MOS and at least thirteen others were sent to Jordan during this period, where they were "held at the GID's main headquarters in Amman, located in the Jandawil district in Wadi Sir. The headquarters, which appear to cover nearly an acre of land, contain a large four-story detention facility that Human Rights Watch visited in August 2007."

Researchers who carried out that visit recorded that "the administrative offices and interrogation rooms are on the second floor of the building, while visiting rooms are on the ground floor. During the period that Human Rights Watch inspected the facility, all of the detainees in custody were held on the second floor. There are also many cells on the ground floor and third floor, however, as well as a small number of cells on the fourth floor, which includes a few collective cells and what the director called the "women's section" of the facility. In addition, the facility has a basement where many prisoners have claimed that they were brought for the most violent treatment. Prisoners in GID detention at Wadi Sir are kept in single-person cells and are prohibited from speaking with one another, but some have managed to communicate via the back window of their cells. (Each cell faces onto the central courtyard, and has a window looking out on the yard.)." Double Jeopardy, 1, 10–11. The Human Rights Watch report is available at http://www.hrw.org/sites/default/files/reports /jordan0408webwcover.pdf.

* This behavior may be the basis for the nickname "I'm-Watching-You," which appears unredacted later in this chapter.

"Why do they call you guys the Arab Legion?" I asked one of the guards later.

"Because we are supposed to protect the entire Arab world," he responded.

"Oh, that's really great," I said, thinking that we'd be just fine if they protected us from themselves.

After they had finished processing me, ███████████████ ███████████ handcuffed me behind my back, blindfolded me, and grabbed me as usual by the back of my collar. We got in the lift and I felt it going up. We must have landed on the third floor. ████████████████████████ led me through a corridor and took a couple turns before a heavy metal door opened. ████████████████████████ uncuffed me and took off the blindfold.

I looked as far as my eyes could reach. It was not far: about 8 or 9 feet to a window that was small and high so detainees could not look outside. I climbed up once, but I saw nothing but the round wall of the prison. The prison was in the shape of a circle. The idea was smart, because if you succeeded in jumping out of the window, you would land in a big arena with a 30 or 40 foot concrete wall. The room looked bleak and stark, though clean. There was a wooden bed and an old blanket, a small sheet, and that was about it. The door closed loudly behind ████████████████████████ and I was left on my own, tired and scared. What an amazing world! I enjoyed visiting other countries, but not this way.

I performed my ritual wash and tried to pray standing, but there was no way so I opted to pray sitting down. I crawled over to the bed and soon trailed off. Sleep was a torture: as soon as I closed my eyes, the friends I was potentially going to be asked about kept coming to me and talking to me. They scared the hell out of me; I woke up numerous times mumbling their names. I was in a no-win situation: if I stayed awake, I was so dead tired, and if slept I got terrorized by nightmares to the point that I screamed out loud.

Around 4:30 p.m., the guard on watch woke me up for food. Meals were served from a chariot that goes through the corridor from cell to cell, with the cook passing by again later to collect the empty plates. Detainees were allowed to keep one cup for tea and juice. When the cook showed up for my plate, he saw that I hardly ate anything.

"Is that all?" As much as I liked the food, my throat conspired against me. The depression and fear were just too much.

"Yes, thanks."

"Well, if you say so!" The cook quickly collected my plate and off he rolled. In jail it's not like at home; in jail if you don't eat, it's OK. But at home your parents and your wife do their best to persuade you. "Honey, just eat a little bit more. Or should I prepare you something else? Please, just do it for my sake. Why don't you tell me what you'd like to eat?" In both cases, though, you more than likely won't eat more—in jail because they scare the hell out of you, and at home because you're spoiled. It's the same way when you feel sick. I remember a very funny case when I was really hurting; it was either a headache or stomach ache.

"I'm in so much pain! Can you please give me some medication?"

"Fuck you, crybaby," the guard said. I burst into laughter because I remembered how my family would be overreacting if they knew I was sick.

After giving my trash back I went back to sleep. As soon as I closed my eyes I saw my family in a dream, rescuing me from the Jordanians. In the dream I kept telling my family that it was just a dream, but they would tell me, "No, it's for real, you're home." How devastating, when I woke up and found myself in the dimly lit cell! This dream terrorized me for days. "I told you it's a dream, please hold me and don't let me go," I would say. But there was no holding me. My reality was that I was secretly detained in a Jordanian jail and my family could not even possibly know where I was. Thank God after a while that dream disappeared, though every once in a while I would still wake up crying intensely after hugging my beloved youngest sister.

The first night is the worst; if you make it through that you're more than likely going to make it through the rest. It was Ramadan, and so we got two meals served, one at sunset and the second before the first light. The cook woke me up and served me my early meal. Suhoor is what we call this meal; it marks the beginning of our fasting, which lasts until sunset. At home, it's more than just a meal. The atmosphere matters. My older sister wakes everybody and we sit together eating and sipping the warm tea and enjoying each other's company. "I promise I will never complain about your food, Mom," I was thinking to myself.

I still hadn't adjusted to Jordanian time. I wasn't allowed to know the time or date, but later when I made friends among the guards they used to tell me what time it was. This morning I had to guess. It was around 4:30 a.m., which meant around 1:30 a.m. back home. I wondered what my family was doing. Do they know where I am?* Will God show them my place? Will I ever see them again? Only Allah knows! The chances looked very low. I didn't eat a lot, and in fact the meal was not

---

* In fact, it would be almost a year before MOS's family learned where he was—and only because a brother in Germany saw an article in Der Spiegel in October 2002 that reported that MOS was in Guantánamo. See "From Germany to Guantanamo: The Career of Prisoner No. 760," Der Spiegel, October 29, 2008.

that big; a pita bread, buttermilk, and small pieces of cucumber. But I ate more than I did the night before. I kept reading the Koran in the dim light; I wasn't able to recite because my brain was not working properly. When I thought it must be dawn I prayed, and as soon as I finished the Muezzin started to sing the Azan, his heavenly, fainting, sleepy, hoarse voice awakening in me all kind of emotions. How could all those praying believers possibly accept that one of their own is buried in the Darkness of the ▇▇▇▇▇▇▇▇▇▇▇▇▇▇▇▇▇▇▇▇ House of Arrest and Interrogation?*

There are actually two Azans, one to wake people to eat the last meal, and the other to stop eating and go to pray. It sounds the same; the only difference is that in the last one the Muezzin says, "Prayer is better than sleeping." I redid my prayers once more and went to bed to choose between being terrorized while awake or asleep. I kept switching between both, as if I were drunk.

That second day passed without big events. My appetite didn't change. One of the guards gave me a book to read. I didn't like it because it was about philosophical differences between all kinds of religions. I really needed a book that would give me comfort. I wished we had a little more peace in the world. I was between sleeping and waking at around 11 p.m. that evening when the guards shouted ▇▇▇▇▇▇▇ and opened the door of my cell.

"Hurry up!" I froze and my feet numbed, but my heart pumped so hard that I jumped off my bed and complied with the order of the guard. The escort guards handcuffed me behind my back and pushed me toward the unknown. Since I was blindfolded I could think about my destination undisturbed, though the pace of the escorting guard was faster than my

---

* See footnote on p. 154.

anticipation. I felt the warmth of the room I entered. When you're afraid you need warmth.

The guard took off both the handcuffs and the blindfold. I saw a big blue machine like the ones in airports for scanning luggage, and some other object to measure height and weight. How relieved I was! They were just going about taking the traditional prisoner data like fingerprints, height, and weight. Although I knew there was no getting around the interrogation session, I both wanted to get through it as soon as possible and was so afraid of that session. I don't know how to explain it, it might not make sense, I'm just trying to explain my feelings then the best way I can.

Another day passed. The routine was no different than the days before, though I gathered one vital piece of information: the number of my cell was ███████████████████████.
After the Iftar fast-breaking meal, the guards would start calling a number, a door would open loudly, and you could hear the footsteps of the taken-away detainees. I figured they were being taken away for interrogation. I imagined I heard the guards shouting my cell number about a hundred times, and after each I went to the toilet and performed a ritual wash. I was just so paranoid. Finally, around 10 p.m. on Saturday, a guard shouted ████████████████████ for real.* I quickly went to the bathroom. Not that I needed to, I really hadn't drunk anything and I had already urinated about half a gallon, but the urge was there. What was I going to urinate, blood?

"Hurry up, we don't have time," said the guard who stood at the opened heavy metal door. Later on, I learned ████████
██
██

---

* MOS arrived in Jordan on Thursday, November 29, so it would now be the evening of Saturday, December 1, 2001.

███

████████████████████ The sergeant handcuffed and blindfolded me, and pushed me off. We took the lift and went one floor down, took a couple of turns, and entered a new area; a door opened and I went down a step. The odor of cigarette smoke hit me. It was the interrogation area, where they smoke relentlessly, like an old train. It's disgusting when the smoke keeps adding up and dominates the odor of a house.

The area was remarkably quiet. The escorting guard dropped me against a wall and retreated.

"What people did you send to Chechnya?" ███████████ ███████████ shouted at a detainee in English.

"I ain't sent nobody," responded the detainee in broken Arabic, with an obvious Turkish accent. I right away knew the setup: This interrogation was meant for me.

"Liar," shouted ████████████████████████.

"I ain't lying," the guy responded in Arabic, although ████████████████████████ kept speaking his loose English.

"I don't care if you have a German or American passport, you're going to tell me the truth," said ████████████████ █████. The setup fit perfectly, and was meant to terrorize me even more. And even though I knew right away it was a setup, it worked.

"Hi, ████████████," said ████████████████████.

"Hi," I responded, feeling his breath right in front of my face. I was so terrorized that I hadn't realized what he was saying.

"So your name *is* ████████████," he concluded.

"No!"

"But you responded when I called you ████████████," he argued. I found it idiotic to tell him that I was so terrorized that I didn't realize what name he called me.

"If you look at it, we all are ████████████," I correctly

answered. ███████████ means "God's servant" in Arabic.* But I actually knew how ████████████████████ came up with that name. When I arrived in Montreal, Canada on November 26, 1999, my friend ████████████ introduced me to his room-mate ██████████████ by my given name. Later on I met another ████████████████████████ who I'd happened to see when I visited the year before. He called me ██████████ and I responded because I found it impolite to correct him. Since then ████████████████ called me ██████████████, and I found it cool. I wasn't trying to deceive ████████████████; after all, ██████████████████ had keys to our common mailbox and always collected my official mail, which obviously bore my given name.

That was the story of the name. Obviously the Americans tasked the Jordanians with investigating why I took the name ████████████ in Canada, but the Jordanians understand the recipe far more than Americans, and so they completely ignored this part of the interrogation.

"Do you know where you are?" asked ██████████████████████.

"In Jordan," I responded. He was obviously shocked. I shouldn't have been informed about my destination, but the Mauritanian interrogator must have been so angry that he didn't exactly follow the orders of the Americans. The initial plan was to send me from Mauritania to Jordan blindfolded and not inform me about my destination, in order to plant as much fear and terror in my heart as possible to break me. But as soon as I answered the question, ████████████████████████ knew that this part of the plan was broken, and so he took off my blindfold right away and led me inside the interrogation room.

It was a small room, about 10 x 8 feet, with an old table and

---

* It appears that the interrogator addressed MOS as "Abdullah," which means "servant of God."

three weathered chairs. ████████████████ was in his

██

███. His assistant ████████████████████ was a █████████

█████████████████████████████████. He was obviously
the type who is ready to do the dirty side of any job. He also
looked ███████████████████. I scanned both back and forth and
wondered about these guys.* The whole problem of terrorism
was caused by the aggression of Israel against Palestinian civilians, and the fact that the U.S. is backing the Israeli government
in its mischiefs. When the Israelis took over Palestine under the
fire of the British Artillery, the invasion resulted in a mass migra-
tion of the locals. Many of them ended up in neighboring countries, and Jordan received the lion's share; more than fifty percent
of Jordanians are of Palestinian origin. To me, these interrogators just didn't fit in the vests they were wearing: it didn't make
sense that Palestinians would work for Americans to defeat the
people who are supposedly helping them. I knew that these two
interrogators standing before me didn't represent any moral values, and didn't care about human being's lives. I found myself
between two supposedly fighting parties, both of which considered me an enemy; the historical enemies were allied to roast
me. It was really absurd and funny at the same time.

████████████████████████ played a vital role in the Americans' War against Terrorism. He was charged with interrogating
the kidnapped individuals the U.S. delivered to Jordan and
assigning them to the different members of his team. He also
personally came to GTMO to interrogate individuals on behalf
of the U.S.†

---

* Context suggests that both the interrogator and his assistant appear to
have Palestinian backgrounds.

† MOS's 2005 ARB testimony indicates that he had three interrogators
during his secret detention in Amman; he profiles the three interrogators

██████████████████████ opened a medium-sized binder; it turned out to be a file on me that the U.S. had turned over to the Jordanians. He started to ask me questions that were not related to each other. It was the first time I ever experienced this technique, the goal of which is to quickly bring the liar into contradiction. But ████████████████████ obviously was not briefed enough about my case and the history of my interrogation: it wouldn't have mattered whether I was lying or telling the truth, because I had been questioned so many times about the exact same things by different agencies from different countries. Should I have lied, I would have been able to lie again and again and again, because I had had enough time to straighten my lies. But I hadn't lied to him—nor did he doubt my truthfulness.

First he showed me the picture of ████████████ ████████ he had been interrogating earlier, and said "If you tell me about this guy, I am going to close your case and send you home." Of course he was lying.

I looked at the photo and honestly answered, "No, I don't know him." I am sure the guy was asked the same question about me, and he must have answered the same because there was no way that he knew me.

████████████ was sitting on ████████████ left and recording my answers. "Do you drink tea?" ██████ ████████████ asked me.

"Yes, I like tea." ████████████ ordered the tea guy to bring me a cup, and I got a big, hot cup of tea. When the caffeine started to mix with my blood I got hyper and felt so comforted. Those interrogators know what they are doing.

"Do you know ████████████ asked ████████ ████████. I had been asked about ████████████ a

in more depth later in this chapter. This one appears to be the senior interrogator who only interrogates him once. ARB transcript, 21.

thousand and one times, and I tried everything I could to convince interrogators that I don't know that guy: if you don't know somebody, you just don't know him, and there is no changing it.* Even if they torture you, they will not get any usable information. But for some reason the Americans didn't believe that I didn't know him, and they wanted the Jordanians to make me admit it.

"No, I don't know him," I answered.

"I swear to Allah you know him," he shouted.

"Don't swear," I said, although I knew that taking the Lord's name in vain is like sipping coffee for him. ▮▮▮▮▮▮▮▮▮
▮▮▮▮▮▮▮▮▮ kept swearing. "Do you think I am lying to you?"

"No, I think you forgot." That was too nicely put, but the fact that the Americans didn't provide the Jordanians with any substantial evidence tied the hands of the Jordanians mightily. Yes, Jordanians practice torture on a daily basis, but they need a reasonable suspicion to do so. They don't just jump on anybody and start to torture him. "I am going to give you pen and paper, and I want you to write me your resumé and the names of all of your friends," he said, closing the session and asking the guard to take me back to my cell.

The worst was over; at least I thought so. The escorting guards were almost friendly when they handcuffed and blindfolded me. There is one common thing among prison guards, whether they are American, Mauritanian, or Jordanian: they all reflect the attitude of the interrogators. If the interrogators are happy the guards are happy, and if not, then not.

---

* This again could be Ahmed Ressam, about whom MOS has by this time been repeatedly questioned. At his 2005 ARB hearing, MOS testified, "Then they sent me to Jordan.... The Jordanians were investigating my part in the Millennium plot. They told me, they are especially concerned about the Millennium plot." ARB transcript, 20.

The escorting guards felt some freedom to talk to me. "Where are you from?"

"Mauritania."

"What are you doing in Jordan?"

"My country turned me over."

"Are you kidding me?"

"No, I'm serious."

"Your country is fucked up." In the Jordanian Prison, as in Mauritania and GTMO, it was extremely forbidden for the guards to interact with detainees. But hardly anybody followed the rules.

"You are starving, man, why don't you eat?" one of the escorting guards asked me. He was right. The shape of my bones was clear, and anybody could tell how serious my situation was.

"I am only going to eat if I get back home. I'm not interested in prison food. I'm interested in my mom's food," I answered.

"God willing, you're going to get out, but for the time being you got to eat." I don't want to make him look good, his type of job already defines his personality, but he felt that his country was not just. I needed any comforting word, and so far he had done a good job with me. Other guards joined us in the corridor and asked him where I'm from.

They opened the door to ███████████████. I felt as though a big burden was taken off my back. "It's only a matter of days, and then they'll send me back home. The DSE was right," I thought. The Jordanians were as confused about the case the U.S. had given them as I was. The U.S. government obviously hadn't given any substantial material to help the Jordanians to do their dirty job. The painful fear started to diminish, and I started to feel like eating.

Sneaky I'm-Watching-You appeared at the bin hole of my cell and gave me thirty numbered pieces of paper. The coordination between the interrogators and guards was perfect. I immediately wrote both assignments. I was tasked by ████ ████████████████████ with writing the names of all my friends, but that was ridiculous: I had so many acquaintances that it would be impossible to include them in less than a big book. So I completed a list of my closest friends and a traditional resumé, using about 10 pages. For the first time I had some relatively good sleep that night.

Some time in the next couple of days ██████████████ ████████████ picked up the written materials and the empty papers as well. He counted the papers thoroughly.

"Is that all you have to write?"

"Yes, Sir!" ████████████████████████████ had been working day and night, and all he was doing was checking on detainees through the bin holes. Most of the time I didn't notice him. Once he caught me having a good time with a guard and he took me and interrogated me about what we were talking about. As to the guard, he disappeared and I never saw him again.

"Put your stuff together," a guard said, waking me in the morning. I grabbed my blanket, my Koran, and the one Library book I had. I was so happy because I thought I was being sent home.

The guard made me hold my stuff and blindfolded me. They didn't send me home; instead I found myself locked in the cellar, ███████████████. The cell there was not clean. It seemed to have been abandoned for a long time. I still wanted to believe in good intentions, and I thought this was the transfer cell for detainees before their release. I was so tired and the cell was so cold that I went to sleep.

Around 4:30 p.m. Iftar was served, and I slowly came to life. I noticed an old paper on the door with the rules of the prison. The guards had clumsily forgotten to tear it off. I wasn't supposed to read the rules, but since nobody is perfect, I had the chance to discover something. The rules stated, among other things, (1) You are only allowed to smoke if you are cooperating; (2) Talking to the guards is forbidden; (3) the ICRC visits the prison every 14 days; (4) Do not talk to the ICRC about your political case.* I was happy, because I would at least be able to send letters to my family, but I missed a vital point: I had been taken temporarily to the cellar to hide me from the ICRC in a Cat-and-Mouse game that lasted eight months, my entire stay in Jordan.

Every fourteen days, the guards would consistently move me from my cell to the cellar, where I would spend a couple of days before they brought me back to my cell. When I discovered the trick, I explicitly asked my interrogator ███████████████ to see the ICRC.

"There is no ICRC here. This is a Military prison," he lied.

"I have seen the clauses of the Rules, and you're hiding me in the cellar every 14 days to prevent me from meeting the Red Cross."

███████████████████ looked at me firmly. "I am protecting you! And you are not going to see the ICRC." I knew then that there was no changing their minds, and ███████████ ██████████████ couldn't even decide the issue. It was way above him. The conspiracy between Mauritania, the U.S., and Jordan to commit the crime was perfect. If my involvement in terrorism were cemented, I would be executed and the party would be over, and who was to know what had happened?

---

* The ICRC is the International Committee of the Red Cross, which has a mandate under the Geneva Conventions to visit prisoners of war, civilians interned during conflicts, and others detained in situations of violence around the world. An internationally acknowledged purpose of these visits is to ensure humane treatment and deter and prevent abuse.

"I'd like to see the Mauritanian Ambassador," I asked the interrogator.

"Impossible."

"OK, what about Mauritanian Intel?" I asked.

"What do you want with them?"

"I would like to ask them about the reason for my incarceration in Jordan. At least you know that I have done nothing against your country."

"Look, your country is a good friend of ours, and they turned you over to us. We can do anything we like with you, kill you, arrest you indefinitely, or release you if you admit to your crime." ▅▅▅▅▅▅▅▅▅▅▅▅▅▅▅▅ both lied and told the truth. Arab countries are not friends. On the contrary, they hate each other. They never cooperate; all they do is conspire against each other. To Mauritania, Jordan is worthless, and vice-versa. However, in my case the U.S. compelled them both to work together.

I tried so many times to contact my family but to no avail, and then I washed my hands of the evils and I prayed to God to take care of my family and make them know where I was. In time, I noticed that I was not the only hidden package: between one and three other detainees were subject to the cellar operation at any one time, and the numbers kept changing as time went by. My whole time in Jordan, I was always in isolation, of course. But I could tell whether there were detainees in the neighboring cells, based on the movements of the food chariot, the guards, and the movement of detainees.

For a while my neighbors were two courageous boys. Although talking was forbidden, those two boys were always shouting, "God's help is coming soon. Remember, God is on our side, and Satan is on theirs!" No matter what the guards did to them, they kept solacing the other detainees and reminding them of God's inevitable relief. You could tell from the accent that they were Jordanians, which made sense, since the locals are more likely to be protected by their families than foreigners. Nonetheless, I have no doubt those boys suffered for what they did.

████████████████████████ I was the only constant in my neighborhood; the cells next to me kept changing owners.* At one point, my next-door neighbor happened to be a young Lebanese nitwit who kept crying and refusing to eat. His story, according to the guards, went like this: He came to Jordan from Lebanon to have some fun. When he bumped into a routine police patrol in downtown Amman, they found an AKM-47 in his trunk and arrested him. Now, having a gun on you in Lebanon is not a big deal, but in Jordan it is forbidden to carry weapons. Taken to jail, the young Lebanese suspect was losing his mind. He kept crying and refusing his food for at least two weeks until his release. Oh, what a relief for me, when they released him! I felt so bad for him. I am sure he learned his lesson, and will think twice about having a weapon in his trunk the next time he comes to Jordan.

████████████████████████. He had been sentenced to one year, and at the end of the year he went crazy. He kept shouting, "I need to see my interrogator!" When I asked the guards why he was doing this, they answered, "Because his sentence is over, but they won't let him go." Sometimes he would start to sing loudly, and sometimes he shouted at the guards, asking for a cigarette. I don't blame him: unless you have nerves of steel, chances are you'll lose your mind in Jordanian custody.

---

* In this section of the manuscript, which MOS heads "My Detainee Neighbors," he is clearly profiling some of his fellow prisoners in Jordan. This redaction, which is preceded by the number 2, appears to introduce a second "neighbor," and the next two redactions seem to introduce two more.

██ kept
coughing the whole time. "He is very old," a guard told me.
"Why did they arrest him?" I wondered.

"Wrong place, wrong time," the guard answered. The older
man was always asking for more food and smokes. After a couple of weeks, he was released. I was happy for everybody released
from that crazy facility.

It is just amazing that the FBI trusts the Jordanians more than
the other American intelligence agencies. When I turned myself
in in the fall of 2001, the FBI confiscated my hard disk, and
when they sent me to Jordan, they sent the contents of my hard
disk to Jordan, too. The DoD has been trying for years to get
that disk. It doesn't make sense that the FBI would cooperate
more with foreign organizations than the domestic ones, but I
do believe that the Intel industry is like any other industry: you
buy the best product for the best price, regardless of the country
of origin. Do the Jordanians offer the best product in this case?
I'm not sure, but they understand the recipe of terrorism more
than Americans. Reportedly without the Jordanians in the field,
the Americans would never have achieved what they have.
However, the Americans over-estimate the capability of the
Jordanians by sending them people from all over the world, as
if the Jordanians were some super Intel Agency.

"I am going to show you some pictures, you tell me about
them," said ████████████████████████████. Lately, he and
████████████████████████████ Jordanian were appointed to
interrogate me; ████████████████████████ was the leader. In
Jordan, they have a technique in which two interrogators or
more interrogate you separately about the same thing, in order

to make sure that you don't change your statements. They rarely sat together and interrogated me.*

"Alright!" I said. ▮▮▮▮▮▮▮▮▮▮▮▮▮▮ started showing me pictures, and as soon as I saw the first one I knew it was from my computer, or more accurately the computer of the company I had been working for. My heart started to pound, and I felt my saliva getting extremely bitter. My face started to turn as red as an apple. My tongue got heavy and twisted. Not because I had done any crimes with my computer; there was really nothing on the hard drive but my business emails and other related data. I remember having over 1500 email messages, and a whole bunch of pictures. But there is more to it when somebody's freedom is violated.

The PC belonged to a company that trusted me, and the fact that a foreign country such as the U.S. was searching the disk and confiscating material was a big burden for the company. The PC held the financial secrets of a company, which the company wouldn't be willing to share with the rest of the world. Moreover, I worked for a family company and the family hardly drew a line between their company and their private lives, which meant that the computer also contained private familial data the family wouldn't share with the world. On top of that, in the office the PC was a shared station, and anybody in the company could and did use it, so there are a lot of data I didn't know of, though I was 100% sure there was no crime behind it, knowing my colleagues and their dedication to their work and life. I personally had emails with my friends in Germany, some of them aren't even Muslims. But I was more worried about my emails with the Muslim friends, especially any of the ones who had

---

* These might be the second and third of the Jordanian interrogators MOS mentioned at his 2005 ARB hearing and briefly profiles later in this chapter. ARB transcript, 21.

ever financially or spiritually helped the oppressed people in Bosnia or Afghanistan, because their messages would be interpreted evilly. Just put yourself in my shoes and imagine somebody storming your house and trying to mess with your whole private life! Would you welcome such an assault?

I started to answer him to the best of my knowledge, especially about my own pictures. He put the pictures I could identify on one side, and the rest on another side. I explained to him that the PC had been used by several colleagues, one of whom scanned all kinds of different pictures for the clients of the Internet café, including all kinds of private family pictures. I was so mad at myself, my government, the U.S., and the Jordanians because I saw how many people's private lives were being violated. I was also confronted in a later session with a couple emails I interchanged with ███████████████████████████. The funny thing was that Mehdi sent an email before I got arrested, and the Mauritanian government interrogated me about it and I explained to them with definite evidence that there was no evil in it.* As soon as I got back to my office I wrote ████████ the following email: "Dear Brother! Please stop sending emails, because the Intel are intercepting our emails and giving me a hard time." I openly didn't want any trouble, and so wanted to close any door that would lead in that direction.

"Why did you write ████████ this email?" asked ████████ ████████████████.

---

* The name "Mehdi" appears unredacted twice in this passage. This is likely Karim Mehdi. Born in Morocco, Mehdi lived in Germany and appears, from Judge Robertson's habeas opinion, to have traveled with MOS to Afghanistan in 1992. Mehdi was arrested in Paris in 2003 and sentenced to nine years in prison for plotting a bombing on Reunion Island. See https://www.aclu.org/files/assets/2010-4-9-Slahi-Order.pdf; http://articles.latimes.com/print/2003/jun/07/world/fg-terror7; and http://news.bbc.co.uk/2/hi/africa/6088540.stm.

I explained the message to him.

"No, it's because you are afraid that the government would learn about your mischiefs with your friend," he commented sillily.

"Well, this message was addressed to both Mehdi and the government. I know my emails are intercepted by the government, and I always assumed that the government got a copy of my email traffic," I said.

"You were using a code when you wrote ███████████ ████████████████████," he said.

"Well, I am sure you have dealt with coded messages in your career, or you have specialists who help you. Go to them first, before you make up your mind."

"No, I want you to explain the code to me."

"There is no code, what you understand is what I meant." But I had another issue with the Jordanian interrogators: my original emails were in German, and the Americans translated them into English and sent them to the Jordanians, who in their turn translated the English versions into Arabic. Under these circumstances, the original text suffered and the space for evil interpretations widened with every translation.

And there was no end to evil interpretations. In the summer 2001 I was tasked by my company to technologically assist the visit of the Mauritanian President to the city of Tidjikja. The family that employed me is from Tidjikja, so it made sense that their interest lay in the well-being of the city. We installed a small media consulting center that operated over the Internet to transmit the visit of the President in real time. The company took many pictures where my colleagues and I appeared close to the president. In the closest one, the President stood behind my neck wondering at me "magically playing with the computer."

"I can tell, you were plotting to kill the President," said ███████████████.

I couldn't help laughing. "So why didn't I kill him?"

"I don't know. You tell me," █████████████████ said.

"Look! If I tried to kill my president in my country, it's none of your business, nor that of the Americans. Just turn me over to my country and let them deal with me." I was both angry and hopeful, angry because the U.S. wanted to pin any crime on me, no matter what, and hopeful because they were going to turn me over to my country to suffer the death penalty. The Americans couldn't possibly have dreamt of a better option. But the Jordanians were fishing on behalf of the Americans, and whenever you notice your interrogator fishing, you can be sure that he is bankrupt.

Though he was as evil as he could be, ██████████████ was sort of a reasonable interrogator, and so he never asked me again about the plot on my President, nor about the pictures in my hard disk. And yet I regretted that I didn't act on the suspicion and make myself look guilty in order to get myself extradited back to Mauritania. It was a crazy and desperate idea, and I don't think that the Mauritanians would have played along because they knew for a fact I hadn't plotted against the president. But when my situation worsened in the Jordanian prison, I thought about confessing that I had an operation going on in Mauritania, and had hidden explosives. The idea was that I would try to be sent back to Mauritania.

"Don't do that! Just be patient and remember that Allah is watching," one of my guards told me when I asked him for advice. By then I had made a lot of friends among the guards; they brought me the news and taught me about Jordanian culture, the torture methods in the prison, and who's who among the interrogators.

It was categorically forbidden for the guards to interact with the detainees, but they always broke these rules. They recounted the latest jokes to me and offered me cigarettes, which I turned down because I don't smoke. They told me about the other detainees and their cases and also about their own private lives, marriage, children, and the social life in Jordan. I learned almost everything about life in Amman from speaking with them. They also brought me the best books from the library—even the Bible, which I requested because I wanted to study the book that must more or less have shaped the lives of the Americans. In Jordan they have a pretty respectable collection, though some of it is meant as propaganda for the King. The best part about the books was that detainees used them to pass messages back and forth, solacing each other by writing good things inside the book. I didn't know any detainees, but the first thing I always did was to sift through a book looking for messages. I memorized all of them.

The guards were picked mostly from the Bedouin tribes that are known for their historical loyalty to the King, and paid miserable wages, about $430 a month, give or take. Although this wage is among the best in Jordan, a guard can't start a family without another support of his own. But when a guard serves for fifteen years, he has the option of retiring with half of his current wage or continuing with that money plus his usual wage. The guards are part of Jordan's Elite Special Forces, and enjoy all kinds of training overseas. There are no females in the Special Forces.

███████████████████ were responsible for moving detainees from one cell to another, to interrogations, to the shower, or to see their parents during the visits that took place on Fridays. I was so frustrated when I had to watch everybody seeing his family, while week after week I was deprived of that right. Lower ranking guards were responsible for the watch, and

██████████████████ for the grocery that took place every Saturday. The responsible ██████████████ would go cell to cell with a list, writing down what each detainee wished to buy. You could buy juice, milk, candy, underwear, a towel, and that was about it; if you had enough money you would get what you ordered, and if not then not. I had about $87 on me when I was sent to Jordan, which seemed to have been enough for my modest groceries. One time, when the ██████████████████ was going around with his list, I spotted my name and my accusation: "Participation in Terrorist attacks."

Every other day the guards offered you a five-minute recreation time. I hardly ever took advantage of it; the fact that I had to be shackled and blindfolded was just not worth it. Every once in a while detainees got their hair cut, and every Sunday the guards gave us cleaning materials to mop our cells, and they mopped the floor. The jail was not dirty.

The prison was run by three individuals: the director of the prison ██████████████████████████████ his two assistants, ██ ██████. They played a role similar to the one ████████████ in GTMO Bay. They are supposedly independent from the Intel community, but in practice both work together and collect Intels, each with its own methods. The director was a very big guy who dressed proudly in his Bedouin-civilian suits. He passed by every morning and asked every single detainee, "How are you doing? Need anything?" He always woke me up asking me the same question.

During my entire eight months in the Jordanian prison I asked him once for a water bottle, which he brought me. I wanted to put the ice-cold water I got from the faucet on the heater in order to warm it up so I could take care of my own hygiene. I do think that it was a good thing for him to check on detainees. However, the chances were really zero that detainees were going to fix any problems with the help of a director who also was actively taking part in torture. The Director made sure that everybody got three meals a day, breakfast around 7 a.m., lunch around 1 p.m., mostly chicken and rice, and dinner, a light meal with tea.

██

were continually patrolling through the corridor and checking on everybody, including whether the guards were following the rules. ████████████████████████ was responsible for what they call External Operations, such as capture and house searches.

Then there were the interrogators. Jordanian Interrogators have been working side-by-side with the Americans since the beginning of the operation baptized the "Global War Against Terrorism," interrogating people both inside and outside Jordan. They have agents in Afghanistan, where they profit from their average Middle Eastern looks. In the beginning the Jordanians were seen as a potential associate for doing the dirty work; the fact that Jordanians widely use torture as a means to facilitate interrogation seemed to impress the American authorities. But there was a problem: the Jordanians don't take anybody and torture him; they must have reason to practice heavy physical torture. As Americans grew hardened in their sins, they started to take the dirty job in their own hands. Nonetheless, being arrested in a Jordanian Jail is an irreparable torture already.

I had three interrogators in Jordan. ████████████████
██
██
████████████████████████████████. He has been leading the interrogators team in Jordan, and interrogating detainees himself in GTMO, and most likely in other secret places in Afghan-

istan and elsewhere, on behalf of the U.S. government. He seems to be widely-known in Jordan, as I learned from a Jordanian detainee in GTMO. ████████████████████████ seemed to be pretty well experienced: he saw my file once and decided it wasn't worth wasting his "precious" time on me, and so he never bothered to see me again.

██

██

█████████████████████████.*

"You know, ███████████████████, your only problem is your time in Canada. If you really haven't done nothing in Canada, you don't belong in jail," concluded ██████████████████ after several sessions.

He was a specialist on Afghanistan; he himself had attended the training camps there as an undercover agent during the war against communism. When I was training in Al Farouq in '91, he was working undercover as a student in Khalden.† He questioned me thoroughly about my whole trip to Afghanistan and showed satisfaction with my answers. That was very much his whole job. In the winter of 2001 he was sent, maybe undercover, to Afghanistan and Turkey to help the U.S. capture Mujahideen, and I saw him when he came back in the summer of 2002 with a whole bunch of pictures. Part of his

---

* Preceded with a "2" in a passage subtitled "Interrogators," this redaction likely introduces the second Jordanian interrogator.

† Court documents indicate that MOS trained at the al-Farouq training camp near Khost, Afghanistan, for six months in late 1990 and early 1991. At the time, both the al-Farouq and Khalden camps were training al-Qaeda fighters for the conflict with the Soviet-backed government in Kabul. As the appellate court reviewing MOS's habeas case wrote, "When Salahi took his oath of allegiance in March 1991, al-Qaida and the United States shared a common objective: they both sought to topple Afghanistan's Communist government." See http://www.aclu.org/files/assets/2010-4-9-Slahi-Order. pdf; and http://caselaw.findlaw.com/us-dc-circuit/1543844.html.

mission was to gather Intels about me from other detainees in Afghanistan, but he didn't seem to have come up with anything. ███████████████████████████ showed me the pictures. I didn't recognize anybody, and felt bad for myself. Why did they show me more than 100 pictures, and I knew none of them? It didn't make sense. Usually, interrogators ask about people that are connected to you. So I decided to recognize at least one picture.

"This is Gamal Abdel Nasser," I said.

"You are making fun of me, aren't you?" said ███████████ ██████████████ angrily.

"No, no, I just thought it looks like him." ███████████ is a former Egyptian president who died before I was born.*

"These people are from the same gang as you are," ████ ██████████████ said.

"Maybe. But I don't know them," I said. He didn't say much after that; ████████████████████ just spoke about his adventure in Afghanistan. "You're courageous," I remarked, to give him fuel for more talk.

"You know, the Americans are using smart weapons that follow their target based on temperature changes. Many brothers have been captured," ██████████████████████ recounted under the thick cloud of his cigarette smoke. I never saw ████████████████████ after that session.

████████████████████; I know his real first name.†

---

* Nasser, Egypt's second president, died in 1970. The redaction here seems especially absurd.

† Numbered "3," this redaction seems to introduce the third Jordanian interrogator, who appears to have been MOS's primary interrogator in Jordan. At his 2005 ARB hearing, MOS said that his main interrogator in Jordan was "young" and "a very bright guy." He testified that this particular interrogator "struck me twice in the face on different occasions and pushed me against concrete many times because I refused to talk to him," and

Boom! He slapped me across the face, and pushed my face against the wall. I was sobbing, maybe more because of frustration than pain.

"You are not a man! I am going to make you lick the dirty floor and tell me your story, beginning from the point when you got out of your mother's vagina," he continued. "You haven't seen nothing yet." He was correct, although he was the biggest liar I ever met. He lied so much that he contradicted himself because he would forget what he had said the last time about a specific topic. In order to give himself credibility, he kept swearing and taking the Lord's name in vain. I always wondered whether he thought I believed his garbage, though I always acted as if I did; he would have been angry if I called him a liar. He arrested big al Qaeda guys who talked about me being the bad guy, and he released them a thousand and one times from the prison when they told the truth. The funny thing was that he always forgot that he arrested and released them already.

"I arrested your cousin Abu Hafs and he told me the whole truth. As a matter of fact, he said 'Don't you put your hands on me, and I'm gonna tell you the truth,' and I didn't, and he did. He told me bad things about you. After that I bid him farewell and secretly sent him to Mauritania, where he was going to be interrogated for a couple of weeks and released. But you're different. You keep holding back Intels. I am going to send you to the secret political prison in the middle of the desert. Nobody is gonna give a shit about you." I had to keep listening to this same garbage over and over; the only thing he changed was the dates of arrest and release. In his dreams, he also arrested ████, ███████████████████████████████, and other individuals

---

"threatened me with a lot of torture and...took me to the one room where they torture and there was this guy who was beaten so much he was crying, crying like a child." ARB transcript, 21.

who had supposedly been providing information about me. Good for him; as long as he didn't beat me or attack me verbally I was cool, and would just listen carefully to his Thousand-and-One-Arabian-Nights tales.

"I've just arrived from the U.S., where I interrogated ██████████████████," he obviously lied.

"Well, that's good, because he must have told you that he doesn't know me."

"No, he said he does."

"Well, that's none of your business, right? According to you, I've done crimes against the U.S., so just send me to the U.S. or tell me what have I done against your country," I remarked sharply. I was growing tired of the futile conversation with him, and of trying to convince him that I had nothing to do with the Millennium Plot.

"I am not working for the Americans. Some of your friends are trying to hurt my country, and I'm asking you indirect questions as an interrogation technique," ███████████████ lied.

"Which friends of mine are trying to hurt your country?" I wondered.

"I cannot tell you!"

"Since I haven't tried to hurt your country, there's no blaming me. I am not my friends. Go and arrest them and release me." But if you are trying to make sense of things, the interrogation room is not for you. Whenever ███████████████ told me he had arrested somebody, I knew that the guy was still free.

Although he used physical violence against me only twice, he kept terrorizing me with other methods that were maybe worse than physical pain. He put a poor detainee next to my interrogation room, and his colleague started to beat him with a hard object until he burst out crying like a baby. How cheap! That was painful. I started to shake, my face got red, my saliva got as bitter as green persimmon, my tongue as heavy as metal. Those are the symptoms I always suffer when I get extremely scared, and the constant fear didn't seem to harden me. My depression reached its peak.

"Do you hear what's happening next door?"

"Yes."

"Do you want to suffer the same?" I almost said yes. It was so hard for me to helplessly listen to somebody suffering. It's not easy to make a grown-up cry like a baby.

"Why? I am talking to you!" I said, showing a fake composure. After all, the brother next door was also talking to his interrogator. ████████████████████ sardonically smiled and continued to smoke his cigarette as if nothing were happening. That night I was very cooperative and quiet; the logical and argumentative human being in me disappeared all of a sudden. ██████████████████████ knew what he was doing, and he had apparently been doing it for a long time.

He would make me pass through the torture row so I would hear the cries and moans and the shouting of the torturers. I was blessed because the guards kept me blindfolded so I couldn't see the detainees. I was not supposed to see them, nor was I interested in seeing a brother, or actually anybody, suffering. The Prophet Mohamed (Peace be upon him) said, "God tortures whoever tortures human beings," and as far as I understand it, the person's religion doesn't matter.

"I am going to send you to the Shark Pool," ███████████████ ██████ threatened me, when I refused to talk to him after he hit me.

"You don't know me. I swear by Almighty God I'll never talk to you. Go ahead and torture me. It will take my death to make me talk, and for your information I'm sorry for every bit of cooperation I have offered in the past," I said.

"First of all, your cooperation was achieved by force. You

didn't have a choice. Nor will you in the future: I am going to make you talk," ██████████████████████ said.

██████████████████████████ started to push me against the wall and hit me on the sides of my face, but I didn't feel any pain. I don't think he hit me with his whole strength; the guy looks like a bull, and one real blow from him would have cost me 32 teeth. As he was hitting me, he started to ask me questions. I don't remember the questions, but I do remember my answers. There was only one answer.

"Ana Bari'a, I am innocent." I drove him crazy, but there was no making me talk.

"I have no time right now, but you're gonna suffer heavily tomorrow, son of a....." he said, and immediately left the room.

The escort took me back to my cell. It was around midnight; I sat on my prayer mat and started reading the Koran and praying until very late. I could hardly concentrate on what I was reading. I kept thinking, What will it be like in the Shark Pool? I had heard of an electrified pool, I knew they used one in Egypt, but "Shark Pool" sounded terrible.

But the rendezvous came and went without me being taken to the torture place, one day, two day, three days! Nothing happened to me, except for no food, not because they didn't give it to me but because I had no appetite, as always when I get depressed. I learned later from the Jordanian detainee in GTMO who spent fifty days in the same prison that there is no such thing as the Shark Pool, but that they do have other painful methods of torture, like hanging detainees from their hands and feet and beating them for hours, and depriving them from sleep for days until they lose their minds.

"In Jordan they don't torture unless they have evidence," █████████████ said. "If they knew what I do, they wouldn't even bother arresting you. The Americans told them to," ██████████████ continued.

"The torture starts around midnight and finishes around dawn. Everybody takes part, the prison director, the interrogators, and the guards," ████████████████ said. ██████████████ information was consistent with what I saw. I personally heard beatings, but I don't know whether the detainees were hung up or not when the beating happened. And I witnessed sleep deprivation more than once.

Late one night when I was talking to some of my guard friends, I kept hearing sounds as if some people were performing harsh training with loud voices to get the whole energy out of their body, like in Kung-Fu. I heard heavy bodies hitting the floor. It was just too noisy, and too close to my ██████████ ██████████████.

"Are you guys training so late?" I asked one of the guards. Before he could say a word, another guy appeared dressed in a Ninja-like suit that covered him from head to toe. The guard looked at him and turned to me, smiling.

"Do you know this guy?" he asked. I forced an official smile.

"No." The new guy took his mask off, and he looked like the devil himself. Out of fear, my smile turned to laughter. "Oh, yes! We know each other," I said.

"██████████████ asks if you guys are training now?" my guard wryly asked the Ninja.

"Yes! Do you want to train with us? We have many detainees enjoying PT," he said sardonically. I knew right away that he meant torture. My laughter faded into a smile, and my smiled into fixed lips over my teeth. I didn't want to reveal my disappointment, fear, and confusion.

"No, I'm just fine," I said. The devil resumed his business, and I asked the guard, "Why do they put on the masks for this type of job?"

"They want to protect their identities. In Jordan, you can get killed for doing such things." He was right: most of the detainees were arrested because they know something, not because of crimes, and so they will be released sooner or later. I wished I hadn't known about that mischief; it was just impossible for me to sleep when I was listening to grown-ups crying like babies. I tried to put every object in my ears and around my head but nothing helped. As long as the torture lasted, I couldn't sleep. The good thing was that the torture wasn't every day, and the voices didn't always reach my cell.

In February 2002, the director of Jordan's Antiterrorism Department was the subject of an assassination plot.* He almost gave his soul back. Somebody planted a time bomb in the chassis of the car of the biggest target of the Islamic movement in Jordan. The bomb was supposed to explode on the way between his home and his office—and it did. But what happened seemed like a miracle. On his way to work, the Director felt like buying cigarettes. His driver stopped in front of a store and left to grab a pack of cigarettes. The director felt like going with his chauffeur. As soon as both left the car, the bomb exploded. Nobody was harmed, but the vehicle was history.

The investigation led to a suspect, but the secret police couldn't find him. But the King of the Fight against Terrorism cannot be messed with; suspects must be arrested and the guilty party must be found. Immediately. The Jordanian secret Agency had to have revenge for the big head. The peaceful brother of the

---

* Press reports document an assassination attempt like the one described here, aimed at General Ali Bourjaq, head of Jordan's antiterrorism unit, on February 20, 2002, in Amman. See, e.g., http://weekly.ahram.org .eg/2002/576/re72.htm.

suspect was to be taken as a pawn and tortured until his brother turned himself in. Special Forces were sent out, arrested the innocent boy in a crowded place, and beat him beyond belief. They wanted to show people the destiny of a family when one of its members tries to attack the government. The boy was taken to the prison and tortured every day by his interrogator.

"I don't care how long it takes, I am going to keep torturing you until your brother turns himself in," his interrogator said. The family of the boy was given the opportunity to visit the boy, not for humane reasons, but because the interrogator wanted the family to see the miserable situation of the boy so they would turn in the suspected son. The family was devastated, and soon the information leaked that the suspect was hiding in his family's house. Late that night, an operation stormed the house and arrested him. The next day his brother was released.

"What will you say if somebody asks you about the bruises and injuries I caused you?" the interrogator asked him.

"I'll say nothing!" answered the boy.

"Look, we usually keep people until they heal, but I'm releasing you. You go ahead and file anything you like against me. I did what I got to do to capture a terrorist, and you're free to go." As to his brother, he was taken care of by the director himself: he kept beating him for six straight hours. And that is not to mention what the other interrogators did to satisfy their chief. I learned all this from the guards when I noticed that the prison had become remarkably crowded. Not that I could see anybody, but the food supply shrunk decidedly; they kept moving detainees to and from their cells; whenever detainees were led past my cell the guards closed my bin hole; and I saw the different shifts of guards more frequently than usual. The situation started to improve in the summer of 2002.

By then, the Jordanians were basically done with me. When

████████████████████ finished my hearing, he handed me my statements. "Read the statements and sign them," he said.

"I don't need to read them, I trust you!" I lied. Why should I read something when I didn't have the option to sign or to refuse? No judge would take into consideration somebody's statements that were coerced in a prison facility such as the Jordanian Military prison.

After about a week ████████████████████ took me to interrogation in a nice room. "Your case is closed. You haven't lied. And I thank you for your cooperation. When it comes to me, I am done with you, but it's the decision of my boss when you'll go home. I hope soon."

I was happy with the news; I had expected it, but not that soon.

"Would you like to work for us?" he asked me.

"I'd like to, but I really am not qualified for this type of work," I said, partly lying and partly telling the truth. He tried in a friendly way to convince me, but I, with the most friendliness I could manage, told him that I was way too much of an idiot for Intel work.

But when the Jordanians shared the result of their investigation with the U.S. and sent them the file, the U.S. took the file and slapped the Jordanians in their faces. I felt the anger of Uncle Sam thousands of miles away, when ████████████████ ██████ came back into his old skin during the last two months of my incarceration in Jordan. The interrogations resumed. I tried all I could to express myself. Sometimes I talked, sometimes I refused. I hunger-struck for days, but ██████████████ ████████████ made me eat under threat of torture. I wanted to compel the Jordanians to send me back home, but I failed. Maybe I wasn't hardcore enough.

GTMO

SECRET//NOFORN 324 PROTECTED

They had no reason to doubt me b/c I never lied to them and ▮ made sure to get me the ▮ i GTMO. I took

"Who do you think you are? I am not telling the truth b/c of ▮ I would cooperate, to my advantage, with every body regardless his gender or his look. Just calm down,

"I am leaving" said. ▮ also was upset b/c I told that ~~doesn't~~ didn't have experience as much

~~SECRET//NOFORN~~ ~~PROTECTED~~

GTMO

February 2003–August 2003

First "Mail" and First "Evidence"...The Night of Terror...The DOD Takes Over...24 Hour Shift Interrogations...Abduction inside the Abduction...The Arabo-American Party

"The rules have changed. What was no crime is now considered a crime."

"But I've done no crimes, and no matter how harsh you guys' laws are, I have done nothing."

"But what if I show you the evidence?"

"You won't. But if you do, I'll cooperate with you."

██████████ showed me the worst people in ██████████. There were fifteen, and I was number 1; number 2 was ██████████ ██████████.*

"You gotta be kidding me," I said.

---

* At his 2005 ARB hearing, MOS told the panel, "Then the FBI at GTMO Bay during the time era of General Miller, they released a list of the highest priority detainees here at GTMO. It was a list of 15 people and I was, guess which number, number ONE. Then they sent a special FBI team and the leader was [redacted] and I worked with him especially for my case....I thought he was just making fun of me when he said I was number ONE in the camp, but he was not lying; he was telling the truth,

"No, I'm not. Don't you understand the seriousness of your case?"

"So, you kidnapped me from my house, in my country, and sent me to Jordan for torture, and then took me from Jordan to Bagram, and I'm still worse than the people you captured with guns in their hands?"

"Yes, you are. You're very smart! To me, you meet all the criteria of a top terrorist. When I check the terrorist check list, you pass with a very high score."

I was so scared, but I always tried to suppress my fear. "And what is your ▮▮▮▮ check list?"

"You're Arab, you're young, you went to Jihad, you speak foreign languages, you've been in many countries, you're a graduate in a technical discipline."

"And what crime is that?" I said.

"Look at the hijackers: they were the same way."

"I am not here to defend anybody but myself. Don't even mention anybody else to me. I asked you about my crime, and not about x's or y's crimes. I don't give a damn!"

"But you are part of the big conspiracy against the U.S."

"You always say that. Tell me my part in this 'big conspiracy!'"

"I am going to tell you, just *sabr*, be patient."

My sessions continued with arguments of this nature. Then one day when I entered the interrogation room ▮▮▮▮▮▮▮ ▮▮▮▮▮▮▮▮▮▮▮▮▮, I saw video equipment already hooked up. To be honest, I was terrified that they were going to show me a video with me committing terrorist attacks. Not that I have done anything like that in my life. But a fellow detainee

as future events would prove. He stayed with me until May 22, 2003."
ARB transcript, 24.

called ▓▓▓▓▓▓▓▓▓▓▓▓▓▓▓▓▓▓▓▓▓▓▓▓ told me that his interrogators forged an American passport bearing his picture. "Look: We now have definitive evidence that you forged this passport and you were using it for terrorist purposes," they told him. ▓▓▓▓▓▓▓▓▓▓▓▓▓ laughed wholeheartedly at the silliness of his interrogators. "You missed that I'm a computer specialist, and I know that the U.S. government would have no problem forging a passport for me," he said. The interrogators quickly took the passport back and never talked about it again.

Scenarios like that made me very paranoid about the government making up something about me. Coming from a third-world country, I know how the police wrongly pin crimes on political rivals of the government in order to neutralize them. Smuggling weapons into somebody's house is common, in order to make the court believe the victim is preparing for violence.

"Are you ready?" said ▓▓▓▓▓▓▓▓▓.

"Y-e-e-s!" I said, trying to keep myself together, though my blushing face said everything about me. ▓▓▓▓▓▓▓▓ hit the play button and we started to watch the movie. I was ready to jump when I saw myself blowing up some U.S. facility in Timbuktu. But the tape was something completely different. It was a tape of Usama bin Laden speaking to an associate I didn't recognize about the attack of September 11. They were speaking in Arabic. I enjoyed the comfort of understanding the talk, while the interrogators had to put up with the subtitles.

After a short conversation between UBL and the other guy, a TV commentator spoke about how controversial the tape was. The quality was bad; the tape was supposedly seized by U.S. forces in a safehouse in Jalalabad.

But that was not the point. "What do I have to do with this bullshit?" I asked angrily.

"You see Usama bin Laden is behind September 11," ▮▮▮▮▮ ▮▮▮ said.

"You realize I am not Usama bin Laden, don't you? This is between you and Usama bin Laden; I don't care, I'm outside of this business."

"Do you think what he did was right?"

"I don't give a damn. Get Usama bin Laden and punish him."

"How do you feel about what happened?"

"I feel that I'm not a part of it. Anything else doesn't matter in this case!" When I came back to ▮▮▮▮▮▮▮ Block I was telling my friends about the masquerade of the "definitive evidence" against me. But nobody was surprised, since most of the detainees had been through such jokes.

During my conversations with ▮▮▮▮▮▮▮ and his associate, I brought up an issue that I believe to be basic.

"Why are you guys banning my incoming mails?"

"I checked, but you have none!"

"You're trying to say that my family is refusing to respond to me?"

The brothers in the block felt bad for me. I was dreaming almost every night that I had received mail from my family. I always passed on my dreams to my next door neighbors, and the dream interpreters always gave me hope, but no mails came. "I dreamt that you got a letter from your family," was a common phrase I used to hear. It was so hard for me to see other detainees having pictures of their families, and having nothing— zip—myself. Not that I wished they never got letters: on the contrary, I was happy for them, I read their correspondence as if it were from my own mom. It was customary to pass newly received mails throughout the block and let everybody read them, even the most intimate ones from lovers to the beloved.

▮▮▮▮▮▮▮ was dying to get me cooperating with him, and

he knew that I had brought my issue to the detainees. So he was working with the mail people to get me something. A recipe was prepared and cooked, and around 5 p.m. the postman showed up at my cell and handed me a letter, supposedly from my brother. Even before I read the letter, I shouted to the rest of the block, "I received a letter from my family. See, my dreams have come true, didn't I tell you?" From everywhere my fellow detainees shouted back, "Congratulations, pass me the letter when you're done!"

I hungrily started to read, but I soon got a shock: the letter was a cheap forgery. It was not from my family, it was the production of the Intel community.

"Dear brothers, I received no letter, I am sorry!"

"Bastards, they have done this with other detainees," said a neighbor. But the forgery was so clumsy and unprofessional that no fool would fall for it. First, I have no brother with that name. Second, my name was misspelled. Third, my family doesn't live where the correspondent mentioned, though it was close. Fourth, I know not only the handwriting of every single member of my family, but also the way each one phrases his ideas. The letter was kind of a sermon, "Be patient like your ancestors, and have faith that Allah is going to reward you." I was so mad at this attempt to defraud me and play with my emotions.

The next day, ███████████ pulled me for interrogation.

"How's your family doing?"

"I hope they're doing well."

"I've been working to get you the letter!"

"Thank you very much, good effort, but if you guys want to forge mail, let me give you some advice."

"What are you talking about?"

I smiled. "If you don't really know, it's okay. But it was cheap to forge a message and make me believe I have contact with my dear family!" I said, handing the strange letter back.

"I don't shit like that," ████████████ said.

"I don't know what to believe. But I believe in God, and if I don't see my family in this life, I hope to see them in the afterlife, so don't worry about it." I honestly don't have proof or disproof of whether ████████████ was involved in that dirty business. But I do know that the whole matter is much bigger than ████████████; there are a bunch of people working behind the scene.* ████████ was in charge of my case through ████████████, but I was taken for interrogation a couple of times by other ████████████████████████████ without his consent or even knowledge. As to letters from my family, I received my first letter, a Red Cross message, on February 14, 2004, 816 days after I was kidnapped from my house in Mauritania. The message was seven months old when it reached me.

"I am gonna show you the evidence bit by bit," said ████████████ one day. "There is a big al Qaeda guy who told us that you are involved."

"I guess you shouldn't ask me questions then, since you have a witness. Just take me to court and roast me," I said. "What have I done, according to your witness?"

"He said you are a part of the conspiracy." I grew tired of the words Big Conspiracy against the U.S. ████████████ could not give me anything to grab onto, no matter how much I argued with him.

As to ████████████, he was not an argumentative guy. "If

---

* People were indeed "working behind the scene." Though the FBI was still leading MOS's interrogation, the DOJ IG found that through the spring of 2003, "Military Intelligence personnel observed many of Slahi's interviews by Poulson and Santiago from an observation booth," and that MI agents were complaining about the FBI's rapport-building approach. The Senate Armed Services Committee reported that military interrogators started circulating a draft "Special Interrogation Plan" for MOS in January 2003. DOJ IG, 298; SASC, 135.

the government believes that you're involved in bad things, they're gonna send you to Iraq or back to Afghanistan," ▮▮▮▮▮▮▮ said.*

"So if you guys torture me, I'm gonna tell you everything you want to hear?"

"No, look: if a mom asks her kid whether he's done something wrong, he might lie. But if she hits him, he's gonna admit it," replied ▮▮▮▮▮▮▮. I had no answer to this analogy. Anyway, the "big al Qaeda" guy who testified against me turned out to be ▮▮▮▮▮▮▮▮.† ▮▮▮▮▮▮▮▮ was said to have said that I helped him to go to Chechnya with two other guys who were among the hijackers, which I hadn't done. Though I had seen ▮▮▮▮▮▮ once or twice in Germany, I didn't even know his name. Even if I had helped them to go to Chechnya, that would be no crime at all, but I just hadn't.

By then I knew about the horrible torture that ▮▮▮▮▮▮ had suffered after his arrest ▮▮▮▮▮▮▮. Eyewitnesses who were captured with him in Karachi said, "We thought he was dead. We heard his cries and moans day and night until he was separated from us." We had even heard rumors in the camp that he died under torture. Overseas torture was obviously a

---

* This may be the agent the DOJ's Inspector General calls Santiago. The IG reported that MOS "identified Santiago as a 'nice guy,'" and recorded that MOS reported to investigators that "Santiago told Slahi he would be sent to Iraq or Afghanistan if the charges against him were proved." DOJ IG, 296.

† The passage likely refers to Ramzi bin al-Shibh. MOS explained at his ARB hearing, and indicates elsewhere in the manuscript as well, that he learned about bin al-Shibh's treatment in CIA black sites from detainees who were captured alongside bin al-Shibh and held with him in secret sites before being transferred to Guantánamo. MOS told the ARB panel that "a Yemeni guy who was captured with Ramiz [sic] told him, "Ramiz was tortured. We would hear his cries every night, we would hear his moans every night." ARB transcript, 25; see also MOS manuscript, 83, 294.

common practice and professionally executed; I heard so many testimonies from detainees who didn't know each other that they couldn't be lies. And as you shall see, I was subject to torture in this base of GTMO, like many other fellow detainees. May Allah reward all of us.

"I don't believe in torture," said ████████████. I didn't share with him my knowledge about Ramzi having been tortured. But because the government has sent detainees including me, ████████████████████████, and ████████████████████████████ overseas to facilitate our interrogation by torture, that meant that the government believes in torture; what ████████████ believes in doesn't have much weight when it comes to the harsh justice of the U.S. during war.

████████████████ finally came forth on his promise to deliver the reasons why his government was locking me up. But he didn't show me anything that was incriminating. In March 2002 CNN had broadcast a report about me claiming that I was the coordinator who facilitated the communication between the September 11 hijackers through the guestbook of my homepage. Now ████████████████████ showed me the report.*

"I told you that you fucked up," ████████████ said.

"I didn't design my homepage for al Qaeda. I just made it a long time ago and never even checked on it since early 1997. Besides, if I decided to help al Qaeda, I wouldn't use my real

---

* This appears to refer to a story CNN aired on March 6, 2002, the transcript of which is titled "Al Qaeda Online for Terrorism." As MOS indicates here, the story suggested that he was "running a seemingly innocuous website" where al-Qaeda was secretly exchanging messages through the website's guestbook. The allegation that MOS ran a website that facilitated al-Qaeda communications does not appear in any of the summaries of evidence against MOS from Guantánamo. See http://transcripts.cnn.com/TRANSCRIPTS/0203/06/lt.15.html.

name. I could write a homepage in the name of John Smith."
██████████ wanted to know everything about my homepage
and why I even wrote one. I had to answer all that bullshit
about a basic right of mine, writing a homepage with my real
name and with some links to my favorite sites.

In one session, ██████████ asked, "Why did you study
microelectronics?"

"I study whatever the heck I want. I didn't know that I had
to consult the U.S. government about what I should or should
not study," I said wryly.

"I don't believe in the principle of black and white. I think
everybody is somehow in between. Don't you think so?"
██████████ asked.

"I've done nothing."

"It is not a crime to help somebody to join al Qaeda and he
ended up a terrorist!" ████████████████████████████████.
I understood exactly what ██████████ meant: Just admit that
you are a recruiter for al Qaeda.

"Might be. I'm not familiar with U.S. laws. But anyway, I
didn't recruit anybody for al Qaeda, nor did they ask me to!" I
said.

As a part of his "showing me the evidences against me,"
██████████ asked a colleague of his for help. ██████████
██████████, a ██████████████████████ who interrogated
me back in ████████████████████████████████.* ██████████
██████████ is one of those guys, when they speak you think
they're angry, and they might not be.

"I am happy that you showed up, because I would like to
discuss some issues with you," I said.

---

* "Mauritania" appears unredacted a few sentences later; the agent is
apparently one of the FBI agents who questioned MOS in Nouakchott in
February 2000.

"Of course, ████████████ is here to answer your questions!" said ████████████.

"Remember when you guys came to interrogate me in Mauritania?" I began. "Remember how sure you were that I was not only involved in Millennium, but that I was the brain behind it? How do you feel now, knowing that I have nothing to do with it?"

"That's not the problem," ████████████ answered. "The problem was that you weren't honest with us."

"I don't have to be honest to you. And here's a news flash for you: I'm not going to talk to you unless you tell me why I am here," I said.

"That's your problem," ████████████ said. You could tell that ████████████ was used to humbled detainees who probably had to cooperate due to torture. He was by then interrogating ████████████.* He spoke very arrogantly; he as much as told me, "You're gonna cooperate, even against your will, ha! ha!" I admit I was rude with him, but I was so angry since he had wrongly accused me of having been part of the Millennium Plot and now was dodging my requests to him to come clean and say he and his government were wrong.

████████████ looked worn out from his trip; he was very tired that day. "I don't see why you don't cooperate," he said. "They share food with you, and speak to you in a civilized way," he said.

"Why should I cooperate with any of you? You're hurting me, locking me up for no reason."

"We didn't arrest you."

"Send me the guy who arrested me, I'd like to talk to him."

---

* Possibly Ramzi bin al-Shibh; see footnote on p. 203.

After that tense discussion, the interrogators left and sent me back to my cell.

"For these next sessions, I have asked for ███████████ to help me in laying out your case. I want you to be polite to him," ███████████ said at our next session.

I turned to his colleague. "Now you're convinced that I am not a part of Millennium. What's the next shit you're gonna pull on me?"

"You know, sometimes we arrest people for the wrong thing, but it turns out they are involved in something else!" ███████████ said.

"And when are you going to stop playing this game on me? Every time there is a new suspicion, and when that turns out to be incorrect, I get a new one, and so on and so forth. Is there a possibility in the world that I am involved in nothing?"

"Of course; therefore you have to cooperate and defend yourself. All I am asking is for you to explain some shit to me," said ███████████. When ███████████ arrived he had a bunch of small papers with notes, and he started to read them to me. "You called ███████████ and asked him to bring you some sugar. When you told him about ███████████████ in Germany, he said, 'Don't say this over the phone.' I wouldn't say something like that to anybody I called."

"I don't care what ███████████ says over the phone. I am not here on behalf of ███████████; go and ask him. Remember, I'm asking you what *I* have done."

"I just want you to explain these conversations to me — and there's much more," said ███████████.

"No, I am not answering anything before you answer my question. What have I done?"

"I don't say you've done anything, but there are a lot of things that need to be clarified."

"I've answered those questions a thousand and one times; I told you I mean what I am saying and I'm not using any code. You're just so unjust and so paranoid. You're taking advantage of me being from a country with a dictatorship. If I were German or Canadian, you wouldn't even have the opportunity to talk to me, nor would you arrest me."

"In asking you to cooperate, we're giving you an opportunity. After we share the cause of your arrest with you, it will be too late for you!" ▓▓▓▓▓▓▓▓▓▓ said.

"I don't need any opportunities. Just tell me why you arrested me, and let it be too late." ▓▓▓▓▓▓▓▓ knew me better than ▓▓▓▓▓▓▓▓▓ did; thus, he tried to calm both of us down. ▓▓▓▓▓▓▓▓▓ was trying to scare me, but the more he scared me, the sharper and less cooperative I got.

The camp was locked down the whole day. Around 10 p.m. I was pulled out of my cell and taken to ▓▓▓▓▓▓▓ building. The room was extremely cold. I hate to be woken up for interrogation, and my heart was pounding: Why would they take me so late?

I don't know how long I'd been in the room, maybe two hours. I was just shaking. I made my mind up not to argue anymore with the interrogators. I'm just gonna sit there like a stone, and let them do the talking, I said to myself. Many detainees decided to do so. They were taken day after day to interrogation in order to break them. I am sure some got broken because nobody can bear agony the rest of his life.

After letting me sweat, or let's say "shake," for a couple hours, I was taken to another room ▓▓▓▓▓▓▓▓▓▓▓▓▓▓ ▓▓▓▓, where ▓▓▓▓▓▓▓▓▓▓▓▓▓▓▓▓ sat. This room was acceptably cold. The military people were watching and listening from another room as usual.

"We couldn't take you during the day because the camp was locked down," said ███████████. "We had to take you now, because ████████████████ is leaving tomorrow."

I didn't open my mouth. ████████████ sent his friends out. "What's wrong with you?" he said. "Are you OK? Did anything happen to you?" But no matter how he tried, there was no making me talk.

The team decided to take me back to the cold room. Maybe it wasn't so cold for somebody wearing regular shoes, underwear, and a jacket like the interrogators, but it was definitely cold for a detainee with flip-flops and no underwear whatsoever.

"Talk to us!" ████████████ said. "Since you refuse to talk, ████████████████ is going to talk to you anyway."

████████████ started his lecture, "We have been giving you an opportunity, but you don't seem to want to take advantage of it. Now it's too late, because I am going to share some information with you."

████████████ put down three big pictures of four individuals who are believed to be involved in the September 11 attack. "This guy is ████████████████████. He was captured ████████████████████████████ and since then I've been interrogating him.* I know more about him than

---

* It appears that this interrogator has been, or claims to have been, questioning Ramzi bin al-Shibh in the CIA black sites. At his ARB hearing, naming bin al-Shibh, MOS described what could be the same exchange with an interrogator this way: "Okay, then his interrogator [redacted] from the FBI asked him to speculate who I was as a person. He said I think he is an operative of Usama bin Laden and without him I would have never been involved in September 11th. That was a big accusation. The interrogator could have lied because they lie all the time, but that is what they said." ARB transcript, 23–24.

he knows about himself. He was forthcoming and truthful with me. What he told me goes along with what we know about him. He said that he came to your house on advice of a guy named ███████████████, whom he met on a train. ████████████████ wanted somebody to help him getting to Chechnya."

"That was around Oct 1999," he continued. "He showed up at your house with these two guys," he said, pointing at ██ ████████████ and ████████████████. "The other guy," he said, pointing at Atta, "was not able to see you because he had a test. You advised them to travel through Afghanistan instead of Georgia, because their Arab faces would give them away and they probably would have been turned back. Furthermore, you gave them a phone contact in Quetta of a guy named ██████ ████████████████. These guys traveled shortly after that meeting with you to Afghanistan, met Usama Bin Laden, and swore a pledge to him. Bin Laden assigned them to the attack of September 11, and sent them back to Germany."

He went on. "When I asked ████████████ what he thinks about you, he replied that he believes you to be a senior recruiter for Usama Bin Laden. That's his personal opinion. However, he said that without you, he would never have joined al Qaeda. In fact, I'd say without you September 11 would never have happened. These guys would have gone to Chechnya and died."

████████████████ excused himself and left. I was kept the rest of the night with ████████████████████████████ ████████████████████████. I was so scared. The guy made me believe I was the one behind September 11. How could that possibly have happened? I was like, Maybe he's right. And yet anybody who knew the basics about the attack, which were published and updated through time, can easily see what a swiss cheese ████████████ was trying to sell me. The guys he mentioned were reportedly trained in 1998, and joined al Qaeda and were assigned to the attack then. How could I possibly have sent them in October 1999 to join al Qaeda, when they not only already were al Qaeda, but had already been assigned to the attack for more than a year?

I was kept up the rest of the night and forced to see pictures of dead body parts which were taken at the site of the Pentagon after the attack. It was a nasty sight. I almost broke down, but I managed to keep myself silent and together.

"See the result of the attack?" ████████████ asked.

"I don't think he foresaw what these were going to do," said ████████████. They were talking to each other, asking and answering each other. I kept myself as the present-absent. They kept sliding those nasty pictures in front of me the whole night. At the break of dawn, they sent me back to a cell in a new block, ████████████. I prayed and tried to sleep, but I was kidding myself. I could not get the human body parts out of my head. My new neighbors, especially ████████████████████ tried to help me.

"Don't worry! Just talk to them and everything is gonna be alright," he encouraged me. Maybe his advice was prudent, and anyway I felt that things were going to get nastier. So I decided to cooperate.

████████████ pulled me to interrogation the next day. I was so worn out. I had no sleep last night, nor during the day.*

---

* A 1956 CIA study titled "Communist Control Techniques: An Analysis of the Methods Used by Communist State Police in the Arrest, Interrogation, and Indoctrination of Persons Regarded as 'Enemies of the State'" had this to say about the effects of sleep deprivation and temperature

"I am ready to cooperate unconditionally," I told him. "I don't need any proof whatsoever. You just ask me questions and I'm gonna answer you." And so our relationship seemed to enter a new era.

During his time with me, ███████████ made a couple of trips, one to ████████████████ and one to ███████████, in order to investigate my case and gather evidence against me. In February 2003, while he was on his trip to ████████████ an

---

manipulation as coercive interrogation methods: "The officer in charge has other simple and highly effective ways of applying pressure. Two of the most effective of these are fatigue and lack of sleep. The constant light in the cell and the necessity of maintaining a rigid position in bed compound the effects of anxiety and nightmares in producing sleep disturbances. If these are not enough, it is easy to have the guards awaken the prisoners at intervals. This is especially effective if the prisoner is always awakened as soon as he drops off to sleep. The guards can also shorten the hours available for sleep, or deny sleep altogether. Continued loss of sleep produces clouding of consciousness and a loss of alertness, both of which impair the victim's ability to sustain isolation. It also produces profound fatigue.

"Another simple and effective type of pressure is that of maintaining the temperature of the cell at a level which is either too hot or too cold for comfort. Continuous heat, at a level at which constant sweating is necessary in order to maintain body temperature, is enervating and fatigue producing. Sustained cold is uncomfortable and poorly tolerated....

"The Communists do not look upon these methods as 'torture.' Undoubtedly, they use the methods which they do in order to conform, in a typical legalistic manner to overt Communist principles which demand that 'no force or torture be used in extracting information from prisoners.' But these methods do, of course, constitute torture and physical coercion. All of them lead to serious disturbances of many bodily processes."

Sleep deprivation has been used specifically in the service of conditioning prisoners to make false confessions. A study by the U.S. Air Force sociologist Albert Biderman of the means by which North Korean interrogators were able to coerce captured U.S. airmen into falsely confessing to war crimes found that sleep deprivation, as a form of induced debilitation, "weakens mental and physical ability to resist." See http://www.theblackvault.com/documents/mindcontrol/comcont.pdf; and http://www2.gwu.edu/~nsarchiv/torturing democracy/documents/19570900.pdf.

agent from the ████████████████████████████████ pulled me to interrogation.

"My name is ██████████████, from ███████. I came here to ask you some questions about your time in ████████████," said ████████████ while flashing his badge. He was accompanied with one female and one male who were just taking notes.*

"Welcome! I'm glad that you have come because I want to clarify some reports you produced about me which are very inaccurate." I continued, "Especially since my case with the U.S. is spinning around my time in ████████████, and every time I argue with the Americans they refer to you. Now I want you guys to sit with the Americans and answer one question: Why are you arresting me? What crime have I done?"

"You have done nothing," ████████████████ said.

"So I don't belong here, do I?"

"We didn't arrest you, the U.S. did."

"That's correct, but the U.S. claims that you pitted them on me."

"We just have some questions about some bad people, and we need your help."

"I'm not helping you unless you tell the Americans in front of me that one or the other of you lied."

The agents went out and brought ██████████████ in, who was probably watching the session through the ██████████████ ██████████.

"You are not honest, since you refuse to answer the ██████

---

* These might be agents of the Canadian Security Intelligence Service (CSIS). The *Toronto Star* has reported that CSIS agents interviewed detainees with ties to Canada in Guantánamo, including MOS, in February 2003. See Michelle Shephard, "CSIS Grilled Trio in Guantánamo," http://www .thestar.com/news/canada/2008/07/27/csis_grilled_trio_in_cuba.html.

questions. This is your opportunity to get help from them," ███████████ said.

"███████████, I know this game better than you do. Stop trying to talk nonsense to me," I said. "Look, you keep telling me the ███████████ say such and such. Now it's you guys' opportunity to face me with my charges," I said.

"We don't accuse you of any crime," said ███████████.

"Then release me!"

"That's not in my hands." ███████████ tried to convince me but there was no convincing me. I was sent back to my cell and taken again the next day, but I just sat there like a stone. I didn't waste a word because I had told them clearly the conditions of my cooperation. The ███████████ also interrogated a teenager ███████████ called ███████████ ███████████ and made the Army take all his belongings. We detainees felt bad for him: he was just too young for this whole campaign.*

When ███████████ came back, he was pissed off because the ███████████ had ignored him and were exposing me to whomever they wanted. Now I knew the ███████████ had no control over my

---

* The teenager is very likely Omar Khadr. In 2010 the Supreme Court of Canada found that Khadr's interrogations by Canadian Security Intelligence Service (CSIS) and the Foreign Intelligence Division of the Department of Foreign Affairs and International Trade (DFAIT) agents in Guantánamo in February and September 2003 and March 2004 violated the Canadian Charter of Rights and Freedoms. The Supreme Court held, "The deprivation of [Khadr]'s right to liberty and security of the person is not in accordance with the principles of fundamental justice. The interrogation of a youth detained without access to counsel, to elicit statements about serious criminal charges while knowing that the youth had been subjected to sleep deprivation and while knowing that the fruits of the interrogations would be shared with the prosecutors, offends the most basic Canadian standards about the treatment of detained youth suspects." The Supreme Court's opinion is available at http://scc-csc.lexum.com/decisia-scc-csc /scc-csc/scc-csc/en/item/7842/index.do.

fate; they didn't have the ability to deal with me, and henceforth I could not really trust them. I don't like to deal with somebody who cannot keep his word. I knew then for a fact that the ████████ was nothing but a step, and the real interrogation was going to be led by ████████████. If you look at the situation, it makes sense: most of the detainees were captured by ████████████ in a military operation, and they wanted to maintain the upper hand. ████████ are only guests in GTMO, no more, no less; the facility is run by █████████████████████ ███████████████████████.

It happened again. When ████████████ went to █████████████ in May 2003, the ████████████ reserved me for interrogation, and they were no luckier than their fellow citizens from ████████████; ███████ was completely overawed by his colleagues from the ████████ command.

████████████ came back from █████████████. "I was ordered to quit your case and go back to the U.S. My boss believes that I'm only wasting my time. The MI will take your case," ████████████ told me. I wasn't happy that ████████████ was leaving, but I wasn't really that upset. ████████████ was the guy who understood the most about my case, but he had neither power nor people who backed him up.

The next day the team organized a pretty lunch party. They bought good food as a good-bye. "You should know that your next sessions will not be as friendly as these have been," ████████████ said, smiling wryly. "You will not be brought food or drinks anymore." I understood the hint as rough treatment, but I still never thought that I was going to be tortured. Furthermore, I believed that ████████████ and his associate ████████████ would inform the proper authorities to stop a crime if they knew one was going to happen.

"I wish you good luck, and all I can tell you is to tell the truth,"  said. We hugged, and bid each other good-bye.*

When I entered the room a desk was prepared with several chairs on the other side of the table. As soon as the guards locked me up to the floor

entered the room

. You

---

* MOS told the Administrative Review Board that his last interview with FBI interrogators took place on May 22, 2003; the DOJ IG report confirms that "in late May 2003 the FBI agents who were involved with Slahi left GTMO, and the military assumed control over Slahi's interrogation." ARB transcript, 25; DOJ IG, 122.

A few days after the military took over MOS's interrogation, an FBI agent circulated a report documenting FBI concerns about the military's interrogation methods in Guantánamo. According to the DOJ IG report, a month later, on July 1, 2003, the FBI's assistant general counsel, Spike Bowman, sent an e-mail to senior FBI officials, "alerting them that the military had been using techniques of 'aggressive interrogation,' including 'physically striking the detainees, stripping them and pouring cold water on them and leaving them exposed (one got hypothermia) and similar measures.' Bowman opined that: 'Beyond any doubt, what they are doing (and I don't know the extent of it) would be unlawful were these Enemy Prisoners of War (EPW). That they are not so designated cannot be license to do something that you cannot do to an EPW or criminal prisoner.' Bowman expressed concern that the FBI would be 'tarred by the same brush' and sought input on whether the FBI should refer the matter to the DOD Inspector General, stating that '[w]ere I still on active duty, there is no question in my mind that it would be a duty to do so.'" ARB transcript, 25; DOJ IG, 122, 121.

could tell they had a head start I didn't. ███████████
███████████ brought heavy binders with them, and were
talking to each other.*

"When is the guy supposed to come?"

"Nine o'clock." Against interrogation customs, ███████████

███

██████. It was a technique used to scare and irritate the detainee.

The door opened. "I am sorry, I was thinking diplomatic
time," the new arrival said. "You know, those of us from
███████████████ are on another time." The ███████████
looking gentleman was dying to impress. I wasn't sure how
much he succeeded. He was a ███████████████████████
███████████. He even brought his McDonald's with him,
but offered nothing to anybody.

"I just arrived from Washington," he commenced. "Do you
know how important you are to the U.S. government?"

"I know how important I am to my dear mom, but I'm not
sure when it comes to the U.S. government." ███████████
couldn't help smiling, although ██████ tried hard to keep █████
frown. I was supposed to be shown harshness.

"Are you ready to work with us? Otherwise your situation is
gonna be very bad," the man continued.

"You know that I know that you know that I have done

---

* MOS described this new DOD team at his ARB hearing, saying it was
led by "a female interrogator" who was "a very beautiful lady and decent
lady" whom he identified, apparently mistakenly, as an FBI agent. In fact,
she may merely have been posing as an FBI agent. The DOJ Inspector General found that "the person who identified herself as 'Samantha' was actually
an Army Sergeant." According to the IG, "On several occasions in early
June 2003 an Army Sergeant on the DIA Special Projects Team at GTMO
identified herself to Slahi as FBI SSA 'Samantha Martin' in an effort to
persuade Slahi to cooperate with interrogators." At his ARB hearing, MOS
said the team included "another weird guy, I think he was CIA or something
but he was very young." ARB transcript, 25; DOJ IG, 296, 125.

nothing," I said. "You're holding me because your country is strong enough to be unjust. And it's not the first time you have kidnapped Africans and enslaved them."

"African tribes sold their people to us," he replied.

"I wouldn't defend slavery, if I were in your shoes." I said. I could tell ███████████ was the one with the most power, even though the government let other agencies try their chances with detainees. It's very much like a dead camel in the desert, when all kinds of bugs start to eat it.

"If you don't cooperate with us we're gonna send you to a tribunal and you're gonna spend the rest of your life in prison," ████ said.

"Just do it!"

"You must admit to what you have done," ████████████ said, gesturing to a big binder in front of ████.

"What have I done?"

"You know what you've done."

"You know what, I am not impressed, but if you have questions I can answer you," I said.

"I have been working along with ████████████ ████████████ on your case. ████████████ are gone. But I'm still here to give you an opportunity."

"Keep the opportunity for yourself, I need none." The purpose of this session was to scare the hell out of me, but it takes more than that to scare me. The ████████████ disappeared for good, and I never saw him again; ████████████ ████████████ kept interrogating me for some time, but there was nothing new. Both ████████ were using dead-traditional methods and techniques I probably mastered better than they had.

"What is the name of your current wife?" ████████████ favorite question. When I arrived in Cuba on August ███, 2002

I was so hurt physically and mentally that I literally forgot the name of my wife and provided a wrong one. ███████████ wanted to prove that I am a liar.

"Look, you won't provide us information we don't already know. But if you keep denying and lying, we'll assume the worst," said ████████████. "I have interrogated some other detainees and found them innocent. I really have a problem sleeping in a comfortable room while they suffer in the block. But you're different. You're unique. There's nothing really incriminating, but there are a lot of things that make it impossible not to be involved."

"And what is the straw that broke the camel's back?"

"I don't know!" ████████████ answered. █████ was a respectable ████████ and I very much respected ████ honesty. █████ was appointed to torture me but ████ ultimately failed, which led to ████ separation from my case. To me ████████████ ████████ was an evil person. ████ always laughed sardonically.

"You're very rude," ████ once said.

"So are you!" I replied. Our sessions were not fruitful. Both ███████████████████████████████ wanted to reach a breakthrough, but there was no breakthrough to be reached. Both wanted me to admit to being part of the Millennium Plot, which I wasn't. The only possible way to make me admit to something I haven't done is to torture me beyond my limit of pain.

"You're saying that I am lying about that? Well guess what, I have no reason not to keep lying. You don't seem any more impressive than the hundred interrogators I have had lately," I said. ████████████ was playing the smart interrogator–bad guy.

"You're funny, you know that?"

"Whatever that means!"

"We're here to give you an opportunity. I've been in the

block for a while, and I am leaving soon, so if you don't cooperate..." ▮▮▮▮▮ continued.

"Bon Voyage!" I said. I felt good that ▮▮▮▮▮ was leaving
because I didn't like ▮▮▮.

"You speak with a French accent."

"Oh, God, I thought I speak like Shakespeare," I said wryly.

"No you speak pretty well, I only mean the accent." ▮▮▮▮▮
▮▮▮▮▮▮▮▮▮ was a polite and honest person. "Look, we have
so many reports linking you to all kinds of stuff. There is nothing incriminating, really. But there are too many little things.
We will not ignore anything and just release you."

"I'm not interested in your mercy. I only want to be released
if my case is completely cleared. I really am tired of being
released and captured in an endless Catch-22."

"You need your freedom, and we need information. You give
us what we need and in return, you get what you need,"
▮▮▮▮▮▮▮▮▮ said. The three of us argued this way for days
without any success.

And then the guy I call "I-AM-THE-MAN" came into play.
It was around noon when ▮▮▮▮▮▮▮▮▮▮▮ joined ▮▮▮▮
▮▮▮▮▮▮▮▮▮ while they were interrogating me. ▮▮▮▮
▮▮▮▮▮▮▮▮▮▮▮▮▮▮ said, gesturing to ▮▮▮▮▮▮▮
▮▮▮.

"This ▮▮▮▮▮ is working for me. He is going to be seeing
you often, among others who are working for me. But you're
gonna see me also." ▮▮▮▮▮▮▮▮▮▮▮ sat there like a stone;
he didn't greet me or anything. He was writing his notes and
hardly looked at me, while the other ▮▮▮▮▮▮▮▮ were asking questions. "Don't make jokes, just answer ▮▮ questions,"
he said at one point. I was like, Oops. ▮▮▮▮▮▮▮▮▮▮▮
▮▮▮▮▮▮▮▮▮▮▮▮▮▮▮▮▮▮▮▮▮▮▮▮▮▮▮▮▮
▮▮▮▮▮▮▮▮▮▮▮▮▮▮▮▮▮▮ was chosen with some

others to do the dirty work. He had experience in MI; he had interrogated Iraqis who were captured during operation Desert Storm. He speaks ████████████████████████ ████████████████████████████████. All he was able to hear was his own voice. I was always like, Is this guy listening to what I am saying? Or let's just say his ears were programmed to what he wanted to hear.*

"I'm an asshole," he said once. "That is the way people know me, and I have no problem with it."

For the next month I had to deal with ████████████████ and his small gang. "We are not ████████████; we don't let lying detainees go unpunished. Just maybe not physical torture," he said. I had been witnessing for the last months how detainees were consistently being tortured under the orders of ████ ████████████████████████.† ████████████████████ was taken to interrogation every single night, exposed to loud music and scary pictures, and molested sexually. I would see ████████████

---

* At his 2005 ARB hearing, MOS described a member of the military interrogation team who was as an army first sergeant, and said, "I don't hate him but he was a very hateful guy." MOS appears to have given the ARB panel this interrogator's real name. I believe this may be the same interrogator he refers to as "I-AM-THE-MAN" in this scene and also by the nickname Mr. Tough Guy, which appears unredacted on page 222. In all there appear to be four interrogators who play major roles in MOS's Special Projects Team. ARB transcript, 25.

† We do not know whom MOS specifically names here. It is a matter of record, however, that military interrogators in Guantánamo were under the command of the Joint Task Force Guantánamo (JTF-GTMO), which was led at this time by General Geoffrey Miller. Their interrogation methods were sanctioned first by the "Counter Resistance Techniques" memorandum that Defense Secretary Donald Rumsfeld signed on December 22, 2002; then by a March 13, 2003, legal opinion written by John Yoo of the Office of Legal Counsel; and finally by another authorization memo that Rumsfeld signed on April 16, 2003. The Senate Armed Services Committee found that General Miller sought official Pentagon approval for, and Rumsfeld personally signed off on, MOS's "Special Interrogation Plan." SASC, 135–38.

████ when the guards took him in the evening and brought him back in the morning. He was forbidden to pray during his interrogation. I remember asking the brothers what to do in that case. "You just pray in your heart since it's not your fault," said the Algerian Sheikh in the block. I profited from this fatwa since I would be exposed to the same situation for about a year. ████████████ was not spared the cold room. █ ████████████ suffered the same; moreover his interrogator smashed the Koran against the floor to break him, and had the guards push his face down against the rough floor. ████████████ also suffered sexual molestation. I saw him taken back and forth almost every night as well. Not to speak of the poor young Yemenis and Saudis who were grossly tortured the same way.* But since I'm speaking in this book about my own experience, which reflects an example of the evil practices that took place in the name of the War Against Terrorism, I don't need to talk about every single case I witnessed. Maybe on another occasion, if God so wills.

When ████████████ informed me about the intentions of his team, I was terrified. My mouth dried up, I started to sweat, my heart started to pound (a couple weeks later I developed hypertension) and I started to get nausea, a headache, a stomach-ache. I dropped into my chair. I knew that ████████████ was not kidding, and I also knew that he

---

* The Schmidt-Furlow report, the DOJ IG report, the Senate Armed Services Committee report, and several other sources all document the sexual humiliation and sexual assault of Guantánamo prisoners, often carried out by female military interrogators. After the release of the Schmidt-Furlow report in 2005, a *New York Times* op-ed titled "The Women of GTMO" decried the "exploitation and debasement of women in the military," noting that the report "contained page after page of appalling descriptions of the use of women soldiers as sexual foils in interrogations." See http://www.nytimes.com/2005/07/15/opinion/15fri1.html.

was lying about physical pain-free torture. But I held myself together.

"I don't care," I said.

Things went more quickly than I thought. ▮▮▮▮▮▮▮▮ ▮▮▮▮ sent me back to the block, and I told my fellow detainees about being overtaken by the torture squad.

"You are not a kid. Those torturers are not worth thinking about. Have faith in Allah," said my next ▮▮▮▮▮▮▮▮ ▮▮▮▮▮▮▮▮▮▮▮▮. I really must have acted like a child all day long before the guards pried me from the cellblock later that day. You don't know how terrorizing it is for a human being to be threatened with torture. One literally becomes a child.

The Escort team showed up at my cell.

"You got to move."

"Where?"

"Not your problem," said the hateful ▮▮▮▮▮ guard. But he was not very smart, for he had my destination written on his glove.

"Brothers pray for me, I am being transferred ▮▮▮▮▮▮▮ ▮▮▮▮▮▮▮▮▮▮▮▮▮▮ was reserved by then for the worst detainees in the camp; if one got transferred ▮▮▮▮▮▮▮▮▮▮▮▮▮, many signatures must have been provided, maybe even the president of the U.S. The only people I know to have spent some time ▮▮▮▮▮▮▮▮▮▮▮▮▮▮ since it was designed for torture were a Kuwaiti detainee and another fellow detainee from ▮▮▮▮▮▮▮▮*

---

* It is now likely around mid-June 2003. MOS told the Administrative Review Board, "Around June 18th, 2003, I was taken from Mike Block and put in India Block for total isolation." Former detainees who were held

When I entered the block, it was completely empty of any signs of life. I was put at the end of the block and the Yemeni fellow was at the beginning, so there was no interaction whatsoever between us. ███████████████████████ was put in the middle but with no contact either. Later on both were transferred somewhere else, and the whole block was reserved for me, only me, ALLAH, ████████████████████, and the guards who worked for them. I was completely exposed to the total mercy ██████████████████████, and there was little mercy.

In the block the recipe started. I was deprived of my comfort items, except for a thin iso-mat and a very thin, small, worn-out blanket. I was deprived of my books, which I owned, I was deprived of my Koran, I was deprived of my soap. I was deprived of my toothpaste and of the roll of toilet paper I had. The cell—better, the box—was cooled down to the point that I was shaking most of the time. I was forbidden from seeing the light of the day; every once in a while they gave me a rec-time at night to keep me from seeing or interacting with any detainees. I was living literally in terror. For the next seventy days I wouldn't know the sweetness of sleeping: interrogation 24 hours a day, three and sometimes four shifts a day. I rarely got a day off. I don't remember sleeping one night quietly. "If you start to cooperate you'll have some sleep and hot meals," ████ ██████████ used to tell me repeatedly.

Within a couple of days of my transfer, ██████████████ from the International Committee of the Red Cross showed up

for a time in India Block describe windowless solitary confinement cells that were often kept at frigid temperatures. See, e.g., James Meek, "People the Law Forgot," *Guardian*, December 2, 2003. The second detainee being held in India Block when MOS arrives seems to be identified in the next paragraph as Yemeni. ARB transcript, 26; http://www.theguardian.com /world/2003/dec/03/guantanamo.usa1.

at my cell and asked me whether I wanted to write a letter. "Yes!" I said. ██████████████ handed me a paper and I wrote, "Mama, I love you, I just wanted to tell you that I love you!" After that visit I wouldn't see the ICRC for more than a year. They tried to see me, but in vain.*

"You're starting to torture me, but you don't know how much I can take. You might end up killing me," I said when ████████████████ and ██████████████ pulled me for interrogation.

"We do recommend things, but we don't have the final decision," ████████████ said.

"I just want to warn you: I'm suffering because of the harsh conditions you expose me to. I've already had a sciatic nerve attack. And torture will not make me more cooperative."

"According to my experience, you will cooperate. We are stronger than you, and have more resources," ████████████ ████ said. ██████████████ never wanted me to know his name, but he got busted when one of his colleagues mistakenly called him by his name. He doesn't know that I know it, but, well, I do.

██████████████ grew worse with every day passing by. He started to lay out my case. He began with the story of ████████████, and me having recruited him for the September 11 attack.†

---

* An October 9, 2003 JTF-GTMO Memorandum for the Record recounts a contentious meeting between a visiting delegation of the International Committee of the Red Cross and Guantánamo commander General Geoffrey Miller. During the meeting, General Miller "informed [ICRC team leader Vincent] Cassard that ISN 760, 558, and 990 were off limits during this visit due to military necessity." MOS is ISN 760. The minutes of the ICRC meeting are available at http://www.washingtonpost.com/wp-srv/nation/documents/GitmoMemo10-09-03.pdf.

† It seems likely from the context here that the interrogator is referring to Ramzi bin al-Shibh.

"Why should he lie to us," ███████████████ said.

"I don't know."

"All you have to say is, 'I don't remember, I don't know, I've done nothing.' You think you're going to impress an American jury with these words? In the eyes of the Americans, you're doomed. Just looking at you in an orange suit, chains, and being Muslim and Arabic is enough to convict you," ██████████████ said.

"That is unjust!"

"We know that you are a criminal."

"What have I done?"

"You tell me, and we'll reduce your sentence to thirty years, after which you'll have a chance to lead a life again. Otherwise you'll never see the light of day. If you don't cooperate, we're going to put you in a hole and wipe your name out of our detainee database." I was so terrified because I knew that even though he couldn't make such a decision on his own, he had the complete back-up of a high government level. He didn't speak from thin air.

"I don't care where you take me, just do it."

In another session when he was talking to me ███████████ ███████████████████████████. "What the fuck do you mean, tea or sugar?"

"I just meant what I said, I was not talking in code."

"Fuck you!" ██████████████ said. I figured I wouldn't degrade myself and lower myself to his level, so I didn't answer him. When I failed to give him the answer he wanted to hear, he made me stand up, with my back bent because my hands were shackled to my feet and waist and locked to the floor. ██████████████ turned the temperature control all the way down, and made sure that the guards maintained me in that situation until he decided otherwise. He used to start a fuss before going to lunch, so he could keep me hurt during his lunch, which took at least two to three hours. ██████████ likes his food; he never missed his lunch. I always wondered how ████████████████ could possibly have passed the Army's fitness test. But I realized he was in the Army for a reason: he was good at being inhumane.

"Why are you in jail?" he asked me.

"Because your country is unjust, and my country isn't defending me?"

"Now you're saying that we Americans are just looking for skinny Arabs," he said. ██████████████ came with him occasionally, and it was kind of a blessing for me. I grew tired of dealing with a lifeless face like ████████████████. When ████████████████ came I felt like I was meeting with a human being. ██████ offered me the appropriate chair for my back pain, while ████████████████ always insisted on the metal chair or the dirty floor.*

"Do you know that ██████████████████████████ is dealing such and such?" ██████ asked me, naming some kind of drug.

"What the hell do you mean?" I asked.

"You know what ██████ means," ████████████████ ████████████ smiled because ██████ knew that I wasn't lying. I really could have been anything but a drug dealer, and ████████████████ was dying to link me to any crime no matter what.

"It's a type of narcotic," ████████████████████ replied.

---

* MOS seems to be contrasting the approaches of two of his interrogators, possibly the female interrogator identified in government documents by the name of Samantha and the interrogator he called "I-AM-THE-MAN."

"I'm sorry, I am not familiar at all with that circle."

███████████ and his bosses realized that it took more
███████████████████████████. And so they decided to
bring ████████ interrogator into play. Sometime ███████
█████████ I was taken ████████████████████ to reservation. The escorting team was confused.

"They said █████████████████████? That's weird!"
said one of the guards.

When we entered the building there were no monitoring guards. "Call the D.O.C.!" said the other.* After the radio call, the two guards were ordered to stay with me in the room until my interrogators showed up. "Something's wrong," said the ███████████ one. The escort team didn't realize that I understood what they were talking about; they always assume that detainees don't speak English, which they typically don't. The leadership in the camp always tried to warn the guards; signs like "DO NOT HELP THE ENEMY," and "CARELESS TALK GIVES SECRETS AWAY," were not rare, but the guards talked to each other anyway.

█████████████████████████ was at one point a regular interrogation booth, then a building for torture, then an administrative building. My heart was pounding; I was losing my mind. I hate torture so much. A slim, small ███████████ entered the room followed by Mr. Tough Guy.† ███████████ ███████████ was a ███████████████████████████ █████████████████████████████████ ███████████████████. Neither greeted me, nor released my hands ██████████████████.

---

* According to the 2003 Camp Delta Standard Operating Procedures, "DOC" is the acronym for the Detention Operations Center, which directs all movements within Guantánamo.

† "Mr. Tough Guy" appears here unredacted.

"What is this?" ███████ asked, showing me a plastic bag with a small welding stick inside.*

"It's Indian incense," I replied. That was the first thing that came to my mind. I thought ████ wanted to give me a treat by burning the incense during the interrogation, which was a good idea.

"No, you're wrong!" ████ almost stuck it in my face.

"I don't know," I said.

"Now we have found evidence against you; we don't need any more," said ████. I was like, What the hell is going on, is that part of a bomb they want to pull on me?

"This is a welding stick you were hiding in your bathroom," ████████████ said.

"How can I possibly have such a thing in my cell, unless you or my guards gave it to me? I have no contact whatsoever with any detainees."

"You're smart, you could have smuggled it," said ███████.

"How?"

"Take him to the bathroom," ████ said. ████████████ ████████████████████████████████ The guards grabbed me to the bathroom. I was thinking, "Are these people so desperate to pull shit on me, I mean any shit?" In the meantime, a ██████ guard was explaining to ████████████████ how these welding sticks end up in the cells; I caught his last words when the guards were leading me back from the restroom. "It's common. The contractors keep throwing them in the toilets

---

* It appears from the redacted pronouns here, and becomes clear from unredacted pronouns later in the scene, that this interrogator is female. In the ARB transcript, MOS indicates that a couple of days after the male first sergeant started interrogating him, a female interrogator joined the team. This seems to be the second of the four interrogators who will carry out the "Special Interrogation Plan." She will become a central character. ARB transcript, 25.

after finishing with them." As soon as I entered, everybody suddenly shut up. ███████ put the welding stick back in a yellow envelope. ████████ never introduced herself, nor did I expect ████ to do so. The worse an interrogator's intention is, the more ███████████ covers his or ████ identity. But those people get busted the most, and so did ████████, when one of her colleagues mistakenly called ████████ by her name.

"How does your new situation look?" ████████ asked me.

"I'm just doing great!" I answered. I was really suffering, but I didn't want to give them the satisfaction of having reached their evil goal.

"I think he's too comfortable," ████████████ said.

"Get off the chair!" ████████ said, pulling the chair from beneath me. "I'd rather have a dirty farmer sitting on the chair than a smart ass like you," ████ continued, when my whole body dropped on the dirty floor. ████████████████████ ████████████████ killing me. Since June 20th I never got relief from them. ████████████████ obviously was getting tired of dealing with me, so his boss offered him fresh blood, manifesting in the person of ██████████████████████ spread the pictures of some September 11 suspects in front of me, namely ████████████████████████████████████ ██████████████████████.

"Look at these motherfuckers," said ████████.

"OK, now tell us what you know about those motherfuckers!" ████ said.

"I swear to God, I will not tell you one word, no matter what."

"Stand up! *Guards!* If you don't stand up, it'll be ugly," ████████ said. And before the torture squad entered the room I stood up, with my back bent because ████████████████ ████████████████████████ didn't allow me to stand up straight.* I had to suffer every-inch-of-my-body pain the rest of the day. I dealt with the pain silently; I kept praying until my assailants got tired and sent me back to my cell at the end of the day, after exhausting their resources of humiliations for that day. I didn't say a single word, as if I had not been there. You, Dear Reader, said more words to them than I did.

"If you want to go to the bathroom, ask politely to use the restroom, say 'Please, may I?'" Otherwise, do it in your pants," ▬▬▬▬ said.

Before lunch ▬▬▬▬▬▬▬▬▬▬ dedicated the time to speaking ill about my family, and describing my wife with the worst adjective you can imagine. For the sake of my family, I dismiss their degrading quotations. The whole time ▬▬▬ ▬▬▬▬▬▬▬▬▬▬ offered me just water and a cold meal; "You are not entitled to a warm meal unless you cooperate," ▬▬▬▬ said once. Whenever they started to torture me I refused to drink or eat. ▬▬▬▬ brought her lunch from outside to frustrate me.

"Yummy, ham is tasty," ▬▬▬ said, eating ▬▬ meal.

That afternoon was dedicated to sexual molestation. ▬▬▬
▬▬▬▬▬▬▬▬▬▬▬▬▬▬▬▬▬▬▬▬▬

▬▬▬▬▬▬▬▬▬▬▬▬▬▬▬▬▬▬▬▬▬

▬▬▬ blouse and was whispering in my ear, "You know how good I am in bed," and "American men like me to whisper in their ears," ▬▬▬▬▬▬▬▬▬▬▬▬▬▬▬▬
▬▬▬▬▬▬▬▬▬▬▬▬▬▬▬▬▬▬▬▬▬

▬▬▬▬▬▬▬▬▬▬▬▬▬▬▬▬▬▬▬▬▬

---

* Very likely because of shackling. Just a few pages before, MOS described how the interrogator "made me stand up, with my back bent because my hands were shackled to my feet and waist and locked to the floor." The Senate Armed Services Committee found that shackling MOS to the floor was prescribed in his "Special Interrogation Plan." SASC, 137.

███████████████████████ "I have a great body." Every once in a while ████████ offered me the other side of the coin. "If you start to cooperate, I'm gonna stop harassing you. Otherwise I'll be doing the same with you and worse every day. I am ███████████████████████ and that's why my government designated me to this job. I've always been successful. Having sex with somebody is not considered torture."*

████████ was leading the monologue ████████████ ████████. Every now and then the ██████████ entered and tried to make me speak, "You cannot defeat us: we have too many people, and we'll keep humiliating you with American ████████."

"I have a █████████████████ friend I'm gonna bring tomorrow to help me," ███ said. "At least ███████ cooperate," said ████████ wryly. ████████ didn't undress me, but ███ was touching my private parts with ███ body.

In the late afternoon, another torture squad started with another poor detainee. I could hear loud music playing. "Do you want me to send you to that team, or are you gonna cooperate?" ████████ asked. I didn't answer. They guards used to call ██████████████████████████████ because most of the torture took place in those buildings, and at night, when darkness started to cover the sorry camp.†

---

* This incident is well documented in the Schmidt-Furlow report, the DOJ IG's report, and elsewhere. Lt. Gen. Randall Schmidt and Lt. Gen. John Furlow, *Army Regulation 15-6: Final Report, Investigation into FBI Allegations of Detainee Abuse at Guantanamo Bay, Cuba Detention Facility* (hereinafter cited as Schmidt-Furlow). Schmidt-Furlow, 22–23; DOJ IG, 124. The Schmidt-Furlow Report is available at www.defense.gov/news/jul2005/d20050714 report.pdf.

† This might be "the Night Club." Elsewhere in the manuscript, MOS refers to a detainee who was "a member of the Night Club" and a guard who was "one of the Night Club attendants." MOS manuscript, 293.

███████████████████████ sent me back to my cell, warning me, "Today is just the beginning, what's coming is worse."

But in order ████████████████████████ to know how much torture a detainee can take, they need medical assistance. I was sent to a doctor, an officer in the Navy. I would describe him as a decent and humane person.*

"██████████████████████████████. I don't examine people with that shit on them," he said to the escorting ███████.

"The gentleman has a pretty serious case of sciatic nerve," he said.

"I cannot take the conditions I am in anymore," I told him. "I am being stopped from taking my pain medication and my Ensure, which were necessary to maintain my head above water," I said. The interrogators would organize the sessions so that they would cover the time when you are supposed to take your medication. I had two prescriptions, tabs for the sciatic nerve back pain and Ensure to compensate the loss of weight I had been suffering since my arrest. I usually got my meds between 4 and 5 p.m., and so the interrogators made sure that I was with them and missed my medication. But look at it, what sense does it make, if the interrogators work on hurting my back and then give me back pain medication, or to give me a bad diet and want me to gain weight?

---

* Court papers filed in MOS's habeas appeal reference records that may be from this exam: "The medical records document increased low back pain 'for the past 5 days while in isolation and under more intense interrogation'" and note that the pain medication prescribed for him could not be administered throughout July 2003 because he was at the "reservation." The June 9, 2010, Brief for Appellee is available at https://www.aclu.org/sites/default/files/assets/brief_for_appellee_-_july_8_2010.pdf.

"I don't have much power. I can write a recommendation, but it's the decision of other people. Your case is very serious!" he told me. I left the clinic with some hope, but my situation only worsened.

"Look, the doctor said I've developed high blood pressure. That's serious; you know that I was a hypotensive person before," I said the next time ███████ called me to interrogation

"You're alright, we spoke with the doctor," the interrogators replied. I knew then that my recipe was going to continue.

The torture was growing day by day. The guards on the block actively participated in the process. The ██████████████ tell them what to do with the detainees when they came back to the block. I had guards banging on my cell to prevent me from sleeping. They cursed me for no reason. They repeatedly woke me, unless my interrogators decided to give me a break. I never complained to my interrogators about the issue because I knew they planned everything with the guards.

As promised, ████████ pulled me early in the day. Lonely in my cell, I was terrified when I heard the guards carrying the heavy chains and shouting at my door "Reservation!" My heart started to pound heavily because I always expected the worst. But the fact that I wasn't allowed to see the light made me "enjoy" the short trip between my freakin' cold cell and the interrogation room. It was just a blessing when the warm GTMO sun hit me. I felt life sneaking back into every inch of my body. I would always get this fake happiness, though only for a very short time. It's like taking narcotics.

"How you been?" said one of the Puerto Rican escorting guards in his weak English.

"I'm OK, thanks, and you?"

"No worry, you gonna back to your family," he said. When he said that I couldn't help breaking in ███████.* Lately, I'd become so vulnerable. What was wrong with me? Just one soothing word in this ocean of agony was enough to make me cry. ████████████████████ we had a complete Puerto Rican division.† They were different than other Americans; they were not as vigilant and unfriendly. Sometimes, they took detainees to shower ████████████████████. Everybody liked them. But they got in trouble with those responsible for the camps because of their friendly and humane approach to detainees. I can't objectively speak about the people from Puerto Rico because I haven't met enough; however, if you ask me, Have you ever seen a bad Puerto Rican guy? My answer would be no. But if you ask, Is there one? I just don't know. It's the same way with the Sudanese people.

"████████████████████ and give him no chair," said the D.O.C. worker on the radio when the escort team dropped me in ████████████████████ ████████████████████ entered the room. They brought a picture of an American black man named ████████████████████."We're gonna talk today about ████████████████████ after bribing me with a weathered metal chair.‡

"I have told you what I know about ████████████████."

"No, that's bullshit. Are you gonna tell us more?"

---

* Is seems possible, if incredible, that the U.S. government may have here redacted the word "tears."

† MOS may be referring here to the particular cellblock in Camp Delta where he encountered the Puerto Rican division.

‡ It soon becomes clear that the lead interrogator is accompanied by another female interrogator, as his interrogator had threatened in the previous session.

"No, I have no more to tell."

The new ▆▆▆▆▆ pulled the metal chair away and left me on the floor. "Now, tell us about ▆▆▆▆▆▆▆▆▆▆ ▆▆▆▆▆▆▆▆!"

"No, that's passé," I said.

"Yes, you're right. So if it is passé, talk about it, it won't hurt," the new ▆▆▆▆▆ said.

"No."

"Then today, we're gonna teach you about great American sex. Get up!" said ▆▆▆▆▆▆. I stood up in the same painful position as I had every day for about seventy days.* I would rather follow the orders and reduce the pain that would be caused when the guards come to play; the guards used every contact opportunity to beat the hell out of the detainee. "Detainee tried to resist," was the "Gospel truth" they came up with, and guess who was going to be believed? "You're very smart, because if you don't stand up it's gonna be ugly," ▆▆▆▆▆▆▆▆▆.

As soon as I stood up, the two ▆▆▆▆▆ took off their blouses, and started to talk all kind of dirty stuff you can imagine, which I minded less. What hurt me most was them forcing me to take part in a sexual threesome in the most degrading manner. What many ▆▆▆▆▆ don't realize is that men get hurt the same as women if they're forced to have sex, maybe more due to the traditional position of the man. Both ▆▆▆▆▆ stuck on me, literally one on the front and the other older ▆▆▆▆ stuck on my back rubbing ▆▆ whole body on mine. At the same time they were talking dirty to me, and playing with my sexual parts. I am saving you here from quoting the disgusting and degrading talk I had to listen to from noon or before until

---

* That position is likely a forced stoop precipitated by the shackling of his wrists to the floor; see footnotes on pp. 225 and 227.

10 p.m. when they turned me over to ████████, the new character you'll soon meet.

To be fair and honest, the ████████ didn't deprive me from my clothes at any time; everything happened with my uniform on. The senior ████████████████ was watching everything ██.* I kept praying all the time.

"Stop the fuck praying! You're having sex with American ████████ and you're praying? What a hypocrite you are!" said ████████████████ angrily, entering the room. I refused to stop speaking my prayers, and after that, I was forbidden to perform my ritual prayers for about one year to come. I also was forbidden to fast during the sacred month of Ramadan October 2003, and fed by force. During this session I also refused to eat or to drink, although they offered me water every once in a while. "We must give you food and water; if you don't eat it's fine." They also offered me the nastiest MRE they had in the camp. We detainees knew that ████████████████ gathered Intels about what food a detainee likes or dislikes, when he prays, and many other things that are just ridiculous.

I was just wishing to pass out so I didn't have to suffer, and that was really the main reason for my hunger strike; I knew people like these don't get impressed by hunger strikes. Of course they didn't want me to die, but they understand there are many steps before one dies. "You're not gonna die, we're gonna feed you up your ass," said ████████████████.

I have never felt as violated in myself as I had since the DoD

---

* Like all interrogations, this session would likely be observed from a monitoring room. The 2003 Camp Delta Standard Operating Procedures mandated that during all interrogations "a JIIF monitor will be located either in a monitor room that is equipped with two-way mirrors and CCTV or in a CCTV only room." SOP, 14.2.

Team started to torture me to get me admit to things I haven't done. You, Dear Reader, could never understand the extent of the physical, and much more the psychological, pain people in my situation suffered, no matter how hard you try to put yourself in another's shoes. Had I done what they accused me of, I would have relieved myself on day one. But the problem is that you cannot just admit to something you haven't done; you need to deliver the details, which you can't when you hadn't done anything. It's not just, "Yes, I did!" No, it doesn't work that way: you have to make up a complete story that makes sense to the dumbest dummies. One of the hardest things to do is to tell an untruthful story and maintain it, and that is exactly where I was stuck. Of course I didn't want to involve myself in devastating crimes I hadn't done — especially under the present circumstances, where the U.S. government was jumping on every Muslim and trying to pin any crime on him.

"We are going to do this with you every single day, day in, day out, unless you speak about ▆▆▆▆▆ and admit to your crimes," said ▆▆▆▆▆.

"You have to provide us a smoking gun about another friend of yours. Something like that would really help you," ▆▆▆▆▆ said in a later session. "Why should you take all of this, if you can stop it?"

I decided to remain silent during torture and to speak whenever they relieved me. I realized that even asking my interrogators politely to use the bathroom, which was a dead basic right of mine, I gave my interrogators some kind of control they don't deserve. I knew it was not just about asking for bathroom: it was more about humiliating me and getting me to tell them what they wanted to hear. Ultimately an interrogator is interested in gathering Intels, and typically the end justifies the means in that regard. And that was another reason why I refused both to drink and to eat: so I didn't have to use the rest room. And it worked.

The extravagance of the moment gave me more strength. My statement was that I was going to fight to the last drop of my blood.

"We're stronger than you, we have more people, we have more resources, and we're going to defeat you. But if you start to cooperate with us, you'll start to have some sleep and hot meals," said ████████ numerous times. "You cooperate not, you eat not, you get remedy not."

Humiliation, sexual harassment, fear, and starvation was the order of the day until around 10 p.m. Interrogators made sure that I had no clue about the time, but nobody is perfect; their watches always revealed it. I would be using this mistake later, when they put me in dark isolation.

"I'm gonna send you to your cell now, and tomorrow you'll experience even worse," said ████████ after consulting with ████ colleagues. I was happy to be relieved; I just wanted to have a break and be left alone. I was so worn out, and only God knew how I looked. But ████████ lied to me; ████ just organized a psychological trick to hurt me more. I was far from being relieved. The D.O.C., which was fully cooperating when it came to torture, sent another escort team. As soon as I reached the doorstep ████████████████████████████ I fell face down, my legs refused to carry me, and every inch in my body was conspiring against me. The guards failed to make me stand up, so they had to drag me on the tips of my toes.

"Bring the motherfucker back!" shouted ████████, a celebrity among the torture squad.* He was about ████████████████,

---

* The third of the four interrogators who will carry out MOS's "Special Interrogation Plan," this masked interrogator is named "Mr. X" in the Schmidt-Furlow, DOJ IG, and Senate Armed Services Committee reports.

(cont'd)

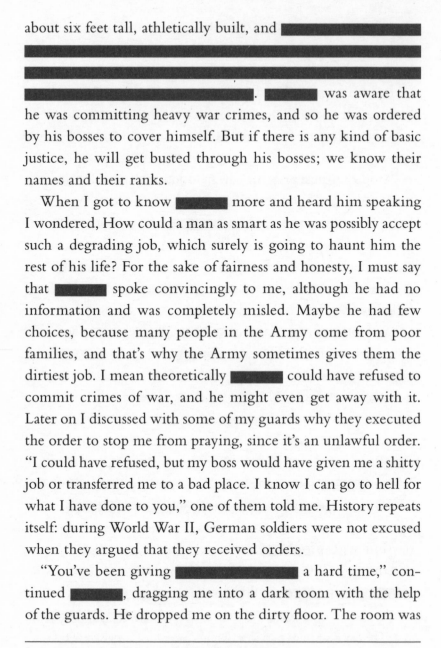

about six feet tall, athletically built, and ███████████
███
███
███████████████████████████████████. ███████ was aware that
he was committing heavy war crimes, and so he was ordered
by his bosses to cover himself. But if there is any kind of basic
justice, he will get busted through his bosses; we know their
names and their ranks.

When I got to know ████████ more and heard him speaking
I wondered, How could a man as smart as he was possibly accept
such a degrading job, which surely is going to haunt him the
rest of his life? For the sake of fairness and honesty, I must say
that ████████ spoke convincingly to me, although he had no
information and was completely misled. Maybe he had few
choices, because many people in the Army come from poor
families, and that's why the Army sometimes gives them the
dirtiest job. I mean theoretically ████████ could have refused to
commit crimes of war, and he might even get away with it.
Later on I discussed with some of my guards why they executed
the order to stop me from praying, since it's an unlawful order.
"I could have refused, but my boss would have given me a shitty
job or transferred me to a bad place. I know I can go to hell for
what I have done to you," one of them told me. History repeats
itself: during World War II, German soldiers were not excused
when they argued that they received orders.

"You've been giving ████████████████████ a hard time," continued ████████, dragging me into a dark room with the help
of the guards. He dropped me on the dirty floor. The room was

---

At his 2005 Administrative Review Board hearing, with characteristic wit,
MOS said this interrogator was always covered "like in Saudi Arabia, how
the women are covered," with "openings for his eyes" and "O.J. Simpson
gloves on his hands." ARB transcript, 25–26.

as dark as ebony. ██████ started playing a track very loudly—I
mean *very* loudly. The song was, "Let the bodies hit the floor."
I might never forget that song. At the same time, ██████
turned on some colored blinkers that hurt the eyes. "If you
fucking fall asleep, I'm gonna hurt you," he said. I had to listen
to the song over and over until next morning. I started
praying.*

"Stop the fuck praying," he said loudly. I was by this time
both really tired and terrified, and so I decided to pray in my
heart. Every once in a while ██████ gave me water. I drank
the water because I was only scared of being hurt. I really had
no real feeling for time.

To the best of my knowledge, ██████ sent me back to my
cell around 5 a.m. in the morning.

"Welcome to hell," said the ████████████ guard when
I stepped inside the block. I didn't answer, and ██████ wasn't
worth it. But I was like, "I think you deserve hell more than I
do because you're working dutifully to get there!"

When ██████ joined the team, they organized a 24-hour shift
regime. The morning shift with ████████████ started
between 7 and 9 a.m. and ended between 3 and 4 p.m.; the
dayshift with ██████ ran between 4:30 and 10 or 11 p.m.;
and the nightshift was with ██████. He always took over when
██████ left; ████ would literally hand me over to him. This

---

* The Senate Armed Services Committee, which reviewed JTF-GTMO
interrogation records, dates what appears to be this interrogation session as July
8, 2003. On that day, the committee found, "Slahi was interrogated by Mr. X
and was 'exposed to variable lighting patterns and rock music, to the tune of
Drowning Pool's 'Let the Bodies Hit [the] Floor.'" SASC, 139.

went on until August 24, 2003; I rarely got a break or relief from even one of the shifts.*

"Three shifts! Is it not too much for a human being to be interrogated 24 hours a day, day after day?" I asked ████ ████████████ was the least of many evils, so I just tried to talk to ████ as a human being. You might be surprised if I tell you that ████ possesses good qualities as a person. As much as I hated what ████ was doing, I must be just, fair, and honest.†

"We could put on more personnel and make four shifts. We have more people," ████████ answered. And that's exactly what happened. The team was reinforced with another ████ ████████████████████, and instead of a three-shift team I had to deal with four fresh people during a 24-hour period.

"You fucked up!" said an escorting guard who by accident had to escort me twice in one day from one building to another. "What are you doing here? You've been in reservation already!"

"I get interrogated for 24 hours."

The guard laughed loudly and evilly repeated, "You fucked up!" I just looked at him and smiled.

On day three of the shifts the escorting team showed up at my door in the early morning, as soon as I fell asleep after a rough, 20-hour interrogation. You know, when you just fall asleep and the saliva starts to come out of your mouth?

"Reservation!" shouted one of the guards. My feet barely carried me. "Hurry up!" I quickly washed my face and my mouth. I tried to use every opportunity to keep myself clean,

---

* Based on MOS's descriptions of the interrogation sessions that follow, I believe the shifts may work like this: morning/early afternoon shift with the male first sergeant/"I-AM-THE-MAN"/Mr. Tough Guy interrogator; late afternoon/evening shift with the Special Projects Team's female interrogator; and overnight with the interrogator known as Mr. X.

† This paragraph could refer to the female member of the Special Projects Team; see footnote on p. 240.

although I was deprived from the right to take a shower like other detainees. The team wanted to humiliate me.

"What a smell!" ███████ used to say when he entered the room where he interrogated me.

"Man, you smell like shit!" said one of the guards more than once. I only got the opportunity to shower and change my clothes when his lowness █████████████ couldn't bear my smell anymore; "Take the guy, give him a shower, he smells like shit," he would say. Only then would I get a shower, for months to come.

"Hurry up!" the guards kept saying. ████████████ ████████████████████████████████. I had a head-ache, nausea, and heartburn from the sleeplessness of the last several days. My eyes were playing games on me. I hated the place where I was going.

The guards dropped me in ██████████████████. Nobody was in the room. I kept dozing off while waiting on ██████████████. Oh, my neck really hurt. I badly wanted him to show up, because I hated to sleep like that: at least he would enjoy depriving me of sleeping. ████████████ is one of the laziest people I ever knew. He didn't take time to read reports, and so he always mistook me for other suspects. Most of the time he came late, but he reserved me early anyway, so I couldn't sleep.*

There really was not a lot of news: ████████████ and I facing each other with the same topics, like the movie *Ground-hog Day*. But I had grown very nervous now that they were depriving me of the sweetness of sleep.

The order of the day always went as follows. ██████████

---

* Because it encompasses lunch, MOS seems to be describing the routine of his first shift/day shift interrogator.

███ started to read some paper crap he brought with him and asked me questions.

"Why the fuck did you go to Canada?"

"I wanted to find a job and have a nice life."

"Fuck you! Stand up!"

"I'd rather stand up like this until death than talk to your ugly face!" When ███████████████ made me stand up, he made sure that the guards maintained his orders while ███████████ was stuffing his big stomach during lunch; whenever I tried to change my inconvenient position, the guards surged from nowhere and forced me to stay as straight as I could. Every interrogator I knew missed a meal sometimes, for whatever reason. ███████████ never missed his meal no matter what.

"If you stop denying what you've done, we'll start to give you hot meals and some sleep. We are stronger than you."

"I don't need what I don't have."

"We're gonna put you in a hole the rest of your life. You're already convicted. You will never see your family."

"It's not in your hands, but if it is, just do it, the sooner the better!"

Sometimes ███████████ went through the propaganda posters of detainees who were supposedly released. "Look at this guy, he's a criminal but he admitted to everything, and now he's able to lead a normal life." I mean, all interrogators lie, but ███████████ lies were more than obvious. Though if another interrogator lies, his appearance changes, but ███████████ recounts a lie as well as the truth: his face always had the same hateful look.

When the pain became unbearable, I became smooth for negotiation, and he agreed to let me sit on the uncomfortable chair. But he soon got shocked when I didn't give him the answers he wanted to hear.

"I am going to do everything I am allowed to to break you!" ▮▮▮▮▮▮▮▮ said angrily. ▮▮▮▮▮▮▮▮▮▮▮▮ threatened me with all kind of horrible scenarios. "You're gonna spend the rest of your life in jail." "We will wipe you out of the database and put you in a hole where nobody knows about you." "You will never see your family again." My answer was always, "Do what you got to do! I have done nothing!" and as soon as I spit my words ▮▮▮▮▮▮▮▮ went wildly crazy, as if he wanted to devour me alive. So I avoided answering him and let him for the most part do the talking. As I say, ▮▮▮▮▮▮▮▮ likes to talk and hates to listen. I sometimes doubted that his ears functioned. He spoke as if he were reading some Gospels.

I was just wondering how he was so sure I was a criminal. "▮▮▮▮▮▮▮▮, what if you are wrong in what you're suspecting me of?" I asked him.

"I would be wasting my time," he answered.

"Fair enough."

"If you provide incriminating information about somebody, say ▮▮▮▮▮▮▮▮▮▮▮▮▮▮▮▮▮▮▮▮▮▮▮▮▮▮▮▮▮▮▮, that leads to his conviction, your life would change to a better one." I didn't answer him, because I didn't have what he was looking for. ▮▮▮▮▮▮▮▮▮▮▮▮ view of justice was very rough: even if I provided him everything he wanted, he would reduce my sentence from the electric chair to life, and then maybe thirty years in prison. I honestly was not interested in his offer.

During his shift, ▮▮▮▮▮ would be reporting to his boss during the breaks. I was not sure who his boss was at that point, probably ▮▮▮▮▮▮▮▮▮▮▮▮▮▮▮▮▮▮▮▮▮▮. But I'm sure that the highest authority in his chain of command in GTMO was ▮▮▮▮▮▮▮▮▮▮▮, and that he was briefed regularly about my case and always gave the orders for what to do next with "that bastard." According to ▮▮▮▮, President Bush

was regularly briefed about my case, and so was ██████████
████████. ████████████████████ even sent his secretary
████████████████████ to check on me in summer 2004. He
asked me some Intel questions. By that time, though the tension
was already relieved.*

I spent the afternoon shift with ████████████. Like I mentioned
before, ████████████ was the least evil of all. ████████ order of day
went as follows. When ████ pulled me to interrogation, ████████
informed the D.O.C. not to give me a chair, so I had to settle
for the dirty floor—but I didn't even get that, because the
D.O.C. always asked the guards to make me stand up until
████████████ arrived. Then ████ decided whether to allow me
to sit or make me stand up during her whole shift, and
after that ████ made me stand up for the rest of the 24 hours.†

---

* As these July 2003 sessions were happening, General Miller was submitting Slahi's "Special Interrogation Plan" to SOUTHCOM commander
General James Hill for approval. On July 18, 2003, Hill forwarded the plan
to Secretary of Defense Donald Rumsfeld. The plan was approved by Deputy Secretary of Defense Paul Wolfowitz on July 28, 2003, and signed by
Rumsfeld on August 13, 2003. For a detailed account of the development
and authorization of MOS's "Special Interrogation Plan," see SASC,
135–41.

† This "her" is unredacted, so it seems clear that the afternoon shift is
with the female member of the interrogation team. Described here as "the
least evil" of the evils he was facing, this is likely the same interrogator he
describes as "the least of many evils" a few pages earlier.

When Defense Secretary Rumsfeld issued his original authorization to
use interrogation techniques beyond those included in the Army Field
Manual, including forced standing, he famously appended the note "I stand
for 8–10 hours a day. Why is standing limited to four hours?" But as Albert
Biderman found in his study of coercive interrogation techniques employed
by North Korean interrogators during the Korean War, "Returnees who
underwent long periods of standing and sitting...report no other experience
could be more excruciating." Biderman explained, "Where the individual
is told to stand at attention for long periods an intervening factor is
introduced. The immediate source of pain is not the interrogator but the
victim himself. The contest becomes, in a way, one of the individual against

I started to recite the Koran quietly, for prayer was forbidden. Once ▮▮▮▮▮▮▮▮ said, "Why don't you pray? go ahead and pray!" I was like, How friendly! But as soon as I started to pray, ▮▮▮▮▮ started to make fun of my religion, and so I settled for praying in my heart so I didn't give ▮▮▮▮ the opportunity to commit blasphemy. Making fun of somebody else's religion is one of the most barbaric acts. President Bush described his holy war against the so-called terrorism as a war between the civilized and barbaric world. But his government committed more barbaric acts than the terrorists themselves. I can name tons of war crimes that Bush's government is involved in.

This particular day was one of the roughest days in my interrogation before the day around the end of August that was my "Birthday Party" as ▮▮▮▮▮▮▮ called it. ▮▮▮▮▮▮▮ brought someone who was apparently a Marine; he wore a ▮▮▮▮▮▮▮ ▮▮ ▮▮▮▮▮▮▮▮▮▮▮▮▮▮▮▮▮▮▮▮▮▮▮▮▮▮▮▮▮▮▮▮▮▮▮▮.

▮▮▮▮▮▮▮ offered me a metal chair. "I told you, I'm gonna bring some people to help me interrogate you," ▮▮▮▮▮▮ said, sitting inches away in front of me. The guest sat almost sticking on my knee. ▮▮▮▮▮▮▮ started to ask me some questions I don't remember.

"Yes or no?" the guest shouted, loud beyond belief, in a show to scare me, and maybe to impress ▮▮▮▮▮▮▮, who knows? I found his method very childish and silly.

---

himself. The motivational strength of the individual is likely to exhaust itself in this internal encounter. Bringing the subject to act 'against himself' in this manner has additional advantages for the interrogator. It leads the prisoner to exaggerate the power of the interrogator. As long as the subject remains standing, he is attributing to his captor the power to do something worse to him, but there is actually no showdown of the ability of the interrogator to do so." See http://www2.gwu.edu/~nsarchiv /torturingdemocracy/documents/19570900.pdf.

I looked at him, smiled, and said, "Neither!" The guest threw the chair from beneath me violently. I fell on the chains. Oh, it hurt.

"Stand up, motherfucker," they both shouted, almost synchronous. Then a session of torture and humiliation started. They started to ask me the questions again after they made me stand up, but it was too late, because I told them a million times, "Whenever you start to torture me, I'm not gonna say a single word." And that was always accurate; for the rest of the day, they exclusively talked.

██████████ turned the air conditioner all the way down to bring me to freezing. This method had been practiced in the camp at least since August 2002. I had seen people who were exposed to the frozen room day after day; by then, the list was long. The consequences of the cold room are devastating, such as ███████tism, but they show up only at a later age because it takes time until they work their way through the bones. The torture squad was so well trained that they were performing almost perfect crimes, avoiding leaving any obvious evidence. Nothing was left to chance. They hit in predefined places. They practiced horrible methods, the aftermath of which would only manifest later. The interrogators turned the A/C all the way down trying to reach 0°, but obviously air conditioners are not designed to kill, so in the well insulated room the A/C fought its way to 49°F, which, if you are interested in math like me, is 9.4°C—in other words, very, very cold, especially for somebody who had to stay in it more than twelve hours, had no underwear and just a very thin uniform, and who comes from a hot country. Somebody from Saudi Arabia cannot take as much cold as somebody from Sweden; and vice versa, when it comes to hot weather. Interrogators took these factors in consideration and used them effectively.

You may ask, Where were the interrogators after installing the detainee in the frozen room? Actually, it's a good question. First, the interrogators didn't stay in the room; they would just come for the humiliation, degradation, discouragement, or other factor of torture, and after that they left the room and went to the monitoring room next door. Second, interrogators were adequately dressed; for instance ██████ was dressed like somebody entering a meat locker. In spite of that, they didn't stay long with the detainee. Third, there's a big psychological difference when you are exposed to a cold place for purpose of torture, and when you just go there for fun and a challenge. And lastly, the interrogators kept moving in the room, which meant blood circulation, which meant keeping themselves warm while the detainee was ██████████ the whole time to the floor, standing for the most part.* All I could do was move my feet and rub my hands. But the Marine guy stopped me from rubbing my hands by ordering a special chain that shackled my hands on my opposite hips. When I get nervous I always start to rub my hands together and write on my body, and that drove my interrogators crazy.

"What are you writing?" ██████████ shouted. "Either you tell me or you stop the fuck doing that." But I couldn't stop; it was unintentional. The Marine guy started to throw chairs around, hit me with his forehead, and describe me with all kinds of adjectives I didn't deserve, for no reason.

"You joined the wrong team, boy. You fought for a lost cause," he said, alongside a bunch of trash talk degrading my family, my religion, and myself, not to mention all kinds of threats against my family to pay for "my crimes," which goes against any common sense. I knew that he had no power, but

---

* Again, likely shackled. See footnote on p. 225.

I knew that he was speaking on behalf of the most powerful country in the world, and obviously enjoyed the full support of his government. However, I would rather save you, Dear Reader, from quoting his garbage. The guy was nuts. He asked me about things I have no clue about, and names I never heard.

"I have been in ███████████," he said, "and do you know who was our host? The President! We had a good time in the palace." The Marine guy asked questions and answered them himself.*

When the man failed to impress me with all the talk and humiliation, and with the threat to arrest my family since the ████████████████ was an obedient servant of the U.S., he started to hurt me more. He brought ice-cold water and soaked me all over my body, with my clothes still on me. It was so awful; I kept shaking like a Parkinson's patient. Technically I wasn't able to talk anymore. The guy was stupid: he was literally executing me but in a slow way. ███████ gestured to him to stop pouring water on me. Another detainee had told me a "good" interrogator suggested he eat in order to reduce the pain, but I refused to eat anything; I couldn't open my mouth anyway.

The guy was very hot when ██████ stopped him because █████ was afraid of the paperwork that would result in case of my death. So he found another technique, namely he brought a CD player with a booster and started to play some rap music. I didn't really mind the music because it made me forget my pain. Actually, the music was a blessing in disguise; I was trying to make sense of the words. All I understood was that the music

---

* The interrogator may be referring to Mauritania, and to then-president Maaouya Ould Sid'Ahmed Taya. See footnotes on pp. 98 and 100.

was about love. Can you believe it? Love! All I had experienced lately was hatred, or the consequences thereof.

"Listen to that, Motherfucker!" said the guest, while closing the door violently behind him. "You're gonna get the same shit day after day, and guess what? It's getting worse. What you're seeing is only the beginning," said ▇▇▇▇▇. I kept praying and ignoring what they were doing.

"Oh, ALLAH help me.....Oh Allah have mercy on me" ▇▇▇▇ kept mimicking my prayers, "ALLAH, ALLAH.... There is no Allah. He let you down!" I smiled at how ignorant ▇▇▇▇ was, talking about the Lord like that. But the Lord is very patient, and doesn't need to rush to punishment, because there is no escaping him.

Detainees knew the policy in the camp: if the MI believes that you're hiding crucial information, they torture you in Camp ▇▇▇▇▇▇▇▇▇▇▇▇▇▇▇▇▇▇▇▇▇▇▇▇, they kidnap you to a secret place and nobody knows what they're doing with you. During my time in ▇▇▇▇▇ Camp two individuals were kidnapped and disappeared for good, namely ▇▇▇▇▇ ▇▇▇▇▇▇▇▇▇▇▇▇▇▇▇▇▇▇▇▇▇▇▇▇▇▇▇▇▇▇▇▇▇ ▇▇. I started to get the feeling that I was going to be kidnapped because I really got stuck with my interrogators, and so I started to gather Intels.

"The camp out there is the worst one," said a young MP.

"They don't get food?" I wondered.

"Something like that," he replied.

Between 10 and 11 p.m., ▇▇▇▇▇ handed me over to ▇▇▇▇▇▇▇▇▇▇ gave orders to the guards to move me to his specially prepared room.* It was freezing cold and full of pictures showing the glories of the U.S.: weapons arsenals,

---

* This seems to be describing a night shift session with Mr. X. The scene is mentioned again in the final chapter.

planes, and pictures of George Bush. "Don't pray! You'll insult my country if you pray during my National anthem. We're the greatest country in the free world, and we have the smartest president in the world," he said. For the whole night I had to listen to the U.S. anthem. I hate anthems anyway. All I can remember was the beginning, "Oh say can you see . . ." over and over. I was happy that no ice-cold water was poured over me. I tried at the beginning to steal some prayers, but ███████ was watching closely by means of ████████████████████████ ██████. "Stop the fuck praying, you're insulting my country!" I was really tired and worn out, and I was anything but looking for trouble, and so I decided to pray in my heart. I was shaking all night long.

Between 4 and 5 a.m., ████████ released me, just to be taken a couple of hours later ██████████████████ to start the same routine over. But the hardest step is the first step; the hardest days were the first days, and with every day going by I grew stronger. Meanwhile I was the main subject of talk in the camp. Although many other detainees were suffering similar fates, I was "Criminal Number One," and I was being treated that way. Sometimes when I was in the Rec yard, detainees shouted, "Be patient. Remember Allah tests the people he loves the most." Comments like that were my only solace beside my faith in the Lord.

Nothing really interesting changed in my routine: cold room, standing up for hours, interrogators repeating the same threats about me being kidnapped and locked up forever.* ██████████

---

* Military, Department of Justice, and Senate investigators have described in more detail several of these threats. According to a footnote in the Schmidt-Furlow report, "On 17 Jul 03 the masked interrogator told that he had a dream about the subject of the second interrogation dying. Specifically he told the subject of the second special interrogation that in the dream he 'saw four detainees that were chained together at the feet. They dug a

made me write tons of pages about my life, but I never satisfied him. One night he undressed me with the help of ▇▇▇▇ ▇▇▇▇▇▇▇▇▇▇▇ a male guard. Expecting the cold room, I had put shorts on over my pants to reduce the cold that was penetrating through my bones, but he was extremely mad, which led him to make a ▇▇▇▇▇▇▇▇ guard undress me. I never felt so violated. I stood up all the night in the ice-cold room praying, ignoring all his barking and ordering me to stop praying. I couldn't have cared less about whatever he was going to do.*

---

hole that was six-feet long, six-feet deep, and four-feet wide. Then he observed the detainees throw a plain, pine casket with the detainee's identification number painted in orange lowered into the ground.' The masked interrogator told the detainee that his dream meant that he was never going to leave GTMO unless he started to talk, that he would indeed die here from old age and be buried on 'Christian...sovereign American soil.' On 20 Jul 03 the masked interrogator, 'Mr. X,' told the subject of the second Special Interrogation Plan that his family was 'incarcerated.'"

The report continues, "The MFR dated 02 Aug 03 indicates that the subject of the second special interrogation had a messenger that day there to 'deliver a message to him.' The MFR goes on to state: 'That message was simple: Interrogator's colleagues are sick of hearing the same lies over and over and over and are seriously considering washing their hands of him. Once they do so, he will disappear and never be heard from again. Interrogator assured detainee again to use his imagination to think of the worst possible scenario he could end up in. He told Detainee that beatings and physical pain are not the worst thing in the world. After all, after being beaten for a while, humans tend to disconnect the mind from the body and make it through. However, there are worse things than physical pain. Interrogator assured Detainee that, eventually, he will talk, because everyone does. But until then, he will very soon disappear down a very dark hole. His very existence will become erased. His electronic files will be deleted from the computer, his paper files will be packed up and filed away, and his existence will be forgotten by all. No one will know what happened to him, and eventually, no one will care.'" Schmidt-Furlow, 24–25.

* Context suggests there are two guards, one male and one female, and that the female guard undresses him. An incident in which MOS was "deprived of clothing by a female interrogator" is recorded in the DOJ IG report; the report suggests the date of that session was July 17, 2003. DOJ IG, 124.

▮▮▮▮▮▮▮▮▮▮▮▮▮▮▮▮▮▮ crawled from behind the scene. ▮▮▮▮▮▮ told me a couple of times before ▮▮▮▮ ▮▮▮▮▮▮▮▮▮▮▮▮ visit about a very high level government person who was going to visit me and talk to me about my family. I didn't take the information negatively; I thought he was going to bring me some messages from my family. But I was wrong, it was about hurting my family. ▮▮▮▮▮▮▮▮▮▮▮▮▮▮▮▮▮▮ was escalating the situation with me relentlessly.

▮▮▮▮▮▮▮▮▮▮▮▮ came around 11 a.m., escorted by ▮▮▮▮▮▮ and the new ▮▮▮▮▮▮▮▮▮▮. He was brief and direct. "My name is ▮▮▮▮▮▮▮▮▮▮▮. I work for ▮▮▮▮▮▮▮▮▮ ▮▮▮▮. My government is desperate to get information out of you. Do you understand?"*

"Yes."

---

* The date, according to the DOJ Inspector General, is now August 2, 2003. The IG reported, "On August 2, 2003, a different military interrogator posing as a Navy Captain from the White House" appeared to MOS. Both the Senate Armed Services Committee report and the DOJ IG report describe the letter he delivered. According to the Senate Armed Services Committee, the letter stated "that his mother had been detained, would be interrogated, and if she were uncooperative she might be transferred to GTMO." The DOJ IG reported that "the letter referred to 'the administrative and logistical difficulties her presence would present in this previously all-male environment,'" and "The interrogator told Slahi that his family was 'in danger if he (760) did not cooperate.'" The DOJ IG and SASC reports and the army's Schmidt-Furlow report all make clear that this interrogator was in fact the chief of MOS's "Special Projects Team," and the Schmidt-Furlow report indicates he presented himself to MOS as "Captain Collins." MOS describes him here as crawling from behind the scene; in his book *The Terror Courts: Rough Justice at Guantanamo Bay* (New Haven: Yale University Press, 2013), Jess Bravin, a reporter for the *Wall Street Journal*, writes that the Special Projects Team chief who carried out this ruse had taken over MOS's interrogation a month before, on July 1, 2003, which is the same day General Miller approved his "Special Interrogation Plan." DOJ IG, 123; SASC, 140; Schmidt-Furlow, 25; Bravin, *The Terror Courts*, 105.

"Can you read English?"

"Yes."

████████████████████ handed me a letter that he had obviously forged. The letter was from DoD, and it said, basically, "Ould Slahi is involved in the Millennium attack and recruited three of the September 11 hijackers. Since Slahi has refused to cooperate, the U.S. government is going to arrest his mother and put her in a special facility."

I read the letter. "Is that not harsh and unfair?" I said.

"I am not here to maintain justice. I'm here to stop people from crashing planes into buildings in my country."

"Then go and stop them. I've done nothing to your country," I said.

"You have two options: either being a defendant or a witness."

"I want neither."

"You have no choice, or your life is going to change decidedly," he said.

"Just do it, the sooner, the better!" I said. ████████████ ████ put the forged letter back in his bag, closed it angrily, and left the room. ███████████████ would lead the team working on my case until August or September 2004. He always tried to make me believe that his real name was ████████████ ████, but what he didn't know was that I knew his name even before I met him: ███████████████.*

---

* The interrogator who posed as "Captain Collins" and led MOS's Special Projects Team has been identified by name in court documents filed in MOS's habeas corpus appeal, in footnotes to the Senate Armed Services Committee report, and in other published sources as Lt. Richard Zuley. In *The Terror Courts*, Jess Bravin describes Zuley as a Chicago police officer and navy reservist. SASC, 135, 136; Bravin, *The Terror Courts*, 100, 105; Brief for Appellee, 23.

*　　*　　*

After that meeting ███████████████████████████, he
was just seeking the required formalities to kidnap me from the
camp to an unknown place. "Your being here required many
signatures. We've been trying for some time to get you here,"
one of my guards would tell me later. ██████████████████
was also putting together a complete team which would execute
the Abduction. All of this was carried out in secrecy; participants knew only as much as they needed to. I know for instance
that ████████ didn't know about the details of the plan.

On Monday August 25, 2003, around 4 p.m. ███████████
reserved me for interrogation ████████████████████.*
By then I had spent the weekend on ████████████, which
was entirely emptied of any other detainees, in order to keep
me isolated from the rest of the community. But I saw it as a
positive thing: the cell was warmer and I could see daylight,
while in ██████████████ I was locked in a frozen box.

"Now I have overall control. I can do anything I want with
you; I can even move you to Camp ██████████████████.

"I know why you moved me to ████████ Block," I said.
"It's because you don't want me to see anybody." ███████████
didn't comment; ██████ just smiled. It was more of a friendly
talk. Around 5:30 p.m., ████████ brought me my cold MRE.
I had gotten used to my cold portions; I didn't savor them, but
I had been suffering weight loss like never before, and I knew
in order to survive I had to eat.

I started to eat my meal. ████████ was going in and out, but
there was nothing suspicious about that, █████ had always been
that way. I barely finished my meal, when all of a sudden

---

* The time of day would make this the afternoon shift, and the redacted
pronouns and later context suggest this is the team's female interrogator.

██████████ and I heard a commotion, guards cursing loudly ("I told you motherfucker...!"), people banging the floor violently with heavy boots, dogs barking, doors closing loudly. I froze in my seat. ██████████ went speechless. We were staring at each other, not knowing what was going on. My heart was pounding because I knew a detainee was going to be hurt. Yes, and that detainee was me.

Suddenly a commando team consisting of three soldiers and a German shepherd broke into our interrogation room. Everything happened quicker than you could think about it. ██████████ punched me violently, which made me fall face down on the floor.

"Motherfucker, I told you, you're gone!" said ██████.* His partner kept punching me everywhere, mainly on my face and my ribs. He, too, was masked from head to toe; he punched me the whole time without saying a word, because he didn't want to be recognized. The third man was not masked; he stayed at the door holding the dog's collar, ready to release it on me.

"Who told you to do that? You're hurting the detainee!" screamed ██████████, who was no less terrified than I was. ██████ was the leader of the assailing guards, and he was executing ██████████████████ orders. As to me, I couldn't digest the situation. My first thought was, They mistook me for somebody else. My second thought was to try to recognize my environment by looking around while one of the guards was squeezing my face against the floor. I saw the dog fighting to get loose. I saw ██████ standing up, looking helplessly at the guards working on me.

"Blindfold the Motherfucker, if he tries to look—"

One of them hit me hard across the face, and quickly put the

---

* It will become clear, and explicit, that this is Mr. X.

goggles on my eyes, ear muffs on my ears, and a small bag over my head. I couldn't tell who did what. They tightened the chains around my ankles and my wrists; afterwards, I started to bleed. All I could hear was ▉▉▉▉ cursing, "F-this and F-that!" I didn't say a word, I was overwhelmingly surprised, I thought they were going to execute me.

Thanks to the beating I wasn't able to stand, so ▉▉▉▉ and the other guard dragged me out with my toes tracing the way and threw me in a truck, which immediately took off. The beating party would go on for the next three or four hours before they turned me over to another team that was going to use different torture techniques.

"Stop praying, Motherfucker, you're killing people," ▉▉▉▉ said, and punched me hard on my mouth. My mouth and nose started to bleed, and my lips grew so big that I technically could not speak anymore. The colleague of ▉▉▉▉ turned out to be one of my guards, ▉▉▉▉▉▉▉▉▉▉▉▉▉▉▉▉▉▉▉▉▉▉▉▉▉▉. ▉▉▉▉ and ▉▉▉▉▉▉ each took a side and started to punch me and smash me against the metal of the truck. One of the guys hit me so hard that my breath stopped and I was choking; I felt like I was breathing through my ribs. I almost suffocated without their knowledge. I was having a hard time breathing due to the head cover anyway, plus they hit me so many times on my ribs that I stopped breathing for a moment.

Did I pass out? Maybe not; all I know is that I kept noticing ▉▉▉▉ several times spraying Ammonia in my nose. The funny thing was that Mr. ▉▉ was at the same time my "lifesaver," as were all the guards I would be dealing with for the next year, or most of them. All of them were allowed to give me medication and first aid.

After ten to fifteen minutes, the truck stopped at the beach, and my escorting team dragged me out of the truck and put me in a high-speed boat. ██████████████████████ never gave me a break; they kept hitting me and ████████████████ ████████ in order to make them stab me.* "You're killing people," said ████████. I believe he was thinking out loud: he knew his was the most cowardly crime in the world, torturing a helpless detainee who completely went to submission and turned himself in. What a brave operation! ████████ was trying to convince himself that he was doing the right thing.

Inside the boat, ████████ made me drink salt water, I believe it was directly from the ocean. It was so nasty I threw up. They would put any object in my mouth and shout, "Swallow, Mother-fucker!," but I decided inside not to swallow the organ-damaging salt water, which choked me when they kept pouring it in my mouth. "Swallow, you idiot!" I contemplated quickly, and decided for the nasty, damaging water rather than death.

████████ and ████████████████ escorted me for about three hours in the high-speed boat. The goal of such a trip was, first, to torture the detainee and claim that "the detainee hurt himself during transport," and second, to make the detainee believe he was being transferred to some far, faraway secret prison. We detainees knew all of that; we had detainees reporting they had been flown around for four hours and found themselves in the same jail where they started. I knew from the beginning that I was going to be transferred to ████████████████████ about a five-minute ride. ████████████ had a very bad reputation: just hearing the name gave me nausea.† I knew the whole long trip

---

* It could be that MOS's escorts are pulling or manipulating his shackles to cause pain.

† The Senate Armed Services Committee found that the military's "Special Interrogation Plan" for MOS included a staged scene in which "military in full riot gear take him from his cell, place him on a watercraft, and drive him around to make him think he had been taken off the island." Afterward, the committee reported, "Slahi would be taken to Camp Echo,"

I was going to take was meant to terrorize me. But what difference does it make? I cared less about the place, and more about the people who were detaining me. No matter where I got transferred, I would still be a detainee of the U.S. Armed Forces; and as for rendition to a third country, I thought I was through with that because I was already sent to Jordan for eight months. The politics of the DoD toward me was to take care of me on their own; "September 11 didn't happen in Jordan; we don't expect other countries to pry Intels off detainees as we do," ███████████ said once. The Americans obviously were not satisfied with the results achieved by their "torture allies."

But I think when torture comes into play, things get out of

where his cell and interrogation room—self-contained in a single trailer-like isolation hut—had been "modified in such a way as to reduce as much outside stimuli as possible." The plan directed that "the doors will be sealed to a point that allows no light to enter the room. The walls may be covered with white paint or paper to further eliminate objects the detainee may concentrate on. The room will contain an eyebolt in the floor and speakers for sound." The SASC also recorded that an August 21, 2003, e-mail from a JTF-GTMO intelligence specialist to Lt. Richard Zuley reported on the final preparations to the Camp Echo hut: "The email described sealing Slahi's cell at Camp Echo to 'prevent light from shining' in and covering the entire exterior of his cell with [a] tarp to 'prevent him from making visual contact with guards.'"

According to the DOJ Inspector General, the original Special Interrogation Plan that General Miller signed on July 1, 2003, "stated that Slahi would be hooded and flown around Guantanamo Bay for one or two hours in a helicopter to persuade him that he had been moved out of GTMO to a location where 'the rules have changed.'" However, the IG reported, military interrogators told investigators that in the end "they did not use a helicopter because General Miller decided that it was too difficult logistically to pull off, and that too many people on the base would have to know about it to get this done." Instead, "on August 25, 2003, Slahi was removed from his cell in Camp Delta, fitted with blackout goggles, and taken on a disorienting boat ride during which he was permitted to hear pre-planned deceptive conversations among other passengers." SASC, 137–38, 140; DOJ IG 122–123, 127.

control. Torture doesn't guarantee that the detainee cooperates. In order to stop torture, the detainee has to please his assailant, even with untruthful, and sometimes misleading, Intels; sorting information out is time-consuming. And experience shows that torture doesn't stop or even reduce terrorist attacks: Egypt, Algeria, Turkey are good examples. On the other hand, discussion has brought tremendously good results. After the unsuccessful attack on the Egyptian president in Addis Ababa, the government reached a cease-fire with Al Gawaa al-Islamiyah, and the latter opted later on for a political fight. Nevertheless, the Americans had learned a lot from their torture-practicing allies, and they were working closely together.

When the boat reached the coast, ▮▮▮▮▮ and his colleague dragged me out and made me sit, crossing my legs. I was moaning from the unbearable pain.

"Uh.... Uh... ALLAH... ALLAH.... I told you not to fuck with us, didn't I?" said Mr. X, mimicking me.* I hoped I could stop moaning, because the gentleman kept mimicking me and blaspheming the Lord. However, the moaning was necessary so I could breathe. My feet were numb, for the chains stopped the blood circulation to my hands and my feet; I was happy for every kick I got so I could alter my position. "Do not move Motherfucker!" said ▮▮▮▮▮, but sometimes I couldn't help changing position; it was worth the kick.

"We appreciate everybody who works with us, thanks gentlemen," said ▮▮▮▮▮▮▮▮▮.† I recognized his voice; although he was addressing his Arab guests, the message was addressed to me more than anybody. It was nighttime. My

---

* Mr. X appears here unredacted in the original.

† Based on court filings in MOS's habeas corpus appeal, this is likely to be Richard Zuley ("Captain Collins"), MOS's Special Projects Team chief. Brief for Appellee, 25.

blindfold didn't keep me from feeling the bright lighting from some kind of high-watt projectors.

"We happy for zat. Maybe we take him to Egypt, he say everything," said an Arab guy whose voice I had never heard, with a thick Egyptian accent. I could tell the guy was in his late twenties or early thirties based on his voice, his speech, and later on his actions. I could also tell that his English was both poor and decidedly mispronounced. Then I heard indistinct conversations here and there, after which the Egyptian and another guy approached. Now they're talking directly to me in Arabic:

"What a coward! You guys ask for civil rights? Guess you get none," said the Egyptian.

"Somebody like this coward takes us only one hour in Jordan to spit everything," said the Jordanian. Obviously, he didn't know that I had already spent eight months in Jordan and that no miracle took place.

"We take him to EEEgypt," said the Egyptian, addressing ████████████████.

"Maybe later," said ███████████.

"How poor are these Americans! They really are spoiling these fuckers. But now we're working with them," said the Egyptian guy, now addressing me directly in Arabic. When I heard Egypt, and a new rendition, my heart was pounding. I hated the endless world tour I was forcibly taking. I seriously thought rendition to Egypt on the spot was possible, because I knew how irritated and desperate the Americans were when it came to my case. The government was and still is misled about my case.

"But you know we're working with Americans in the field," said the Egyptian. He was right: Yemeni detainees had told me that they were interrogated by ████████████ and Americans at the same table when they were captured in Karachi and afterward transferred to a secret place on September 11, 2002.*

After all kinds of threats and degrading statements, I started to miss a lot of the trash talk between the Arabs and their American accomplices, and at one point I drowned in my thoughts. I felt ashamed that my people were being used for this horrible job by a government that claims to be the leader of the democratic free world, a government that preaches against dictatorship and "fights" for human rights and sends its children to die for that purpose: What a joke this government makes of its own people!

What would the dead average American think if he or she could see what his or her government is doing to someone who has done no crimes against anybody? As much as I was ashamed for the Arabic fellows, I knew that they definitely didn't represent the average Arab. Arabic people are among the greatest on the planet, sensitive, emotional, loving, generous, sacrificial, religious, charitable, and light-hearted. No one deserves to be used for such a dirty job, no matter how poor he is. No, we are better than that! If people in the Arab world knew what was happening in this place, the hatred against the U.S. would be heavily watered, and the accusation that the U.S. is helping and working together with dictators in our countries would be cemented. I had a feeling, or rather a hope, that these people would not go unpunished for their crimes. The situation didn't make me hate either Arabs or Americans; I just felt bad for the Arabs, and how poor we are!

---

* MOS may be referring here to detainees who were captured along with Ramzi bin al-Shibh on September 11, 2002, and also held for a time in CIA custody before being transferred to Guantánamo. See footnote on p. 197.

All these thoughts were sliding through my head, and distracted me from hearing the nonsense conversations. After about forty minutes, I couldn't really tell, ▇▇▇▇▇▇▇▇▇ instructed the Arabic team to take over. The two guys grabbed me roughly, and since I couldn't walk on my own, they dragged me on the tips of my toes to the boat. I must have been very near the water, because the trip to the boat was short. I don't know, they either put me in another boat or in a different seat. This seat was both hard and straight.

"Move!"

"I can't move!"

"Move, Fucker!" They gave this order knowing that I was too hurt to be able to move. After all I was bleeding from my mouth, my ankles, my wrists, and maybe my nose, I couldn't tell for sure. But the team wanted to keep the factor of fear and terror maintained.

"Sit!" said the Egyptian guy, who did most of the talking while both were pulling me down until I hit the metal. The Egyptian sat on my right side, and the Jordanian on my left.

"What's your fucking name?" asked the Egyptian.

"M-O-O-H-H-M-M-EE-D-D-O-O-O-U!" I answered. Technically I couldn't speak because of the swollen lips and hurting mouth. You could tell I was completely scared. Usually I wouldn't talk if somebody starts to hurt me. In Jordan, when the interrogator smashed me in the face, I refused to talk, ignoring all his threats. This was a milestone in my interrogation history. You can tell I was hurt like never before; it wasn't me anymore, and I would never be the same as before. A thick line was drawn between my past and my future with the first hit ▇▇▇▇▇ delivered to me.

"He is like a kid!" said the Egyptian accurately, addressing his Jordanian colleague. I felt warm between them both, though not for long. With the cooperation of the Americans, a long torture trip was being prepared.

I couldn't sit straight in the chair. They put me in a kind of thick jacket which fastened me to the seat. It was a good feeling. However, there was a destroying drawback to it: my chest was so tightened that I couldn't breathe properly. Plus, the air circulation was worse than the first trip. I didn't know why, exactly, but something was definitely going wrong.

"I c....a...a...a...n't br...e...a...the!"

"Suck the air!" said the Egyptian wryly. I was literally suffocating inside the bag around my head. All my pleas and my begging for some free air ended in a cul-de-sac.

I heard indistinct conversations in English, I think it was ▇▇▇▇▇ and his colleague, and probably ▇▇▇▇▇▇▇▇▇▇▇▇▇▇. Whoever it was, they were supplying the Arab team with torture materials during the 3 or 4 hour trip. The order went as follows: They stuffed the air between my clothes and me with ice-cubes from my neck to my ankles, and whenever the ice melted, they put in new, hard ice cubes. Moreover, every once in a while, one of the guards smashed me, most of the time in the face. The ice served both for the pain and for wiping out the bruises I had from that afternoon. Everything seemed to be perfectly prepared. People from cold regions might not understand the extent of the pain when ice-cubes get stuck on your body. Historically, kings during medieval and pre-medieval times used this method to let the victim slowly die. The other method, of hitting the victim while blindfolded in inconsistent intervals, was used by the Nazis during World War II. There is nothing more terrorizing than making somebody expect a smash every single heartbeat.

"I am from Hasi Matruh, where are you from?" said the Egyptian, addressing his Jordanian colleague. He was speaking as if nothing was happening. You could tell he was used to torturing people.

"I am from the south" answered the Jordanian. I tried to keep my prayers in my heart. I could hardly remember a prayer, but I did know I needed the Lord's help, as I always do, and in that direction went my prayers. Whenever I was conscious, I drowned in my thoughts. I finally had gotten used to the routine, ice-cubes until melted, smashing. But what would it be like if I landed in Egypt after about twenty-five hours of torture? What would the interrogation there look like? ████ ████████████████████ an ████████████████████ described his unlucky trip from Pakistan to Egypt to me; so far everything I was experiencing, like the ice-cubes and smashing, was consistent with ██████████████████ story. So I expected electric shocks in the pool. How much power can my body, especially my heart, handle? I know something about electricity and its devastating, irreversible damage: I saw ████████ ██████████ collapsing in the blocks a couple of times every week with blood gushing out of his nose until it soaked his clothes. ██████████████████████ was a Martial art trainer and athletically built.

I was constructing the whole interrogation over and over, their questions, my answers. But what if they don't believe me? No, they would believe me, because they understand the recipe of terrorism more than the Americans, and have more experience. The cultural barrier between the Christian and the Muslim world still irritates the approach of Americans to the whole issue considerably; Americans tend to widen the circle of involvement to catch the largest possible numbers of Muslims. They always speak about the Big Conspiracy against the U.S. I personally had been interrogated about people who just practiced the basics of the religion and sympathized with Islamic movements; I was asked to provide every detail about Islamic movements, no matter how moderate. That's amazing in a country like the U.S., where Christian terrorist organizations such as Nazis and White Supremacists have the freedom to express themselves and recruit people openly and nobody can bother them. But as a Muslim, if you sympathize with the political views of an Islamic organization you're in big trouble. Even attending the same mosque as a suspect is big trouble. I mean this fact is clear for everybody who understands the ABCs of American policy toward so-called Islamic Terrorism.

The Arabo-American party was over, and the Arabs turned me over once more to the same U.S. Team. They dragged me out of the boat and threw me, I would say, in the same truck as the one that afternoon. We were obviously riding on a dirt road.

"Do not move!" said ▆▆▆▆▆, but I didn't recognize any words anymore. I don't think that anybody beat me, but I was not conscious. When the truck stopped, ▆▆▆▆ and his strong associate towed me from the truck, and dragged me over some steps. The cool air of the room hit me, and boom, they threw me face down on the metal floor of my new home.

"Do not move, I told you not to fuck with me, Motherfucker!" said ▆▆▆▆, his voice trailing off. He was obviously tired. He left right away with a promise of more actions, and so did the Arab team.

A short time after my arrival, I felt somebody taking ▆▆▆▆ ▆▆▆▆▆▆▆▆▆▆▆▆▆▆ off my head. Removing these things was both painful and relieving, painful because they had started to penetrate my skin and stick, leaving scars, and relieving because I started to breathe normally and the pressure around my head went away. When the blindfold was taken off I saw a ██ ██. I figured he was a Doctor, but why the heck is he hiding behind a mask, and why is he U.S. Army, when the Navy is in charge of the medical care of detainees?

"If you fuckin' move, I'm gonna hurt you!" I was wondering how could I possibly move, and what possible damage I could do. I was in chains, and every inch in my body was hurting. That is not a Doctor, that is a human butcher!

When the young man checked on me, he realized he needed more stuff. He left and soon came back with some medical gear. I glimpsed his watch: it was about 1:30 a.m., which meant about eight hours since I was kidnapped from ████████████ Camp. The Doctor started to wash the blood off my face with a soaked bandage. After that, he put me on a mattress — the only item in the stark cell — with the help of the guards.

"Do not move," said the guard who was standing over me. The Doctor wrapped many elastic belts around my chest and ribs. After that, they made me sit. "If you try to bite me, I'm gonna fuckin' hurt you!" said the Doctor while stuffing me with a whole bunch of tablets. I didn't respond; they were moving me around like an object. Sometime later they took off the chains, and later still one of the guards threw a thin, small, worn-out blanket onto me through the bin hole, and that was everything I would have in the room. No soap, no toothbrush, no iso mat, no Koran, nothing.

I tried to sleep, but I was kidding myself; my body was conspiring against me. It took some time until the medications started to work, then I trailed off, and only woke up when one of the guards hit my cell violently with his boot.

"Get up, piece of shit!" The Doctor once more gave me a bunch of medication and checked on my ribs. "Done with the motherfucker," he said, showing me his back as he headed toward the door. I was so shocked seeing a Doctor act like that, because I knew that at least fifty percent of medical treatment is psychological. I was like, This is an evil place, since my only solace is this bastard Doctor.*

I soon was knocked out. To be honest I can report very little about the next couple of weeks because I was not in the right state of mind. I was lying on my bed the whole time, and I was not able to realize my surroundings. I tried to find out the *Kibla*, the direction of Mecca, but there was no clue.

---

* MOS's habeas appeal brief refers to medical records from what could be this exam, describing a corpsman "who treated his injuries while cursing him" and citing "medical records confirming the trauma to Salahi's chest and face, as '1) Fracture ?? 7–8 ribs, 2) Edema of the lower lip.'" Brief for Appellee, 26.

SIX

GTMO

September 2003–December 2003

First Visit in the Secret Place...My Conversation with My Interrogators, and How I Found a Way to Squinsh Their Thirst...Chain Reaction of Confessions...Goodness Comes Gradually...The Big Confession...A Big Milestone

Back in ▋▋▋▋▋▋▋▋▋ the *Kibla* was indicated with an arrow in every cell. Even the call to prayer could be heard five times a day in ▋▋▋▋▋▋▋▋.* The U.S. has always repeated that the war is not against the Islamic religion — which is very prudent because it is strategically impossible to fight against a religion as big as Islam — and back there the U.S. was showing the rest of the world how religious freedom ought to be maintained.

---

* Defense Department publicity materials for Guantánamo indeed emphasize protections for religious expression in Guantánamo; see, e.g., "Ten Facts about Guantanamo," which states, "The Muslim call to prayer sounds five times a day. Arrows point detainees toward the holy city of Mecca." See http://www.defense.gov/home/dodupdate/For-the-record /documents/20060914.html. Here MOS seems to be contrasting the situation as he experienced it when he was held in Camp Delta with the situation in his Camp Echo cell.

But in the secret camps, the war against the Islamic religion was more than obvious. Not only was there no sign to Mecca, but the ritual prayers were also forbidden. Reciting the Koran was forbidden. Possessing the Koran was forbidden. Fasting was forbidden. Practically any Islamic-related ritual was strictly forbidden. I am not talking here about hearsay; I am talking about something I experienced myself. I don't believe that the average American is paying taxes to wage war against Islam, but I do believe that there are people in the government who have a big problem with the Islamic religion.

For the first couple of weeks after my "Birthday Party" I had no clue about time, whether it was day or night, let alone the time of day. I could only pray in my heart lying down, because I could not stand straight or bend. When I woke up from my semi-coma, I tried to make out the difference between day and night. In fact it was a relatively easy job: I used to look down the toilet, and when the drain was very bright to lightish dark, that was the daytime in my life. I succeeded in illegally stealing some prayers, but ████████████████████████ busted me.

"He's praying!" ████████████████████████. "Come on!" They put on their masks. "Stop praying." I don't recall whether I finished my prayer sitting, or if I finished at all. As a punishment ████████████████ forbade me to use the bathroom for some time.

As soon as the assessing doctor reported that I was relieved from my pain, it was time to hit again before the injuries healed, following the motto "Strike While the Iron's Hot." When I heard the melee behind the door, and recognized the voices of both ████████████████ and his Egyptian colleague, I drowned in sweat, got dizzy, and my feet failed to carry me.*

---

* MOS's habeas appeal brief describes what could be the same scene: "After Salahi had been in isolation for a few days, Zuley told him he had

My heart pounded so hard that I thought it was going to choke me and fly off through my mouth. Indistinct conversations involving ████████████ and the guards took place.

"████████████████, let mee geet him," said the Egyptian guy in his stretched-out English to ████████████. "I wish ████████████████ let me in to have a little conversation with you," said the Egyptian in Arabic, addressing me.

"Stand back now; let me see him alone," ████████████ said. I was shaking, listening to the bargaining between the Americans and the Egyptians about who was going to get me. I looked like somebody who was going through an autopsy while still alive and helpless.

"You are going to cooperate, whether you choose to or not. You can choose between the civilized way, which I personally prefer, or the other way," said ████████████████ when the guards dragged me out of my cell to him. In the background the Egyptian guy was barking and threatening me with all kinds of painful revenge.

"I am cooperating," I said in a weak voice. It had been a while since I had talked the last time, and my mouth was not used to talking anymore. My muscles were very sore. I was scared beyond belief. The Halloween-masked ████████████ was literally stuck on me, moving around and ready to strike at an eye's wink.

"No, quit denying. We are not interested in your denials. Don't fuck with me," ████████████ said.

"I'm not."

"I am going to appoint some interrogators to question you. You know some of them, and some you don't."

---

to 'stop denying' the government's accusations. While Zuley was talking, the [redacted] man was behind the tarp, cursing and shouting for Zuley to let him in." Brief for Appellee, 26–27.

"OK!" I said. The conversation was closed. ███████ ████████████ ordered the guards to put me back in my cell, and he disappeared.

Then nothing short of a "miracle" happened: ██████████ ███ made it to the "far faraway secret place."

"You've been causing me so much trouble—nah, well, in Paris it wasn't that bad but in Mauritania the weather was terrible. I sat at the table across from ████████, and when I asked him, 'Who recruited you for al Qaeda?' His answer was you. And the same with ██████████████. ███████████ are working with us now. You know, you are a part of an organization which the free world wants to wipe out of the face of the earth," said ██████████████.

I was listening carefully, and wondering, Free world? I was saying to myself, Do I really have to listen to this crap? ████████████████ was accompanied by the same ████████ ████████████████ had brought about two months ago to molest me sexually.*

"You know, in jail the one who talks first wins. You lost and ████████████████ won. He said everything about you," ████████████████. "The good thing is, we don't have to dirty our hands with you; we have Israelis and Egyptians doing the job for us," ████ continued, while taunting me sexually by touching me everywhere. I neither talked nor showed any resistance. I was sitting there like a stone.†

---

* The tone of this interrogation session suggests the lead interrogator may be the same "hateful" first sergeant whom MOS identified in his 2005 ARB hearing as a member of the Special Projects Team. The second interrogator in this scene appears to be the female interrogator who assisted in the earlier sexual assault.

† Threatening prisoners with the specter of abusive interrogations by Israeli or Egyptian agents apparently was commonplace. In 2010 a former Guantánamo military interrogator named Damien Corsetti testified at the

"Why is he shaking so much?" asked the ████████.

"I don't know," ███████████████ answered.

"But his hands are sweating like crazy!"

"If I were him, the same would be happening to me," said ████████. "You think this place is like ████████, where you survived every attempt ███████████████████, but you won't survive here if you keep playing games with us," he said.

"Like what?" I wondered.

"Like your trip to Slovenia. You only told me about it because you knew I knew about it. Now: are you going to cooperate with us?" he asked.

"I *was* cooperating," I said.

"No, you weren't, and guess what? I am going to write in my report that you're full of shit, and other people are going to take care of you. The Egyptian is very interested in you!"

Meanwhile the ████████ stopped molesting me since I showed no resistance. "What's wrong with him?" █████ wondered once more.

"I don't know. But maybe he is too relaxed in this place. We should maybe take away some of his sleep," said █████████
██
██
█████████. I've never seen a human being as emotionless as he was. He spoke about keeping me from sleeping without a single change in his voice, face, or composure. I mean, regardless of our religion or race, we human beings always feel more or less

---

military commissions trial of Omar Khadr that during his time at the Bagram air base, interrogations included threats of sending detainees to Israel and Egypt. See http://www.thestar.com/news/canada/omarkhadr /2010/05/05/interrogator_nicknamed_the_monster_remembers_omar _khadr_as_a_child.html.

bad for somebody who is suffering. I personally can never help breaking into tears when I read a sad story or watch a sad movie. I have no problem admitting this. Some people may say that I am a weak person; well, then, let me be!

"You should ask ██████████████████ to forgive you the lies, and start everything over," said the ███████. I didn't say anything. "Start small. Give us a piece of information you never said before!" ██████ continued. I had no response to that malicious, nonsense suggestion either.

"Your mom is an old lady. I don't know how long she can withstand the conditions in the detention facility," ████████████ said. I knew that he was talking out of his tail. But I also knew that the government was ready to take any measures to pry information out of me, even if it would take injury to my family members, especially when you know that the ████████████████ government is cooperating blindly with the U.S. I mean the U.S. government has more power over ████████████████ than over U.S. nationals, that's how far the cooperation goes. A U.S. citizen cannot be arrested without due process of law, but ████████████████ can—and by the U.S. government!* I always said to my interrogators, "Let's say I am criminal. Is an American criminal holier than a non-American?" And most of them had no answer. But I am sure that Americans are not much luckier. I've heard of many of them getting persecuted and wrongly arrested, especially Muslims and Arabs, in the name of the War Against Terror. Americans, non-Americans: it is as the German proverb puts it, Heute die! Morgen du! Today Them, Tomorrow You!

It was very hard to start a conversation with ████████████████

---

* The reference here might be to the Mauritanian government and its close cooperation with the U.S. government, and to MOS's own arrest in Mauritania at the behest of the United States.

███; even the guards hated him. Today I couldn't get anywhere with him; I just couldn't find a handrail in the train of
his speech. And as to the other ████████████ was only sent to
harass me sexually, but I was at a stage where I had no feeling
████████████████████████. Thus, ████ mission was dead
before it was born.

"You know how it looks when you feel our wrath," ████
█████████████ said, and left me with many other threats
including sleep deprivation and starvation, which I believed to
be true and serious. The guards put me roughly back in my cell.

Over the next several days, I almost lost my mind. Their
recipe for me went like this: I must be kidnapped from ████
█████████████ and put in a secret place. I must be made to
believe I was on a far, faraway island. I must be informed by
█████████████ that my mom was captured and put in a special facility.

In the secret place, the physical and psychological suffering
must be at their highest extremes. I must not know the difference between day and night. I couldn't tell a thing about days
going by or time passing; my time consisted of a crazy darkness
all the time. My diet times were deliberately messed up. I was
starved for long periods and then given food but not given time
to eat.

"You have three minutes: Eat!" a guard would yell at me,
and then after about half a minute he would grab the plate.
"You're done!" And then it was the opposite extreme: I was
given too much food and a guard came into my cell and forced
me to eat all of it. When I said "I need water" because the food
got stuck in my throat, he punished me by making me drink
two 25-ounce water bottles.

"I can't drink," I said when my abdomen felt as if it was going
to explode. But █████████████ screamed and threatened me,

pushing me against the wall and raising his hand to hit me. I figured drinking would be better, and drank until I vomited.

All the guards were masked with Halloween-like masks, and so were the Medics, and the guards were briefed that I was a high-level, smart-beyond-belief terrorist.

"You know who you are?" said ███████████ friend. "You're a terrorist who helped kill 3,000 people!"

"Indeed I am!" I answered. I realized it was futile to discuss my case with a guard, especially when he knew nothing about me. The guards were all very hostile. They cursed, shouted, and constantly put me through rough Military-like basic training. "Get up," "Walk to the bin hole." "Stop!" "Grab the shit!" "Eat." "You got two minutes!" "You're done!" "Give the shit back!" "Drink!" "You better drink the whole water bottle!" "Hurry up!" "Sit down!" "Don't sit down unless I say it!" "Search the piece of shit!" Most of the guards rarely attacked me physically, but ██████████ hit me once until I fell face-down on the floor, and whenever he and his associate grabbed me they held me very tight and made me run in the heavy chains: "Move!"

No sleep was allowed. In order to enforce this, I was given 25-ounce water bottles in intervals of one to two hours, depending on the mood of the guards, 24 hours a day. The consequences were devastating. I couldn't close my eyes for ten minutes because I was sitting most of the time on the bathroom. Later on, after the tension was relieved, I asked one of the guards, "Why the water diet? Why don't you just make me stay awake by standing up, like in ███████████?"

"Psychologically it's devastating to make somebody stay awake on his own, without ordering him," said █████████ ████. "Believe me, you haven't seen anything. We have put detainees naked under the shower for days, eating, pissing, and shitting in the shower!" he continued. Other guards told me about other torture methods that I wasn't really eager to know about.

I was allowed to say three sentences: "Yes, sir!" "Need my interrogator!" and "Need the medics." Every once in a while the whole guard team stormed my cell, dragged me out, put me facing the wall, and threw out whatever was in my cell, shouting and cursing in order to humiliate me. It wasn't much: I was deprived from all comfort items that a detainee needs except for a mattress and a small, thin, worn-out blanket. For the first weeks I also had no shower, no laundry, no brushing. I almost developed bugs. I hated my smell.

No sleep. Water diet. Every move behind my door made me stand up in a military-like position with my heart pounding like boiling water. My appetite was non-existent. I was waiting every minute on the next session of torture. I hoped I would die and go to heaven; no matter how sinful I am, these people can never be more merciful than God. Ultimately we all are going to face the Lord and beg for his mercy, admitting our weaknesses and our sinfulness. I could hardly remember any prayers, all I could say was, "Please, God, relieve my pain..."

I started to hallucinate and hear voices as clear as crystal. I heard my family in a casual familial conversation that I couldn't join. I heard Koran readings in a heavenly voice.* I

---

* This is corroborated chillingly in government documents. According to the Senate Armed Services Committee, on October 17, 2003, a JTF-GTMO interrogator sent an e-mail to a GTMO Behavioral Science Consultation Team (BSCT) psychologist that read, "Slahi told me he is 'hearing voices' now....He is worried as he knows this is not normal....By the way...is this something that happens to people who have little external stimulus such as daylight, human interaction, etc???? seems a little creepy." The psychologist responded, "Sensory deprivation can cause hallucinations, usually visual rather than auditory, but you never know....In the dark you create things out of what little you have." SASC, 140–41.

heard music from my country. Later on the guards used these hallucinations and started talking with funny voices through the plumbing, encouraging me to hurt the guards and plot an escape. But I wasn't misled by them, even though I played along.

"We heard somebody—maybe a genie!" they used to say.

"Yeah, but I ain't listening to him," I responded. I just realized I was on the edge of losing my mind. I started to talk to myself. Although I tried as hard as I could to convince myself that I was not in Mauritania, I was not near my family, so I could not possibly hear them speaking, I kept hearing the voices constantly, day and night. Psychological assistance was out of the question, or really any medical assistance, beside the asshole I didn't want to see.

I couldn't find a way on my own. At that moment I didn't know if it was day or night, but I assumed it was night because the toilet drain was rather dark. I gathered my strength, guessed the *Kibla*, kneeled, and started to pray to God. "Please guide me. I know not what to do. I am surrounded by merciless wolves, who fear not thee." When I was praying I burst into tears, though I suppressed my voice lest the guards hear me. You know there are always serious prayers and lazy prayers. My experience has taught me that God always responds to your serious prayers.

"Sir," I said, when I finished my prayers. One of the guards showed up in his Halloween mask.

"What?" asked the guard with a dry, cold emotion.

"I want to see ██████████████████. Not ██████████ ████; I want the guy ████████████████████," I said.

"You mean ████████████████?" Oops, the guard just made a big mistake by revealing the real name of ████ ██████████████. In fact I was already familiar with the name, because I saw it a long time before on a file ██████████

carried, and if you can put two and two together the puzzle is solved.*

"Yes, ████████████████████████, not the ████████████████." I really wanted to speak to somebody who was likely to understand me, rather than ████████████████, who hardly had an understanding for anything. But ████████████ ████████████ didn't show up, ████████████████ did.

"You asked for ████████████████████?"

"I did."

"And you asked not to see me?"

"I did."

"Well, I work for ████████████████████, and he sent me!" said ████████████████ dryly.

"OK, I have no problem with cooperating with you just as I would with ████████████████████. However, I would also like Mr. ████████████████ to take part in the interviews," I said.

"I am not the one who decides about that, but I guess it would be no problem," he said.

"I am starving, I want you to tell the guards to give me some food."

"If you start to cooperate, you'll get more food. I am going to come later today to interview you. I just want to tell you that you made the right decision."

---

* The Schmidt-Furlow report places the date of this session as September 8, 2003, noting that interrogation records show that on that date "the subject of the second special interrogation wanted to see 'Captain Collins'" and that the interrogation team "understood that detainee had made an important decision and that the interrogator was anxious to hear what Detainee had to say." It appears that another member of the Special Projects Team continued to lead the interrogation instead. Schmidt-Furlow, 25.

*   *   *

Confessions are like the beads of a necklace: if the first bead falls, the rest follow.

To be honest and truthful, I am telling many things here that I had been holding back merely because of fear. I just couldn't find any common ground to discuss my case comfortably in a relaxed environment. I had no crimes to confess to, and that is exactly where I got stuck with my interrogators, who were not looking for innocent undertakings. They were looking for evil enterprises. But through my conversations with the FBI and the DoD, I had a good idea as to what wild theories the government had about me.

"We know you came to Canada to plot to harm the U.S.," said ███████████████████.

"And what was my evil plan?"

"Maybe not exactly to harm the U.S., but to attack the CN Tower in Toronto?" he said. I was thinking, Is the guy crazy? I've never heard of such a tower.

"You realize if I admit to such a thing I have to involve other people! What if turns out I was lying?" I said.

"So what? We know your friends are bad, so if they get arrested, even if you lie about ███████ it doesn't matter, because they're bad." I thought, "What an asshole! he wants to lock up innocent people just because they're Muslim Arabs! That's Nuts!" So ████████████████ very much told me a precise crime I could admit to which would comply with the Intel theory.

"Back in the states, if I recommend somebody to a good school and he ended up shooting and killing people, is that my fault?" ████████ asked me once.

"No!"

"So, if you have recruited people for al Qaeda, it's not your fault if they become terrorists!" said ██████████.

"The only problem is that I haven't, regardless of the consequences."

██████ was clearer. "We don't give a shit if you helped ████████████ and two other hijackers go to Chechnya. We only give a shit if you sent them to your ████████████ ████████." So, according to ██████, I could stop the torture if I said I recruited ██████████████ and two hijackers. To be honest with you, they made me believe I recruited ██████████ ██████; I thought, God, I might have recruited the guy before I was born!

"Looks like a dog, walks like a dog, smells like a dog, barks like a dog, must be a dog," ██████ used to say repeatedly during his sessions with me. It sounded awful, I know I am not a dog, and yet I must be one. The whole police theory of doing every trick to keep people in jail by pinning things on them doesn't make sense to me. I believe simply that an innocent suspect should be released. As the just, legendary Arabic King Omar put it, "I would rather release a criminal than imprison an innocent man."

██████████████████████ explained the ██████████████ the most: ████████ said that you helped him go to Chechnya by suggesting that he and his friends transit through Afghanistan, because Georgia was sending Mujahideen back. Furthermore, when I asked ████████████ what he thinks you do for al Qaeda, he said that you're an al Qaeda recruiter."

"I believe that without you September 11 would never have happened," ████████████████████ concluded. According to his theory I was the guy; all I needed to do was to admit it.

Many interrogators asked me, "What do you know about al Qaeda cells in Germany and Canada?" To be honest with you, I'd never heard of such a thing; I know al Qaeda organizations, but I don't know about al Qaeda cells in other countries, though that doesn't necessarily mean there aren't.

██████████████████ pushed the issue even more into the light. "You are a leader, people like you, respect you, and follow you," he said to me multiple times. As you can see, my recipe was already cooked for me. I am not only a part of an al Qaeda cell in both Germany and Canada, but I am the leader.

I argued the case of █████████ with ████████████ many times. "According to you, I recruited ███████ and his two friends for al Qaeda," I said.

"Yes."

"Okay, but that allegation requires many other things and coincidences."

"Like what?" he said.

First, I explained, I supposedly knew ████████ and ████████ himself said he has seen me only once, and that is not enough for knowing somebody, let alone recruiting him. Second, I must have recruited ███████ without his knowledge, because all he claims is that I told him how to get to Chechnya. "According to you," I told him, "And maybe to him, too, I told him to travel through Afghanistan, so what guaranteed that he was going to stay in Afghanistan? And if he miraculously stayed in Afghanistan, what guaranteed that he was going to train? And if he decided to train, what guaranteed that he was going to meet al Qaeda's criteria? And if by chance he met al Qaeda's criteria, what told me that he was ready to be a suicide bomber, and was ready to learn how to fly? This is just ridiculous!"

"But you are very smart," ████████ said.

"Under these circumstances, I agree with you that I'm beyond smart: I am a psychic! But what makes you guys think that I'm so evil?"

"We just don't know, but smart people don't leave any traces. For instance, we had an ███████████████████ who had been working for Russia for 20 years without being noticed," said ███████.*

"We have people who still believe that you conspired with ██████████████████ said ████████████ when I told her not to ask me about ███████████████████ because the FBI had settled his case since he had started cooperating.†

"Obviously there is no way out with you guys," I addressed ██████████.

"I'm telling you how!" ██████ responded.

Now, thanks to the unbearable pain I was suffering, I had nothing to lose, and I allowed myself to say anything to satisfy my assailants. Session followed session since I called ██████ ████████████.

"People are very happy with what you're saying," said ██ ███████████ after the first session. I answered all the questions he asked me with incriminating answers. I tried my best to make myself look as bad as I could, which is exactly the way you can make your interrogator happy. I made my mind up to spend the rest of my life in jail. You see most people can put up with being imprisoned unjustly, but nobody can bear agony day in and day out for the rest of his life.

---

* The reference here might be to Robert Hanssen, an FBI agent who spied for Soviet and then Russian intelligence services from 1979 until his arrest and conviction in 2001.

† This may refer to Ahmed Ressam and his cooperation with U.S. authorities. See footnote on p. 66.

██████████████████ started to take the shape of a human being, though a bad one. "I write my report like newspaper articles, and the members of the community submit their comments. They're really happy," ████████████ said.

"So am I," I said. I was wondering about the new, half-happy face of ███████████████████████ is an angry person; if he talks to you he always looks at the roof, he hardly ever looks anybody in the eyes. He can barely lead a dialogue, but he's very good when it comes to monologues. "I divorced my wife because she was just so annoying," he once said to me.

"Your request to see ██████████████████ is not approved, in the meantime I am working on your case," he said.

"Alright!" I knew that ████████████████ was a trial, and that the DoD still wanted me to deal with the "bad guy."

"████████████████████████████████," he said.

"But since you don't know my limit, you drove me beyond it," I responded. When I started to talk generously to ████████████████, ████████████████ brought ██████████ back into the picture; for some reason the team wanted █████ back, too.

"Thank you very much for getting the ██████████ back," I said.

████████████ looked both sad and happy. "I enjoy talking to you, you're easy to talk to, and you have pretty teeth," █████ told me before I was kidnapped from ████████████████. ████████ was the closest person to me; █████ was the only one I could relate to.*

"I can never do what ███████████████████ is doing; all he's

---

* The redacted pronouns and the descriptions "the person closest to me" and "the only one I could relate to" suggest that this may be the female member of the Special Projects Team who previously led the second-shift interrogations. See footnote on p. 240.

worried about is getting his job done," said ▓▓▓▓▓ commenting ▓▓▓▓▓▓▓▓▓▓ methods when ▓▓▓▓▓▓▓ was absent. ▓▓▓▓▓▓▓▓▓▓▓▓▓▓▓ were now interrogating me in turn. They dedicated the whole time until around November 10, 2003, to questioning me about Canada and September 11; they didn't ask me a single question about Germany, where I really had the center of gravity of my life. Whenever they asked me about somebody in Canada I had some incriminating information about that person, even if I didn't know him. Whenever I thought about the words, "I don't know," I got nauseous, because I remembered the words of ▓▓▓▓▓▓▓▓▓▓, "All you have to say is, "I don't know, I don't remember, and we'll fuck you!" Or ▓▓▓▓▓▓▓ "We don't want to hear your denials anymore!" And so I erased these words from my dictionary.

"We would like you to write your answers on paper; it's too much work to keep up with your talk, and you might forget things when you talk to us," said ▓▓▓▓▓▓▓▓.

"Of course!" I was really happy with the idea because I would rather talk to a paper than talk to him; at least the paper wouldn't shout in my face or threaten me. ▓▓▓▓▓▓▓▓ drowned me in a pile of papers, which I duly filled with writings. It was a good outlet for my frustration and my depression.

"You're very generous in your written answers; you even wrote a whole bunch about ▓▓▓▓▓▓▓▓▓, whom you really don't know," ▓▓▓▓▓▓▓▓ accurately said, forgetting that he forbade me to use the words "I don't know."

"▓▓▓▓▓▓▓▓ reads your writing with a lot of interest," said ▓▓▓▓▓▓▓▓. I was extremely frightened, because this statement was ambiguous. "We're gonna give you an assignment about ▓▓▓▓▓▓▓▓. He is detained in Florida and they cannot make him talk; he keeps denying everything. You better provide us a Smoking Gun against him," said ▇▇▇▇▇▇▇▇▇▇▇. I was so sad: how rude was this guy, to ask me to provide a smoking gun about somebody I hardly know?

"All I can say is that Ahmed L. is a criminal and should be locked up the rest of his life.* I'm ready to testify against him in court," I said, though I was not ready to lie in court to burn an innocent soul.

"▇▇▇▇▇▇▇▇▇▇ is facing the death penalty if we can make him guilty of drug smuggling," ▇▇▇▇▇▇▇▇▇▇▇ said once, showing me his picture. I burst out laughing as soon as I saw the expression on his face and the Bob Barker–Calvin Klein prison uniform.†

"What are you laughing at?" ▇▇▇▇▇▇▇▇▇▇ asked me. "It's just funny!"

"How can you laugh at your friend?" I felt guilty right away, even though I knew I was not laughing at him. After all, my situation was worse than his. I was laughing at the situation: I could read everything that was going on in his head just from the expression on his face. I'd been made to take that same picture many times, in Senegal, in Mauritania, in Germany, in Jordan, in Bagram, and in GTMO. I hate the pose, I hate the look, I hate the height measure. Let me tell you something, whenever you see that bleak-looking face in a jail uniform,

---

* "Ahmed L." appears in the manuscript unredacted. This could refer to Ahmed Laabidi, a Tunisian national who lived in Montreal in 2000 and was later detained in the United States on an immigration violation. Laabidi was held in U.S. immigration custody and then deported to Tunisia in September 2003. See footnote on p. 294 for more on Laabidi.

† Bob Barker Company, Incorporated, which identifies itself as "America's Leading Detention Supplier," is a major supplier of prison uniforms for the U.S. Department of Defense. See http://news.google.com/newspapers?nid=1454&dat=20020112&id=6gJPAAAAIBAJ&sjid=Ux8EAAAAIBAJ&pg=5765,3098702.

posing in front of a height measure scaled on a wall, you can be sure that is not a happy person.

In fact, I really felt bad for that poor guy. He had sought asylum in Canada for a certain time but the Canadians refused his petition, partly because they considered him as Islamist. ████████████████ was willing to try his chances in the U.S., where he faced the harsh reality of the highly electrified environment against Muslims and Arabs, and where the U.S. gave him asylum in a high-level security prison and now was trying to link him to any crime. When I saw his face, I knew he was like, "Screw these Americans. How much I hate them! What do they want from me? How did I end up in jail when I came here seeking protection?"

"I talked today with the Canadians and they told me they don't believe your story about ████████████████ being involved in drug smuggling into the U.S., but we know he is," he told me once.

"I can only tell you what I know," I said.

"But we want you to give an evidence linking ████████████ ████████ to the Millennium Plot. Things like, he supports the Mujs or believes in Jihad are good, but not good enough to lock him up the rest of his life," he told me.

"Oh, yes, I will," I said. He handed me a bunch of papers and I went back in my cell. Oh, my God, I am being so unjust to myself and my brothers, I kept thinking, and then repeating "Nothing's gonna happen to us....*They'll* go to hell....Nothing's gonna happen to us....*They'll*...." I kept praying in my heart, and repeating my prayers. I took the pen and paper and wrote all kinds of incriminating lies about a poor person who was just seeking refuge in Canada and trying to make some money so he could start a family. Moreover, he is handicapped. I felt so bad, and kept praying silently, "Nothing's gonna happen to you dear brother…" and blowing on the papers as I finished. Of course it was out of the question to tell them what I knew about him truthfully, because ▮▮▮▮▮▮▮▮▮▮ already gave me the guidelines: "▮▮▮▮▮▮▮▮▮▮ is awaiting your testimony against ▮▮▮▮▮▮▮▮ with extreme interest!" I gave the assignment to ▮▮▮▮▮▮▮▮▮▮, and after evaluation, I saw ▮▮▮▮▮▮▮▮ smiling for the first time.

"Your writing about Ahmed was very interesting, but we want you to provide more detailed information," he said. I thought, What information does the idiot want from me? I don't even remember what I've just written.

"Yes, no problem," I said. I was very happy that God answered my prayers for ▮▮▮▮▮▮▮▮ when I learned in 2005 that he was unconditionally released from custody and sent back to his country. "He's facing the death penalty," ▮▮▮▮▮ used to tell me! I was really in no better situation.

"Since I am cooperating, what are you going to do with me?" I asked ▮▮▮▮▮.

"It depends. If you provide us a great deal of information we didn't know, it's going to be weighed against your sentence. For instance, the death penalty could be reduced to life, and life to thirty years," he responded. Lord have mercy on me! What harsh justice!

"Oh, that's great," I replied. I felt bad for everybody I hurt with my false testimonies. My only solaces were, one, that I didn't hurt anybody as much as I did myself; two, that I had no choice; and three, I was confident that injustice will be defeated, it's only a matter of time. Moreover, I would not blame anybody for lying about me when he gets tortured. Ahmed was just an example. During this period I wrote more than a thousand pages about my friends with false information. I had to wear the suit the U.S. Intel tailored for me, and that is exactly what I did.

At the beginning of this phase of cooperation the pressure hardly relieved. I was interrogated ████████████████████ ████████████████████████████. It was so rude to question a human being like that, especially somebody who is cooperating. They made me write names and places ████████████ ████████████████████████. I was shown thousands of pictures. I knew them all by heart because I had seen them so many times; everything was deja-vu. I was like, What ruthless people!

The whole time, the guards were driven madly against me.

"Show him no mercy. Increase the pressure. Drive the hell out of him crazy," said ██████████████████████. And that was exactly what the guards did. Banging on my cell to keep me awake and scared. Taking me violently out of my cell at least twice a day for cell search. Taking me outside in the middle of the night and making me do PT I couldn't due to my health situation. Putting me facing the wall several times a day and threatening me directly and indirectly. Sometimes they even interrogated me, but I never said a word to my interrogators because I knew the interrogators were behind everything.

"You know who you are?" said ██████████████████.

"Uh..."

"You are a terrorist," he continued.

"Yes, Sir!"

"If we kill you once it wouldn't do. We must kill you three thousand times. But instead we feed you!"

"Yes, Sir."

The water diet kept working on me harshly. "You haven't seen nothing yet," they kept telling me.

"I am not looking forward to seeing that. I'm just fine without further measures."

The guards were working in a two-shift routine, day shift and night shift. Whenever the new shift showed up, they made their presence known by banging heavily on the door of my cell to scare me. Whenever the new shift appeared my heart started to pound because they always came up with new ideas to make my life a living hell, like giving me very little food by allowing me about 30 seconds to one minute to eat it, or forcing me to eat every bit of food I got in a very short time. "You better be done!" they would shout. Or they made me clean the shower excessively, or made me fold my towels and my blanket in an impossible way again and again until they were satisfied. To forbidding me any kind of comfort items, they added new rules. One: I should never be lying down; whenever a guard showed up at my bin hole, I always had to be awake, or wake up as soon as a guard walked into my area. There was no sleeping in the terms that we know. Two: My toilet should always be dry! And how, if I am always urinating and flushing? In order to meet the order, I had to use my only uniform to dry the toilet up and stay soaked in shit. Three: My cell should be in a predefined order, including having a folded blanket, so I could never use my blanket.

That was the guards' recipe. I always showed more fear than I felt as a self-defense technique. Not that I would like to play the hero; I'm not, but I wasn't scared of the guards because I just knew they had orders from above. If they reported back that "detainee wasn't scared!" the doses would have been increased.

Meanwhile, I had my own recipe. First of all, I knew that I was really just a stone's throw away from ██████████████

████.* The Interrogators and the guards always hinted at the "God-forsaken nowhere" I was in, but I ignored them completely, and when the guards asked me "Where do you think you are?" I just responded, "I'm not sure, but I am not worried about it; since I am far from my family, it doesn't really matter to me where I am." And so I always closed the door whenever they referred to the place. I was afraid that I would be tortured if they knew I knew where I was, but it was kind of solacing, knowing that you are not far from your fellow detainees.

Once I figured out how to tell day from night, I kept count of the days by reciting 10 pages of the Koran every day. In 60 days I would finish and start over, and so I could keep track of the days. "Shut the fuck up! There is nothing to sing about," said ████████ when he heard me reciting the Koran. After that I recited quietly so nobody could hear me. But my days of the week were still messed up; I failed to keep track of them until I glimpsed ████████████ watch when he pulled it out of his pocket to check the time. He was very vigilant and careful but it was too late, I saw MO████████████████, but he didn't notice. Friday is a very important Muslim holiday, and that was the reason I wanted to keep track of the weekdays. Besides, I just hated the fact that they deprived me of one of my basic freedoms.

I tried to find out everybody's name who was involved in my torture — not for retaliation or anything like that; I just didn't want those people to have the upper hand over any of my brothers, or anybody, no matter who he is. I believe they should not only be deprived of their powers, but they should also be locked up. I succeeded in knowing the names of the ████████████

---

* MOS may be referring to the distance between the isolation cell where he is being held and the main detention blocks of Camp Delta, where he was held previously.

██████████████████████ two of my interrogators, two of the guards, and other interrogators who weren't involved directly in my torture but could serve as witnesses.

When I first met Americans I hated their language because of the pain they made me suffer without a single reason; I didn't want to learn it. But that was emotion; the call of wisdom was stronger, and so I decided to learn the language. Even though I already knew how to conjugate "to be" and "to have," my luggage of English was very light. Since I wasn't allowed to have books, I had to pick up the language mostly from the guards and sometimes my interrogators, and after a short time I could speak like common folk: "He don't care, she don't care, I ain't done nothin', me and my friend did so and so, F—this and F—that, damn x and damn y..."

I also studied the people around me. My observations resulted in knowing that only white Americans were appointed to deal with me, both guards and interrogators. There was only one black guard, but he had no say. His associate was a younger, white ██████████████ but the latter was always in charge. You might say, "How do you know the ranks of the guards, when they were covered?" I wasn't supposed to know who was in charge, nor should they have given me a hint as to who the boss was, but in America it's very easy to notice who the boss is: there's just no mistaking him.

My suspicion of me being near ██████████████████ was cemented when one day I got some of the diet I was used to back in ████████████. "Why did they give me a hot meal?" I asked the sarcastic head guard. "Doctor said we had to." I really looked like a ghost, just bones, no meat. In a matter of weeks I had developed grey hair on the lower half of the sides of my head, a phenomenon people in my culture refer to as the extreme result of depression. Keeping up the pressure was vital in the process of my interrogation. The plan worked: the more pressure, the more stories I produced and the better my interrogators felt toward me.

And then, slowly but surely, the guards were advised to give me the opportunity to brush my teeth, to give me more warm meals, and to give me more showers. The interrogators started to interrogate me ███████████████████████████ ███████████████████████████ was the one who took the first steps, but I am sure there had been a meeting about it. Everybody in the team realized that I was about to lose my mind due to my psychological and physical situation. I had been so long in segregation.

"Please, get me out of this living hell!" I said.

"You will not go back to the population anytime soon." ██████████ told me. Her answer was harsh but true: there was no plan to get me back.* The focus was on holding me segregated as long as they could and gathering information from me.

I still had nothing in my cell. Most of the time I recited the Koran silently. The rest of the time I was talking to myself and thinking over and over about my life and the worst-case scenarios that could happen to me. I kept counting the holes of the cage I was in. There are about four thousand one hundred holes.

Maybe because of this, ██████████ happily started to give me some puzzles that I could spend my time solving. "If we discover that you lied to us, you're gonna feel our wrath, and we're gonna take everything back. This can all go back to the old days, you know that," ██████████ used to tell me whenever he gave me a puzzle. My heart would pound, but I was like,

---

* "Her" appears here unredacted.

What a jackass! Why can't he let me enjoy my "reward" for the time being? Tomorrow is another day.

I started to enrich my vocabulary. I took a paper and started to write words I didn't understand, and ███████████████████ explained them to me. If there is anything positive about ████████████ is his rich vocabulary. I don't remember asking him about a word he couldn't explain to me. English was his only real language, though he claimed to be able to speak Farsi. "I wanted to learn French, but I hated the way they speak and I quit," he said.

████████████████████████ wants to see you in a couple of days," ████████████ said. I was so terrified; at this point I was just fine without his visit.

"He is welcome," I said. I started to go to the toilet relentlessly. My blood pressure went crazily high. I was wondering what the visit would be like. But thank God the visit was much easier than what I thought. ██████████████████ came, escorted by ████████████. He was, as always, practical and brief.

"I am very happy with your cooperation. Remember when I told you that I preferred civilized conversations? I think you have provided 85% of what you know, but I am sure you're gonna provide the rest," he said, opening an ice bag with some juice.

"Oh, yeah, I'm also happy!" I said, forcing myself to drink the juice just to act as if I were normal. But I wasn't: I was like, 85% is a big step coming out of his mouth. ████████████████ advised me to keep cooperating.

"I brought you this present," he said, handing me a pillow. Yes, a pillow. I received the present with a fake overwhelming happiness, and not because I was dying to get a pillow. No, I took the pillow as a sign of the end of the physical torture. We have a joke back home about a man who stood bare naked on the street. When someone asked him, "How can I help you?" He replied, "Give me shoes." And that was exactly what happened to me. All I needed was a pillow! But it was something: alone in my cell, I kept reading the tag over and over.

"Remember when ███████████ told you about the 15% you're holding back," said ████████ a couple of days after ████████████ visit. "I believe that your story about Canada doesn't make sense. You know what we have against you, and you know what the FBI has against you," he continued.

"So what would make sense?" I asked.

"You know exactly what makes sense," he said sardonically.

"You're right, I was wrong about Canada. What I did exactly was...."

"I want you to write down what you've just said. It made perfect sense and I understood, but I want it on paper."

"My pleasure, Sir!" I said.

I came to Canada with a plan to blow up the CN Tower in Toronto. My accomplices were ████████████████ ████████ *and* ████████. ████████ *went to Russia to get us the supply of explosives.* ████████████ *wrote an explosives simulation software that I picked up, tested myself, and handed in a data medium to* ████████████. *The latter was supposed to send it with the whole plan to* ████████ *in London so we could get the final fatwa from the Sheikh.* ████████ *was supposed to buy a lot of sugar to mix with the explosives in order to increase the damage.* ████████████ *provided the financing. Thanks to Canadian Intel, the plan was discovered and sentenced to failure. I admit that I am as guilty as any other participants and am so sorry and ashamed for what I have done. Signed, M.O. Slahi*

When I handed the paper to ██████████████████████ read it happily.

"This statement makes perfect sense."

"If you're ready to buy, I am selling," I said. ██████████████ could hardly hold himself on the chair; he wanted to leave immediately. I guess the prey was big, and ██████████████ was overwhelmed because he reached a breakthrough where no other interrogators had, in spite of almost four years of uninter- rupted interrogation from all kinds of agencies from more than six countries. What a success! ██████████████████ almost had a heart attack from happiness.

"I'll go see him!"

I think the only unhappy person in the team was ██████████, because ████ doubted the truthfulness of the story.

Indeed the next day ██████████████████████ came to see me, escorted as always by his ██████████████████. "Remember when I told you about the 15% you were holding back?"

"Yes, I do."

"I think this confession covered that 15%!" I was like, Hell, yes!

"I am happy that it did," I said.

"Who provided the money?"

"████████████ did.

"And you, too?" ██████████████████ asked.

"No, I took care of the electrical part." I don't really know why I denied the financial part. Did it really make a difference? Maybe I just wanted to maintain the consistency.

"What if we tell you that we found your signature on a fake credit card?" said ██████████████████. I knew he was bullshit- ting me because I knew I never dealt with such dubious things. But I was not going to argue with him.

"Just tell me the right answer. Is it good to say yes or to say

no?" I asked. At that point I hoped I was involved in something so I could admit to it and relieve myself of writing about
every practicing Muslim I ever met, and every Islamic organization I ever heard of. It would have been much easier to admit
to a true crime and say that's that. "This confession is consistent with the Intels we and other agencies possess," ▆▆▆▆▆▆▆
▆▆▆▆▆▆▆ said.

"I am happy."

"Is the story true?" asked ▆▆▆▆▆▆▆▆▆.

"Look, these people I was involved with are bad people anyway, and should be put under lock and key. And as to myself,
I don't care as long as you are pleased. So if you want to buy, I
am selling."

"But we have to check with the other agencies, and if the
story is incorrect, they're gonna find out," ▆▆▆▆▆▆▆▆▆▆▆

"If you want the truth, this story didn't happen," I said sadly.
▆▆▆▆▆▆▆▆▆ had brought some drinks and candies that I
forced myself to swallow. They tasted like dirt because I was
so nervous. ▆▆▆▆▆▆▆ took his ▆▆▆▆▆ outside and pitted
him on me. ▆▆▆▆▆▆▆▆▆ came back harassing me and
threatening me with all kinds of suffering and agony. ▆▆▆▆▆
▆▆▆▆▆▆▆▆▆▆▆▆▆▆▆▆▆▆▆▆▆▆▆▆▆▆▆▆▆▆▆▆
▆▆▆▆▆▆▆▆▆▆▆▆▆▆▆▆▆▆▆▆▆▆▆▆▆▆▆▆▆▆▆▆
▆▆▆▆▆▆▆▆▆▆▆▆▆.

"You know how it feels when you experience our wrath,"
▆▆▆▆▆▆▆▆▆ said. I was like, what the heck does this asshole
want from me? If he wants a confession, I already provided one.
Does he want me to resurrect the dead? Does he want me to
heal his blindness? I am not a prophet, nor does he believe in
them. "The Bible is just the history of the Jewish people, nothing more," he used to say. If he wants the truth, I told him I

have done nothing! I couldn't see a way out. "Yes! . . . Yes! . . . Yes!"
After ███████████████ made me sweat to the last drop in my
body, ███████████████████████ called him and gave him advice
about the next tactics. ████████████ left and ███████████████
continued.

"███████████████████████ has overall control. If he is happy
everybody is. And if he isn't, nobody is." ███████████████████
started to ask me other questions about other things, and I
used every opportunity to make myself look as bad as I could.
"I'm going to leave you alone with papers and pen, and I want
you to write everything you remember about your plan in
Canada!"

"Yes, Sir."

Two days later they were back at my door.

"Get up! Get your hands through the bin hole!" said an
unfriendly-sounding guard. I didn't welcome the visit: I hadn't
missed my interrogators' faces over the weekend, and they
scared the hell out of me. The guards shackled me and took me
outside the building where █████████████████████████ were
waiting for me. It was my first time seeing the daylight. Many
people take daylight for granted, but if you are forbidden to see
it, you'll appreciate it. The brightness of the sun made my eyes
squint until they adjusted. The sun hit me mercifully with its
warmth. I was terrified and shaking.

"What's wrong with you?" one of the guards asked me.

"I am not used to this place."

"We brought you outside so you can see the sun. We will
have more rewards like this."

"Thank you very much," I managed to say, though my mouth
was dry and my tongue was heavy as steel. "Nothing is gonna
happen to you if you tell us about the bad things. I know you're

afraid that we will change our opinion toward you," said ███████████████████████ while ███████████████████ was taking notes.

"I know."

"Let's talk hypothetically. You understand hypothetical?" ████████████████████████ said.

"Yes, I do."

"Let's assume you've done what you confessed to."

"But I haven't."

"Just let's assume."

"Okay," I said. As high-ranking as ██████████████████████ was, he was the worst interrogator I've ever met. I mean professionally. He just jumps back and forth without focusing on any specific thing. If I had to guess, I would say his job was anything but interrogating people.

"Between you and ██████████████████, who was in charge?"

"It depends: in the mosque I was in charge, and outside he was in charge," I answered. The questions assumed that Hannachi and I are members of a gang, but I didn't even know Mr. ██████████████████, let alone conspire with him as part of a corps that never existed.* But anyway I could not tell some-

---

* "Hannachi" might refer to Raouf Hannachi, a Tunisian-born Canadian citizen who also lived in Montreal in 2000. It appears from MOS's 2008 Detainee Assessment and from MOS's habeas corpus decision that confessions like those MOS is describing here became part of the government's allegations against him. Both Hannachi and Ahmed Laabidi appear in both the 2008 Detainee Assessment and Judge James Robertson's 2010 habeas memorandum order; in both the government portrays MOS, Hannachi, and Laabidi as members of a Montreal cell of al-Qaeda, with Hannachi as the cell's leader and Laabidi as the cell's financier. A footnote to Judge Robertson's opinion specifically notes that MOS's statement under interrogation that "Laabidi [is] a terrorist who supported use of suicide bombers" came in an interrogation session dated September 16, 2003 — right around the time of the scene MOS describes here. The 2008 Detainee Assessment is available at http://projects.nytimes.com/guantanamo

thing like that to ███████████████████; I had to tell him
something that made me look bad.

"Have or haven't you conspired with those individuals as you
admitted?"

"You want the truth?"

"Yes!"

"No, I haven't," I said. ████████████████████ and ████████
████████████ tried to play all kinds of tricks on me, but first of
all I knew all the tricks, and second I had already told them the
truth. So it was futile to play tricks on me. But they drove me
into the infamous Catch-22: if I lie to them, "You'll feel our
wrath." And if I tell the truth, it will make me look good,
which would make them believe I am withholding information
because in their eyes I AM A CRIMINAL and I wasn't yet able
to change that opinion.

███████████████████ handed me a printed version of the
so-called Witness Protection Program. He obviously forgot to
disable the date printout footnote, so I could read it. I wasn't
supposed to know the date, but nobody is perfect.

"Oh, thank you very much," I said.

"If you help us, you'll see how generous our government is,"
███████████████ said.

"I'll read it."

"I think this is something for you."

"Sure." ███████████████████ gestured to the guards to
take me back in my cell. They were still holding me all this
time ████████████████████.*

/detainees/760-mohamedou-ould-slahi. Detainee Assessment, 10; Memorandum Order, 26–28.

★ MOS indicates later in the manuscript that he remained in the same
cell he was delivered into at the end of his staged abduction through the
time of the manuscript's creation. There are no indications that he has been
moved since. A 2010 *Washington Post* report described a "little fenced-in

As soon as the interrogation team left, one of the guards was opening my cell and shouting, "Get up Motherfucker." I was like, Oh my God, again? ███████████████████████

████████ took me out of the cell and made me face the wall.

"You fucking pussy. Why don't you admit?"

"I've been telling the truth."

"You ain't. Interrogators never ask if they don't have proof. They just wanted to test you. And guess what? You failed. You blew your chance," he continued. I was sweating and shaking, and I showed even more fear than I really felt. "It's so easy: we just want you to tell us what you've done, how you've done it, and who else was involved with you. We use this information to stop other attacks. Is that not easy?"

"Yeah, it is."

"So why do you keep being a pussy?"

"Because he's gay!" said ████████████████████████.

"You think the ███████████████ just gave you the Witness Protection information for fun? Hell, we should kill you, but we don't; instead, we're gonna give you money, a house, and a nice car, how frustrating is that? In the end, you are a terrorist," he continued. "You better tell them everything the next time they come. Take a pen and paper and write everything down."

The Interrogators and guards believed the Witness Protection Program is a U.S. specialty, but it isn't. It's practiced all over the world; even in the darkest dictatorship countries, criminals can profit from such a program. ██████████████████████ provided me stories about other criminals who became friends of the U.S.

---

compound at the military prison" that matches the description of his living situation at the time the manuscript was written. See Peter Finn, "For Two Detainees Who Told What They Knew, Guantanamo Becomes a Gilded Cage," *Washington Post*, March 24, 2010, http://www.washingtonpost .com/wp-dyn/content/article/2010/03/24/AR2010032403135.html. MOS manuscript, 233.

government, such as ████████████████████████ and another communist who fled the Soviets during the Cold War. I was really not enlightened by any of this, but I took the papers anyway: something to read beside the pillow tag. I kept reading and reading and reading it again because I just like to read and I had nothing to read.

"You remember what you told ████████████████, when he told you you're hiding 15%," ████████ said in our next session.

"Yeah, but you see I can't argue with ████████████████. Otherwise he gets mad." ████████████ took a printed version of my confession and started to read it, smiling.

"But you're not only hurting yourself. You're hurting other innocent people."

"That's correct. But what else should I do?"

"You said you guys wanted to mix sugar with explosives?"

"Yes, I did." ████████████ smiled.

"But that's not we wanted to hear when we asked you what you meant by 'sugar.' As a matter of fact, ████████████████████ ████████████████████████████████████."

"████████ I really don't know that," I said.

"You cannot possibly lie about something as big as that," ████████ said. "We have a highly qualified expert who could come and question you. What do you think about ████████ ████████?"

"████████████ I'm dying to take one!" I said, though my heart was pounding because I knew I might fail the test even if was telling the truth.

"I'm gonna organize a ████████████ for you as soon as possible."*

---

* Context, including the unredacted word "poly" a bit farther into this passage, suggests that the subject of this conversation and the long redaction

"I know you want to make yourself look good," I said.

"No, I care about you. I would like to see you out of jail, leading a normal life. There are some detainees I want to see stay here the rest of their lives. But you, no!" ▆▆▆▆▆▆▆ genuinely.

"Thank you very much." ▆▆▆▆▆▆ left with that promise and I retreated back to my cell, completely depressed.

"Remember that the ▆▆▆▆▆▆ is decidedly important in your life," said ▆▆▆▆▆▆▆▆▆ shortly before he left one of his sessions, trying with the help of his executioner ▆▆▆▆▆▆▆▆▆ to pry nonexistent information out of my mouth. He scared the hell out of me, because my whole life was now hanging on a ▆▆▆▆▆▆.

"Yes, Sir, I know."

"Who would you like to have with you during the ▆▆▆▆▆▆," asked ▆▆▆▆▆▆ a couple of days before the ▆▆▆▆.

"I think ▆▆▆▆▆▆▆▆ wouldn't be a good idea, but I would be just fine if you would be here!"

"Or the other ▆▆▆▆," ▆▆▆▆▆▆▆.

"Yeah," I said reluctantly. "But why don't you just come?"

"I'll try, but if not me, it will be the ▆▆▆▆▆."

"I am very scared because of what ▆▆▆▆▆▆▆ said," I told ▆▆▆▆ the day before the test.

---

that follows could be the polygraph exam MOS describes toward the end of his ARB testimony. After recounting the boat trip and its aftermath, MOS stated, "Because they said to me either I am going to talk or they will continue to do this, I said I am going to tell them everything they wanted. . . . I told them I was on my own trying to do things and they said write it down and I wrote it and I signed it. I brought a lot of people, innocent people with me because I got to make a story that makes sense. They thought my story was wrong so they put me on [a] polygraph." ARB transcript, 27.

"Look, I've taken the test several times and passed. All you need to do is clear your mind and be honest and truthful," ▇▇▇▇▇▇ answered.

"I will."

▇▇▇▇▇▇▇▇▇▇▇▇▇ "Guess what?" said ▇▇▇▇▇▇▇▇, looking at me through the cage of my cell. I quickly stood up at the bin hole.

"Yes, Sir!" I thought ▇▇▇▇ was one of the guards. ▇▇▇▇▇▇▇ startled, and ▇▇▇▇▇ looked at me, smiling.

"Oh, it's you! I am sorry, I thought you were one of the guards. You came for the ▇▇▇▇▇▇▇▇▇, didn't you?"

"Yes, in a couple of hours I'll be back with the guy with the ▇▇▇▇▇▇▇▇. I just want you to be prepared."

"OK, thank you very much." ▇▇▇▇ left. I performed a ritual wash and managed to steal a prayer off the guards, I don't remember whether I performed it formally or informally. "Oh, God! I need your help more than ever. Please show them that I am telling the truth. Please give not these merciless people any reason to hurt me. Please. Please!" After the prayer I exercised a kind of yoga. I never really practiced that meditation technique before, but now I sat on my bed, put my hands on my thighs, and imagined my body connected to the poly.*

"Have you done any crimes against the U.S.?" I asked myself.

"No." Would I really pass? Screw them! I've done no crimes; why should I be worried? They're evil! And then I thought, No, they're not evil: it's their right to defend their own country. They're good people. They really are! And then again, Screw them, I don't owe them anything. They tortured me, they owe me! I did the ▇▇▇▇▇▇▇ with all the possible questions.

"Did you tell the truth about ▇▇▇▇▇▇▇▇▇▇▇▇.

---

* "Poly" appears here unredacted.

299

"No." Oh, that's a big problem, because ▓▓▓▓▓▓▓ said, "When we catch you lying you're gonna feel our wrath." Screw ▓▓▓▓▓▓▓; I'm not gonna lie to please him and destroy my own life. No way. I'm gonna tell the truth no matter what. But what if I fail the test, even after answering truthfully? OK! No problem, I'm gonna lie. But what if the ▓▓▓▓ shows my new lies? Then I'm really gonna be stuck in a cul-de-sac. Only God can help me: my situation is serious and the Americans are crazy. Don't worry about that, just take the ▓▓▓▓ and you're gonna be alright. I was going to the bathroom so often that I thought I was going to urinate my kidneys.

The doorbell rang and ▓▓▓▓▓▓▓ surged through with the ▓▓.

"My name is ▓▓▓▓▓▓▓▓. Nice to meet you."

"Nice to meet you," I said, shaking his hand. I knew he was dishonest about his name. He unluckily chose the wrong name, ▓▓▓▓▓▓▓▓, which I knew to be a generic name. But I really didn't care. After all, what interrogator is honest about anything? He could as well have introduced himself as ▓▓▓▓▓▓▓ with the same effect. "You will be working with me today. How are you?"

"I am very nervous," I answered.

"Perfect. That is the way you should be. I don't like relaxed detainees. Give me a minute, I am going to install the ▓▓▓▓▓▓." In fact ▓▓▓▓ and I helped him ▓▓▓▓▓▓▓▓▓▓▓▓▓▓▓▓▓▓▓.

"Now, I want you to sit and look at me the whole time while I am speaking to you." ▓▓▓▓▓▓▓ was not exactly the evil-looking interrogator. He was, I think, skeptical but fair.

"Have you taken ▓▓▓▓▓▓▓▓▓ before?"

"Yes, I have!"

"So you understand the ▮▮▮▮▮▮▮▮▮▮▮▮▮▮▮▮▮▮▮▮
▮▮▮▮▮▮▮▮▮▮."

"I guess I do."

But anyway, ▮▮▮▮▮▮▮▮▮▮▮▮▮▮▮▮▮▮▮▮▮▮▮▮

SEVEN

GTMO

2004-2005

The Good News...Goodbye Like Family Members...
The TV and the Laptop...The First Unofficial Laugh-
ter in the Ocean of Tears...The Present Situation...
The Dilemma of the Cuban Detainees

I am happy and ██████████████████ is very pleased," said
██████████ when ██████ showed up the day after the
█████████████████, accompanied by a ████████████ white ██████████
in ██████ late twenties.*

"What does 'pleased' mean?" I asked ████████████. I had an
idea, but I wanted to be clear since the word was a quotation
from ████████████████████.

"Pleased means very happy."

---

* In *The Terror Courts*, Jess Bravin published details of a polygraph examination of MOS that he dates to October 31, 2004. Bravin reported that
MOS answered "No" to five questions about whether he knew about or
participated in the Millennium and 9/11 plots, and whether he was concealing any information about other al-Qaeda members or plots. The results,
according to Bravin, were either "No Deception Indicated" or "No Opinion"—results that Lt. Col. Stuart Couch, the Military Commissions prosecutor assigned to MOS's case, considered potentially exculpatory
information that would need to be shared with defense attorneys if MOS
was ever charged and prosecuted. Bravin, *The Terror Courts*, 110–11.

"Ah, OK. Didn't I tell you that I wasn't lying?"

"Yes, I'm glad," said ███████ smiling. ██████████ happiness was obvious and honest. I was hardly happier about my success than ██████████.* Now I could tell that the resented torture was heading the other direction, slowly but surely. And yet I was extremely skeptical, since I was still surrounded by the same people as I had been since day one.

"Look at your uniform and ours. You are not one of us. You are our enemy!" █████████████████ used to say.

"I know."

"I don't want you to forget. If I speak to you, I speak to my enemy."

"I know!"

"Don't forget."

"I won't!" Such talk left no doubt that the animosity of the guards had been driven to its extreme. Most of the time I had the feeling that they were trained to devour me alive.

██████████ introduced █████ company to me. "This is another interrogator you can ████████████████████████ like me."

The new interrogator █████████████████████████ was quiet and polite. I can't really say anything negative about ████████████████████████ was a workaholic, and not really open to other people. █████████████████ literally followed the orders of █████ boss ████████████████, and sometimes even worked like a computer.

"Do you know about █████████████████ travel to Iraq in 2003?" █████ asked me once.

---

* The redacted pronouns and tone of this conversation suggest that the lead interrogator might be the female member from the special interrogation team. In this scene she seems to be introducing a new interrogator who will be working with MOS as well; redactions hint that this interrogator, too, might be female.

"Come on, ▇▇▇▇ you know that I turned myself in in 2001. How am I supposed to know what went on in 2003? It doesn't make sense, does it?" I said.

▇▇▇▇▇▇ smiled. "I have the question in my request."

"But you know that I've been in detention since 2001!" I said. ▇▇▇▇▇▇ was very careful, too careful: ▇▇▇▇▇▇ used to cover ▇▇▇ rank and ▇▇▇ name all the time, and ▇▇▇ never made any reference to ▇▇▇ beliefs. I personally was content with that, as long as ▇▇▇ didn't give me a hard time.

"I like the way you make connections," ▇▇▇▇▇▇▇▇ said, smiling at me in that session. Interrogators have a tendency to enter the house through the window and not the door; instead of asking a direct question, they ask all kinds of questions around it. I took it as a challenge, and for the most part I would search out the direct question and answer that. "Your question is whether or not...," I would say. And ▇▇▇▇▇▇ seemed to like that shortcut.

But has there ever, in all of recorded human history, been an interrogation that has gone on, day in and day out, for more than six years? There is nothing an interrogator could say to me that would be new; I've heard every variation. Each new interrogator would come up with the most ridiculous theories and lies, but you could tell they were all graduates of the same school: before an interrogator's mouth opened I knew what he ▇▇▇▇▇▇ was going to say and why he ▇▇▇▇▇▇ was saying it.*

"I am your new interrogator. I have very long experience doing this job. I was sent especially from Washington D.C. to assess your case."

---

* Context suggests that the redactions in this sentence may be "or she." If so, this would be a particularly absurd example of the effort to conceal the fact that the U.S. deployed female interrogators.

"You are the most important detainee in this camp. If you cooperate with me, I am personally going to escort you to the airport. If you don't cooperate, you're gonna spend the rest of your life on this island."

"You're very smart. We don't want to keep you in jail. We would rather capture the big fish and release the small fish, such as yourself."

"You haven't driven a plane into a building; your involvement can be forgiven with just a five-minute talk. The U.S. is the greatest country in the world; we would rather forgive than punish."

"Many detainees have talked about you being the bad person. I personally don't believe them; however, I would like to hear your side of the story, so I can defend you appropriately."

"I have nothing against Islam, I even have many Muslim friends."

"I have helped many detainees to get out of this place; just by writing a positive report stating that you told you the whole truth....."

And so on, in an endless recitation that all the interrogators recited when they met with their detainees. Most detainees couldn't help laughing when they had to hear this *Groundhog Day* nonsense; in fact, it was the only entertainment we got in the interrogation booth. When his interrogator told him, "I know you are innocent," one of my fellow detainees laughed hard and responded, "I'd rather be a criminal and sitting home with my kids." I believe anything loses its influence the more we repeat it. If you hear an expression like, "You are the worst criminal on the face of the earth" for the first time, you'll most likely get the hell scared out of you. But the fear diminishes the more times you hear it, and at some point it will have no effect at all. It may even sound like a daily compliment.

And yet let's look at it from the interrogator's perspective. They were literally taught to hate us detainees. "Those people are the most evil creatures on earth…Do not help the enemy… Keep in mind they are enemies…Look out, the Arabs are the worst, especially the Saudis and the Yemenis. They're hardcore, they're savages….Watch out, don't ███████████████████ unless you secure everything…" In GTMO, interrogators are taught more about the potential behavior of detainees than about their actual Intelligence value, and so the U.S. Interrogators consistently succeeded in missing the most trivial information about their own detainees. I'm not speaking about second hand information; I'm speaking about my own experience.

"███████████ spoke about you!" ███████████ said to me once.

"███████████ doesn't know me, how could he possibly have spoken about me? Just read my file again."

"I am sure that he did. I'm gonna show you!" █████ said. But █████ never did because █████ was wrong. I had ████████ of such and worse examples depicting the ignorance of interrogators about their detainees. The government would hold back basic information from its interrogators for tactical reasons, and then tell them, "The detainee you are assigned to is deeply involved in terrorism and has vital information about coming and already performed attacks. Your job is to get everything he knows." In fact, I hardly met a detainee who was involved in a crime against the United States.

So you have interrogators who are prepared, schooled, trained, and pitted to meet their worst enemies. And you have detainees who typically were captured and turned over to U.S. forces without any proper judicial process. After that, they experienced heavy mistreatment and found themselves incarcerated in another hemisphere, in GTMO Bay, by a country that claims to safeguard human rights all over the world—but a country that many Muslims suspect is conspiring with other evil forces to wipe the Islamic religion off the face of the earth. All in all, the environment is not likely to be a place of love and reconciliation. The hatred here is heavily watered.

But believe it or not, I have seen guards crying because they had to leave their duties in GTMO.

"I am your friend, I don't care what anybody says," said one guard to me before he left.

"I was taught bad things about you, but my judgment tells me something else. I like you very much, and I like speaking with you. You are a great person," said another.

"I hope you get released," said ███████ genuinely.

"You guys are my brothers, all of you," another whispered to me.

"I love you!" said a ███████ corpsman once to my neighbor, a funny young guy I personally enjoyed talking to. He was shocked.

"What...Here no love...I am Mouslim!" I just laughed about that "forbidden" love.

But I couldn't help crying myself one day when I saw a German-descendent ███████ guard crying because ███████ got just a little bit hurt. The funny thing was I hid my feelings because I didn't want them to be misinterpreted by my brethren, or understood as a weakness or a betrayal. At one point I hated myself and confused the hell out of myself. I started to ask myself questions about the humane emotions I was having toward my enemies. How could you cry for somebody who caused you so much pain and destroyed your life? How could you possibly like somebody who ignorantly hates your religion? How could you put up with these evil people who keep hurting your brothers? How could you like somebody who works day and night to pull shit on you? I was in a worse situation than a slave: at least a slave is not always shackled in chains, has some limited freedom, and doesn't have to listen to some interrogator's bullshit every day.

I often compared myself with a slave. Slaves were taken forcibly from Africa, and so was I. Slaves were sold a couple of times on their way to their final destination, and so was I. Slaves suddenly were assigned to somebody they didn't choose, and so was I. And when I looked at the history of slaves, I noticed that slaves sometimes ended up an integral part of the master's house.

I have been through several phases during my captivity. The first phase was the worst: I almost lost my mind fighting to get back to my family and the life I was used to. My torture was in my rest; as soon as I closed my eyes, I found myself complaining to them about what has happened to me.

"Am I with you for real, or is it a mere dream?"

"No, you're really at home!"

"Please hold me, don't let me go back!" But the reality always hit me as soon as I woke up to the dark bleak cell, looking around just long enough to fall asleep and experience it all again. It was several weeks before I realized that I'm in jail and not going home anytime soon. As harsh as it was, this step was necessary to make me realize my situation and work objectively to avoid the worst, instead of wasting my time with my mind playing games on me. Many people don't pass this step; they lose their minds. I saw many detainees who ended up going crazy.

Phase two is when you realize for real that you're in jail and you possess nothing but all the time in the world to think about your life—although in GTMO detainees also have to worry about daily interrogations. You realize you have control over nothing, you don't decide when you eat, when you sleep, when you take a shower, when you wake up, when you see the doctor, when you see the interrogator. You have no privacy; you cannot even squeeze a drop of urine without being watched. In the beginning it is a horrible thing to lose all those privileges in the blink of an eye, but believe me, people get used to it. I personally did.

Phase three is discovering your new home and family.

Your family comprises the guards and your interrogators. True, you didn't choose this family, nor did you grow up with it, but it's a family all the same, whether you like it or not, with all the advantages and disadvantages. I personally love my family and wouldn't trade it for the world, but I have developed a family in jail that I also care about. Every time a good member of my present family leaves it feels as if a piece of my heart is being chopped off. But I am so happy if a bad member has to leave.*

"I'm going to leave soon," ██████████ said a couple of days before ████ left.

"Really? Why?"

"It's about time. But the other ████████████████ is going to stay with you." That was not exactly comforting, but it would have been futile to argue: the transfer of MI agents is not a subject of discussion. "We're gonna watch a movie together before I leave," ████████ added.

"Oh, good!" I said. I hadn't digested the news yet.

██████████ most likely studied psychology, and came from the west coast, maybe California ████████████████████ ████████████████████ early twenties ████████████ ████████████████. I think that ████████ comes from

---

* MOS adds a note here in the margin of the handwritten original: "Phase four: getting used to the prison, and being afraid of the outside world."

a rather poor family. The ████████████████ provides a great deal of opportunity for people from the lower classes, and most of the ████████████████ people I've seen are from the lower class. ████████████████████ and has a rather shaky relation ██████ ████████████████████ has a very strong personality, ██████ looks at ████████████ and ██████ ideas very highly. At the same time ████████████ likes ██████ job, and might have been forced to step over the red line of ██████ principles sometimes. "I know what we are doing is not healthy for our country," ██████ used to tell me.

████████████ was my first real encounter with an American ████████████████████████ you are so foul-mouthed! I feel ashamed for you," I wondered once. ██████ smiled.

"It's because I've been most of the time ██████████████████ ████." At first I had a problem starting a conversation with a foul-mouthed ██████████, but later I learned that there was no way to speak colloquial English without F—ing this and F—ing that. English accepts more curses than any other language, and I soon learned to curse with the commoners. Sometimes guards would ask me to translate certain words into Arabic, German, or French, but the translation spun around in my head and I could not spit it out; it just sounded so gross. On the other hand, when I curse in English I really have no bad feeling whatsoever, because that's the way I learned the language from day one. I had a problem when it comes to blasphemy, but everything else was tolerable. The curses are just so much more harmless when everybody uses them recklessly.

████████████ was one of my main teachers of the dictionary of curse words, alongside ████████████████████████████████ ████████████████████████ has been through some bad relationships; ██████ had been cheated on and some bad things like that.

"Did you cry when you knew?" I asked ██████.

"No, I didn't want to ███████████████████████
████████████████████████████. I have a problem when it
comes to crying."

"I see." But I personally don't see the problem: I cry whenever I feel like it and it makes me stronger to admit my
weakness.

████████████ was misused by ████████████ and his colleague ██████████████████████████ and some other
behind-the-scenes guys. I know that I am looking for excuses
to acquit ████████████████████ was old enough to know
that what █████ was doing was wrong, and █████ could have
both saved █████ job and had the other higher-ranking officers fired. ████████████ certainly contributed to the pressure to
which I had been subjected. But I do also know that ██████████
doesn't believe in torture.

I used to make fun of the signs they put up for the interrogators and the guards to raise their morale, "Honor bound to
defend freedom." I once cited that big sign to ████████████.

"I hate that sign," █████ said.

"How could you possibly be defending freedom, if you're
taking it away?" I would say.

The bosses had noticed the close relationship developing
between ██████████ and me, and so they separated █████ from
me when I was kidnapped. The last words I heard were, "You're
hurting him! Who gave you the orders?" █████ shouts fading
away as ████████ and ██████████████████████ dragged me
out of the room in ████████████████. And when they decided
to give me a chance at a halfway humane interrogation,
████████████ appeared in the picture again. But this time █████ was
somewhat unfriendly to me, and used any opportunity to make
my statements look stupid. I couldn't understand █████ behavior. Was it in my favor, or was █████ just pissed off at everybody?

I'm not going to judge anybody; I'm leaving that part to Allah. I am just providing the facts as I have seen and experienced them, and I don't leave anything out to make somebody look good or bad. I understand that nobody is perfect, and everybody does both good and bad things. The only question is, How much of each?

"Do you hate my government?" ███████ asked me once while sifting through a map.

"No, I hate nobody."

"I would hate the U.S. if I were you!" ████ said. "You know, nobody really knows what we're doing here. Only a few people in the government know about it."

"Really?"

"Yes. The President reads the files of some detainees. He reads your case."

"Really?"

████████ enjoyed rewarding rather than punishing detainees. I can say without a doubt that ███████ didn't enjoy harassing me, although ████ tried to keep ████ "professional" face; on the other hand, ████ very much enjoyed giving some stuff back. ████ was even the one who came with most of the ideas related to literature that I was given to read.

"This book is from █████████████ said one day, handing me a thick novel that was called something like *Life in the Forest.**
It was historical fiction, written by a British writer, and it covered a great deal of the medieval European history and the Norman invasion. I received the book gratefully and read it hungrily, at least three times. Later on, ████ brought me several

---

* The description suggests the book might be Edward Rutherfurd's historical novel *The Forest*, which was published in 2000.

Star Wars books. Whenever I finished one, ▮▮▮▮ traded it for a new one.

"Oh, thank you very much!"

"Did you like the Star Wars?"

"I sure do!" In truth, I didn't really like the Star Wars books and their language, but I had to settle for any books they gave to me. In prison you have nothing but all the time in world to think about your life and the goal thereof. I think prison is one of the oldest and greatest schools in the world: you learn about God and you learn patience. A few years in prison are equivalent to decades of experience outside it. Of course there is the devastating side of the prison, especially for innocent prisoners who, besides dealing with the daily hardship of prison, have to deal with the psychological damages that result from confinement without a crime. Many innocent people in prison contemplate suicide.

Just imagine yourself going to bed, putting all your worries aside, enjoying your favorite magazine to put you to sleep, you've put the kids to bed, your family is already sleeping. You are not afraid of being dragged out of your bed in the middle of the night to a place you've never seen before, deprived of sleep, and terrorized all the time. Now imagine that you have no say at all in your life—when you sleep, when you wake up, when you eat, and sometimes when you go to the toilet. Imagine that your whole world comprises, at most, a 6 by 8 foot cell. If you imagine all of that, you still won't understand what prison really means unless you experience it yourself.

▮▮▮▮▮▮▮▮ showed up as promised a few days later with a laptop and two movies, and told me. "You can decide which one you'd like to watch!" I picked the movie *Black Hawk Down*; I don't remember the other choice.

The movie was both bloody and sad. I paid more attention to the emotions of ███████ and the guards than to the movie itself. ███████ was rather calm; ██████████████ every once in a while paused the movie to explain the historical background of certain scenes to me. The guards almost went crazy emotionally because they saw many Americans getting shot to death. But they missed that the number of U.S. casualties is negligible compared to the Somalis who were attacked in their own homes. I was just wondering at how narrow-minded human beings can be. When people look at one thing from one perspective, they certainly fail to get the whole picture, and that is the main reason for the majority of misunderstandings that sometimes lead to bloody confrontations.

After we finished watching the movie, ███████ packed ████ computer and got ready to leave.

"Eh, by the way, you didn't tell me when you're going to leave!"

"I am done, you won't see me anymore!" I froze as if my feet were stuck on the floor. ███████ didn't tell me that ████ was leaving *that* soon; I thought maybe in a month, three weeks, something like that—but today? In my world that was impossible. Imagine if death were devouring some friend of yours and you just were helplessly watching him fading away.

"Oh, really, that soon? I'm surprised! You didn't tell me. Good-bye," I said. "I wish everything good for you."

"I have to follow my orders, but I leave you in good hands." And off ████ went. I reluctantly went back to my cell and silently burst in tears, as if I'd lost ████████, and not somebody whose job was to hurt me and extract information in an end-justifies-the-means way. I both hated and felt sorry for myself for what was happening to me.

"May I see my interrogator please?" I asked the guards, hoping they could catch ▮▮▮▮▮▮▮ before they reached the main gate.

"We'll try," said ▮▮▮▮▮▮▮. I retreated back in my cell, but soon ▮▮▮▮▮▮ showed up at the door of my cell.

"That is not fair. You know that I suffered torture and am not ready for another round."

"You haven't been tortured. You must trust my government. As long as you're telling the truth, nothing bad is gonna happen to you!" Of course ▮▮▮▮ meant The Truth as it's officially defined. But I didn't want to argue with ▮▮▮ about anything.

"I just don't want to start everything over with new interrogators," I said.

"It's not gonna happen," ▮▮▮▮▮▮▮ said. "Besides, you can write me. I promise I'll answer every email of yours," ▮▮▮▮ continued.

"No, I will not write you," I said.

"OK." ▮▮▮▮▮▮ said. "Are you alright?" ▮▮▮ asked.

"I'm not, but you may surely leave."

"I am not leaving until you assure me everything's alright," ▮▮▮ said.

"I said what I had to say. Have a good trip. May Allah guide you. I'll be just fine."

"I am sure you will. It will take at most a week and you'll forget me." I didn't speak after that. Instead I went back and lay myself down. ▮▮▮▮▮▮ stayed a couple of minutes repeating ▮▮▮▮▮▮▮ "I am not leaving until you assure me everything is alright."

After ▮▮▮ left, I never saw ▮▮▮ again or tried to get in contact with ▮▮▮▮. And so the chapter of ▮▮▮▮▮▮ time with me was sealed.

"I heard yesterday's goodbye was very emotional. I never

thought of you this way. Would you describe yourself as a criminal?" ▮▮▮▮▮▮▮▮ said the next day.

I prudently answered, "To an extent." I didn't want to fall in any possible trap, even though I felt that he was honestly and innocently asking the question, now that he realized that his evil theories about me were null. "All the evil questions are gone," ▮▮▮▮▮▮▮▮▮▮ said.

"I won't miss them," I said.

▮▮▮▮▮▮▮▮▮▮▮▮▮▮ had come to give me a haircut. It was about time! One of the measures of my punishment was to deprive me of any hygienic shaves, toothbrushing, or haircuts, so today was a big day. They brought a masked barber; the guy was scary looking, but he did the job. ▮▮▮▮▮▮▮▮ also brought me a book he promised me a long time ago, *Fermat's Last Theorem*, which I really enjoyed—so much so that I hungrily read it more than twice. The book is written by a British journalist and speaks about the famous De Fermat theorem that says the equation $A^n + B^n = C^n$ has no solution when n is greater than two. For more than three hundred years, mathematicians from all around the world were boxing against this harmless-looking theorem without succeeding in tackling it, until a British Mathematician in 1993 came up with a very complicated proof, which was surely not the one De Fermat meant when he wrote, "I have a neat proof but I have no space on my paper."

I got a haircut, and later on a decent shower. ▮▮▮▮▮▮▮▮ was not a very talkative person; ▮▮▮▮▮ asked me just one question about computers.

"Are you going to cooperate with the new ▮▮▮▮▮?"

"Yes."

"Or anybody who's going to work with ▮▮▮▮?"

"Yes."

*   *   *

The guards wanted to be baptized with the names of characters in the *Star Wars* movies. "From now on we are the ████████ and that's what you call us. Your name is Pillow," ████████████ said. I eventually learned from the books that ████████████ are sort of Good Guys who fight against the Forces of Evil. So for the time being I was forced to represent the Forces of Evil, and the guards the Good Guys.

"████████████, that's what you call me," he said. I also called him ██ ██ ██ was in his early forties, married with children, small but athletically built. He spent some time working in the ████████████ ████████████, and then ended up doing "special missions" for the ████████ "████████████████████████████████ ████████. I've been working ████████████████████████████," he told me.

"Your job is done. I am broken," I answered.

"Don't ask me anything. If you want to ask for something, ask your interrogator."

"I got you," I said. It sounds confusing or even contradictory, but although ████████████ was a rough guy, he was humane. That is to say his bark was worse than his bite. ████████████ understood what many guards don't understand: if you talk and tell your interrogators what they want to hear, you should be relieved. Many of the other nitwits kept doubling the pressure on me, just for the sake of it.

████████████ was in charge of all the other guards. "My job is to make you see the light," said ████████████, addressing me for the first time when he was watching me eating my meal.

Guards were not allowed to talk to me or to each other, and I couldn't talk to them. But ▮▮▮▮▮▮▮▮▮▮ was not a by-the-book guy. He thought more than any other guard, and his goal was to make his country victorious: the means didn't matter.

"Yes sir," I answered, without even understanding what he meant. I thought about the literal sense of the light I hadn't seen in a long time, and I believed he wanted to get me cooperating so I could see the daylight. But ▮▮▮▮▮ meant the figurative sense. ▮▮▮▮▮ always yelled at me and scared me, but he never hit me. He illegally interrogated me several times, which is why I called him ▮▮▮▮▮▮▮▮▮▮▮▮▮▮▮▮▮▮▮▮▮▮▮▮ wanted me to confess to many wild theories he heard the interrogators talking about. Furthermore, he wanted to gather knowledge about terrorism and extremism. I think his dream in life was to become an interrogator. What a hell of a dream!

▮▮▮▮▮▮▮▮▮ is an admitted Republican, and hates the Democrats, especially Bill Clinton. He doesn't believe that the U.S. should interfere in other countries' business, and instead should focus more on internal issues—but if any country or group attacks the U.S., it should be destroyed ruthlessly.

"Fair enough," I said. I just wanted him to stop talking. He is the kind of guy who never stops when he gets started. Gosh, he gave me an earache! When ▮▮▮▮▮ first started talking to me I refused to answer, because all I was allowed to say was, "Yes, sir, No Sir, Need Medics, Need Interrogators." But he wanted a conversation with me.

"You are my enemy," ▮▮▮▮▮ said.

"Yes, Sir."

"So let's talk as enemy to enemy," ▮▮▮▮▮ said. He opened my cell and offered me a chair. ▮▮▮▮▮ did the talking for the most part. He was talking about how great the U.S. is, and how powerful; "America is this, American is that, We Americans are so and so..." I was just wondering and nodding slightly. Every once in a while I confirmed that I was paying attention, "Yes, sir...Really?...Oh, I didn't know...You're right...I know..." During our conversations, he sneakily tried to make me admit to things I hadn't really done.

"What was your role in September 11?"

"I didn't participate in September 11."

"Bullshit!" he screamed madly. I realized it would be no good for my life to look innocent, at least for the time being. So I said, "I was working for al Qaeda in Radio Telecom."

He seemed to be happier with a lie. "What was your rank?" he kept digging.

"I would be a Lieutenant."

"I know you've been in the U.S.," he tricked me. This is a big one and I couldn't possibly lie about it. I could vaguely swallow having done a lot of things in Afghanistan, because Americans cannot confirm or disconfirm it. But the Americans could check right away whether or not I had been in their own country.

"I really haven't been in the U.S.," I answered, though I was ready to change my answer when I had no options.

"You've been in Detroit," he sardonically smiled.

I smiled back. "I really haven't." Though ████ didn't believe me, he didn't push the matter further; ████ was interested in a long-term dialogue with me. In return for my confessions ████ gave me extra food and stopped yelling at me. Meanwhile, in order to maintain the terror, the other guards kept yelling at me and banging the metal door to my cell. Every time they did, my heart started to pound, though the more they did such things, the less effect it had.

"Why are you shaking?" ████ asked me once when he took me out for conversation. I both hated and liked when he was on duty: I hated him interrogating me, but I liked him giving me more food and new uniforms.

"I don't know," I answered.

"I am not gonna hurt you."

"OK." It took some time until I accepted talking to ███████. He started to give me lessons and made me practice them the hard way. The lessons were proverbs and made up of phrases he wanted me to memorize and practice in my life. I still do remember the following lessons: 1) Think before you act. 2) Do not mistake kindness for weakness. 3) ████████ questions always in mind when you are asked about somebody. Whenever ███████ judged me to have broken one of the lessons, he took me out of my cell and strew my belongings all over the place, and then ██████ asked me to put everything back in no time. I always failed to organize my stuff, but he would make me do it several times, after which I miraculously put all my stuff back in time.

My relationship with ██████████ developed positively with every day that went by, and so with the rest of the guards, too, because they regarded him highly.

"Fuck it! If I look at Pillow I don't think he is a terrorist, I think he's an old friend of mine, and I enjoy playing games with him," he said to the other guards. I relaxed somewhat and gained some self-confidence. Now the guards discovered the humorous guy in me, and used their time with me for entertainment. They started to make me repair their DVD players and PC's, and in return I was allowed to watch a movie. ██████████ didn't exactly have the most recent PC model, and when ████████ ██████████ asked me whether I had seen ████████ PC, I answered, "You mean that museum piece?"

██████████ laughed hard. "Better hope he doesn't hear what you said."

"Don't tell him!"

We slowly but surely became a society and started to gossip about the interrogators and call them names. In the mean time, ▬▬▬ taught me the Rules of chess. Before prison, I didn't know the difference between a pawn and the rear end of a knight, nor was I really a big gamer. But I found in chess a very interesting game, especially the fact that a prisoner has total control over his pieces, which gives him some confidence back. When I started playing, I played very aggressively in order to let out my frustration, which was really not very good chess playing; ▬▬ was my first mentor and ▬▬ beat me in my first game ever. But the next game was mine, and so were all the other games that followed. Chess is a game of strategy, art, and mathematics. It takes deep thinking, and there is no luck involved. You get rewarded or punished for your actions.

▬▬▬▬▬▬▬▬▬▬▬▬▬▬ brought me a chessboard so I could play against myself. When the guards noticed my chessboard, they all wanted to play me, and when they started to play me, they always won. The strongest among the guards was ▬▬▬▬. He taught me how to control the center. Moreover, ▬▬▬▬ brought me some literature, which helped decidedly in honing my skills. After that the guards had no chance to defeat me.

"That is not the way I taught you to play chess," ▬▬▬ commented angrily when I won a game.

"What should I do?"

"You should build a strategy, and organize your attack! That's why the fucking Arabs never succeed."

"Why don't you just play the board?" I wondered.

"Chess is not just a game," he said.

"Just imagine you're playing against a computer!"

"Do I look like a computer to you?"

"No." The next game I tried to build a strategy in order to let ▓▓▓▓▓▓ win.

"Now you understand how chess must be played," he commented. I knew ▓▓▓▓▓▓▓ had issues dealing with defeat, and so I didn't enjoy playing him because I didn't feel comfortable practicing my newly acquired knowledge. ▓▓▓▓▓▓▓ believes there are two kinds of people: white Americans and the rest of the world. White Americans are smart and better than anybody. I always tried to explain things to him by saying, for instance, "If I were you," or "If you were me," but he got angry and said, "Don't you ever dare to compare me with you, or compare any American with you!" I was shocked, but I did as he said. After all, I didn't have to compare myself with anybody. ▓▓▓▓▓▓▓ hated the rest of the world, especially the Arabs, Jews, French, Cubans, and others. The only other country he mentioned positively was England.

After one game of chess with him, he flipped the board. "Fuck your Nigger chess, this is Jewish chess," he said.

"Do you have something against Black people?" I asked.

"Nigger is not black, Nigger means stupid," he argued. We had many discussions like that. At the time we had only one Black guard who had no say, and when he worked with ▓▓▓▓▓ they never interacted. ▓▓▓▓▓▓ resented him. ▓▓▓▓▓▓ had a very strong personality, dominant, authoritarian, patriarchal, and arrogant.

"My wife calls me asshole," he proudly told me. ▓▓▓▓▓▓ listened mostly to Rock-n-Roll music and some type of country. His favorite songs were "Die Terrorist Die," "The Taliban Song," and "Let the Bodies Hit the Floor."

▓▓▓▓▓▓▓▓▓▓▓▓▓▓▓▓▓▓▓▓▓▓▓▓▓▓▓▓▓▓▓▓▓▓▓▓
▓▓▓▓▓▓▓▓▓▓▓▓▓▓▓▓▓▓▓▓▓▓▓▓▓▓▓▓▓▓▓▓▓▓▓▓
▓▓▓▓▓▓▓▓▓▓▓▓▓▓▓▓▓▓▓▓▓▓▓▓▓▓▓▓▓▓▓▓▓▓▓▓

███████████████████████████████████████

███████████████████████████████████████

███████████████████████████████████████

███████████████████████████████████████

████████ I never had the chance to see his face because he left

███████████████████████████████████████

████████. But that was OK with me; I really wasn't interested in seeing anybody's face at that point. In the beginning, he was rough with me: he used to pull me hard and make me run in the shackles, screaming loudly "Move!"*

"You know who you are?" he asked me.

"Yes, Sir!"

"You are a terrorist!"

"Yes, Sir!"

"So let's do some math: if you killed five thousand people by your association with al Qaeda, we should kill you five thousand times. But no, because we are Americans we feed you and are ready to give you money if you give us information."

"That's right, Sir!" But after ████████████████ ordered the guards to be friendly with me, ████████████ started to treat me like a human being. I enjoyed discussing things with him because his English was decent, although he was always "right" in his position.

"Our job is to accommodate you!" he used to tell me sarcastically. "You need a house maid." Since guards copy each other,

---

* In this section, which MOS headed "Guards," he introduces several characters. Everything from the opening of the section to this multiline redaction appears to refer to guard number one, clearly a leader on the guard team. Redactions make it difficult to distinguish among the several guards that follow, though this redaction likely marks the introduction of guard number two, whose tour apparently ended before the Special Projects Team interrogators permitted MOS's guards to remove their masks in his presence.

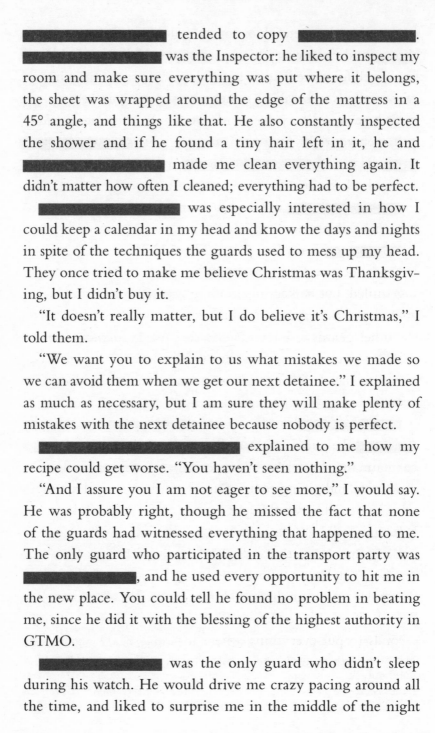 tended to copy ████████████.

████████████ was the Inspector: he liked to inspect my room and make sure everything was put where it belongs, the sheet was wrapped around the edge of the mattress in a 45° angle, and things like that. He also constantly inspected the shower and if he found a tiny hair left in it, he and ████████████ made me clean everything again. It didn't matter how often I cleaned; everything had to be perfect.

████████████ was especially interested in how I could keep a calendar in my head and know the days and nights in spite of the techniques the guards used to mess up my head. They once tried to make me believe Christmas was Thanksgiving, but I didn't buy it.

"It doesn't really matter, but I do believe it's Christmas," I told them.

"We want you to explain to us what mistakes we made so we can avoid them when we get our next detainee." I explained as much as necessary, but I am sure they will make plenty of mistakes with the next detainee because nobody is perfect.

████████████ explained to me how my recipe could get worse. "You haven't seen nothing."

"And I assure you I am not eager to see more," I would say. He was probably right, though he missed the fact that none of the guards had witnessed everything that happened to me. The only guard who participated in the transport party was ████████████, and he used every opportunity to hit me in the new place. You could tell he found no problem in beating me, since he did it with the blessing of the highest authority in GTMO.

████████████ was the only guard who didn't sleep during his watch. He would drive me crazy pacing around all the time, and liked to surprise me in the middle of the night by banging the metal door to my cell and making me take a shower and clean everything perfectly. I should not feel rested in my cell for more than an hour: that is one of the most important methods in breaking somebody in detention, because you must hate your life, your guards, your cell, your interrogators, and even yourself. And that is exactly what ███████████ ██████ did until ████████████████ and ███████████████ ordered otherwise.

███████████████ was a white man in his twenties, very tall, lazy, non-athletic looking.*

"███████████ is my best friend," he told me once.

"How do you know ███████████?" He didn't answer me, he just smiled, but he kept mentioning ███████ and how he had abused me. I always changed the subject because I didn't want the other guards to know that beating me was something normal. I was glad my guards didn't know everything that happened to me; I didn't need the gang to be encouraged to do crimes.

███████████████ was the most violent guard. In Building ██████████ the guards performed regular assaults on me in order to maintain the terror. They came in a big masked team, screaming and giving contradictory orders so I wouldn't know what to do. They would drag me out of my cell and throw my belongings all over the place.

"Get up...Face the wall...You've been resting lately too much...You have a Pillow...Ha Ha!...Look inside his cell... The piece of shit might be hiding something...We found two kernels of rice hidden beneath his mattress...You have twenty seconds to put everything where it belongs!" The game was over when they made me sweat. I knew the guards didn't have

---

* This redaction may introduce the third guard that MOS is profiling.

the order to beat me, but this guard used every opportunity to hit me and claw me deeply. I don't think that he is the smartest guy, but he was well trained in how to beat somebody without leaving irreparable injuries. "Hitting in the ribs is painful and doesn't leave permanent scars, especially when treated right away with ice-cubes," one of the guards told me. ████████ ████ was both violent and loud, but thank God, he was very lazy; he only barked at the beginning of the shift and after a short time he disappeared from the stage to watch a movie or go to sleep.

████████████████████ didn't have any bad feelings about his job; on the contrary, he was rather proud of what he was doing, and he was mad at the fact that he was taking care of the dirty part of the job and he wanted to be rewarded adequately. "Fuck the interrogators: we do the work and they take the credit," ████████████ told me once.

He also didn't get along with ██████████████, the only guy that outranked him. "██████ is a pussy!" he described him once. But ███████████████ was not a social person anyway. He could not lead a normal conversation like everybody else. He rarely spoke, and when he did, it was about his wild sex experiences. One common thing among the guards is that most of them never understood the fact that some people don't have sex outside marriage.

"You're gay," was the usual response.

"That is OK with me, but I cannot have sex outside marriage. You may consider me an idiot, but that's OK!"

"How can you buy a car without test-driving it?"

"First of all, a woman is not a car. And I am doing it because of my religion." Even ███████████ interrogator ███████ shocked me once when ██████ said, "I wouldn't marry anybody before test driving him." But I still do believe that some Americans don't believe in premarital sex.

███████████████████████████████████████

███████████████████████████████████████
███████████████████████████████████████

███████ about himself.* He told me he had been tasked to gather Intels about me before my kidnapping from ████████████, and gave evidence of this by accurately recounting details of my special situation. I had never noticed him in the blocks of ████████████████ nor was I supposed to. ████████████ was mostly partnered with ████████████████; at the beginning, and in the decisive period, ██████████ was in charge. ██████████████ was in good physical shape, unlike his friend ████████████.

████████████ moderately and dutifully followed the rules he was given by ████████████████ and the rest of the ████████████████ and his associate delivered my water diet, gave me PTs, forbade me to pray or fast, and kept giving me a "Party-shower." ████████████████ was even the one who came up with that annoying ██████████████████████████ ██████ every piece in a defined place, toilet and sink always dry, so I ended up having to use my uniform because I had no towel. ████████████████████████████████ ██████████████████████████████████ Nonetheless, I can tell you truthfully that ██████████ didn't enjoy bothering me or torturing me.

"Why did you forbid me to pray when you knew it's an illegal order?" I asked him when we became friends.

"I could have but they would have given me some shitty job."

---

* This redaction appears to introduce the fourth guard that MOS profiles in this section.

He also told me that ███████████████████ gave him the order preventing me from practicing any religious activities. ████████████████ said, "I'm going to hell because I forbade you to pray."

████████████████ was so happy when he was ordered to treat me nicely. "I really enjoyed being here with you more than being at home," he genuinely said. He was a very generous guy; he used to give me muffins, movies, and PS2 games. Before he left he asked me to choose between two games, Madden 2004 and Nascar 2004. I chose Nascar 2004, which I still have. Above all, ████████████████ was a hell of an entertainer. He tended to stretch the truth, and he would tell me all kinds of stuff. Sometimes he gave me too much information, things I didn't want to know, nor was I supposed to know.

████████████████ was a big gamer. He used to play video games all the time. I'm terrible when it comes to video games; it's just not for me. I always told the guards, "Americans are just big babies. In my country it's not appropriate for somebody my age to sit in front of a console and waste his time playing games." Indeed, one of the punishments of their civilization is that Americans are addicted to video games.

And Americans worship their bodies. They eat well. When I was delivered to Bagram Air Base, I was like, What the heck is going on, these soldiers never stop chewing on something. And yet, though God blessed Americans with a huge amount of healthy food, they are the biggest food wasters I ever knew: if every country lived as Americans do, our planet could not absorb the amount of waste we produce.

They also work out. I have a big variety of friends who come from all backgrounds, and I really had never heard any other group of mortals speaking about the next workout plan.

"Is that a homosexual magazine?" I asked one of the guards

who was holding a man fitness magazine with those oversized guys. You know, those guys who keep working out until their necks disappear, and their heads barely fit between their overgrown shoulders.

"What the fuck are you talking about? This is a workout magazine," he responded. American men are more intolerant toward male homosexuals compared to German men, and they work out as if they're preparing for a fight.

"When I hug my wife, she feels secure," ████████████ ████ told me once.

"My wife always feels secure; she doesn't need a hug to be calmed," I answered.

████████████████ was like anybody else: he bought more food than he needed, worked out even during duty, planned to enlarge his member, played video and computer games, and was very confused when it comes to his religion.

"Pillow, I am telling you, I really don't know. But I am Christian and my parents celebrate Christmas every year," he told me, adding, "My girlfriend wants to convert to Islam but I said no."

"Come on, ████████████, you should let her choose. Don't you guys believe in freedom of religion?" I replied.

████████████████ had all the qualities of a human being; I liked conversing with him because he always had something to say. He liked to impress the females on the island. And he especially resented ████████████████████; I really can't blame him!

Everyone resented him.* He was lazy and on the slower side. Nobody wanted to work with him, and they talked ill about him all the time. ████████████████████ didn't have any initiative or personality of his own, and he used to copy every

---

* The passage from here to the section break seems to refer to a fifth guard.

other guard. When he started working on the team he was quiet; he just served me my food and dutifully made me drink water every hour. And that was cool. But he quickly learned that I could be yelled at, have food taken from, and made to do harsh PTs I didn't want to do. He couldn't believe that he was entitled to so much power. He almost went wild making me stand up for hours during the night, even though he knew I suffered from sciatic nerve. He made me clean my cell over and over. He made me clean the shower over and over.

"I wish you'd make a mistake, any mistake, so I can strike," he used to say while performing some corny fake martial arts he must have learned for purposes of his mission. Even after ▓▓▓▓▓▓▓▓▓▓ ordered the guards to be nice to me, he became worse, as if trying to catch up on something he missed.

"You call me Master, OK?" he said.

"Oh, yes," I answered, thinking, Who the heck does he think he is? When he saw the other guards playing chess with me, he wanted to play, too, but I soon discovered how weak a person can be in chess. Moreover, he had his own rules, which he always enforced, him being the Master, and me the detainee. In his chess world the king belonged to his own color, breaking the basic rule in chess that states that the king sits on the opposite color when the game begins. I knew he was wrong, but there was no correcting him, so with him I had to play his version of chess.

Around March ▓▓ ▓▓▓▓▓▓▓▓▓ gave me a TV with an integrated VCR to watch the movies they would give me. ▓▓▓▓▓▓▓▓▓ himself gave me the movie *Gladiator* from his personal collection. I like that movie because it vividly depicts how the forces of evil get defeated at the end, no matter how strong they seem. On advice and approval, ██████████████ and ███ colleague got me many interesting movies.*

In my real life I was not a big fan of movies; I don't remember watching a single movie all the way through since I turned eighteen. I do like documentaries and movies based on true stories, but I have a problem giving up my mind and going with the flow of the acting when I know that everything that happens in the movie is fake. But in prison, I'm different: I appreciate everything that shows regular human beings wearing casual clothes and talking about something besides terrorism and interrogation. I just want to see some mammals I can relate to.

The Americans I met watch movies a lot. In America it's like, "Tell me how many movies you've seen, and I'll tell you who you are." But if Americans can be proud of something, they have the right to be proud of their motion picture industry.

Of course, the TV had no receiver, because I was not allowed to watch TV or know anything that happened outside my cell; all I was allowed to watch were the movies that had been approved ████████████████████████. It is so evidently unjust to cut off a person from the rest of the world and forbid him to know what's going on in the outside world, regardless of whether or not he is involved in criminal activities. I noticed that the TV/VCR combo had an FM Radio receiver that could receive local broadcasts, but I never touched it: although it is my basic right to listen to whatever radio I wish, I find it so

---

* This would likely be March 2004—more than seven months after MOS was dragged into the isolation cell in Camp Echo. The paragraph may refer to "Captain Collins," who appears from later passages to have remained in control of Slahi's interrogation until he was transferred to Iraq in the summer of 2004, and the new female interrogator. See footnote on p. 347.

dishonest to stab the hand that reaches out to help you. And regardless of what ████████████████████████████ have done to me, I found it positive that they offered me this entertainment tool, and I would not use it against them. Moreover, ██████████████████ got me a laptop, which I mightily enjoyed. Of course one of the main reasons for the laptop was to make me type my answers during interrogations to save both time and manpower ████████████████████████████. But I had no problem with that idea; after all, I wanted to deliver my words and not their interpretation thereof.

"Look, I got some Arabic Music," said ██████████████████ handing me an Audio CD.

"Oh, fine!" But the CD was not even close to the Arabic language: it was Bosnian. I laughed wholeheartedly. "Close enough. It's Bosnian music," I said when the CD started to play.

"Is it not the same, Bosnian and Arabic?" asked ████████████ ██████. That is just one example of how little Americans know about Arabs and Islam. ██████████████████ is a member of ████████ and not just anybody; ██████████████ is supposedly armed with basic knowledge about Arabs and Islam. But ████████████ and the other interrogators always addressed me, "You guys from the middle east...," which is so completely wrong. For many Americans, the world comprises three places: The U.S., Europe, and the rest of the world, the Middle East. Unfortunately, the world, geographically speaking, is a little bit more than that. In my job in my country, I had to make some calls to the U.S. for professional purposes. I remember the following conversation:

"Hello, we are dealing with office materials. We are interested in representing your company."

"Where are you calling from?" asked the lady at the other end.

"Mauritania."

"What state?" asked the lady, seeking more precise information. I was negatively surprised at how small her world was.

The confusion ████████████████████████ was as obvious as his
ignorance about the whole terrorism issue. The man was completely terrified, as if he were drowning and looking for any
straw to grasp. I guess I was one of the straws he bumped into
in his flailing, and he grasped me really hard.

"I don't understand why people hate us. We help everybody
in the world!" he stated once, seeking my opinion.

"Neither do I," I replied. I knew it was futile to enlighten
him about the historical and objective reasons that led to where
we're at, and so I opted to ignore his comment; besides, it was
not exactly easy to change the opinion of a man as old as he was.

Many young men and women join the U.S. forces under the
misleading propaganda of the U.S. government, which makes
people believe that the Armed Forces are nothing but a big
Battle of Honor: if you join the Army, you are a living martyr;
you're defending not only your family, your country, and
American democracy but also freedom and oppressed people all
around the world. Great, there is nothing wrong with that; it
may even be the dream of every young man or woman. But the
reality of the U.S. forces is a little tiny bit different. To go
directly to the bottom line: the rest of the world thinks of
Americans as a bunch of revengeful barbarians. That may be
harsh, and I don't believe the dead average American is a
revengeful barbarian. But the U.S. government bets its last
penny on violence as the magic solution for every problem, and
so the country is losing friends every day and doesn't seem to
give a damn about it.

"Look, ████████████, everybody hates you guys, even your

traditional friends. The Germans hate you, the French hate you," I said once to █████████████████.*

"Fuck all of them. We would rather have them hate us, and we'll whup their asses," ███████ replied. I just smiled at how easy a solution can be made.

"That's one way to look at it," I answered.

"Fuck them Terrorists."

"OK," I would say. "But you should find the terrorists first. You can't just go wild and hurt everybody in the name of terrorism." He believed that every Arab is a terrorist until proven innocent.

"We need you to help us lock up ██████████████ for the rest of his life," he said.

"I am. I've been providing enough Intels to convict him."

"But he keeps denying. He is dealing with other agencies that have different rules than we do. I wish I could get my hands on him: things would be different then!"

I was like, "I hope you never get your hands on anybody."

"All he says is that he did the operation on his own, and that's it," ██████████ said.

"Oh, that's very convenient!" I said wryly. Lately I had started to copy ██████████████████████, using the exact same phrases as ██████████████████████. He used to tell me "All you can say is I don't know, I don't remember. That's very convenient! You think you are going to impress an American jury with your charisma?" He always liked to quote the U.S. President, saying "We will not send you guys to court and let you use our justice system, since you're planning to destroy it."

"Is that part of the Big Conspiracy?" I wryly wondered.

"Al Qaeda is using our liberal justice system," he continued.

---

* Here and for the next several paragraphs, MOS appears to be recalling a previous conversation or conversations with one of his interrogators.

I really don't know what liberal justice system he was talking about: the U.S. broke the world record for the number of people it has in prison. Its prison population is over two million, more than any other country in the world, and its rehabilitation programs are a complete failure. The United States is the "democratic" country with the most draconian punishment system; in fact, it is a good example of how draconian punishments do not help in stopping crimes. Europe is by far more just and humane, and the rehab programs there work, so the crime rate in Europe is decisively lower than the U.S. But the American proverb has it, "When the going gets rough, the rough get going." Violence naturally produces violence; the only loan you can make with a guarantee of payback is violence. It might take some time, but you will always get your loan back.

As things improved, I asked ███████████████████ to transfer me to another place because I wanted to forget the bad memories I experienced where I was. ███████████████████ tried to meet my request; he promised me the transfer many times, but he failed to keep his promises. I don't doubt his seriousness, but I could tell there was some kind of power struggle in the small island of GTMO. Everybody wanted the biggest portion of the pie, and the most credit for the work of ████████ ████. He genuinely promised me many other things, but couldn't hold those promises either.

One amazing thing about ██████████████████████ was that he never brought up the story of my torture. I always expected him to open the topic, but nothing like that happened: Taboo! Personally I was scared to talk about it; I didn't feel secure enough. Even if he had brought the topic up, I would have dodged talking about it.

But at least he finally told me where I was.

"I have to inform you, against the will of many members in

our team, that you are in GTMO," he said. "You've been honest with us and we owe you the same." Although the rest of the world didn't have a clue as to where the U.S. government was incarcerating me, I had known since day one thanks to God and the clumsiness of the ██████████. But I acted as if this was new information, and I was happy because it meant many things to me to be told where I am. As I write these lines, I am still sitting in that same cell, but at least now I don't have to act ignorant about where I am, and that is a good thing.

██████████████████ the U.S. Army released the first letter from my family.* It was sent through the International Committee of the Red Cross. My family wrote it months before, in July 2003. It had been 815 days since I was kidnapped from my house and had all contacts with my family forcibly broken. I had been sending many letters to my family since I arrived in Cuba, but to no avail. In Jordan I was forbidden even to send a letter.

████████████████ was the one who handed me that historical piece of paper, which read:

Nouakchott, ████████████████

In the Name of God the most Merciful.

Peace be with you and God's mercy.

From your mom ██████████████████████

After my greeting I inform you of my wellbeing and that of the rest of your family. We hope you are the same way. My health situation is OK. I still keep up with my schedule with the Doctors. I feel I am getting better. And the family is OK.

---

* Earlier in the manuscript, MOS indicates that he received the first letter from his family on February 14, 2004.

As I mentioned everybody sends his greeting to you. Beloved son! As of now we have received three letters from you. And this is our second reply. The neighbors are well and they send their greetings. At the end of this letter I renew my greeting. Peace be with you.

Your Mom ████████████

I couldn't believe that after all I had been through I was holding a letter from my mom. I smelled the odor of a letter that had touched the hand of my mom and other members of my beloved family. The emotions in my heart were mixed: I didn't know what to do, laugh or cry. I ultimately ended up doing both. I kept reading the short message over and over. I knew it was for real, not like the fake one I got one year ago. But I couldn't respond to the letter because I was still not allowed to see the ICRC.

Meanwhile, I kept getting books in English that I enjoyed reading, most of them Western literature. I still remember one book called *The Catcher in the Rye* that made me laugh until my stomach hurt. It was such a funny book. I tried to keep my laughter as low as possible, pushing it down, but the guards felt something.

"Are you crying?" one of them asked.

"No, I'm alright," I responded. It was my first unofficial laughter in the ocean of tears. Since interrogators are not professional comedians, most of the humor they came up with was a bunch of lame jokes that really didn't make me laugh, but I would always force an official smile.

██

████████████████████████ came one Sunday morning and waited outside the building. ████████████████ appeared before my cell ████████████████████. I didn't recognize him, of

343

course; I thought he was a new interrogator.* But when he spoke I knew it was him.

"Are ███████████████████?"

"Don't worry. Your interrogator is waiting on you outside." I was overwhelmed and terrified at the same time; it was too much for me. ███████████████ led me outside the building; I saw ███████████████ looking away from me, shy that I see his face. If you deal with somebody for so long behind a face cover, that is how you know him ██████████. But now if he ██████████ takes off the face cover you have to deal with his features, and that is a completely different story for both sides. I could tell the guards were uncomfortable to show me their faces.

███████████████████ put it bluntly. "If I catch you looking at me, I'm gonna hurt you."

"Don't you worry, I'm not dying to see your face." Through time I had built a perception about the way everybody looked, but imagination was far from the reality.

██████████ prepared a small table with a modest breakfast. I was scared as hell; for one, ██████████ never took me outside the building, and for two, I was not used to my guards' "new" faces. I tried to act casually but my shaking gave me away.

"What's wrong with you," ██████████ asked.

"I am very nervous. I am not used to this environment."

"But I meant it for your good," ██████ said. ███████████ was a very official person; if ██████ interrogates you, she does it officially, and if ██████ eats with you, ██████ does it as part of ██████ job, and that was cool.† I was just waiting for the breakfast

---

* This could be one of MOS's guards, appearing unmasked for the first time.

† "She" appears unredacted; this might be the businesslike female interrogator introduced at the beginning of the chapter.

to be done so I could go back to my cell, because ▓▓▓▓▓▓▓
had brought me the movie *King Henry V* by Shakespeare.

"▓▓▓▓▓, may I watch the movie more than once?" I asked.
"I am afraid I am not going to understand it right away."

"Yes, you can watch it as many times as you wish."

When ▓▓▓▓▓▓▓▓▓▓▓▓ brought the TV ▓▓▓▓▓▓▓ briefed
the guards to let me watch a movie only once, and then the
party is over. "You're allowed to watch your movie only once,
but as far as we're concerned you can watch it as many times as
you wish, as long as you don't tell your interrogator about it.
We really don't care," ▓▓▓▓▓▓▓▓▓ told me later.

"No, if ▓▓▓▓▓▓▓ said so, I am going to stick with it. I am
not gonna cheat," I told him. I really didn't want to mess with
a comfort item I had just gotten, so I chose to treat everything
carefully. But I did ask for one thing.

"▓▓▓▓▓, can I keep my water bottle in my cell, and drink
whenever I choose?" I was just tired of the lack of sleep; as soon
as I closed my eyes, the heavy metal door opened and I had to
drink another bottle of water. I knew ▓▓▓▓▓▓▓ was not the
right person to ask to take the initiative; ▓▓▓▓▓▓▓▓▓ had
literally been following the orders of ▓▓▓▓▓▓▓▓▓▓▓. But
to my surprise, ▓▓▓▓▓▓▓ came the next day and briefed the
guards that the water bottle now belonged in my cell. You cannot imagine how happy I was to be able to decide the time and
the amount of water I could drink. People who never have been
in such a situation cannot really appreciate the freedom of
drinking water whenever they want, however much they want.

Then, in July 2004, I found a copy of The Holy Koran in my
box of laundry. When I saw the Holy Koran beneath the clothes
I felt bad, thinking I had to steal it in order to save it. But I
took the Koran to my cell, and nobody ever asked me why I
did so. Nor did I bring it up on my own. I had been forbidden

all kinds of religious rituals, so I figured a copy of the Koran in my cell would not have made my interrogators too happy. More than that, lately the religious issue had become very delicate. The Muslim chaplain of GTMO was arrested and another Muslim soldier was charged with treason—oh, yes, *treason.** Many Arabic and religious books were banned, and books teaching the English language were also banned. I sort of understood religious books being banned. "But why English learning books?" I asked ███████████.

"Because Detainees pick up the language quickly and understand the guards."

"That's so communist, ███████████████" I said. To this date I have never received any Islamic books, though I keep asking for them; all I can get are novels and animal books. ███████ ███████████ my prayers started to be tolerated. I had been gauging the tolerance toward the practice of my religion; every once in a while I put the tolerance of the ███████████████ to the test, and they kept stopping me from praying. So I would pray secretly. But on this day at the very end of July 2004, I performed my prayer under the surveillance of some new guards

---

* Three Guantánamo-based personnel who were practicing Muslims were arrested in September 2003 and accused of carrying classified information out of the prison. MOS may be referring here specifically to army chaplain Captain James Yee, who was charged with five offenses including sedition and espionage, and Senior Airman Ahmad al-Halabi, an Arabic-language translator who was charged with thirty-two counts ranging from espionage and aiding the enemy to delivering unauthorized food, including the dessert baklava, to detainees. The sedition and spying cases collapsed. All charges against Yee were eventually dropped, and he received an honorable discharge; al-Halabi pled guilty to four counts, including lying to investigators and disobeying orders, and received a "bad conduct" discharge. See, e.g., http://usatoday30.usatoday.com/news/nation/2004-05-16 -yee-cover_x.htm; and http://usatoday30.usatoday.com/news/washington /2004-09-23-gitmo-airman_x.htm.

and nobody made a comment. A new era in my detention had emerged.

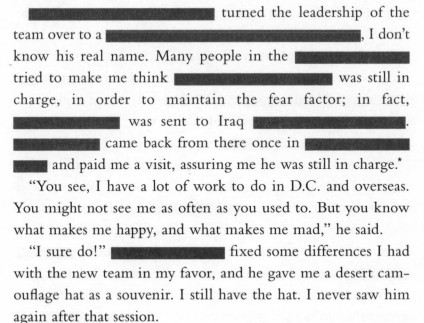

███████████████████████ turned the leadership of the team over to a ███████████████████████████████, I don't know his real name. Many people in the ████████████████ tried to make me think ███████████████████████ was still in charge, in order to maintain the fear factor; in fact, ████████████████ was sent to Iraq ███████████████████. ██████████████ came back from there once in ████████████ ████████ and paid me a visit, assuring me he was still in charge.*

"You see, I have a lot of work to do in D.C. and overseas. You might not see me as often as you used to. But you know what makes me happy, and what makes me mad," he said.

"I sure do!" ██████████████████████ fixed some differences I had with the new team in my favor, and he gave me a desert camouflage hat as a souvenir. I still have the hat. I never saw him again after that session.

Finally, in September 2004, the ICRC was allowed to visit after a long fight with the government. It was very odd to the ICRC that I had all of sudden disappeared from the camp, as if the earth had swallowed me. All attempts by ICRC representatives to see me or just to know where I was were thoroughly flushed down the tube.

The ICRC had been very worried about my situation, but they couldn't come to me when I needed them the most. I cannot blame them; they certainly tried. In GTMO, the ███████████████████████ is integrally responsible for both detainees' happiness and their agony, in order to have total control

---

* This might be referring to the Special Projects Team chief, "Captain Collins." In April 2004, General Miller left Guantánamo to assume command of prison and interrogation operations in Iraq; it appears from this passage that the chief of MOS's Special Projects Team was also reassigned to Iraq.

over the detainees. ██████████ and his colleague ██
██████████████████ categorically refused to give the ICRC
access to me. Only after ████████████ left was it possible for
the ICRC to visit me.

"You are the last detainee we had to fight to see. We have
been able to see all other detainees," said ██████████.
████████████████████████ tried to get me talking
about what happened to me during the time they couldn't have
access to me. "We have an idea because we have talked to other
detainees who were subject to abuse, but we need you to talk
so we can help in stopping further acts of abuse." But I always
hid the ill-treatment when the ICRC asked me about it because
I was afraid of retaliation. That and the fact that the ICRC
has no real pressure on the U.S. government: the ICRC tried,
but the U.S. government didn't change its path, even an inch. If
they let the Red Cross see a detainee, it meant that the operation
against that detainee was over.

"We cannot act if you don't tell us what happened to you,"
they would urge me.

"I am sorry! I am only interested in sending and receiving
mail, and I am grateful that you're helping me to do so."
██████████ brought a very high level ICRC ██████████
from Switzerland who has been working on my case; ██████████
tried to get me talking, but to no avail.

"We understand your worries. All we're worried about is
your well-being, and we respect your decision."

Although sessions with the ICRC are supposedly private, I
was interrogated about the conversations I had during that first
session, and I truthfully told the interrogators what we had said.
Later on I told the ICRC about this practice, and after that
nobody asked me what happened in our sessions. We detainees
knew that the meetings with ICRC were monitored; some

detainees had been confronted with statements they made to the ICRC and there was no way for the ████████████████ to know them unless the meeting was monitored. Many detainees refused to talk to the ICRC, and suspected them to be interrogators disguised in ICRC clothes. I even know some interrogators who presented themselves as private journalists. But to me that was very naïve: for a detainee to mistake an interrogator for a journalist he would have to be an idiot, and there are better methods to get an idiot talking. Such mischievous practices led to tensions between detainees and the ICRC. Some ICRC people were even cursed and spit on.

Around this same time, I was asked to talk to a real journalist. ██████████████████████ time had been a hard time for everybody; he was a very violent person, and he decidedly hurt the already damaged image of the U.S. government.* Now many people in the government were trying to polish the reputation it had earned from its mischief toward detainees. "You know many people are lying about this place and claiming that detainees get tortured. We'd like you to talk to a moderate journalist from *The Wall Street Journal* and refute the wrong things we're suspected of."

"Well, I got tortured, and I am going to tell the journalist the truth, the naked truth, without exaggeration or understatement. I'm not polishing anybody's reputation," I said. After that the interview was completely canceled, which was good because I didn't want to talk to anybody anyway.

Gradually I was introduced to the "secret" new boss. I don't exactly know why the team kept him secret from me and tried to make me believe the ██████████████████████ was still in charge, but most likely they thought that I would be less cooperative

---

* Possibly referring to General Miller's era, which encompassed his "special interrogation."

when somebody other than ██████████████ took over. But they were wrong: I was interested more than anybody in the Intel community in bringing my case into the light. ██████████ had been counseled to work on my case from behind the scenes, which he did for a certain time, and then he came and introduced himself. I don't know his real name, but he introduced himself as a ██████████ is ████████████████████ ██ ██ ██

rather humble. He tried everything in the realm of his power to make my life in custody as easy as possible.

I asked him to end my segregation and let me see other detainees, and he successfully organized several meetings between me and ████████████████████████████████, mainly to eat together and play chess. ██████████████ was not my first choice, but it was not up to me who I could meet, and in any case, I was just dying to see some other detainee I could relate to.

In early summer ████████ they moved ██████████████ next to my hut, and we were allowed to see each other during recreation.* ██████████████ is on the older side, about

---

* Press reports have identified a detainee who became neighbors with MOS as Tariq al-Sawah. A 2010 *Washington Post* article indicated that MOS and al-Sawah occupied "a little fenced-in compound at the military prison, where they live a life of relative privilege—gardening, writing and painting." In a 2013 interview with *Slate*, Col. Morris Davis, who served as chief prosecutor of the Guantánamo military commissions in 2005 and 2006, described meetings with both MOS and Sawah in the summer of 2006. "They're in a unique environment: They're inside the detention perimeter, there's a big fence around the facility, and then they're inside what they call the wire, which is another layer within that, so it's a manpower-intensive effort to deal with two guys," he said. Davis suggested in that interview that this living arrangement has remained unchanged. See http://

███████████ old. ████████████ did not seem to have
passed detention's shock sanely; He suffered from paranoia,
amnesia, depression, and other mental problems. Some interrogators claimed that he was playing a game, but to me he was
completely out of his mind. I really didn't know what to believe,
but I didn't care too much; I was dying to have company, and
he was sort of company.

There is a drawback to detainees being together, though, especially if you know the detainee only from the camp: We detainees tend to be skeptical about each other. But I was very relaxed
in that regard because I really didn't have anything to hide.

"Did they tell you to gather Intels from me?" he asked me
once. I wasn't shocked, because I assumed the same about him.
"████████, relax and just assume that I am only here to spy
on you. Just keep your mouth shut and don't speak about anything you're not comfortable speaking about," I told him.

"You have no secrets?" he wondered.

"No, I don't, and I allow you to provide anything you may
learn about me," I said.

I do remember the first day in August when ██████████ surged
through the door smiling and greeted me, "Salamu Alaikum."

"Waalaikum As-Salam! Tetkallami Arabi?" I answered her
greeting, asking if ███ spoke Arabic.*

---

www.washingtonpost.com/wp-dyn/content/article/2010/03/24/AR2010
032403135_pf.html; and http://www.slate.com/articles/news_and_politics
/foreigners/2013/04/mohamedou_ould_slahi_s_guant_namo_memoirs
_an_interview_with_colonel_morris.html.

  * The "her" appears unredacted. This section seems to introduce, and
center on, a new female lead interrogator. See footnote on p. 362, citing
records indicating that MOS had a female interrogator in late 2004.

"I don't." In fact ███████ had already used all the Arabic ████ knew, namely the Greeting, Peace be upon you. ███████ and I started to talk as if we had known each other for years. ███████ studied Biology and joined ███████████ recently as an enlisted person, most likely to pay her college tuition. Many Americans do; college education in the U.S. is sinfully high.

"I am going to help you start your garden," ██████ said. A long time before, I had asked the interrogators to get me some seeds in order to experiment around, and maybe succeed in growing something in the aggressive soil of GTMO. "I have experience in gardening," ████ continued. And indeed ██████ seemed to have experience: ████ helped me to grow sunflowers, basil, sage, parsley, cilantro, and things of that nature. But as helpful as ████ was, I kept giving ████ a hard time about one single bad experience ████ made me do.

"I have a problem with crickets that keep destroying my garden," I complained.

"Take some soap and put it in water and keep spraying it lightly on the plants every day," ██████ suggested. And I blindly followed ███ advice. However, I noticed that my plants were growing unhappy and sort of sick. So I decided to spray only the half of the plants with the diluted soap and watch the results. It didn't take long to see the soap was responsible for the bad effects, and so I completely stopped the story of soap.

After that I kept telling ██████, "I know what you studied: You studied how to kill plants with diluted soap!"

"Shut up! You just didn't do it right."

"Whatever."

██████████ had introduced ███████ to me, and

from then on ▉▉▉ took my case in hand entirely. For some reason the ▉▉▉▉▉▉▉▉▉▉▉▉▉▉ thought that I would disrespect ▉▉▉, and were skeptical as to whether ▉▉▉ was the right choice. But they had no reason to worry: ▉▉▉▉▉▉ treated me as if I were ▉▉▉ brother, and I as if ▉▉▉ were my sister. Of course some might say that all that interrogators' stuff is a trick to lure detainees to provide them information; they can be friendly, sociable, humane, generous, and sensitive but still they are evil and ungenuine about everything. I mean, there is a good reason to doubt the integrity of interrogators, if only due to the nature of the interrogators' job. The ultimate goal of an interrogator is to get Intel from his target, the nastier the better. But interrogators are human beings, with feelings and emotions; I have been uninterruptedly interrogated since January 2000, and I have seen all kinds of interrogators, good, bad, and in between. Besides, here in GTMO Bay everything is different. In GTMO, the U.S. government assigns a team of interrogators who stick with you almost on a daily basis for some time, after which they leave and get replaced with a new team, in a never ending routine. So whether you like it or not, you have to live with your interrogators and try to make the best out of your life. Furthermore, I deal with everybody according to what he shows me, and not what he could be hiding. With this motto I approach everybody, including my interrogators.

Since I have not had a formal education in the English language, I needed and still do a lot of help honing my language skills. ▉▉▉▉▉▉ worked hard on that, especially on my pronunciation and spelling. When it comes to spelling, English is a terrible language: I don't know any other language that writes *Colonel* and pronounces it *Kernel*. Even natives of the language have a tremendous problem with the inconsistency of the sounds and the corresponding letter combinations.

On top of that, prepositions in English don't make any sense; you just have to memorize them. I remember I kept saying "I am afraid from...," and ██████████ jumping and correcting me: "afraid *of.*" I am sure I was driving ████ crazy. My problem is that I had been picking the language from the "wrong" people — namely, U.S. Forces recruits who speak grammatically incorrectly. So I needed somebody to take away the incorrect language from me and replace it with the correct one. Maybe you *can* teach an old dog new tricks, and that is exactly what ██████████ duly tried to do with me. I think ████ was successful, even though I gave ████ a hard time sometimes. ████ once forgot that ████ was around me and said something like, "Amana use the bathroom," and I went, "Oh, is 'Amana' one of the words I missed?"

"Don't even go there!" ████ would say.

██████████ taught me the way Americans speak English. "But British people say so and so," I would say.

"You're not British," ██████████ would say.

"I am just saying that there are different ways to pronounce it," I would answer. But ████ failed to give me the Grammar Rules to follow, which is the only way I can really learn. Being a native speaker, ██████████ has a feel for the language, which I don't. Besides ████ mother-tongue, ██████████ also spoke Russian and proposed to teach me; I was eager but ██████████ didn't have enough time, and with time I lost the passion. A person as lazy as me won't learn a new language unless he has to. ██████████ was dying to learn Arabic but ████ didn't have time for that either. ████ job kept ████ busy day and night.

By this time, my health situation was way better than in Jordan, but I was still underweight, vulnerable, and sick most of the time, and as days went by, my situation decidedly worsened. Sometimes when the escorting team led me past the wall mirror I would get terrorized when I saw my face. It was a very pitiful sight. Although the diet kept getting better and better in the camp, I couldn't profit from it.

"Why don't you eat?" the guards always asked.

"I am not hungry," I used to reply. Then one day my interrogator ██████████ just happened to witness one time when I got my lunch served.

"May I check your meal?"

"Yeah, sure."

"What the hell do they serve you? That is garbage!" said ███████.

"No, it's okay. I don't like speaking about food," I said. And I really don't.

"Look it may be OK for you, but it's not OK by my standards. We've got to change your diet," ██████ said. And nothing short of a miracle, ███████████ managed in a relatively short time to organize an adequate diet, which decidedly improved my health situation.

██████████ also turned out to be a religious person when measured at American standards. I was very excited to have somebody I could learn from.

"██████████, can you get me a Bible?"

"I'll see if I can," ██████ said, and indeed, ███████████ brought me ██████ own Bible, a Special Edition.

"According to your religion, what is the way to heaven?" I asked ██████████.

"You take Christ as your Savior, and believe that he died for your sins."

"I do believe Christ was one of the greatest prophets, but I don't believe that he died for my sins. It doesn't make sense to me. I should save my tail on my own, by doing the right things," I replied.

"That is not enough to be saved."

"So where am I going after death?" I wondered.

"According to my religion, you go to hell." I laughed whole-heartedly. I told ▨▨▨▨▨▨, "That is very sad. I pray every day and ask God for forgiveness. Honestly, I worship God much more than you do. As a matter of fact, as you see, I am not very successful in this worldly life, so my only hope is in the afterlife."

▨▨▨▨▨▨ was both angry and ashamed—angry because I laughed at ▨▨ statement, and ashamed because ▨▨ couldn't find a way to save me. "I am not gonna lie to you: that's what my religion says," ▨▨▨ said.

"No, I really don't have any problem with that. You can cook your soup as you please. I am not angry that you sent me to hell."

"What about the Islamic belief? Do I go to heaven?"

"That's a completely different story. In Islam, in order to go to heaven, you have to accept Mohamed, the natural successor of Christ, and be a good Muslim. And since you reject Mohamed you don't go to Heaven," I honestly answered.

▨▨▨▨▨▨ was relieved because I also sent ▨▨▨ to hell. "So, let's both of us go to Hell and meet over there!" ▨▨▨▨▨ said.

"I'm not willing to go to Hell. Although I am an admitted sinner, I ask God for forgiveness." Whenever we had time, we discussed religion and took out the Bible and the Koran to show each other what the Books say.

"Would you marry a Muslim?"

"Never," ▨▨▨ replied.

I smiled. "I personally wouldn't have a problem marrying a

Christian woman as long as she doesn't have anything against my religion."

"Are you trying to convert me?" ████████ asked emotionally.

"Yes, I am."

"I will never, never, never be a Muslim."

I laughed. "What are you so offended about? You're sort of trying to convert me, and I don't feel offended, since that's what you believe in."

I continued. "Would you marry a Catholic, ████████?"

"Yes, I would."

"But I don't understand. It says in the Bible that you cannot marry after a divorce. So you are a potential sinner." ████████ was completely offended when I showed ████ the verses in the Bible.

"Don't even go there, and if you don't mind, let's change the topic." I was shocked, and smiled a dry smile.

"Oh, OK! I'm sorry about talking about that." We stopped discussing religion for the day and took a break for the next few days, and then we resumed the dialogue.

"████████, I really don't understand the Trinity doctrine. The more I look into it, the more I get confused."

"We have the Father, the Son, and the Holy Spirit, three things that represent the Being God."

"Hold on! Break it down for me. God is the father of Christ, isn't he?"

"Yes!"

"Biological Father?" I asked.

"No."

"Then why do you call him Father? I mean if you're saying that God is our father in the sense that he takes care of us, I have no problem with that," I commented.

"Yes, that's correct," ▆▆▆ said.

"So there is no point in calling Jesus 'the Son of God.'"

"But he said so in the Bible," ▆▆▆▆▆ said.

"But ▆▆▆▆▆, I don't believe in the 100 percent accuracy of the Bible."

"Anyway, Jesus is God," ▆▆▆ said.

"Oh, is Jesus God, or Son of God?"

"Both!"

"You don't make any sense, ▆▆▆▆▆▆, do you?"

"Look, I really don't understand the Trinity. I have to research and ask an expert."

"Fair enough," I said. "But how can you believe in something you don't understand?" I continued.

"I understand but I cannot explain it," ▆▆▆▆▆ replied.

"Let's move on and hit another topic." I suggested. "According to your religion I seem to be doomed anyway. But what about the bushmen in Africa who never got the chance to know Jesus Christ?" I asked.

"They are not saved."

"But what did they do wrong?"

"I don't agree that they should suffer, but that's what my religion says."

"Fair enough."

"But how about Islam?" ▆▆▆▆▆ asked.

"In the Koran it says that God doesn't punish unless he sends a messenger to teach the people."

▆▆▆▆▆▆▆▆▆▆▆▆▆▆▆▆

▆▆▆▆▆▆ was one of those guys who you like the first time you meet.* ▆▆▆▆▆▆▆▆▆▆▆▆▆▆

▆▆▆▆▆▆▆▆▆▆▆▆▆▆▆▆

---

* It appears that the interrogator enlists a colleague to help with the theological discussion.

███

███

███

████████████████████████ He is more of a lover than a hater. █████████████████████████ are good friends, and he was fighting for the betterment of our condition.

██████████████ introduced him to me as a friend and someone to help ████████ my thirst for information about Christianity. Although I enjoyed getting to know ████████████, he didn't help me understand the Trinity. He confused me even more, and my lot with him was no better: he, too, sent me to hell. ██████████████████ ended up arguing with ██████████ because they had some difference in their beliefs, although both were Protestant. I realized that they could not help me understand, and so I dismissed the topic for good, and we started to talk about other issues.

It's very funny how false the picture is that western people have about Arabs: savage, violent, insensitive, and cold-hearted. I can tell you with confidence is that Arabs are peaceful, sensitive, civilized, and big lovers, among other qualities.

"████████, you guys claim that we are violent, but if you listen to the Arabic music or read Arabic poetry, it is all about love. On the other hand, American music is about violence and hatred, for the most part." During my time with ██████████, many poems went across the table. I haven't kept any copies; █████ has all the poems. █████ also gave me a small Divan. █████ is very surrealistic, and I am terrible when it comes to surrealism. I hardly understood any of her poems.

One of my poems went

███

███

███

———————————————————————
———————————————————————
———————————————————————
———————————————————————
———————————————————————
———————————————————————
———————————————————————
———————————————————————
———————————————————————
———————————————————————
———————————————————————
———————————————————————
———————————————————————
———————————————————————
———————————————————————
———————————————————————
———————————————————————
———————————————————————
———————————————————————
———————————————————————

—by Salahi, GTMO

All this time I kept refusing to talk about the way I had been treated, which ███████████ understood and respected. I didn't want to talk, first, because I was afraid of retaliation, and second, because I was skeptical about the readiness of the government to deal with things appropriately, and third, because the Islamic religion suggests that it is better to bring your complaints to God rather than disclosing them to human beings. But ████████████ kept patiently trying to persuade me; furthermore, ████████████ explained to me that ████ must report any misbehavior by ████ colleagues to ████ superiors.

After thoroughly contemplating the options, I decided to talk to ████████████. When ████ heard my account, ████████

brought ███████████████████████████████ who interrogated me about the issue after having sent the guards away.
███████████████████████ prudently wanted to avoid any
possible leak and spread of the story. I have no idea what happened after that, but I think there is sort of an internal DOD
investigation, because I was asked some questions about my
story in a later time.*

"You are a very courageous guy!" ███████████ used to tell me
in relation with my story.

"I don't think so! I just enjoy peace. But I certainly know
that people who torture helpless detainees are cowards." ██████

██
██
██
██
██
██
██

---

* The Schmidt–Furlow report records that on December 11, 2004, "after
months of cooperation with interrogators," "the subject of the second special interrogation notified his interrogator that he had been 'subject to
torture' by past interrogators during the months of July to October 2003."
A footnote elaborates: "He reported these allegations to an interrogator.
The interrogator was a member of the interrogation team at the time of the
report. The interrogator reported the allegations to her supervisor. Shortly
after being advised of the alleged abuse, the supervisor interviewed the
subject of the second special interrogation, with the interrogator present,
regarding the allegations. Based on this interview, and notes taken by the
interrogator, the supervisor prepared an 11 Dec 04 MFR addressed to JTF-
GTMO JIG and ICE. The supervisor forwarded his MFT to the JTF-
GTMO JIG. The JIG then forwarded the complaint to the JAG for
processing IAW normal GTMO procedures for investigating allegations of
abuse. The JAG by email on 22 Dec 04 tasked the JDOG, the JIG, and the
JMG with a review of the complaint summarized in the Dec 04 MFR and
directed them to provide any relevant information. The internal GTMO
investigation was never completed." Schmidt-Furlow, 22.

██

██

████████████████████████████

Not long after that, ███████████ took a leave for three weeks. "I'm going to Montreal with a ████████████ friend of mine. Tell me about Montreal." I provided ██████ with everything I remembered about Montreal, which wasn't much.

When ███████████ came back, ██████ hardly changed out of ██████ travel clothes before ██████ came to see me; ██████ was genuinely excited to see me again, and so was I. ████████████ said that ██████ enjoyed ██████ time in Canada and that everything was alright, but ██████ was probably happier to be in GTMO. ████████████ was tired from the trip, so ██████ stayed only for short time to check on me, and off ██████ went.

I went back to my cell and wrote ████████████ the following letter.

"Hi, ████████████ I know you were in Canada ████████████

██

██

██

██

████████████████████████████ I haven't asked you about it, but I don't appreciate somebody lying to me and taking me for an idiot. I really don't know what you were thinking when you made up that story to mislead me. I don't deserve to be treated like that. I chose to write and not talk to you, just to give you the opportunity to think about everything, instead of making you come up with inaccurate answers. Furthermore, you don't have to give me any answer or comment. Just destroy this letter and consider it non-existent. Yours truly Salahi."

I read the letter to the guards before I handed the sealed envelope to ███████ and asked ████ not to read it in my presence.

"Wha' the? How the hell do you know that ███████ was with ██████████████?" the guard on duty asked me.

"Something in my heart that never lies to me!"

"You don't make any sense. Besides, why the fuck should you care?"

"If you cannot tell whether ████████████ had some intimacy with a man, you ain't no man," I said. "I don't care, but I don't appreciate when ████████████ uses my manhood and plays games on me, especially in my situation. ████████ might think I am vulnerable but I am strong."

"You're right! That's fucked up."

████████ came the next day and confessed everything to me.

"I am sorry! I just figured we had a close relationship, and I thought it would hurt you ████████████████████ ██████████████████

"First I thank you very much for being forthcoming. I'm just confused! Do you think I'm looking forward ████ ██████████████? I'm not! For Pete's sake, you are a Christian ████████████ who is engaged in a war against my religion and my people! Besides, I am ████████████████ ████████████ inside this prison."

████████████ always tried after that to tell me that ████ didn't think that ████ would continue ████████████████ ████████████. But I didn't make any comment about the issue. All I did was I handcrafted a bracelet and sent it to him as the ████████████████████████████ who I liked and who had helped me in many issues.

*　　*　　*

"We are desperate to get information from you," said ▮▮▮ ▮▮▮▮▮▮▮▮▮▮▮▮▮▮ when he first met with me.

It was true: when I arrived in the camp in August 2002, the majority of detainees were refusing to cooperate with their interrogators.

"Look, I told you my story over and over a million times. Now either you send me to court or let me be," they were saying.

"But we have discrepancies in your story," the interrogators would say, as a gentle way of saying, "You're lying."

Like me, every detainee I know thought when he arrived in Cuba it would be a typical interrogation, and after interrogation he would be charged and sent to court, and the court would decide whether he is guilty or not. If he was found not guilty, or if the U.S. government pressed no charges, he would be sent home. It made sense to everybody: the interrogators told us this is how it would go, and we said, "Let's do it." But it turned out either the interrogators deliberately lied to encourage detainees to cooperate with them, or the government lied to the interrogators about the procedure as a tactic to coerce information from the detainees.

Weeks went by, months went by, and the interrogators' thirst for information didn't seem close to being satisfied. The more information a detainee provided, the more interrogators complicated the case and asked for more questions. All detainees had, at some point, one thing in common: they were tired of uninterrupted interrogation. As a newcomer, I first was part of a small minority that was still cooperating, but I soon joined the other group. "Just tell me why you arrested me, and I'll answer every question you have," I would say.

Most of the interrogators were coming back day after day empty-handed. "No information collected from source," was what the interrogators reported every week. And exactly as ███████████████████ said, the ███████████ was desperate to get the detainees talking. So ██████████ built a mini ████████████ inside the bigger organization. This Task Force, which included the U.S. Army, the U.S. Marines, the U.S. Navy, and civilians, had the job of coercing information from detainees. The operation was clouded with top secrecy.

██████████ was a very distinguished character in this sub-███████ group. Although ██████████ was a smart person, they gave him the dirtiest job on the Island, and shockingly brainwashed him into believing he was doing the right thing. ██████████ was always wrapped in a uniform that covered him from head to toe, because ██████████ was aware that he was committing war crimes against helpless detainees. ██████████ was The Night Owl, The Devil Worshipper, Loud Music Man, the Anti-Religion Guy, the interrogator par excellence. Every one of those nicknames had a reason.

██████████ used to keep detainees who were not allowed to sleep "entertained." He deprived me of sleep for about two months, during which he tried to break my mental resistance, to no avail. To keep me awake, he drove the temperature of the room crazily down, made me write all kinds of things about my life, kept giving me water, and sometimes made me stand the whole night. Once he stripped me naked with the help of a ██████████ guard in order to humiliate me. Another night, he put me in a frozen room full of propaganda pictures of the U.S., including a picture of George W. Bush, and made me listen to the National Anthem over and over.

██████████ was serving several detainees at the same time; I could hear many doors slamming, loud music, and detainees coming and leaving, the sound of their heavy metal chains giving them away. ██████████ used to put detainees in a dark room with pictures that were supposed to represent devils. He made detainees listen to the music of hatred and madness, and to the song "Let the Bodies hit the Floor" over and over for the whole night in the dark room. He was very open about his hatred toward Islam, and he categorically forbade any Islamic practices, including prayers and mumbling the Koran.

Even with all that, on around ██████████████████ the special team realized that I was not going to cooperate with them as they wished, and so the next level of torture was approved. ████████████████████████████ and another guy with a German shepherd pried open the door of the interrogation room where ██████████ and I were sitting. It was in ██████████ Building. ██████████████ and his colleague kept hitting me, mostly on my ribs and my face, and made me drink salt water for about three hours before giving me over to an Arabic team with an Egyptian and a Jordanian interrogator. Those interrogators continued to beat me while covering me in ice cubes, one, to torture me, and two, to make the new, fresh bruises disappear.

Then, after about three hours, Mr. X and his friend took me back and threw me in my present cell.* "I told you not to fuck with me, Motherfucker!" was the last thing I heard from ██████████. Later on, ██████████████████████ told me that ██████████ wanted to visit me for friendly purposes, but I didn't show any eagerness, and so the visit was cancelled. I am still in that same cell, although I no longer have to pretend I don't know where I am.

They finally allowed doctors to see me around March 2004, and I was able to get psychological assistance for the first time

---

* "Mr. X" appears here unredacted.

that April. Since then I have been taking the anti-depressant Paxil and Klonopin to help me sleep. The doctors also prescribed a multi-vitamin for a condition that was due to a lack of exposure to the sun. I also got some sessions with some psychologists who were assessing me; they really helped me, though I couldn't tell them the real reason for my sickness because I was afraid of retaliation.

"My job is to help your rehabilitation," one of my guards told me in the summer of 2004. The government realized that I was deeply injured and needed some real rehab. From the moment he started to work as my guard in July 2004, ▇▇▇▇▇▇▇ related to me right; in fact, he hardly talked to anybody beside me. He used to put his mattress right in front of my cell door, and we started to talk about all kinds of topics like old friends. We talked about history, culture, politics, religion, women, everything but current events. The guards were taught that I was a detainee who would try to outsmart them and learn current events from them, but the guards are my witnesses, I didn't try to outsmart anybody, nor was I interested in current events at the time because they only made me sick.

Before ▇▇▇▇▇▇▇ left he brought me a couple of souvenirs, and with ▇▇▇▇▇▇▇ and ▇▇▇▇▇▇▇ dedicated a copy of Steve Martin's *The Pleasure of My Company* to me.

▇▇▇▇▇▇▇ wrote, "Pill, over the past 10 months I have gotten to know you and we have become friends. I wish you good luck, and I am sure I will think of you often. Take good care of yourself. ▇▇▇▇▇▇▇"

▇▇▇▇▇▇▇ wrote, "Pillow, good luck with your situation. Just remember Allah always has a plan. I hope you think of us as more than just guards. I think we all became friends.

▇▇▇▇▇▇▇ wrote, "19 April 2005. Pillow: For the past 10 months I have done my damnedest to maintain a

Detainee–Guard relationship. At times I have failed: it is almost impossible not to like a character like yourself. Keep your faith. I'm sure it will guide you in the right direction."

I used to debate faith with one of the new guards. ▮▮▮▮▮▮▮▮ was raised as a conservative Catholic. He was not really religious, but I could tell he was his family's boy. I kept trying to convince him that the existence of God is a logical necessity.

"I don't believe in anything unless I see it," he told me.

"After you've seen something, you don't need to believe it," I responded. "For instance, if I tell you I have a cold Pepsi in my fridge, either you believe it or you don't. But after seeing it, you know, and you don't need to believe me." Personally, I do have faith. And I picture him, and these other guards, as good friends if we would meet under different circumstances. May God guide them and help them make the right choices in life.

Crisis always brings out the best and worst in people — and in countries, too. Did the Leader of the Free World, the United States, really torture detainees? Or are stories of torture part of a conspiracy to present the U.S. in a horrible way, so the rest of the world will hate it?

I don't even know how to treat this subject. I have only written what I experienced, what I saw, and what I learned firsthand. I have tried not to exaggerate, nor to understate. I have tried to be as fair as possible, to the U.S. government, to my brothers, and to myself. I don't expect people who don't know me to believe me, but I expect them, at least, to give me the benefit of the doubt. And if Americans are willing to stand for what they believe in, I also expect public opinion to compel the U.S. government to open a torture and war crimes investigation. I am more than confident that I can prove every single thing I have written in this book if I am ever given the opportunity to call witnesses in a proper judicial procedure, and if military personnel are not given the advantage of straightening their lies and destroying evidence against them.

Human beings naturally hate to torture other human beings, and Americans are no different. Many of the soldiers were doing the job reluctantly, and were very happy when they were ordered to stop. Of course there are sick people everywhere in the world who enjoy seeing other people suffering, but generally human beings make use of torture when they get chaotic and confused. And Americans certainly got chaotic, vengeful, and confused, after the September 11, 2001 terrorist attacks.

At the direction of President Bush, the U.S. began a campaign against the Taliban government in Afghanistan. On September 18, 2001, a joint resolution of Congress authorized President Bush to use force against the "nations, organizations, or persons" that "planned, authorized, committed, or aided the terrorist attacks on September 11, 2001, or harbored such organizations or persons." Then the U.S. government started a secret operation aimed at kidnapping, detaining, torturing, or killing terrorist suspects, an operation that has no legal basis.

I was the victim of such an operation, though I had done no such thing and have never been part of any such crimes. On September 29, 2001, I got a call on my cellphone and was asked to turn myself in, and I immediately did, sure I would be cleared. Instead, Americans interrogated me in my home country, and then the U.S. reached a joint agreement with the Mauritanian government to send me to Jordan to squeeze the last bits of information out of me. I was incarcerated and interrogated under horrible conditions in Jordan for eight months, and then the Americans flew me to Bagram Air Base for two weeks of interrogation, and finally on to the Guantánamo Navy Base ▉▉▉▉▉▉▉▉▉▉, where I still am today.

So has the American democracy passed the test it was subjected to with the 2001 terrorist attacks? I leave this judgment to the reader. As I am writing this, though, the United States and its people are still facing the dilemma of the Cuban detainees.

In the beginning, the U.S. government was happy with its secret operations, since it thought it had managed to gather all the evils of the world in GTMO, and had circumvented U.S. law and international treaties so that it could perform its revenge. But then it realized, after a lot of painful work, that it had gathered a bunch of non-combatants. Now the U.S. government is stuck with the problem, but it is not willing to be forthcoming and disclose the truth about the whole operation.

Everybody makes mistakes. I believe the U.S. government owes it to the American people to tell them the truth about what is happening in Guantánamo. So far, I have personally cost American taxpayers at least one million dollars, and the counter is ticking higher every day. The other detainees are costing more or less the same. Under these circumstances, Americans need and have the right to know what the hell is going on.

Many of my brothers here are losing their minds, especially the younger detainees, because of the conditions of detention. As I write these words, many brothers are hunger-striking and are determined to carry on, no matter what.* I am very worried about these brothers I am helplessly watching, who are practically dying and who are sure to suffer irreparable damage even

---

* MOS completed this manuscript in the fall of 2005; the last page is signed and dated September 28, 2005. One of the largest Guantánamo hunger strikes started in August 2005 and extended through the end of the year. See, e.g., http://www.nytimes.com/2005/09/18/politics/18gitmo .html?pagewanted=1&_r=0; and http://america.aljazeera.com/articles /multimedia/guantanamo-hungerstriketimeline.html.

if they eventually decide to eat. It is not the first time we have had a hunger strike; I personally participated in the hunger strike in September 2002, but the government did not seem to be impressed. And so the brothers keep striking, for the same old, and new, reasons. And there seems to be no solution in the air. The government expects the U.S. forces in GTMO to pull magic solutions out of their sleeves. But the U.S. forces in GTMO understand the situation here more than any bureaucrat in Washington, DC, and they know that the only solution is for the government to be forthcoming and release people.

What do the American people think? I am eager to know. I would like to believe the majority of Americans want to see Justice done, and they are not interested in financing the detention of innocent people. I know there is a small extremist minority that believes that everybody in this Cuban prison is evil, and that we are treated better than we deserve. But this opinion has no basis but ignorance. I am amazed that somebody can build such an incriminating opinion about people he or she doesn't even know.

Author's Note

In a recent conversation with one of his lawyers, Mohamedou said that he holds no grudge against any of the people he mentions in this book, that he appeals to them to read it and correct it if they think it contains any errors, and that he dreams to one day sit with all of them around a cup of tea, after having learned so much from one another.

331

personality, very confident, knows what he is supped to do, and doesn't respect his less comptent superiors. Before ▮▮ left he so bought me a couple of souvenirs, and dedicated to me The Pleasure of My Company by Steve Martin, with ▮▮ ▮▮▮ and ▮▮▮ ▮▮▮ wrotes " Pill, over the past 10 months I have gotten to know you and we have become friends. I wish you good luck and I am sure I will think of you often. take good care of yoursef. ▮▮ - ". ▮▮▮▮ wrote: " Pillow, Good Luck with your situation. Just remember Allah always has a plan. I hope you think of us as more than just guards. I think we all became friends. ▮▮ ". ▮▮ ▮▮ wrote: " Pillow 19 APRIL, 2005 For the past 10 months I have done my damnest to Detainee Guard relationship. At time I have failed. It is almost impossible not to like a charachter like yourself. Keep your ferith + I'm sure it will guide you in the right direction. _ ▮▮ " . That was not exactly a bad time. ② ▮▮

▮▮▮▮▮▮▮▮▮▮▮▮▮▮▮▮

Religions, Islam, Christianity and Judaism as the Middle Eastern culture as well. He found found in me the bright address as I did in him. We had been discussing all the time, without any prejudices or any taboos. We had been even hitting, some tins, Racism in the U.S when the other his other black colleague ▮▮▮ worked with him, ▮▮ is proud on his ▮▮▮ all he reads, watches is mostly ▮▮▮ and that why ▮▮▮ and I always started a friendly discussion with him. ▮▮▮ suspected me of having some tines, instigated the discussion, and

Editor's Acknowledgments

That we are able to read this book at all is thanks to the efforts of Mohamedou Ould Slahi's pro-bono lawyers, who fought for more than six years to have the manuscript cleared for public release. They did this quietly and respectfully, but also tenaciously, believing—and ultimately proving—that the truth is not incompatible with security. Time will only underscore what an accomplishment this has been, and how much readers everywhere owe a debt of gratitude to Nancy Hollander and Theresa M. Duncan, his lead attorneys; to their private co-counsel Linda Moreno, Sylvia Royce, and Jonathan Hafetz; and to their co-counsel Hina Shamsi, Brett Kaufman, Jonathan Manes, and Melissa Goodman of the National Security Project of the American Civil Liberties Union and Art Spitzer of the ACLU of the National Capital Area.

I owe my own profound thanks to Nancy Hollander and the rest of Mohamedou Ould Slahi's legal team, and above all to Mohamedou Ould Slahi himself, for offering me the opportunity to help bring these words to print. Every day I have spent reading, thinking about, and working with Mohamedou's manuscript has illuminated in some new way what a gift their trust and confidence has been.

Publishing material that remains subject to severe censorship restrictions is not for the faint of heart, and so I am especially grateful to all those who have championed the publication of Mohamedou's work: to Will Dobson and *Slate* for the chance to present excerpts from the manuscript and the space to put those excerpts in context; to Rachel Vogel, my literary agent, to Geoff Shandler, Michael Sand, and Allie Sommer at Little, Brown, and to Jamie Byng and Katy Follain at Canongate for their vision and patient navigation of a variety of publication challenges; and to everyone at Little, Brown/Hachette, Canongate, and all the foreign language publishers of *The Guantánamo Diary* for making it possible for this once-suppressed but irrepressible work to be read around the world.

Anyone who has written about what has happened in Guantánamo owes a debt to the ACLU's National Security Project, whose Freedom of Information Act litigation unearthed the trove of secret documents that stands as the stark historical record of the United States' abusive post-9/11 detention and interrogation practices. I am grateful for that record, without which the cross-referencing, corroboration, and annotation of Mohamedou's account would not have been possible, and even more grateful for the opportunities the ACLU has given me over the last five years to explore, absorb, and write about that indispensible record.

I am indebted to many who shared their time, insights, experiences, and ideas with me as I was working with this manuscript. I cannot mention them all, but I cannot fail to mention Hahdih Ould Slahi, for helping me understand Mohamedou's experience from his family's perspective, and Jameel Jaffer, Hina Shamsi, Lara Tobin, and Eli Davis Siems, for their constant support, thoughtful counsel, and careful readings of edited versions of this book.

Finally, I am forever indebted to Mohamedou Ould Slahi, for the courage to write his manuscript, for the integrity, wit, and humanity of his writing, and for the faith he has shown in all of us, the reading public, in committing his experiences to print. May he at least, and at last, receive the same honest judgment he has afforded us.

Notes to Introduction

1 Transcript, Administrative Review Board Hearing for Mohamedou Ould Slahi, December 15, 2005, 18. The ARB transcript is available at http://www.dod.mil/pubs/foi/operation_and_plans/Detainee/csrt_arb /ARB_Transcript_Set_8_20751-21016.pdf, 184–216.

EDITOR'S NOTE ON THE INTRODUCTION: None of Mohamedou Ould Slahi's attorneys holding security clearances has reviewed this introduction, contributed to it in any way, or confirmed or denied anything in it. Nor has anyone else with access to the unredacted manuscript reviewed this introduction, contributed to it in any way, or confirmed or denied anything in it.

2 Letter to attorney Sylvia Royce, November 9, 2006, http://online .wsj.com/public/resources/documents/couch-slahiletter-03312007.pdf.

3 Transcript, Combatant Status Review Tribunal Hearing for Mohamedou Ould Slahi, December 8, 2004, 7–8. The CSRT transcript is available at http://online.wsj.com/public/resources/documents/couch -slahihearing-03312007.pdf.

4 ARB transcript, 14, 18–19, 25–26.

5 ARB transcript, 26–27.

6 Department of Defense News Briefing, Secretary Rumsfeld and Gen. Myers, January 11, 2002, http://www.defense.gov/transcripts/transcript .aspx?transcriptid=2031.

7 Department of Defense Press Release, April 3, 2006, http://www .defense.gov/news/newsarticle.aspx?id=15573.

8 John Goetz, Marcel Rosenbach, Britta Sandberg, and Holger Stark, "From Germany to Guantanamo: The Career of Prisoner No. 760," *Der Spiegel*, October 9, 2008, http://www.spiegel.de/international/world/from -germany-to-guantanamo-the-career-of-prisoner-no-760-a-583193.html.

9 CSRT transcript, 3–4.

10 ARB transcript, 15–16.

11 Memorandum Order, *Mohammedou Ould Salahi v. Barack H. Obama*, No. 1:05-cv-00569-JR, 13–14. The Memorandum Order is available at https://www.aclu.org/files/assets/2010-4-9-Slahi-Order.pdf.

12 ARB transcript, 19.

13 Goetz et al., "From Germany to Guantanamo."

14 "Keep the Cell Door Shut: Appeal a Judge's Outrageous Ruling to Free 9/11 Thug," Editorial, *New York Daily News*, March 23, 2010, http://www .nydailynews.com/opinion/cell-door-shut-appeal-judge-outrageous-ruling -free-9-11-thug-article-1.172231.

15 Memorandum Order, 4.

16 The Reminiscences of V. Stuart Couch, March 1–2, 2012, Columbia Center for Oral History Collection (hereafter cited as CCOHC), 94, 117, http://www.columbia.edu/cu/libraries/inside/ccoh_assets/ccoh_10100507 _transcript.pdf.

17 CIA Office of the Inspector General, "Counterterrorism Detention and Interrogation Activities, September 2001–October 2003," May 7, 2004, 96. The CIA OIG report is available at http://media.luxmedia.com/aclu /IG_Report.pdf.

18 Bob Drogin, "No Leaders of Al Qaeda Found at Guantanamo," *Los Angeles Times*, August 18, 2002, http://articles.latimes.com/2002/aug/18 /nation/na-gitmo18.

19 ARB transcript, 23–24.

20 The National Commission on Terrorist Attacks upon the United States, *The 9/11 Commission Report* 165–166. The 9/11 Commission report is available at http://govinfo.library.unt.edu/911/report/911Report.pdf.

21 CCOHC interview with V. Stuart Couch, 90.

22 Memorandum Order, 19.

23 Jess Bravin, "The Conscience of the Colonel," *Wall Street Journal*, March 31, 2007, http://online.wsj.com/news/articles/SB117529704337355155.

24 U.S. Senate Committee on Armed Services, "Inquiry into the Treatment of Detainees in U.S. Custody," November 20, 2008, 140–41. The committee's report is available at http://www.armed-services.senate .gov/imo/media/doc/Detainee-Report-Final_April-22-2009.pdf.

25 Transcript of interview with Lt. Col. Stuart Couch for *Torturing Democracy*, http://www2.gwu.edu/~nsarchiv/torturingdemocracy/interviews /stuart_couch.html.

26 Bravin, "The Conscience of the Colonel."

27 CCOHC interview with V. Stuart Couch, 95.

28 Colonel Morris Davis, interview by Larry Siems, *Slate*, May 1, 2013, http://www.slate.com/articles/news_and_politics/foreigners/2013/04 /mohamedou_ould_slahi_s_guant_namo_memoirs_an_interview_with _colonel_morris.html.

29 Order, *Salahi v. Obama*, 625 F.3d 745, 746 (D.C. Cir. 2010). The decision is available at http://caselaw.findlaw.com/us-dc-circuit/1543844 .html.

30 Ibid., 750, 753.

372

responded the detainee in broken Arabic with his obvious Turkish accent. I right away knew the setup. This interrogation was meant for me in the first place. "Liar!" shouted ▮▮▮ "I ain't lying" responded the guy in Arabic, although ▮▮▮ kept speaking his loose English. "I don't care if you have a German or American passport you're going to tell me the truth!" said ▮▮▮ Now, I knew that the ▮▮▮ The setup fitted perfectly and meant to terrorize me even more. Although I knew right away it was a setup but the scaring effect was not affected. "Hi ▮▮▮ said ▮▮▮ "Hi" I responded feeling his breath right in front of my face. I was so terrorized that I couldn't realize what he was saying. "So your name is ▮▮▮" he concluded "No!" "But you responded when I called you ▮▮▮" he argued. I didn't really realize that he had called me ▮▮▮ but I found it idiot to tell him that I was so terrorized that I couldn't realize what name he call me "If you look at it we all are ▮▮▮" I correctly answered. ▮▮▮ means in Arabic God's servant. However, I knew how ▮▮▮ came up with the name of ▮▮▮. The story of the Name ▮▮▮: When I arrived in Montreal / Canada on 26 NOV 1999 my friend ▮▮▮ introduced me to his roommate ▮▮▮ with my civilian name. When I later on met with another ▮▮▮ who happened to see a year before with me, he called me ▮▮▮ and I responded b/c I found it impolite to correct him. Since then ▮▮▮ called me ▮▮▮

About the Authors

Mohamedou Ould Slahi was born in a small town in Mauritania in 1970. He won a scholarship to attend college in Germany and worked there for several years as an engineer. He returned to Mauritania in 2000. The following year, at the behest of the United States, he was detained by Mauritanian authorities and rendered to a prison in Jordan; later he was rendered again, first to Bagram Air Force Base in Afghanistan, and finally, on August 5, 2002, to the U.S. prison at Guantánamo Bay, Cuba, where he was subjected to severe torture. In 2010, a federal judge ordered him immediately released, but the government appealed that decision. The U.S. government has never charged him with a crime. He remains imprisoned in Guantánamo.

Larry Siems is a writer and human rights activist and for many years directed the Freedom to Write Program at PEN American Center. He is the author, most recently, of *The Torture Report: What the Documents Say about America's Post-9/11 Torture Program*. He lives in New York.